WORLD CLOTHING AND FASHION

WORLD CLOTHING AND FASHION

An Encyclopedia of History, Culture, and Social Influence

Volume 1

Mary Ellen Snodgrass

SHARPE REFERENCE
an imprint of M.E. Sharpe, Inc.

SHARPE REFERENCE

Sharpe Reference is an imprint of M.E. Sharpe, Inc.

M.E. Sharpe, Inc.
80 Business Park Drive
Armonk, NY 10504

Cover images (clockwise from top left): Jonathan C. Katzenellenbogen/Getty Images; DeA Picture Library/
The Granger Collection, NYC; The Granger Collection, NYC; Sanjit Das/Bloomberg via Getty Images;
Michael Smith/Getty Images; The Granger Collection, NYC—All rights reserved.

Library of Congress Cataloging-in-Publication Data

Snodgrass, Mary Ellen.
World clothing and fashion: an encyclopedia of history, culture, and social influence / Mary Ellen Snodgrass.
    pages cm.
Includes bibliographical references and index.
ISBN 978-0-7656-8300-7 (hardcover: alk. paper)
1. Clothing and dress—History—Encyclopedias. 2. Fashion—History—Encyclopedias. I. Title.

GT507.S6 2013
391.009′03—dc23   2013019775

Printed and bound in the United States

The paper used in this publication meets the minimum requirements of
American National Standard for Information Sciences—Permanence of
Paper for Printed Library Materials,
ANSI Z 39.48.1984.

CW (c) 10 9 8 7 6 5 4 3 2 1

Publisher: Myron E. Sharpe
Vice President and Director of New Product Development: Donna Sanzone
Executive Development Editor: Jeff Hacker
Project Manager: Laura Brengelman
Program Coordinator: Cathleen Prisco
Editorial Assistant: Meredith Day
Text Design and Cover Design: Jesse Sanchez
Typesetter: Nancy Connick

Clothes make the man. Naked people
have little or no influence on society.

Mark Twain

Fashion has to do with ideas,
the way we live, what is happening.

Coco Chanel

Contents

x   **Contents**

Topic Finder

Accessories and Adornments
Accessories
Amulets
Appliqué
Badges and Insignias
Beads and Beading
Belts and Suspenders
Body Painting
Body Piercing
Canes and Swagger Sticks
Cosmetics
Crowns and Tiaras
Embroidery
Eyeglasses
Fans, Hand
Feathers
Flowers
Gloves
Hairdressing
Handbags
Handkerchiefs
Hats, Men's
Hats, Women's
Headdress, Formal
Headdress, Functional
Jewels and Jewelry
Livery and Heraldry
Monogramming
Nail Art
Ribbons and Embellishments
Shell Ornaments
Symbolic Colors, Patterns, and Motifs
Ties and Cravats
Umbrellas and Parasols
Wigs

Art and Media
Advertising
Art and Media, Fashion
Art Nouveau and Art Deco Fashion
Catalogs, Clothing and Fashion
Costume Design, Film
Costume Design, Theater
Dolls, Fashion
Elle
Esquire
Fashion Plates
Glamour
Godey's Lady's Book
GQ
Harper's Bazaar
Museums, Clothing and Textile
Photography, Fashion
Pin-Up Girls
Seventeen
Town & Country
Vanity Fair
Vogue
Women's Wear Daily

Biographies
Armani, Giorgio
Avedon, Richard
Balenciaga, Cristóbal
Balmain, Pierre
Beaton, Cecil
Beene, Geoffrey
Blass, Bill
Bloomer, Amelia
Brummell, Beau
Burberry, Thomas
Cardin, Pierre

Clothing Types (Functions, Purposes, Groups)

Clothing Items and Parts

Corsets and Girdles
Denim and Jeans
Dresses and Dressmaking
Fasteners
Hats, Men's
Hats, Women's
Hosiery, Men's
Hosiery, Women's
Knitwear
Lingerie
Padding
Petticoats
Pockets
Robes
Shirts and Blouses
Shoes, Men's
Shoes, Women's
Skirts
Sleepwear
Sleeves and Cuffs
Slippers
Sweaters
Swimwear
T-Shirts
Trousers
Tunics and Togas
Undergarments
Veils and Veiling
Vests

Fabrics, Fibers, Materials
Calico
Cotton and Cotton Products
Denim and Jeans
Dyeing
Embroidery
Felt
Fibers, Natural
Fibers, Synthetic
Fur
Feathers
Flowers
Hides
Lace and Tatting
Lacing
Leather and Suede
Linen

Microfiber
Motley
Nylon
Patchwork
Patterns
Polyester
Printing, Textile
Rayon
Satin
Silk and Sericulture
Spandex
Velcro
Velvet
Wool and Wool Products
Whalebone
Yarn

Historical Periods and Styles
Amerindian Clothing, Pre-Columbian
Amerindian Clothing, Post-Contact
Belle Époque Fashion
Byzantine Clothing
Edwardian Styles and Fashions
Elizabethan Styles and Fashions
Greek Clothing, Ancient
Hippie and Mod Fashion
Medieval European Clothing
Mesopotamian Clothing
Napoleonic Styles and Fashions
Noble, Princely, and Chivalric Attire
Prehistoric Clothing
Roaring Twenties Styles and Fashions
Roman Clothing, Ancient
Victorian Styles and Fashions
Vintage Clothing

Holiday and Event Costumes
Coming-of-Age Attire
Costume Parties
Dance Costumes
Divinities
Formal Attire, Female
Formal Attire, Male
Halloween Costumes
Holiday Costumes
Mardi Gras and Carnival Costumes
Masks and Masking

Motley
Pageantry
Priestly Attire
Ritual Garments
Wedding Dress

Manufacturing, Production, Care
Cotton and Cotton Products
Dry Cleaning
Dyeing
Fibers, Synthetic
Ironing
Knitwear
Laundry
Looms
Microfiber
Needle and Thread
Nylon
Printing, Textile
Sewing Machines
Spinning, Textile
Storage, Clothing
Sweatshops
Textile Manufacturing
Weaving

Merchandising and Commerce
Advertising
Bond Clothing Stores
Boutiques
Catalogs, Clothing and Fashion
Cotton Trade
Department Stores
Dolls, Fashion
Education, Fashion
Fashion Plates
Gap
Gimbel Brothers
Knockoff Fashions
L.L. Bean
Labels
Lord & Taylor
Macy's
Mail Order
Marks & Spencer
Merchandising
Ready-to-Wear

Retail Trade
Silk Trade
Standard Sizing
Textile Trade
Wool Trade

Regional, National, and Cultural Styles
African American Clothing and Fashion
African Clothing, Northern
African Clothing, Sub-Saharan
American Western Clothing
Amerindian Clothing, Pre-Columbian
Amerindian Clothing, Post-Contact
Arctic Attire
British Clothing and Fashion
Central American, Mexican, and Caribbean Clothing
Chinese Clothing
Clan Attire
Coming-of-Age Attire
Customs, Lore, and Myth
Divinities
Eastern European Clothing
Ethnic and National Dress
Feminist Styles and Fashions
French Clothing and Fashion
Greek Clothing, Ancient
Indian and Pakistani Clothing
Italian Clothing and Fashion
Japanese Clothing and Fashion
Jewish Religious Attire
Korean Clothing and Fashion
Latino Styles and Fashions
Mesopotamian Clothing
Middle Eastern Clothing
Muslim Religious Attire
Pacific Island Clothing
Persian/Iranian Clothing
Roman Clothing, Ancient
Russian Clothing and Fashion
Social Status
South American Clothing
Southeast Asian Clothing
Spanish and Portuguese Clothing
Symbolic Colors, Patterns, and Motifs

Techniques, Trades, Professions

Appliqué
Batiking
Beads and Beading
Body Painting
Body Piercing
Cobblery
Costume Design, Film
Costume Design, Theater
Couturiers
Dresses and Dressmaking
Dyeing
Embroidery
Fashion Design
Haberdashers
Hairdressing
Haute Couture
Knitting and Crocheting
Lacing
Models and Modeling
Printing, Textile
Silk and Sericulture
Spinning, Textile
Tailoring
Tie-Dye
Weaving

Trends and Movements

Art Nouveau and Art Deco Fashion
Bohemian Style and Fashion
Color Trends
Customs, Lore, and Myth
Dress Codes and Conventions
Dress Reform
Eco-fashion
Ethnic and National Dress
Eton Style
Feminist Styles and Fashions
Gendered Dressing
Globalization
Hippie and Mod Fashion
Nudity and Nudism
Orientalism
Rationing
Social Status
Sumptuary Laws
Symbolic Colors, Patterns, and Motifs
Teen Trends
Unisex Clothing
Vintage Clothing

Preface

World Clothing and Fashion examines the nature of apparel and the fashion industry from rawhide to ready-to-wear. For the convenience and edification of the teacher, student, researcher, clothier, and trend spotter, 313 major entries survey milestones in the history of attire—the advance of the human wardrobe from needle-and-thread repair in cave dwellings to Syrian weaves, Roman cosmetics, and Plains Indian moccasins.

Entries cover the merchandising of style at boutiques and resale shops, tinkerings with spinning wheels and looms, and the exploitation of children in hosiery mills and immigrant workers in sweatshops. Clothing controversies—sumptuary laws, dress codes, veiling, body piercing, whalebone, swimwear, school uniforms, knockoffs, pin-up girls, feathers, and eco-fashion—convey the immediacy of concerns that body coverings retain dignity and propriety as well as respect for sources.

The headword list encompasses marketers (Lord & Taylor, department stores), styles (art nouveau and art deco, Bohemian), advances (standard sizing, textile printing), and period dress (Edwardian, Byzantine). Summations of national costume—Mesopotamian, Russian, Korean, Arctic, Caribbean—parallel essays on ethnic identity, such as masks and masking, togas and tunics, Muslim and Jewish religious attire, ritual garments, and African American fashion.

Details of global needs—armor, boots, vests, hats, belts—contrast methods of supplying body protection with helmets, blankets, police uniforms, and leather. For different reasons, museums and movies capture glamour with crowns and tiaras, jewelry, fans, canes and swagger sticks, and lingerie. Artisanal and industrial production ranges from knitting, patchwork, tailoring, haberdashery, cobblery, and dressmaking to wool cloth manufacture, sewing machines, tie-dye, yarn, and spandex. All find coverage in this work.

In addition to individual looks in corsetry and padding, specialized forms of dress and adornment shape the human image with princely and priestly attire, body painting, monogramming, club attire, ties and cravats, and occupational uniforms. The aesthetics of wardrobe impact the study of circus costumes, motley, courtship attire, burial garb, and unisex jeans and T-shirts. Life-changing issues emerge under the headings of rationing, disguise, clothes for the elderly, academic garb, divinities, and protective and orthotic dress.

The blending of cultures through voyages, trade, and exploration results in historical appreciation of amulets, Latino styles, Middle Eastern apparel, space suits, and globalization. Entries on mail order, modeling, fashion dolls, and silk trade delineate the selling of commodities. From the runway and the mall, outfits and accessories pass to consumers through retail trade, catalogs, vintage shops, and patterns. Technological improvements precede major changes in texture and convenience, the contributions to couture by wigs, the Jacquard loom, nylon, Ultrasuede, orientalism, and microfiber.

Peripheral issues stress the centrality of grooming to well-being, the focus of essays on hairstyles, sleepwear, dry cleaning, rainwear, and leisure and prison attire. An overview of couture enumerates the apparel changes wrought by reformer Amelia Bloomer, couturier Charles Frederick Worth, feminist Coco Chanel, trendsetter Levi Strauss, and mod merchant Mary Quant, among others. A conclusive analysis of world clothing also requires perusal of accessories, batiking, livery, royal apparel, and badges and insignias, and the evidence of social status recorded in ciphers.

Research involves lengthy reading in humanistic topics, beginning with prehistoric use of skins and shells and incorporating divinities, nuptials, dance, maternity wear, baby clothes, national costumes, and teen trends. In addition to the biographies of photographer Richard Avedon and designer Liz Claiborne, wardrobe study requires knowledge of leather merchant Guccio Gucci, fashion illustrator Erté, innovator Gianni Versace, and wedding specialist Vera Wang. The basics of apparel history derive from the commentaries of *GQ* and *Godey's Lady's Book* as well as articles from *Women's Wear Daily, Vogue, Seventeen,* and *Vanity Fair.* Primary sources extend over time from the period survey *The Mirror of the Graces* to autobiographies by American designer Bill Blass and Hollywood film costumer Edith Head.

Rounding out the two-volume reference source, study aids clarify individual garment parts, period shifts, and national costumes:

- A glossary of 82 terms defines stitching strategies of laidwork and shirring, the purpose of the tabard and clan sett, philosophies of the Empire silhouette and ready-to-wear, creation of faience and hairwork, and the historical significance of the fibula, Hays code, extrusion, and collective costuming. Global wardrobe commentary clarifies resist dyeing, tawing, tumplines, and the bon ton. Detailing—trompe l'oeil, foulard, ombré, deconstruction, cloisonné—gives insight into the influence of history, the arts, and couture on period attire.
- A chronology covers events from 100,000 B.C.E. to the present day. Entries recognize the importance of twining and netting bark and hemp to industrialized weaving. Landmarks note the first use of natural fibers, goat fleece, lacing, the *bliaut,* veiling of women, rhinestones, the Hudson's Bay blanket, "little black dress," and gendered color coding. Within events are the achievements of memorable people: Chinese emperor and silk promoter Shi Huangdi, king and military outfitter Xerxes, velvet appreciator Akbar the Great, navigator and ethnographer Christopher Columbus, yarn producer Richard Arkwright, tutu maker Barbara Karinska, tie designer Jesse Langsdorf, chemist Hazel Bishop, and dye master Miriam C. Rice.
- An exhaustive index alphabetizes key entries on people and peoples, materials, events, businesses, issues, inventions, concepts, ethnic and religious groups, geographic locations, institutions, laws, and social movements.

While compiling these two volumes, I sought input from merchants, chemists, archivists, travelers, hunters, farmers, and reference librarians, the backbone of research. Historical societies, university libraries, the Library of Congress, book and film reviewers, and specialists in apparel history and marketing filled in details. I found particularly helpful the databases of Alexandria Street Press and the writings of Elizabeth Barber, Valerie Steele, Donna Kooler, Deborah Landis, Fiona McDonald, Sheila Paine, Ulinka Rublack, Alexandra Palmer, Giorgio Riello, Francesca Sterlacci, Carl Waldman, Ann Pollard Rowe, Daniel Hill, Valerie Cumming, and Colin Gale. One of the most unusual sources, Deb Salisbury's *Elephant's Breath and London Smoke,* entertained as well as enlightened.

Acknowledgments

Appalachian State University Library, Boone, North Carolina

David O. McKay Library, Brigham Young University, Rexberg, Idaho

Hugh Snodgrass, adhesives chemist, Hickory, North Carolina

L.L. Bean Customer Service, Freeport, Maine

Lotsee Patterson, professor emerita, Oklahoma University, Norman, Oklahoma

Martin Otts, Patrick Beaver Library, Hickory, North Carolina

Mary Canrobert, *Charlotte Observer* feature writer and former resident of Suzhou, China

Ronald Key, volunteer dentist, Gambia

My unending gratitude to Martin Otts and Mark Schumacher for running down sources and bibliography and to Eileen Lawrence and Stephen Rhind-Tutt for the use of Woman and Social Movements and Anthropology, two databases hosted by Alexandria Street Press. A special salute to Mary Canrobert for emails supplying details about Chinese apparel and department stores. Blessings on editor Jeff Hacker and my publicist, Joan Lail, for dissuading me from folly.

Introduction

Apparel history crops up in unexpected places, revealing the economical and psychological impact of wardrobe on all aspects of living, throughout history. From swaddling and coming of age to nuptials and grave goods, the story of garments discloses facets of human need and individuality that leap off the hanger. A survey of how people dress themselves and their families picks up details from unusual sources, including purple dye from shellfish, the smuggling of athletic shoes through border patrols, rue to mourn the beheading of Charles II, and jaguar pelts that honor combat bravery.

A thorough examination of attire reflects on human life for proof of vanity in the Amazon basin, concern for soldier safety among Julius Caesar's troops, and adaptability in the era of Rosie the Riveter, as well as ventures into outer space in pressurized suits that mimic earthly atmosphere. The adorning of celebrants at crownings and feast days typically drew on skilled goldsmiths and dressmakers along with shapers of boned collars and weavers of daisy chains. The importance of duck down for warmth in Arctic lands compared with the weaving of grass skirts in the Society Islands and the styling of hair with mud among the Rendille of East Africa.

The art of dressing has conferred dignity from prehistory, inspiring early clothiers to fasten hide cloaks with lianas and shield heads from the sun with woven beach hats. Burial attire graced the deceased with delicate embroidery and beading, moccasins and feather mantles, and the gilded glories of pharaonic Egypt and the Inca Empire. Into the current age, advisories on what to wear and how to groom the face, hands, and hair prepare travelers and company agents for global adventures in lands where dress takes on a variety of meanings and nuances.

Overall, clothing history encompasses every aspect of human endeavor, from *quinceañeras* and debutante balls to suitable gear for mines, fortresses, and retirement homes. Along with hygiene and makeup, wardrobe selection emphasizes care of the body and self-expression through the choice of textures, colors, and designs. Global interest in seasonal changes of fashion fuels a long-lived business that involves factory-made leisure wear as well as the artistry of knitting, crochet, and embroidery. Enthusiasm for something new, something different, something fun to wear continues to draw humankind to the marketplace for a glimpse of fashion's latest.

A-Z ENTRIES

Academic Garb

The symbolism of academic regalia identifies academics and professionals with formal robes, scarves or hoods, and tasseled caps in significant color combinations. Both mythic and emblematic of *sacra* (holy things), the *supertonic* (cassock or soutane), soutane, and surplice (short yoked robe) or cotta of academics and clergymen from medieval universities set the tone and style for the British and North American *vestimentum clausum* ("closed clothing," or academic dress), signifying affiliation.

From the founding of Oxford University around 1096, students donned the black academic gown for conferences with advisers, communal dining, and exams. For undergraduates at Queen's College, Oxford, the tabard signified professionals in training, called tabarders. At Merton College, scholars also adopted the hood and fur tippet (stole), a practical outfit for cold weather that extended from the head to the shoulders for doctors of philosophy. Until the 1200s, gowns remained undifferentiated for advanced-degree students. The colleges that made up universities chose a uniform gown to indicate medicine, law, theology, and arts. In 1222, Stephen Langton, the archbishop of Canterbury, added the *capa clausa* (closed cope) with slits for armholes and a clasp at the throat as an indication of decorum.

The Faculty of Theology donned robes in designated colors at early European universities, such as black at Cambridge, Oxford, and the Sorbonne (Paris), and white at the universities of Coimbra (Portugal), Perpignan (southern France), and Salamanca (Spain), the first medieval schools to prescribe scholarly garb. Doctors of theology chose scarlet or purple, colors approved after 1243 by Pope Innocent IV and promoted in 1334 by Pope Benedict XII for doctors of law in Paris. Over the surplice, academics wore the secular tabard marked by university crest and coat of arms. Wearing the regalia obliged graduates to honor higher learning and treasure academic achievement.

Evolving Emblems and Styles

At Peterhouse College, Cambridge University, in 1344, masters and scholars donned the surplice. Monks received colored college gowns, black for Black Friars and gray for Grey Friars. Under sumptuary laws from 1350 to 1500, campus rules prohibited ornamentation of the capa clausa. Taste dictated the lining of the bachelor's robe with inexpensive black lamb's wool or badger fur.

During the Renaissance, university faculties adopted dignified robing for formal occasions, a distinction that authorities discouraged in public to prevent clashes of town and gown. In the mid-fifteenth century, academia made extensive shifts in style. The corded bonnet or round cap replaced the pileus (skullcap). The hood advanced from rainwear to an element of formalism, but without shoulder pieces. And by 1463, scholars abandoned the formal cape and liripipe (tippet), replacing them with the paneled scarf. Late in the 1400s, comfort and convenience dictated shortening the robe from ankle to knee length and replacing sleeves with side slits, which freed the arms.

In 1500, academics replaced the closed gown with the tabard, yoked habit, or sleeved tunic, left open to reveal the fur lining. Bag sleeves displayed embroidery. Hem-length tubular glove sleeves opened at the elbow to free the arms.

By 1520, the University of Paris adopted an Italian *pileus quadratus* (square cap), predecessor of the modern mortarboard. In the time of England's

Faculty and fellows at a British university pose in formal academic attire for commencement exercises. The black gown originated at Oxford University in the eleventh century. Colors, piping, and emblems may designate school, academic field, or degree. *(Christopher Furlong/ Getty Images)*

King Henry VIII (r. 1509–1547), gowns of ottoman silk featured light balloon sleeves of lawn. The Elizabethan era brought the display of winged sleeves, a contemporary fashion, and black silk linings for wool robes, a somber offshoot of the Reformation.

At convocations, commencements, ritual oaths, processions, and pageants, full-dress uniforms marked membership in the academic community and lent sobriety, pomp, and pride to faculty and school. In the 1670s, Oxford graduates posed in academic dress for painted miniatures. Students at Columbia (New York) and Princeton (New Jersey) universities in the mid-1700s followed the Renaissance custom of wearing robes to class. New York University added three stripes to the sleeves, a trend that spread to smaller colleges.

Presidents of academic institutions began wearing official medallions. Investiture of a president introduced an emblematic robing in the leader's unique colors, as with the purple robe and white hood at Saint Michael's College in Colchester, Vermont. At the state memorial service for General Richard Montgomery, a hero of the American Revolution, on February 19, 1776, students and faculty of the College of Philadelphia wore academic gowns as a gesture of respect and patriotism.

In addition to representing institutional values, academic robes incited power struggles, as with the Puritan abandonment of academic regalia during the English Commonwealth (1649–1660). The subordination of Ingolstadt University to Bavarian law in 1804 banished academic robing and replaced regalia with civil-service uniforms. After 1895, colleges reclaimed their control of academia and signified excellence with logos, arms, seals, and emblems, such as the matching crowns on the robes of Columbia University and, at Rutgers (New Jersey), the italic Q (for Queen's College, its original name) alongside "1766" (the school's founding date).

The class of 1899 at the University of Mississippi introduced traditional caps and gowns. That same year, portrait artist John Singer Sargent painted Martha Carey Thomas, the president of Bryn Mawr College (Pennsylvania), in a black academic robe, a token of the rise of women in academia. In 1932, the American Council on Education standardized length, colors, and styles and declared dark suits and dresses appropriate to wear under the gown. The guidelines remained authoritative but not binding on formal academic robing for students and professors.

Contemporary Attire

Materials today tend toward silk faille, cotton broadcloth, Russell cord, bengaline, and light wool flannel, with black-tipped ermine or rabbit fur, lace, cording, tassels, and gold buttons adorning the outfit. In China, the winged hat tops a distinctive *shangfu* (court robe) with a round collar, identifying the scholar or official. Similarly, French academic regalia mimic the magistrate's robe with a button-front gown, lace jabot, and train in black. Fringed sashes, gilt stripes, and colored bands in front indicate academic discipline, such as rose for science, pink for medicine, yellow for the humanities, scarlet for law, and purple for theology. In New Zealand, a broader range of colors offers baby blue for law, royal blue for philosophy and science, crimson for biology, burgundy for business, and white for music.

Current styles bear national and ethnic details, as in the case of *songket* or brocade fabric in Malaysia, black vested suits worn with robes in Portugal, ermine copes in Ireland, top hats in Finland and Sweden, a biretta and embroidered cuffs for Spanish academic gowns, and school colors and sashes for Filipino robes. U.S. graduates wear the bordered cowl or hood with chevrons and gold honor cords around the neck to denote achievement. African American traditions add African kente cloth to the medieval European stole. At the University of Jordan, okra velvet parallels black in a somber duo.

At more than 400 U.S. universities, PhD candidates typically wear black with velvet bands on the sleeves and hoods trimmed in velvet or piping. Graduates furl their hoods at the bottom to reveal satin linings, often in school colors, such as cherry and white at Temple University (Pennsylvania) and green and gold at the University of Vermont. Mortarboard caps feature a folding skullcap and the graduate tassel in black or school colors.

See also: Robes; Symbolic Colors, Patterns, and Motifs.

Further Reading

Bolman, Lee G., and Joan V. Gallos. *Reframing Academic Leadership.* San Francisco: John Wiley & Sons, 2011.

Harris, April L. *Academic Ceremonies: A Handbook of Traditions and Protocol.* Washington, DC: CASE Books, 2005.

Manning, Kathleen. *Rituals, Ceremonies, and Cultural Meaning in Higher Education.* Westport, CT: Greenwood, 2000.

Accessories

Whether carried or worn, accessories, the complements of ensembles, intensify their overall appearance, utility, and social impact. As early as 100,000 B.C.E., African nomads covered their naked bodies and those of their young in fur pelts and hides, securing these with the first accessories—sashes made from vines and animal gut. The Neolithic Tuareg of the Sahel beautified themselves with shell pendants, Africa's first artistic jewelry. From 18,000 B.C.E., Paleolithic Chinese in the area of Beijing further individualized dressing by adorning their hair and attire with animal fangs and bones, clamshells, pebbles, and stone beads, amulets that shielded them from harm.

Stone Age clothiers devised accessories that transformed appearance, such as the palm frond fan in India and the Gansu shell dressing for beards in north-central China. In Crete, Canaan, and Assyria, aprons enhanced the sacred nature of ritual attire. Germanic tribes, Polynesians, and Australian Aborigines increased their status by topping their heads with horn and feather head-dresses. Globally, bearers of status draped their shoulders with blankets and barkcloth cloaks, adaptable wraps that identified clan leaders and war chiefs.

By 3000 B.C.E., accessories acquired more socioeconomic meaning. Chinese petroglyphs pictured jade earrings, documenting the early use of semiprecious stones as a maiden's jewelry. Crude accessories gave way to carved and beaded hair ornaments and sashes, which distinguished a national costume. With similar ethnic pride, subjects of the Egyptian pharaoh Khati after 2345 B.C.E. fanned themselves with sacred ibis feathers and displayed the solar disc of Ra and the ankh (key of life) on garments and tiaras as proofs of loyalty and faith. In 1323 B.C.E., Tutankhamen demonstrated his royal power with the royal collar, crown, crook, and scepter.

Mesopotamian accessories around 745 B.C.E. included feather coronets and horsehair fly whisks. In ancient Greece, the herald bore a staff as both walking stick and symbol of office. On battlefields throughout the Roman Empire, centurions wore feathered aigrettes (ornamental tufts) and wielded the *vitis* (swagger stick) to emphasize legionary authority.

Medieval Trends and Baubles

During the early Middle Ages, the buckle contributed style to ordinary belts and cloaks. Byzantine women favored crosses on long chains and fastened to their belts the chatelaine—literally "castle mistress"—a cord suspending seals, keys, thimble, needle-and-thread kit, and scissors. Men in Constantinople went through fads of domed hats, Spanish felt hats, and Phrygian skullcaps. Japanese aristocrats fastened hand fans to belts much as the Chinese tied coin pouches at the waist.

As fashion spread along the Silk Road, European leather shops imported Arabian belts and handbags adorned with gold leaf. During epidemics, owners of fashionable handkerchiefs and purses stuffed them with fragrant petals and herbs, believed to provide protection against contagion. Accessories sold in 1431 by haberdashers included riding gloves, eyeglasses, shoe-roses, women's mourning hoods and linen headdresses, men's turbans and tasseled hats, and decorative caps, embellishments favored by young dandies.

The sixteenth century elevated accessories to prime importance in status dressing. In 1520, women's stomachers, barbes (wimples) and gable hoods, and starched tie-on ruffs, as well as men's leather codpieces with trunk hose, garters, and feathered berets, increased the theatricality of Iberian, French, and Tudor court fashions. Fasteners such as tiny buttons, ribbon ties for trunk sleeves, and gilded lacing advanced from necessities to adornments.

In the Western Hemisphere, accessories for Amerindians included prayer feathers tied to the neck and each foot of the Hopi, Zuni sashes dyed with cochineal, Navajo serapes, and rawhide thongs bearing Sauk medicine bags, Creek buffalo tails, and Cherokee pouches, forerunners of the sewn-in pocket. The Wampanoag of Massachusetts carved shells for wampum belts, which owners traded like currency. The Tlingit of Alaska whittled cedar headdresses and, for realistic detail, attached mountain goat, dog, or coyote hair. Trappers and traders imitated native dress by adopting beaver caps, blanket shawls, and fringed gloves.

According to the sixteenth-century Spanish conquistador Hernán Cortés, the Maya of Mesoamerica accessorized loincloths and tunics with ostrich plumes, fans, and agave-stitched headdress. Labrets and tongue jewelry provide evidence of ritual bloodletting. Feathers of flamingos, macaws, and quetzels suspended from pierced nasal cartilage served as facial accessories. In South America, body paint among the Tupi of Brazil took the shape of clan insignia.

Secondary Adornments

European fashion in the 1700s favored women's tie-on pockets and the tucker, a frill or lace draped over a low neckline, in addition to soft drawstring reticules in colors matching pumps and parasols. English optician George Adams framed the first lorgnette, eyeglasses on a handle, which the fashionable carried as hand and eye jewelry. Dandies preferred the quizzing glass (monocle), a stylish single lens attached to a neck strap and raised in a flamboyant gesture of curiosity, concern, or disapproval.

In Western Europe, the Napoleonic era (1799–1815) elevated buff gloves and the paisley shawl into the must-have accessories for women's afternoon and evening attire. In the mid-nineteenth century, swag shops displayed a variety of second-hand shawls, silk purses, handkerchiefs, suspenders, bow ties, gloves, turbans, and fur muffs and tippets. Fashionable women called attention to their graceful necks with cameos on ribbons. They tucked combs into their hair and hat pins into their bonnets and added beads, flowers, and plumes to poufs and fascinators, lacy or crocheted head coverings. Civilian males postured in public with swagger sticks, homburg hats, and equestrian boots.

Early twentieth-century accessories ranged from the flapper's cloche or headband over bobbed hair to the suave cigarette holder and netted cocktail hat. Men flaunted fraternity jewelry and monogrammed cigarette cases and protected their eyes from glare with sunglasses. Long chains, fedoras, and clocked hose accessorized 1930s ensembles. During the Nazi occupation of France during World War II, the suppression of fashion led women to treasure handbags, taffeta and rayon gloves and hats, and crocheted or knitted shawls, small bits of luxury extracted from rationed markets.

The late 1940s in the United States debuted bobby socks and letter sweaters for teens, and wide belts, Stetson women's hats, lockets, and clutch and cocktail bags for adult women. A decade later, pin-on corsages of cherries, acorns, or holly brightened jackets and hats. Businessmen appeared more dignified when wearing horn-rimmed glasses made from tortoise shell or high-impact plastic.

Ensembles in the 1960s made bright-colored hose and boots the focus of legwear with miniskirts, with pillbox hats and Pierre Balmain watches being the appropriate accessories for Chanel suits. Hippies popularized wire granny glasses, peace symbol jewelry, and tie-dyed headbands. Fashions of the disco set in the 1970s followed with platform shoes, hoop earrings, and spiked false eyelashes. Japanese fabric engineer Issey Miyake experimented with handbags and totes shaped from equilateral triangles.

The remainder of the twentieth century brought media attention to leotards and leggings with Spandex, fleece vests, sunglasses, aviator glasses, men's earrings, digital watches, running shoes, and a revival of fishnet hose. Early 2000s accessories ranged from sedate parkas, scarves, and hoodies to high-heel boots, sequined sweaters, and "bling," the pop term for sparkly jewelry and chic cell phones. Labeled goods—Gucci or Burberry handbags and Rolex or Omega watches—continued to inspire knockoffs.

See also: Belts and Suspenders; Canes and Swagger Sticks; Fans, Hand; Feathers; Gloves; Handbags; Handkerchiefs; Hats, Men's; Hats, Women's; Jewels and Jewelry; Ribbons and Embellishments; Shell Ornaments; Ties and Cravats.

Further Reading

Beaujot, Ariel. *Victorian Fashion Accessories.* New York: Bloomsbury, 2012.

Genova, Aneta. *Accessory Design.* New York: Fairchild, 2012.

Peacock, John. *Fashion Accessories: The Complete 20th Century Sourcebook.* New York: Thames & Hudson, 2000.

Stall-Meadows, Celia. *Know Your Fashion Accessories.* New York: Fairchild, 2003.

Advertising

The premier, time-honored method of marketing goods and services to consumers, advertising has promoted person-to-person sales since ancient times—papyrus ads in Egypt, Greece, and Arabia and wall blurbs in ancient Rome announcing a new fulling (dry cleaning) shop, which whitened clothes with ammonia and fuller's earth.

History to Twentieth Century

For the preliterate in medieval Europe, sales techniques for clothing and accessories included pictorial signage over cobbleries and hatters' and jewelers' workshops. In the 1400s, luxury wholesalers Francesco di Marco Datini in Avignon and Andrea Barbarigo in Venice enriched themselves through marketing campaigns for fashionable European leather goods.

In 1672, publication of the French gazette *Mercure Galant* merged journalism with fashion. Expansion of literacy in Europe and the Americas in the 1700s enabled sellers to print their offerings on handbills and in single columns of newspapers such as Benjamin Franklin's *Pennsylvania Gazette,* John Peter Zenger's *New-York Weekly Journal,* and David Chambers Claypoole and John Dunlap's *Pennsylvania Packet,* America's first successful daily.

The 1800s, an age of sales pioneering, encouraged mail order by printing items and prices alongside company addresses. The debut of Boston publisher John Lauris Blake's *Ladies' Magazine* in 1828 provided marketers with a means of communicating directly with female consumers about up-to-the-moment styles. The shift to paid print advertising began on June 16, 1836, with the French weekly *La Presse,* which was able to lower the cost of an annual subscription from 80 francs to 40 francs.

In Philadelphia in the early 1840s, Volney B. Palmer brokered space in newspapers to clothiers. In Puteaux, France, Charles-Louis Havas, the pioneer of Agence France-Presse, translated foreign ad copy for publication in the French media. His employee, Paul Julius von Reuter, established Reuters, Germany's first global ad brokerage, in Aachen. Bernhard Wolff applied the same sales method at Vossische Zeitung in Berlin.

Contemporaneous with ad brokering, postal reform acts discounted mailing costs for magazines and newspapers, flyers, coupons, and samples. The tedious labor of fashion advertising on a flatbed press in the 1850s involved sheet-by-sheet printing. Processors of *Godey's Lady's Book* folded each of the pages, sewed them into books, and addressed the books for mailing. The steam press increased output to 750 sheets per hour, greatly expanding the circulation of style monthlies, which offered home sewing machines for $15. In the 1870s, halftone photography engulfed viewers in the realism of live models posing in chic outfits.

Advertising focused attention on the materials and workmanship of clothing, as in the drawings of women's fur wraps in *Puck's Magazine.* Late in the nineteenth century, department stores offered economical wardrobes at one price for brides, businessmen, and schoolchildren. Ad copy promoted simplicity as the hallmark of children's comfort

and well-being. As listed by Lord & Taylor in Manhattan in 1872, the attire of the crawling baby began with drawers, calico wrappers, quilted and rubber bibs, and short gowns with pantaloons. Rather than utilitarian purpose or economy, Macy's in New York, Marshall Field's in Chicago, and Wanamaker's in Philadelphia advertised the height of style.

According to an industry newsletter, *The Boot and Shoe Recorder,* in the 1890s, in-house advertising expanded business. As women's hemlines rose and society paid more attention to footwear, shoe stores publicized complete service, which included tinting, button replacement, and repair. Packaging of new shoes contained leaflets listing prices for staining and dyeing, re-soling, replacing canvas and suede insoles, re-heeling, and reconditioning fine footwear to prevent slips and falls. The seller's willingness to extend service indicated faith in shoe quality and a concern for customer comfort and safety.

In the four decades from 1880 to 1920, advertising volume rose fifteenfold, from $200 million to around $3 billion. Street graphics, billboards, and art posters pushed a variety of products, notably seasonal department store clearance sales and women's couture in Erté's art nouveau style.

Niche marketing in the *American Journal of Nursing, Corset and Underwear Review,* and the *Journal of Obstetrics and Gynecology* in 1908 featured maternity and post-mastectomy bras, uplift breast supports, and corsets, a forerunner of campaigns for better prenatal care in *Good Housekeeping, Hygeia,* and *Parents Magazine.* At the other end of the sales spectrum, the Sears, Roebuck catalog brought concise ads to rural America for buttons, aprons, snowsuits, long johns, and brogans. In 1897, copy identified denim pants as Kentucky jeans and offered mechanics' overalls, apron overalls, and riding overalls as well as denim yard goods and brownie suits for children.

Through the work of professional women in connecting female consumers with the best in attire for the household, clothing ads underscored body image and women's control of household expenditures. In 1905, advertisers accentuated drawings in *Harper's Bazaar* of the trendy Lohengrin suit from $15 to $35. Details listed long coats for as little as $12, sturdy lace-up shoes for $2.50, hair switches for $1.50, and knitted wool arctic socks for 25¢ per pair.

Advanced Print Ads

In contrast to economical appeals, publisher Condé Nast achieved class-conscious success through technology, which made *Vanity Fair* the third-largest U.S. magazine in terms of revenue by 1926. Thanks to high-speed color printing on coated stock, in 1932 the company debuted a color cover and double-page fashion spreads. The column "For the Well Dressed Man" advised women on shopping trends and how to purchase men's clothes for business and travel among peers in the corporate world.

A "Smart Set" column and "On and Off the Avenue" explained how to coordinate attire for hostessing, the female contribution to men's success. Sketches of modish ensembles for men, women, and children hyped the latest cuts and hemlines. Photographs by Man Ray and Edward Steichen portrayed the fashion pacesetters of the day—George Gershwin, Greta Garbo, Gertrude Lawrence, and Gloria Swanson—in formal cutaway coats, lounging garments, and sportswear for sailing and motoring.

Ads for leather fashions acquired pizzazz with offerings of Siberian pony, walrus, dolphin, sea leopard, and zebra leather shoes. Sketches of buttoned spats added "ankle dress" to ordinary oxford lace-ups. Contrasting leather pumps called spectators increased the appeal of two-tone lace-ups with zigzag and punched designs for men and women.

In 1922, a new wrinkle in on-site advertising, scented leathers, took on the flower aromas of rose and violet. Less gimmicky media blurbs began to balance bobbed hair with tight cloches, sack dresses, flapper beads, and T-strap shoes. Glamour sketches illustrated shoes made with luxury fabrics, detachable kilts, beaded ornaments, "boudoir novelties," nonslip rubber heels, safe treads, expandable side gores, and flexible arch construction that spared the working woman end-of-the-day fatigue. Advertising copy focused psychological

salesmanship on the "particular woman" with the adjectives "youthful," "smart," "charming," and "elegant," terms not typically applied to descriptions of menswear.

After 1927, celebrity ads popularized the Charles Lindbergh look in sheepskin jackets, helmets, and goggles worn over leather-seated jodhpurs. Specialty leathers offered the conformity to feet necessary for lightweight ballet slippers, leather-trimmed Keds and basketball shoes, chamois Turkish boudoir slippers, sport moccasins, and bathing shoes, which protected soles from sharp shells and rocks. Shoe stores touted novelty straps, fringe, ties, buckles, and tassels as well as matching handbags and caps for adults and children.

During the 1930s, merchants targeted children by featuring the styles favored by school-age buyers. Advertisers surveyed the field for fads, including permanent waves and hair coloring. After 1936, Bass Weejun penny or tassel slip-on loafers appealed to chic college students and to younger businessmen, who abandoned wing tips in favor of a comfortable moccasin.

During World War II, pin-up posters pictured Betty Grable and Esther Williams in one-piece bathing suits, a must-have for teens and college girls. Graphic designers and layout artists filled the first 100 glossy, oversized pages of *Harper's Bazaar* with advertisements of consumer goods, from garter belts to Helena Rubinstein diet systems. Women adapted factory overalls to leisure wear in California-style sports slacks and man-tailored lounging pajamas, as pictured in *Life* magazine. Flight crews posed at high altitudes in leather aviator jackets fitted at the waist and wrist and zipped up to a fur or shearling collar, a garment that became part of the motorcycling attire of the 1940s as these airmen returned home.

In 1948, a Bond Company flagship store erected a spectacular sign in New York's Times Square that featured seven-story images of a nude male and female above a 28-foot by 132-foot (8.5-meter by 40.2-meter) waterfall, a hint at honeymooners at Niagara Falls. At the demand of guests at the posh Hotel Astor across the street, Bond advertisers clothed the nude figures in gold neon drapery. For six years, the sign circulated 50,000 gallons

(190,000 liters) of water spiked with antifreeze to prevent icing and scrolled a message over 23,000 light bulbs and neon tubes claiming "Every Hour 3,490 People Buy at Bond."

Magazine ads flaunted "Dior's daring neckline" and the "I dreamed I . . ." campaign for Maidenform bras, which ran for two decades. The successful "man in the gray flannel suit" and his off-hours pose as an avid sportsman placed a model amid other males who admired the fit and cut of his wardrobe and the reasonable cost of investment dressing. Full-page examples from *Life* magazine flaunted such celebrities as Giants quarterback Chuck Conerly, television star Ed Herlihy, and Giants catcher Wes Westrum.

For the sporting consumer, Harley-Davidson issued its 1912 catalogs with 1,216 items. Copy featured leather jackets, Koveralls, Kant Leak suits, gloves, puttees, and leather-bound hat brims and goggles. Tanned gaiters shielded the calf from spurts of engine oil. As an on-the-road ad, the basic togs of the motorcycling outfit, including the peaked cap, brandished the company's winged logo.

Electronic Media

Beginning in the 1920s, electronic media invigorated consumer advertising with the human voice, music, and live modeling by posed families and individuals touting glamour and romance. Radio blitzes such as fashion talks by *Harper's Bazaar* and voiceover jingles backed name-brand goods, from Buster Brown shoes for children to Pendleton woolens. In the late 1940s, commercial television juxtaposed niche marketing alongside age-appropriate viewing, thus allying cowboy hats and boots with the popular *Howdy Doody* show from 1947 to 1960 and premiering the first women's seamless hosiery on the soap operas *Search for Tomorrow* (1951–1986) and *As the World Turns* (1956–2010).

In the latter part of the twentieth century, celebrity ads, appeals to nonwhite audiences, and sexually explicit photography added clout to straight sales. Ads for Mary Quant defined the miniskirt of the 1960s. Black comedian Richard Pryor made a fashion statement in 1977 with his denim leisure suit, a short-lived quirk in men's tailoring. French film icon Brigitte Bardot promoted the flared look in designer jeans by sporting a tight fit. Actor Tom Selleck popularized scruffy machismo chic in his television hit *Magnum P.I.* (1980–1988).

In the late 1980s, cable television introduced channels devoted exclusively to advertising and call-in purchasing, which treated the viewer to a stream of blurbs for loungewear, jewelry, and accessories. In 1982, the Home Shopping Network offered live showings of fashions and beauty products, sold by interactive order centers. In July 1986, QVC began showcasing Joan Rivers Classics, Affinity diamonds, and Bob Mackie Wearable Art, mostly to women. By 1998, department store owners acknowledged that females purchased 89 percent of men's clothing, an increase from 60 percent in 1956.

Ads featuring couturiers Gloria Vanderbilt, Jordache, Oscar de la Renta, Sergio Valente, and Yves Saint Laurent keyed chic looks to denim, bringing back pleated pants from 1940s zoot suits and dressing women informally in a softer silhouette. Bullying and strong-arm robbery among youth as a result of some fashion campaigns raised an outcry from parents and educators about the snob appeal of designer apparel such as leisure wear and athletic shoes. Feminists alerted the public to the damage young girls incurred by dieting and starving themselves to achieve a size 0, an idealized female shape featured in print and electronic ads.

The floundering economy of the early 2000s required new strategies that balanced direct mail, print catalogs, and electronic media sales. Aiming ad copy at buyers from Fortune 500 companies, on advice from the management of Williams-Sonoma, the 2012 L.L. Bean catalog promoted more than 16,000 products in the United States and 160 countries. The modern facility that replaced the original L.L. Bean store mounted ads in *Field & Stream, The New Yorker, The New York Review of Books, Outdoor Life,* and *Sports Afield,* advertising camera and shooting vests, backpacks, moccasins, and ragg sweaters for men and women.

See also: Dolls, Fashion; Fashion Plates; *Godey's Lady's Book; GQ; Harper's Bazaar; Vanity Fair; Vogue.*

Further Reading

Diamond, Jay, and Ellen Diamond. *Fashion Advertising and Promotion.* New York: Fairchild, 1996.

Nieder, Alison A. *Fashion of the 20th Century: 100 Years of Fashion Ads.* London: Taschen, 2009.

Tungate, Mark. *Adland: A Global History of Advertising.* Philadelphia: Kogan Page, 2007.

———. *Fashion Brands: Branding Style from Armani to Zara.* 3rd ed. Philadelphia: Kogan Page, 2012.

African American Clothing and Fashion

African American attire features the historic influence of garments from the Sahel and sub-Saharan Africa. West African abductees entered slavery in feathered headdress, skins, and body paint and scarification. At the coastal barracoons in Nigeria and Angola, captives bound for the Americas suffered public nudity that began with head shaving to rid them of lice and daubs of tar over wounds. In 1789, Igbo memoirist Olaudah Equiano proposed that British investors cease trafficking in slaves and focus instead on manufacturing garments from African cotton and indigo.

Slave Attire

Installed at Jamaican and Barbadian mansions and Guyanese sugar plantations, slaves made homespun yard goods and secretly fabricated amulets, such as the Yoruban magic square appliquéd on the *agbada* (gown). In Brazil, Haiti, and Louisiana, voodoo shamans brandished *gris-gris,* animistic amulets modeled on Maasai, Akan, or Gyaman symbolism. Ghanaian body art featured the same Asante talismans stamped with bark dye on *adinkra* story panels made from "Negro cloth," an unbleached osnaburg.

At North American slave pens in Charleston, South Carolina, and Annapolis, Maryland, bondsmen from West Africa lost native garments bearing clan and religious ciphers. From their new owners, they received allotments of clothing suited to their employ. At Great Hopes Plantation near Williamsburg, Virginia, butlers and carriage drivers sported tricorn hats and household livery, which bore the braid trim and gold buttons common to British uniforms.

Kitchen staff maintained cleanliness and order with mobcaps or turbans, drawstring blouses, and long skirts and aprons. Framework wardrobes consisted mainly of the loose trousers or skirts and drop-shoulder shirts suited to heavy labor. Head wraps and straw or felt hats warded off heatstroke.

To discourage runaways, slave owners supplied skimpy work clothes and insubstantial footwear hand sewn from cowhide and lined with cardboard. Those who achieved self-liberation relied on gifts from women's sewing societies or goods purchased at used clothing outlets. Upon the flight of Anna Murray and Frederick Douglass to Philadelphia in 1838, Murray made her own bridal fashion with a plum-colored dress. Refugees who served in the Union Army after 1862 received a $3 clothing allowance to buy pants, shirts, and boots from sutlers. Following emancipation, the New York African Society for Mutual Relief dispatched boxes of clothing for children enrolled in freedmen's schools.

Freedom's Wardrobe

Black seamstresses in New Orleans thrived on white clientele seeking the height of nineteenth-century styles and mulatto women soliciting respect. City fashions, borne by steamboat, spread north throughout the Mississippi Valley. One Washington, D.C., dressmaker, Elizabeth Hobbs Keckley, made a gown for First Lady Mary Todd Lincoln to wear to the inaugural ball on March 6, 1865, as well as outfits for Mary Anna Custis Lee and Varina Howell Davis, first lady of the Confederacy.

As discussed in *Ringwood's Afro-American Journal of Fashion* and *Half-Century Magazine,* black fashion became the freedman's preoccupation. Throughout Reconstruction, black churches offered services and social events at which members could dress in African American style. Ensembles featured the hairdressing, bold colors, and patterns from nature derived from African ancestry. The baptism of African Americans into fundamentalist faiths required total immersion in rivers or streams. Prospective members attended the ceremony in white headcloths and gowns sashed at the waist, the style once worn by Egyptian priests.

During the Pan-African movement begun in 1887, entertainers set the tone of black pride and extravagance in the arts, a free-spirited philosophy that influenced the Harlem Renaissance. Flapper Josephine Baker frolicked on stage in fan earrings, long beads, and her famous jungle skirt shaped from mock bananas. In Greenwich Village in 1922, poet Claude McKay posed in a Sudanese turban and robe while proffering a royal staff. At Harlem's Cotton Club into the 1930s, band leader Duke Ellington and his musicians performed jazz in top hats and tuxedos, an upgrade from the self-abnegating costumes of minstrel shows.

A rebellion against fabric rationing in March 1942 caused ghettoized black hipsters in Chicago, Los Angeles, Detroit, and Memphis to turn to exhibitionism. They flaunted reddish conked (straightened) hair processed in lye and slicked up the back with Murray's Pomade. Urban "zoot-suiters" dressed in duo-toned knob-toed oxfords, overpadded jackets, and baggy "reet-pleat" pants with pegged cuffs and accessorized with long pocket chains, monogrammed belts, and fedoras. In dancehall displays of the Lindy and bebop, their garish combinations of red, plum, aqua, and yellow mocked the somber gray and navy suits of white businessmen and the uniforms of soldiers.

Black Fashion Power

A glossy pocket digest, *Jet,* published weekly by Chicago entrepreneur John Harold Johnson, surveyed hair, clothing, and shoe styles. The debut of the magazine on November 1, 1951, issued positive images of black Americans in "The Week's Best Photos" and images of high-society brides and grooms, "Beauty of the Week," and "Woman of the Year." Covers featured such black entertainers as Dorothy Dandridge and Harry Belafonte in Caribbean beachwear, Patti La Belle with big hair, the Jackson Five in sequined ice cream suits, and Diana Ross and the Supremes in tight jumpsuits

and sheaths split to the hip. *Jet's* photo backlog amassed the world's largest collection of African American images.

Johnson focused on black culture and its impact on world art and aesthetics. In 1958, he and his wife, Eunice Walker Johnson, initiated Ebony Fashion Fair, the world's largest itinerant fashion show. Held in black towns, the production featured animal prints, boxy Ethiopian hats, and feathered headdress along with the Fashion Fair line of black cosmetics, launched in 1973. Black-owned media exposure helped introduce African American models to high-fashion catwalks and the covers of *Vogue, GQ, Sports Illustrated,* and *Harper's Bazaar,* beginning in 1965 with Donyale Luna and including Beverly Johnson, Naomi Sims, Iman Abdulmajid, Tyra Banks, and Naomi Campbell.

During the Black Power movement of the mid-1960s, reformer and poet LeRoi Jones (later Amiri Baraka) launched the Black Arts movement in Harlem. Trendsetters promoted African anticolonialism by refusing to conform to white notions of beauty and style. Activist model Tyson Beckford shaved his head for fashion shots. Supporters such as singer Marvin Gaye and Black Panther leaders Bobby Seale and Huey Newton wore Yoruban braids or full Afros, black berets, *kufis* (round caps), circle beards, and African medallions. Female contemporaries such as radical scholar Angela Davis, poet Audre Lorde, actor Pam Grier, and singer Tina Turner adopted tie-up shirts, turbans, hoop earrings, and such traditional accessories as fright wigs and polychromatic kiffa beads, first shaped in glass in Mauritania, West Africa, around 1200.

North, Central, and South American consumers revived the Ghanaian textiles and geometric styles that the Akan, Ga, Asante, Abron, and Ewe of the Volta River basin hand-loomed in the 1000s. Communities patronized boutiques selling black fashions and accessories as well as holiday attire for Kwanzaa, the first Afrocentric celebration in the Western Hemisphere, instituted in 1966. Ritual robes and shirts tended toward yellow, red, green, and black, colors common to Caribbean, African, and South American flags.

In the 1970s, an affinity for all things African resulted in more Ethiopian-style cornrowing of children's and men's hair and the application of the Jheri curl, a glossy permanent treatment that actor Samuel L. Jackson modeled in the film *Pulp Fiction* (1994). Jamaican Rastafarians sported untrimmed beards, Kenyan dreadlocks, and badges and skullcaps. Women indoctrinated into Islam adopted the hijab as a symbol of modesty and female submission. Teens involved in hip-hop music in the 1980s popularized the high-top fade, a male hairstyle closely shaved at the bottom and rising to a full-length crown. Women invested in clip-on extensions and fusion weaves.

Phat Farm, FUBU, Rocawear, Baby Phat, and other African American labels marked distinctive urban styles for youths and adults, notably denim, tie-dye, and platform shoes. In 2005, singer Beyoncé Knowles began designing ready-to-wear for the House of Deréon. After the death of singer Michael Jackson in 2009, boys and girls adopted his signature fedora.

In the second decade of the twenty-first century, African folk weaving and motifs influenced couturier and multicultural ready-to-wear dashikis (tunics), boubous (loose gowns), and *tignons* (turbans). Apple Bottoms and Dana O marketed jeans and lingerie accommodating black tastes and camisoles revealing breasts. Variations on academic and pulpit robes decorated the European stole with the complex patterns and bold colors of kente cloth. Traditional cotton *bògòlanfini* (mud cloth), dating back to the 1100s, retains the zigzags, rectangles, and star patterns in the earthy colors of Nigeria and southeastern Mali.

See also: African Clothing, Sub-Saharan; Hairdressing; Models and Modeling.

Further Reading

Bailey, Eric J. *Black America, Body Beautiful: How the African American Image Is Changing Fashion, Fitness, and Other Industries.* Westport, CT: Praeger, 2008.

McCollom, Michael. *The Way We Wore: Black Style Then!* New York: Glitterati, 2006.

Reed Miller, Rosemary E. *The Threads of Time, The Fabric of History: Profiles of African American Dressmakers and Designers from 1850 to the Present.* Washington, DC: Toast and Strawberries, 2003.

African Clothing, Northern

North African clothing history covers a range of materials and styles. Around 88,000 B.C.E., Algerian hunter-gatherers in the Tassili n'Ajjer mountain range dyed shell beads and disks with red ochre to create a colored accessory and wearable currency emulated by the Moroccan Tuareg after 80,000 B.C.E. Paleolithic clothiers combined pelt garments with woven belts and accessories. Egyptian fiber vestiges from 6500 B.C.E. indicate pre-knitting yarn crafts adopted from North African Berber cameleers traveling the Sahara Desert from the area of Morocco southeast to Mali on the Niger River.

Northwest Africans of the Capsian culture (10,000–6000 B.C.E.) reddened corpses with ochre to brighten the afterlife. At Ait Khabbach, female Moroccans painted themselves yellow and red with saffron and henna and shielded soldiers from injury with guardian symbols inscribed on the right hand.

Because Egyptians respected the dead, textile makers wove ramie bast into shrouds that restored the shape of shriveled corpses. Thus, more North African clothing survived in Nile-side tombs and on mummies, as with ribbon fillet securing the hair and waist ties binding the linen tunic. The pharaoh depended on ties to hold his false beard to the ears.

Embroidery figured in eastern Mediterranean trade linens. At Abydos in Asia Minor, needleworkers from 5500 B.C.E. assembled floss tinted with imported Assyrian woad (*Isatis tinctoria*), indigo (*Indigofera tinctoria*), or madder (*Rubia tinctorum*), which dyed thread a rust hue. By 5000 B.C.E., North African farmers crossbred wild flax to rid fibers of insects and lint.

Around 4000 B.C.E., the cultivation of henna (*Lawsonia inermis*) and sumac (*Rhus coriaria*) extended the seamstress's palette with reddish-brown for dyeing wool and leather as well as hair. Dye processors at Athribis in Lower Egypt discovered how to make henna colorfast in linen corpse wraps by adding metallic salt mordants. Later technology produced green and purple linen yarn by mixing Arabian or Libyan yellow turmeric (*Curcuma longa*) with Yemenite indigo or local reds.

Farther west, Algerians, Tunisians, and Moroccans tinted wool shawls with herb bunches to yield red, yellow, or orange concentric geometrics. From 4000 B.C.E., clothiers wove linen strips for corpse wraps and dyed ordinary skirts and tunics indigo blue. Some priests enveloped themselves in leopard or panther skins, ceremonial capes and vestments garnished with imported foxtails and charms, and white sandals plaited of papyrus. Court cloaks from 3400 B.C.E. displayed sophisticated understanding of patchwork and padding.

During the desertification of the Sahara after 3200 B.C.E., intense heat drastically altered lifestyles. Egyptian courtiers cooled themselves with hand fans and went to their graves bald, but wearing helmet-like head coverings and false beards. After 3150 B.C.E., Pharaoh Menes's *pschent* (double crown) represented his dual sovereignty over Upper and Lower Egypt, signified by the red Egyptian corona and the white Nubian dome. Feathered fans remained the accessories of the vizier and courtiers.

A bas-relief from 2500 B.C.E. pictured Egyptians defeating their Libyan neighbors, men wearing distinctive full beards, shoulder locks, pendants, and chest bandoliers. Two centuries later, chroniclers pictured the nearly nude Libyans cloaked in leather on one shoulder. Historical detail proved that Libyans neither made nor purchased woven goods.

Social Status in the Ancient World

From 2200 B.C.E., while commoners dressed in hemp bag tunics, triangular undergarments, and rush sandals, Pharaoh Pepi II displayed priestly authority with splendid ritual aprons. Grave goods of deceased aristocrats included ostrich shell chokers, faience amulets, and nail treatment with tinted lotions and henna. Sweeping in from the Levant, upland Hyksos chariot warriors covered their skulls in caps pieced from boar tusk scales.

Around 2000 B.C.E., Nile Valley slaves abandoned the weaving of coarse palm fronds, reeds, and rushes and operated flax and wool mills that enlarged the textile industry. In 1897 B.C.E., Senusret II wore beaded chest jewelry of cloisonné (vitreous enamel) inlaid with lapis lazuli and turquoise. Shrines to the goddess Isis issued temple workers white tunics stitched with emblems. Israelites fleeing from bondage into the Sinai after 1523 B.C.E. took with them linen technology that supplied their tabernacle with drapes and Aaron's priestly attire.

In 1323 B.C.E., Tutankhamen's court raiment included a kingly collar, crown, crook, and flail, symbols of inherited power, sovereignty, herding, and agriculture. After 1187 B.C.E., Ramses III, the last great pharaoh, wore a quilted tunic, evidence of sophisticated needlework. Courtiers displayed prominence with feather or palm leaf fans. Noblewomen applied honeyed lotions to the hands and slept in silk gloves to soften skin. Security guards laced a version of the Greek boot with thongs.

The djellaba (an outer robe with knit leggings) and kaffiyeh (wound cloth turban) have long provided the Berbers of Morocco, Algeria, and Tunisia with protection from desert sands and mountain cold. *(Independent Picture Service/UIG via Getty Images)*

Around 800 B.C.E., North Africans traded slaves and gold with Carthaginians for luxury fabrics. Greco-Roman cultural intermingling influenced north Mediterranean dress, as with the placement of the Libyan aegis on statues of Athena, the addition of Libyan leather goods to Greek military dress, and the sale of garnets delivered by Berber caravan from the Niger in Mali to Carthage on the Gulf of Tunis.

Outside Influence

The colonization of North Africa by Romans after 49 B.C.E. resulted in the destruction of Libyan religious statuary, the record of their clothing and accessories. Newcomers injected European styles into common dress, particularly the thigh-length cotton tunic, which locals wore unbelted and flowing. Egyptians entwined ivy collars Roman-style with narcissus, lotus buds, and pomegranate blossoms. The wealthy looked to Phoenician middlemen as dealers in purple textiles, the key luxury item in the Mediterranean microcosm.

Algerian and Tunisian peasants admired the stringent Donatists, fourth-century C.E. Christians who limited their outerwear to rough Numidian wool capes. Christian Copts knitted reinforced sandal socks and displayed their faith with gold symbols painted on slippers. According to Greek, Roman, and Byzantine eyewitnesses, only the Berbers continued to shave their heads and drape themselves in animal pelts and soft tanned goatskins topped with rough shoulder wraps.

From Arabia across Libya, Algeria, and Tunisia to the Atlantic coast, the imposition of Muslim dress codes after 634 supplanted clan lifestyle with sweeping religious regulations. Severe Muslims inflicted a minority image on Zoroastrians, Jews, and Christians. Under the Pact of Umar I in 637, non-Muslims lived and worshiped unmolested in the central Maghreb only if they dressed austerely and wore a waist cord and patchwork headdress as evidence of submission.

For Muslims, devotion to Allah required *tiraz,* the stitching of scripture on the ritual *rida* (cloak) and everyday garments. Leatherworkers inserted holy phrases from the Koran in men's belt channels as divine protectors for newly converted Muslims.

Adherence demanded the storage of men's shoes with soles down to spare heaven an insult. During the detailing of men's wardrobes, women's attire in the second century of Muslim control received scant mention.

Blended Cultures

After 711, only Sharifan Morocco and Berber tribes maintained the Phoenician and Byzantine elements of traditional dress. The flat, untailored Algerian or Tunisian burnoose (hooded cloak) and Moroccan djellaba, derivatives of the hooded Roman *paenula* (traveler's cloak), dominated desert wear, especially in the Atlas Mountains of Morocco, Algeria, and Tunisia. Under Sharia (Muslim law), Jews and Christians in 850 received a humbling directive ordering the wearing of a patch-like white badge shaped like an ape or pig. The suppression of colorful garments in 1009 under al-Rahman Sanchuelo of Córdoba forced North Africans to adopt the undyed Berber turban.

Under the Almohad caliphate (1130–1269), Moroccan males sported varied turban shapes, both round and ovoid, with pendant cloth hanging down the back. In contrast to the tiaras of noblewomen, Moroccan and Algerian peasant women adopted a modest form of veiling that they removed indoors or for mourning. Only female slaves remained exempt from restrictive headgear. From 1184, Tunisian Jews converting to Islam obeyed distinctive dress codes requiring yellow apparel and turbans. Violators could suffer stoning.

After the Mamluks subdued Egypt on May 2, 1250, punitive regulations regarding burkas and the black mesh *miqna'a* (face covering) forced women to remain out of sight. Across the Sahara, females draped the lower face in a *litham* (mouth veil) or pulled on a head sack with eyeholes. Because of the recapture of Moorish Spain by Christians on January 2, 1492, Jews lost their wardrobes and jewelry to pillagers. Sephardic Jewish and Muslim embroiderers and weavers retreated from Andalusia across North Africa to ply their trades free of coercion.

According to the *Descrittione dell'Africa* (*Description of Africa,* 1550) by Moorish chronicler Leo Africanus, peasants in the early sixteenth century dressed in simple white wool and silver anklets, while wealthy Moroccans at Fez flaunted broad-sleeved Venetian jackets and turbaned caps. Key to the era's style, imported luxury fabrics complemented linen pantaloons and boots. Noblewomen covered robes and trousers with an enveloping linen body wrap secured at the shoulder with the Roman fibula (pin). For accessories, they decked wrists and arms in gold ornaments, which laws reserved for Muslims.

Under control of Ottoman Turks at Algiers and Tunis, Arab weavers marketed silks and woolens. Tailors sought *catifa* (wool velvet) for sewing short cloaks, part of the uniform of Turkish janissaries. Gilded silk imported from Almería, Málaga, and Murcia in Spain supplied North Africans with material for the corselets and whirling skirts of Jewish and Ibero-Moroccan women.

From the 1600s, Algerians required Jews to wear black shoes rather than typical Islamic yellow. At Fez, Marrakesh, and Meknes, Moroccan Jews had to remove their shoes on the streets while passing a mosque. Koranic obligation required elite Muslims to dress servants in fine livery and to distribute alms and clothing to beggars at the gate.

Trade Goods in the Modern Era

In the 1800s at Naqada, Egypt, weavers stylized historical and religious motifs in cotton and silk for the burka and aba (man's gown). At Tripoli, corsairs traded with Libyan Muslims finery confiscated from captives in exchange for rations and munitions. Burglars sorted stolen garments, shoes, and cosmetics into those suitable for resale to Jews and to Arabs.

Under the rule of Ahmad Bey in the 1820s, Tunisians feted Mamluk visitors by presenting them with ceremonial robes, jewelry, and diamond-encrusted swords much envied at Istanbul. The cosmopolitan nature of the North African coast drew Sicilian net-fishers, Maltese laborers, and Greek, Spanish, Maltese, and Tuscan traders, including peddlers of Iberian woolens and merchandisers of cotton and silk handkerchiefs.

Outsiders shaped North African dress more overtly in the mid-1800s. In Tunis, the foreign population doubled to 15 percent. French nuns influenced Tunisian peasants by feeding and clothing some 800 destitute schoolchildren in uniforms donated by Europeans. Foreign observers noted the dominance of loose robes, the woman's patchwork dress, winding headcloths for men, and unisex cork-soled sandals. As rail and steamer transportation through the Suez Canal reduced the cost of British cottons and woolens, French accessories, and Syrian yarns and silks, coastal Tunisians and Moroccans sold fewer fezzes, leather shoes, and textiles and imported more European styles.

Cosmopolitan Wardrobes

At Tangier during the 1850s, while Jewish Moroccan women continued submitting to modest Arab veiling, the harem of Sultan Abd al-Rahman ibn Hisham puzzled over the bonnet and corset of bourgeois European visitors. Urbanites gossiped about the immodesty of Christians associated with Italian rebel Giuseppe Garibaldi.

Simultaneously, daring Jewish males flouted sumptuary laws by refusing to abandon European dress for dark caps and patches. Only elderly rabbis continued to don traditional anti-Semitic garb. By the 1870s, Catholic émigrés to Tunisia rapidly altered dress codes and behavior patterns from dominant Muslim austerity to a creolized culture.

Differentiation of origins and tribes required minute observations of robes, turbans, and hairstyles. The identification of outside influences became crucial to decolonization during the late 1950s, when North Africans acclimated to the withdrawal of Italians from Libya, the British from the Suez Canal, and the French from Algeria, Tunis, and Morocco. The modernization of dress and behavior caused scrutiny of minutiae in fabrics and styles reflecting Koranic teachings, particularly the public dress of Muslim women and the clothing of the Egyptian poor. Youth influenced by the media questioned adult customs. By 1962, universal education of Berbers further altered traditions with the introduction of a broader worldview.

In the 2010s, King Mohammed VI of Morocco dresses like a Westerner except on religious holidays, when he wears a white robe, cloak, and turban. In the mountains of Algeria and Morocco, the djellaba with knitted leggings and a skullcap or a kaffiyeh (a scarf often wrapped around the head) remains the favored outfit of Berber herders. Rural Berber women maintain the traditional burka accessorized with a black *bedla* (head scarf), painted leather bag, and silver bracelets. In Tunis, men favor the red felt *chechiya* (cap) as national dress. In western Egypt, rayon has replaced cotton and silk in shawls traded to Sudan and Libya and sold to tourists. The traditional white turban pairs with a *jellabiya*, a long, full caftan that offers wide sleeves containing pockets to hold cash, keys, or tobacco.

Moroccan urbanites favor the short-sleeved cotton *thobe*, a collarless Arab caftan worn with sandals. In the M'zab region of north-central Algeria, clothiers mark the *gandura* (man's tunic) with protective symbols. Female garments vary by tribe: women at Daqahliya Oasis east of Cairo follow traditional patterns of bodice embroidery; at Bahariya Oasis in western Egypt, females mark their native bodice with shoulder tassels. In contrast to rural apparel, at urban centers from Marrakech to Cairo, local people shopping at souks (open-air markets) purchase Western suits and ties as well as jeans, T-shirts, and running shoes.

See also: Burka; Cotton and Cotton Products; Ethnic and National Dress; Priestly Attire; Ritual Garments; Textile Trade.

Further Reading

Becker, Cynthia. *Amazigh Arts in Morocco: Women Shaping Berber Identity.* Austin: University of Texas Press, 2006.

Naylor, Philip Chiviges. *North Africa: A History from Antiquity to the Present.* Austin: University of Texas Press, 2009.

Stillman, Yedida Kalfon. *Arab Dress, A Short History: From the Dawn of Islam to Modern Times.* Ed. Norman A. Stillman. Boston: Brill, 2003.

African Clothing, Sub-Saharan

- -

The history of sub-Saharan African dress reflects the struggle of tribal custom and self-awareness against change. After 180,000 B.C.E., early *Homo sapiens* in central Africa and present-day Ethiopia on Africa's horn turned natural materials into garments. From 42,000 B.C.E., bushmen, the hunter-gatherers of the areas now known as Angola, Botswana, Lesotho, Mozambique, Namibia, South Africa, Swaziland, and Zimbabwe, protected the male groin with a thong breechcloth held in place by a cord or sinew waistband. Batwa herders indigenous to Rwanda turned goatskins and hammered barkcloth into rudimentary attire.

By 2000 B.C.E., African clothiers added woven yarns to workable materials that included feathers, fur, and young leaves of the tropical raffia (*Raphia vinifera*), which processors braided, twined, or knotted into apparel. In the Zambezi River valley after 1200 B.C.E., *conus* (sea snail) shell necklaces dotted with metal beads and imported glass ornaments and amulets adorned the San at the neck and waist. The blend of coastal and foreign elements established the reliance of natives on long-distance barter.

Emulating fabric artisans in Egypt's Lower Nile Valley, Nubian crafters after 800 B.C.E. plied sophisticated East African trades. Accessory makers turned ostrich feathers into fans and fashioned rings, armlets, pendants, and earrings out of faience (tin-glazed ceramic) beads. From the 590s B.C.E., Kushite men and women in the same region covered the lower body in knee-length linen or leather kilts and long wrap skirts, but left the chest bare.

Less easily dated, the fabric arts of sub-Saharan Africa rely on pictographs, oral history, and eyewitness accounts from outsiders. Dynastic dance wear in Equatorial Africa, Congo, and Sudan featured braid and patches sewn on hammered barkcloth, a flat fabric also tucked under the chin as a rain shield. Around Mounts Kenya and Kilimanjaro, upland Kenyan and Tanzanian farmers pressed into commercial centers to buy the leather apparel marketed by plains cattlemen. During the voyage of Persian navigator Sataspes in 480 B.C.E. to reconnoiter West Africa, he reported on diminutive natives dressed in palm leaf garments.

By the mid-400s B.C.E., weavers in Meroë, Nubia (Sudan), crafted gold jewelry from local ore and wove lengths of cotton for export. After

100 C.E., traders on the Red Sea coast at Axum imported refined fabrics and clothing from Asia that served as models for African entrepreneurs. Textile crafts advanced in Central Africa with the weaving of raffia palm fronds while clothiers in Madagascar loomed flax and jute into cloth. By 550, Nubian flax workers turned rough stalks into fine linen.

Historic Changes

In the seventh century, the spread of Islam by missionaries and traders introduced African males to standard Arab dress, the long collarless silk tunic. The Asante of Ghana followed Islamic injunctions against idolatry and stitched magic numbers and Koranic phrases on robes and warriors' shirts. Other peoples of Africa retained ancient practices. Ugandans fashioned their garments from the hammered bark of fig bushes. At Gabon, maskers donned animistic facial coverings and headgear dedicated to harmony and balance.

Nigerians introduced woven fibers in the 800s, three centuries before cotton processing began in Mali, and turned fabric rectangles into wrappers, a body drape passed over the shoulder and under the arm for fastening at the waist. In Ghana in the 1000s, the development of kente cloth by Akan, Ga, Asante, and Ewe of the Volta River basin applied basketry skills to hand looming. Based on spider webs, the bright geometrics, emblematic of peace and purity, took shape from woven strips whipstitched together in the Malian style pioneered by Tellem cliff dwellers.

By century's end, the Bonoman of Ghana and the Ivory Coast profited from trade in kente cloth, which they valued as currency. In Central Africa, Maasai runners sprinkled their feet with granulated bark and cut shoes from raw cowhide or sheepskin. With beads imported from India, they outlined leather capes in simple chevrons.

In the 1100s at San in southeastern Mali, Bamanan hunters evolved a camouflage tunic or shirt from *bògòlanfini* (mud cloth), a fabric hand-loomed by rural women in zigzags, boxes, and starbursts. Apprenticed girls hand-painted lengths in shades of brown with fermented pond sledge and the tannic acid from leaf tea. Dressing women in mud

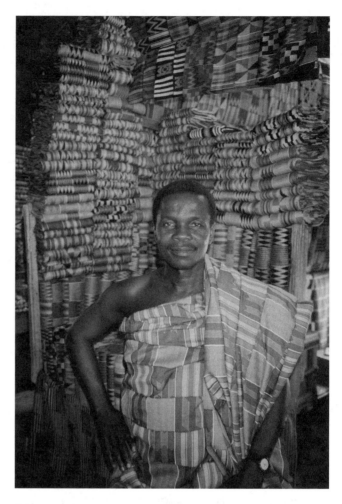

A kente cloth merchant displays his wares at a market in Accra, Ghana. Developed a thousand years ago from basket craft, the loomed geometric designs symbolize peace, purity, vitality, and other qualities in specific colors and patterns. *(Jonathan C. Katzenellenbogen/Getty Images)*

cloth protected them from harm before marriage, after childbirth, during female genital circumcision, and at interment.

Intercontinental commerce expanded the world's awareness of African fabric art. Malian clothiers sold cotton mud cloth garments on the global market. Cultural exchange across the Sahel during the thirteenth century introduced sub-Saharan Africa to iron daggers, woven wool and silk, and apparel from Tunisian ports. Within the century, African cloth manufacturers emulated Arab and European techniques that sold well to Niger River societies.

In February 1353, on a caravan over the Sahara Desert to Mali, Moroccan travel writer Ibn Battuta reported that European and Indian fabrics and yarns had reached imperial Mansa warehouses at Timbuktu. Dealers even bartered goods woven with gold and silver thread, a product of the Byzantine Empire. Observing the Zagawa in the Islamic empire of Kanem-Bornu northeast of Lake Chad, Ibn Battuta found them prospering from the dyeing of cotton cloth with indigo and the export of fancy stitchery through the Sahara to Tripoli.

Fifteenth-century Congo River basin crafts featured Kasai embroiderers who produced Kasai velvet or Kuba cloth, cut-pile damask stitched with raffia. Local people turned the cloth into dance skirts and royal regalia encrusted with cowries, feathers, beads, and couching, and paired outfits with copper masks. Portuguese merchants imported more sophisticated Indian and European weaves that dealers sold in the African interior. Kenyan, Comoro Island, and Cameroon raffia workers supplied markets with tie-dyed garments.

By the mid-1400s along the Sahel, warriors of the Songhai Empire topped combat tunics with iron breastplates and carried leather or copper shields. Their dye masters excelled at processing indigo and the dun yellow of *Anogeissus leicarpus,* a tree rich in tannic acid. After 1463, under reformer king Muhammad Rumfa in Kano, Nigeria, Hausa dye works produced trade goods for sale at the Kurmi Market and on the Mediterranean coast. Reports from Portuguese navigator Vasco da Gama on Christmas 1497 at Natal on Durban Bay, South Africa, noted that native women adorned their lower lips with labrets. On March 2, 1498, he admired the fine wardrobes of residents of Mozambique, who maintained intercontinental commerce with Arabs traversing the Indian Ocean.

In 1493, a royal wardrobe at Kukya, the capital of Gao on the Niger River, passed to the progressive Songhai king Askia Muhammad the Great 210 luxurious ensembles of wool and silk imported from North Africa and cottons woven and glazed at Tera. He promoted the marketing of local gold jewelry, leather goods, and cottons and linen.

After 1600, the Fon of Benin beaded crowns and appliquéd canvas and leather gowns, pants, and headgear with mythic nature shapes and embroidered names or magic charms. The Chokwe of Angola, Congo, and Zambia excelled at curved barkcloth head coverings and ancestral dance masks carved from wood that they believed protected observers from epidemics and other catastrophes. Among the Hausa of northern Nigeria, fabric art copied Arabic battle dress for both horsemen and their mounts.

In the 1700s, Benin warehouses distributed Indian calico and chintz, fine linen, silk kerchiefs, white muslin, and wool yard goods. In February 1772, Tegbessou, the king of Dahomey at Whydah, Benin, expected European ambassadors to bring gifts of silk damask from India for his interpreters and security guard. Among the coastal Swahili on Africa's southeastern shore, fashionable Muslims flaunted in public the finest quality silk turbans and sashes.

According to trader John Adams's *Sketches Taken During Ten Voyages to Africa Between the Years 1786 and 1800* (1822), Guineans north of Sierra Leone marketed bandannas and an unusual trade item, kidskin dyed in indigo in starburst patterns. By the late 1820s, the Yoruba at Abeokuta, Nigeria, produced their own gifts of indigo-dyed *adire* cloth, handspun shirting sewn into women's wrappers. The Hausa version, *adire alabere,* displayed the tie-dyeing of locally woven cotton or wild silk, a commodity shipped west to the Gold Coast and Senegal.

The Fate of Native Fabrics

Nineteenth-century missionaries, who equated Western fabrics and designs with evidence of Christian conversion, orchestrated Africa's reclothing and the initiation of capitalism, especially in the Congo and Nyasaland. Among indigenous art fabrics, the clergy denounced Liberian tie-dye and men's broadcloth suits, Bobo maskers in Burkina Faso, Asante cotton robes of *adinkra* stamped with bark dye, and the Oba coral bead netting in Benin. From outside Africa, Christian instructors inveighed against Nigerian crinolines and high heels and the cotton sheeting imported from Mumbai (Bombay), India, to Africa's east coast.

Culture clash engendered a hodgepodge of customs blended from new and old. In female academies at Botswana, young Tswana girls learned to sew European fashions. In Zanzibar, slaves wrapped themselves in *merikani* (American cloth) and spent their lives with bare feet and shaved heads as marks of humility before masters.

In 1861, outside Lagos, Nigeria, British ambassador Richard Burton approved Nigerian men's styles consisting of loose cotton knee breeches and a cloth flung over one shoulder. The ensemble came to identify black ministers whom the Anglican hierarchy rejected for pulpit service. At Freetown, Sierra Leone, in 1887, West Indian diplomat Edward Wilmot Blyden, the "Father of Pan-Africanism" and author of *African Life and Customs* (1908), established the Dress Reform Society to promote dressing in tribal costumes rather than British suits, starched collars, vests, and neckties, all superfluous in an equatorial climate.

Into the 1890s, the disruption of indigenous fabric arts slowed production and customary barter with *adire eleko,* a Yoruba specialty dyed with a cassava starch-resist method at Lagos and Abeokuta. For the Egungun masquerade ritual, native consumers valued the cloth, which processors figured by scraping a comb over the surface. In Cameroon, King Ibrahim Njoya, a proponent of Bamum turbans, robes, and sandals, encouraged grasslands weavers to continue making *ndop* cloth, an indigo fabric woven on a treadle loom. Wearers folded ndop into body wrappers combined with leopard skins to assert royal status. On the Ivory Coast, a ceremonial mask knitted and braided with sisal captured the ivory, orange, and brown colors of Africa.

From 1900 until after World War I, the suppression of African textile arts coincided with the flaunting of European poplin suits, silk shirts, shoes, and panama hats by young Congolese in Brazzaville and Kinshasa as proof of status. Students in British West Africa attended class in European school uniforms, socks, and shoes—cold weather outfits. In Zambia, the size of a man's wardrobe in imported or mail-order ready-to-wear determined his prestige and status.

The Great Depression of the 1930s in the South African Transkei ended reliance on imported cottons for braided skirts and white sheeting for cloaks and breast ties. Penury returned the hum-

blest in Pondoland, South Africa, to animal pelts. Ignoring Christian proselytizers, pagans retreated to the loincloth with a wool blanket bunched over one shoulder.

The diminution of native crafts continued until the rise of anticolonialism and rebellion against white overlords in the 1940s and 1950s. During World War II, middle-class consumers in the Belgian Congo abandoned unrealistic hopes that salaried jobs and a cash economy would raise black Africans to equality with whites. Blacks in the African interior began wearing with pride the dashiki (tunic), boubou (caftan), sash, head wrap, and bags made from traditional mud cloth and kente cloth, or factory simulations. On the Gold Coast in 1953, women shielded their heads from the sun with bright scarves and turbans borne proudly.

Obligatory Western shirts and trousers failed to erase centuries of African attire. Into the 1970s, enforced dress codes caused riots in Uganda. Among the Maasai of Tanzania, the red tribal *lubega* (one-shoulder toga) and bare backsides maintained ancient traditions along with red ochre body paint to respect tradition and combat lice. From another perspective, women encountered violence in Ethiopia, Zambia, Zanzibar, and Malawi for flaunting miniskirts, wigs, painted nails, complexion lighteners, and lipstick, all symbols of Western decadence. In Ghana, leader Kwame Nkrumah set a flexible standard by varying his selection of native kente costumes and Western suits depending on the occasion and international expectation.

African apparel has remained much in evidence in the 2010s. West African festivals and weddings call for lavish dressing among women. Village and kinship groups in Gambia, Senegal, and Nigeria purchase print fabric from the same bolt, but design dresses, *bubas* (blouses), pants or skirts, boubous, infant slings, and turbans to suit the individual. The system allies women by pattern and vivid colors while encouraging competition and flair in personal ensembles. Men complement bold female attire with the sedate navy or black dashiki, a collarless pullover shirt embroidered with gilt thread. Guineans have popularized polished cotton and brocade. Ghanaians have perpetuated a tradition of black prints on red or white backgrounds.

In modern-day Eritrea and Sudan along the Red Sea, Beja and Bedouin men retain the Arab *thobe,* a long-sleeved cotton, silk, or linen robe left unbelted for wearing over sandals. For monarchs or imams, the *bisht* (cloak) enhances dignity. In Tanzania, Kenya, Uganda, and the Comoros Islands, a similar ankle-length *kanzu* (tunic) topped with a sport coat or blazer adds gravitas to the appearance of men of all faiths. Ugandan clothiers at Mende adorn the sleeves and neckline with emblematic embroidery, a beautification captured in photographs of weddings and receptions.

Tanzanian designs display a collar tassel attached to a polyester tunic and a matching cylindrical *kofia* (cap) usually imported from China, Arabia, or the United Arab Emirates. For formal occasions, both Kenyan and Tanzanian men accessorize the kanzu with a jacket or cloak and cap. Christian men in Kenya and Nigeria prefer drawstring trousers and the dashiki featuring bright colors and elaborate needlework on neckline and sleeves and the matching cap.

See also: Beads and Beading; Breechcloths; Cotton and Cotton Products; Cotton Trade; Ethnic and National Dress; Ritual Garments; Textile Trade.

Further Reading

Allman, Jean Marie, ed. *Fashioning Africa: Power and the Politics of Dress.* Bloomington: Indiana University Press, 2004.

Gillow, John. *African Textiles: Color and Creativity Across a Continent.* New York: Thames & Hudson, 2009.

Gott, Suzanne, and Kristyne Loughran. *Contemporary African Fashion.* Bloomington: Indiana University Press, 2010.

Kriger, Colleen E. *Cloth in West African History.* Lanham, MD: AltaMira, 2006.

Rabine, Leslie W. *The Global Circulation of African Fashion.* New York: Bloomsbury, 2002.

American Western Clothing

Utilitarian Western attire adapted to the exigencies of the American frontier. Before extensive settlement west of the Mississippi in the mid-nineteenth century, mountain men Kit Carson and Jim Beckwourth emulated American Indian dress by turning bighorn sheep, pronghorn, mule deer, and whitetail deer hides into coats and pants. A single hide provided material for carriers for percussion caps and patch knives, drawstring pouches, tomahawk sheaths, fringed gloves, and moccasins with double rawhide soles to cushion the arch.

Doeskin shaped into a cone for smoke curing over a buffalo chip fire produced the softest apparel for breeches and a knee-length hunting shirt, a loose tunic that the trapper or hunter smeared with buffalo grease for waterproofing. A dressier buckskin hunting shirt contained a cavalry bib and double row of buttons. Scraps of buckskin became "wangs" (patches) for repairing torn clothing and replacing moccasin soles.

From military stores in Philadelphia, explorers Meriwether Lewis and William Clark in 1804 received linen and wool overalls to supplement their buckskin travel attire. Standard issue included linen frock fatigues and caps, tricorn hats, flannel drawers, worsted stockings, blue handkerchiefs, gloves, and half gaiters. Members of the expedition wore cloth shirts as nightgowns and switched black high-top leather boots daily between left and right feet for even wear. Shoshone women mended expeditionary moccasins and sewed lynx fur into Clark's cap and glove linings.

Shoshone guide Sacagawea bartered beads with Mandan, Hidatsa, Shoshone, Salish, and Nez Percé for skins to make pullover shirts and beaver pelts for felted waterproof hats. At the height of the expedition, members replaced leather breechcloths and leggings rotted by rain. On the return route, as the party approached the last segment on the lower Missouri River, they traded with woodsmen for woven American flannel and linen shirts and hats.

After the Civil War, army and railroad scouts William Frederick "Buffalo Bill" Cody, Texas Jack Omohundro, and Wild Bill Hickok continued dressing in the buckskin coats and leggings of Western Indian tribes. For hunting jackets, they selected three hides, one for the bodice and two for the sleeves, and fastened the front with skin buttons. For protection, they padded the back and upper thigh sections of pants and the soles of moccasins with extra skins. The attire created the illusion of authenticity in the first Wild West shows in the 1880s, which opened with a procession of cowboys and Indians and included trick-riding cowgirls in fringed split skirts.

Herding Apparel

Outfitting the cowboy required an appreciation for herding in the wild. A cotton bandanna absorbed sweat and covered the lower face during wildfires and dust storms. To prevent snow blindness, herders daubed under the eyes with a mix of grease and soot. A saddle blanket doubled as a warm cape and hood; an oilskin slicker shielded the body against hail or snow. A tall-crowned Stetson hat protected the head from sun and doubled as a ladle for dipping water from springs for horse and rider.

With canvas or denim pants, herders wore hide or leather chaps that fit over boots to ward off snakebite, cactus thorns, and brambles. South American kidskin developed a reputation for scuffing that occurred during the goat's encounters with cactus; this marring of the leather limited its use to mundane bags, caps, suspenders, rain capes, and work gloves.

The invention of barbed wire in the 1860s added to the imperfections in cheap hides and complicated the job of hide sorting. In Alta California, driers on the Pacific shore enlisted the work of vultures to strip rotting flesh from the skins. Tall-masted ships carried salted leather to booteries in Boston and Lynn, Massachusetts, the leather-working centers of North America.

Worn by Southwesterners, the head-to-toe denim outfit earned the designation "Texas tuxedo." Boys dressed like their fathers in homespun pullover shirts, jeans or other long pants, knit stockings, and boots. Bootmakers attached both inlaid and onlaid leather appliqués to boot vamps and uppers. Decorative leather boots with pointed toes and stacked Cuban heels set the dress style for frontiersmen and politicians.

The Settler's Wardrobe

Approaching the American frontier, where dry goods emporiums were scarce, settlers carried fabric for sewing clothes and sewing kits for mending worsted stockings, long canvas aprons, whale-boned jackets, linsey underwear, and round-toed lace-up boots. To make the most of materials, Oregon women unraveled old sweaters to knit into stockings. They restyled adult clothes for children and fashioned baby coats and children's overcoats from the canvas covers of Conestoga wagons, which sun and weather had softened. Sunbonnets with wide bills and neck drapings protected skin from sun and windburn.

Wood pegs held the family wardrobe on cabin walls. Discarded sheeting trousers and women's taffeta dress-up ensembles supplied thread and fabric for sturdier shirts and shifts as well as patches for hand-me-downs. The dominant pattern for new dresses attached Victorian leg-of-mutton muslin sleeves to a collarless bodice with a dropped shoulder line. For maternity wear, the seamstress added fabric gussets at the waist of the long pleated skirt.

Out of modesty, women wore shawls over blouses and skirts or dresses of calico and feed sack material, and, while riding horseback, covered their legs and russet shoes with blankets. Bibi bonnets with lined or ruched brims and straw hats shielded the complexion. For the industrious spinner of thread and weaver of homespun, sales of pioneer goods at stores brought 50 cents for hemp or linen, 75 cents for flannel, and up to $1.50 for woven cotton broadcloth or wool gabardine or serge, typically dyed butternut yellow or walnut brown.

The typical silhouette for girls featured the serviceable gingham or homespun linsey-woolsey long-sleeved dress over petticoats, pantalettes, knit wool stockings, and leather button-up shoes. Special occasions called for cambric shawl collars pinned at the neck, kid gloves, and dusters (loose coats) of brilliantine, a mixed-fiber fabric. Saloon girls sported lace, flounces, and bustiers, a mockery of patriarchal control in the Eastern states.

From Frontier to Fashion

Jeans and denim vests over flannel shirts outfitted miners during the California Gold Rush of 1849, when panners chose durable garments made with fabric more easily washed and dried than wool. The influx of miners brought new demands for boots and brogans on the frontier, where hard labor and panning in creeks rapidly broke down leather shoes and dissolved insoles. Wise pioneers carried their own shoe repair kits, which included scraps of suede, rawhide, and leather for patches and babiche for lacing.

Cobblers newly arrived to Canada and the United States found opportunities in repairing casual and sport shoes and handbags. After Norman leatherworker François Byssot built the first tannery in 1668 at Pointe-Lévy, Québec, French Canadian cobblers bought his cow and porpoise hides to make ankle boots and muffs. Shoemakers sold imported and ready-made shoes and winter boots to farm women and work and safety boots, brogans, and gaiters to their husbands. Asian immigration in California in the 1880s produced Chinese and Japanese cobbleries, where artisans repaired leather goods and trained apprenticed leatherworkers.

Dude ranches, Southwestern artists, and the cowboy films of the 1930s contributed to the cachet of denim pants, leather aprons, and the Stetson hat as inexpensive, functional ready-to-wear items for riding, horseshoeing, wagoneering, and climbing. Cattle herding and other ranch work spawned the rodeo, a demonstration of roping, bulldogging, barrel racing, and bronc and bull riding. Demand for typical dress in hide chaps over jeans and fringed gloves gave jobs to Cheyenne and Sioux buckskin workers.

Durable Western outfits gained pizzazz from Spanish-style hats, ponchos, spurred boots, reatas, and quirts plaited out of rawhide. Costuming influenced the movie industry with simulations of Native American hide garments and accessories. By the mid-1990s, as designers modified Western attire with more expensive materials, fashion dictated greater harvesting of Argentine, Brazilian, Bolivian, and Paraguayan tegus and Southeast Asian lizards for cowboy boots.

See also: Boots; Denim and Jeans; Hats, Men's; Hides; Leather and Suede.

Further Reading

Foster-Harris, William. *The Look of the Old West.* New York: Skyhorse, 2007.
George-Warren, Holly, and Michelle Freedman. *How the West Was Worn: A History of Western Wear.* New York: Harry N. Abrams, 2001.
Krohn, Katherine. *Calico Dresses and Buffalo Robes: American West Fashions from the 1840s to the 1890s.* Minneapolis, MN: Twenty-First Century Books, 2012.
Lindmier, Tim. *I See by Your Outfit: Historic Cowboy Gear of the Northern Plains.* Glendo, WY: High Plains, 1996.

Amerindian Clothing, Pre-Columbian

Amerindian dress in prehistory relied entirely on natural materials. In the Great Basin of the North American continent, the distinctive geometrics of Pueblo stitchery on skin breechcloths, sashes, and mantas (blanket capes) predated Columbus's contact with the New World. In what is now the southwestern United States, the Navajo developed a unique form of embroidering feathers into animal pelts to make blanket robes.

Archaeological evidence in the Southwest—primitive nets of cedar bark and yucca fiber braided, knotted, and twisted in prehistory—links the first woven blankets with a gift from the mythic creator, Spider Man. Across the Great Plains, buffalo blankets adapted quickly into winter robes, which converted from bedrolls to cloaks and back to bedrolls as the day progressed. The Crow, Cheyenne, Sioux, Kansa, and Arapaho of the southern Plains rode horseback on rawhide saddle blankets. Along the Colorado River, the Mojave stitched rabbit skins into blanket robes.

From 7000 B.C.E., the Anasazi of the Great Basin decorated elk hide robes with rabbit fur and eagle and turkey feathers. In the Southeast, the Green Corn Dance concluded with gifts to the male participants of blue or white shaved crane or egret feathers to adorn their headdresses. Among Plains tribes, eagle and hawk feathers, symbols of communication with deities and of speed and courage, contributed stature and dignity to ritual attire. At kiva spiritual ceremonies, Pueblo participants attached prayer feathers to the neck and each foot. The Hopi dressed kachina dolls, masks, and prayer sticks with feathers, the emblems of prayer. For the dead, they tied an eagle feather to the top of the head as a token of the spirit's departure from the body to the afterlife.

Dance regalia often featured owl feather

headdresses, swan feather fans and wands, or red caps made from woodpecker pelts and long black and white feathers. War bonnets contained 30 feathers around the head and more feathers in the parallel trailers. Additions to the war bonnet denoted kills in combat. Among the Maidu of California, women adorned themselves for ritual in dance plumes or feather bunches. Men topped their heads with plumed crowns, headdresses made of wood bases, feathers and quills, and sturdy rawhide fasteners.

Pueblo Indians of Arizona and New Mexico so prized feather adornment that they collected 219 different species of feathers as demonstrations of tribal pride and tradition. Among the tribes west of present-day Santa Fe, New Mexico, embroidering animal pelts with feathers produced unusual blankets and serapes (shoulder wraps). Just as initiates to the Ghost Dance received eagle feathers, Lakota parents presented a single eagle feather or plume as a gift in an adoption.

Hide and Woven Costume

In the "hide age," indigenous Americans chose materials for clothes and footwear from the pelts or skins of antelope, bison, cattle, deer, elk, and Rocky Mountain goats. The Native American breechcloth covered the groin with an undergarment and two flaps, a back panel and front apron. Northeastern Abenaki cinched their loincloths with rawhide belts. The Pueblo of the Great Basin used rust, red, green, and black yarn to embroider breechcloths, which they finished with tassels.

From 1200 B.C.E., the Olmec of present-day Veracruz, Mexico, loomed breechcloths of cotton and woven plant leaves. The Aztec later traded similar garments with Spaniards for Iberian fabrics. From 1000 to 1550 C.E., the Mississippi Indians at Etowah made short-fiber yarns from mammal fur and turkey down to prevent fraying in belts, sashes, shoes, medicine bags, and breechcloths. Around 600 C.E., the abbreviated breechcloth that Choctaw men attached to wide leather belts served as athletic shorts for playing chunkey, a rowdy ball game.

Native American embellishment of buckskin

left materials and patterns up to women. Huron breechcloths displayed fur strip appliqué, painting, and fringe. The Seminole of Florida embellished the tapered loincloth with zigzag appliqués. On the Great Plains, Blackfoot women stitched ribbon chevrons on men's breechcloths, which reached to the ankles.

The three blanket types of the Deep Southwest consisted of Navajo, Pueblo, and Chimayo or Old Rio Grande style. From the 500s, Pueblo tribes, the descendants of the ancient Basketmaker, wove their handspun cotton into blankets and infant carriers on upright home looms. Hopi and Zuni needleworkers embroidered distinctive geometric stitchery on agave and cotton kilts and mantas, which they suspended from the front door frame in winter to block cold wind. They chose cotton because it surpassed wool in strength when wet and did not pill or mat. Pueblo weavers pressed weft threads so tightly that the cloth could store water as well as canvas.

Body Embellishment

For body painting and tattooing, Native Americans typically chose celestial symbols, including comets, lightning, and moons, as well as the number of kills in battle. At potlaches (gift-giving ceremonies), families identified their membership in clans with paint. In the Great Basin, Navajo, Pima, and Walapai chose iron oxide as a skin emollient and sun shield as well as a treatment for wounds. Hopi clowns, the Koshari and Tsukuwimkya, accentuated grotesquery with painted dots and stripes of soot or corn smut.

Plains tribes—Blackfoot, Cheyenne, Comanche, Sioux—decorated themselves and their horses with dramatic emblems. The Blackfoot applied paint before prayers accompanying medicine bundle ceremonies. The Dakota daubed the critically ill with red, a practice similar to that of the Arunta of Australia. Colorants marked a liminal state that preceded departure to the land of the dead. Among the Nootka, the topping of body paint with mica flakes added glitter to matte tones.

Among the Kuna of Panama and the Achual, Karaja, Shipibo, Txukarramae, and Warran Indians of the Amazon and Orinoco rivers in

South America, the use of annatto (*Bixa orellana*), charcoal, and huito (*Genipa americana*) produced a palette of red, black, and gray that warded off biting insects. The Bororo of present-day Mato Grosso, Brazil, used geometric lines and motifs to identify themselves as belonging to a clan. For their neighbors, the Caiapó (or Kayapo), black body dye camouflaged hunters in the rain forest. The Xinguano, relatives of the Caiapó, painted themselves for wrestling matches. Containers of pigments proved valuable as commodities for trade with Andean tribes.

In the Amazon rain forest, Yanomami natives used skin designs in purple, red, and white clay as their only written communication. Black visage and torso coverings implied the facing of death in combat. Women chose black cheek paint to show sorrow. The Kadiwéu and Tirió of Mato Grosso covered female cheeks with geometric motifs. The Camayura used red and black dyes mixed with fish oil to transform hair and face. In what is now Tabasco, Mexico, the Tenosique turned themselves into jaguars by daubing their bodies with clay, adding ashen rings as spots on fur.

In what is now Ecuador, nudity and body painting became the normal dress of Indians. The Valdivia painted their torsos with wide colored bands and incorporated hairstyles with face art by applying a dressing of achiote and wax. Early tribes patterned themselves with roller stamps or clay stamps. From as early as 1500 B.C.E., the Machalilla inscribed circles and stripes over the face and body. After 900 C.E., the Chorrera embellished their naked skin with a painted-on vest and wrap skirt or pants.

Protecting the Young

Across the Western Hemisphere, indigenous people adorned themselves with protective jewelry and needlework that warded off curses and assuaged fears. Examples include the hematite jewelry of the Cahokia mound builders of modern Illinois from 400 C.E., beaded medicine wheels dangling from the head of an Iroquois cradleboard, shell or bead talismans suspended from the Inuit *amauti* (parka), and beneficent spiders embroidered on the clothing of Mexica children. Among the Huichol in the

Sierra Madres of present west-central Mexico, to defend wearers from accidents and disease, women outlined peyote visions and hallucinations in woven and embroidered patterns on peasant blouses, belts, and bags. They wove five-petal blossom patterns into fabric, depicting stylized peyote buttons, and applied the design to deer hide.

In the Pacific Northwest, styles of swaddling shaped infant posture. Chinook and Kwakiutl mothers attached stones to the skull to flatten it, broaden the face, and slant the forehead, a custom also adapted by the Hopi, Ute, and Osage with tight bindings and flat wood slabs. Among the Makah and Nootka, leg bindings above and below the calf created bulges, a valued curve in the lower leg.

The Apache wove cradleboards out of flexible cattail, dogwood, tule, and willow and enhanced infant comfort with a footrest and face shade. The Cayuse differentiated male and female designs by providing the male baby with a slot in the lacings for urinating. A mother could attach the carrier with burden straps, or she could suspend the child down her back with a tumpline fastened around her forehead. For long journeys, the baby carrier swung from the pommel of a saddle or nestled against hide coverings of a travois. Comanche babies wore rabbit fur garments and slept in a cradleboard spiked at the top to protect the child's head if the carrier fell.

Hopi and Navajo carriers attached the infant to a pine frame with buckskin straps. The Iroquois opted for a solid wood board and padded the base with cattail down, cliff rose and juniper bark, rabbit fur, or smoked sphagnum moss, providing both a mattress and disposable diaper and bib. Amulets and umbilical cord pouches entertained the infant while a jogging gait rocked the child to sleep. For lengthy stops, the mother leaned the cradleboard against trees or rocks or suspended it from tree branches.

By the time a baby could sit up unaided, Amerindian mothers weaned them from cradleboards and encouraged creeping and walking. For rest periods, the babies napped in animal pelt sacks. Boys of the Apache, Navajo, and Shoshone typically played naked or wore buckskin loincloths.

Caddo girls wore downsized versions of the necklaces, grass aprons, dresses, buckskin leggings, and moccasins of adult females.

Mesoamerica and South America

In a style similar in purpose to that of North American tribes, a Mesoamerican or South American mother positioned her infant in a *rebozo* (shawl or sling) that tied at the shoulder into a cocoon and left the mother's hands free for work. In Central America, when there was no adult available to supervise, the Maya swaddled children from birth to protect them from rolling into a fire pit or drowning in a puddle. A Nahua figurine from 1350 C.E. depicted the bindings securing a child to a cradleboard that left feet and legs free to move.

Stately adornments for Mesoamerican warriors and aristocrats applied the iridescent green quetzal tail to robes, parasols, fans, and crowns. The Mexica specialized in red arara and blue and crimson parrot feathers, later adding quetzal and troupial feathers. For gifts to kings, the Maya traded quetzal feathers with Central American tribes. The Aztec paid taxes in Tenochtitlan with feathers and incorporated feather lore in myths and art featuring Quetzalcoatl, the feathered serpent.

In present-day Ecuador from 355 B.C.E., the Jama-Coaque created distinctive attire for high-status natives. Pottery depicted them in full masks and headdresses with earflaps and pectorals. Loincloths and matching wristbands and anklets completed the ensemble. The feet remained bare.

In the Andes of western South America, from the twelfth century C.E., the Inca collected fine multicolored feathers to adorn valuable feather cloth and cover it like velvet. Warehouses stored a supply of tiny hummingbird feathers and valued most the iridescent types that added a gold or greenish-gold sheen. The women who wove the feathers at the Temple of the Sun held religious rank approaching that of a royal lineage. The emperor guarded feather cloth and restricted its distribution to those who received royal permission to wear it. Blue and yellow feather cloth panels, aprons, and crowns accented in red, fashioned from macaws and tanagers, accompanied royal mummies to the grave.

See also: American Western Clothing; Arctic Attire; Body Painting; Body Piercing; Breechcloths; Customs, Lore, and Myth; Dance Costumes; Fur; Hides; Ritual Garments.

Further Reading

Anawalt, Patricia Rieff. *Indian Clothing Before Cortés: Meso-american Costumes from the Codices.* Norman: University of Oklahoma Press, 1981.

Brasser, Theodore. *Native American Clothing: An Illustrated History.* Buffalo, NY: Firefly, 2009.

Mann, Charles C. *1491: New Revelations of the Americas Before Columbus.* New York: Alfred A. Knopf, 2005.

Amerindian Clothing, Post-Contact

From contact with Europeans after 1492, Amerindians adapted indigenous clothing with new materials and styles. Native clothing styles impressed European settlers with their uniqueness. The centuries since have produced an array of ethnic styles and innovative stitchery, such as the application of porcupine quills to deerskin by the native peoples of Alberta, Canada, and the embroidery of the hair drop, a scalp ornament quilled by Kiowa, Sioux, and Blackfoot Plains Indians to secure a buffalo tail.

History

Upon his arrival in present-day Porto Seguro, Brazil, on April 22, 1500, Portuguese navigator Pedro Álvares Cabral found Tupi maidens and warriors painting themselves with geometric lines in black and red dye as a pastime. The inland Bororo used body art as a means of claiming clan membership.

According to Bernal Díaz del Castillo, the chronicler of Hernán Cortés's conquest of Mexico that began in 1519, the Aztec *maxtlatl* (loincloth) consisted of enough fabric to gird the waist. Designed from two pieces—a narrow strip of grass, maguey fiber, Spanish moss, or hide stabilized at the waist by a band or belt—the simple garment also served the Delaware of the lower Hudson Valley of New York and the Cahuilla and Maidu of California. Along the Mississippi River, the Osage and Missouria supported their deer hide breechcloths with belts woven of bison wool. In the Mississippi and Ohio valleys, French *coureurs de bois* (woods runners) emulated Cree dress by adopting breechcloths and leggings.

When Francisco Pizarro encountered the Inca of Peru in August 1526, native men customarily tied the *huara* (loin covering) with string and displayed a fringed apron that hung below a tunic. Around 1527, Spanish explorer Álvar Núñez Cabeza de Vaca noted the cotton, linen, and wool blankets and serapes, shoulder blankets worn by Pueblo men. In July 1540, explorer Francisco Vásquez de Coronado described how Zuni women used one blanket to wrap the body, knotting the ends over the left shoulder and leaving the right arm free. A sash secured the open side. To retain the bright reds obtained from cochineal insects, launderers washed blankets in *amole,* a natural soap acquired from agave or yucca bulb or root.

From the late 1500s, blankets became the elements of interracial negotiation and introductory capitalism. With the Spaniards' introduction of the *churro* (sheep) via Coronado, Navajo looming developed the wool saddle blanket (folded square) as well as the tasseled wearing blanket, serape, poncho, and manta, self-fringed in natural shades of brown, cream, and tan, for wearing over breechcloths. The bright patterns of black, blue, white, and yellow added colors to drab hogans. Overnight guests could go outdoors and wrap themselves in blankets for sleeping under the stars.

In 1581, colonial artist John White painted a Roanoke Indian wearing a wide fringed loincloth. The apron spread from across the hips to midthigh. The arrival of merino sheep with Mexican explorer Juan de Oñate at what is now El Paso, Texas, in April 1598 contributed to Navajo blanket technology, which gradually overtook basketry and pottery as crafts. Anthropologists surmise that native weavers also unraveled European goods and used the yarn for their own blankets. To enhance the finished piece, weavers embellished blankets at center with beaded blanket strips or medallions and traded them at the great Santa Fe marketplace.

In November 1620, the Pilgrims first saw the Wampanoag at Plymouth clad in hide breechcloths and wampum belts, a beaded trade item valued like currency. In 1674, Gabriel Díaz Vara Calderón, the bishop of Cuba, reported that the Calusa and Tequests, hunter-gatherers of Florida, made their loincloths of palmetto brush, bark bast, animal skins, or woven palm, a style echoed by the Arawak of Haiti that Columbus encountered on December 16, 1492.

As depicted in a statue in Bismarck, North Dakota, Sacagawea, the Shoshone guide and interpreter for the expedition of Meriwether Lewis and William Clark (1804–1806), carried her infant son, Jean Baptiste Charbonneau, in a blanket shawl papoose. The traditional carrier kept him warm and safe over 5,000 miles (8,000 kilometers) from Fort Mandan, North Dakota, along the Missouri River to the Pacific Ocean and back.

Materials from Nature

Newcomers to the Americas discovered the value of native materials for men's footwear, such as sisal or agave twine for Andean sandals and woven leather for Central American huaraches. Among the Aztec of Mexico, low-cost *cactli* (heeled sandals) of yucca offered flexibility to warriors and members of the upper class. For combat, soldiers added the hide shin guard, a Central American version of the greave.

Costumes among the Zuni of New Mexico differentiated members of the badger, corn, coyote, dogwood, and sun clans. For Pacific Northwest tribes, the clan symbol connected a human genealogy to an animal totem or symbol of a progenitor, such as the salmon or whale. Examples include the Tlingit carved headdress and cape interwoven of yellow cedar bark with dog or coyote hair and the wool of the white mountain goat.

In Oklahoma, feathers lined capes for warmth. The Sioux, Kansa, Crow, Cheyenne, and Arapaho of the southern Plains attached rawhide fringe to ceremonial feather fans. South of the Great Lakes, the Iroquois sported the *gus-to-weh,* a hide skullcap layered in short turkey feathers and topped with an eagle feather. As Europeans began settling Canada, they emulated native chiefs in displaying plumage as a token of rank rather than as a fashion statement.

For adults, Mesoamerican natives esteemed long feathers of the cormorant, egret, flamingo, macaw, Muscovy duck, parrot, and tanager. Some decorated the nose cartilage with feathers that imitated mustaches. According to sixteenth-century Spanish eyewitness Abbé Francisco Clavigero, author of *History of Mexico* (1787), the Maya of Central America sewed ostrich plumes and macaw and hummingbird feathers into garments, fans, and ceremonial headdress with agave thread.

To the east of Tenochtitlan, Aztec infantry wore the *ehuatl,* a sleeveless, thigh-length feathered tunic of blue, red, violet, yellow, and white. Only the king's ehuatl bore red spoonbill feathers. Because of the demand in Spain for feather adornment, the Araucani of Chile traded ostrich plumes for grain, iron, knives, and wine.

The Pawnee of Oklahoma used this painted buckskin shirt in the spiritual Ghost Dance ritual of the late nineteenth century. On the Great Plains and across the frontier, native peoples relied heavily on buckskin and other hides for fashioning their attire. *(The Granger Collection, NYC—All rights reserved)*

Buckskin Styles

On the northern Plains of North America, women scraped deer hides to make soft breechcloths, the least binding costume for hot weather. Decoration of buckskin clothing left materials and styles to women's imagination, as with the painted designs, fur strip appliqué, and fringe on Huron loincloths. Across the frontier, the skin loincloth served as daily attire. For the Yokut of San Joaquin, California, the best material for comfort, a strip 10 inches (25 centimeters) wide cut from a deer's neck to its tail, yielded a generous length that paired with a mountain lion pelt for a shoulder wrap in winter. The Yurok along the Klamath River preferred rabbit skin.

A variant style worn by the Salish of Montana reversed the tuck by bringing the cloth over the front of the band to form a neat crotch shield. The Seminole of Florida tailored the breechcloth from hide or coarse strouding cloth; the ends, decorated with appliqué and beaded zigzags, tapered to points reaching to the mid-thigh. Among Pueblo tribes, the Hopi and Zuni adorned breechcloths with geometric embroidery. For Abenaki ritual regalia, an apron panel adorned with fancy stitches, quilling, beading, or painting bore images from nature or symbolic shapes.

Blackfoot breechcloths extended to the ankles to display ribbon appliqué in a chevron pattern. The Pueblo of the Great Basin embellished breechcloths of loomed fabric with red, green, rust, and black embroidery and tassels on the four corners. Mojave women's aprons duplicated the modesty shield of men's loincloths.

Adaptations suited underwear to lifestyle in the finely beaded groin cloth of the Kickapoo, the wool squares covering Piegan Blackfoot loins, and the trade-cloth body covering of the Apache. A Bannock breechcloth fit under a sash. For cold weather, the Fox supplemented their summer undergarment with leggings, moccasins, and a buffalo robe. Among the Western Shoshone, winter required both breechcloths and rabbit-skin blankets for males. Farther south, Aztec mourners burned loincloths and mantles of the dead and smeared the ash on the faces of deceased warriors.

The Medicine Bag

American Indian tribes put their faith in medicine bags of one form or another—a potent buckskin pouch, embroidered bandolier bag, animal paw, snakeskin vessel, or part of a birch bark apron. In varying sizes, sacks held a ceremonial bundle, including such items as magical feathers, raven skin, shells, crystals, pebbles, holy soil, juniper branches, tobacco, and animal parts. Some amulets represented sacred visions of a totemic animal.

Animistic religions placed trust in the natural powers of fetishes, such as the claws of a bear, a turtle's heart, or the fangs of a wolf or coyote killed during a boy's first hunt, a rite of passage. Individuals placed the personal items most meaningful to spirituality and genealogy in buckskin bags, gathering the mystical objects that connected one to divinity, region, and clan. Thus, the personal pouch represented in size and bulk the beliefs of its owner, such as the bags in which Clatsop and Crow girls bore their umbilical cords. The pouch held power for only one person, who never willingly parted with it.

The stitching, fringing, quilling, fur, cording, and beading of the medicine sack among the Sioux and Shoshone constituted an act of love by the female needleworker toward husbands and sons. Women's medicine bags contained amulets and miniature medicine wheels emulating the great circle of creation, which conferred energy, purity, and predictive powers on their users. The Lakota turtle amulet pouch imparted fertility and courage to the female who attached it to a belt. Midwives tucked into their pouches symbols of vigilance, charms against labor pain and birth trauma, and sage leaves for smudging (burning) to cleanse the air. Families included their medicine bags in clan heritage and passed the tribal pouches to successive generations as emblems of values and continuity.

Blankets

The first encounters of Europeans with Amerindians disclosed the value of smoked elk hides for blankets. Further observation of indigenous tribes revealed the tanning of deerskin ground cloths by the Great Lakes Huron and the weaving of wool and cotton yarns by Tarahumara treadle loomers to make *fresadas* (hairy coverlets) and *jergas* (fringed blankets) in the area of Chihuahua, Mexico. Other varieties included the buffalo blankets used by the Mandan of South Dakota and blanket coats with leggings that clothed the southeastern Cherokee. The Western Shoshone made blankets from rabbit skins.

In Manitoba, the Cree and Salteaux decorated buffalo hide with an eight-pointed star design incorporated into ritual. After acquiring woven goods from Europe, native designers adapted their sewing of black, red, white, and yellow yarns on hides into star blankets. In Ontario and Quebec, the Cree crafted blankets with a netting needle or shuttle. To the northwest, blankets bore appliqués and shell designs of totemic significance.

The Pacific Coast Salish turned babiche, a spiral of rabbit fur sliced from whole pelts, into fur blankets, which they traded to the Kutenai and Kwakiutl. Raiding parties sought out the tasseled blanket above plainer styles. Special blankets made of the black, brown, or white hair of *Oreamnos americanus* (mountain goat) shrouded the Salish dead.

Chilkat, Haida, and Tsimshian weavers evolved a complicated matrix that produced contoured dancing blankets that chiefs fastened with bone or wood blanket pins. Each shoulder wrap displayed clan insignia as well as animal and bird faces in traditional black, blue, ecru, and yellow. A distinctive style of blanket robes, raven's tail weaving generated black-on-white geometrics through twining, a technique that evolved from Yakutat basketry. Linear motifs depicted fish flesh, fireweed leaves, clamshells, waves, tattoos, and the tail of Raven, the trickster.

French merchants dispatched from Montreal introduced Canadian Haida, Kwakiutl, and Kutenai, and tribes along the Ohio and Mississippi valleys, to felted, wool, or wool-and-cotton blankets. The original "chief's blanket," a white or cream blanket, appealed to Indians as winter camouflage and accounted for 60 percent of fur trades. Knowledgeable go-betweens judged the mind-set of aborigines by the way they draped their wearing blankets.

One blanket, generally cream fabric striped in bright colors of green, indigo, red, and yellow, sufficed to make a blanket coat, shaped into a caped and hooded long-sleeved overcoat. The Canadian Métis, people of mixed-blood origins, turned blankets into a *capote*, a fringed Indian blanket coat introduced by the French *coureurs de bois,* or woodsmen, which they wore with pointed caps.

During this era, male and female Ojibwa wrapped themselves in blankets for overcoats, which they tied at the waist. In 1670, the Hudson's Bay Company, the world's oldest merchandiser, began trading blankets with Cree, Northern Algonquin, Iroquois, Slave, Eskimo, and Ottawa in exchange for furs. The Shasta and Yavapai acquired woven blankets by bartering leftover hides to Europeans. The swap introduced tribes on the shores of Lake Michigan and Lake Superior, along the Yukon River, and into the Northwest Territories to lightweight bedding and woven textiles less cumbersome and more easily maintained than the fur of buffalo, lynx, marten, mink, muskrat, otter, or sable. In the Southwest, tribes traded silver and turquoise jewelry for blankets to give as gifts, wear at naming ceremonies and weddings, add to dowries, and warm the spirit of the deceased on the journey into the afterlife. In hard times, Indians learned that blankets served as secure currency and pawn items.

In the 1700s, Navajo women devised a two-piece ensemble made of small blankets stitched at the shoulders and sides. A single small blanket swaddled an infant or toddler. The Crow and Nez Percé made the blankets into leggings edged with horsehair fringe. Northwestern shore tribes adorned blanket capes with abalone and dentalium shell buttons and flannel appliqué. They valued blankets for funeral gifts and symbols of affection and respect.

European Materials

The blending of American and European materials rapidly diversified Native American folk styles. Stroud cloth imported from Stroud Valley, England, provided tribes with cheap red fabric blankets bearing a white selvage. Cherokee women fashioned the stroud blanket into a wraparound skirt to replace deerskin. Cherokee males folded stroud blankets into breechcloths. Sioux men turned the stroud blanket into beaded leggings.

Influenced by missionary needleworkers, indigenous peoples of the Western Hemisphere adapted appliqué to crafts, as with reverse appliqué cutouts, layers, and *molas* (designs) adorning Kuna Indian *camisas* (blouses) in the San Blas Islands east of Panama. Similar handwork embellished folk blouses and skirts among the Seminole of Florida, and the ribbon shirts, pectorals, belts, and leggings sewn with deer thongs used for powwows and dancing among Great Lakes Ojibwa, Huron, Iroquois, Ottawa, Sioux, and Potawatomi.

In the 1870s, the U.S. Army's roundup of native tribes limited access to hunting, forcing indigenous peoples to abandon cultural dress and adopt the woven fabrics of their white captors. In 2003, to preserve the spiritual heritage of Native Americans in 562 federally recognized tribes, exemptions for the ownership of eagle feathers enabled the Sioux to observe traditional ritual.

See also: Arctic Attire; Beads and Beading; Blankets; Customs, Lore, and Myth; Fur; Hides; Ritual Garments; Weaving.

Further Reading
Brasser, Theodore. *Native American Clothing: An Illustrated History.* Buffalo, NY: Firefly, 2009.

National Museum of the American Indian. *Identity by Design: Tradition, Change, and Celebration in Native Women's Dresses.* New York: Collins, 2007.

Paterek, Josephine. *Encyclopedia of American Indian Costume.* New York: W.W. Norton, 1996.

Williams, Colleen. *What the Native Americans Wore.* Philadelphia: Mason Crest, 2002.

Amulets

A talisman or good luck charm, an amulet adorns ensembles and fills pouches worldwide to ensure magic, blessing, or protection from ill fortune or harm. In Egypt after 2345 B.C.E., the pharaoh Khati proclaimed that god made magic to ward off evil. As examples, the sacred ibis feather served as both a decoration and a fan that repelled poisonous asps and, in death, the worms that devoured

corpses. More common, the Egyptian ankh (key of life) promoted benevolence and longevity when sewn on fillets and tunics. Two eyes painted or appliquéd to apparel placed the wearer under the protection of sun and moon. The girdle of Isis safeguarded the wearer with the goddess's holy blood; the Isis collar strengthened the heart and breast. Adherence to Ra, the sun god, required a circle with a dot at the center, a common symbol on jewelry that promised eternal life.

Around 2000 B.C.E., the Bhutanese or Tibetan *dzi* bead, a talisman carved from agate in Mesopotamian style, safeguarded the wearer from evil. In Japan and China, shamans fashioned protective attire and adorned it with bells and metal appliqué to defeat hexes. In Africa, the Kushites of Nubia turned crocodile or hippopotamus leather and gold pendants of Isis, Horus, rams' heads, cats, and birds into auspicious amulets. Hausans of the Sahara and Sahel in northern Africa embroidered or painted the six-pointed star and triangular charms on capes as a potent fetish. West African Yoruba needleworkers sewed magic squares on gowns as protections to women.

From about 1300 B.C.E., when Moses led the Hebrews out of slavery in Egypt to liberation in Canaan, scriptural injunction commanded the wearing of *tefellin,* or phylacteries, leather boxes bound to the forehead and arm. Each bore biblical texts on papyrus or parchment, reminders that God demands truth and righteousness. Red thread outlined kabbalistic decor as an emblem of worthy passions and goodness. The engraving of the word *shaddai* (almighty) on jewelry represented the Hebrew concept of God as defender.

As mentioned by the poet Hesiod, Greek magical thinking from around 700 B.C.E. linked divine aid to gemstones—Aries with red jasper, Zeus with chalcedony, Helios with bloodstone, Bacchus with amethyst, and Demeter with green jasper. In Rome, infants wore amber as a source of strength and wellness. Girls relied on a leather or metal *bulla,* a bubble-shaped Etruscan-style capsule containing charms and suspended on a thong or chain around the neck. In 330 C.E., Constantine I the Great, the first Christian emperor, blessed his robes, scepter, and livery with the sign of the Christian cross, the prime fetish of the new faith.

Amulets worldwide attested to creativity in stitchery, leatherwork, netting, and metal craft.

Indonesians marked their daughters with amulet boxes bearing umbilical cords. As girls advanced toward puberty, they wore silver modesty shields, pendants covered in hearts, lotus, stars, grids, labyrinths, and crosses as auspices of purity and virginity.

Celts trusted in the power of mistletoe and the green four-leaf clover. Needleworkers embroidered vines and leaves on linen robes, cloaks, shawls, and stoles for shamans to enfold spirits and project the wearer to a higher plane. Indian talismans—the *aum* (Sanskrit for A, U, and M), *bindi* (dot), mandala (circle), lamp, lotus, conch, swastika, wheel, lingam (coital symbol), flames, red ribbon—evolved into emblems revered by the Roma (Gypsies), who applied occult shapes to garments, jewelry, leather pouches, pocket charms, and forehead markings.

Throughout the Middle Ages, jewelers and needleworkers created objects and designs intended to heal, strengthen, or shield the wearer from attack, such as the endless knot, a Sanskrit symbol revered in China, Mongolia, and Tibet, and the Coptic cross of Egypt. A common amulet, the *hamsa,* a depiction of the right palm, a protector on necklaces and key chains, deflected the evil eye from Muslims, Jews, Buddhists, and Christians. Islamic appliqué incorporated prayers, numerology, and signs, notably fertility symbols stitched on children's bonnets.

Magic apparel boosted confidence, as garments made from the hide of the unborn kid in Arabic faith. Throughout the Crusades, soldiers on both sides wore prayer shawls that conferred blessing. The advance of bubonic plague at Sussex, England, resulted in the creation of aromatic amulets—rose petals, cloves, vinegar, lavender, sage, juniper, rue, artemisia—in pouches and pockets and around the neck, a vulnerable part of the anatomy. Faith in the power of herbs to ward off infection yielded the children's rhyme "Ring around the rosie, pocket full of posies."

Natural charms shielded people from particular threats. Seagoing men treasured the birth caul in pockets and bags as a defense against scurvy and drowning. Yorkshire folk bore potatoes in their pockets for warmth and tucked dog's tongues into their neck pouches to treat scrofula, a tubercular condition. Faith in magic squares in Turkey and India took the form of grids of sacred numbers worn by handicapped children and women in labor and warrior shirts embroidered with protective rectangles.

In Western Europe, needle cases on chains took the shape of a good luck piece to shield the mother of the house. Afghan needlework marked bodices, cuffs, and stockings with the pre-Islamic meandering cross-stitch, Fatima's hand, and a triangle to acknowledge the mother of sons.

Diasporas bore alien forms of magic, such as the Chinese hat amulet and infant jackets and shoes embroidered with defensive animal shapes, jade Buddhas, bells to scare away evil spirits, and a number of longevity symbols. Scots immigrants brought to North America faith in moleskin, which women wore over the chest to prevent breast cancer. For pregnant women, otter skin garments ensured the birth of a healthy child. In the Appalachian Mountains, British newcomers valued asafetida, a noxious plant worn in a neck pouch for its supernatural powers against pneumonia. Another amulet, a garter made from cork pieces strung on silk ribbons, prevented muscle spasm.

See also: Accessories; Appliqué; Customs, Lore, and Myth; Embroidery; Jewels and Jewelry.

Further Reading

Bohak, Gideon. *Ancient Jewish Magic: A History.* New York: Cambridge University Press, 2008.

Leslie, Catherine Amoroso. *Needlework Through History: An Encyclopedia.* Westport, CT: Greenwood, 2007.

Paine, Sheila. *Amulets: Sacred Charms of Power and Protection.* Rochester, VT: Inner Traditions, 2004.

Appliqué

To amplify themes and symbolism on apparel and to adorn and repair garments, artistic needlework attaches ribbons, accents, and other ornamentation to plain fabric. Such adornments are referred to as appliqués.

A single piece, the appliqué follows the technique of patchwork: blind hemming or fancy stitching holds the onlaid piece to the surface, for example, a heraldic badge on a crusader's surcoat.

In reverse appliqué or underlaid work, stitching displays contrasting fabric under a space cut into the surface of the upper layer. The first examples probably patched apparel to extend its use. The needleworker pinned the shape on the base fabric, basted it into place, then stitched the edge to the foundation.

Appliqué with leather and felt dates to 300 B.C.E. among Siberians, Turks, and Uzbeks for bags adorned with tassels. From Kashmir and Yarkand, the *numdah* method of appliquéing several layers of felt, cotton, or wool produced a two-toned look. A dazzling array of appliquéd designs stitched in gold, called *resht,* passed from Resht in Iran along the Silk Road to Scandinavia and Western Europe.

Celtic, Anglo-Saxon, and Viking needleworkers adorned outfits with appliqués of the Viking raven, the Norse oak tree, a Celtic cross intersected with a halo, the sacred pillar, and ancient runes that predated Christianization. Congregations took pride in hand-decorated chasubles and stoles. Families treasured appliquéd garments as heirlooms and wore them until they turned to rags.

In medieval France, Germany, Iberia, Italy, Scandinavia, and Switzerland, intarsia embroidery inlaid Arabic geometric appliqués on plain wool, silk, linen, or gilded leather. The method stressed dual or treble tones and revealed heraldic crests and nature designs on both sides of hats, cloaks, and shawls. A model of Swedish quilting from 1303 added shapes within quartered roundels.

The early Renaissance brought new patterns and uses to needlework. By the 1400s, needleworkers abandoned crewel embroidery with thick wool yarn in favor of sturdy appliqué on apparel and ruching, a three-dimensional appliqué made with gathered strips. In Western Europe, needleworkers ornamented clothing and vestments with Christian lambs, crosses, lilies, and Pentecostal flames.

Immigrant Irish, Scots, English, Amish, and Pennsylvania Dutch brought traditional folk art and latticing to the Americas. Quilting turned sophisticated patterns into symmetrical fabric art typically applied in nine segments, three to a row, or 16 segments, four to a row. The style, pieced from ribbon, cast-off garments, hosiery, curtains, and bed hangings, emulated the patterns and primary colors of Jacobean embroidery as well as the Amish Garden of Eden and the wishing wells, log cabins, and bear paws of the frontier. Irish needleworkers introduced Carrickmacross whitework, the fine appliqué of dainty white organdy flowers and ribbons on white net handkerchiefs and wedding veils.

The invention of pin-making machines in 1832 increased the availability of affordable sewing notions for detailed work. Strips of velvet, satin, or corded bindings sewed to bodices, collars, and cuffs in contrasting colors transformed calico or linen garments into dressier outfits. *Godey's Lady's Book,* the most popular women's magazine of nineteenth-century America, suggested methods of attaching a sheet of paper to a three-dimensional surface and rubbing with nutmeg to acquire a pattern for appliqué.

North American garments acquired panache from *broderie perse* (Persian embroidery), the sewing of cretonne or chintz starbursts, flower baskets, trees of life, hearts, rosettes, tulips, Stars of Bethlehem, and medallions on baby bibs, hats, vests, and jackets. The method enabled families to put scraps to good use as inexpensive adornment for unbleached muslin. *Ladies Home Journal* published pattern ideas in the 1890s. By edging appliqués with satin, blanket, or buttonhole stitches, needleworkers turned decoration into a work of art. They sometimes documented marriages with monogramming and summarized historical events, such as the evolution of the American flag and eagle as national emblems.

In the 1900s, insubstantial dye methods dimmed enthusiasm for tedious needlework that rapidly faded in strong light. Young girls favored sewing machine stitchery to handwork. Advanced electric sewing machines made patching and decorative attachments available to the home seamstress for securing appliqués with buttonhole or satin stitches.

The Great Depression revived interest in appliqué for extending the use of garments and individualizing the wardrobe. The poor fashioned tobacco, feed, and flour sacks into folk art garments. Hippies of the 1960s returned quilting and appliqué to fashion in shirts and maxi skirts.

In the 1970s, hobby stores began marketing bags of appliqué fabrics, embroidery hoops, and fine cotton, silk, and monofilament polyester threads. Rather than the traditional oval-eyed embroidery needle, crafters now chose straw needles, long bodkins with round eyes suitable for soft-edged appliqué. Beginners applied designs to cloth or felt with iron-on fusible tape to make tote bags, skirts, visors, and sun hats. Skilled needleworkers introduced stained glass or art glass appliqué by stitching bold colored designs with thick black edges or bias strips.

See also: Badges and Insignias; Embroidery; Livery and Heraldry; Patchwork.

Further Reading

Brackman, Barbara. *Clues in the Calico: A Guide to Identifying and Dating Antique Quilts.* Lafayette, CA: C&T, 2009.
———. *Encyclopedia of Appliqué.* Lafayette, CA: C&T, 2009.
Cluckie, Linda. *The Rise and Fall of Art Needlework: Its Socio-Economic and Cultural Aspects.* Bury St. Edmunds, UK: Arena, 2008.
Kooler, Donna. *Donna Kooler's Encyclopedia of Quilting.* Little Rock, AR: Leisure Arts, 2010.
Leslie, Catherine Amoroso. *Needlework Through History: An Encyclopedia.* Westport, CT: Greenwood, 2007.

Aprons

A decorative accessory and utilitarian shield of the body and clothes from dirt, splatters, heat, or dangerous objects, the apron finds uses in the home, laboratory, bakery, workshop, and factory. Historically, the apron has adapted to specialized needs, such as the vintner's bib front, dairy worker's oiled apron, fishmonger's oilskin, gardener's lap cover, and x-ray technician's lead shield. More inclusive models have ranged from the baker's and stonemason's wraparound garment protectors and photography darkroom coat aprons to the full-body glassmaker's pinafore.

Both the welder and the pitch worker have worn a jumper fitted over the bodice or tied with straps at the neck. Nurses and greengrocers popularized the white apron as a model of hygiene.

Before a wedding, Bantwane women of Botswana traditionally offered a bride aprons made of the front and rear ox hide or goatskin as well as a shoulder blanket as gifts.

Aprons in History

From ancient times, Cretan goddesses wore holy aprons, as did Assyrian priests and Egyptian pharaohs. The ritual lambskin apron, such as that worn by Canaanite priest Melchizedek in 2200 B.C.E., served a hygienic purpose during sacrificial slaughters. Following the Israelites' flight from Egypt around 1520 B.C.E., Aaron, the high priest, sashed his breastplate and ephod, or sleeveless apron, over a sleeveless floor-length tunic as part of temple dress.

Roman consumers valued *linum usitatissimum* (the Latin name for flax, meaning "very useful linen") for weaving into aprons and towels, which seamstresses easily repaired with patchwork. In the Ural Mountains, maidens declared their willingness to marry by donning a string apron, a parallel of the Tibetan nuptial apron. Polynesian males adopted the loincloth topped by a fringed overskirt or apron. Persian men wore a similar style in the public bath or wrestling ring.

In the Balkans, Serbian women adopted pairs of front and back aprons of linen or hemp as modesty shields. During the lighting of Sabbath candles, Ashkenazi Jewish women wore aprons as supernatural protectors of the female head of household. Russian attire for the women of Archangel and Novgorod topped a collarless, cuffless linen blouse with pinafore, triangular vest, apron, and belt. Serfs tied lengths of cloth around the waist and used them as breadbaskets or carriers for pome fruit.

During the Jacobean era in England and Scotland (1603–1625), garment covers protected women's court gowns from frequent laundering just as apron skirts shielded the equestrienne's clothes from mud. Pregnant women tied aprons under their laced vests and A-line jackets. Professionals advertised their industry with the barber's checked apron, the butcher's green cover-up, the nanny's black apron, the apothecary's brown fustian chest protector, and the mason's white tool carrier.

Aprons in America

In the Atlantic Coast states, colonial housewives sewed neckerchiefs to match their tea aprons and edged both with tatting. American abolitionists formed sewing societies to collect disguises for runaway slaves consisting of straw hats, work aprons, and tool belts. A laborer's apron from the forge, bakery, or slaughterhouse gave convincing evidence of the wearer's employment. Freedwomen in New Orleans sported immaculate aprons and matching *tignons* (turbans) as proof of their liberation from bondage.

Westerners carried leather and cloth for making vests, chaps, and long canvas aprons, inexpensive, functional attire for leather repairing, horseshoeing, wagoneering, and tending to farm chores. Housewives stitched pockets onto waistbands to hold kitchen implements, knitting needles, and baby needs. A posthumous inventory of the garments owned by a Connecticut lady in 1727 listed 11 nightcaps, nine petticoats, seven gowns, five hoods, four pairs of stockings, two bonnets, two pairs of shoes, and 21 aprons.

In the 1800s, seamstresses upgraded the workhouse pinafore by making gauzy or satin aprons to accompany long bustled dresses or morning gowns or to adorn a maid's uniform. As skirts widened, aprons, dickeys, and pelisses increased in fullness to provide better coverage.

During the Belle Époque (1871–1914), chic aprons and hemispheric overskirts rounded out plain dress styles with fancy stitches on taffeta or velvet. The invention of the sewing machine and Butterick patterns gave homemakers an easy way to turn cloth scraps into quilted or appliquéd aprons. Instructions in *Woman's Home Companion* suggested mother-and-daughter aprons as an introduction to shared kitchen work.

In the early 1900s, girls accessorized special-occasion dresses with sheer camisoles, pinafores, and flounced aprons. For working-class females, the Sears, Roebuck catalog featured aprons and "hooverettes" (wrap aprons) as well as rickrack and bias trimming to transform feed sacks into farm, shop, and home necessities. Farm wives evolved the cobbler's or canning apron as a high-necked bodice shield with hemline pockets for carrying poultry feed, eggs, garden vegetables, or kindling. Kindergarten teachers found the cobbler style useful for keeping tissues, chalk, and classroom supplies handy.

The smocking machine, invented in the 1940s, added decorative stitchery to glamour aprons used as accessories to evening gowns. During World War II, factory women stitched industrial aprons from rubberized canvas to wear with denim overalls and leather gloves. The first sewing of polyvinyl chloride garments in the 1950s made plastic clothing protectors a boon to hairdressers and dockworkers. Half-aprons smartened the housedress while warding off flour smudges and lint. Television chefs wore impeccable aprons as emblems of their profession and dedication to cleanliness.

The dress and hostess apron defined the suburban homemaker as reflected on such popular television series as *Father Knows Best* (1954–1963), *Leave It to Beaver* (1957–1963), and *The Donna Reed Show* (1958–1966). For Lord & Taylor, Claire McCardell designed the long-skirted kitchen dinner dress, a pioneer-style calico with detachable scalloped apron. Skimpier versions attaching waistbands to toweling associated garment protection with a place to wipe wet hands. Message aprons sported upbeat and feminist slogans, such as "Home Body" and "Don't Iron While the Strike Is Hot," as well as the logos of barbecues and food-service venues.

In the 1970s, men's stores popularized the canvas grilling apron and matching chef's hat. Late in the twentieth century, antiquing buffs collected vintage aprons as models of utility and nostalgia. In 2012, Victoria's Secret advertised a skimpy lace apron for seductive home wear. Elizabeth Scokin introduced Haute Hostess Aprons, a blend of glamour with women's traditions.

See also: Amerindian Clothing, Post-Contact; Breechcloths.

Further Reading

Cheney, Joyce. *Aprons: Icons of the American Home.* Philadelphia: Running Press, 2000.

Geisel, EllynAnne. *The Apron Book: Making, Wearing, and Sharing a Bit of Cloth and Comfort.* Kansas City, MO: Andrews McMeel, 2006.

Arctic Attire

In the far north, the challenge of maintaining body warmth while ventilating perspiration requires innovative attire. Over millennia of surviving gales and blizzards, the High Arctic people living from eastern Siberia to Greenland and from southeastern Labrador to the Queen Elizabeth Islands west of Thule made annual clothing replacement the basis of female training. After 5000 B.C.E., the shrinkage of glaciers moderated the climate, allowing Paleo-Eskimo or Denbigh tundra dwellers greater mobility to fish lakes and rivers for char and trout, hunt reindeer, and craft skin apparel using chipped stone implements.

Early History

From Alaska to northern Greenland and across the Hudson Bay, Siberian migrants established a maritime economy based on caribou, seal, walrus, fish, and birds. For weathering harsh cold, the Inuit and Aleut chose caribou skins and dense seal fur as lightweight, waterproof blankets. For rain capes, the Tlingit of Alaska interwove yellow cedar bark with dog or coyote hair and the wool of the white mountain goat.

Girls and women prioritized the making of men's parkas (tunics) from caribou skins and seal fur, a compact pelt that easily shed water and retained its minimal weight. Among the Aleut of Alaska, women painted their parkas with clan symbols as testimonials of belonging. Young seamstresses saved the sewing of blankets, baby swaddling, stuffed skin balls, and doll clothes until high winter.

To supply women with food and materials, boys and men followed a yearly cycle. Tracking caribou began in October. Seal hunting occupied males in late November, followed by ice fishing in late December and polar bear and basking seal hunting in March. The rest of the year, men and women hunted birds, sea mammals, and small game.

Around 2500 B.C.E., the Pre-Dorset of Ellesmere Island west of Greenland set tiny chert cutters in whalebone or ivory handles for cleaning and shaping pelts. The Kachemak of Alaska's Pacific coast preferred the stone *ulu* (a semicircular knife) for making precise cuts in pelts and sea mammal gut skins. Turned inward, skins covered the mouths of small children and formed mittens and socks to encase fingers and toes in delicate rabbit and wolverine hair.

Arctic scavengers used bird feathers as parka linings, an extra layer that trapped body warmth. Siberian Yup'ik, Chukchi, and Koryak Eskimo scraped and soaked sea mammal intestines into a pliant material and adorned the seams with crested auk feathers. Two months' work yielded a garment that lasted five months.

From around 1500 B.C.E., processors' kits included chert, burins, and quartz, the primary

An elder Inuit woman displays some of the elements common to Arctic attire: a parka with wolf-fur hood and fine stitchery, often a unique clan design. Pelt, fur, feathers, bark, and layered fabric serve the paramount needs of warmth and waterproofing. *(Hinrich Baesemann/picture-alliance/dpa/AP Images)*

sewing supplies among the Thule, Paleo-Indians of Arctic Canada, to scrape off blubber and meat, separate skins, and join them into garments. Bow drills penetrated walrus tusks to make buttons and toggles. Pelts formed both inner and outer tunics. Waterproof gut linings supplied raincoats and slickers. The waste fed sled dogs.

One ring-headed pin unearthed in Newfoundland in 1960 established the presence of Vikings and their sewing styles among the Dorset Eskimo, ancestors of the Inuit, around 1000 C.E. The miniaturized sewing tools of the Dorset attest to control and skill in cutting and stitching hides. The whalebone sewing needles, whetting stones, thimbles, microblades, and utility knives of upper Canada stocked needlework cases, which kinship groups employed each autumn for communal sewing and clothing repair.

Innovation and Embellishment

Women cataloged materials for best use, reserving up to eight caribou pelts for one adult's tunics, pants, boots, and mittens. By turning fur inward, the wearer captured pockets of air for trapping body heat. Two-layered Arctic qiviut, or musk ox fur, proved ideal for shoulder blankets to ward off mosquitoes.

Less common pelts of bear, eider duck, fox, dog, marmot, squirrel, wolf flanks and legs, otter, swan foot skin, and wolverine added variety to fabrics for specific uses, such as wolf pelt capes and scarves. Ruffs of the Siberian husky, wolf, or wolverine kept the neck dry. For more casual attire, the Arctic hare, similar to a long-haired rabbit, provided a blue pelt. Puffin skins supplied pelts for Aleut ritual dress. Seal pelts entered service after scraping, washing, stretching, and drying. Drying racks kept skins from curling until they could air-dry.

As technology improved after 500 B.C.E. along the Bering Sea, stitchery turned into an art form. Sewing required the twining of the seal esophagus for thread. On the Punuk Islands in the Bering Sea, the Neolithic Okviks' uses of Siberian and silver foxes, sea otters, and ringed seals turned a profit from their customers, Russian-American farmers, whalers, and Aleut trappers on Attu Island and the

Pribilofs. Thule utilitarians shaped caribou parkas with appliquéd dyed skins, incorporated fringe and bristle, attached ivory buttons and scrimshaw engravings, and sewed sealskin boots with fine waterproof stitches.

The visored helmet, a major contribution to family stability of the Inuit, enabled hunters to remain outdoors during extreme weather, which increased in severity during the Little Ice Age, beginning in the Atlantic around 1250 and lasting for 350 years. The eye-slitted head protector gained enhancement from sea mammal ivory, loon beaks, painting, and sea lion whiskers. For walking, wives carved the snow creeper (crampon), a serrated piece of bone or ivory attached by leather straps to the boot for added traction during the stalking of seals over ice.

The Arctic Inuit carried a blanket on hunting expeditions. By bouncing one hunter from a taut blanket, the hunting party gave him the height to look for caribou. As whaling died out in the early 1900s, the Inuit hunted seals and trapped foxes for clothing materials. The fox market collapsed in the 1930s.

Mother and Child

The roomiest parkas enabled women to carry infants under wraps and suckle them without exposing tender skin to harsh weather. The subarctic Kutchin wrapped infants in delicate rabbit skin robes and suspended them from the mother's shoulders with a beaded baby belt. Arctic child care required suspending the naked infant from a skin sling under the anorak to facilitate breastfeeding and warming with the mother's body heat, a system introduced to North America by Norse Greenlanders.

The Baffinland, Iglulik, Kotzebue, or Caribou Eskimo mother tucked her newborn into her wolf or wolverine fur hood, where thongs or toggled cords held the baby securely. For nursing, the mother lowered the child through her elongated armhole to her breast. A small cap shielded the infant's head from the cold.

An alternate carrier for daily use throughout Alaska, Greenland, Labrador, northern Canada, and Russia, the Quebec Inuit *amauti* (parka)

consisted of a caribou hide, ground squirrel skin, or sealskin coat, hood, and built-in infant pouch. Complete coverage protected the child from wind, snow, and frostbite while the mother hunted, fished, or picked berries. The large shoulder piece enabled the wearer to shift the infant from facing the back to facing upward in the front for feeding or tending without exposure to wind or snow.

Footwear

The Inuit styled durable mukluks, calf-high boots made from fox, rabbit, or raccoon fur, hand-scraped reindeer pelts, and bearded sealskin, which contoured easily to the shape of the feet. Farther south, Athapascan imitators made similar insulated high-top fur-trimmed shoes from buckskin, moose hide, and caribou or the skins of salmon. Hay inner soles and linings of rabbit fur increased warmth and comfort.

Shoemakers chose specific materials—tough, de-haired sealskin for soles with gathered toes, flexible harp sealskin at the arch, and ringed sealskin uppers stitched with sinew or cordage taken from both sides of caribou spines. The thinnest pelts provided suede nap of the calf, deer, goat, or lamb for gloves and shoes and for lining capes and coats. Loon and duck skins made warm, pliant summer moccasins.

Linings of feathers, fox belly fur, grass, moss, and auk, guillemot, and ptarmigan down and skins insulated Arctic garments, such as trackers' boots and the short house pants made from caribou leg skins and worn by women over sealskin stockings. When hunters broke through melting ice, they removed their duffle socks, beat them with a stick to remove excess water, allowed them to freeze, and pounded the remaining ice out of the undercoat before putting the socks on again.

The Aleut and Inuit made indoor slippers of smoked rabbit skin and outdoor boots of caribou, walrus, or seal with the fur facing outward to protect the feet from slipping on ice. In the 1960s, global fashions in sealskin created a shortage of materials for clothes and boots, forcing seamstresses to put every scrap to good use. Women softened the materials by chewing them. For adornment, they added dog and wolverine pelts and seal gut skins. As a cash economy brought changes in traditional lifestyles, most young women lost the training in fur sewing that had readied their mothers and grandmothers for supplying the family with boots and apparel.

See also: Amerindian Clothing, Pre-Columbian; Fur.

Further Reading

Issenman, Betty Kobayashi. *Sinews of Survival: The Living Legacy of Inuit Clothing.* Vancouver, UBC Press, 1997.

King, J.C.H., Birgit Pauksztat, and Robert Storrie, eds. *Arctic Clothing of North America—Alaska, Canada, Greenland.* Montreal: McGill-Queen's University Press, 2005.

Oakes, Jill, and Rick Riewe. *Alaska Eskimo Footwear.* Fairbanks: University of Alaska Press, 2007.

Armani, Giorgio (1934–)

Internationally renowned for his innovations in menswear, Italian fashion designer Giorgio Armani earned his reputation—and built a multibillion-dollar label—on the strength of his distinctive luxury attire and accessories, as well as ensembles for sports, cinema, and stage.

The son of Maria Raimondi and accountant and shipping manager Ugo Armani, he was born in Piacenza, Italy, on July 11, 1934. In addition to periods of hunger during World War II, he suffered an eye injury from exploding ordnance. Because of his father's postwar imprisonment for complicity with Fascists, Armani and his family moved north to Milan, where Giorgio took refuge in Hollywood movies.

After medical training at the University of Milan, photography studies, and service in the Italian army medical corps infirmary in Verona, Armani found work as a window dresser in a Milan department store. At age 20, he began selling menswear and soon advanced to assistant buyer, developing a flair for confident attire on business trips to England, India, Japan, and the United States. At age 30, he began designing for the Nino Cerruti label, paring down traditional tailoring to free menswear of the stiffness and artifice dictated by seasonal fashions.

Armani sketched androgynous designs that

would age well and serve the buyer in even small details of wear and upkeep. To free consumers of discomfort in double-breasted blazers, he lengthened the cut, removed padding from shoulders, relaxed pockets, and stripped linings. With a repositioning of buttons, reshaping of lapels, and softening of trousers, he established the natural fit of casual chic in neutral mineral tones.

On the advice of his mentor and partner, architect Sergio Galeotti, and with an investment of $10,000, Armani in 1973 established a freelance design house called Giorgio Armani S.p.A. (the letters refer to a partnership), the precursor to his label of ready-to-wear for men and women. One of his major successes, the bomber jacket, treated leather as a workable fabric. Another success, unadorned women's business suits in menswear crepe and serge, accorded purchasers elegance and aplomb. After his line turned a profit in 1975, he expanded to underwear, swimsuits, shoes and handbags, jeans, and fragrances, which he sold at his Milan boutique on Via St. Andrea.

Armani's designs gained cachet on the shoulders of such celebrities as Los Angeles Lakers basketball coach Pat Riley and actors Russell Crowe, Whoopi Goldberg, Jack Nicholson, Cate Blanchett, Jodie Foster, John Travolta, and Michelle Pfeiffer. His stress-free luxuries—felt hats, suede sweatshirts, and the pairing of T-shirts with wrinkle-free jackets and sloping cardigan sweaters—appeared in magazines, his Hollywood boutique, media ads, and the films *American Gigolo* (1980) and *The Untouchables* (1987). For the television series *Miami Vice* (1984–1990), Armani provided wedge-shaped, slim-hipped power suits for actor Don Johnson. As a result, Armani became the most popular European designer in America.

Following the death of his business partner from AIDS on August 14, 1985, Armani ventured on alone. His antifashion philosophy, consistent in its embrace of youthful ease and simplicity, extended to skiwear, eyeglasses, socks, and watches sold in the United States, China, and boutiques in 37 other countries. With the help of his sister Rosanna Armani and her daughters, Roberta and Silvana, Armani expanded his line to include cosmetics, hotels, and restaurants. By 1999, he operated 2,000 stores. In 2002, *Forbes* magazine named him the Most Successful Italian Designer.

After the death of model Ana Carolina Reston from anorexia in 2006, Armani refused to hire dangerously thin models. The designer's public persona gained prestige from four honorary doctorates and an appointment to the United Nations High Commission for Refugees and a global initiative to fight AIDS in Africa. Two arrests for bribing tax officials did little to tarnish his reputation, but his emphasis on rabbit pelt in designs angered People for the Ethical Treatment of Animals and other anti-fur advocates in 2008. That same year, he created a spangled matador's jacket, pants, and cloak in satin for torero Cayetano Rivera Ordóñez to wear in the 2008 celebration of the Corrida Goyesca, a bullfight and culture festival in the southern Spanish town of Ronda, again touching on a sensitive subject for animal rights activists.

Armani's diverse contributions to celebrity costume design include stage outfits for pop singer Lady Gaga, a gray cotton-and-linen suit and trench coat for soccer superstar David Beckham, and sweat suits for Italian athletes at the 2012 Summer Olympics. His business conglomerate, generating some $2 billion annually, operates 13 factories and employs 4,700 garment specialists. His Emporio Armani stores opened in October 2012 in airport boutiques in Frankfurt, Taiwan, Geneva, Warsaw, Rome, Macau, Taipei, and Tenerife.

See also: Fashion Design; Italian Clothing and Fashion.

Further Reading

Celant, Germano, and Harold Koda. *Giorgio Armani.* New York: Guggenheim Museum, 2000.

Giorgio Armani S.p.A. www.armani.com/giorgioarmani

Molho, Renata. *Being Armani.* Milan, Italy: Baldini Castoldi Dalai, 2008.

White, Nicola. *Giorgio Armani.* London: Carlton Books, 2000.

Armor

The armoring of combat forces shields the body and head from direct weapon attack, ammunition, shrapnel, projectiles, and flying debris.

In 2500 B.C.E. at Ur, Sumerian soldiers under Prince Eannatum of Lagash introduced armored cloaks and helmets to shield against blows of the battle-ax to the neck and body. By 2000 B.C.E., the world's armies had adopted some mix of head and torso armor. In 1700 B.C.E., the Chinese added bronze neck escutcheons and padded jackets stuffed with cotton, a form of chest guard adopted independently by the Aztec in 1500 B.C.E.

Around 1450 B.C.E., Mycenaean soldiers protected their heads from slashing blades with caps pieced from boar tusk scales, a 30-to-35-pound (14-to-16-kilogram) armor style also worn by the upland Hyksos of Egypt. Similar boar tusk apparel molded to the bodies of infantrymen around 1200 B.C.E. in Homeric Greece countered the stones of slingers.

After 800 B.C.E. in Assyria, India, Byzantium, Japan, Korea, Iran, Mongolia, Persia, Tibet, and the Ukraine, flexible lamellar armor introduced advanced technology—the boiling of leather and cutting it into small hide scales. This labor-intensive task raised the price of outfitting an army but produced more durable fighting gear. The Chinese protected armies with similar laminar armor after 771 B.C.E. For other East Asian combatants—among the Siberian Chukchi, Chinese Lolo, and Gilbert Islanders—a variety of scales, fashioned from such materials as fish skin, limestone, cord, coconut shell, wood, and metal coins and disks, served as deflectors in torso coverings.

Etruscans armored the shoulder and sternum with dense linen. The armored phalanx, a Greek tactic requiring armor made from linen glued into plates, proved decisive against Persian archers at the Battle of Marathon, northeast of Athens, on September 12, 490 B.C.E. The Chinese produced their own fabric armor from quilted cotton and positioned it over a hemp tunic. A later version connected turtle shells with cords.

Chain Mail

The earliest pattern mail, which protected Romanians and Slovakians around 300 B.C.E., derived from Celtic experiments with metal scales, a shift in combat dress that added weight as well as flexibility and protection from lance points.

The design, particularly in Chinese stone armor, compromised warriors by placing stress on the shoulders. After 100 B.C.E., Parthians and Scythians devised the cataphract, an assault cavalryman and horse covered in scale armor. Horse armor alone weighed more than 100 pounds (45 kilograms).

In battle against the Carthaginians from 264 to 146 B.C.E., early Roman infantrymen topped leather underwear with leather *squamata* (scale) armor. In the first century B.C.E., contact with Germanic forces along the Rhine introduced Romans to the *lorica hamata*, a torso covering of bronze or iron rings riveted in place. To shield the thighs, infantrymen wore a kilt of *pteruges* (flaps), a series of leather strips studded or plated with metal.

By 75 C.E., Roman armorers introduced *segmentata*, metal bands attached individually to a leather body, a rapidly assembled plating that influenced battle gear from Iberia to Britain. Soldiers fastened their breastplates over a wool tunic and neck scarf to prevent abrasions. Because the segmented armor required constant maintenance, by 383, according to military historian Publius Vegetius's *De re Militari* (*On Armies*), coats of ring mail appear to have been standard issue, adding 43 pounds (20 kilograms) to the weight of a legionary. Hun invasions in the early fifth century pitted them against the Alans of Iran, horse archers reinforced with lamellar armor plating. The combined attack of Alanic and Gothic lancers routed the Romans by easily piercing their chain mail.

Medieval Enhancements

In the seventh century, Persians shielded the torso in hauberks, coats of mail made of iron rings and strips and split front and back for cavalry use. For warmth and additional protection, soldiers topped hauberks with densely quilted silk battle caftans or surcoats. The creation of armor from small metal rings simplified fitting a warrior for battle, a cost savings that Charlemagne adopted in 773 when outfitting Frankish troops in the iron mail *byrnie,* a combat shirt. At the Battle of Hastings in 1066, William the Conqueror's Normans wore the *coif,* a head-to-shoulder protector. Their English

adversaries fired crossbows and turned their backs to reload, revealing shields suspended from a cord around the neck.

From the Mali and Songhai of West Africa to the Norse of Scandinavia, the loose mail style remained a battle standard for centuries until the advance of longbows and 28-inch (71-centimeter) arrows, which penetrated chain mail. Armoring styles tended toward lengthening of coverage over the back, arms, and upper hands. Psychological tactics involved polishing armor to reflect sunlight and disorient the enemy. On July 4, 1187, Saladin, the Kurdish commander of Saracens, outsmarted European Christians at the Battle of Hattin in Palestine by luring them into the hot sun to wear down the Crusaders from the heat of their metal armor.

Against lances, maces, war hammers, and unfletched bolts from the crossbows of Arabs and Turks, warfare during the Third Crusade (1189–1192) created the need for plate armor, sturdy stallions to bear the weight, and squires to attend to armor and mounts. Troops adopted sleeveless brigandines or jacks, canvas, felt, or leather torso coverings lined with steel plates. Knights shielded their hands with plated gauntlets, but the throat remained a vulnerable point, where an arrow pierced Richard the Lionheart in Châlus, France, on March 25, 1199.

At the Siege of Calais from September 1, 1346, to August 3, 1347, the gusseted gloves of Edward, the Black Prince, featured knuckle spikes for hand-to-hand combat. Steel or leather gorgets worn under the breastplate and back plate safeguarded the throat. Subsequent versions of armor grew in size with plated cuisses (thigh shields), metal tubes or scaled joints and plates for the elbows and forearms, hinged wrist guards, and thumb shields for protection in sword fighting and attack by pole arms.

Scandinavian improvements in modular fit over the torso and legs reduced the need for padding. For cold weather, warriors placed the quilted *jupon* (jacket) on the outside of armor. By 1490, armorers in Brescia and Milan, Italy, and Augsburg, Nuremberg, and Innsbruck, Germany, encased horse soldiers in individually fitted full armor suits weighing 50 to 90 pounds (23 to 41 kilograms).

Modern Arms and Armor

The advent of the harquebus, musket, and matchlock long guns required a thickening of armor plating to withstand bullets. Armorers lightened the load by deleting greaves from the shins and replacing them with jackboots reinforced with chain mail and iron sole plates. During the seventeenth century, heavier firearms ended the era of the fully armored infantry.

With increases in firepower, armor returned to use during World War I. German companies wore armored head coverings open over the eyes. Three-pound (1.4-kilogram) canvas brigandines from Wilkinson Sword Company in London, forerunners of the flak jacket, and mail-fringed steel helmets improved the Allies' chances of surviving shrapnel from exploding grenades. Soft body armor of kapok, sisal, hemp, flax, hair, cotton, or silk slowed projectiles to protect soft tissue.

Flight crews during World War II wore Wilkinson's tapered cotton aprons and vests filled with steel to shield the major organs from antiaircraft fire. By 1941, a British manganese steel chest plate weighing 2.75 pounds (1.25 kilograms) attached to webbed straps and curved over the torso to ward off machine-gun fire. By the Korean War, nylon duck and Doron laminated fiberglass ballistic vests attached to groin aprons armored with ceramic plates; this armor stopped shrapnel and .45-caliber bullets, but not rifle fire. The chest protector remained in use during the Vietnam War, when DuPont chemist Stephanie Kwolek developed Kevlar.

Into current times, U.S. troops in the Middle East wear the light, strong Kevlar vest. Kevlar greaves equipped with ceramic, plastic, and metal can deflect ammunition from Kalashnikov assault rifles. Civilian armored equipment remains practical, as with firefighters' mail gloves, bulletproof vests for police use, diving suits for protection from shark attack, welding hand shields, oven gloves, and metal gauntlets used for the shucking of oysters.

See also: Badges and Insignias; Boots; Disguise and Spy Wear; Gloves; Helmets, Military; Linen; Patchwork; Uniforms, Law Enforcement; Uniforms, Military; Vests.

Further Reading

Alexander, David. *The Arts of War: Arms and Armour of the 7th to 19th Centuries.* New York: Oxford University Press, 1993.

Bull, Stephen. *An Historical Guide to Arms and Armor.* Ed. Tony North. New York: Facts on File, 1991.

Ford, Roger, R.G. Grant, Adrian Gilbert, Philip Parker, and Richard Holmes. *Weapon: A Visual History of Arms and Armor.* New York: DK, 2010.

Gabriel, Richard A. *Soldiers' Lives Through History: The Ancient World.* Westport, CT: Greenwood, 2007.

Art and Media, Fashion

Based on an ambiguous nexus between elaboration and utility, fashion exhibits an art of the moment. For preindustrial civilization among the Harappa of the Punjab and the Maori and Lapita of the Pacific, from 3300 to the 100s B.C.E., the body supplied a canvas on which to apply paint, tattoos, feathers, fillets, and piercing. Customized jewelry, amulets, and headdress expressed social status, ethnicity, and celebration.

Sixth-century B.C.E. Ethiopian sculpture reflected ethnic attitudes toward the human form. The unstructured linen and wool draping featured in classical Greek sculpture by Phidias and Praxiteles in the 400s B.C.E. and Egyptian Fayum funerary portraits after 50 B.C.E. dominated poses as indications of dignity and self-confidence. For the realistic portraits, tomb effigies, cameos, and panel art of Imperial Rome until 450 C.E., hairstyles and hair ornamentation attested to the importance of grooming and creativity to ideal beauty.

Painters and engravers made clothing and gesture the focus of portraits and murals, especially as historical records of the ruling classes of China's Song dynasty (960–1279), iconic Russian hagiography of the early 1300s, and the royal Bourbon and Tudor courts of France and England. Sixteenth-century Venetian costume books by Fernando Bertelli and Cesare Vecellio surveyed the intricacies of lacing, slashed sleeves, ruffs, petticoats, and starched collars and their contribution to European ideals of refined elitism. In 1805, the image of Beau Brummell signaled the rise of the dandy with his stand-up collar, neck cloth, Hessian boots, top hat, and cane, a look that influenced Regency portraiture.

After 1391, the concept of clothing as a commodity influenced the first fashion dolls and fashion plates, forerunners of decades of modeling in magazines with social clout such as *Mercure Galant*, *The Lady's Magazine*, *Journal der Luxus un der Moden*, *Godey's Lady's Book*, and *Art et Décoration*. As guides to the fashionable, *Vanity Fair*, *Vogue*, *Harper's Bazaar*, *Paris-Match*, *Elle*, *Glamour*, *GQ*, and *Bild-Zeitung* promoted adaptations of art deco, impressionism, and orientalism to investment dressing. Poster art by Giovanni Boldini, Auguste Toulmouche, James Tissot, Jean Beraud, and Alfred Stevens reinterpreted male-female relationships in social and intimate settings to underscore the role of style in human interaction.

The Industrial Age and rise of mass print media exploded the exclusionary concept of fashion as the province of the prestigious few. In place of the static grandeur of sculptural evening costumes from the late 1850s by Charles Frederick Worth, Coco Chanel liberated fashion to keep pace with feminist achievement and representations of self. At the beginning of the 1900s, rather than merely decorate feminine contours for the sake of the vain plutocrat, Chanel produced day dresses and suits that defined and elevated modern women. Functional ensembles introduced the glamour of active women, the result of generations of feminism that freed females from their role as sex objects.

Fashion art during the Jazz Age, in keeping with technology, shifted from static mannequins in department store windows to bodies in motion. During fashion week, magazine journalists camped out in Paris to note what American social lion Wallis Warfield Simpson purchased and to photograph the look of the times. Movie news-reels replicated the fluid flapper style in fringed, sequined chemises and boas and athletic males dancing, cycling, riding horseback, and playing golf. Subsequent experiments with jersey knits and bias couture by Madeline Vionnet for dance ensembles yielded the stretchy, body-revealing apparel of the second half of the 1900s.

Reverence for design inspired artistic displays at clothing museums and photographic retrospectives of major couturiers. By aligning displays in chronological order, such as the inaugural gowns of U.S. first ladies at the Smithsonian Institution, art historians laid out graphic statements about period details and visions of femininity. Exhibits of male clothing from the grandeur of court ensembles under Louis XIV to the formation of the business ideal of Nino Cerruti informed viewers of the evolution of a gendered self-image. The gradual repackaging of men retrieved them from popular styles entailing effete exhibitionism to a crisp, sober image of efficient professionalism.

Hollywood and commercial film contributed to perceptions of period costumes as manifestations of time and place. From the lavish ensembles and wigs in *Cleopatra* (1963), moviegoers absorbed the pageantry of the historical alliance of Republican Rome's general Mark Antony and the Egyptian queen. *Doctor Zhivago* (1965) used screen costume to reflect Russian folk attire and the brutal shift from Bolshevik militarism to a gray Soviet uniform. The British television series *Downton Abbey* (2010–) informed drama fans of the role of couture, furs, and jewelry in periods of rapid social and economic change among England's aristocracy during the early twentieth century.

From art history to grand portraiture to modern mass media, clothing design has advanced through aesthetic phases, illuminating the interrelation of the human form and body coverings. In the early twenty-first century, an indistinct merger of up-to-the-minute silhouettes with electronic imagery kept runway modeling and stage, television, and film costuming in public debate. Energized by synthetic fabrics and technology, fashion art and media recorded the zeitgeist as it modified wardrobe, from street savvy to the red-carpet promenade.

See also: Art Nouveau and Art Deco Fashion; Dolls, Fashion; Fashion Plates; Museums, Clothing and Textile; Photography, Fashion.

Further Reading

Geczy, Adam, and Vicki Karaminas, eds. *Fashion and Art.* New York: Bloomsbury, 2012.

Mackrell, Alice. *Art and Fashion: The Impact of Art on Fashion and Fashion on Art.* 2nd ed. London: Batsford, 2005.

Wolbers, Marian Frances. *Uncovering Fashion: Fashion Communications Across the Media.* New York: Fairchild, 2009.

Art Nouveau and Art Deco Fashion

During the rise of haute couture, elements of art deco and art nouveau directed fashion decor toward romanticism from about 1880 to 1920. Chief influences derived from the vivid colors of European painting and graphics and the energy of Japanese block prints and Chinese scroll painting. Stylists and goldsmiths promoted elegance in wardrobe and accessories through fashion plates and media coverage. Bold parabolas and operatic flourishes manifested the rebellion of artists Antoni Gaudí, Alphonse Mucha, Gustav Klimt, and Louis Comfort Tiffany, who sought to liberate art from immobile, two-dimensional surfaces.

Garment designers relished Battenburg and polychrome Courseulles lace inserts, set-in cummerbunds, Chantilly chemisettes, asymmetric overlays, couching, and diamante (spangled) and pin-tucked edging. Overdresses shifted hues with misty netting and tulle atop pastels and foam lace. Ruffled tiers and sequined trains added drama to formal wear, such as the elongated pink moiré and silver court ensemble by Russian designer Nadezhda Lamanova, the couturier of Romanov courtiers enraptured by French styles in the late 1890s.

Transcending national borders, accessory makers contributed nuanced picture hats, feathered muffs, and scrolled stockings that turned wearers into objets d'art. Jewelers flourished creating diamond dog collars, pierced wedding bands, peacock-hued enamel brooches, Cornish combs, and a Westphalian tiara edged with the Greek meander. From the late nineteenth century, French modelier René Lalique dazzled the jewelry market with naturalistic bangles and filigreed brooches pulsating with iridescent insects, reptiles, and stylized vines and ferns.

In 1898, leading Paris designer Charles Frederick Worth patterned satin velvet with art nouveau arabesques and paisleys. In the early 1900s, couturiers Paul Poiret, Jacques Doucet, and Jeanne Paquin supplied ready-to-wear featuring art deco, impressionist, and Eastern touches, which knockoff artists duplicated in the medium price range. *Harper's Bazaar* featured theatrical fashion plates by fantasists George Barbier, Edmund Dulac, and Gustav Michelson. For Ballets Russes performances of *Cléopatre* (1909), *The Firebird* (1910), and *L'Après-midi d'un Faune* (1912), artist Léon Bakst of Grodno, Belarus, supplied imaginative harem pants, overskirts, belly dance ensembles, and Turkish slippers in smoldering colors.

In 1915, the Russian-born French fashion artist Erté created exotic covers for *Vogue* that introduced the consumer to medieval wimples and snoods, negligees with feathery marabou, and beaded harem dresses reflecting the mythic qualities of goddesses. During World War I, the closure of Paris fashion houses gave *Vogue* editor Edna Woolman Chase an edge on shaping global aesthetics. She and British editor Alison Settle championed American designs and the sinuous grace and mystery of art deco ensembles.

Contributing to a trend in artistic apparel, illustrators Tom Keogh and Bernard Blossac relieved fashion plates of their sterility by emphasizing fantasy over realism. Jazz Age styles of the 1920s featured sequins and fringe on chemise dresses, sparkly cloches, and hinged pendants on jewelry that created a titillating shimmy for dancing. Asymmetric ruffles accentuated the hipline. In 1922, Nadezhda Lamanova costumed a Moscow stage performance of *Princess Turandot* with sensuous paisleys and stylized geometrics, a seductive challenge to Soviet austerity.

In 1934, filmmaker Cecil B. DeMille turned costuming for the biopic *Cleopatra* (1934) into fashion news. By garbing star Claudette Colbert in sculptured wigs, winged crests, and spangles, he launched a fad for vampish glamour in satin and velvet. From Buenos Aires to Madrid, department stores marketed replicas of screen costumes. Poster art and billboards turned art nouveau into the wardrobe aesthetic of consumers at all levels in Europe, India, Southeast Asia, Brazil, and Africa. Analysts described the era's flair as *l'esprit nouveau* (the new spirit).

At the height of the Great Depression, French designer Jeanne Lanvin gave an *Arabian Nights* aura to a supple satin evening gown with matching velvet cape. The revival of the world economy in the late 1930s produced a demand for ephemeral fabrics from Wiener Werkstätte, cosmetics, and powdered-enamel dispensers. Art deco dressing in lush tunics and silk pajamas with fringed tassels flourished in western Australia, New Zealand, Shanghai, and Hong Kong as evidence of modernization. Showcased in *Mademoiselle* and *Vogue,* streamlined apparel and glamorous beauty aids satisfied female shoppers who had suffered the absence of beauty in their lives during hard times.

Art deco artistry maintained its influence on apparel in subsequent decades. In 1960, couturier Cristóbal Balenciaga accessorized the royal wedding ensemble of King Baudouin of Belgium to Queen Fabiola with an art deco tiara. Yves Saint Laurent's 1967 line featured an African art deco collection. Designer Emilio Pucci swirled leisure wear and scarves with black and metallic stripes and Egyptian chevrons on short and long evening gowns. His color blocking in afternoon ensembles and sportswear brightened Vogue, McCalls, and Spadea pattern catalogs. In 1977, the cult disco movie *Saturday Night Fever* popularized art nouveau elements in polyester shirts.

In 2008, Ralph Lauren tinged his hunting lodge collection with art deco velvet evening

The high-waisted corsetless gowns introduced by French fashion designer Paul Poiret typified the flowing, colorful art nouveau style for women around the turn of the twentieth century. *(ullstein bild/The Granger Collection, NYC—All rights reserved)*

wear and cloches topped with pheasant feathers. Jill Milan, Karl Lagerfeld, and Donatella Versace reprised the operatic aesthetics of the previous century in Egyptian column dresses and armlets, high-low gowns, and lightning bolt designs in lustrous fabrics. At the Bangalore fashion show in January 2013, designer Ritu Kumar of Delhi, India, garnished artistic designs with mixed patterns and pendant tassels on Empire dance dresses and traditional tunics polished with art deco braid. Cosmetic artist Laura Mercier re-created the art deco face with heavy black eyebrows, platinum eye shadow, porcelain foundation, and bold red lips.

See also: Erté; Pucci, Emilio; Worth, Charles Frederick.

Further Reading

Battersby, Martin. *Art Deco Fashion: French Designers 1908–1925.* New York: St. Martin's, 1984.

Fischer, Lucy. *Designing Women: Cinema, Art Deco, and the Female Form.* New York: Columbia University Press, 2003.

Lussier, Suzanne. *Art Deco Fashion.* Boston: Bulfinch, 2003.

Weber, Edith. *Art Nouveau & Art Deco Fashion Postcards.* Atglen, PA: Schiffer, 2009.

Athletic Shoes

Early exercise footwear spawned the modern athletic shoe that now dominates work and leisure apparel worldwide. From the 1830s, advances in shoe soles by the Liverpool Rubber Company applied flexible synthetics to the canvas upper of the British sand shoe, later known as a plimsoll (high-top). After 1864, track and field competitors chose low-top kangaroo leather athletic footwear, the ancestor of the running shoe. Difficulties with durability during marathons forced designers to reevaluate the toe cap, lacing, outsole, and heel to devise sturdier foot protection and a sole that bent at the ball of the foot.

In 1907, Chicago sports promoter Albert Spalding invented high-cut footwear specifically for basketball with gum rubber reinforcements and rigid heel counters (posts) perpendicular to soles. For after-school and after-work hours, basketball shoes combined leather-trimmed canvas or suede uppers with a buffed outsole and rubber toe cap for stylish and protective footwear for sports. Air-plumped gum rubber reduced weight in shoes previously made from dense tire rubber. The lighter shoes gripped a polished floor and enhanced sliding and pivoting, the essentials of the game.

U.S. Rubber in Naugatuck, Connecticut, marketed Keds, a popular and inexpensive brand of canvas sneakers that debuted in 1916. After World War I, the brand seized the emerging American market for sports apparel, especially for outdoor wear in summer. In Europe, Adidas and Puma both got their start in 1921 in Bavaria with brothers Adolf and Rudolph Dassler. In America that same year, the term "chucks" was attached to Converse high-tops, manufactured in Malden, Massachusetts, and touted by Charles Taylor, a basketball star for the Columbus Bull Dogs.

During the Great Depression, vented soles and traction treads increased the appeal for athletics by releasing perspiration and increasing foot-to-floor friction. Sports teams generated a demand for footwear designed for football, racquet sports, soccer, weight lifting, and wrestling. In the mid-twentieth century, U.S. children wore athletic shoes as daily school and play footwear. Because of natural attrition, team players replaced worn shoes after 500 miles (800 kilometers) of use.

Japanese entrepreneur Khachiro Onitsuka of Kobe increased traction by fitting the sole of the Tiger sports shoe with suction cups and a separate compartment for the big toe. By 1957, competitive American manufacturers hastened output to 1.2 billion shoes per year. The emergence of Reebok in Bolton, England, in 1958 preceded a global range of athletic shoes for baseball, bowling, boxing, car racing, cricket, football, ice hockey, lacrosse, rugby, soccer, tennis, and track. Each suited the type of exertion, as with rigid soles for cycling and enhanced support for aerobic dance and rope jumping.

By 1960, the term "sneakers" replaced earlier slang for Keds rubber-soled shoes. The style flourished in India as gym wear for schoolchildren. The following year, investor Paul Kidd of New Balance advanced biomechanical research that resulted in the Trackster, a running shoe with an elevated wedge heel to distribute weight for stability and to synchronize arch flexion during forward motion. In 1968, Puma introduced Spikes running shoes, the first sneaker with adjustable Velcro® closures. The style boosted jogging, a health regimen popularized in the 1970s.

Title IX legislation in 1972, which barred gender discrimination in federally funded athletic programs, boosted brand loyalty for outdoor footwear among active women, including lighter models made from DuPont Kevlar, a strong, flexible, composite. Nike, which led the change, pictured women not merely posing in shoes, but competing in track and field, race walking, cross-country, climbing, trail running, and cycling. Manufacturers began advertising lightweight styles of running shoes and sports-specific socks that catered to women's narrow heels and provided extra strapping and arch and heel support.

To extend marketability, sales staffs observed customers on treadmills to assess foot anatomy, arch stability, and gait during aerobic training. In the late 1980s, such popular names and logos as Air Jordan, Air Force 1, Dunk, and Terminator appealed to the fashionable youth who could afford expensive footwear for individual sports, cross training, and image. As designers increased choices, children and teens generated more demand for skateboard shoes featuring flexible grooves, neoprene bumpers, and padded tongue and collar to protect ankles.

The Pump, a Reebok innovation, added an air sac to the sneaker tongue for personalized fit. The comfy air pocket supplied women with more flexible ankle support than the leather strips around the collars of men's athletic shoes. Ethylene vinyl acetate and polyurethane energized the midsole to cushion shock and prevent sprains and stress fractures. Ripple soles fostered safety on frozen ground and asphalt and concrete surfaces. By 1997, as designers researched female athletic needs, women invested more money in sports footwear than men.

The rivalry among Adidas, Puma, and Nike for athletic shoe contracts influenced the buying for the 2012 Summer Olympics in London for national teams, who displayed the logos of supplier sponsors. In 2013, to compete with Nike, Adidas,

the world leader in soccer shoes, energized its athletic footwear with more bounce. Nike retaliated by hyping its Vapor Laser Talon, a running shoe built by a three-dimensional printer. Other innovations have included gel pads and shoes that look and respond like bare feet.

Keds has advertised its Green Label line as an ecological contribution to recycling. By using 20 percent reclaimed rubber, nontoxic dyes, and laces made from polyethylene terephthalate (PET) water bottles, the company upgraded its claim that Keds wash and air-dry easily and that they withstand normal athletic punishment from children and adults.

See also: Shoes, Men's; Shoes, Women's; Sports Attire, Competitive; Sports Attire, Recreational; Sweatshops; Uniforms, Sports.

Further Reading

Cardona, Melissa. *The Sneaker Book: 50 Years of Sports Shoe Design.* Atglen, PA: Schiffer, 2005.

Unorthodox Styles. *Sneakers: The Complete Collectors' Guide.* London: Thames & Hudson, 2005.

Werd, Matthew B., and E. Leslie Knight, eds. *Athletic Footwear and Orthoses in Sports Medicine.* Lakeland, FL: Springer, 2010.

Avedon, Richard (1923–2004)

A behind-the-camera star of contemporary media for 60 years, Richard Avedon won acclaim as a fashion and portrait photographer who helped establish a uniquely American style in postwar popular culture.

A native New Yorker born on May 15, 1923, he and his twin, Frank, were the sons of Anna Polonsky and Jacob Israel "Jack" Avonda, a Russian-Jewish retailer of women's clothes. Richard owned a box camera at age 10 and collected magazine photos that covered the walls of his room. In 1942, he left Columbia University to enter the Merchant Marines. He married model and actor Dorcas "Doe" Nowell two years later.

With a minimalism honed in service, Avedon began shooting ads for Bonwit Teller department store, which opened the way to jobs for such popular magazines as *Look, Life, Junior Bazaar, Rolling Stone, Egoïste, Harper's Bazaar,* and *Vogue.* His early work involved arranging models Dorian Leigh and Jean Shrimpton in surrealistic displays of luxury ensembles. A fashion shoot of Doe in Paris depicted her posed in a fur-lined coat and hat by Christian Dior. Other photographs showcased women laughing, smoking, primping, leaping, brooding, gambling, carousing, and touring the pyramids of Giza.

For *Harper's Bazaar* editor Diana Vreeland, Avedon debuted new models with inventive glamour shots on shores and dunes and at an arcade and circus. By reducing details with strobe lighting on empty backdrops and asking personal questions, he elicited the spontaneous vitality and sensuality of such celebrities as Mae West, Marlene Dietrich, and Gloria Vanderbilt, and models Suzy Parker, Dovima Horan, and Audrey Hepburn, whom he lionized for her natural beauty and grace. In the 1950s, Avedon arranged on-site projects for art director and mentor Alexey Brodovitch. The photographer inserted dramatic elements of wind, water, buildings, animals, and traffic into advertisements for André Perugia shoes, Tom Brigance bathing suits, and dresses and coats by Pierre Cardin, Coco Chanel, Cristóbal Balenciaga, Kimberly Goldson, and Dior.

In the 1960s, Avedon shot a poster series of the Beatles and a groundbreaking nude portrait of model Christina Paolozzi Bellin for *Harper's.* For Giorgio Ungari's fashions, Avedon pictured Twiggy and Penelope Tree in gleeful and contemplative moods. In January 1965, he debuted the fashion looks of black model Donyale Luna in apparel by Paco Rabanne. Avedon's assignments included portraits of *Vogue's* 10 best-dressed women and campaigns for designer Gianni Versace and Carnaby Street.

In the 1980s, Calvin Klein requested glimpses of denim on teen model Brooke Shields, an early example of Avedon's "shockvertising." Avedon enlivened promotion of Dior's line with a whimsical series of family photos. In 1989, the photographer accepted an honorary PhD from the Royal College of Art in London and a lifetime achievement award from the Council of Fashion Designers of America, two honoraria given, in part, for his exhibit *In the American West.* Subsequent honorary degrees from Kenyon College in Ohio and the Parsons School of Design in New York preceded his election in 2001 to the American Academy of Arts and Sciences.

Weary of fashion, at age 69, Avedon became the first photographer on staff at the *New Yorker.* His innovative views of actors Marilyn Monroe, Tilda Swinton, Lauren Hutton, Sophia Loren, and Charlize Theron provoked varied reader response. The year before his death on October 1, 2004, from a brain hemorrhage, he received a special 150th Anniversary Medal and fellowship from the Royal Photographic Society. *The New York Times* memorialized Avedon as "the Eye of Fashion."

See also: Photography, Fashion.

Further Reading

Avedon, Richard. *Evidence, 1944–1994.* New York: Random House, 1994.

Avedon, Richard, and Judith Thurman. *Richard Avedon: Made in France.* San Francisco: Fraenkel Gallery, 2001.

Squiers, Carol, and Vince Aletti, eds. *Avedon Fashion 1944–2000.* New York: Harry N. Abrams, 2009.

Baby Clothes

Fashions for babies throughout history have reflected adult attitudes toward themselves and their children. From ancient times, swaddling in soft cloth strips restrained the baby's limbs during sleep. In 4000 B.C.E., migrants carried babies in animal pelt backpacks or bound to carriers or rigid cradleboards to straighten the child's spine. Swaddling safeguarded babies from falls or other endangerment. In ancient Rome, swaddling began immediately after birth in a ritual acknowledging the infant's need for adult protection.

As early as 1200 B.C.E., in southern Greece, Lacedaemonian infants tended to be naked and barefoot. In Athens, cloth drapings served babies as diapers and swaddling. Prestigious families fastened a fine white shawl or purple scarf around the newborn with a gold band. A conical cap covered the baby's head to the ears in cold weather.

Korean mothers secured their infants in a soft-sided fabric rectangle quilted for warmth and wound under the baby's bottom to the parent's torso. In Africa, working women varied this design with a loose sling or double-strapped pouch tied to the mother's abdomen, a style still found in China, Russia, and Turkey.

European Bindings

In the Middle Ages, swathing posed a serious concern in an era of high infant mortality. Wrapping and tying began with the knotting of the clout (diaper). When a newborn survived the initial months, parents offered the bindings to kin as auspicious clothing. In the 1100s, smocking honeycombed the christening gowns of infants.

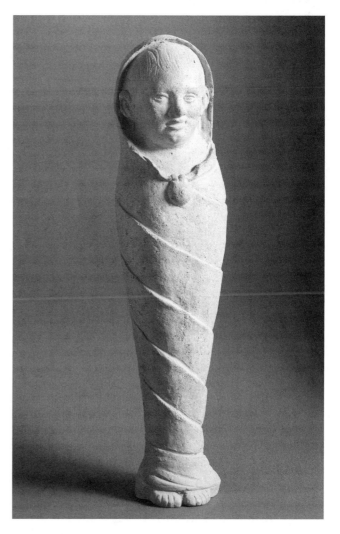

An Etruscan votive statue from about 1900 B.C.E. depicts an infant in swaddling wraps. Throughout history and across the globe, mothers have used swaddling to protect their babies from injury, keep them warm, and restrain the limbs during sleep. *(De Agostini/Getty Images)*

Renaissance swaddling among the wealthy featured exquisite linen bands and bearing cloths (mantles) decorated with cutwork, satin stitching, metallic thread, and needle lace. Throughout the 1600s, the French lashed infants to the parent's thigh with arms crossed over the chest and lower limbs left free. Infant hygiene required the removal of wrappings several times daily and at night for bathing.

Farther north, English parents condemned Renaissance-style swaddling from neck to fingertips as child abuse because of the absence of cuddling. On the advice of philosopher John Locke and child care expert William Cadogan, mothers made sleeveless flannel vests attached to a loose skirt and either a gauze scarf, muslin cap, or wicker eyeshade to protect the head from dust. The complete outfit included a long overgown and nightcap constructed of a double thickness of fabric.

Advisories from the 1770s rebuked parents for constraining babies in tight clothing and for using straight pins as fasteners. In 1781, the London Foundling Hospital introduced the foundling dress, a gown with ties down the back similar to contemporary surgical gowns. The English created orthopedic attire to straighten posture and prevent crawling, an animal behavior that appalled parents in the Age of Reason.

First Fashions

Parents began abandoning tight wraps and instead dressed both genders in sashed frocks. Clothing makers favored linen, batiste, gingham, challis, sateen, net, calico, and sheer silk for unisex outfits and undershirts. Harness bands or leading strings on toddlers helped parents guide children through the first steps.

For outdoor walks, parents draped infants in netted throws, attached embroidered covers to diapers, and tied quilted bibs around the neck for drooling teethers. Embroidered linen or wool mitts kept babies warm, as did capes with velvet trim and cotton earmuffs on wire frames to encircle the ears. Matched with a lace collar, the crocheted or tucked bonnet displayed artistry with drawn thread work, French knotting, satin stitchery, and lace edgings.

In the latter part of the nineteenth century, satin-edged wool knit or crocheted blankets and cashmere *pelisses* (caped cloaks) covered infants by day and quilted bunting (sleepbags) with attached pillows by night. Underneath, crib babies wore suede bibs lined in wool, rib knit undershirts, and lacy drawstring gowns and sacks.

Button-up one-piece pajamas and flannel baby slips and princess-style gowns with inset lace panels increased warmth, especially for night and nap wear. Nickel-plated crib pins protected diapered babies from sharp points. Rubber diaper covers spared contamination from soiled diapers. Concern for hygiene in the 1890s encouraged mothers to burn used diapers rather than wash them.

Babies in Style

The Victorian rage for orientalism impacted baby fashions in the form of kimono robes and matching diaper covers in cotton or silk. Pantalettes, skirts, and gauze caps with deep eyelet trim over elegant knitted booties in fine wool softened the ornate silhouette of previous centuries. Baby sacks, kimonos, and gowns maintained the eyelet, silk crepe, and embroidered organdy of adult Edwardian dress, but with more satin edging, tatting, and chintz insets and less fancy embroidery of the nineteenth century.

Bellybands covered the umbilicus until it healed. Cotton or wool diapers required frequent changing. All-in-one booties and socks and one-piece rompers with padded groin linings simplified the job of dressing infants. Rubber and metal garters secured baby stockings under two-strap corduroy overalls.

As World War I approached, baby clothes exhibited military motifs, as with soldiers and cannon decorating the top of a diaper shirt. Chambray rompers and Russian-style Cossack collars on tunics and banded pants over felt shoes highlighted the chic baby outfit. Nightgowns featured drawstring hems and machine-knit mittens that nestled feet and hands. Fleece carriage blankets derived from a period interest in lambskin, astrakhan, and fake fur.

Buttons on christening dresses and slips and two-piece crawler suits replaced some of the ribbon ties of previous generations. Poufy crowns attached to long knit scarf ends relieved bonnets of infantilizing ribbon ties. Russian-style dresses with box pleats created a smooth line without the gathers that dominated torso coverings in the 1800s. Bonnets exhibited elegant chiffon ruching, bobbin lace, angora, and Teneriffe lace (webwork) and flat knitted braid. High-top flannel booties in pearlized cotton embroidery and dentelle edging matched the high tone of head wear.

Ready-to-Wear

In the 1920s, working mothers limited the amount of time spent on making and repairing baby clothes. Marketers of ready-to-wear stressed individualized baby wardrobes to suit their personalities. Clothiers displayed outfits by length, 24–26 inches (61–66 centimeters), the standard height up to six months. Designers introduced tasseled booties for infants and reshaped the baptismal dress with eyelet trim rather than lace.

Gowns and shirts featured colored collars against white bodices, slash pockets, and appliqués in duck, dog, and bird shapes. Rompers in vertical stripes echoed the styling of baseball uniforms. The snapped crotch eased the chore of diaper changing. For cold weather, bright-colored quilted bootees lined in cotton batting and pompom tams replaced lace and embroidery.

During the 1930s, for the first time, mass-produced baby togs came in standard sizing. Designers perpetuated the simple silhouette marked by sedate detail and smocking on rayon knit. Zip-up crib covers and lined bathrobes featured snuggly fleece and corduroy.

Infant suits bore appliquéd bibs and two-color sailor tops with button-on shorts. For crawlers, corduroy overalls with bib fronts offered no-iron ease for mothers. One-piece suits opened at the waist with a buttoned band extending over the front. Tweed pompom caps with earflaps upgraded fabrics for babies from lawn and batiste to lightweight wool.

Baby shoes tended toward silk moccasins and slippers edged in rabbit fur. Baby swimsuits added open mesh bibs to knit bottoms with bound elastic legs. For girls, ruffled straps on sunsuits sported rickrack trim in primary tones. Matching organdy hats with picot edging on the circular brim shaded the face.

War Years and After

The 1940s increased comfort and simplicity with technological advances in weaving, knitting, and trims. Designers stereotyped the color coding of pink for girls and blue for boys. For bassinet babies, wool bunting with a separate hood and shoulder flaps provided more coverage from drafts. Layettes (complete outfits) consisted of shaped diapers, snap-up diaper covers, and machine-made caps, sweaters, sleepbags, and booties with coordinated detailing. Popular infant gifts included monogrammed bracelets, lockets, and necklaces.

The postwar baby boom, the period from 1946 to 1964 that produced 76 million babies, heightened demand for infant wear and diaper services. The market debuted unique designs not based on adult attire. For outdoors, carriage suits enclosed the feet in soft corduroy. Banded neck, sleeves, and leg openings sustained the shape of knit creepers. Little girls' outfits matched short tops with snap-leg panties to cover diapers. Boys' fashions added the miniature bow tie to three-piece cotton suits with coordinated blanket.

The wool snowsuit combined a straight jacket with wool leggings flared at the bottom to cover booties. Baby hats abandoned a tight skull fit in favor of long pointed crowns, billed Eton caps, and pompom beanies. For indoor play, babies wore knit booties with moccasin soles.

Polio epidemics in 1949 and 1950 increased parental concern for straight legs and feet. Introductory walking shoes extended the sole up the heel to support ankles. The high-top look became common footwear to accompany twill overalls and coveralls with contrasting roll-up cuffs.

Technological Advances

Children's fashions in the 1960s and 1970s mimicked adult leisure wear. Young parents experimented with global styles of cradleboards, hip or chest carriers, Chinese pouches, and slings to keep the newborn near an adult. Sleepers and fleece pajamas with ankle ribbing offered a tighter fit than elastic. Synthetic pull-on slippers came in animal shapes and emulated train cars with wheels on the sides. For toddlers, nylon bodysuits stretched with the crawler.

Changes in baby clothes, such as Velcro®-fastened waterproof cotton diaper covers invented in Japan in the 1960s, down-filled polyester mittens, fleece snowsuits with toggle buttons, and high-impact plastic helmets, reflected the manufacturing advances of the 1980s and 1990s. Velveteen rompers and dresses and eyelet pinafores over bloomers and matching blouses in easy-care fabrics ended the need for dry cleaning and ironing. For precrawlers, one-piece sweat suits or snap-crotch "onesies" worn with open-toed sandals featured Bugs Bunny and Care Bear decals.

All-natural disposable diapers with Velcro tabs or tapes relieved the eco-friendly parent of guilt for choosing convenience over washables. Some diapers came with leg gathers and emollient lotions to prevent diaper rash. Sizing allowed parents to purchase fitted diapers for preemies and newborns. Leakproof liners and diaper covers extended protection with polyurethane linings.

Preemie sizes in drawstring gowns, leggings, lap-shoulder shirts, and skullcaps suited special sizing needs. Footed blanket sleepers, side-snap shirts, drool bibs, and zip-up sleepbags bore flame retardants that lasted the life of the garments. Prewalker Uggs, fleece slippers with elastic closures, and leopard-patterned tights protected the crawler from rug burn. More fashionable footwear emulated that of adults with cross-laced espadrilles, ballet flats, aqua shoes, sparkle sneakers, silver-toed Mary Janes, and gladiator sandals.

Into the twenty-first century, baby clothes maintained hip details, including bodysuits, jeggings (jean leggings), slippers with animal faces and ears, and felt riding boots. Denim in skirted overalls, miniskirts, pull-on jeans, roll-up pants, sunsuits, jumpers, and knickers teamed with sherpa rain jackets, puff-sleeve T-shirts, flutter sleeve tees, glitzy shirts, and polka-dotted hoodies. Swimsuits featured neon and citrus colors as well as animal prints with matching coverups, elastic headbands with bows, and plastic sunglasses.

See also: Children's Clothing, Boys; Children's Clothing, Girls.

Further Reading

Chudacoff, Howard. *Children at Play: An American History.* New York: NYU Press, 2007.

Cook, Daniel Thomas. *The Commodification of Childhood: The Children's Clothing Industry and the Rise of the Child Consumer.* Durham, NC: Duke University Press, 2004.

MacPhail, Anna. *The Well-Dressed Child: Children's Clothing, 1820–1940.* Atglen, PA: Schiffer, 1999.

Paoletti, Jo B. *Pink and Blue: Telling the Boys from the Girls in America.* Bloomington: Indiana University Press, 2012.

Badges and Insignias

From early history, sewn or appliquéd badges, patches, and insignias have symbolized authority and alliance with institutions, belief systems, and agencies. Examples of societies that used official insignia to inform the preliterate include the early Egyptians, Persians, Macedonians, Romans, Hebrews, Goths, Vandals, and Native Americans, among whom the Pueblo cultures of the Great Basin from 7000 B.C.E. used eagle feathers. As early as 1800 B.C.E., the Minoans of Crete employed the chevron as an insignia. After 1319 B.C.E., Egyptians marked the pharaoh Horemheb's scepter with the *was* (power) glyph, symbolizing control.

The coiled dragon signified rank in China as early as 4700 B.C.E. On court robes and slippers in imperial China from 221 B.C.E., the dragon and phoenix indicated sources of power. After 9 C.E., China's Xin dynasty emperors issued badges to military commanders. A ranking of symbols reserved the five-clawed dragon for the emperor.

Byzantine needlework combined artistry with religious and governmental authorization, such as identification of priests and pilgrims. Fur also outlined official emblems and crests, the forerunners of heraldic coats of arms. After 306, Constantine I the Great, the first Christian emperor, chose the cross as an official emblem and applied it to his jewelry and clothing along with appliqués of the Lamb of God. The emperor's subjects emulated his designs as good luck amulets. They economized by buying used garments and removing emblems and geometrics to appliqué over cheap cotton, linen, and wool attire.

Formalizing Insignias

Around 500 in Constantinople, security guards increased the visibility of imperial insignia. Their armored breastplates fastened over short, shirt-shaped Coptic tunics of linen or wool and war kilts embroidered or appliquéd with royal cyphers. Decoration on the neckline, sleeves, hem, wristbands, and side slits ranged from resist-dye or batiking in gold, yellow, orange, or red to loomed roundels or stripes and a kilt of fringed leather straps embossed with insignia.

After 1096, embroidered shield covers displaying chivalric crests and insignia, forerunners of heraldic coats of arms, gained popularity among European troops during the First and Second Crusades. English officers adorned the right shoulder with a cross worked in white silk. The French adopted a similar insignia in red. The Flemish chose green. Ordinary soldiers replicated the designs in worsted yarn.

Into the thirteenth century, soldiers promoted unity by attaching military emblems to war kilts, such as those worn by crusaders. Unlike true heraldry, the early patterns of Kazakhs and Picts lacked the authority of the heraldic device or badge, as with the clan symbols identifying warriors in ancient Greece and the *kamon* or *mon* (round emblem) worn by Japanese clans from the 1100s.

Artistry

In European courts, the early Renaissance saw the elevation of embroidery to high art on crests, livery cyphers, and heraldry. Emblems identified the Lancaster and York dynasties during the Wars of the Roses from 1455 to 1485. By the 1600s, soldiers and rescue workers identified their allegiances with embroidered, enamel, silver, or brass cap badges displaying corps and regiment. Common symbols on service caps, glengarries, tams, bonnets, and officers' hats ranged from eagles, stags, lions, and thistles to scrolls, swords and anchors, and crowns.

The eighteenth century saw the formalization of military insignia, such as the sash and stars on epaulets worn by officers of the Continental Army during the American Revolution. In 1784, formation of the Highland Society of Edinburgh promoted Scots culture through Gaelic language and clan symbolism. In the late 1700s, Highlanders chose specific twill weaves, contrasting squares, and colors produced by natural local dyes as a form of heraldry. The first tailored regimental tartan and

kilt with sewn-in box pleats at the back dated to 1792. By wearing plaids in blankets, kilts, sashes, and wraps woven in their district, Scots exhibited their belonging to an extended family.

Twentieth-century insignia makers marked members and followers of authority figures with identifiable symbols, such as the silver vest buttons of Eton students, swastikas on Hitler Youth, affiliation pins worn by registered nurses, shoulder patches attached to the uniforms of the NASA Apollo 17 Skylab crew, and shields borne by police officers, treasury and Interpol agents, and Royal Canadian Mounted Police indicating jurisdiction. Business contributed iron-on badges for airline crews and gas station attendants, and hats for Jaguar owners. After 1966, Mao Zedong conferred the red-and-gold metal Chairman Mao badge in China. Hollywood movies marked Western lawmen with marshal's and sheriff's badges and soldiers with military insignia.

See also: Appliqué; Livery and Heraldry; Symbolic Colors, Patterns, and Motifs; Uniforms, Military.

Further Reading

Gaylor, John. *Military Badge Collecting.* London: Secker & Warburg, 1983.
Rosignoli, Guido. *World Army Badges and Insignia Since 1939.* Poole, Dorset, UK: Blandford, 2003.

Balenciaga, Cristóbal (1895–1972)

An artistic Basque minimalist, Cristóbal Balenciaga Eizaguirre dominated haute couture of the mid-twentieth century with flowing, sculptured lines that flattered female gestures and movements.

Born in a fishing village in the northern Spanish province of Gipuzkoa on January 21, 1895, Balenciaga studied tailoring with his widowed mother, Martina Eizaguirre, a seamstress for wealthy clients. Apprenticed at age 12, he learned his trade at a high-end tailor shop in San Sebastián, a seaside resort in the western Pyrenees. He eventually mastered the classic silhouette from Spanish Renaissance paintings by Diego Velázquez, Francisco de Zubarán, and Francisco Goya featuring the drama of the bullfight, Catholic ritual, and flamenco dancing.

In 1914, Balenciaga worked for a tailor in Bordeaux. A patron of his mother, the Marquesa de Casa Torres, financed his business at a shop in Madrid after he copied a suit made by Christoff von Drecoll of Vienna. At age 24, Balenciaga opened his own boutique, Balenciaga y Compañia, in San Sebastián. From branches in Barcelona and Madrid, he outfitted Spain's Queen Victoria Eugénie, Queen Mother María Cristina, and Infanta Isabel Alfonsa. In 1927, Balenciaga established the House of Eisa, named for his mother, which he operated with the aid of his sister Agustina and niece Tina.

In 1937, during the Spanish Civil War, because of the exile of court ladies, Balenciaga moved his operation to Paris. At his Avenue George V studio, he presented a first live model show on August 5, 1937, introducing aloof linear originals based on historic designs. In his limited annual production of 356 designs, he gained a reputation for exquisite embroidery and passementerie (stitched braid). His supporters included Carmel Snow, editor of *Harper's Bazaar,* who wore his work almost exclusively, and Carmen Polo, wife of Spanish dictator Francisco Franco.

Clients weary of artificial hourglass designs continued to seek Balenciaga's feminine shapes during World War II, when they risked travel through bombed-out towns to view the latest garments. His business courted a reputation for *le plus cher, et clientèle le plus riches* (the most expensive clothes and the wealthiest buyers). In June 1940, Balenciaga joined major Paris couturiers Elsa Schiaparelli and Jeanne Lanvin in retreating to Biarritz, a French resort town north of his birthplace in Spain.

Under the protection of Franco, Balenciaga reopened Eisa in September 1940 and showed cycling skirts, blazers, bloomers, and stockings. His dressmakers slimmed down silhouettes to accommodate fabric rationing and employed prints to appeal to American buyers. To ensure employment for seamstresses, Balenciaga kept the business open during the Nazi occupation by remaining apolitical.

In 1945, Balenciaga dressed some of the 200 fashion dolls showcased in the Théâtre de la Mode, a traveling style show touting the best of Paris. Called "fashion's Picasso," the designer pioneered theatrical outfits—the loose back of the barrel line jacket and the demi-fitted square coat, an uncluttered garment featuring a yoke cut in one piece with the sleeves. By elevating a distinctive bias collar, his coats set off nape and collarbone. His seven-eighths–length sleeves showcased dainty hands and wrists, bracelets, and rings.

In contrast to the girlish shape promoted by competitor Christian Dior, Balenciaga in 1951 introduced modernistic silhouettes recalling the smock top and the middy. Balenciaga and his staff of 232 debuted the tunic, a classic silhouette falling straight from broadened shoulders. In 1953, he designed the balloon jacket, a cocoon for the upper body that set the head on top of a fabric pedestal.

His uncluttered lines flattered self-assured women, including actor Ava Gardner, playwright Claire Boothe Luce, American First Lady Jacqueline Kennedy, and Wallis Warfield Simpson, the duchess of Windsor. Actor Ingrid Bergman wore Balenciaga fashions in the historical film *Anastasia* (1956), which featured Bergman in a navy velvet suit and a princess line gown with a stole of slipper satin.

The media lauded Balenciaga's boxy chemise and applauded his bubble skirts, peacock tail dress, and trapeze or baby doll dress. A triumph of 1957, the semi-fitted sack displayed the female form in unconfining lines that welcomed jewelry and gloves. His distinctive concepts earned him a Chevalier de la Légion d'honneur from the French government for innovative haute couture and architectonic style.

In 1959, Balenciaga chose another historic look, the Empire line, originally introduced by the Empress Joséphine of France in the late eighteenth century. Balenciaga's contributions to the style included the dramatic shape of a high-waisted kimono with a bias rolled collar and cantilevered cut, a semitransparent overdress, and innovative uses of crepe de chine, flocked organdies, boucles, wools, organzas, velvets, silk gabardines, and *poult-de-soie* (corded taffetas). In collaboration with Abraham, Gustav Zumsteg's silk company in Zurich, Balenciaga evolved silk gazar, a matte high-twist material for shaping afternoon dresses, suits, and evening gowns and capes.

To secure the best in haute couture, Balenciaga shopped for accessories and embellishments that complemented his abstract, monochromatic styles, such as a cascade of ermine tails on the train of a simple black velvet gown. In 1960, Balenciaga designed a wedding ensemble for Fabiola de Mora y Aragón, the granddaughter of the couturier's first patron, for Fabiola's marriage to King Baudouin I of Belgium on December 15, 1960. Paired with an art deco tiara, the austere white silk and mink dress and train expressed the bride's selfless perspective. The Balenciaga house maintained its reputation for surprising the public by introducing avant-garde over-the-knee boots by Renato Mancini and designing Air France stewardess uniforms adaptable to a range of climates.

In 1968, Balenciaga retired and mentored André Courrèges, Oscar de la Renta, Hubert de Givenchy, and Emanuel Ungaro. In his last months, Balenciaga designed a wedding ensemble for Duchess María of Cadiz, the granddaughter of Spanish leader Francisco Franco. After the designer's death in Jávea, Spain, on March 23, 1972, Nicolas Ghesquière continued to direct the Balenciaga House couture and original line of perfumes.

See also: Fashion Design; Spanish and Portuguese Clothing.

Further Reading

Balenciaga. www.balenciaga.com

Descalzo, Amalia, Pierre Arizzoli-Clémentel, Miren Arzalluz, and Lourdes Cerrillo Rubio. *Balenciaga.* London: Thames & Hudson, 2011.

Golbin, Pamela. *Balenciaga Paris.* London: Thames & Hudson, 2006.

Jouve, Marie-Andrée, and Jane Brenton. *Balenciaga.* New York: Assouline, 2005.

Miller, Lesley Ellis. *Cristóbal Balenciaga (1895–1972): The Couturier's Couturier.* New York: Harry N. Abrams, 2007.

Walker, Myra. *Balenciaga and His Legacy.* New Haven, CT: Yale University Press, 2006.

Balmain, Pierre (1914–1982)

A fashion dressmaker and structural master of ball and bridal gowns, Pierre Alexandre Claudius Balmain sculpted suave lines to flatter female curves.

Born on May 18, 1914, in Saint-Jean-de-Maurienne, Savoie, he was the son of wholesale draper Maurice Balmain and retailer Françoise Ballinari Balmain. During his first year of elementary school at Chambéry, he recovered from his father's death by arranging and measuring fabrics that his mother and maternal aunts, Marie and Marthe, sewed into ensembles at their boutique, the Galeries Parisiennes.

During matriculation in architecture at l'École des Beaux Arts in Paris, Balmain sold design sketches to Swiss couturier Robert Piguet at Redfern. While living at the Cité Universitaire, Balmain abandoned architecture at age 20 and petitioned designer Edward Molyneux for a position in dress design. As an introduction to elite clients, Balmain acquainted himself with the wardrobe tastes of Princess Marina of Greece, the duchess of Kent.

Following service in the French Air Force from 1936 to 1939, Balmain designed for Lucien Lelong during the Nazi occupation of Paris and made garments for his neighbors, Gertrude Stein and Alice B. Toklas. In 1942, although Balmain felt unfulfilled by his experience with Lelong, he received Gestapo permission to attend the Barcelona International Exhibition as the Lelong emissary and sold 360 of his black crepe afternoon dresses.

After World War II, following his desire for creative freedom, Balmain, along with Cristóbal Balenciaga and Christian Dior, revived Parisian haute couture for royalty and celebrities. With just 600,000 francs, he established his own label on October 12, 1945. His collections showcased ample bustlines and nipped-in waists above the bell skirts of embroidered gowns and suits, which he made for Wallis Warfield Simpson, the duchess of Windsor. Fashion commentary in *Vogue* on his dresses for Helena Rubinstein noted his nuanced detail in paillettes, bows, trim, fur muffs and hoods, the game pocket on a corduroy hunting suit, and the silk plaque embroidered on an ivory grosgrain summer dress and petticoat. In October 1946, a Balmain wedding ensemble became one of the first Paris fashions imported into postwar Toronto, Canada.

After scouting design possibilities in Australia, Balmain opened a U.S. boutique in 1949. Under the Jolie Madame label, he marketed sportswear, full back coats, Cossack capes, jacketed sheath day dresses, and stoles that suited the American lifestyle. By 1951, his clothes began earning acclaim, appearing in 16 Hollywood films and in the private wardrobes of such stars as Mae West and Vivien Leigh. Key to his supple drapery, choices of silk georgette with elastic threads created classical Greek fluidity. His retro eighteenth-century gowns featured a bustier bodice, padded hips, and an underskirt visible through the divided overskirt.

Balmain's global visibility advanced with his quiet luxury and elegant bridal dresses sold at Eaton's in Toronto and worn in 1950 by Patrice Wymore, the bride of actor Errol Flynn. His imported originals featured subtle tones in contrasting fabric cut to hug the torso and complementary costume jewelry. Screen wear for Marlene Dietrich included a long mink stole in *No Highway in the Sky* (1951). For Katharine Hepburn, he created a wardrobe for her role in the Broadway comedy *The Millionairess* (1952). Following the design of an ivory satin and taffeta dress with embroidered pearl and sequin apron, Balmain accepted the 1955 Neiman Marcus award.

As of 1956, the golden era of haute couture, the House of Balmain employed 600 seamstresses in 12 ateliers. His team customized designs for a cocktail dress shown in Ontario and modified it to client taste with custom embroidery, making it impossible to replicate.

At a peak of refinement in the late 1950s, Balmain designed stage costumes for film glamour icons Brigitte Bardot and Sophia Loren, couture for model Ruth Ford and socialite Bronwen Astor, and exotic stage gowns and a mink-edged gold peplum jacket for dancer Josephine Baker. In 1958, critics credited Balmain's costuming of actor Kay Kendall for her success in *The Reluctant Debutante* (1958). As personal couturier for Queen Sirikit of Thailand, he produced state gowns for her New York visit in 1960 and a sailor suit for her appearances on the royal barge. For First Lady Jacqueline Kennedy, he shaped a ladylike princess line ivory dress with a demure bodice covered in glittering embroidery.

After looking back on his life and career in a memoir titled *My Years and Seasons* (1964), Balmain entered a period of even greater panache and notoriety for long, uncluttered silhouettes in sumptuous fabrics. Three years after upgrading TWA stewardess uniforms for Singapore Airlines in 1968, he redefined the national *kebaya* (blouse-dress) into a two-piece uniform batiked in a navy Indonesian paisley. After he dressed Nicaraguan first lady Hope Portocarrero Debayle, she appeared on the 1968 International Best-Dressed List Hall of Fame.

In the 1970s, after a brush with bankruptcy, Balmain established a ready-to-wear division. In the Paris Originals series, patterns included pantsuits, trench coat, culotte dress, cocktail dress with cape sleeves, and Greek revival gown. In 1980, he received a Tony nomination and a Drama Desk Award for wardrobes he designed for the Cole Porter musical *Happy New Year* (1980).

Three years after Balmain died in Paris from liver cancer on June 29, 1982, the Musée de la Mode et du Costume honored his work with a 40-year retrospective. In the early twenty-first century, celebrities Angelina Jolie, Gwyneth Paltrow, Penélope Cruz, and Kate Moss have reclaimed his couture gowns as retro chic.

See also: Fashion Design; French Clothing and Fashion.

Further Reading

Balmain, Pierre. *My Years and Seasons*. London: Cassell, 1964.

House of Balmain. www.balmain.com/en

Palmer, Alexandra. *Couture & Commerce: The Transatlantic Fashion Trade in the 1950s*. Vancouver, UBC Press, 2001.

Shaeffer, Claire B. *Couture Sewing Techniques*. Newtown, CT: Taunton, 2011.

Batiking

One of Asia's major art forms, batiking—Javanese for "writing with dots"—is a dyeing method that involves melted beeswax, paraffin, or wood sap as dye repellants to shape traditional motifs. The finished fabric incorporates mystical folk beliefs and tropical patterns on silk or cotton. Unlike tie-dyeing, which requires boiling fabric in dye, the more subdued batik technique appears to have begun in 300 B.C.E. in Egyptian linen shops in the manufacture of mummy wrappings and grave goods.

In the mid-500s, Byzantine tunics carried the resist-dye decor in gold, yellow, red, and orange. By permeating linen with wax and using a pointed stylus, the designer could scratch a pattern to dye with a contrasting color. In the final stage, the dyer dried the fabric, then dissolved the wax with heat or solvent to reveal fine detailing.

In the seventh century, China's batiking influenced designs in India, Ceylon, the Philippines, and Japan, where chrysanthemum and cherry blossoms dominated motifs on formal waistcloths. Over caravan routes of the Silk Road, batiking spread westward, especially the intersecting circle pattern popularized in the 1200s.

Inscribed with a bamboo or wood canting (tracer) filled with molten wax, Javanese patterns indicated a class structure headed by the sultan and aristocracy. The style combined intricate Hindu scrolling, blossoms, palms, birds, butterflies, fantasy figures, the tree of life, and greenery on densely woven fabric. Hindu mythography took shape in yellow, cream, brown, indigo, red, white, green, and black as well as a sprinkling of gold dust glued with albumin or linseed oil for gilded batik. Another method, ikat (binding) technology, involved the bunching of silk threads for resist dyeing on velvet.

For formal national costume, Malaysian batik since the 1200s has depicted calligraphy and geometrics rather than people and animals, a forbidden form of idolatry under Islamic aesthetics. In the 1400s, the Chinese Buddhist trade influenced design at Batavia and contributed the *kebaya,* a traditional Balinese or Indonesian outfit for women that placed a long-sleeved, collarless tunic over a straight wrap skirt. By the seventeenth century, court audiences required formal dress in batik for ministers, priests, and dancers. In 1677, China introduced varied fabrics and patterns by exporting silk batiks to Java, Sumatra, Persia, and Hindustan. Patterns indicated source, as with the dark, somber designs of Surakarta and Yogyakarta in central Java and the richer, more colorful Chinese patterns produced in Ceribon and Pekalongan, Java.

Under Dutch colonial entrepreneurs, Javanese factories expanded traditional prints with international styles. By 1835, Indonesian batik artists traveled to Holland to teach Dutch fabric makers the wax repellant method. A stylized Dutch pattern originated in 1840 indicated the arrival of European influence in Java, where outsiders observed the meticulous application of color to cloth.

Early in the twentieth century, Malaysian crafters modernized batiking by applying patterns with copper and wood blocks, which reduced the need for the canting and introduced silk screening as a print method. The batik screens at the 1900 Exposition Universelle in Paris won acclaim for artist Chris Lebeau at the Dutch booth and prompted German fabric makers to mass-produce batiks.

The 1890s saw the replacement of traditional Javanese borders with European lace, arches, bouquets, fairies, and flowering vines. Migration from Indonesia spread hand-drawn batiking crafts to Malaysia, the Caribbean, and Australia for maternity outfits, infant slings and clothing, blouses and shirts, sarongs, shawls and scarves, turbans, and shrouds.

World turmoil influenced shifts in batik production in the 1930s to high-end luxury textiles with an art deco flair. The postwar boom saw a rise in demand for the wax dye process in a multitude of styles and colors. In 1955, President Sukarno suggested another change in design to "Batik Indonesia," a style that celebrated the end of Dutch colonialism and the freedom and unity of the republic of Indonesia. Sukarno banned imitation batik and commissioned artist Go Tik Swan to design a nationalistic batik.

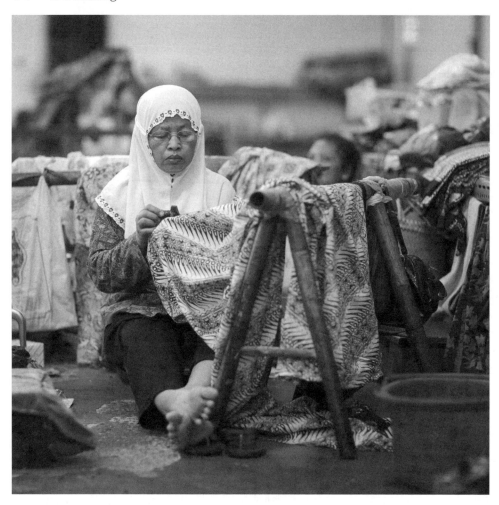

A woman in Indonesia practices the ancient dyeing technique of batiking. In traditional Javanese batik, hand-rendered designs may represent Hindu gods, social class, or aspects of nature and daily life. One bolt can take up to five months to complete. *(Thomas Koehler/Photothek via Getty Images)*

In 1970, Iwan Tirta, an attorney and art historian of Javanese-Sumatran descent, researched batik for its cultural and historical significance as a court art. He wanted to introduce handmade Asian styles to the pages of *Vogue* as a means of preserving ancient techniques and making Indonesia competitive in the global fashion market. In 1986, First Lady Nancy Reagan chose an artistic Tirta butterfly batik for a state gown. President Bill Clinton wore a Tirta shirt to the 1994 Asia-Pacific Economic Cooperation Summit. As a cultural ambassador, Tirta showed clothing collections in Beijing, Barcelona, and Madrid.

Today, batik belongs to the world. In banks and hotel and restaurant chains, high-fashion wall hangings replicate sophisticated designs dating to the Middle Ages that calm and bemuse. Flight attendants in Indonesia, Malaysia, and Singapore wear batik uniforms as models of folk culture, although the fabric derives from contemporary computerized design methods. Nelson Mandela, another Tirta customer, popularized the Madiba batik silk shirt as a personal favorite. In 2009, within months of Tirta's death at age 75, the United Nations Educational, Scientific and Cultural Organization (UNESCO) declared batik a model of cultural heritage.

See also: Color Trends; Dyeing; Symbolic Colors, Patterns, and Motifs.

Further Reading

Elliott, Inger McCabe. *Batik: Fabled Cloth of Java.* North Clarendon, VT: Tuttle, 2010.

Harper, Donald J., Rudolph G. Smend, and Leo Haks. *Batik: From the Courts of Java and Sumatra.* Singapore: Periplus, 2004.

Hillmer, Paul. *A People's History of the Hmong.* St. Paul: Minnesota Historical Society Press, 2010.

Maxwell, Robyn. *Textiles of Southeast Asia: Tradition, Trade and Transformation.* Hong Kong: Periplus; North Clarendon, VT: Tuttle, 2003.

Beads and Beading

Beadwork has adorned clothing, amulets, jewelry, and knitting as well as weaving virtually throughout the world since ancient times. Natufian artisans around 98,000 B.C.E. at Skhul Cave on Mount Carmel in present-day Israel pierced sea snail shells with a drill point for stringing on vines or sinew as necklaces and anklets. Crafted in Algeria around 88,000 B.C.E. and Morocco around 80,000 B.C.E., shell beads and disks dyed red with ochre manifested the human need for personal adornment and protection of the living and dead.

Idiosyncratic beadwork developed rapidly after the evolution of the bow drill and needle-and-thread technology, beginning in Gujarat, India, in 5000 B.C.E. with polished gemstones. Hindu worshippers wore devotional beads and preserved choice shapes and colors as charms against evil and envy. From 4500 B.C.E., Syrians at Tell Hamoukar carved beads from obsidian, a smooth volcanic glass. Thai metalsmiths added tin to copper to produce bronze beads. Chinese jewelers favored porcelain, enamel, and cloisonné (vitreous enamel). Japanese bead makers worked in stone, bone, and jade.

After 3000 B.C.E., artisans applied beadwork to clothing, headdresses, or shoes using beads of horn, teeth, ivory, wood, seeds, nuts, coral, ochre, or mother-of-pearl in spherical, cylindrical, and amorphous shapes. Mesopotamian workers began shaping decorative clay and glass beads over flame after 2350 B.C.E. and turned steatite (soapstone) into ceramic beads. From onyx, sardonyx, and agate, they produced the goat eye bead popularized in Afghanistan and Bactria as protection from the evil eye.

After 2000 B.C.E., Indian jewelers cut ostrich eggshell into disks and hoarded agate dzi stones or evil-eye beads seized by soldiers deployed to Persia. After 1897 B.C.E., makers of cloisonné adorned the pectoral of Senusret II of Egypt with beads and inlays of lapis lazuli and turquoise. Around 600 B.C.E., Egyptian jewelers added faience beads, a tin-glazed ceramic, in red, blue, and green.

The Trade

As trade items, personal adornment, and curiosities, beads are a common archaeological find. Phoenician and Roman exporters hired Syrian and Alexandrian artisans to shape mosaic beads from blown glass for sale along Mediterranean shores and into the Far East. By 700 B.C.E., Buddhist and Hindu mystics chanted verses of sutras and the name of the divine while gripping knotted and beaded *malas* (prayer garlands). Each string consisted of a set number of beads, such as the 32 units of the Hindu Saiva rosary, and specialized shapes to enhance ritual or meditation. Christian and Greek Orthodox ascetics adopted the practice of "telling beads" around 200 C.E.

The Indian trade in etched beads and metal and glass tubes, barrels, and discs flourished after 500 along routes to Southeast Asia, Arabia, and Africa. From 800 to 1000, Bedouins, Celts, and Vikings included beading in grave goods to shield corpses from grave robbers. When natural fibers rotted, only the location and pattern of beadwork preserved the design over skeletal remains. In the 1100s, West Africans carried on trade with Arabs across the Sahara Desert using cylindrical glass beads as currency.

From 1291, Venetian bead makers copied the carved gems and glass that Marco Polo brought back from his travels across Asia, along with the Buddhist chant *Om mani padma hom*. At glass furnaces, Murano replicators molded crystal, milk glass, foil, and aventurine (gold striped quartz) or blew air bubbles through molten silica to create the thread holes. By 1308, a guild standardized bead manufacture and protected consumers from inferior imports. In the 1390s, Venetians perfected the striated chevron and star or Rosetta beads from contrasting colors, the forerunner of millefiori beads.

By 1500, Venice dominated beadwork markets. Christian monasticism promoted the bead industry after Dominic of Prussia, a Carthusian monk, initiated the saying of the rosary as an official form of Roman Catholic prayer. From the sixteenth century, Dutch, Spanish, and Portuguese explorers of Africa and southern Asia carried aggry, or trade beads, and eye (dotted) beads to barter for slaves, ivory, and spices. The Asante of Ghana, who had no glassmaking technology, prized the beads and used them for currency, amulets, waistbands, board game markers, and court necklaces. At Benguela, Angola, natives made their own version of slave beads by cutting disks from land snail shells as a trade medium with Portuguese sailors.

Beadwork and Fashion

In the nineteenth century, Europeans embraced beadwork from foreign ports. Designers applied beading to crochet to produce bracelets, chokers, hat pins, collars, coin purses, and evening bags. Dutch needleworkers published the first patterns for beaded purses in 1824. In the early 1900s, a Bohemian bead industry expanded the global jewelry trade with aluminum and steel spheres, which contributed a silvery glint to glass and ceramic beadwork.

Today, silversmiths in Nepal, Bangladesh, and Sri Lanka profit from the global demand for high-fashion beads. Sub-Saharan Africa and India maintain beadwork as a cultural expression of monarchy, piety, clan identity, and status. The Bamileke of western Cameroon shape elephant masks from cowries and glass beads for use in ancestral masquerade. South African artisans dress dolls and make animals out of beads for addition to necklaces, pins, and bracelets. Bondo women of Orissa, India, wear cloth skirts and beaded breastplates and dress their hair in strands of seed beads.

Beading hobbyists buy quality materials from Japan or the Czech Republic according to standard size and appearance. The most common surfaces range from opaque and translucent to metallic. More expensive beads come in transparent, lined, iridescent, or pearlized hues. Stringing on thread, wire, or monofilament requires thin beading needles, such as those used by Mexican artisans to connect amber, coral, and alabaster beads. Jewelry makers apply earring hooks or hoops and necklace clasps to finished work.

See also: Amulets; Burial Garb; Divinities; Indian and Pakistani Clothing; Jewels and Jewelry; Mesopotamian Clothing; Shell Ornaments.

Further Reading

Dubin, Lois Sherr. *The History of Beads: From 100,000 B.C. to the Present.* New York: Harry N. Abrams, 2009.

Francis, Peter, Jr. *Beads of the World: A Collector's Guide with Revised Price Reference.* 2nd ed. Atglen, PA: Schiffer, 1999.
Geary, Theresa Flores, and Debra Whalen. *The Illustrated Bead Bible: Terms, Tips & Techniques.* New York: Sterling, 2008.
Simak, Evelyn. *African Beads: Jewels of a Continent.* Denver: Africa Direct, 2010.

Beaton, Cecil (1904–1980)

Costume and stage designer, photographer, writer, and illustrator Cecil Walter Hardy Beaton set style trends and helped revolutionize fashion journalism from the 1920s to the 1970s.

Born at Hampstead in northeast London on January 14, 1904, to Esther "Etty" Sisson and timberman Ernest Walter Hardy Beaton, he learned to take pictures and process film from his nanny at age nine. After schooling in art, history, and architecture at Harrow and Cambridge, he apprenticed under portrait photographer Paul Tanqueray and studied surrealism before manipulating the image and reputation of patrician society.

On the staff of *Vogue* and *Vanity Fair* from 1927, Beaton produced youthful, ebullient fashion photographs, featuring gowns with trains by Elsa Schiaparelli and the House of Worth and chiaroscuro portraits of actors Marlene Dietrich and Greer Garson. Beaton designed Egyptian headdresses for Tallulah Bankhead's stage appearance in *Antony and Cleopatra* (1937) and posed Wallis Warfield Simpson in her blue silk crepe wedding dress with shirred bust and buttoned waist by Main Rousseau Bocher. A photo with anti-Semitic scribble in the margin on January 24, 1938, forced Condé Nast to fire Beaton from his post at *Vogue*. During the Nazi bombing of London in 1940–1941, Beaton served as a home-front photographer for the British Ministry of Information.

Redeemed in part by his war portraits, Beaton began designing haute couture textiles in 1948 and went to work for *Harper's Bazaar.* He created costumes and sets for drama, ballet, and opera, beginning with a Broadway revival of Oscar Wilde's social drama *Lady Windermere's Fan* (1946) and elegant at-home coat, furs, bonnets, and diamond parure for Ralph Richardson and Vivien Leigh in *Anna Karenina* (1948). The

In a career spanning half a century, Cecil Beaton pioneered fashion photography for top magazines beginning in the 1920s and earned fame as a costume designer for stage and film. Credits include *My Fair Lady* on Broadway and the big screen.

designer summarized his views on a half century of style and tastes in *The Glass of Fashion* (1954), which glorified the trendsetting of Christian Dior and Yves St. Laurent.

Beaton received Tony Awards for costume design in the Broadway musicals *My Fair Lady* (1957) and *Saratoga* (1959), a late Victorian period piece for which he made some 200 costumes, including a panniered, off-the-shoulder gown for Carol Lawrence. For Julie Andrews in *My Fair Lady,* he designed a ball gown of elegant simplicity, a frothy satin delicacy topped with ivory chiffon and gold fringe and beaded with rubies, crystals, pearls, and rhinestones. For the biographical musical *Coco* (1969), he dressed Katharine Hepburn in the nimble "new woman" suits that designer Coco Chanel had popularized.

Beaton won Academy Awards for Belle Époque wardrobes in the films *Gigi* (1958) and *My Fair Lady* (1964). His camera framed shots of an off-the-shoulder ball gown for Leslie Caron and the memorable black-and-white picture hat and crystal collar and tiara worn by Audrey Hepburn. The French presented him a Legion of Honor in 1960.

The designer's gift for costume history buoyed Giacomo Puccini's opera *Turandot* (1961) at the Metropolitan Opera House with glittering robes and pelerines in red, orange, gold, and pink for Birgit Nilsson and Anna Moffo, fur hat and cloak for Franco Corelli, and plated armor for Chinese palace guards. He engaged Russian costume maker Barbara Karinska to supply the demimonde in Giuseppe Verdi's *La Traviata* (1966) with tiered, aproned, and overskirted ball gowns in dominant purple and red. For the film *On a Clear Day You Can See Forever* (1970), Beaton adorned Barbra Streisand's classic profile in an elaborate turban surrounded by medallions and draped across the forehead in pearls.

At the height of stardom in 1972, Beaton received a knighthood. After a stroke paralyzed his right side in 1974, he continued designing with only his left hand. He died from heart failure on January 18, 1980, willing his extensive papers to Princeton and Cambridge universities.

See also: Costume Design, Film; Costume Design, Theater; Photography, Fashion.

Further Reading

Beaton, Cecil. *The Unexpurgated Beaton.* New York: Random House, 2002.

Garner, Philippe, and David Alan Mellor. *Cecil Beaton: Photographs 1920–1970.* New York: Stewart, Tabori & Chang, 1995.

Pepper, Terence. *Beaton: Portraits.* New Haven, CT: Yale University Press, 2004.

Beene, Geoffrey (1925–2004)

Unconventional American designer Geoffrey Beene pioneered Yankee pragmatism in clothing for men and women throughout the postwar era. He was especially known for his offbeat use of fabrics and materials, and for freeing women's clothes from the restrictive, form-fitting lines of his contemporaries.

A native of Haynesville, Louisiana, he was born Samuel Albert Bozeman, Jr., to Eva Lorene Waller and car salesman S.A. Bozeman on August 30, 1925. The cotton growing on his grandfather's 1,000-acre (400-hectare) plantation, part of his earliest memories, introduced him to the texture of pure fiber. He bought his first Simplicity pattern and began sewing beach pajamas at age eight. During the Great Depression, he salvaged pieces of fabric to study.

Like his physician grandfather and two uncles, Beene studied on scholarship at the Tulane University School of Medicine. In 1946, he entered the army and received a medical discharge for worsening asthma. He moved to California to rest and study at the University of Southern California, but abandoned academia to dress windows in Los Angeles for I. Magnin.

At age 20, Beene settled in New York City's West Village and entered the Traphagen School of Fashion for a year before studying design in Paris at Académie Julian and l'École de la Syndicate d'Haute Couture, and in New York at the Harmay dress salon and Teal Traina clothing firm. Under the aegis of art director Alexey Brodovitch, Beene took his grandfather's middle name and launched his designs in *Harper's Bazaar* and *Vogue.* He showcased his line at his 550 Seventh Avenue showroom in Manhattan.

Beene gained recognition for his unconstructed, free-flowing garments. Patronized by first ladies Pat Nixon, Nancy Reagan, and Jacqueline Kennedy, he created a princess-line wedding ensemble for the White House nuptials of Lynda Bird Johnson in 1967. Beene revived lace in wool jersey and flannel dresses and added black patent bows to worsted jumpers, ostrich feathers at the hemline of a wool crepe cocktail dress, and a tank top to an evening dress.

Beene's "Alice Capone" pinstriped suits anchored a unique Mafia-style collection in the 1960s. By the end of that decade, he was designing slimline wallets, scuffs, slippers, sweaters, luggage, fedoras, and Van Heusen dress shirts for men. He injected denim fabrics into his 1970 line of evening couture and sold his radical, streamlined ensembles in Japan and Europe. The following year, his Beene Bag collection consisted of mid-priced sportswear, including voluminous wool jersey pants, sequined biker's jersey, ombré silk chiffon, spiral-seamed dresses, and evening wear featuring cartoon characters.

Beene's inventiveness ranged from quilted faille jackets, bow ties, elbow-length gloves with polka dots, and bias trim to innovative bustiers, stomachers, nude chiffon insets, hip-banded jersey dresses, and hooded jumpsuits. By 1976, his lines appeared in Brussels, Milan, Rome, Vienna, Munich, and Paris on the bodies of models leaping and dancing rather than treading the runways. His injection of imaginative materials—horsehair insets, plastic tube detailing, oversized rickrack, quilted ticking, zippered dresses and bolero jackets, trapunto hems, rubber and net back harnesses, blanket coats, sable with corduroy, gingham with satin, and strapless gowns in sweatshirt fleece—relieved the earnest self-consciousness of haute couture.

For his command of minimalism, Beene won a total of eight Coty awards, a 1965 Neiman Marcus honorarium, Fashion Center Walk of Fame, a 1996 Chicago Historical Society award, an honorary PhD from the Rhode Island School of Design, a Silver Slipper Award from Houston's Museum of Fine Arts, and the designation of an "American Original" from the Smithsonian Institution. In 1988, Bergdorf Goodman sponsored a 25-year retrospective of Beene's career at the National Academy of Design. At his death from cancer and pneumonia in Manhattan on September 28, 2004, the Council of Fashion Designers of America honored his career by establishing a Geoffrey Beene lifetime achievement award.

See also: Fashion Design.

Further Reading

Beene, Geoffrey. *Beene by Beene.* New York: Vendome, 2005.
Geoffrey Beene. www.geoffreybeene.com
Hastreiter, Kim. *Geoffrey Beene: An American Fashion Rebel.* New York: Assouline, 2008.

Belle Époque Fashion

From 1871 to the outbreak of the Great War in Europe in 1914, the conspicuous consumption of lush Belle Époque fashions demonstrated the optimism, vibrance, and affluence accrued during a quarter century of peace. French haute couture, especially that of dynamic designer Paul Poiret, featured oriental evening dress and opera capes in alternating weaves of cut velvet and silk satin trimmed in silk fringe and tassels. Subsequent innovations involved elegant touches to apron-shaped overskirts, bustles, and oversized gigot (leg of mutton) sleeves in taffeta or velvet. Ensembles suited evenings at cabarets, burlesque halls, casinos, dining at Maxim's in Paris, viewing Serge Diaghilev's Ballets Russes, or strolling through the Exposition Universelle of 1889.

An affectation of the period, a mock-ballerina outfit featured a bodice of bastard velvet (plush) or beggars' velvet (a cotton and linen blend) stitched over layered skirts made from some 20 yards (18 meters) of tulle. For enhancement, dressmakers chose ottoman velvet for its colorful patterns or mirror velvet, a heavily ironed fabric that gave the impression of reflecting light. The heaviest grade, Utrecht velvet (furniture plush) of wool pile on a linen base, displayed a brushed nap woven from goat hair, suited to handbags and hats. A master at late-nineteenth-century aesthetic dressing, Irish author Oscar Wilde revived brown velvet knee breeches and the doublet, combined with a pea-green coat, which he claimed was the most beautiful attire for a male.

In one example of period elegance, in 1888, English-born designer Charles Frederick Worth completed an imperial Russian court dress of a silk velvet bodice and train over a silver moiré skirt. To build a national reputation for fine fabrics and haute couture, Worth encouraged Emperor Alexander II to buy French goods from Lyons and Tulle. In 1898, Worth designed an evening gown from satin velvet woven with swirls and paisleys, a classic art nouveau design.

The fashion media highlighted pleasure, dance, sports, fun, and theatrical and fashion art and the photographs of Alfred Stieglitz and Antonie van Horn. Costume party attire featured art deco mock-ups of diamond-decked harlequins, gypsy skirts, Carnival masks, and whimsical butterfly wings and antennae. For shock effect, men posed as sugar daddies in top hat and tux; women revealed their ankles beneath rising hemlines. Dancer Isadora Duncan shocked audiences by performing barefoot in a transparent silk tunic.

From September 1913, an American version of the British *Vanity Fair*—originally called *Dress & Vanity Fair*—appealed to the smart set of the Gilded Age with photos of the lives and wardrobes of celebrities. Articles for the affluent, well-bred woman set a premium on female self-satisfaction, economic optimism about capitalism, and French-inspired modernist fashions available at *les grands magasins* (department stores). In a retort to low-brow American interest in self-improvement, *Vanity Fair* ridiculed advice on how the average man could refine and dress himself to get ahead in business and romance.

Urbane-style commentary featured more advertisements than publications from previous eras, projecting the image of self-confident wearers of blouses and hobble skirts, boater hats, ski pants and jodhpurs, lawn tennis dresses and slacks, dance wear, tuxedos, and flamenco skirts. An undercurrent of gay fashion concealed itself beneath the cliché of the dapper bachelor. A witty commentary on gender boundaries pictured comedienne Fanny Brice in tails, white tie, and top hat.

Rather than chide the reader into fashion sense, advertisers featured smart advertisements for Arrow, "the aristocrat of collars," Dobbs hats that "foreshadow the vogue," Lissue handkerchiefs from the "best men's furnishers," Whalley-Ford brogues "for town and country," and John Shannon's "incontestably correct" top coats and ulsters. Additional men's furnishings—Waltham watches, Kaiser cravats, Harris tweed golf knickers and matching belted jackets—completed the wardrobe of the well-rounded gentleman.

Clothiers and milliners worked toward pleasing the moneyed class while excluding all others. Style columnists made no effort to hide the era's celebration of modernity, elitism, and the chic form of *la femme parisienne,* epitomized by the narrow-waisted Gibson Girl. In 1913, the *Vanity Fair* article "The Dance Craze in Paris Creates New Types of Gowns" explained how the Argentine tango and the *thé dansant* (tango tea) influenced the seductive way people dressed, walked, and conversed—a fair assessment of the impact of the arts on behavior and wardrobe during the Belle Époque.

See also: French Clothing and Fashion; Haute Couture; Worth, Charles Frederick

Further Reading

Blackman, Cally. *100 Years of Fashion Illustration.* London: Laurence King, 2007.

Holmes, Diana, and Carrie Tarr. *A "Belle Epoque"? Women in French Society and Culture, 1890–1914.* New York: Berghahn, 2006.

Tierney, Tom. *Great Fashion Designs of the Belle Epoque: Paper Dolls in Full Color.* Mineola, NY: Dover, 1982.

Welters, Linda, and Abby Lillethun, eds. *The Fashion Reader.* 2nd ed. New York: Berg, 2011.

Belts and Suspenders

The first wardrobe accessories, flexible torso ties and straps have secured garments from prehistory to the present. As early as 100,000 B.C.E., nomads from Africa fastened hide and fur garments around the midriff with woven vines, yucca fiber, babiche (rabbit fur strips), or dried animal gut. Around 3300 B.C.E., Ötzi the Iceman, a corpse frozen in a glacier in the Italian Alps, secured his goat leather loincloth and tool pouch with a calfskin belt.

From 1600 B.C.E., traditional Chinese ensembles, called Hanfu, included knee-length tunics sashed at the midline. Native Americans fastened loincloths with strips of rawhide, wampum, and bison wool. Belts kept early tools and weapons handy, as well as spare ammunition, small game and fish, and pouches of seeds and jerky for snacks. During famines, non-Muslim African men wrapped their abdomens tightly in utilitarian leather hunger belts, which inhibited hunger spasms. Assyrian robes tied by elegant sashes with long, knotted tassels identified the elite.

In the early 500s B.C.E., Greeks relied on the woolen Doric chiton for daily dress. Men bound them with wide belts; women double-belted their waists. Roman women shaped tube dresses with belts or sashes under the bosom, in an X over the chest, or pulled tight at the waist to facilitate the blousing of cloth according to fashion. Roman officials mimicked legionaries by cinching their girth with thick military belts. Slaves and workers wore simple tunics raised over cord belts to bare the legs for work.

Evolving Styles

After 500 C.E., at Sutton Hoo in Suffolk, England, a female cadaver went to her grave wearing a homemaker's belt and chatelaine (key ring), a symbol of womanly authority. Japanese noblemen used their belts as a place to hang hand fans. During the spread of Christianity in the early 800s, abbey leatherworkers received dispensation from Charlemagne to hunt deer in royal preserves for the making of suede and leather pouches and breech girdles (belts). In the 1100s, citizens of Constantinople replaced wide buckled belts with more fashionable slender cording, cloth sashes, chains, and braided leather. In contrast, Russian men's fashions sported a heavy belt over linen shirt-tunics.

Crusaders displayed loyalty with the commander's crest tied with a belt and buckle, symbols of union. From the 1200s to the 1400s, full military attire required the baldric, a shoulder-to-hip strap passed across the torso to hold a saber, knife, or powder horn. During the same period, Chinese merchants sold silk belts and coin pouches to the Western world, which valued the soft, sleek fabric. In 1552, English boys' charity schools required belted, ankle-length blue coats, a long-lived tradition.

Cloth suspender straps, commonly known as braces, made their appearance with hooks and eyes around 1787. By 1800, waistbands pierced with holes anchored the end pieces. Women's basques, form-fitting torso shapers, held up stockings with detachable suspenders. For leisure dress in the 1820s, conservative Europeans standardized a businessman's uniform—a hip-length jacket with wide lapels and linen, moleskin, or wool trousers held up by braces.

Leicester manufacturer Albert Thurston invented the 1.125- to 1.5-inch (2.86- to 3.81- centimeter) shoulder harness in 1822 out of hand-stitched catgut or leather dressed with silk in woven patterns and polished brass fittings. Cloth suspenders or galluses with a back fork and adjustable midline clasps expanded with the waist for sitting and standing, especially in high-waisted pleated pants raised over a paunch. Worn at the midsection and attached above the main pleat, suspenders remained securely on the shoulders and encouraged erect posture.

In 1853, when Levi Strauss commercialized jeans, he included suspender buttons rather than belt loops for shoulder straps, which Americans called galluses. After 1857, American men abandoned suspenders for belted trousers that emphasized the midline. American versions used lighter leather and knitted ends for wearing with cummerbunds and waistcoats. Suave dressers matched the figures on braces with neckties and foulards.

Modern Innovations

During the American Civil War, shortages of leather for belts, suspenders, and holsters worsened in the nonindustrial South. By 1911, however, U.S. manufacturers began closing the commercial gap with German, French, and English accessory suppliers. American inventiveness added the slide fastener for adjusting suspender lengths. Competitive prices for men's and boys' suspenders started at 21 cents per pair.

Before World War I, young men held up thigh-high hosiery with sock suspenders equipped with metal and rubber clasps. Adult males collected a range of suspenders for sporting events and for business suits to keep the vest in line with trousers. Englishwomen's liberty bodices connected a knitted torso cover to stocking suspenders, which buttoned to the lower edge. In combat, the wide saber belt became standard equipment for Russian and Prussian fighters. During the 1920s, suspenders with elastic garters held cuffed socks and cable-knit kneesocks in place. Prices began at 25 cents for hosiery suspenders and 50 cents for cross-back suspenders.

Hickok Manufacturing in Rochester, New York, added a new dimension to men's waist accessories in 1922 with the monogrammed watch chain and slide, which attached to the belt and sold for $1.50. D-ring or web belts cinctured the short pants of schoolboys. In the 1930s, men's fashions embraced the colonial safari jacket and hacking jacket, two banded sporting coats that placed belt and buckle front and center. The House of Gucci in Rome exploited the demand by crafting matched belts, wallets, shoes, and gloves.

During World War II, rationing regulations in England and the United States funneled leather to military use rather than civilian suspenders and belts. Garment makers narrowed the belt as a way to comply. The demand for sophisticated leather belts and elasticized suspenders generated a postwar boom in monogrammed haberdashery goods. The high-waisted Hollywood look introduced longer-rise trousers held up by a narrow belt buckled to the side.

In midcentury, leather suspenders remained popular on American college campuses. Girls' school uniforms combined blouses with plaid skirts and suspenders. At mid-century, adult women favored the contour belt, which conformed to feminine curves. In the 1970s, stylish disco dancers wore jeans with suspenders. And in the 1980s, adult fashion saw a comeback of suspenders and restored trousers to the natural waist, a boon to shorter men. Victoria's Secret popularized women's stretch lace garter belts as fantasy items.

In Europe and North America, fashions in the early twenty-first century featured large-buckle python, lizard, crocodile, and snakeskin belts as well as conservative styles of double-layered leather to coordinate shirt and tie with trousers. Belts matched the shoe color and buckles reflected the metal of men's rings and watches. By 2010, one-quarter of American public school systems had standardized dress codes, which outlawed studded punk belts for girls and required boys to wear belts at the waistline to prevent their pants from sagging.

See also: Accessories; Hosiery, Men's; Trousers.

Further Reading

Bridges, John. *A Gentleman Gets Dressed Up: What to Wear, When to Wear It, How to Wear It.* Rev. ed. Nashville, TN: Rutledge Hill, 2003.
Leurquin, Anne. *A World of Belts: Africa, Asia, Oceania, America.* Milan, Italy: Skira, 2005.

Blankets

A personal drape, buggy wrap, or sleeping bag, the blanket illustrates the flexibility of flat, shapeless garments to meet a variety of needs, including personal and tribal identity, as well as warmth. The earliest fur wraps, blankets covered the shoulders, tucked under limbs, and tied into place with fibrous twine or leather thongs, as in the poncho-shaped night wrappings of ancient Germanic tribes. Blanket layering pressed varied materials into use, such as the barkcloth capes of Polynesians and Australian Aborigines.

In about 1400–1200 B.C.E., Asian nomads traded felt to Mongolian cavalry for making into saddle blankets, which doubled as night garments around campfires. Persian and Eastern Asian men and women wore a thin peplos (blanket shawl). Chinese, Japanese, and Siberian potentates added fur to blanket linings to increase the warmth and status of woven wraps.

Ancient Greek literature describes blankets as integral to ritual, notably as gifts to the Pythia, the priestess at the Temple of Apollo at Delphi. The Greeks bought cloth blankets at the Athens market, which sold the work of Megarian slaves. Distinguished males displayed their authority by letting their blanket wraps trail behind them. For weddings, the groom wore only the pallium (blanket cloak) to greet his bride, who came to his home in full dress with a blanket shawl covering her head as a display of modesty.

In the early Buddhist period after 600 B.C.E., weavers in India specialized in unique textiles, including the deerskin patchwork blanket, luxurious goat-hair festival blanket, long ewe-hair blanket, fluffy Nepalese blanket, and a blanket left hairy on both sides. Felted fibers served the poor as blankets. Among residents of Kangra, India, women wore blankets skewered at the shoulders and tied at the waist. Afghan women of Lampaka made their dresses from blankets. Indian hermits and Jains wove garment blankets from camel, goat, and human hair. Pilgrims distinguished themselves in black blanket wraps.

In Republican Rome, the cotton, flax, or long-napped winter wool pallium, like the cloak of Arab bedouins, served as a shoulder wrap when pinned with a brooch over a tunic by day and a cape by night for the traveler or soldier on guard duty. For running, the wearer folded the pallium to a smaller size, attaching weights to ensure that the blanket stayed in place on the left shoulder. A white pallium shrouded corpses, which families bore to the crematory on a deathbed.

Roman matrons valued the *palla,* a short wool, linen, or silk wrap that they bordered, tasseled, or fringed for decoration. The flexible garment doubled as a head shawl for mourning, a modest covering for breastfeeding, or a baby veil. During palla cleaning at the fuller's shop, slaves washed and brushed the surface to enhance the nap. At processionals to the temples of Diana or Venus, women bore new pallas to drape around the goddess's shoulders.

In the early Middle Ages, around 500 C.E., Vikings made felt into cloak blankets, their night cloaks on board longboats. Travelers wrapped themselves in cloak blankets and slept in leather sleeping bags or tents. Poor Vikings kept warm in a wrap of skins or wadmal, a homespun wool common to Greenland, Iceland, Norway, and Sweden. After 1100, Scots wore clan tartans of a similar homespun, which they called *hodden.* Thrown over hay, the tartan served as a comfortable bedroll easily assembled the next day into a cloak and kilt.

In the 1580s, Scots employed the brown plaid (shoulder blanket), a camouflage garment the color of heather in which Highlanders wrapped themselves to wait out storms and snow. Saxon families warded off the cold in blankets lined with the pelts of badgers, cats, European beavers, or rabbits. Wolf fur offered an alternative lining, but required cleansing and airing to remove the feral odor. Saxons sprinkled the wraps with fragrant herbs and evergreen needles to deter fleas. Tattered blankets served the poor as fabric for making leg bindings reaching to the arches of the feet.

After the arrival of Normans in England in 1066, the wealthy stored blankets in chests as protection from moths and thieves. Hospices such as Sancta Maria Nuova, founded in Florence in 1285, furnished paupers with blanket wraps. For prisoners at Newgate in London, the only way to acquire a blanket was to pay one cent per week per covering.

In Renaissance Europe, blankets became standard wraps in clinics and hospitals, where laundries sanitized infected garments by scalding before washing. Highland Scots developed the plaid, an over-the-shoulder cloak gathered at the front into a kilt, part of the national Scots costume. For travel and marching, regiments added the shaggy rug, a coarse mantle that held in body heat in rainy or snowy weather.

After the chartering of the Hudson's Bay Company in 1670, blankets dominated trade on the North American frontier. In 1780 at Witney, Oxfordshire, Thomas Empson expanded the range of commercial goods by weaving a durable trade blanket. Two years later, napping machines raised the surface to give greater comfort and to encourage the shedding of dirt. Because of a shortage of coats during the War of 1812, British units stationed near Sault Sainte Marie, Ontario, had to wrap themselves in blankets called Mackinaws. During the American Civil War, Confederate soldiers and casualties suffered more than the Union enemy from a lack of blankets while hovering over campfires and hospital stoves.

In 1909, the opening of the Pendleton Woolen Mills on the Oregon Trail in Pendleton, Oregon, supplied the U.S. Army and local tribes with plaid blankets, robes, and shawls. Market researcher Joe Rawnsley interviewed tribes from Washington State south to Arizona and New Mexico to collect designs and color combinations. He found that men favored felt edging and women preferred fringed blankets.

Contemporary blanket manufacture involves advanced weaving of synthetic lap robes and down or polyester batting in shoulder wraps for the elderly. NASA scientists invented Mylar space blankets that reflect back body heat. Used as thermal wraps, these were adapted for use as warmers for premature infants.

See also: Accessories; Wool and Wool Products.

Further Reading

Berlant, Anthony, and Mary Hunt Kahlenberg. *Walk in Beauty: The Navajo and Their Blankets.* Layton, UT: Gibbs Smith, 1991.

Henderson, John. *The Renaissance Hospital: Healing the Body and Healing the Soul.* New Haven, CT: Yale University Press, 2006.

Johnston, Ruth A. *All Things Medieval: An Encyclopedia of the Medieval World.* Santa Barbara, CA: Greenwood, 2011.

Tichenor, Harold. *The Blanket: An Illustrated History of the Hudson's Bay Blanket.* Toronto: Madison, 2002.

Blass, Bill (1922–2002)

An American original, Bill Blass shaped movable, elegant day wear with impeccable tailoring. His sophisticated designs for both men and women eventually found expression as well in luggage, perfume, and even chocolate, as part of the Bill Blass Limited brand.

The son of hardware merchant Ralph Aldrich Blass and dressmaker Ethyl Easter Keyser, he was born William Ralph Blass on June 22, 1922, in Fort Wayne, Indiana. After his father's suicide in 1927, the five-year-old immersed himself in art and Hollywood film. In his mid-teens, Blass began selling original designs to Kalmour, a New York firm specializing in Celanese rayon evening dresses.

After settling in Manhattan in 1939, Blass learned his trade at Parsons School of Design. The following year, at age 18, he became the first male to win an award from *Mademoiselle*. After he began sketching sportswear for sportswear designer David Crystal, he developed his belief that style is personal but fashion is not.

Following service in U.S. Army counterintelligence in France, Sicily, Germany, and North Africa during World War II, Blass began designing men's and women's fashions for Anne Klein, Anna Miller Fashion House, and Maurice Rentner, who specialized in women's plus sizes. In 1959, he established his own label, Bill Blass Limited, marked by his signature double B. His creations ranged from men's shoes and bowties, furs, bathing suits, rainwear, hosiery, eyeglasses, watches, and luggage to American Airlines uniforms, Barbie doll outfits, and Ford Continentals.

By mingling in the social scene, Blass built his fame on classic architectural lines in cashmere, tweed, sable trim, relaxed zip-front dresses, and baby-doll evening ensembles. He sketched urbane coatdresses and holiday sweaters with taffeta skirts for clients Nancy Kissinger, Jacqueline Kennedy, Barbra Streisand, Nancy Reagan, Estée Lauder, Jane Seymour, and Gloria Vanderbilt and customized double-breasted blazers for Senator Jacob Javits. Blass's eye for detail brought into the mainstream hand-knit raglan sweaters, color-blocked suits, smocked jackets, patchwork fur, men's kilts, and original animal print textiles. *Ebony* magazine featured Blass's side-button coat, jeweled lace dresses with scalloped hems and oversized turbans, and a velvet theater coat with gold frog closures.

Blass modeled his own menswear, popularizing the debonair fitted suit coat with angled pocket flaps in glen plaid. To standard male apparel, he added heathered vests, Dacron tuxedos, and an eight-button blazer with purple silk lining. Key to his view of the well-dressed male, dark shirts and plain ties updated the garish 1950s look.

In 1972, the designer introduced a medium-priced line under the name Blassport and set about determining what buyers wanted by traveling the world. He increased profits with trunk shows, which he declared more timely and less theatrical than runway shows. For the seamstress, he published two-piece dress and coat patterns with McCall's and Vogue. For the young, he exploited jeans with easy-fit styles in spandex.

Following a stroke that forced his retirement at age 77, Blass began composing a memoir, *Bare Blass* (2002). He died of throat cancer in New Preston, Connecticut, on June 12, 2002. His accolades included seven Coty awards, a plaque on the Fashion Walk of Fame, and a lifetime achievement citation from the Fashion Institute of Technology.

See also: Fashion Design.

Further Reading

Bill Blass. www.billblass.com

Blass, Bill. *Bare Blass.* New York: HarperCollins, 2002.

O'Hagan, Helen, and Kathleen Rowold. *Bill Blass: An American Designer.* New York: Harry N. Abrams, 2002.

Bloomer, Amelia (1818–1894)

Women's rights advocate and platform speaker Amelia Jenks Bloomer did not invent the article of women's clothing called "bloomers"—long, billowy trousers worn under a short skirt—but she wore them often in the early 1850s as an expression of her radical feminism and the women's dress reform movement. The outfit came to be called a "bloomer suit," later shortened to "bloomer," a term of ridicule in the press.

A native of Homer, New York, she was born on May 27, 1818, to Presbyterian clothier Ananias Jenks. Amelia and her five siblings attained an education from homeschooling and absorbed feminist ideals from their mother, Lucy Webb Jenks.

After working as a tutor and governess in Waterloo, Amelia married Quaker town clerk and publisher Dexter Chamberlain Bloomer, who appointed her postmaster of Seneca Falls. Dexter hired Amelia as a journalist for the *Seneca Falls County Courier* and, in 1854, for the reform weekly *Western Home Visitor.*

On July 19–20, 1848, at age 30, Bloomer involved herself in emerging East Coast feminism by attending the Woman's Rights Convention at Seneca Falls. In her biweekly newsletter, *The Lily: A Ladies' Journal, Devoted to Temperance and Literature,* she voiced progressive opinions on slavery, employment, divorce, women's education, the right to petition, taxation without representation, and prohibition. She also issued a temperance paper called *The Water Bucket* and led suffrage and temperance rallies in Iowa and Nebraska.

Dress Reform

A disciple of suffragist pacesetters Susan B. Anthony and Elizabeth Cady Stanton, Bloomer pioneered feminist advocacy of comfortable women's attire. The concept first impacted female fashions in 1824 at the New Harmony Commune in Indiana by Scots freethinker and lecturer Fanny Wright. In France, nonconformist author George Sand promoted the cause by adopting pants for public wear. In 1847, Bloomer made her first written opposition to women's lacings and fashionable petticoats.

In December 1849, Bloomer supported British actor Fanny Kemble of Lennox, Massachusetts, in the wearing of "pantelettes," a diversion from standard female costume. In 1850 at Beaver Island, New York, Mormon reformer Elvira Field Strang contributed her own design for the pantaloon outfit, which followers called the "Mormon dress." Critics spurned such attire as Muslim exotica worn by kept women and odalisques in Algerian and Turkish harems. Conservative males feared a power clash with assertive, pants-wearing females.

In spring 1851, Bloomer's advocacy of "The Move Toward Rational Dress" influenced activist Elizabeth Smith Miller to design Turkish trousers or billowy pantaloons. Secured at the ankle, the pants appeared under a knee-length dress or belted tunic worn without a corset or stays. Summer heat moved polemicists to action in Lowell, Massachusetts, where they held a Bloomer Ball on July 22, 1851, a formal introduction of feminist dress. At Seneca Falls, both Stanton and Bloomer, along with notable female athletes and patients at water cure spas, modeled tidy, convenient harem pants for the public, which deemed them immodest. A stir in the streets of Manhattan received notice on September 18, 1851, in the New York press. Advocates of dress reform referred to the outfits as "the American costume" and the "freedom dress," but the *New York Tribune* popularized the name "bloomers."

In the 1850s, feminist Amelia Bloomer wore and promoted the billowy pantaloons that would take her name—bloomers—as an expression of women's independence and for comfort. The press responded with outrage, and the style passed by decade's end. *(The Granger Collection, NYC—All rights reserved)*

Controversial Pantaloons

The pantaloon captured attention, partly from a fashion article in the September 1851 issue of *Harper's New Monthly Magazine,* which suggested the pairing of the pantsuit with a waistcoat. That same month, *Godey's Lady's Book* rejected a pro or con stance in favor of calling the "freedom dress" a fashion freak. Six American "Bloomer girls" strolled Piccadilly in London and lectured on the value of free physical movement, drawing 700 male gawkers.

Journalists dubbed dress reform a form of "Bloomerism" and referred to violators of gendered attire as "Bloomerites." Opponents charged pantaloon wearers with enticing men with a show of ankles and knees. Amelia Bloomer, meanwhile, continued agitating for dress reform and labeled as misogynistic the prank of mailing petticoats to progressive male politicians who countenanced women's demands for comfortable clothes.

By 1852, high-profile suffragist Susan B. Anthony had adopted bloomers, but kept her dress length below the knee for a campaign in Auburn, New York. While Unitarian theologian Antoinette Brown Blackwell found bloomers too undignified for a pulpit minister, feminist reformers Sara Ann Barlow Gillett and Mary Edwards Walker, Universalist preacher Olympia Brown, and lecturers Elizabeth Buffum Chace and Angelina Grimké Weld applauded the shift from hoops and corsets for active mothers and working women. Promoters reminded hecklers that women's bloomers were sparing on fabric use, unlikely to drag mud and muck into the house, less likely than skirts to cause falls and burns at the fireside, and appropriate for gardening and horseback riding.

Supporters and Opponents

The uproar created by Bloomer's two-piece dress and trousers and her editorials on gender roles amazed the journalist, whose readership rose to more than 6,000 curious about the "new gospel." The fashion in dresses with trousers became the butt of barroom ditties, vaudeville performances, and media satire on defeminized, cigar-puffing women. The style lasted to the end of the 1850s, when crinolines relieved the misery of hoop skirts and bustles.

In 1855, Bloomer stopped publishing *The Lily* and moved with her husband to Council Bluffs, Iowa. She kept her pantaloons and short dresses, which she loaded around the hem with shot to keep her skirts from blowing about. In Iowa, Bloomer continued writing on social reform and women's rights while serving as president of the state suffragist society. At the time of her death from heart disease in Council Bluffs on December 30, 1894, Amelia Bloomer remained an icon of women's dress reform.

See also: Dress Reform; Feminist Styles and Fashions.

Further Reading

Bloomer, D.C. *Life and Writings of Amelia Bloomer.* Whitefish, MT: Kessinger, 2010.

Fischer, Gayle V. *Pantaloons and Power: Nineteenth-Century Dress Reform in the United States.* Kent, OH: Kent State University Press, 2001.

Petrash, Antonia. *More Than Petticoats: Remarkable New York Women.* Guilford, CT: TwoDot, 2002.

Rappaport, Helen. *Encyclopedia of Women Social Reformers.* Santa Barbara, CA: ABC-CLIO, 2001.

Bodices

The torso covering of female apparel derived from the medieval kirtle, the bodice enhances the womanly ensemble from shoulders to midriff or hip. The Japanese *happi* (short coat) of the 700s C.E., a fitted torso with flared skirt, prefigured the Chinese *jifu* (dragon robe). After 1421, Chinese women of the Ming dynasty went to their graves in dragon robes—tight, long-sleeved bodices attached to a gathered peplum skirt of contrasting fabric. In India, only high-caste Dheda women of Gujarat could afford fitted bodices.

For the tailored look in Europe around 1450, the bodice dominated fashion. Seamstresses laced the front across the chest like a vest and inserted padding, reeds, wood or ivory busks, or whalebone to prevent wrinkling. The tight-laced look framed the torso of Marie d'Anjou, the queen consort of France's Charles VII.

In the 1500s, when removable sleeves accessorized the bodice, European women wore one or more bodices both as a complement to the wheel farthingale skirt and as a bosom shaper, a forerunner of the brassiere. In the mid-1600s, Dutch, Flemish, and German fashions added ruffs to the necklines of the *Mieder*, a bodice with pointed waist. The back-laced court bodice featured a deep stomacher, a triangular panel variously graced with stitchery, lace, gemstones, and appliqué.

A century later, sleeveless bodices paired with flowing artist's sleeves over ample skirts. By the late 1700s, the simple bodice acquired a finished look. The fashionable woman maintained a collection of separate fichus, long sleeves, border trims, chain lacings, filigree neck cloths, Levetes (crossed straps), or partlets, a collared or ruffled yoke extending to the mid-chest. Pregnant women preferred the jump, an adjustable bodice that replaced boned stays.

In the 1800s, the Austrian and Bavarian national costume teamed the maid's gathered dirndl skirt and apron with a deep-cut vest-corset over a blouse, a common costume for folk dancing, processions, and beer halls. In the 1870s, the outfit made fashionable the *Landhausmode* (country manor style). A French variant, the *fanfreluche* (frilled) bodice, topped the corset with a gathered shoulder and chest covering. For Bulgarian women, the tight bodice featured a stomacher made of large gold coins.

For the rest of Europe, the nineteenth century introduced males to the Brummell bodice, a waist-whittling corset stiffened with whalebone. Women emulated men's tailcoats and vests with the torso-hugging casaquin bodice and the frock-backed coat-bodice. A slenderizing military style, the cuirasse or Joan of Arc bodice extended boned sides past the hips. A retro fad, the Marie Stuart bodice carried boning to a deep-pointed waist in front. The Circassian bodice extended folds from the shoulders that crossed surplice style at the midline, a modest look for maidens, widows, and elderly women.

In the mid-1800s, the female bodice, worn over a camisole, developed such variations as the high-buttoned amazon corsage; ruched Canadian-style gathered bag bodice pouched over the midline;

square-necked Agnes Sorel bodice; form-fitting casaque bodice; deep-bosomed antique bodice; pleated Grecque or draped Norma corsage; and wide-lapelled Anglo-Greek bodice. In the late 1880s, the bébé bodice with a sash preceded the Empire bodice, formed by a pair of draped scarves, and the baby bodice, which featured ribbons threaded through the bohemian neckline.

According to a fashion report from the *Australian Journal* of November 1890, the women of Sydney imitated Western fashion with bridal gowns featuring the fitted Elizabethan bodice, brocade train, and clusters of ostrich feathers. Bridesmaids and guests chose pointed bodices adorned with rose sprays and gold passementerie. In the outback, Aborigines fashioned a bodice from bamboo and bark fastened with brass wire rings for wearing over a petticoat.

Twentieth-century bodices abandoned lacing for simpler designs to accompany straight skirts. The elasticized bust bodice, patented in 1902, contoured and supported the breasts with steel uprights, cotton net, and goose quills. In 1918, the bodice topped a tunic to form the faddish chemise, a popular flat-bosomed style for dancing. Glamorous Hollywood sportswear and relaxed evening dress introduced the halter bodice, which tied around the neck.

Late in the twentieth century, the cotton or silk *choli* (vest bodice), reputedly introduced to India by a daughter of Mughal emperor Aurangzeb, extended to the bottom of the rib cage or waist for pairing with harem pants and belly dance attire. Tokyo-based fabric engineer Issey Miyake contributed the fiberglass bodice, one of his many experiments in synthetic materials. In Gujarat, India, elite women still flaunt the open-back bodice and skirt as a mark of distinction. In the early 2000s, a light-emitting diode (LED)–embedded bodice featured a small screen that scrolled tweets. Skin-baring styles offered diagonal slashing and V-necks open to the waist.

See also: Brassieres; Corsets and Girdles.

Further Reading

Ambrose, Bonnie Holt. *The Little Bodice Book: A Workbook on Period Bodices.* New York: Costume & Fashion, 1995.

Steele, Valerie, ed. *The Corset: A Cultural History.* New Haven, CT: Yale University Press, 2004.

Summers, Leigh. *Bound to Please: A History of the Victorian Corset.* New York: Bloomsbury, 2001.

Body Painting

A short-term alteration of the color of skin, tongue, teeth, and nails, body painting disguises reality while satisfying ritual and whimsy through an ancient art. Unlike scarification, branding, or tattoo, body paint provides only a short-term change in appearance, such as for Mardi Gras, Carnival, or Halloween. Ancient Egyptians painted newborns with a protective coating of white clay. In southern Sudan, the Nuba enlarged the eyes and broadened the nose with color patterns.

Red ochre (iron oxide) and yellow ochre (limonite) appear to be the earliest body art materials. Among sadhu (ascetic) shamans, devotional marks of sandalwood, ash, and ochre paste indicated sect and caste and prepared the body for possession by a sacred spirit. Because of tribal body art among the Karo of southern Ethiopia, a shared identity from gray and ochre clay, chalk, charcoal, and iron oxide markings enabled the individual to merge with the group mentality for worship, coming of age, parturition, war, or death.

Throughout history, in areas of the Middle East, North Africa, and India, where henna grew wild, celebrants of the Hindu festival of lights, Eid al-Fitr to end Ramadan, Hindu and Sikh celebration of wives, Muhammad's birthday, Persian New Year, Passover, and Purim have incorporated body art into ritual. On the Night of the Henna, artistic application of oil and ground henna leaves to nails, hands, eyebrows, and feet celebrate fertility, luck, or prosperity. Additives—clove, coffee, lac (mealybug secretions), saffron, tea, and tamarind—vary the colorings.

Body painters have been motivated by a wide variation in purpose across cultures. Nomadic Wodaabe men of southwestern Niger covered their faces with iron oxide for pageants. The Surma on the Ethiopian-Sudanese border painted their own faces to emulate their friends' designs. On palms and soles, the paste darkened to red-brown through oxidation, revealing the intricacy of lines and calligraphy.

For distinguished members of other cultures—Maasai warriors, Lapita chiefs, New Guinean ancestor worshippers, Australian Aborigine seers, Myanmar dancers, Kabuki actors, Semang magicians—body designs made with ochre, berry juice, chalk, limestone, hematite, and ground copper established status as well as spiritual oneness with the divine. Mesopotamian figures exhibited an ancient tradition of body art. Around 5000 B.C.E.

The art of skin decoration with henna has been practiced for thousands of years from North Africa to India wherever the plant (*mehndi* in Sanskrit) is native. In Hindu tradition, the hands and feet of wedding couples are adorned for prosperity, fertility, and love. *(Giorgio Majno/ Photographer's Choice/Getty Images)*

in northern Mesopotamia at Chagar Bazar (present-day Syria), Neolithic Halaf women painted their breasts for religious purposes. Additional examples from Ur in southern Mesopotamia in 4500 B.C.E. depict Ubaid females adorned in iron oxide and manganese oxide.

In reaction to the lip, cheek, eye, and nail art of Egyptian pharaohs, a cultural art dating to 4000 B.C.E, the acerbic prophet Jeremiah in about 600 B.C.E. thundered his disapproval of the application of lead carbonate to the skin. In Jeremiah 16:6, 18–20, he damned self-adornment with paint as savage and disrespectful of the body, which God made in his own image. In the fourth century C.E, Saint Basil the Great of Caesarea and Christian missionaries echoed Jeremiah's shaming of native body art, thus ending millennia of paint methods and motifs. By 1000 C.E., orthodox Christianity banned body art as pagan. In the Middle East, European outsiders especially criticized the use of body art to demarcate a female life passage from menarche and virginity to marriage, pregnancy, and menopause.

When Julius Caesar's army approached Britannia in 54 B.C.E., the Celts appeared naked and painted blue with woad (*Isatis tinctoria*) as a form of psychological warfare, a strategy they shared with insurgent Gauls, Picts, Saxons, and Visigoths. Subsequent Roman authors investigated Celtic and Thracian body painting, particularly outlining totemic animals in pigment. After Roman occupation influenced Celtic apparel, body art gave way to the drawing of the same figures on shields.

Body painting returned to vogue in the twentieth century as an expression of allegiance and ethics. In the 1960s, protesters applied body paint to make a political, social, or economic statement, symbolized by sunflowers, peace symbols, rainbows, and animal shapes. This form of public statement has continued into the twenty-first century, using various imagery. Sports enthusiasts today paint letters and team colors on their faces and torsos. For the military, camouflage paint in green, tan, and black conceals light-colored skin on the face, neck, and hands. At street fairs and festivals, face painting allows children to select color combinations and designs. Teenagers and adults also indulge in body painting as a transitive form of artistic self-expression.

See also: Disguise and Spy Wear; Holiday Costumes; Pageantry.

Further Reading
DeMello, Margo. *Encyclopedia of Body Adornment.* Westport, CT: Greenwood, 2007.
Jablonski, Nina G. *Skin: A Natural History.* Berkeley: University of California Press, 2006.
Miczak, Marie Anakee. *Henna's Secret History: The History, Mystery & Folklore of Henna.* Lincoln, NE: iUniverse, 2001.

Body Piercing

A means of altering and beautifying the human form, non-normative body piercing accommodates jewelry, feathers, teeth, horn, bamboo skewers, and leather adornments. Global practices encompass a variety of flesh shaping, including clavicle and chest piercing, scarification, tongue and nipple splitting, eye and scrotal implants, stapling and pocketing, subdermal tattooing, transdermal silicone injections, and the attachment of horns to the forehead. As a form of blood ritual, piercing and flesh slicing attest to self-mortification as a form of repentance, spiritual healing, submission, or even depression.

Body piercing is central to some young practitioners during rites of passage. Young brides in India, Nepal, and Tibet undergo septum piercing for bridal adornment, and Fulani initiates of West Africa undergo ear piercing in order to receive large brass hoops denoting adulthood. Less invasive than female genital mutilation, chastity piercing, earlobe cropping, and tooth filing, piercing dates to 3500 B.C.E. in the burial ornamentation of mummies and the bone and labrets (plates) and wood spools worn by male Amerindians of the American Northwest. The recovery of Ötzi the Iceman from a glacier in the Italian Alps produced evidence of earlobe plugs dating to around 3300 B.C.E.

An Olmec aristocrat depicted on a cave mural at Oxtotitlan, Mexico, dating to 1500 B.C.E. wore a jade septum ring. Other images of Olmec self-adornment offer profiles bearing one or more nose beads and a leaf ornament. After 1000 B.C.E., Hindu scripture in the canonical Yajurveda depicts Lakshmi, the goddess of beauty and prosperity, undergoing the *karna veda* (sacramental piercing) of ears and nose as a toddler. The ritual enhanced female fertility and reduced birth pangs.

Data and images of the Maya and natives of Costa Rica and Guatemala after 500 describe gold and turquoise ear flares, a symbol of aristocratic superiority. The arrival of Hernán Cortés at Tenochtitlan in 1519 introduced Spanish conquistadores to the Aztec use of labrets and tongue jewelry as testimonials of ritual bloodletting. Sixteenth- and seventeenth-century explorers of the Amazon and West Africa reported on the insertion of thickeners under the skin, thorn piercings of Wodaabe women of Niger, and the stretching of earlobes and lips with bone and ivory labrets, a practice of Suyá males of central Brazil during puberty rites and after marriage. Rural Persians under Safavid rule from 1501 to 1722 popularized the nose ring.

In the late eighteenth century, Captain James Cook surveyed similar skin and scalp modification in the South Pacific. Portuguese sailors testified to the carved ivory earplugs of Polynesians of the Marquesas Islands, weighted torture devices inserted in Indian fakirs, and nose bones and spikes sported by male Asmat of Irian Jaya, Indonesia. Missionaries to Papua New Guinea and Borneo met natives who adorned their ears with leopard claws and bear teeth. Missionaries also encountered the shamans of Aranda, Australia, who wore septal bones of hawks or kangaroos, scarified their features with flint or glass, and pierced their tongues with spear points as evidence of magical powers.

In 1834 on the Upper Missouri River in North Dakota, artist George Catlin observed wooden skewers and hooks piercing the chests and backs of Mandan for the Okipa (creation) ceremony and Sioux for the Sun Dance. The test of manhood and endurance involved the lifting of Mandan males by the skewers to a lodge beam while buffalo skulls on skewers weighted their calves and thighs.

In the West, fans of body modification increased in number during the late 1940s, beginning with the self-identification of gay men with a single earring. American and European women joined proponents of ear piercing in the 1960s and popularized hoop earrings. The light metal circlets relieved the discomfort of screw-back earrings while imparting a bohemian flair to costume jewelry.

In the mid-1970s, British punk nonconformists turned body jewelry into exhibitionism with the implanting of safety pins, cheek plugs, and chains in the flesh. Aficionados drew attention to the counterculture with more bizarre piercings— in the uvula and the webbing between fingers and toes—as well as the scalpel widening of ear piercings and insertion of tapers to enlarge the openings. Spurious articles, books, and Internet postings by Doug Malloy of Los Angeles in the late 1970s fabricated histories of body piercing in the ancient world.

In the United States, health concerns about the transmission of AIDS, staphylococcus, and hepatitis from septic needles influenced passage of stricter state laws, notably requiring parental permission and outlawing genital piercing of young teens as a form of molestation. By the end of the twentieth century, however, adolescents, college students, rock musicians, and runway models rallied behind the body transformation phenomenon with multiple earrings and posts, metal tunnels, and studs through the eyebrows, tongue, lips, oral mucus membranes, nipples, umbilicus, and genitals.

In the twenty-first century, obsession with three-dimensional body art spawned a piercing industry. To avoid nickel allergy, piercers added to gemstones and metal materials such as Plexiglas, thermoplastics, porcelain, acrylics, and surgical tubing. The purposes of altering flesh or nails ranged from self-expression, identification with a subculture, and mimicry of celebrities to the celebration of a lifestyle change, rebellion against home and sect authority, and recovery from sexual abuse.

At a vegetarian festival on October 19, 2012, religious extremists at a Kathu shrine in Phuket, Thailand, expressed loyalty to a Chinese shrine by piercing their cheeks and lips with knives, beaded skewers, double-headed axes, and pistols. Currently, conservative school districts forbid any body art other than the adornment of pierced ears. Jewish, Islamic, and Mormon precepts denounce aesthetic piercings as violations of the body.

See also: Amerindian Clothing, Pre-Columbian; Body Painting; Jewels and Jewelry.

Further Reading

Angel, Elayne. *The Piercing Bible: The Definitive Guide to Safe Body Piercing.* New York: Random House, 2009.

DeMello, Margo. *Encyclopedia of Body Adornment.* Westport, CT: Greenwood, 2007.

Rush, John A. *Spiritual Tattoo: A Cultural History of Tattooing, Piercing, Scarification, Branding, and Implants.* Berkeley, CA: Frog, 2005.

Bohemian Style and Fashion

The dress of an unconventional subculture, Bohemian styles reflect adventure, ethnic dress, and raffish idiosyncrasies. The attire of the nonconformist or expatriate intellectual entered clothing history in the 1830s and heightened with the advance of industrialism. The disheveled wardrobe included dowdy secondhand ensembles, wanton posture, and eccentric embellishments of flowing hair with fresh flowers.

The artistic whims of the pre-Raphaelite Brotherhood, epitomized after 1848 by models Jane Morris and Elizabeth Siddal, depicted embroidered shawls and mismatched scarves layered over kimonos and the medieval *bliauts* (lace-up dresses) of females such as those painted by Dante Gabriel Rossetti, John Millais, and William Morris. By freeing women's portraiture from corsets, hoops, and layered petticoats, the pre-Raphaelites advanced a romantic disorder in historical and literary figures, including Pandora and Persephone from Greek mythology, Arthurian maidens, and Ophelia, the tragic drowning victim in Shakespeare's *Hamlet*.

Influenced by the antimaterialist tastes of the nomadic Rom, Rossettian attire epitomized *haut bohème* (high Gypsy) style. Couturiers emulated the bangles, paisleys, and contrived layers that repudiated Victorian codes of genteel decorum.

Socialism in the 1890s inspired men's luxuriant hair and voluminous cloaks and reform dress among female suffragists. In the early 1900s, Russian radicals flaunted Bohemian dress in defiance of extravagance in the imperial court of Czar Nicholas II.

Exhibitionism weakened American Bohemianism with studied theatrics rather than authenticity. Greenwich Village women flaunted the sack dress and smocks in chartreuse and magenta, leopard skin coats, vamp makeup, and Parisian pumps with white anklet socks. After World War I, cafe society popularized down-and-out Chelsea-style dirndl skirts and kerchiefs. Loose gowns, wide silk ties, and baggy, threadbare suits of the Lost Generation personified the alternatives styles of Isadora Duncan, Ernest Hemingway, Vanessa Bell, Rupert Brooke, and Gertrude Stein.

To express sympathy with the post–World War II destitute, European men in the late 1940s adopted trousers and knit jerseys paired with scruffy navy pea coats, watch caps, and sandals. In 1953, women's wear designer Hubert de Givenchy launched the jumper, cropped top, and pedal pushers. The avant-garde spurned the capitalist uniform by flaunting beards and berets, Eastern European peasant styles, leotards, cowboy boots, and caftans with flat ballet slippers.

The 1960s spread the beatnik combination of stressed jeans or prairie skirts with turtlenecks and patchwork vests, the elements of vagrant style dressing. Anti-establishment philosophies—pacifism, civil rights, feminism, and gay rights—found expression in long hair. Students exploited youthful disgruntlement with granny glasses, braless fishnet tops, hemp belts and sandals, paisley head rags, Navajo headbands, handkerchief hems, and Birkenstock earth shoes.

Military elements interposed reminders of the Vietnam War. Mounting protests by the counterculture and disaffected rock-and-roll bands inspired the addition of denim and leather vests, distressed camouflage field jackets, Marine fatigue caps, and the pairing of army boots or bare feet with ankle-length skirts. Copycat ready-to-wear promoted beads, tie-dye tunics and dashikis, and bell-bottoms.

Businessmen in the 1990s donned collarless shirts, drawstring pants, no socks, huaraches, and Timberlands for casual Fridays and the weekend. In the early 2000s, boho chic stressed individualism by layering florals, ruffled skirts, and batiked or lace tops, accessorized with hoop earrings and boots. Fantasy touches of brothel stereotypes—bustiers, lace-up bodices and shoes, flounced petticoats, peignoirs—echoed the sexual freedom of cancan dancers and uninhibited 1920s shabby chic. Rave-goers added funky dancewear, neon-colored hair with glitter makeup, and running shoes.

In 2012, the Manhattan Vintage Show displayed retro styles once strutted on runways in London and Milan. Bohemian dress revived the bravado of men's leather hats and satchels, Nehru jackets, and chambray shirts and pants. Women took comfort in smocked waists and elastic or drawstring necklines in plums and purples that allowed the wearer to raise or lower the top for effect. Three-tiered gauzy skirts eased with gathers added swish to the walk.

Beading in hairstyles, pull ties, belts, and sandals drew the eye to natural cording and earthy wood or shell ornaments. Bowknot or halter dresses plunged necklines to reveal tattoos. Garnishing with men's leather bracelets and women's studded bags with bamboo handles, amber necklaces, collections of Indian bangles, and fishnet stockings contributed to the overall look of the free thinker.

See also: Hippie and Mod Fashion; Vintage Clothing.

Further Reading

Nicholson, Virginia. *Among the Bohemians: Experiments in Living, 1900–1939.* New York: William Morrow, 2002.

Stover, Laren, with Paul Gregory Himmelein and Patrisha Grainger Robertson. *Bohemian Manifesto: A Field Guide to Living on the Edge.* New York: Bulfinch, 2004.

Wilson, Elizabeth. *Bohemians: The Glamorous Outcasts.* New York: Taurisparke, 2003.

Bond Clothing Stores

A middle-class U.S. shopping haven, Bond Clothing stores met the needs of average men with affordable suits, shoes, and accessories from the early to mid-twentieth century. The store dates back to Charles Anson Bond, the mayor of Columbus, Ohio, and his haberdashery at 237 North High Street. In 1915, Bond, Lester Cohen, and Mortimer Slater founded the nation's first men's clothing chain on Euclid and East Ninth Street in Cleveland, Ohio. The company marketed $15 men's suits, tailored primarily by Jewish seamstresses. By 1917, the Cleveland store reported a capital stock of $1.75 million.

From the beginning, the Bond stores presented goods in elegant surroundings. In Pittsburgh, designers introduced the Bond Company's signature lighting by installing hanging lamps. Within a decade, the company opened an opulent haberdashery in Washington, D.C. Comprising 28 stores in the 1930s and 1940s, Bond was the largest retail chain for men's clothing in America. Its employment rolls exceeded 4,000. Boosting sales among working-class men, the company's budget service offered a 10-payment plan.

In 1933, under president and board chair Barney Smith Ruben, the company moved its manufacturing from New Brunswick, New Jersey, to a new factory in Rochester, New York, which eventually hired 2,500 employees. Men on the way up visited Bond stores for everything from Western-style sport coats, double-breasted business suits, and tuxedos and formal accessories to uniform jackets for Senate pages and gangster blazers. To increase cash flow, Ruben altered the stipulations of the 10-payment plan to thirds—one-third at the time of purchase and two equal payments over the next two months.

Throughout the Great Depression and World War II, the Bond chain dominated the sale of two-pant men's suits in the United States. Store architecture emphasized spectacle, as exemplified by a Vitrolite pigmented glass façade erected over the Toledo store in 1936. The Detroit location flaunted Armstrong linoleum, a custom flooring chosen for its masculine appeal. In 1940, the glass and steel edifice on State Street in Chicago became one of the most photographed commercial façades of the era because of designer Morris Lapidus's use of light. Aggressive investment in California seized market share in Oakland and San Francisco.

Throughout the tenuous period of World War II, the Bond Company sponsored local radio news. In 1942, Bond supplied the U.S. military with uniform coats, pants, and overcoats. On V-J Day, August 14, 1945, a photo picturing a sailor kissing a nurse in front of the Union Square store in New York City added the Bond brand to classic American iconography. Company history acquired additional fame from ads presented by journalist Mike Wallace on metropolitan news in New York and the work of comedian Joan Rivers as fashion coordinator for the entire chain.

Until a union law protecting the Amalgamated Clothing Workers of America lowered the company's profits, Barney Ruben aimed to expand the business into the world's largest factory. In 1946, the company demolished its Cleveland anchor and rebuilt in art moderne style a four-story pink marble and steel showplace inspired by Hollywood depictions of department stores. Lighted mirrored columns extended from the first floor to the third-floor open terrace. Spotlights illuminated a canopy pocked with large circular holes that directed beams to the sky.

To combat the post–World War II slump in clothing sales, Bond offered women's coats and suits and family apparel. The company's focus on Hopalong Cassidy shirts for $2.95 in its 1950 Chicago Christmas clothing ads illustrated Bond's intent to draw younger shoppers to its stores. The company encouraged salesmanship with high pay, sales meetings and competitions, and loudspeaker announcements to shoppers.

In 1956, some 100 outlets sold Bond goods in major U.S. cities, with subsidiary stores in 50 smaller municipalities. Company officials chose ideal locations, such as the terra cotta–fronted store at Scollay Square in Boston, the Beverly Hills store on Wilshire Boulevard in Los Angeles, and the three-story Bond store on Peachtree Street in Atlanta.

In 1959, a five-day strike in Washington, D.C., expressed disgruntlement at a contract impasse involving Bond retail clerks. Officials took out full-page ads in the Washington papers reassuring workers that their jobs were secure. In 1969, to support sales with quality alterations, the company imported 13 Turkish tailors to replace dwindling skilled labor from Europe. The Bond Company remained in business until its sale to foreign investors in 1975.

See also: Retail Trade.

Boots

Functional footwear protecting the ankle and lower leg, boots increase the range of wearers into high grass, over unstable ground and swales, and amid hazards from rocks and animals.

In the first millennium B.C.E., shoemakers invented the first models by joining leggings to shoes or moccasins. Mukluks, foot wraps, and leggings from Thule in the far north protected the feet from extreme cold and the rough edges of ice. Among the Aleut, Yupik, and Inuit, sewers stitched in tiny intervals to make caribou and sealskin boots watertight.

Fur on the sole increased stability on ice. Alaskan boot styles featured bearded seal, sea lion, or walrus soles tied with leather thongs to the calf. Dress boots for men and women bore dyed appliqué, decorative stitchery, and rabbit, fox, or raccoon fur. Similar styles prevailed among Scandinavian Sami and Siberians.

Ancient Styles

Etruscan, Persian, and Greek bootmakers developed civilian styles from the military. Soles and uppers consisted of one piece sewn down front and back. Etruscans favored an unadorned boot with a loose top reaching to the knee. Elitist Persian mode offered a banded top tied at the ankle. For height, Greek females elevated the open-toed half-boot or buskin, a cork or wood-soled shoe with fur ankle decor originating in Phrygia. Egyptians adapted the Greek boot with a laced model that provided loops to hold thongs. Women preferred their high-top footwear in green.

Roman legionaries laced open-toed *caligae* (marching boots) up the front of the calf, a style that women adopted. In Britannia, quartermasters bought Celtic cowhide for airy netted caligae, the iron hobnailed footwear distributed to marching units the rank of centurion and below. Soldiers and urban peace officers developed a lethal kick by which the hobnails inflicted harm on an attacker. Imperial footwear followed ordinary styles but added rich embellishments, jewels, and gold leaf. Saxon boots accommodated the foot with ankle-hugging lacing down to the toes. The thong tied over the instep for security.

In northern Britain around 1000, Scots fashioned a low boot from rawhide to use in torturing captives. After soaking the vamp in water and tying the boots to prisoners' feet, they heated the soles over coals to compress the feet and dislocate bones as the hide shrank.

Medieval Europe

Norman insurgents in 1066 introduced to England the wide half-boot with a studded band above the ankle. Northampton gained fame as a shoemaking center after King John bought a pair of flat-soled boots there around 1199. His successor, Henry III, adorned his boots with gold bands crisscrossed over the instep and marked by the lions of his royal insignia. Henry's successors introduced the buttoned boot, with closures up the center or outer leg.

Around 1200, Mongol insurgents introduced Asian ankle boots to Russia, China, and India. The camel riders of North Africa preferred boots for desert travel. For royal Chinese courts, noblemen developed the embroidered silk high-heel boot into a decorative art.

In 1396, French Crusaders fighting the Ottoman Turks at Nicopolis, Bulgaria, had to lop the points from *poulaines* (peaked shoes) to speed their flight from a massacre. In the 1400s, armorers adapted the poulaine with the riveted metal plates of the *sabaton,* an armored style prohibited in Nuremberg by the 1453 sumptuary laws. Turned-up toes leaned left or right. Fold-down collars of lighter leather presaged the flamboyance of seventeenth-century cavalier boots.

Around 1500, Englishwomen accentuated the tasteful use of Spanish leather or velvet with buskins, knee-high boots with a turn-back collar revealing a fur lining. Men's buckskin boots bore jingly heel spurs for riding and ties across the front of the calf that left open much of the top portion.

Dress boots featured toe buckles, lacing, buttons, and latchets (straps) that secured the fit over the instep. Elizabethan riders and hunters popularized the thigh boot with a turn-down collar. In 1580, bootmakers farmed out a proliferation of orders to outworkers, men and women who labored at piecework in home workshops, such as stitching the edge binding on a high boot to hold a drawstring.

As a replacement for pull-on boots, the square-toed brogue, a heavy walking shoe, came into fashion in the 1600s. Orders from armies enabled Northampton factory managers to hire journeymen for multiple tasks, from cutting and stitching to tacking, polishing, and buffing of regulation cuffed boots. Early-seventeenth-century men's footwear favored waxed leather walking boots that encouraged lengthening the stride in a show of masculinity. A heel guard of hardened leather extended the life of buckskin vamps from spur and stirrup wear.

Effeminate vs. Masculine

During the Restoration era in England (after 1660), men's boots lost their effeminate detailing. Straight thigh-high riding boots of heavy black leather featured a square toe and polished gloss. Fancier styles sported a brown or white cuff to match knee breeches. In 1688, Massachusetts shoemaking regulations forbade oversized boots of thin Spanish leather, a design popularized by dandies in England.

In contrast to English disdain for effete footwear, the French preferred high heels, broad toes, and suede vamps either buttoned on the outside or laced at the front. Cuffs spread as wide as a waistband and flaunted lace or fringe. By the 1770s, Hessian boots with notched tops and Wellingtons with pull-on loops offered a choice of foot fashion for morning wear. Because footwear did not indicate left and right, consumers reversed boots daily to extend their use.

At Williamsburg, Virginia, George Wilson set up a factory in the 1760s and advertised in the *Virginia Gazette* "Boots and Shoes for Gentlemen," a separate enterprise from fashioning military and women's footwear. The price rose 25 percent from 16 to 20 shillings for top-grade calfskin boots made to measure.

From Labrador and Newfoundland, manufacturers acquired sealskin for popular women's styles. The outbreak of the American Revolution strained the shoemaking industry to provide boots for soldiers and temporarily ended manufacture of women's foot fashions. The landing of British Redcoats in October 1776 resulted in the Continental Army's caching of boot leather in the New York highlands. Booteries in Virginia and the Carolinas began competing with New England factories. The Continental Congress passed strong measures to halt profiteering and protect shoemaking supplies to keep the patriots in combat boots. Despite quick action, as of December 4, only 66 percent of soldiers at Fort Ticonderoga wore shoes for duty. Marching units left bloody tracks from gashes in soldiers' feet. By December 20, the rise in pleurisy rates depleted the fighting force, causing the commissariat to impound shoes and stockings.

High Style

Following the French Revolution in 1789, London cordwainers popularized spurred boots. After 1804, men adapted the velvet brodequin (wood-soled boot) edged at the top with a fringe. At the height of the Napoleonic Wars, the demand for repair of Hessian and Wellington boots increased the cobblery business, especially in the securing of leather straps with rivets and washers.

More significant to employment, combat at century's end disposed men's civilian styles toward tassels and military detailing in Hessian boots, Prussian bluchers (or derbies) with bellows tongue and open lacing, and Wellingtons, popular with students at Eton. For weight in the heel of military shoes, manufacturers added clay to the leather. Coachmen and postilions wore winged jackboots, a cavalry boot lined in leather and reinforced with chain mail and iron sole plates.

In 1810, urban men popularized the Coburg or Oxonian, a side-slit or lace-up introduced at Oxford University during a student rebellion against boots and high-tops. Fops exhibited their fashion savvy in shiny patent-leather riding boots with tassels on the front and noisy iron horseshoes on the heels. American men preferred Joseph Walker's wood pegs to rivets for nonslip boot soles.

In London, engineer and inventor Marc Isambard Brunel determined to improve military provisioning, which cost English taxpayers £150,000 annually for shoes. In 1810, Brunel began employing wounded veterans to cut uppers with a press and rivet soles with his patented invention. His factory teams produced soldiers' shoes and boots at the rate of 400 pairs per day, removing clay from the heels and studding them with nails or pins.

Workhouses taught orphaned and delinquent boys to make simple boots, which the British and U.S. navies bought during the War of 1812. At war's end, Brunel faced warehouses full of unsold footwear, which he contracted to the Prussian army in 1819 at the height of national reform. As tastes returned to civilian day wear, the Wellington replaced the Hessian boot in popularity. From the 1860s on the American frontier, cowboys stipulated pointed toes and smooth soles to slip into stirrups and the elevated heel for riding.

Boots in War and Peace

Prince Albert, Queen Victoria's husband, popularized the high Balmoral boot, a welt toe and closed vamp with lacing in six eyelets that produced a trim fit and even lacing. Both Wellingtons and galoshes came in rubber for use as sturdy, inexpensive working boots. From the onset of the Crimean War in 1853 through World War I, bootmakers returned to overwork and low wages while laboring at military contracts for riveted, iron-plated ammunition boots, an advance of the late 1880s, and the leather laced tank boot featuring a waterproof strapped upper, a style later preferred by tank commander George Patton. Outside military camps, prostitutes of the 1890s cozened submissive clients with thigh-high laced leather boots, either flat-heeled or platform-soled.

The Joseph Williams factory, the prize footwear producer in England's shoemaking capital of Northampton, offered a wide range of calf-high tops, long boots, and galoshes with lacings or elastic inserts and top-grain walking shoes. While the Balmoral still dominated sales to business and professional men, the twentieth century brought demands for rubber Wellingtons made in Hood, Massachusetts, and for British-made acid-proof

The leather cowboy boot, now an American art form, dates to the cattle drives of the 1860s to 1880s. A tall shaft protected the legs from rocks, burrs, snakebite, and mud. A smooth sole slid easily into stirrups; a strong tapered heel kept the foot secure in them. *(Greg Ward/ Dorling Kindersley/Getty Images)*

India rubber shoes and calf-high cuffed Russian Cossack boots with heels cut and layered on a revolution press. In the 1910s, younger men favored mid-calf lace-up boots with buckles at the top and triple-stitched high-button shoes for school and college.

By 1917, sales to Belgian and French dough-boys of heavy American Pershing boots (trench boots) ended the domination of the russet (unpolished) marching boot, which remained out of favor until the Korean War. The British firm of Howlett & White in Norwich made 30,000 canvas fatigue shoes; the nearby Edwards & Holmes factory concentrated on Cossack boots. From 1917 to 1919, steam-powered Russian factories dedicated their efforts to turning out military boots for infantrymen, who sometimes fought barefoot for lack of footwear. Erich Maria Remarque's novel *All Quiet on the Western Front* made symbolic use of German side-seamed, wood-bottomed boots, a necessity during trench warfare. For parade dress, officers sported polished riding boots, giving an impression that belied the privations of World War I.

After 1940, mass orders of lace-up combat boots with a high-top buckled cuff and the fully laced Corcoran (jump or paratrooper boot) increased total U.S. factory output by more than 40 percent, from 102 million pairs in 1940 to 143 million by the middle of World War II. Speeding manufacture was the one-piece sole and heel molded from recycled rubber, a reliable construction that inspired men to continue wearing them in civilian life.

For mountainous terrain, soldiers wore high lace-ups with heavy hobnailing for traction. Troops bound for North Africa received regulation suede boots with crepe soles suited to desert sand. For jungle warfare, the military pierced the instep of the combat boot with vents to prevent jungle rot, a severe fungal infection that could lead to amputation. From 1941 to 1945, Russian soldiers donned simple felt boots and German soldiers wrapped their legs in thick green felt puttees above lace-up combat boots.

By 1950, machines molded soles directly on uppers, an innovation the British military adopted in 1961. Old men popularized the crepe-soled chukka boot (turf buck), a low boot of calf, suede, or crocodile replicating World War II British military footwear from the desert campaign. The

Dingo Company introduced the straps and rings of the harness boot with a leather heel for stability.

See also: Equestrian Attire; Lacing; Leather and Suede; Shoes, Men's; Shoes, Women's; Uniforms, Military.

Further Reading

Beard, Tyler. *Cowboy Boots.* Salt Lake City, UT: Gibbs Smith, 2004.
DeMello, Margo. *Feet and Footwear: A Cultural Encyclopedia.* New York: Macmillan, 2009.
Montgomery, David R. *Crafts and Skills of the Native Americans: Tipis, Canoes, Jewelry, Moccasins.* New York: Skyhorse, 2009.
Riello, Giorgio. *A Foot in the Past: Consumers, Producers, and Footwear in the Long Eighteenth Century.* New York: Oxford University Press, 2006.

Boutiques

A one-of-a-kind retail shop, the boutique sparked the shopping tastes of British and American women from the early 1900s into the twenty-first century. Unlike department stores, the "concept shop" derived from the Italian *bottega,* a studio or dressmaker's atelier specializing in the work of a single artisan, such as shell jewelry at shops in Papeete, Tahiti. In an informal atmosphere, owners stressed offbeat merchandise with such whimsical store names as The Honey Chile in Wilmington, North Carolina, and Arsenic et Vieilles Dentelles (Arsenic and Old Lace) in Saint Paul de Vence, France.

Boutique minimalism focused on specialty requests or age groups, such as tuxedos and hand-cobbled shoes at Boyds in Philadelphia, camo gear at Club Monaco in Toronto, Rag & Bone men's shirts at Odin in New York City, Japanese denim for men at The Archive in San Francisco, and Latina teen finery at V-Chic Boutique in Amarillo, Texas. In 1909, French designer Jeanne Lanvin opened the Heart House of Lanvin, where she marketed mother-and-daughter outfits. In 1927 in Paris and the 1930s in Manhattan, designer Elsa Schiaparelli anticipated boutique commerce with tastemaking salons selling cubist sweaters.

The 1940s saw the rise in swank apparel as disparate as maternity outfits from The Stork Set in Washington, D.C., and the capri pants found at Emilio Pucci's Capri resort wear emporium in Capri, Italy. In the 1950s, gay men patronized specialty shops in Los Angeles and Palm Springs and Pierre Cardin's Adam boutique in Paris. Small, informal businesses offered exclusive patrons customized services, including seasonal collections, mail delivery, coordinated ensembles, and tailoring of short-run patterns, colors, and textures, such as the Mediterranean border prints displayed in fabric shops in the 1960s in Athens, Greece.

Women in Buenos Aires, Zurich, and Rome perused the 1960s couture fashions houses of Hubert de Givenchy. In 1966, Yves Saint Laurent opened Rive Gauche, the first small couture shop in London. André Courrèges adapted downsized shopping in 1967 with 65 boutiques in Asia, Europe, and the United States. In London, tourists popularized the specialty stores on Carnaby Street and Kings Road.

The 1970s sharpened the focus, decor, and layout of specialty shops, as with the svelte menswear designer Nino Cerruti, marketed at Hitman in Milan and the basic sailors' sweaters and mackintoshes displayed in coastal shops in Quebec. Ralph Lauren adapted the scaled-down merchandising of jeans in 1971 with his Beverly Hills boutique, the first freestanding store owned by an American couturier. Stores around the world followed the trend, raising profits for Victoria's Secret lingerie in Edmonton, Gianni Versace leather and knits in Milan, and Vera Wang wedding attire in Sydney, Australia, and Shanghai, China.

The proliferation of boutiques in the 1980s fostered adventuresome devotees, such as fans of the cotton sweaters and travelers' sportswear in Chico's chain. Tokyo's Harajuku mall increased teen traffic by offering chained and zippered goods, dog collars, and dark Goth attire at punk outlets and headrags and bling (costume jewelry) at hip-hip shops. In 1997, Berlin shoppers at Friedrichstrasse chose among shops retailing Gucci leather goods, Louis Vuitton handbags, and Akkesoir jewelry and hats. Retro chic of the 2000s introduced vintage boutiques specializing in secondhand glamour from the past. The Chinese promoted boutique shopping at Triple-Major in Beijing, a dealer in socks, toboggans, and cardigans.

See also: Retail Trade; Vintage Clothing.

Further Reading

Lester, Richard. *Boutique London: A History: King's Road to Carnaby Street.* Woodbridge, UK: ACC, 2010.

Palmer, Alexandra, and Hazel Clark. *Old Clothes, New Looks: Second Hand Fashion.* New York: Berg, 2005.

Vernet, David, and Leontine de Wit. *Boutiques and Other Retail Spaces: The Architecture of Seduction.* New York: Routledge, 2007.

Brassieres

From ancient times, bandeau, bodice, and corset-style brassieres have molded and repositioned female breasts for maximum style and function. Although the term "brassiere" did not enter the English language until 1810 in *The Spectator,* the concept dates to Egyptian shoulder harnesses as early as 3000 B.C.E. Evidence of Mongolian silk bras with back strings and Minoan athletic bandeaux in 1000 B.C.E. suggests that breast support was more prevalent in the ancient past than fashion history generally records.

After 200 B.C.E., Greek women crossed extensions of the *zoné* (girdle) over the bosom as an external breast support. Roman females wore the linen, wool, or leather *strophium* (breast band) under the *tunica intima* (foundation tunic). For flair, they topped their ensembles with crisscross cording or straps that anticipated twentieth-century European lingerie that separated the breasts. Around 300 C.E., Roman athletes worked out in garments resembling bikinis while running and exercising with barbells.

From the mid-1300s, Chinese women wore a strapped, diamond-shaped *dudou,* a sternal apron that tied around the neck. Western intimate apparel favored the French *cotte,* which flattened the breasts, and the corset, a midriff support that boosted the bosom. In the 1400s, the addition of the laced basquine (underbodice) to the hooped petticoat or farthingale increased the natural presentation of the female torso. The discovery of fifteenth-century linen breast bags at Lengberg Castle in East Tyrol, Austria, boosted the historic study of medieval lingerie.

During the Renaissance, European women paired the chemise with torso-hugging bodices, breast shapers that showcased the female chest. In the fervor of the French Revolution of 1789, women reclaimed the Greek zoné, which rounded the breasts under high-waisted muslin Empire dresses. By 1800, more natural breast definition supplanted the mono-bosom for display of individual breasts in gusseted silk cups. Functional brassieres and drawers enabled women to develop athletic skills at lawn tennis and cycling.

Modern Commodities

From 1885, manufacturers accommodated mastectomy patients with prosthetic breasts contoured from rubber to resemble a human shape and feel. Parisian lingerie expert Herminie Cadolle, founder of the Fashion Form Brassière Company, designed the *corselet-gorge* (breast corset) in 1889 out of elasticized cloth. She displayed a two-piece waist cinch and bra at the Paris Exposition Universelle under the name *bien-être* (well-being). Her company marketed the beribboned top portion—the *soutien-gorge* (breast support)—to royalty, actresses, the duchess of Windsor, designer Coco Chanel, and spy Mata Hari.

Popularized in the Belle Époque by the Charles B. DeBevoise Company of New York City, "bust girdles," "breast retainers," and "bust bodices" engineered like boned camisoles appeared in fashion advertisements from 1904. The company specialized in fitting stout figures and equipping workaday models with underarm shields and girlish cotton lace models with satin straps. French couturier Paul Poiret promoted flexible, unboned brassieres as less rigid and more liberating than unwieldy corsets for wearing under the era's simpler straight dress.

By 1907, the brassiere with mesh net cups applied kinetics to comfort and posture control, an improvement noted in *Vogue* magazine. By 1914, a factory in Stuttgart, Germany, had begun mass-producing brassieres. On February 12, 1914, bohemian inventor Mary Phelps "Polly" Jacob patented a wraparound breast garment she had fashioned four years earlier from ribbon, cord, and two silk handkerchiefs. After 1920, after Lucien and DeVer Warner purchased Jacob's patent, the company boosted bra sales by 80 percent.

A more substantial button-front model, the Symington Side Lacer, added reinforcement to minimize breasts. The boyish cut accommodated the lacy styles of designer Coco Chanel, who favored the androgynous silhouette in flapper dresses styled for dancing the vigorous Charleston and seductive tango. After World War I, home crafters prized patterns for the crocheted cotton brassiere secured with ribbon.

In 1921, London-born dressmaker Lucy Duff-Gordon urged modern women to expand their lingerie wardrobes with the uplifting breast bandeau and sport brassiere. Later in that decade, Ida and William Rosenthal, owners of the Maidenform Company in Bayonne, New Jersey, extended the varieties of silk, chiffon, and batiste bras for upthrust and breastfeeding. Maidenform marketed the concept throughout the Western Hemisphere and Europe, but the concept failed in China because of criticism of passé style and unhealthful restriction.

After 1932, lingerie ads shortened "brassiere" to "bra." Advertising began defining cup sizes as A, B, C, and D and picturing cotton lace and net as well as adjustable hook-and-eye closures. Elastic bras from Gossard in Chicago ended dependence on boning for support. In 1936, after Iranian women adopted modern Western dress, Reza Shah Pahlavi added the brassiere to the female dress code.

Wartime and Postwar Lingerie

In Paris from June 14, 1940, to August 25, 1944, Alice Cadolle kept her lingerie business alive during the Nazi occupation by cutting the salon's curtains into usable fabric. Rationing during World War II limited the amount of rubber and metal available for corsets and popularized the use of cotton-backed satin or drill broche (tapestry), the quartermaster's choice for the Women's Royal Naval Service. Simplicity patterns, advertised in *Harper's Bazaar,* encouraged women to make their own bras, thereby saving $1.25 for a ready-made item from Formfit or 98 cents for the Dickee-Bra combination bra and collar. As bras gained popularity, film actors Lana Turner and Jane Russell publicized the full figure in cone-shaped cups that lifted and outlined the breasts in posters and photos circulated among U.S. soldiers in *Yank, the Army Weekly.*

In Paris, during a postwar return to style and sensuality, designer Simone Pérèle began offering hand-sewn satin bras under the So French label. At Empreinte in Brest, France, owner Jean le Her resculpted the silhouette with the deeper pointed cup. At Kyoto, Japanese entrepreneur Koichi Tsukamoto, founder of Wacoal, introduced breast supports to Japanese and Thai women. In 1946, Frederick Mellinger, founder of Frederick's of Hollywood, patented the push-up bra and marketed the Wonderbra, a favorite of the "sweater girl." His boutique and catalog gained customers for bustiers and strapless bra and panty sets.

At mid-century, consumers chose from a wide variety of models and colors in washable power net and nylon. Styles from Berlei, Triumph, and Marquise introduced padded, strapless, and plunge fronts, revealing cleavage gaps. To the active woman, Vanity Fair from Reading, Pennsylvania, merchandised the V-back, an athletic bra. Glamour seekers found erotic styles from Movie Star, located in New York City. DuPont's invention of Lycra in 1959 encouraged new silhouettes and uplift devoid of rubber, a breakthrough for lingerie pioneer Pérèle.

Marks & Spencer, the British department store chain, advertised the bra slip, a hybrid undergarment featuring underwired uplift. Maidenform touted the health benefits of the sleep bra, a boon to women with dense breast tissue. In 1962, Delightform proclaimed Dacron polyester ideal for the permanently stiffened soft-cup bandeau, which sold for $2.95. In the 1970s, shelf, jogging, basque, and balconette models and T-shirt bras featuring a seamless surface enhanced smoother fashion trends. French backless models from designer Charles Pasquier for Aubade in Paris initiated a line of teaser bras, reflecting burlesque styles and erotic costumes from the film *Emmanuelle* (1974).

The exercise wear of the 1980s demanded stretch leotards and microfiber bodysuits. Pérèle accommodated the fashionable woman with the original coordinated lingerie, a concept expanded in America by Gossard. The Chinese, who standardized the boyishly plain *xiaomajia* (little vest) for East Asian women throughout the twentieth century, monopolized global bra manufacture.

In the early 2000s, women had a wide choice of bareback, demi-cup, T-back, transparent, and self-adhesive silicone bras as well as built-in support in camisoles, halters, and tank tops. The addition of gel pads to straps eased shoulder discomfort in full-figured women. Bioform bras molded from plastic and Ultimo models padded with silicone gel aided older women in restoring sagging bosoms to youthful uplift.

See also: Bodices; Corsets and Girdles; Feminist Styles and Fashions; Lingerie; Maternity Clothes; Pin-Up Girls; Undergarments.

Further Reading

Farrell-Beck, Jane, and Colleen Gau. *Uplift: The Bra in America.* Philadelphia: University of Pennsylvania Press, 2002.

Fields, Jill. *An Intimate Affair: Women, Lingerie, and Sexuality.* Berkeley: University of California Press, 2007.

Williams, Florence. *Breasts: A Natural and Unnatural History.* New York: W.W. Norton, 2012.

Breechcloths

A simple loincloth and a symbol of male dignity and decency, the breechcloth (or breechclout) provided support and covering for active men. The purpose of concealing nudity was twofold—to set the human apart from the animal kingdom and to socialize the body for presentation in the community.

From antiquity, a loincloth of 10–12 feet (3–3.7 meters) became standard dress on Pacific isles and in Vietnam, Bangladesh, Malaysia, Crete, India, Ceylon, and Madagascar. African hunter-gatherers may have pioneered the thong breechcloth. As far back as 42,000 B.C.E., San Bushmen of Angola, Botswana, Lesotho, Mozambique, Namibia, South Africa, Swaziland, and Zimbabwe shaped a piece of skin like a T for desert wear. As a fastener, they threaded cord or sinew through the top. The San extended waist ties for wrapping around the middle. The long aprons passed between the legs and looped under the tie in back and over a thong, exposing the buttocks.

Europeans in frozen and moderate climates made their own style of men's underwear. Ötzi the Iceman, a cadaver dating to 3300 B.C.E. found frozen in a glacier in the Italian Alps in 1991, wore a calf belt that secured his goat-leather loincloth, a tailored garment consisting of strips cross-stitched with sinew. From 1570 B.C.E., Aegean men of the Minoan and Mycenaean cultures wore belted loincloths with back flaps and codpieces, a military crotch protector and modesty shield later replaced by the kilt. From the same era, during desert warfare, Nubian mercenaries in the Egyptian army wore loincloths made from cowhide.

According to the *Shoku Nihongi* (*Japanese Chronicles,* 797), a state history commissioned as an official record, Japanese men wore a *fundoshi* (thong breechcloth) as underwear. After winding a cloth around the waist and knotting it at the lower back, males brought the remaining flap between the legs to thread through the wrapping and drape in front and double back to twist at the rear. The wrap developed into an all-round swimsuit, taiko drummer's uniform, and ritual garment for the biennial *hadaka matsuri* (naked festival). From before 250 C.E., ritual sumo dancers adapted an ornate cotton or silk fundoshi called a *mawashi.*

Variations in size and shape of the breechcloth suggest differing attitudes toward modesty and utility, as with the rectangular loincloth of Borneo and the triangular Javanese and Sumatran version. In India, the *kaupina* (thong) on ritual statues of Shiva consisted of a cloth rectangle securely tied with four waist strings. A more enveloping garment in India, Bangladesh, the Maldives, and Pakistan, the *dhoti* (shorts) required nearly 5 yards (4.6 meters) of cloth to pleat around the legs and torso and knot at the waist. In Egypt, abbreviated triangular underwear of linen served men and women of the servant class. In Oceania, ancient Polynesians recognized a chief's oversized loincloth as a symbol of power.

In the "hide age," the Native American breechcloth covered the groin with an undergarment and two flaps, a back panel and front apron. Indigenous Americans chose materials from the pelts or skins of antelope, bison, cattle, deer, elk, and Rocky Mountain goat. Northeastern Abenaki cinched loincloths with rawhide belts.

From 1200 B.C.E., the Olmec of Veracruz, Mexico, wove breechcloths of cotton and woven plant leaves, which the Aztec later traded with Spaniards for Iberian fabrics. Around 600 C.E., the abbreviated breechcloth that Choctaw men from Tennessee to Mississippi attached to wide leather belts served as athletic shorts for the rowdy ball game of chunkey. From 1000 to 1550 C.E., the Mississippi Indians at Etowah made short-fiber yarns from mammal fur and turkey down to prevent fraying in belts, sashes, shoes, medicine bags, and breechcloths.

When Francisco Pizarro encountered the Inca of Peru in 1526, native men tied the *huara* (loin covering) with string and displayed a fringed apron that hung below a tunic. In 1674, Gabriel Díaz Vara Calderón, the Bishop of Cuba, reported that the Calusa and Tequests, hunter-gatherers of Florida, made their loincloths of palmetto brush, bark bast, animal skins, or woven palm, a style echoed by the Arawak of Haiti that Columbus encountered in 1492.

According to Bernal Díaz del Castillo, the chronicler of Hernán de Cortés's conquest of Mexico in 1519, the Maya *maxtlatl* (loincloth) consisted of enough fabric to gird the waist. Designed from two pieces—a narrow strip of grass, maguey fiber, Spanish moss, or hide stabilized at the waist by a band or belt—the simple garment served the Delaware of the lower Hudson Valley of New York and the Cahuilla and Maidu of California. Along the Mississippi River, the Osage and Missouria supported their deer hide breechcloths with belts woven of bison wool. In the Mississippi and Ohio valleys, French *coureurs de bois* (woods runners) emulated Cree-style dress by adopting breechcloths and leggings.

Across the frontier, the skin loincloth served as common daily attire. For the Yokut of California, the best material for comfort was a strip 10 inches (25 centimeters) wide of deer hide. The Seminole of Florida tailored breechcloths from hide or coarse strouding cloth, tapered to points reaching mid-thigh. On the Northern Plains, women scraped deer hides to make soft breechcloths, the least binding costume for hot weather. Trade in red flannel gave needleworkers a soft, pliant fabric for shaping undergarments, such as those worn by White Bull, Sitting Bull's nephew, along with navy trade cloth leggings. In the Black Hills of South Dakota, White Bull claimed that the combined colors of loincloth and leggings gave him courage and increased his competitiveness in combat.

See also: Amerindian Clothing, Pre-Columbian; Undergarments.

British Clothing and Fashion

A touchstone of world couture, Britain has a history of influencing style at all socioeconomic levels. From 3500 B.C.E., stag hides provided material for unisex gillies, a loose footbag laced at the ankle with a drawstring. By 1900 B.C.E., British herders established the rudiments of wool weaving and export, which undergirded island wealth and fashion prestige.

From 200 B.C.E., Celtic monarchs displayed bronze diadems, a royal style still in use for European monarchs. Druid priests expressed reverence for trees by wearing plain white linen tunics and bare feet for processions featuring mistletoe and oak garlands. The arrival of Roman legionaries introduced classical style in military dress and the everyday linen tunic and wool cloak, as well as the carving of coral and shells into buttons and cameos. On the invasion of Britannia in 54 B.C.E. by Julius Caesar's landing force, Romans gawked at Celtic Britons lining the shore. Painted blue with woad (*Isatis tinctoria*), they intimidated their enemy with a bold display of nudity and totemic animals tattooed with colored pigments.

Keen on tapping international markets, millers established linen works near Roman forts. Agrarian Celts sold cowhide to the Romans and learned how to tan and cobble leather into netted bags and unisex boots with thongs tied over the arch. After 75 C.E., British soldiers adopted segmented armor, a leather basis fitted with metal bands, worn over wool tunics. British women learned to grind seaweed and minerals into makeup and to spin fibers by Mediterranean methods.

After the departure of Roman occupation forces in 450, the manufacture of felt hats introduced a new skill to British clothiers. While Irish and Scots cobblers fashioned the one-piece turnshoe for peasants, Saxon shoemakers shaped military boots to the foot and ankle with tight lacing. Fifth-century goldsmiths equipped King Hengist with a jeweled crown.

Dyers' guilds blended blue woad with yellow weld to create Lincoln green, the color associated with Robin Hood legends. After 800, Viking spinners processed long-hair fleece into wool yarn for clerical and court robes and cloaks. From the late ninth century to the early 1000s, the royal courts of Alfred the Great and Edward the Confessor elevated gloves to distinguishing elements of British attire.

Post-Saxon Britain

The invasion of William the Conqueror at Hastings in 1066 replaced Celtic boot styles with Norman half-boots, banded above the ankle and at the instep, and introduced the buttoning of boots up the inner or outer leg. For hosiery, Scots yarn makers flourished at turning Stamford fleece into wool thread for export to stocking knitters in Belgium, Flanders, and Italy. French influence promoted linen for unisex tunics, jumpers, overshirts, and bodices.

By 1199, Northampton anchored British shoemaking, a stabilizer of the export economy. In the thirteenth century, patchwork gained renown as a cottage craft. In the early 1300s, King Edward III fostered the weaving of camlet from angora and silk or wool, claiming the use of ermine trim and pelts for his court.

British vestments and academic regalia set a sober tone in the robes, tabards, hoods, and skull caps of clergy, surgeons, and academics at Cambridge and Oxford. The 1400s introduced the British concept of clerical austerity in black cassocks, habits, and kirtles, a humble investiture that contrasted the flagrant ostentation of Rome's Borgia popes. Aristocratic dress, on the other hand, featured boxy headdress and oversized veils, the beginning of two centuries of excess in upscale finery.

Early Renaissance status dressing equipped the urban male with wigs, satin linings for embroi-dered coats, and the ivory, ebony, or whalebone walking cane garnished with a knob of precious metal. Seamstresses created a niche market for needle weaving and embroidery on blouses and aprons. Sixteenth-century crafts developed crochet and knitting into marketable commodities. Court livery in England and Ireland required the work of embroiderers to add royal crests and insignia to tunics. While the elite Tudor court flaunted velvet boots, workingmen wore brogues to protect the feet during hard labor.

Infant garments of the early seventeenth century featured fine English stitchery, brocades, and laces on swaddling, coverlets, and bonnets. Women followed Continental trends in satin and calico from India. The return of Charles II to the throne in 1661 revived British zeal for regal crests, signets, buttons, and dynastic cyphers. Gentlemen began emulating France's Louis XIV by wearing the lion's head peruke, an expensive wig graced with side locks.

Couture as Business

In 1700, while boned corsets, muslin petticoats, ruffled underskirts and aprons, and fans advanced women's fashion consciousness, the garnished frock coat defined the ensemble of the gentrified male. By mid-century, tailors for the London rake tightened the bodice and sleeves to create the macaroni coat, a subset of self-expressive couture for men. In contrast, staid professional men accepted the boned pointed collar and silk umbrella as standards of the workday uniform.

The British East India Company directed unprocessed calico or muslin from India to a London factory for petticoats and sturdy, dull-finished cretonne for women's and children's smocks. With the import of Saxony wool, Tibetan goat hair, and Australian and Dublin fleece, Lancashire mills elevated cotton folk textiles and wool shawls and tartans to world prominence. Scots mills at Galashiels supplied tweed for top-quality suits and coats and for export to North American clothiers. Welsh hatters turned fleece into the tall black hat, a part of women's national dress.

Late eighteenth-century styles depicted in *The Lady's Magazine* informed the fashion-minded of trends in gauze ribbon, fur muffs, curled feathers, and fringed cloaks. The Napoleonic influence from France added to women's hats the feather cockades of British dragoons and grenadiers and periwigs to men's daily headdress. Women's evening wear incorporated cap sleeves, hooded pelisses, turbans, tasseled fans, and cameos and jet beads on ribboned chokers. In the Caribbean, traveling *revendeuses* (saleswomen) dressed in light cotton dresses and blouses with skirts for the trek inland with imported European goods.

In 1800, trendsetter Beau Brummell refined the male haircut with neat cropping and restrained forehead curls. He instructed his tailors and shirt makers in supplying trousers with ankle buttons, as well as in the making of tucked linen collars, starched cravats, buff brocade vests, and long black nankeen breeches. For outerwear, he modeled the double-breasted, split-tail cutaway riding coat accessorized with suede gloves, low-heeled black riding boots, black evening cape, tall round hat, and gold-topped cane.

In the 1830s, British "bobbies" set the tone and style of global police with a navy tunic and domed hat with chin strap. Colonial rubber provided the sole for the sand shoe, high-top athletic footwear that preceded running shoes and sneakers. Welsh flannel mills supplied material for shirts, infant wear, and the fringed shawl, a dominant element of the traditional costume. Scots ready-to-wear filled cargoes bound for Australia.

Textile manufacture fueled the Industrial Revolution. The velvet collar and wide lapels defined the fastidious male topcoat, paired with moleskin or wool trousers. By mid-century, British entrepreneurs had seized the market in silk and were equipping factories at Northampton and Stafford to mechanize shoemaking, two major contributions to the economy. Colonial dignitaries as far south as Cape Town, South Africa, emulated British Eton-style school adoptions of braided, uncuffed jackets worn with vests, pinstriped pants, and ties.

Comfort Fashions

The early 1860s extended trends in women's mascara, horsehair and linen crinolines, and paisley shawls with tea gowns and men's ascots and felt hats with Scots plaids. After decades of debutante dress in tulle and feathered headdress over form-fitting gowns and trains, fashion pioneers rejected the corseted hourglass silhouette for women. Feminists furthered casual dress for horseback riding, lawn tennis, cycling, golf, sailing, and croquet and contributed American pantalettes, advocated by British actor Fanny Kemble and suffragist Hannah Tracy Cutler.

British men relieved the tedium of bankers' suits, ties, and bowler hats with tweed Ulsters, Newmarket vests, knickers, canvas gaiters, and flat caps for birding, skeet shooting, and hiking. In 1870, coat-maker Thomas Burberry addressed the needs of the skier, bicyclist, hunter, and fisherman by making gabardine outerwear and trench coats. His modest beginning yielded a half century of advances in wool motoring dusters, motorbike jackets, pullover pants, women's heathered toppers and hats, skiing and skating suits, handbags, gloves, and umbrellas.

The working class produced its own unique looks. Women adopted the housekeeper apron with full skirt, bib, and deep pockets. The Pryce Jones catalog from Powys, Wales, featured linen shirt fronts to tuck into women's jumpers and knee-length gymnasium costumes with belts for swimming and exercise. On the docks and in mining towns, laborers cropped the sleeves and legs of long johns, creating the forerunners of T-shirts, a British invention.

The late Industrial Revolution resulted in distribution of British cottons and woolens and rubber shoes to North Africa, through the Suez Canal, and along the coasts of East Africa, Arabia, India, Indonesia, and China. Boys modeled the khaki choke-collar tunic and knickers of the Boy Scouts, founded in 1907. British enclaves favored men's jodhpurs for riding and fashionable tailored suits, starched collars, vests, neckties, and homburgs for business and evening wear.

The fashion magazine *Dress & Vanity Fair* crusaded for Edwardian era designs. The old money class continued buying luxury custom garments from dressmakers and tailors. The industrial class settled for ready-to-wear available at Hamilton's, Harrod's, Marks & Spencer, and Liberty of London department stores. Mail order dispatched men's sweater vests and house frocks, boiler suits, and slips in synthetic Crimplene, Marspun, Terylene, and Tricel.

The closure of Paris salons during World War I gave American designers an edge in the British Isles, where *Vogue* editor Alison Settle and cover illustrator Erté promoted the allure of art deco styles. Men's footwear patterned dress shoes after the trim Balmoral boot introduced by Prince Albert. The wraparound puttee for soldiers established a fashion adopted by other Allied forces. For everyday wear, stores stocked Cossack boots and the canvas fatigue shoe, a foot-easing product from Norwich. Factories profited from export of the acid-proof India rubber shoe and calf-high cuffed Russian Cossack boot for wet weather and hiking.

Twentieth-Century Transition

Depression-era fashions required more home sewing of art deco dresses and peplum suits, the styles that clothed female stars of Hollywood films. The 1930s lured British men from the suit coat to safari and hacking jackets, zippered leather motorcycle jackets, and toggled wool duffels. Women finished out the decade in quilted hip-length car coats and artificial silk stockings imported from the Continent.

Rationing at the height of World War II forced the British to give up three male prerogatives: the leather belt and the breast pocket with its foulard. Adults economized with pea

The Burberry trench coat, a standard of British style since the early twentieth century, established its reputation for warmth and durability as military attire during World War I. Burberry today is a luxury fashion retailer with more than 500 stores globally. *(The Granger Collection, NYC—All rights reserved)*

coats, utility work attire, rayon hose, gauze lingerie, and crepe-soled chukka boots kept spiffy at home with repair and reinforcement. By 1947, the end of rationing returned nylon hose, anoraks, and raincoats to popularity as well as men's nylon-wool lined Gannex mackintoshes and topcoats.

At mid-century, British women experimented with polyester pleat skirts, slickers, smoking jackets, and maxi coats over long skirts. Men gave brief popularity to viscose ties and the Nehru jacket, a variance from blazers and sport jackets with lapels. Pierre Cardin channeled French style into British ready-to-wear, launching a demand for women's jumpsuits, thigh-high boots, and gold lamé apparel and men's unitards, leather wristwatches, and zippered vests and knickers.

In the 1960s, Carnaby Street, Knightsbridge, and Kings Road boutiques led the Western world in marketing Welsh couturier Mary Quant's short skirts and hot pants, zippered pantsuits, chemises, polyvinyl chloride rainwear, and bell-bottoms—hallmarks of London mod style. For footwear, Quant popularized patterned tights, flats, go-go boots, and Cuban heels. Twiggy's modeling of A-line dresses introduced a sought-after female silhouette.

The styling of British rock bands in the 1960s and 1970s brought fad fame to Mao suits and Nehru collars. The punk era, begun in 1975, extended exhibitionist teen attire with scalpel art and implants in the flesh of safety pins, labrets, cheek plugs, and chains. In the 1980s, British teens purchased high-waisted diesel jeans off the German black market.

Green industry in 1991 yielded British Lyocell or Tencel, a rayon denim synthesized from regenerated cellulose dissolved from waste paper and tree-farmed beech and eucalyptus trunks. A twentieth-century miracle fiber, it yielded imitation chino cloth, leather, linen, silk, and suede for rough sports as well as upscale women's apparel.

The 2000s placed the British ahead in footwear trends with Dr. Scholl's massaging gel exercise sandal. In 2010, couturier Alexander McQueen adapted denim for use as jeggings, a cross between skinny jeans and leggings. Airing of the Master-piece Theater series *Downton Abbey* (2010–) piqued demand for retro Edwardian luxuries in beading, tiaras, pearls, lace gloves, and tea gowns from a more genteel era.

See also: Brummell, Beau; Clan Attire; Edwardian Styles and Fashions; Elizabethan Styles and Fashions; Marks & Spencer; Quant, Mary; Tailoring; Victorian Styles and Fashions.

Further Reading

Bolton, Andrew. *AngloMania: Tradition and Transgression in British Fashion.* New York: Metropolitan Museum of Art, 2005.

Hawkins, Stan. *The British Pop Dandy: Masculinity, Popular Music, and Culture.* Burlington, VT: Ashgate, 2009.

McDermott, Catherine. *Made in Britain: Tradition and Style in Contemporary British Fashion.* London: Mitchell Beazley, 2002.

Shannon, Brent Alan. *The Cut of His Coat: Men, Dress, and Consumer Culture in Britain, 1860–1914.* Athens: Ohio University Press, 2006.

Brummell, Beau (1778–1840)

A trendsetting dandy in Regency England, George Bryan "Beau" Brummell modeled gentlemanly attire featuring somber colors, spotless linens, and an immaculate necktie. Sartorial historians credit Brummell with inventing modern men's pants and suits, the collar and tie, and introducing questionably groomed men to regular bathing and manicures. Brummell's high standards elevated English tailoring to the best in understated men's wear.

A Londoner born on June 7, 1778, to William "Billy" Brummell, the sheriff of Berkshire, and his mistress, a Miss Richardson, Beau Brummell trained under his father in genteel behavior and manners. During his education at Eton and Oriel College, Oxford, Brummell established a reputation for individual taste and for the choice of a fastidious knotted muslin cravat, which he tied in unequal lengths and fastened with a buckle.

At age 16, disappointed by academia, Brummell joined the Tenth Royal Hussars, the regiment of the future George IV. Brummell achieved the rank of lieutenant over the Light Dragoons within 10 months. Throughout a close friendship with the prince regent, Brummell squandered on fine dining and wardrobe the £21,650 legacy left by his father, an inheritance nearing $4 million in present-day value. During a severe backlash against eighteenth-century male finery, Brummell impressed upon the prince regent the need to adapt to the times with statelier, less ostentatious apparel. As a model, Brummell chose the comfortable riding attire of the country gentleman.

In mentoring the prince, Brummell referred to the egalitarianism in apparel and luxuries that followed the French Revolution of 1789. In place of tricorn hats, bouffant wigs with pigtails, flowered vests, bows under the chin, tight knee breeches, and colored hose, Brummell kept to simplicity and dark colors. He earned a reputation as a dilettante, wit, and dictator of fashion. At age 18, he resigned his commission and settled in stylish Mayfair.

Daily dressing in the Hanoverian era kept Brummell occupied from two to six hours, depending on his engagements. From 1800, he patronized the tailors John, Schweitzer and Davidson, and the Austrian couturier Jonathan Meyer. With the latter, Brummell invented one-seam trousers, closed at the ankle by buttons and loops, the forerunner of braided military trousers and tuxedo pants.

To exude manliness, Brummell kept his dark hair neatly cropped, curled at the forehead, and devoid of powdered wigs and fragrances. To achieve a refined look, he hired a seamstress to make his shirts. He ordered his fine linen collars starched and gradually lowered his chin on them to form creases. Any that crimped awry he discarded.

Brummell concentrated on fastidious dress in a buff brocade vest over precisely tucked shirt collar and starched cravat measuring 1 foot by 5 feet (30 centimeters by 152 centimeters). Over long black nankeen trousers, he chose the double-breasted, split-tail cutaway riding coat with a wide collar of woolen broadcloth, an outfit identified as *style à l'anglaise* (the English style). His accessories included impeccable suede gloves, low-heeled black riding boots, black evening cape, and tall round hat. A gold-headed cane replaced the dress sword, which London ordinances had outlawed.

Brummell obsessed over hygiene, particularly teeth brushing, bathing and exfoliating, and shaving, which he performed in the presence of his imitators. Tailors and haberdashers presented him the latest men's fashions in hopes that his celebrity would attach to understated garments. At White's, Brummell's gentleman's club, in ballrooms, and at the opera, he stood rather than dance and projected pithy critiques of the company's fashions. His appearance and deportment educated less stylish gentlemen on fine fashion and influenced the preference of Lord Byron for Irish linen shirts, cambric shirt fronts, and bleached damask linen for night clothes.

Ruined by cricket, gambling, and a public insult to the prince regent in July 1813, Brummell worked harder at courting approval and patronage with continued excess. When creditors threatened at his door, he exiled himself to the port of Calais, France, on May 16, 1816, to avoid debtor's prison. He left his material goods in London to be auctioned.

Brummell lived on the proceeds of a British ambassadorship, which he held at Caen for two years. In 1835, his friends retrieved him from a French debtor's prison and installed him at the Hôtel d'Angleterre. At Caen, obese, toothless, slovenly, broke, and paralyzed by a stroke, he regressed in grooming and cleanliness. On March 30, 1840, in the tertiary stage of syphilis, he died in a lunacy ward of Bon Sauveur Asylum.

See also: British Clothing and Fashion; Business Attire; Eton Style; Ties and Cravats.

Further Reading
Cole, Hubert. *Beau Brummell.* London: Granada, 1977.

Downing, Sarah. *Fashion in the Time of Jane Austen.* Long Island City, NY: Osprey, 2011.

Hawkins, Stan. *The British Pop Dandy: Masculinity, Popular Music, and Culture.* Burlington, VT: Ashgate, 2009.

Kelly, Ian. *Beau Brummell: The Ultimate Dandy.* London: Hodder & Stoughton, 2005.

Burberry, Thomas (1835–1926)

The founder of Great Britain's widest-selling brand of luxury clothing, Thomas Burberry accomplished his design goal of making comfortable, functional, popular outerwear. He is also known as the inventor of gabardine, a tightly woven fabric that outfitted polar explorers in the early twentieth century and in more casual outerwear for later generations.

A native of Surrey, England, Burberry was born on August 27, 1835. He learned the draper's and dressmaking businesses at a local shop in his teens. At age 21, he established his own clothing concern, T. Burberry & Sons at Winchester Street in Basingstoke. Focusing on skiers, cyclists, hunters, and fishermen, he produced durable, breathable garments guaranteeing freedom of movement and impermeability by wind and rain.

In 1879, Burberry developed waterproof worsted wool yarn into twill with a diagonal ribbing suitable for rip-proof pocket linings and windbreakers. Demand for the new fabric led him to open a mill dedicated to its production on London Street in Basingstoke.

In his shop at 30 Haymarket, Burberry and his sons, Thomas Newman Burberry and Arthur Michael Burberry, began selling the Tielocken coat, a forerunner of the trench coat popularized by military officers during the Boer War. In 1901, Burberry established the mounted knight logo and the Latin motto *Prorsum* (Forward) as his trademark. During World War I, he set the rainwear styles of the United Kingdom's Royal Air Force and Royal Marines with belted pilot coats featuring buckled cuffs, epaulets, D rings, and storm flaps over pockets. The company offered free renewal of waterproofing. European and American men popularized the brand for leisure wear.

Three years after the armistice, Burberry standardized his iconic red, black, white, and beige plaid lining, a pattern he used in scarves, handbags, umbrellas, and luggage lining. By outfitting Field Marshal Herbert Kitchener, South Pole explorers Roald Amundsen and Ernest Shackleton, and Boy Scouts founder Robert Baden-Powell, Burberry found prominent models to display his hooded rainwear, double-breasted aviator suits, and belted, shawl-collared ski suits with elastic ankle cuffs.

In 1910, Burberry designed wool dusters for motorists. His double-buttoned motorbike jacket and pullover pants ensured windproofing. He added to his lines women's heathered toppers and hats and belted gabardine skiing and skating suits with deep zippered patch pockets. He outfitted the royal household and security guards of George VI and Edward VII in greatcoats and the colonial mounted police in rainwear. For service to the crown, he earned posthumous royal warrants from Queen Elizabeth II and Prince Charles.

Following Burberry's death at Basingstoke on April 4, 1926, his trench coats took on a life of their own. Sold in New York City and Paris, the famous "Burberry" appeared in such film classics as *Casablanca* (1942) and *Breakfast at Tiffany's* (1961) and in the wardrobes of models and celebrities everywhere. The company continues to flourish from the sale of infant wear, fur-lined raglan raincoats, cotton rainwear, polo coats, topcoats, tweed capes, women's suits, sweaters, belts, caps, rain boots, shoes, hosiery, and gloves.

See also: British Clothing and Fashion; Fashion Design; Rainwear.

Further Reading

Burberry Group. www.burberry.com

Okonkwo, Uche. *Luxury Fashion Branding: Trends, Tactics, Techniques.* New York: Palgrave Macmillan, 2007.

Smith, Nancy MacDonell. *The Classic Ten: The True Story of the Little Black Dress and Nine Other Fashion Favorites.* New York: Penguin, 2003.

Tungate, Mark. *Fashion Brands: Branding Style from Armani to Zara.* 3rd ed. Philadelphia: Kogan Page, 2012.

Burial Garb

Uniquely human in presentation and purpose, grave goods and winding sheets display the respect of mourners for the dead while manifesting elements of piety, kinship, prosperity, and hope for an afterlife. Votive and sacrificial jewelry, slave wrappings, beadwork, blankets, money pouches, prayer beads, weapons, and armor attested to status as well as needs in the netherworld.

Artifacts found in Qafeh, Israel, are evidence that the sprinkling of red ochre dye, shell necklaces, hunting trophies, and blossoms in 98,000

B.C.E. expressed the blessings of surviving Neanderthals. Items dating to around 58,000 B.C.E., found in Shanidar, Iraq, show that Neanderthal funeral preparations included the distribution of carved stones and the pollen of cornflower, thistle, ragwort, grape hyacinth, hollyhock, and yarrow, perhaps as a sacred or preservative offering.

Neolithic funeral customs attested to the formalizing of morals and ethics. After 12,000 B.C.E., Mesopotamian burial rites involved gifts of beads and pendants carved from basalt (volcanic rock). Around 8000 B.C.E., on the eastern Peloponnese, ancestors of the Greeks at Argolid appear to have introduced cremation to the European continent as a means of disposing of corpses, thus leaving no clue to burial dress. From 6000 B.C.E. in south-central Anatolia, at present-day Catal Höyük, fabric workers wove yarn into shrouds to clothe corpses painted in part with plaster and ochre.

Ancient Status Burials

With the rise of urbanization after 5000 B.C.E., goods in royal and warrior tombs varied in quality and profusion according to gender, clan, and socioeconomic position of the deceased. Worn by men and women during the rule of Egyptian king Menes in the Early Dynastic period around 3150 B.C.E., helmet-like head coverings and a variety of false beards promoted the dignity of the courtier before burial. At Mycenae after 1650 B.C.E., rich families laid corpses in state in shrouds or wedding dresses, crowning heads with gold elliptical diadems. Mourners interred the remains of King Agamemnon and other men with gold death masks and knee bands and inlaid bronze daggers.

Corpses of Mycenaean women wore gilt headbands, spiral and hoop earrings, and shrouds appliquéd with gold discs. Female bodies lay alongside mirrors, rock crystal, faience, and additional luxury items. Children's hands bore a layer of gold leaf. Similarly identified by caste, Etruscan and Sicilian burials differentiated social levels in buttons, rings, and fibulas, the primary fastener of dresses and mantles.

Clay stamps of the Hassuna people spread red ochre designs over the Assyrian dead. Around 1500 B.C.E., ancestors of the Danes at Jutland and the Germans in Slesvig placed decorative felt caps and prestigious iron and bronze belts and thick-headed pins on the deceased for mound burials. Fiber-work notions, ring pins, and bear claw necklaces accompanied Angle, Frisian, Jute, Celtic, and Saxon corpses to burial in Scandinavia, Great Britain, and Germany. Grave inventories noted pocket items—whetstones, wire spirals, scissors, tweezers, sickle-shaped cutting blades and seam rippers, and weaving tools—for use in the afterlife. Items made of precious metals removed from circulation the region's wealth.

About 530 B.C.E., the Hochdorf chieftain's monument in present-day Baden-Württemberg, Germany, illustrated a Celtic prince's inhumation. Grave goods consisted of a birch bark Phrygian hat, cloth bag, wood combs, bracelet and torque, gilt dagger and knife, amber jewelry and fibulas over sumptuously dyed woven dress and blanket, and leather buskins ornamented with gold collar and vamp plaques. At Vergina, Macedonia, in 336 B.C.E., mourners crowned Philip II, their assassinated king, with a gold diadem and robed him in royal purple embellished with gold, an appropriate shroud for the father of Alexander the Great.

After 500 C.E., the dead at Sutton Hoo in Suffolk, England, bore ceremonial sword, shield, and crested helmet featuring a face mask with long ear guards and engraved brows, nose, and mustache. A female corpse in embroidered dress bore silver buckles, purse, and chatelaine, the belt and key ring of the lady of the house. Other tumuli in the area contained brooches, gilded studs, and combs.

Norse and Viking ship burials from 750 to 1100, such as the Oseberg ship in Tønsberg, Norway, bore the remains of women along with their brooches, cording, ribbons, chains, and hooks to hold sewing and weaving supplies in addition to spindles, tweezers, fire-making steels, skewers, cosmetic brushes, and keys. The range of tools suggests the family's dependence on women for domestic skills.

In West Africa, a Malian necropolis at Timbuktu yielded the cotton shrouds of saints. A dignitary interred in a seated position at Igbo Ukwu, a textile center at Anambra, Nigeria, around 800 went to his grave in rich garments adorned with noble regalia. Additional grave goods included bronze pendants, fly whisks, a horned death mask, and greaves covered in thousands of glass beads.

Royalty and Commoners

Interments worldwide revealed the tenor of the social order. At the Hippodrome in Constantinople on January 13, 532, the Empress Theodora refused to flee racing factions and declared herself ready to accept death and burial in a purple winding sheet, the royal burial attire in the Byzantine Empire. Some medieval Catholic nuns preserved their novitiate veils to wear as burial garments. In West Africa, Portuguese explorers observed the use of elaborately woven shrouds adorned with intricate netting, openwork, and brocade. The Canadian Ice Man, a mummified male from pre-Columbian British Columbia who died around 1450, went to his grave in a fur robe made from 95 gopher or squirrel hides stitched with sinew, a testimony to the era's use of small animals for fur garments.

Seventeenth-century customs involved body preparers in swaddling and sewing corpses in winding sheets, concealing all but the face. Commoners went to the grave in shrouds but without coffins. A more elaborate shroud consisted of a long-sleeved, full-length white night garment embellished with embroidering or smocking at the neck. Families stitched the attire long in advance, sometimes including shrouds in trousseaus. Individual expressions of emotion involved tucking herb sprigs into the shroud. Rue symbolized regret, yew represented mourning, and rosemary promised remembrance.

More detailed burial attire enhanced the theme of purity with white stockings, gloves, muffler, and cap. After 1607, James I of England commissioned a sculptor to depict his deceased two-day-old Sophia Rosula Stuart under a rich brocade coverlet. As though napping, she lay wrapped in lace swaddling and capped with a bonnet. In 1666, the English parliament passed the Burial in Woollen Act, requiring the making of shrouds from English wool, a defense against the importation of foreign fabrics for internment.

North American Shrouding

In the late eighteenth century, before the development of professional undertaking in North America, extended families in Appalachia prepared corpses for the grave. Women or nurses washed the remains and dressed the body in a plain linen or waxed cerecloth dress or tunic. For shaping, the preparer pinned the garment and knotted it below the feet.

In Ontario, pioneer preparers of the dead covered the shroud with a linen winding sheet and added copper pennies on the eyelids and a muslin face cloth to conceal the deceased from staring eyes. Plains Indians tended to wrap corpses in buckskin and leave them in tree limbs or rock crevices until the decomposition of mortal remains to Mother Earth freed the skeleton for reclamation. Preparers of African and Caribbean slaves in the New York African Burial Ground from 1712 to 1794 respected ethnic customs of the Akan, Asante, Twi, and Senegalese. The remains of twenty-seven individuals pinned into shrouds in cedar or pine coffins bore marks of an Akan *sankofa* symbol of return. Grave goods consisted of a silver pendant, sacral engravings, a waist string of 111 cowries and glass and amber beads, quartz crystal, musket ball, clay pipe, and coins.

After morticians claimed the urban funeral business in the 1800s, garments or ensembles replaced the impersonal shroud and winding sheet. Apparel for viewing the deceased in "wake rooms" grew more elaborate and lifelike. To protect and honor the dead, gravesites acquired iron fencing, family monuments, landscaping, and elaborate edging, such as that initiated in 1831 at Boston's Mount Auburn Cemetery, now a National Historic Landmark.

Around 1910, rural residents in Ontario retained folk customs in concealing the eyes under wet cotton wool and tying a handkerchief into a 3-inch (7.6-centimeter) band to secure the chin with mouth closed during rigor mortis. Preparers discreetly covered the naked corpse with a sheet or blanket during washing with linen cloths and burned the fabric afterward. Three feet (91 centimeters) of calico bound the torso from waist to thighs. Cotton wool packed body orifices. Dressed in white socks and nightgown with ankles bound in white tape but with chin and eyelids stripped of coverings, the body lay in state in a homemade log coffin for viewing.

Modern Quandaries

During the Vietnam War, the U.S. military restored bodies as closely as possible to a normal state. During the Tet Offensive in early 1968, morticians received more than 100 remains daily to recondition torn flesh with wax, tissue fillings, and cosmetics. Quartermasters provided freshly ironed and creased uniform pants and full-dress coat with appropriate medals. Packed in ice, the remains made the journey under honor guard from Southeast Asia to home cemeteries.

The rise of tomb raiding in China, Italy, Guatemala, Afghanistan, Iraq, and Peru in the 2000s resulted in the unearthing of ancient mummies in burial garb, filigree nose rings, and ceremonial masks for sale to museums and antiquities traffickers. In 2005, U.S. Immigration and Customs Enforcement agents in Miami, Florida, confiscated 322 Andean grave goods from 500 B.C.E. that included winding sheets of Peruvian and Colombian royalty and pre-Inca gold jewelry and emerald beads. Upon repatriation of the smuggled antiquities in 2011, Peruvian president Ollanta Humala thanked the U.S. government for respecting ancient South American artifacts.

See also: Beads and Beading; Mourning Attire.

Further Reading

Eicher, Joanne Bubolz. *The Visible Self: Global Perspectives of Dress, Culture, and Society.* 3rd ed. New York: Fairchild, 2008.

Richardson, Ruth. *Death, Dissection, and the Destitute.* 2nd ed. Chicago: University of Chicago Press, 2000.

Robben, Antonius C.G.M. *Death, Mourning, and Burial: A Cross-Cultural Reader.* Malden, MA: Wiley-Blackwell, 2004.

Burka

Islamic veiling of women's bodies—epitomized by the burka (or burqa), a full outer garment and face covering especially common in South Asia—derives from cultural traditions older than scripture. From the settlement of the Indus Valley in 3300 B.C.E. and throughout the Mughal Empire (1526–1757), women hid their feminine features under a facial veil, long scarf, or the end of a sari or shoulder wrap, a forerunner of the burka. By cloaking the face and neck, females concealed their identity from elders, fathers-in-law, and other respected males. Among Muslims, veiling of the face accentuated piety and propriety while securing for the female a small space she could call her own.

In Arabia, Bahrain, Kuwait, Oman, and Yemen, the *niqab* (mask) covered the entire face, leaving only an eye slit or two eyeholes. A more complicated version curtained the eye slit with sheer layers. The mask came in black, blue, gray, pearl, or white and displayed gilding, colorful edging, and silk embroidery. Worn with the abaya (sleeved cloak) or the chador (full-body cloak), the niqab virtually obliterated the woman from view. The full-body burka, another extreme form of female seclusion, enshrouded the entire female body, even the eyes, lest womanly beauty tempt a male onlooker. Afghans developed their own full-body cloak, the *chadri* (body covering), which obscured the eyes behind a fabric grill. Women expressed their need for beauty and gender liberation by developing eyeliner to high style.

Origin

Late in a ministry begun in 610, the Prophet Muhammad acquiesced to the pressure of peers by requiring his 13 wives to cloak themselves and accept chaperonage and isolation under the power of the husband to guard family honor. One interpretation of Muslim veiling described Muhammad's quandary at the crush of men at his mosque and the endangerment of his wives by lustful strangers. His rationalization of male unease at female sexual enticement derived from the moral weakness of the woman and the possibility that her sexuality could shame or even ruin a household. In imitation of the prophet's household, devout Muslim women adopted restrictive garb in honor of Muhammad's wives.

Muhammad's favorite wife, nine-year-old Aisha bint Abu Bakr, whom he married in spring

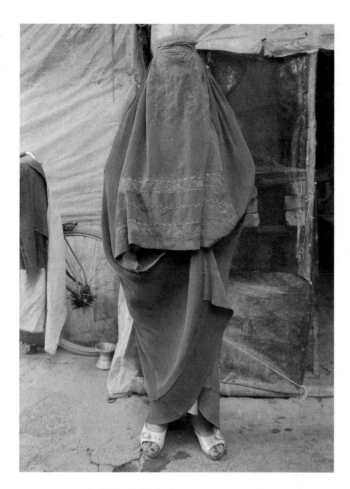

Adhering to radical Islamic tradition—and the fundamentalist dictates of the ruling Taliban—a woman in Afghanistan leaves home wearing the full-body cloak and face covering called the burka (Arabic for curtain or veil) or *chadri*. *(Adek Berry/AFP/Getty Images)*

Obedience and Independence

Before suppression of women under the Umayyad dynasty, an apocryphal revolt at Mecca by Aisha bint Talhah, Aisha bint Abu Bakr's niece and protégé, involved the refusal of the younger Aisha to obey the order of her husband, Musab bin al-Zubair, that she take the veil. She reasoned that female beauty, a gift from God, should be celebrated, not hidden. Musab reputedly prepared a grave to bury his wife alive. In terror, she gave in to his order and wore the veil.

By the second century of Islam, middle- and upper-class women routinely veiled themselves and equipped every Islamic bride's trousseau with head coverings, masks, and body wraps. Some women carried concealment further by covering their hands with black mesh gloves.

During the proselytizing of Iran in 637 C.E., the custom of female seclusion spread to other Muslim enclaves, mostly in cities. In Al-Andalus (Muslim Iberia) from 756 to 1212, however, Spanish Muslim women adhered less to the hijab (head covering) and adapted their own wardrobes without male dictates. Their Maghrebi counterparts in Morocco and what is now Algeria followed more liberal interpretations of veiling until the rise of the Almohad dynasty in 1121, when traditionalists enforced strict rules of modesty.

In 870, the governor of Mecca curtained off a section of the mosque for women. Customs involving female immurement applied only to the upper class, which could afford to dress in ladylike burkas because their servants performed domestic labor. In contrast, the wearing of a head or face covering remained incompatible with the lives of nomads and herding clans, who could not afford the expensive niqab. At the time, prices ranged from one week's to one month's pay for a working-class family.

Baghdad writer Abu Muhammad al-Washsha, author of *Kitab al-zarf wa'l-zurafa'* (*Book on Elegance and Elegant People,* ca. 930), characterized the most fashionable female attire as the veils of Nishapur, Iran, which outranked sheer fabric produced farther north at Jurjan and Sarakhs. From the 900s to the 1500s, when the Muslim female routinely covered her face with the niqab, Bedouin women,

621, adopted full body screening in the *taqanna'a* (mantle). Five years later, a revelation alerted Muhammad to the need for women to envelop themselves in a protective wrap called a *jalabib* (loose robe), a sequestering of the body leaving only the face and hands in view. In Sura 24:31, the Koran mentions the two forbidden areas of female allure—the eyes and the breasts—but leaves unclear the style of covering women should choose.

Islamic segregation of women from public life began after Muhammad's death on June 8, 632, when Aisha barred women from the mosque. After 634, Umar bin al-Khattab, the second caliph, corroborated Aisha's belief that women should pray at home rather than in a gathering of males. Because of the crouching position demanded by Muslim prayer, the prohibition shielded women from viewing men's posteriors and private parts.

entertainers, beggars, maidservants, and rural females remained exempt from veiling. To avoid harassment and jeering, wise outsiders covered their hair and faces on approach to a metropolitan area.

The Hijab and the Outside World

When European warriors returned from the First Crusade to the Holy Land in 1099, they brought with them the reputed veil of the Virgin Mary, housed in a crypt at La Sainte-Chapelle in Paris, and a linen gauze veil of 3.3 yards (3 meters), allegedly belonging to Saint Anne, Jesus's maternal grandmother, a relic embroidered in gold and silk venerated in Apt, France. More significant to the history of costume, the veterans imported the Islamic custom of veiling the woman's head and bosom with the hijab or jalabib, a symbol of privacy and morality in a public place or at worship. French women adapted the Eastern style in fine linen head veils spread over neck and shoulders. European versions of Arabic burkas shielded the skin from sun, grit, and wind, while indicating modesty and devotion and concealing the face during marital deceptions and illicit assignations.

After the Mamluks seized power in Egypt in 1250, laws regarding burkas and confinement at home increased the punishments for disobedience. When women allowed their wrists to show in the market, clerks had the right to shun them. To protect themselves from public humiliation and their husbands from dishonor, females adopted the *miqna'a* (face covering) of black mesh. Alternatives included the burka, a white *qina* (half veil) extending from the top of nose to mid-chest, or the *sha'riyya,* a goat hair or horsehair net covering forehead and eyes, which became the primary face shield of medieval Muslim women. Less common were the face mask, the Saharan *litham* (mouth veil), extending under the eyes, and the head sack with eyeholes cut out, an enveloping façade held in place by a cloth *isaba* wound around the head turban style.

From east to west, in waves of gendered controversy, questions of the burka and obedience to paternalism sparked contention as well as scriptural exegesis. In 1332, with adherence to ancient customs waning, Moroccan traveler Ibn Battuta was astonished to view the sexual freedom of Turkish women, who went about unveiled in public. After 1501, Persia's Safavid Empire pressured urban women to cover their faces.

In the nineteenth century, veiling began to disappear among non-Muslim peoples as a result of interaction with Christians and Jews. Westernization accompanied the adoption of modern lifestyles and costume as emblems of status and prestige. In contrast, followers of Muslim folk dress clung more steadfastly to the medieval burka. As thicker materials gave way to gauze veils, however, Muslim women gradually revealed their facial features. Turkish women adapted the veil to European millinery by attaching the transparent covering to hats. Influenced by the colonization of Algeria and Morocco, the French in Marseilles and Nice debated both the repugnance of female subjugation and the allure of orientalism.

As Western women gained economic and political independence, Middle Eastern society pressed troubling questions about gender stereotypes and clothing statutes in the Ottoman Empire. Táhirih, a martyred poet, theologian, and human rights advocate, shocked males in 1848 by ripping off her veil and condemning Iranian males for suppressing women through religious tyranny, gender superstition, and polygamy. Persecutors at Tehran strangled the 36-year-old reformer with her burka, cast her remains in a well, and threw rocks at her corpse.

During national efforts to throw off British colonialism, Egyptian nationalist Qasim Amin, an attorney and author of *Tahrir al mara'a (The Emancipation of Women,* 1899) and *Al mara'a al jadida (The New Woman,* 1900), declared the burka a gross misinterpretation of Koranic scripture for the sake of male ego and blamed Islamic decadence for the British usurpation of Egypt. In the name of progress and universal education, Amin called for *sufur* (unveiling), a liberation of women from purdah, or virtual internment, beginning with his own daughters.

Amin's arbitrary scuttling of centuries of female isolation brought swift rebuttal from Cairo financier Muhammad Tal'at Harb, author of *Tarbiyat al-Mar'ah wa-al-Hijab* (*The Education of Women and Veiling*, 1899) and *Fasl al-Khitab fi al-Mar'ah was al-Hijab* (*The Final Word Concerning Women and Veiling*, 1901), who declared female character innately inferior. Additional input into the controversy arose from a flurry of women's magazines published in the early 1900s. Feminist supporters demonstrated in Damascus by dropping their veils in public. During the disputation over Amin's philosophy and Harb's rebuttal, middle-class women championed the burka, which allowed them a greater range from home and protected them from molestation.

In 1923, Egyptian feminist Huda Sha'arawi tossed her veil into the Mediterranean Sea and, while retaining the head scarf, staged subsequent dramatic unveilings in the Cairo train station. Her actions influenced wealthy and professional women to abandon face concealment and embrace unrestrictive European dress. As the thickness and coverage of veils lessened, a 20-year-old Lebanese reformer, Nazira Zayn al-Din of Beirut, issued *Al-Sufur wa al-hijab* (*Unveiling and Veiling*, 1928), a radical defiance of religious patriarchs that ignited controversy in Lebanon and Syria for a decade. Singer and film star Umm Kulthum furthered the liberalization of women's costume in the 1930s by posing unveiled for publicity photos. By the 1950s, only the Egyptian lower middle class retained its obedience to the traditional burka.

The founder and first president of the modern Turkish republic, Mustafa Kemal Ataturk, demeaned the burka as a model of paganism and an obstacle to modernization. In 1934, the year Turkish women gained the vote, President Ataturk secularized the dress code by prohibiting religious costume, especially the turban and veil. In 1936, under Reza Shah Pahlavi, ruler of Iran and a disciple of Ataturk, the Women's Awakening revolted against the burka because it limited respiration, exercise, schooling, and full citizenship.

The outlawing of the veil terrified older women, who feared the power of police to strip them in public. They also lacked the funds to outfit themselves in Western dress, which they viewed as vulgar and unseemly. As unveiled females began challenging Islamic customs in Egypt, Lebanon,

Syria, and Tunisia, the women of Fez, Morocco, began wearing the *litham,* a wispy face covering made of sheer black silk chiffon. Only Saudi Arabia clung to the medieval burka and enforced the female dress code by law and domestic violence.

The uneven ruling on veiling through the Muslim world left pockets of conservatism, particularly in Indonesia and the Philippines, where men valued female obedience as an honor to marriage and acknowledgement of male supremacy. In the 1960s, the French prohibition of veiling in Algeria caused women to flaunt their veils as emblems of nationalism and defiance of European colonialism. After the rise of Mohammad Reza Shah Pahlavi to power in Iran in 1941, a variety of head coverings prevailed. Among veiled and unveiled women, a third class, those in the scarf, maintained Muslim custom while promoting choice. Devout women defended the burka in a rejection of Western morals and clothing. Simultaneously, conservative merchants championed the 5- to 6-yard (4.6- to 5.5-meter) chador, the focus of their commerce.

A conservative backlash in 1979 resulted in open conflict between religious zealots and Iranian women over veiling, an era depicted in Marjane Satrapi's *Persepolis* (2000). Liberal Muslim women risked public mockery and mauling by street thugs. Other Iranian women demonstrated against the unchaste Western dress worn by civil employees and university students and donned the chador out of ethnic pride and cultural authenticity. In July 1980, a religious regime demanded the return to veiling as a symbol of chastity and obedience. Ironically, unveiled women lost their jobs, while obedient women found places in universities and positions in industry.

Iran's Islamization movement failed in its overall objective to return to the burka and hijab because women seized control of Muslim fashions and designed alternatives to the unappealing dress of old. Female garment makers liberalized ensembles to include ankle-length trousers, bright-colored scarves, and transparent fabrics over subtly made-up faces. In 1996, the emergence of the Taliban in Kabul, Afghanistan, began a five-year return to punitive veiling and purdah for Afghan women. In

2005, fundamentalist clergy insisted that Muslim women observe veiling if they worked with men in public offices and that they cease seeking schooling or medical treatment at hospitals.

Islamic feminists responded to the Taliban's antiwoman stance with demands for the right to pursue education, medical care, and careers and to create their own dress code, such as the Indian trend toward pairing knee-length burkas with leggings. In 2010, a parallel move by Iranian president Mahmoud Ahmadinejad toward reveiling head to foot victimized women with fines and punishments. Within months, Syrian law under President Bashar al-Assad rescinded a ban on teachers wearing the niqab. In April 2011, French law outlawed the niqab for concealing the identity of suspects, felons, and terrorists. The subject of veiling remained a thorny issue worldwide and a contributor to power struggles between East and West.

See also: Gendered Dressing; Middle Eastern Clothing; Muslim Religious Attire; Veils and Veiling.

Further Reading

Ahmed, Leila. *A Quiet Revolution: The Veil's Resurgence, from the Middle East to America.* New Haven, CT: Yale University Press, 2011.

Shirazi, Faegheh. *The Veil Unveiled: The Hijab in Modern Culture.* Gainesville: University Press of Florida, 2001.

Stillman, Yedida Kalfon. *Arab Dress, A Short History: From the Dawn of Islam to Modern Times.* Ed. Norman A. Stillman. Boston: Brill, 2003.

Business Attire

The rise of the merchant class in the Middle Ages imposed a dress code for business that initiated a distinct capitalistic style. Sometimes, however, antipathies between countries and peoples hampered commercial negotiations and affected clothing or adornment. In Arab lands during the ninth century, for example, foreign merchants dressed in the style of their homelands but were required to display an animal stamp or tattoo on the hand, a form of humiliation for Christians and Jews. Failure to identify non-Muslim affiliation could result in hand amputation.

In the 1100s, sumptuary laws failed to stem the sale of luxury clothing to the competitive middle class. Tradesmen emulated royalty in the display of badges and lineage on garments, especially the Scottish plaid and North African tribal headdress. After 1328, King Edward III of England and his consort, Queen Philippa of Hainault, fostered luxury damask and imported silk velvet for meetings with foreign dignitaries. Educators and administrators in Austria and Germany added linen band collars and knit gloves to professional apparel.

To accessorize tailored bespoke suits and shirts, European haberdashers from the early fifteenth century supplied businessmen with leather belts and suspenders, shoelaces, gloves, caps, and bags. Larger firms stocked handkerchiefs, hosiery, felt hats, canes, eyeglasses, and rainwear as well as rental attire for receptions. In addition to apparel, men brought garments for monogramming and purchased saddle soap and shoe polish, shoehorns, and brushes to maintain leather, woolens, and suede.

Hard times in the mid-1660s from the Great Plague and the Great Fire of London reduced the outfits of the court of Charles II to modest tunics, shirts, and knee breeches. The three-piece look established the pattern for future male wardrobes. After the American and French revolutions, self-restraint in office dress retained monochromatic midnight blue or gray as base colors. By the 1790s, to present a V-shaped torso, daring Englishmen added the buff or gray linen vest under the slim-lined business jacket. Essential to self-presentation, improved hygiene upgraded the commercial class from previous standards.

Nineteenth Century

After 1803, the Savile Row tailors who once outfitted cavalry officers furnished London civilians, surgeons, and merchants traveling to the Maghreb and the Caribbean with custom-made frock coats, boot-length trousers, and overcoats. Consumers chose fabrics and detailing to accommodate the law office, assembly, shop, or pulpit. Double and single vents and slash pockets made accessories available to the circuit rider or sales representative on horseback. The detachable wing collar, invented in 1827, fastened to a band with studs and offered a quick method of refreshing regency ensembles without changing shirts.

After 1837, the Victorian era introduced the lighter hip-length jacket complemented by French ruffled shirtfronts, bow ties, lace jabots, and gaiters. Jewelers showcased the discreet gold tie bar, cuff links, and pocket watch and fob on an Albert chain swagged across vest pockets. Vests developed contours and points accentuating the four-in-hand and a slim waistline, which European men engirthed in corsets. The Chesterfield coat updated the surtout with a trimmer fit and prestigious detailing with velvet collar and lapels.

In the late nineteenth century throughout the British Empire and in Japan, the fastidious silhouette for banking, shipping, and government preserved the starched collar and impeccable tie complementing the tailored suit. Coats supplied inner waist pockets to secure business cards and tickets. Men accessorized suits with vests, neckties, umbrellas, Balmoral boots, and homburgs. For train travel and office-to-office visits, the rain cloak and felt hat shielded the proper suit from the elements. For mid-level managers, department stores advertised one-price wardrobes.

Hints at the emergence of ethnic- and gender-neutral business wear arose globally in 1890s with the appearance of Indian maharajahs and Saudi sheikhs in sack suits and the tailoring of women's coatdresses and suits along the lines of menswear. Rising hemlines revealed sturdy lace-up and buttoned boots for women employed in medical offices, food service, and social work. Transatlantic dealings with North American capitalists introduced British businessmen to the lounge suit, an efficient silhouette devoid of the tails of the English morning coat.

Twentieth Century

Edwardian men's fashions popularized imperial collars, cutaway coats, and cuffed trousers with knife creases over laced derby shoes or bluchers, the appropriate complements to the overcoat or Inverness cape and bowler. Advertisers inserted hints on how to pack for business travel and what

underwear and hosiery complemented double-breasted patterned or plaid ensembles. The invention of the Rolex wristwatch for noncombat use in 1915 contributed a major shift in the male ensemble by rendering the vest obsolete. Inner jacket pockets accommodated the commuter with safe storage of fountain pens, passports, checkbooks, and tickets.

During the hard-pressed 1930s, men's furnishing stores reduced the business ensemble from three to two pieces by excluding the vest entirely. Shoe stores featured the Bass Weejun penny or tassel loafer as appropriate for the starter business wardrobe. Businesswomen established their own trends in white collars and suits with matching shoes, hats, handbags, and gloves, the uniform of IBM keypunch operators in Stockholm, Sweden. On White House business before and during World War II, First Lady Eleanor Roosevelt paired her tweed suits with sleeveless jerseys.

Postwar women's knit suits and sweater sets for the office departed from stereotypical male serge, such as that worn by Brazilian cash register salesmen in Rio de Janeiro, office staff in Brisbane, and typewriter representatives in Buenos Aires. Administrators and clergy demonstrated seriousness with slimmer, natural-shoulder suits and horn-rimmed glasses. Frequent departures from the office required balmacaan or trench raincoats, functional outerwear with zip-out linings. For workday uniforms at gas stations and on airlines, managers and pilots received iron-on badges and insignia as a shortcut to monogramming.

In the 1950s, the advancement of female executives introduced a bifurcated fashion world based on gendered needs. Women edged into the boardroom in man-style business suits and silk blouses with flowing neckties. For long days consisting of meetings and travel, sensible oxfords and pumps replaced high heels.

In the 1960s, hippies coined the term "suit" to identify a conformist male capitalist clad in pinstripes, button-down shirt, rep tie, and wing tips. Western men's office and marketplace wear featured the two-button charcoal or navy business suit worn with a white or pastel shirt, tie, leather belt, and black oxfords. Mail-order apparel from

Chicago-based Lands' End modeled images of standard office and shop apparel and supplied both tailoring and monogramming.

By 1968, *Gentleman's Quarterly* (later *GQ*) magazine alerted the savvy male dresser to shifts away from felt hats and lace-up shoes to bare heads and slip-ons, the choices of the youthful up-and-comer in the tech corridor. Couturier Giorgio Armani lightened the 1970s male silhouette by removing shoulder pads and deconstructing jackets for wear with more deeply colored shirts, a merchandising success from Arrow. Armani's women's lines featured the crepe, tweed, and serge staples of menswear in blazers, skirts, and slacks. Flowing ties emulated the staunch man's tie but manifested women's tastes in color and pattern. Alternative dressing offered women tortoise sunglasses, silk blazers, and mix-and-match linen and polyester crepe pieces available at Marks & Spencer, Lord & Taylor, Bloomingdale's, Dillard's, and Saks.

International Business

By the 1980s, Western businesswomen began building high-level business careers with limited jewelry and natural makeup, especially for association with Middle Eastern, Chinese, Kenyan, South African, Caribbean, Latin America, or French executives. Awkward shoulder pads disappeared late in the decade, replaced by relaxed, interchangeable Donna Karan and DKNY blazers and slacks. Nino Cerruti debuted an Italian office ideal for the professional man with the svelte Italian cut that raised jacket armholes and tailored seams toward the torso. Western European, Scandinavian, and Asian office styles of neat ties, buttoned jackets, long-sleeves shirts, and polished shoes identified the deliberate competitor for transnational commerce.

Calvin Klein rebelled against business-as-usual dressing in the 1990s by pairing dark T-shirts or turtlenecks with sports coats, a pared-down image favored by high-tech icons Steve Jobs of Apple and Mark Zuckerberg of Facebook. Company representatives traveling to Japan found relaxed business attire unacceptable in a land where men revered the tradition of impeccable white shirts with dark suits and the removal of shoes for meetings and business dinners. Individualized female attire in Tokyo enabled Japanese executives to display ties and pins to advantage on drop-shoulder suits. Chinese women made a similar move toward the refined boardroom pantsuit.

Following the relaxing of dress codes in Hawaii and the South Pacific in 1966, the growth of corporate casual and dress-down Fridays at century's end promoted a revamping of the business wardrobe. Employees invested in knit polo and collarless shirts, sweaters, Levi's Dockers, and huaraches for men, especially electronics and entertainment executives on the North American West Coast and offices in Uruguay. For U.S. East Coast women, Liz Claiborne or Jones of New York knit tees, cowl-neck sweaters, and blouses with loafers complemented high-style chino or denim slacks.

On informal occasions, unisex perquisites included pocket or belt security for cell phones and iPads and tees or V-neck sweaters over long-sleeved shirts, especially in tropical locales and information-technology workplaces. Still taboo in serious working environments, fad attire—spandex, tank tops, sequins, flip-flops, flashy costume jewelry, exposed tattoos, extreme piercings—attested to poor judgment and too casual an attitude toward the job.

In the twenty-first century, investment dressing worldwide still benefits the rising star in government, law, finance, and innkeeping. While Central American, Cuban, Dominican, and Filipino offices accept the pleated guayabera for less formal meetings and discussions, for example, Europeans expect understated business suits with minimal accessorizing as indicators of personal taste and company status. Women follow trends in shoulder bags, flats, and power skirt suits that maintain a feminine edge, particularly in style-conscious Israel and Arab nations.

See also: Coats and Jackets; Feminist Styles and Fashions; Social Status; Vests.

Further Reading

Anawalt, Patricia Rieff. *The Worldwide History of Dress.* New York: Thames & Hudson, 2007.

Antongiavanni, Nicholas. *The Suit: A Machiavellian Approach to Men's Style.* New York: HarperBusiness, 2006.

Bixler, Susan, and Nancy Nix-Rice. *The New Professional Image: Dress Your Best for Every Business Situation.* 2nd ed. Avon, MA: Adams Media, 2005.

Morrison, Terri, and Wayne A. Conaway. *Kiss, Bow, or Shake Hands: The Bestselling Guide to Doing Business in More Than 60 Countries.* Avon, MA: Adams Media, 2005.

Byzantine Clothing

Unlike the draped Greek and Roman silhouettes, Byzantine fashion introduced splendid costumes constructed along the body's natural lines as emblems of social, economic, religious, or political prominence. After the Council of Nicaea chose the cross as the emblem of Christianity in 325 C.E., Constantine I the Great, the first Christian emperor of Rome, used the shape on clothing as the official cypher of his rule. Crosses dominated apparel and jewelry for the next millennium. He began transferring power in 330 to Turkey and establishing a more Asian court at Constantinople (present-day Istanbul).

As in the last century of the Roman Empire, design followed the lead of the imperial court with gorgeous patterns and needlework that sometimes covered the foundation material. Linings and edges tended toward black-spotted white ermine or light gray miniver, a form of vair (squirrel) spotted with black lamb's wool.

Ready-to-wear goods and textiles formed the largest body of commodities of the Byzantine economy and drew tourists to artisans' stalls and shopping centers in Antioch and Constantinople to buy apparel and jewelry. Fabrics advanced from plain Egyptian linen and wool or wool blended with linen or cotton from Italy to cut velvet from Cairo, angora from Ankara, cashmere from Kashmir and Nepal, and jewel-toned, bordered, and embroidered Syrian silk, the patterned adornment of nobles and the upper class.

Although Byzantine clothing remained simple in shape, the exotic weaves, selvages, and patterns from Palestine to as far east as China initiated diverse choices in the look and feel of ensembles and accessories. As in the early Roman Empire, Byzantine law reserved for ambassadors and aristocrats the use of Tyrian purple, a deep, reddish plum color derived from the murex sea snail. The colors blue, green, red, and white symbolized horse-racing teams and, eventually, political parties. In the 1100s, Tabriz fabric with Kufic script from Persia offered variety as well as Arabic mystique.

Silver-gilt threads and brilliant hues—indigo (deep blue), kermes (red), madder (raspberry), murex (plum), weld (yellow)—outlined detailed hearts and moons, stylized lotus leaves and palm fronds, medallions, and fantastic animals. The most elaborate patterns drew on chariot racing, hunting, military engagements, and religious scenes, for example, the Annunciation and Pentecost. To these elegant fabrics, wearers attached borders, cuffs, facings, and linings.

Because of the era's self-indulgence in rich dress, Bishop Asterius of Amasea on March 24,

An engraving of eighth-century empress Irene the Athenian (right) and her attendant illustrates defining elements of Byzantine women's dress: a shapeless, ankle-length *stola* of elaborate fabric, often imported, topped with a cowl or headdress. *(Dea Picture Library/De Agostini/Getty Images)*

399, condemned the narcissistic practice in his homily "The Rich Man and Lazarus." He proclaimed vain clothing a frivolous, effeminate practice, especially with garments depicting holy events. After the fall of Rome in 476, the Byzantines gravitated toward more Eastern unisex shapes and adornments from Syria, India, and China.

Byzantine women overlaid the linen *camisa* (chemise) and the round- or boat-neck tunic with a *stola* (overdress), over which they could layer a short shirt for warmth or display. The bell-sleeved stola flared at the hip for ease in walking and remained open at the neck for breastfeeding. In cool weather, prestigious women added the mantle, a shaped overgarment topped with a cowl or hood. Unlike immodest bare-armed Roman dress, Byzantine costumes took on headscarves, cloth belts or sashes, and wrist-length sleeves for propriety. Poorer women wore no jewelry and bought garments of undyed linen, cotton, or wool. For convenience during domestic labor, thrifty women tied up flowing sleeves.

The twelfth century saw major changes in the cut of garments for both men and women. The fitted silhouette of the laced *bliaut* (dress) added low-torso interest with a pleated skirt or slit riding habit bunched at the hip. A sheer train, short mantle, soft slippers, and narrow girdle of leather, silk cord, or metal disks emphasized the natural feminine shape that togas and tunics had concealed under surplus fabric.

By the 1400s, the dalmatic (robe) departed completely from the Roman toga and prefaced the front-opening Armenian, Georgian, and Ottoman or Seljuk Turk caftan. At the same time, *superhumerals* (shoulder wraps) lengthened into the cope, a semicircular cape falling to elbow length and fastened with a buckle, filigree brooch, or clasp. Senior court officials wore blue shoes. Green shoes indicated the uniform of the imperial valet, a staff eunuch. Shoulder-length curls and red leather shoes or knee-high boots completed the imperial wardrobe.

See also: Medieval European Clothing; Roman Clothing, Ancient.

Further Reading

Garland, Lynda, ed. *Byzantine Women: Varieties of Experience, 800–1200.* Burlington, VT: Ashgate, 2006.

Jeffreys, Elizabeth, John Haldon, and Robin Cormack, eds. *The Oxford Handbook of Byzantine Studies.* New York: Oxford University Press, 2008.

Krueger, Derek, ed. *Byzantine Christianity.* Minneapolis, MN: Fortress, 2010.

Calico

An inexpensive colorfast fabric that originated in Calicut, India, calico featured bright floral prints stamped on light, soft cotton grown in Gujarat. The arrival of cotton on the market introduced a pliant summer fabric in naturalistic patterns to compete with linen, the dominant choice in yard goods among Arabs, Dutch, Huns, Vikings, Welsh, and Franks. First woven in the eleventh century as material for women's saris, calico block-printed with a lotus design on a neutral background became an Indian trade item to Egypt in the 1400s.

During the Mughal Empire after 1526, Portuguese spice buyers used coarse calico as a barter medium. From the 1600s, cotton prints tinged with gold tinsel became popular goods imported to England, Holland, France, and Thailand on Dutch and Portuguese merchant vessels. The expenditure of Europeans on Asian calico raised concerns about an imbalance of trade generated by cheap foreign commodities.

After September 1676, England competed with foreign markets after inventor William Sherwin devised a colorfast dyeing process at Westham, Essex, for printing calico. At Essex and a second facility at Bartholomew's Close in London, Sherwin's workers employed a hand-cranked rolling press, the first cylindrical textile press in Europe. Ready-made goods provided even poor consumers with coifs, caps, hoods, and neck cloths at the price of a few pennies.

As European competition increased, Gujarati fabric printers maintained profits by designing textiles to appeal to Turks, Iranis, Arabs, Abyssinians, East Africans, and Persians for handkerchiefs and vests. In North America, the Hudson's Bay Company began stocking calico apparel after 1678 to trade with Native Americans for hides and furs. Under colonial trade laws protecting the silk and wool industries, France in 1686 banned imported glazed patterned chintz from use in clothing, bedding, and upholstery except at the court of Louis XIV at Versailles.

In 1700, the British East India Company imported unprocessed calico rather than *indienne ordinaire,* the common orangey-red, black, and cream fabric from India. By 1719, Peter Mauvillon's calico factory in southwest London produced domestic textiles for petticoats. English and Scots mills bleached and dyed coarse yardage into sturdy, dull-finished cretonne for women's and children's smocks or glazed it into chintz featuring vibrant foliage and blossoms.

Dressmakers featured cream-based repeated flower patterns in elegant women's day dresses, caracos (peplum jackets), and basques, men's banyans (dressing gowns), and the lining of men's coats and vests. The *robe à l'anglaise* (closed gown) featured a low-necked bodice, elbow-length sleeves, and a panniered calico skirt over a muslin petticoat. To meet demand, English drapers requested that Indian mills produce more family designs—heraldic crests, swags, flowers, ferns, and birds. Indian textile specialists complied by emulating hand-painted Chinese silks with polychromatic floral cottons.

After European mills duplicated the Indian processing of chintz, import bans ceased in 1759. In the 1780s, U.S. importers applied the term "muslin" to British calico, which they bought by the bolt from Lancashire. Fabric designers gradually reduced the size of prints to small flower sprigs and altered the backgrounds from cream to darker colors.

Printing with copper rollers in 1783 replaced wood block printing by hand from the previous century and lowered the price of processing. German industrialist Christophe-Philippe Oberkampf prowled auctions of the British and French East India Company in London to acquire plain Indian calico to print at his factory at Jouy-en-Josas in north-central France. By the time of the French Revolution in 1789, some 59 percent of the clothing owned by Parisian women was cotton. By comparison, the servant class dressed in 57 percent calico apparel.

While serving as an explorer of the Missouri River on August 18, 1805, and as the territorial governor of Missouri in 1810, William Clark relied on a cask of 48 ruffled calico shirts as durable bribes to the native peoples. He also bartered calico garments in exchange for Indian ponies, a mule, moccasins, and food. In the 1830s and 1840s, trans-Mississippi settlers paid 50–75 cents per yard for calico piece goods to replace women's clothes worn out by the journey.

A pioneer seamstress often outfitted whole families from the yardage on a single bolt, varying individual men's yoke shirts and women's dresses with piping, ruching (gathered strips), cambric collars embroidered with whitework, drop-shoulder sleeves, and bag pockets. The typical woman's dress consisted of a loose calico blouse over a long gathered skirt. For growing girls, a front yoke provided ease during growth spurts; a false hem allowed for lengthening, extending the use of a skirt. When the garments were threadbare, the seamstress recycled the calico by cutting out patches for mending and figures to appliqué on other sewing projects.

American quilters from New England south to the Carolinas preferred calico and chintz appliqué for vivid bedding, aprons, sunbonnets, and rag dolls. In 1850, when colonial traders in East Africa exploited a fad for bright calico among the Nyamwezi women of Tanzania, calico production reached 600 million yards (550 million meters). During the American Civil War, fabric shortages along the Atlantic Coast raised the price of calico to $5 per yard. In 1880, calico caravans crossed the Sahara Desert to transport Mediterranean fabrics from Tripoli to Kano, Nigeria. Today, Nigerian designers still make up sample gowns, dresses, and blouses in calico, the fabric of choice of Yemi Osunkoya of the Kosibah fashion house.

See also: American Western Clothing; Appliqué; Cotton and Cotton Products; Cotton Trade; Printing, Textile; Textile Manufacturing.

Further Reading

Brackman, Barbara. *Clues in the Calico: A Guide to Identifying and Dating Antique Quilts.* Lafayette, CA: C&T, 2009.

Jenkins, David, ed. *The Cambridge History of Western Textiles.* New York: Cambridge University Press, 2003.

Krohn, Katherine. *Calico Dresses and Buffalo Robes: American West Fashions from the 1840s to the 1890s.* Minneapolis, MN: Twenty-First Century Books, 2012.

Canes and Swagger Sticks

An aid to walking and self-defense, the cane and swagger stick eventually acquired panache as a masculine wardrobe accessory. From prehistory, the stick or staff has provided a stabilizing point for the upright walker, particularly over uneven turf, in water of imperceptible depth, and on inclines. In 1323 B.C.E., Egyptian monarch Tutankhamen went to his tomb in the Valley of the Kings with a box of monogrammed scepters, crooks, and staffs of office made from carnelian, faience, ebony, ivory, and gilded wood.

Over time, multipurpose canes have facilitated the movements and behaviors of men and women. In ancient Greece, the *keryx* (herald) carried his walking staff as a symbol of his role as an intermediary protected by Zeus and Hermes. In an ominous myth, Oedipus (literally "swollen foot") struck Laius, a fellow traveler, with a walking cane, setting in motion a tragedy that cost the life of Oedipus's mother/wife, Jocasta, and brought about the exile of Oedipus and his sisters/daughters, Ismene and Antigone.

Roman centurions applied the *vitis* (swagger stick) to leading marching squadrons and punishing soldiers. Until the disbandment of the Praetorian Guard by Constantine I in 312 C.E., the head of the imperial security force carried an *imperatoris insigne* (military stick) as part of his uniform. The Roman augur carried a *lituus* (rod), a symbol of divination adopted in Christendom as the emblem of the episcopal office. On a more practical note, Roman pedestrians considered the walking stick essential for foot travel.

During the Crusades and into the late Middle Ages, travelers to Rome, Christian shrines, or the Holy Land carried the palmer's crutch or *bourdon* (stave) as the pilgrim's badge. The staff served as a third leg, interpreted as the support of the Holy Trinity. For professional men, the symbolic wand, judicial cane, regimental or pace stick, or baton lent an air of authority to the church usher, magistrate, military drill instructor, and music conductor. A bishop displayed his pastoral office with the crozier, a symbol of the Good Shepherd, or a tau-shaped staff, the insignia of authority over Eastern Orthodoxy.

In 1500, the British walking cane distinguished the stylish urban male, who equipped himself with an ivory, whalebone, or ebony support topped with an engraved knob. When European men abandoned the sword in the late 1600s for holstered pistols, they also adopted the nonaggressive hiking stick or rattan carried under the arm. The cane functioned as an elongation of the arm for brushing aside tree limbs and shrubbery, warding off barking dogs, and retaining balance on snow and ice. Proud ex-soldiers leaned on canes as evidence of combat wounds.

Both men and women purchased umbrellas to serve the dual purpose of walking supports and protection from rain. Horseback riders preferred the leather crop, a short whip for controlling a mount. In the Western Hemisphere and Australia, the crop took the form of a quirt, a braided cowhide whip, or short kangaroo hide staff carried as an ornament to formal riding attire and applied to livestock as a goad. The Irish and Scots adopted the shillelagh and *kebbie*, respectively, oak or blackthorn staffs with a knotty handle brandished like a cudgel for stick fighting.

In the 1700s, manufacturers equipped the heavily varnished walking stick with a wrist strap and ferrule, a metal tip that prevented the wood from splintering. For stability, the feeble or handicapped adopted a cane shaped like a T or an upside down J. Importers of East Asian goods sold at sixpence each the Chinese *jambee* (bamboo cane) or pale yellow Japanese whanghee (jointed bamboo root) featured in *Tatler* magazine.

Late in the eighteenth century, canes acquired an unsavory reputation. The fitting of the Malaysian dragon's blood cane or a stout "Penang lawyer" (palm stick) with a concealed dagger, spike, or rapier produced the swordstick, a suitable weapon for urban self-defense in dangerous neighborhoods. After 1818, the first police officers in Dublin, London, and Paris twirled their canes or billies as evidence of authority in the street.

In the Victorian Age, a carved cane with an ornamental ivory, bone, horn, or gold-plated handle became a standard gift to a retiring official. After 1840, the hand-carved cane contributed to European and American folk art a number of hidden caches of whiskey, medicine, drawing materials, derringers, smuggled items, and safety matches. In 1846, exporters in Canton, China, sold 1.2 million canes, laurel sticks, and bamboos. By 1847, Paris offered a variety of whips and sticks from 165 manufacturers.

A variant from the late nineteenth century, pairs of trekking poles extended or retracted according to the needs of the hiker to relieve stress on the lumbar region, knees, and ankles. The 1894 Montgomery Ward catalog offered a cheap convenience to the stroller—straps to bind the cane to a closed umbrella at 23 cents per pair.

In the early twentieth century, military officers abandoned the crop and swagger stick, symbols of authority that drew derision in peacetime use. In 1921, blind walkers emulated James Biggs of Bristol, England, who warned oncoming traffic of his disability by painting his cane white. During the Great Depression, actor Fred Astaire popularized the dress cane as an accessory for top hat and tails, popularized in the film *Top Hat* (1935). Late in the twentieth century, rehabilitation therapists replaced the rubber-tipped cane for the disabled with a quad cane, which ends in a more stable quadrangular plate and four feet.

See also: Accessories; Umbrellas and Parasols.

Further Reading

Amato, Joseph Anthony. *On Foot: A History of Walking.* New York: NYU Press, 2004.

Dike, Catherine. *Canes in the United States.* Louisville, KY: Minerva Books, 2003.

Cardin, Pierre (1922–)

A fashion structuralist, Pierre Cardin applied geometric shapes and modern technology in pioneering unisex garment design. A successful entrepreneur as well as a couturier, he was among the first Westerners to merchandise his many branded products—from clothing and perfume to housewares and kitchen appliances—in China and Eastern Europe.

He was born Pietro Cardin at his family's vacation home in San Biagio di Callalta northeast of Venice, Italy, on July 2, 1922. His parents, Alessandro and Maria Montagner Cardin, formerly wealthy wine merchants, had lost their fortune during World War I, fled Mussolini's Blackshirts, and reared their 11 children in St. Etienne southwest of Lyons, France.

During his youth, Cardin rejected his father's insistence that he study architecture and instead made dresses for his neighbor's dolls. While completing middle school in 1936, he apprenticed in apparel design under master tailor Louis Bompuis. At age 17, following the Nazi invasion in May 1940, Cardin fled by bicycle some 150 miles (240 kilometers) to work in Vichy tailoring men's suits for Manby.

Cardin escaped compulsory factory labor for the Germans in the early 1940s by studying accounting at night and working as a secretary for the Red Cross in Vichy and Paris under General Pierre Verdier. When the war was over, Cardin advanced from the houses of Jeanne Paquin and Elsa Schiaparelli to a supervisory post for Christian Dior, for whom Cardin designed the "bar look" with fitted basques and black maxi skirts. Cardin's ventures included sewing late Renaissance ruffs, cloaks, gauntlets, and masks for Jean Cocteau's film *La Belle et la Bête* (*Beauty and the Beast,* 1946).

By age 28, Cardin left an attic shop to open his own house, with a staff of 20, at the Maison de Couture on rue Richepanse in Paris. In addition to his first showing of 20 dresses, he costumed the casts of a production of *Casanova* and other theatricals for the Comédie-Française. His fanciful designs for women featured tailored suits, bubble hoods, caped coats, and deep collars, hints of his later contributions to fashion.

A career coup, the creation of 30 costumes for *Le bal oriental* at Palazzo Labia in Venice in 1951 prefaced the designer's move into haute couture for women at the Faubourg Saint-Honoré. His debut of the bubble dress in 1954 and the opening of his boutique, Eve, earned him fame for the cosmos look in modular fur coats, flounced cocktail dresses, and kilt skirts reminiscent of Roman scale armor. In 1957, he paired Eve with Adam, a men's boutique that featured avant-garde ties and the collarless button-up jacket he designed for the Beatles.

After 1959, Cardin scandalized his profession by launching an egalitarian ready-to-wear line sold in the Printemps department chain. His affordable women's wear ranged from the circular raincoat, tulip skirt, harem jump suit, and slotted afternoon dress to pointed shoulder pads, wimples, zippered thigh-high boots, and oversized aviator goggles reminiscent of fictional space suits. For men, he offered the gold lamé suit, zippered vest and knickers, unitard, and leather-encased wristwatches, casual wear that influenced styles in the Americas and Great Britain.

Cardin introduced French couture in Japan with lectures at Bunka Fukusou fashion college in the late 1950s and designed uniforms for Pakistan International Airlines that blended tradition with futurism. He presented his youthful line at L'Espace Cardin in Paris and began designing for television, notably, costumes for the British series *The Avengers* (1961–1969). In 1966, he introduced a children's line of parkas and play clothes. His innovations used carpentry nails, hammered metal, and vinyl to shape helmets, catsuits, and batwing shirts for clients such as First Lady Jacqueline Kennedy, baseball star Joe DiMaggio, and actors Jeanne Moreau, Mia Farrow, and Lauren Bacall.

For the *Barong Tagalog,* a national costume for Filipino men, Cardin tapered the tunic shirt, opened the front, broadened the sleeves, and reduced the white-on-white embroidery. In 1979, he became the first Western couturier to open a shop in Moscow. His other projects involved him in the Maxim's hotel and restaurant chains in 1981, transportation design for the American Motors Corporation Javelin car and Atlantic Aviation jet, architectural restoration, polyurethane furniture, and the arts. He published an autobiography, *Past, Present and Future,* in 1990 and two years later received a designation from the French Academy of Fine Arts as the top-ranking couturier in France.

Currently, a staff of some 200,000 works for Cardin at 840 factories producing 1,000 products, including the uniforms he designed for Chinese civil servants and the People's Liberation Army. His honors include the Order of Cultural Merit of Monaco, Basilica Palladiana and Lion of Veneto from Venice, Golden Spinning Wheel Award, three Gold Thimbles from Cartier, and a Goodwill Ambassador for UNESCO.

See also: Fashion Design; French Clothing and Fashion.

Further Reading

Hesse, Jean-Pascal. *Pierre Cardin: 60 Years of Innovation.* New York: Assouline, 2010.

Längle, Elisabeth. *Pierre Cardin: Fifty Years of Fashion and Design.* New York: Vendome, 2005.

Pierre Cardin. www.pierrecardin.com

Carnival Costumes

See Mardi Gras and Carnival Costumes

Cassini, Oleg (1913–2006)

Achieving fame as a film costumer and creator of the "Camelot look" for First Lady Jacqueline Kennedy in the early 1960s, Oleg Cassini elevated American couture with ladylike applications of Empire lines, sheath dresses, and A-line skirts.

Born Oleg Cassini Loiewski de Capizucchi in Paris on April 11, 1913, he was the son of Russian-Jewish diplomat Alexander Loiewski, a dandy and clotheshorse, and Russian-Italian countess Marguerite Cassini, a hat designer. After the seizure of the Loiewski ancestral estate near Saint Petersburg following the Russian Revolution of 1917, the family fled through Denmark and Switzerland to Florence, Italy, where they abandoned their Russian surname.

While attending an English Catholic school, Cassini observed fashion at his mother's dress shop, the Maison de Couture. During recuperation from a leg injury, he absorbed himself in Native American lore, history, and the novels of James Fenimore Cooper. On recovery, he excelled at track, skiing, horseback riding, fencing, and tennis, and at sketching French couture twice yearly in Paris during his mother's examination of fashions. He studied at the Accademia di Belle Arti Firenze under Giorgio de Chirico, an artist and set and costume maker for the Russian Ballet.

In her signature Oleg Cassini dress and pillbox hat, First Lady Jacqueline Kennedy wowed the press and established herself as an international glamour icon during a European tour in spring 1961. Cassini's 300 designs for her set the trend in "Camelot" fashion. *(Rue des Archives/The Granger Collection, NYC—All rights reserved)*

With training in couture from designer Jean Patou, Cassini began costuming film actors and opened a boutique in Rome. At age 23, he emigrated to Washington, D.C., to draw political cartoons. Resettled in Hollywood, California, under a seven-year contract with Paramount Pictures, he worked as assistant costumer to the great Edith Head. In 1941, he made plunging necklines for Veronica Lake, a sarong for Dorothy Lamour, and a draped slip-dress and mermaid gown of garnet velvet for his wife, Gene Tierney, star of *The Shanghai Gesture*.

During his five years of service as a U.S. Cavalry officer in World War II, Cassini received U.S. citizenship. He continued in the film, television, and Broadway industries through the twentieth century with knit suits, sheaths, and cocktail dresses for such clients as Grace Kelly, Suzy Parker, Marilyn Monroe, and Nancy Kwan. In 1952, he established a couturier salon in New York City on Seventh Avenue and sold ready-to-wear to Dorothy Shaver, the president of Lord & Taylor. Seamstresses purchased Simplicity patterns of his recognizable surplice tops and one-shoulder cocktail dresses.

Beginning in 1961, Cassini designed 300 outfits for Jacqueline Kennedy that included uncluttered boxy suits, a leopard coat, day dresses, state gowns, a pillbox hat with muff, and accessories that established her image as cosmopolitan wife of the U.S. president. *Vogue* featured her inaugural gown, a brocade dinner suit, and a riding habit with boots. With exquisite apparel for trips to India, Paris, and Vienna, the sophisticated first lady transformed fashion worldwide, a feat Cassini summarized in *A Thousand Days of Magic: Dressing Jacqueline Kennedy for the White House* (1995). Key to his creation of dignified state dress, he envisioned the clear geometrics and intense hues as viewed by the camera from a distance.

In addition to women's wear, Cassini shifted men's shirts from white to deep hues and paired the tuxedo with a turtleneck. He created colored tennis outfits, maillot swimsuits, and the Nehru jacket modeled by Johnny Carson, Peter Lawford, Mario Andretti, Kenny Rogers, and Mike Douglas. For his seven decades of success at designing apparel, eyeglasses, fashion dolls, and fake fur that required no slaughter of animals, he earned the Chicago Gold Coast Award, an honorary PhD from the International College of Fine Arts, and the Council of Fashion Designers of America Board of Directors Special Tribute. He died from a ruptured aneurysm on March 17, 2006.

See also: Fashion Design.

Further Reading

Cassini, Oleg. *In My Own Fashion: An Autobiography.* New York: Simon & Schuster, 1987.

Cassini, Oleg, Liz Smith, and Suzy Menkes. *The Wedding Dress.* New York: Rizzoli, 2011.

Oleg Cassini. www.olegcassini.com

Catalogs, Clothing and Fashion

The nineteenth century introduced consumers to the ease of retail shopping by mail-order catalog. Entrepreneur Pryce Jones in Newtown, Wales, began the retailing of wool flannel goods by leaflet in 1851 and expanded the service to Canada. In New York City in 1860, pattern dealers William Jennings Demorest, his wife, milliner Ellen Louise Demorest, and her sister Kate offered French styles in a quarterly catalog, *Mirror for Fashions,* which also marketed accessories by mail.

With the expansion of railroads across the North American West and the advent of free rural mail delivery, access to the latest styles united the frontier with the cosmopolitan East. Settlers chose from garments and technological advances—rubberized rainwear, eyeglasses, and factory-made baby clothes—at prices far lower than those of local dry goods stores. For the agrarian population, Samuel Carley's company in Montreal initiated mail-order shopping in 1871 with specials on kid gloves.

In the United States, Montgomery Ward of Chicago introduced remote purchasing in 1872 with corded pants for men and boys and hosiery for the whole family. By the 1890s, the company's one-page catalog grew to 540 pages and pictured 20,000 items, including fringe, fur, and oiled boots. Its universal appeal enabled the company to outsell such specialty catalogs as those of the Kalamazoo Corset Company and Alaska Furs and Fur Garments of Juneau.

In Winnipeg, Manitoba, the Timothy Eaton Company competed for North American sales from 1884 with a 34-page catalog. The 1887–1888 issue presented seasonal collars and cuffs, suspenders, and dress patterns as well as advice on "healthy corsets" steam molded from coraline, an elasticized cotton. For rural girls growing up in isolated areas, the catalog suggested the leather-bodied "beauty doll" and a trunk for storing home-sewn doll wardrobes. The trendy Welland Vale catalog of St. Catherines, Ontario, pictured female cyclists modeling straw boaters, waists, riding skirts, long socks, and athletic shoes suitable for exercise. Males could choose from trouser guards, caps, and toe clips.

Mail-Order Competitors

In the United States, Sears, Roebuck's catalog competed directly with Montgomery Ward after 1888, earning the name the "Consumer's Wishbook." The first Sears catalogs, written entirely by company founder Richard Sears, pictured watches, jewelry, sewing machines, and the basics of sewing and apparel—buttons, rickrack and bias trim, long underwear, brocade corsets, high-top shoes, rain capes, and croquet sandals. The Montgomery Ward catalog touted patent leather high-top shoes, half-boots with elastic inserts, slippers with leather foxing (appliqué), and inexpensive gaiters at 5 cents per pair.

By 1895, the Montgomery Ward catalog prioritized fashion hairpieces—the La Toska foundation bang, princess and feather bangs, Emma waves, and switches up to 26 inches (66 centimeters) in length. Men's toupées ranged in price from $5.50 to $21. Sears, Roebuck sold forehead puffs, curly Parisian bangs, Alice waves, ventilated wigs, "black Negro" and masquerade wigs, and toupées and toupée paste. A Toronto competitor, the Robert Simpson Company, published a 346-page catalog that listed falls, cluster locks, and such styling accoutrements as hair ornaments, feather bands, and boudoir caps.

At a time when women made the majority of mail orders, competition improved catalog quality and taste, beginning in 1896 with the initial catalog from the Hudson's Bay Company of Winnipeg, which offered blankets and hiking boots. Henry Morgan's in Montreal displayed some 1,000 hat styles from London, New York, and Paris. More variety followed from Woodward's of Vancouver, the "Great Mail Order House of the West," a source of regional work clothes for lumbering and herding, and Compagnie Paquet of Quebec, wholesalers of children's play clothes, mittens, and moccasins.

In 1897, Sears featured its shoe section in color and extended men's services with free swatches of suit material and garments for big and tall customers. The company extended dividends and proposed club purchasing, a method for consumers to earn discounts by submitting a group order. Sears's money-back guarantee in 1903 convinced some consumers to trust mail service. To elevate their prestige with Western goods, consumers as far away as Zambia depended on mail-order ready-to-wear.

Wartime Shopping

Leather and hide met consumer demand in the 1910s, when Goodwin's in Montreal listed aviation caps, hockey boots, alligator and goat leather bags, and lined gloves. Harley-Davidson's catalog from Milwaukee, Wisconsin, accentuated cycling goggles, hats, tanned gaiters, and puttees. Eddie Bauer of Bellevue, Washington, and P.T. Legaré of Quebec joined the coterie of mail-order dealers in 1920 with such staple items as oiled rain gear, tennis togs, and fur robes. As a source of women's well-being, Eaton's promoted tanning in swimsuits, an item opposed by the French Canadian Catholic clergy for revealing female breasts and hips.

In the 1920s, shoe and rainwear catalogs celebrated the end of World War I leather shortages. Live model photos manifested women's love of variety, from the low, curve-heeled, one-strap Mary Jane and the welted felt house slipper to the "radio boot" with a wide astrakhan cuff for wet weather. High-fashion poses flaunted the T-strap with wood heels and silk stockings in a selection of colors to complement the leg under shorter skirts. In contrast, Eaton's Winnipeg catalog in the 1930s revived respect for the pioneer, forester, and miner with utility overalls and rugged milkmaid shoes and brogans.

During rationing in World War II, mail-order catalogs encouraged patriotism with the "V for Victory" concept, which backed government control of rubber, leather, and metal for combat use. Rural seamstresses studied catalog pages for outfits to copy at home with fabric recycled from curtains and tablecloths. Hamley & Company of Pendleton, Oregon, remained cognizant of Western needs in 1942, when its catalog featured cowboy belts, chaps, and fringed unisex riding gear.

At war's end, the Vermont Country Store evolved a client base seeking the old-fashioned values of the previous century in sleepwear and underclothes. Dupuis Frères lured Quebec shoppers with yard goods, embroidery needles, crochet yarn, maternity belts, and baby shoes. In the 1950s, Sears, which merged with Simpson's, featured winter weight jeans with flannel linings to match flannel shirts. In 1958, the Army and Navy catalog from Regina, Saskatchewan, discounted wartime overstocks of Orlon socks and sweaters and silk ties, priced at $1.

Modern Merchandising

Beginning in the 1960s, world merchandisers found better ways to communicate with shoppers. On the high end of fashion, pin-up poses in the catalogs of Frederick's of Hollywood and Victoria's Secret of Columbus, Ohio, flaunted seductive panties, Wonderbras, bustiers, kimonos, and honeymoon nighties. J.C. Penney in Plano, Texas, and Lands' End in Dodgeville, Wisconsin, emulated the Sears model in 1963 by adopting mail order as a merchandising tool. Norm Thompson Outfitters of Hillsboro, Oregon, added a specialty catalog in 1965 offering outdoor sweaters, slacks, and jackets.

Throughout the apparel industry, phone-in orders rid mail order of the time lag until letters reached headquarters. Toll-free telephone numbers enabled shoppers to question agents about sizing and quality. Nonetheless, the decline of mail-order shopping preceded the end of the Dupuis catalog in 1963, Eaton's publications in 1976, Army and Navy direct mail in 1985, and the Sears catalog legacy in 1993.

As more direct marketing turned to gifts and gimmicks, e-commerce through Amazon, eBay, and Yahoo! debuted a cheaper, more personalized method of exhibiting apparel and shoe selections. In 1998, Sears posted an interactive Christmas catalog, Wishbook.com. Electronic search engines simplified the task of locating the latest fashion trends, a strategy employed by Bloomingdale's of New York City, Neiman Marcus of Dallas, Texas, and the Marks & Spencer department store chain in the United Kingdom and Ireland.

The economic recession during the 2010s increased the use of direct mail and print catalogs for browsing paired with Internet offerings. Dispatched to 160 countries, the 2012 L.L. Bean catalog promoted more than 16,000 garments, specializing in the needs of hikers, fishers, and hunters, such as ragg sweaters and leak-proof waders. By 2015, U.S. economic forecasts predict online retail sales of $279 billion, a boon for UPS and FedEx delivery services.

See also: Mail Order; Merchandising; Patterns; Retail Trade.

Further Reading

Cherry, Robin. *Catalog: The Illustrated History of Mail Order Shopping.* New York: Princeton Architectural Press, 2008.
Hill, Daniel Delis. *As Seen in Vogue: A Century of American Fashion in Advertising.* Lubbock: Texas Tech University Press, 2004.

Central American, Mexican, and Caribbean Clothing

The collision of East and West in the late fifteenth century shaped Caribbean, Mexican, and Central American clothing styles from a blend of ethnic and utilitarian apparel. Around 4000 B.C.E., Pipil-speaking hunter-gatherers of what is now

Nicaragua relied on animal pelts for clothing. The Tolupanes (or Xicaques) of Honduras hammered bark into fabric for clothing. Shell carvings found in Cuba and Haiti indicate the use of natural materials to make amulets. Carib artisans of the southern Caribbean introduced a multiple-shuttle technique for netting.

Ancient Apparel

After 1600 B.C.E., the Olmec of south-central Mexico and Belize as far south as Costa Rica flourished at mask making and garnishing attire with blue and crimson parrot feathers. They crafted jewelry and trade items from jadeite, a distinctive burial ornament and source of death masks. On Mexico's Pacific coast, the Mixtec valued turquoise masks and jaguar claws as symbols of authority.

From 1500 B.C.E., the backstrap loom occupied the hands of female Maya weavers of the southern Sierra Madre in making streamers to weave into the plaits of brides. Woven materials included rabbit hair, caterpillar filament, and hummingbird feathers for wedding attire in Chiapas. Agave and yucca fibers served desert nomads as materials for braiding sandals and weaving bags.

From 1200 B.C.E., Nahua speakers of Guatemala and Honduras braided sandals and wove breechcloths and aprons of plant fiber and cotton. The formation of sheets of vegetal fiber from agave spikes and fig tree bark formed a sacred paper covering for priests. On the Gulf Coast, the Olmec began extending the breechcloth around 1150 B.C.E. into an apron or hip cloth held in place by a belt. For ritual ball games, the Olmec of Veracruz padded shorts at the hip. After plunging the ball through a ring, winning players received from spectators rewards of clothing and jewelry.

For twisting, braiding, and weaving, Mexican farmers cultivated white or brown cotton, both long- and short-staple forms of pliant cellulose. Among the Zapotec of Oaxaca after 500 B.C.E., capes supplemented minimal breechcloths and skirts. Natives embellished rectangular mantles with maguey embroidery, seashells, copper, and pearls. For jewelry, women garnished their bodies with glass beads and hoop earrings.

Nahua warriors of Mexico, El Salvador, Guatemala, Nicaragua, and Panama covered themselves from head to foot in jaguar bodysuits topped with eagle headdresses. Claws, tail, and teeth honored the military elite with evidence of combat with fierce beasts. Kings displayed jaguar pelts and sat on thrones carved in the shape of giant cats. Peacetime among Nahua peasants called for a sleeveless bodice to complement the breechcloth and deerhide moccasins. In Costa Rica, gold and turquoise ear flares designated high social status.

In the early Classic period around 300 C.E., the Maya of Guatemala denoted male virility with the belted *maxtlatl* (loincloth) of grass or maguey fibers and female powers with elaborate headdresses and parasols. By 692, a Guatemalan queen, Lady K'abel, went to her grave at El Peru-Waka with a jade icon and alabaster soul jar depicting a female face. Another artifact, a jade-surfaced helmet, denoted her warrior status.

After 900, female citizens superintended Maya dress and commodity apparel with spinning wheels and looms. They set up dye vats for tie-dyeing the Guatemalan skirt and twill *xicolli* (sleeveless jacket) that Maya males wore with fringe and quetzal or macaw feathers stitched with agave thread. The most common womanly apparel included the hand-spun *huipil* (rectangular wrap), a sashed cotton tunic left open on the sides and adorned at the yoke with colored wax, feathers, and metallic stitchery. A *corte* (sarong) covered the lower female body to the feet.

Emulating ancient body painting, the Kuna islanders of San Blas east of Panama after 1200 invented a clothing style opulent with layered stitchery. For reverse appliqué, tinters colored geometric pieces in natural annatto (*Bixa orellana*), carmine (*Dactylopius coccus*), charcoal, and huito (*Genipa americana*). A palette of red, black, and gray defined *mola* (blouse) folk motifs. Kuna design featured extensive latticing and borders on wrap skirts, aprons, and head scarves. Nose rings, ankle and arm beads, and earrings completed the Kuna ensembles.

Around 1250, the loincloth style of classical Teotihuacan underwent modification by the Toltec of south-central Mexico. By shaping the long wrapper into a complex Aztec knot modeling male genitals, the wearer asserted virility. In pre-Hispanic Mesoamerica at Tlatilco and Chichén Itzá, men added gravitas to the wardrobe with capes tied at the neck and extending to the feet. Women achieved a parallel stateliness in the *quechquemitl,* a bodice made by joining two cloth strips to create triangles front and back.

Post-Columbian Attire

Upon arrival on October 12, 1492, on the island he would name San Salvador, Genoan navigator Christopher Columbus took note of cotton growing wild in the Bahamas. He observed Lucayan Taíno natives adorned in red body pigments, parrot feathers, and tooth necklaces. The Taíno returned the curiosity by noting what heavy outfits the Spaniards wore. When entertaining Guacanagaríx, chief of Marién, Hispaniola, aboard the Spanish flagship *Santa Maria,* Columbus impressed him with gifts of expensive Spanish clothing.

Farther west, Columbus observed nudity on Trinidad on July 31, 1498. On August 14, 1502, his fourth voyage took him to Trujillo, Honduras, and fishing villages along the Miskito Coast, where natives appeared the least impressed by Spanish dress. Explorers of Central America discovered the panama hat, a straw head covering extended over the ears and neck like wings, a protective style that survived from 4000 B.C.E. At Tenochtitlan, Spanish explorer Hernán Cortés observed labrets and nose and tongue piercings.

The devastation from influenza and measles carried by the Spanish reduced the indigenous Honduran population from an estimated 825,000 to 50,000. As a result of virtual genocide, regional survivors lost carving, plaiting, and weaving skills as Spaniards subsumed their culture. The Caquetio, miners and lumberers in Curaçao, Bonaire, and Aruba, reverted to Stone Age attire.

During the colonial period, beginning in the 1530s, bondage in the Yucatán, Haiti, Santo Domingo, Puerto Rico, Cuba, and Jamaica under Queen Isabella's trustee system of *encomienda* rapidly depleted the Arawak, Carib, Ciboney, Galibi, and Taíno. As black slaves replaced Indian press gangs, the styles of West Africa, modified by innovations from Spain, Italy, Britain, Holland,

Portugal, and France, replaced native apparel. Among surviving garments, the *rebozo* (shawl) and *quachtli* (cotton mantle) retained their importance to Mexican mestizas, while black wool overpants worn by French sailors influenced the dress code of Guatemalan males.

At the saltworks on Saint Eustatius and Saint Martin in the 1630s, Dutch investors worked indentured Europeans alongside indigenous slaves but supplied less clothing to the latter. Field hands wore little more than body oil to enhance their skin, creating an impression of health and vigor. At Saba, Saint Croix, Guyana, and the British Virgin Islands, the 75 percent death rate of indentured whites and aborigines in the sugar industry in 1660 resulted in importation of the first slaves through triangle trade with West Africa.

Cotton dominated all levels of regional apparel production. After the Spanish began exporting cotton from Barbados in 1650, they introduced the horizontal and treadle loom. From age 12 through old age, fabric workers shaped the traditional tasseled headband, infant swaddling, and burial wrappings. Irish manufacturers of low-grade cottons supplied planters with substandard tunics, pants, and shirts for laborers performing the grueling work in sugar mills. Colonial overlords in Mexico and Cuba promoted the embroidery and pleating of the guayabera shirt, a male uniform for rituals, parties, and business meetings.

From the sixteenth to the eighteenth centuries, piracy favored the loose, mismatched outfits, knife scabbards, and bare feet common to harbor towns in Cuba, Santo Domingo, Jamaica, St. Barts, and Tortuga. In the 1720s in Barbados, St. Lucia, and Dominica, Welsh buccaneer Bartholomew Roberts flaunted the luxury fabrics, leather tricorn hats and thigh-high boots, ribbons, periwigs, and gold chains and earrings outlawed by English sumptuary laws. Impressed sailors wore the remains of navy-issue canvas doublets and breeches, linen shirts, cotton drawers and stockings, and knitted wool caps.

Captive white women held for ransom pieced together blouses, skirts, and petticoats from a tumble of trunks and hampers washed up on shore from foundering vessels. This motley look set the tone for island dress and the female streetwear of mainland Salvadorans and Costa Ricans. Meso-american men made their fashion statement with the red cummerbund and cowboy hat.

As prosperity influenced Caribbean black women, they accessorized calico blouses and African-style skirts and dresses with kidskin slippers and the French Creole *tignon* (turban). The head wrap warded off the sun while absorbing perspiration and adding stature. At harbors in the late 1700s, itinerant *revendeuses* (saleswomen) loaded mules with European woven goods and trim for importation to country estates. After the French Revolution of 1789, Napoleonic Civil Code repressed island mulattos by banning French-style clothing. By the mid-1800s, Cuban planters and slaves relied on imported British calico because island plots produced mainly sugar cane and vegetables but no fiber for weaving.

Post-Slavery Era

During the 1880s, Caribbean patronage guaranteed black hirelings a monthly wage plus food and clothing. At religious enclaves in Martinique, Jamaica, Cuba, and Mexico, missionaries insisted on long dresses, pants, and stockings for children, even though the climate encouraged lighter apparel. Parents tolerated the imposed wardrobe because religious workers supplied families with free shoes, a scarce commodity to the Tarahumara of the Sierra Madre. The proselytizing of Panamanians initiated the annual Carnival, a pre-Lenten celebration marked by street and nightclub dancing in traditional attire and river floats featuring festival royalty in fantasy costumes.

In El Salvador, Costa Rica, and Jamaica, community celebrations of festivals and weddings brought out the most treasured ensembles along with palm leaf hats and rope sandals. Salvadoran men wore striped ponchos over *kushmas* (chaps), a common legging for field-workers. Women displayed heirloom shawl pins and silver earrings. Guatemalan weavers gave as gifts shawls, belts, blouses, and handkerchiefs.

Caribbean fashion featured the white cotton shift garnished with lace and satin ribbon threaded through eyelet trim. West African heritage promoted the white chemise complementing the plaid full skirt and matching turban. Men flaunted floral shirts open to the waist of tight cotton pants. On Guadeloupe and Martinique, children adapted the look for a standard Carnival pirate costume by adding a head bandanna and eye patch.

European colonists quickly adapted their multilayered wardrobes to the tropics and adopted the hand fan as a necessary solution to heat and insects. Daily rains required quick-dry linen suits and shirts and dresses of cotton or silk featuring flounced overskirts. At the same time that indentured Chinese brought silk to the region, settlers from India introduced madras, a light cotton in bright plaids.

In 1881, engineers and workers on the Panama Canal fashioned the modern panama hat, a brimmed straw head covering whose predecessors dated to the seventeenth century in Ecuador. Mesoamerican entrepreneurs began marketing the unisex hat to California and Cuba in the mid-1800s, but the canal project—and a visit by President Theodore Roosevelt in 1904—popularized the style in the United States. At St. Kitts, Indonesian immigrants introduced batiking on cotton head wraps in the 1880s. During the same period, universal education introduced British dress codes for students, encumbering the children of Barbados and the British Leewards with wool shorts and kneesocks and leather oxfords.

Late twentieth-century American influence popularized day wear such as camp shirts, guayaberas, and tees with light shorts and khakis, much of it made in the *maquilas* (factories) of Honduras for export to Korea and the United States. For informal evening occasions, male tourists added V-neck sweaters and jackets. The availability of European and American fashion magazines offered seamstresses ideas for ensembles emulating haute couture, but in the lighter fabrics necessary in equatorial heat. Designer Claudia Pegus introduced Trinidadians and Tobagans to Sea Island cotton (*Gossypium barbadense*), a soft fiber grown commercially throughout the West Indies. Her innovative blend of European couture with island silhouettes resulted in beachwear, halter tops, bikinis, and palazzo pants for women and sheer,

Distinctive elements of the Rastafarian religious and cultural movement, born in Jamaica during the 1930s, include long dreadlocks and hats and clothes in red, green, black, and gold (the colors of the Pan-African movement and the Ethiopian flag). *(Gavin Hellier/Robert Harding World Imagery/Getty Images)*

open-throat shirts, hoodies, and drawstring pants for men as well as traditional ruffled evening dresses and wedding ensembles.

In the 1980s, Rastafarians in Antigua and Jamaica displayed cornrows, dreadlocks, and natural-fiber psychedelic tees and the rastacap or kufi crocheted in Afrocentric colors—red, green, gold, and black. In Cuba, severe economic shortfalls prevented the government from clothing female laborers, a subsidy begun in 1964; instead, the Castro regime encouraged home sewing. In similar straits, Honduran commercial farmers purchased used clothing, rubber boots, and sandals for refurbishing.

Today, kinship groups in El Salvador and Haiti share clothing with less fortunate relatives. The clothing trade encourages self-sufficiency by marketing fair trade palm hats and fans from Belize, St. Barts, and Trinidad and fragrant vetiver grass bags and dolls from Dominica. The palmetto bonnets, sisal carryalls, lantana straw hats, and leather sandals from Nassau retain West African styles and motifs from slave times.

See also: Amerindian Clothing, Pre-Columbian; Amerindian Clothing, Post-Contact; Cotton Trade; Ethnic and National Dress; Latino Styles and Fashions; Ribbons and Embellishments.

Further Reading

Anawalt, Patricia Rieff. *Indian Clothing Before Cortés: Mesoamerican Costumes from the Codices.* Norman: University of Oklahoma Press, 1981.

Evans, Susan Toby, and David L. Webster, eds. *Archaeology of Ancient Mexico and Central America: An Encyclopedia.* New York: Garland, 2001.

Root, Regina A., ed. *Latin American Fashion Reader.* New York: Berg, 2005.

Chanel, Coco (1883–1971)

A touchstone of elegant women's leisure wear and tailored office wear, the Parisian couturier Coco Chanel changed the female silhouette from fussy to relaxed and self-confident. Her simple but chic designs in the mid-twentieth century, including the "little black dress," reflected the new social freedom of women, and her branded accessories and perfumes—including the world-famous Chanel No. 5 scent—earned a reputation for chic luxury.

She was born Gabrielle Bonheur Chanel on August 19, 1883, to journeyman Albert Chanel and laundress Eugénie "Jeanne" Devolle at a convent hospital in Saumur, France. Jeanne's death from consumption in 1895 broke up the couple's six children. Abandoned with her two sisters, Chanel entered a Cistercian orphanage in Aubazine in south-central France and learned to sew.

Six years later, at a shelter for orphaned teens in Moulins, Chanel obtained work as a seamstress and modiste (hat and dress designer), followed by stints as a hosiery shop clerk and cabaret singer in Moulins and Vichy. She picked up the nickname Coco for songs associated with her nightclub performances.

With the aid of model/actress Gabrielle Dorziat, Chanel began selling hats at her Paris millinery near the Tuileries Gardens. In 1913, a lover named Arthur Edward "Boy" Capel bankrolled Chanel's boutique at Deauville on the Normandy coast, where the designer's sister Antoinette and aunt, Adrienne Chanel, strolled through town modeling slim jackets, sailor blouses, crewneck sweaters, and espadrilles. The youth and vigor of her garments won notice in *Harper's Bazaar*.

In 1916, Chanel opened a business at Biarritz, a locale unaffected by World War I. She experimented with knit jersey, a comfortable fabric for women's travel suits, worn with low-heeled pumps. Two years later, she became one of the first designers featured in *Women's Wear Daily*. She invested in properties adjacent to her Paris boutique and merchandised jewelry, accessories, and hats to accompany her original garments.

After Capel died in a car crash in 1919, Chanel suffered depression, which she relieved in part by sun bathing. In December 1920, she assisted ballet promoter Sergei Diaghilev in costuming dancers for *Le Sacre du Printemps* (*The Rite of Spring*), beginning her career as a stage costumer. She admired the androgynous flapper chemise but became better known for Slavic beading, Russian tunic blouses, and the silk crepe "little black dress," a staple sheath she created in 1926 to the delight of editors at *Vogue*. In 1929, she debuted the Chanel bag, a small purse of quilted jersey or leather with thin straps that freed the hands.

In 1931, Chanel accepted a contract with MGM to costume film stars Gloria Swanson and

A pioneer of twentieth-century women's fashion, French designer Coco Chanel brought a relaxed elegance to leisure and business attire. Her "little black dress" reflected a new social freedom and confidence; her perfume line became a global leader. *(The Granger Collection, NYC—All rights reserved)*

Ina Claire. She popularized stretchy knits and influenced singers Maria Callas and Edith Piaf and actors Greta Garbo, Marlene Dietrich, and Clara Bow to base their wardrobes on black. Photographer Richard Avedon inserted dramatic elements in advertisements for Chanel, who marketed a one-of-a-kind collection of platinum and diamond jewelry. By 1935, Chanel employed 4,000 workers.

Disillusioned with Hollywood vulgarity, Chanel began designing for filmmaker Jean Renoir and playwright Jean Cocteau. During World War II, however, she put her career on hold and retreated to the Hotel Ritz in Paris, where she became the mistress of a German SS intelligence officer. Postwar proceeds from her perfumes made her phenomenally wealthy.

Following a nine-year retreat to Switzerland to escape blame for collaborating with the Nazis, Chanel returned to haute couture in 1954. Her suave women's wear contrasted Christian Dior's "New Look," a return to fabric stiffening, bust padding, and midriff cinches. Her defiance of confining female attire produced modernist elements—the black and beige sling back, pearls and diamond cuff bracelet, soft tweed suits with handy pockets, collarless jackets, chain belts, white-collared black pullovers, pea coats, bell bottoms, and cashmere cardigans.

French patriots shunned Chanel for her wartime anti-Semitism and allegiance to Germany, but her clothes found buyers in the United Kingdom and United States. For the biographical musical *Coco* (1969), Cecil Beaton dressed Katharine Hepburn in Chanel's chic "New Woman" suits. Still actively creating a spring line, Chanel died in her sleep on January 10, 1971.

In the 2000s, repro factories copied Chanel's ensembles, marked by the interlocking double C, her logo. A long list of empowered women from the twentieth century honor Chanel for streamlining female fashion.

See also: Fashion Design; French Clothing and Fashion.

Further Reading

Chanel. www.chanel.com

Charles-Roux, Edmonde. *Chanel and Her World: Friends, Fashion, and Fame.* New York: Vendome, 2005.

Madsen, Axel. *Coco Chanel: A Biography.* New York: Bloomsbury, 2009.

Picardie, Justine. *Coco Chanel.* New York: HarperCollins, 2009.

Children's Clothing, Boys

Evolving globally from unisex outfits, boys' attire developed distinct masculine shapes and details. From prehistory, parents outfitted infants in practical day wear or allowed them to go naked, the practice in the Pacific and Caribbean isles. Magical thinking and male gender roles came into evidence early on. Clothing for Korean boys dating to 3000 B.C.E. includes animal fangs tied at the midline to scare off danger. The Hmong of Southeast China supplied homespun pants and tunics during lessons for boys on hunting, plowing, planting crops, and harvesting.

Evolving Styles for Toddlers to Teens

During the Middle Ages in Europe, the A-line shift and gown for boys closed in front with a braid and buttons and remained loose at the bottom to aid the child in gaining stability. After learning to walk, the Renaissance Italian boy graduated to the braided cap, soled hose, and "long clothes," a frock or *giornee* (overgown), a unisex tabard or cloak left open on the sides. In coastal South America during the early 1500s, Inca boys wore cotton tunics and grass sandals stitched with yarn. Chinese farm boys received hemp shirts and pants for fieldwork. Ukrainian families embroidered homespun linen tunics, the mainstay in the wardrobes of young men.

When English boys reached the "breeching" age, a traditional rite of passage achieved sometime between ages 4 and 6, they graduated from lacy dresses to smocks over adult-style linen or light wool knee pants and trousers. In mid-eighteenth-century France, tailored frock coats, silk dressing gowns, and wigs for boys echoed the ornate styles of their fathers. Later that century, European boys played in comfortable two-piece outfits, kneesocks, and buckle shoes. In Alaska,

Inuit boys stayed warm in caribou hide or sealskin snowsuits.

For toddlers in towns and cities of Western Europe and the Americas, eighteenth-century front- or side-laced turnshoes in kid leather extended support up the ankle. Elite children's shoes featured soft leather soles and uppers with square toes for wearing with ribbed knit socks or full-length cotton or linen stockings. Ankle boots in natural leather featured tongue construction gathered at the front for extra toe room. A softer version paired leather toes with fabric uppers tightened at the ankle with a drawstring, a common clothing fastener of the era.

In the nineteenth century, throughout Northern Europe and Russia, two-piece outfits combined long-sleeved smocks with leggings. According to Regency portraits (1811–1820), the high-waisted denim "skeleton suit," a one-piece play outfit, contained a set-in waistband attached to a gathered bodice and pants. By 1872, as boys ventured from home to outdoor play, their clothing followed Empire patterns in a masculine blue chambray.

In the Americas and Europe, department stores promoted the sale of complete schoolboy wardrobes for a single price. Vests completed the ensembles with manly buttons and miniature watch pockets. Pull-on boots with brass- or copper-plated toes, elastic side panels, and pull-on straps emulated men's styles and paired with ready-to-wear stockings.

Early Twentieth Century

In North America and Europe around 1917, gray, white, or khaki sailor suits, Norfolk-style canvas jackets, Buster Brown and navy pea coats, denim knee pants and shorts, double-breasted wool serge coats, and lace-collared Fauntleroy and side-buttoned shirts continued the differentiated attire of male youths. Tweed suits with matching dickey and belt, jodhpurs, denim and khaki uniform shirts and jackets, flat leather caps, and berets with navy emblems further epitomized young masculine style. Undershirts with drawstring necklines, flared cuff mittens, and gloves with wrist snaps detailed the style of cold weather attire.

Post–World War I accessories for boys included clocked (detailed) socks, black stockings, Civil War kepis (visor caps), and fleece-lined aviator caps. Suspenders with elastic garters held cuffed socks and cable knit kneesocks in place. Canvas jackets, fake fur cap and coat ensembles, mesh stockings, and fleece-lined undershirts insulated the body in Scandinavia. Lapp boys wore high-neck knit pullovers banded in traditional symbols at the neck, shoulders, cuffs, and waist.

In the 1920s, button-sided overalls, long tunic and trouser outfits, and linen shirts with chambray button-on shorts added fashion notes to U.S. boys' wardrobes. As they acquired independence, American youths discovered a gendered panache in navy gabardine suits, wool knickers, riding pants, and denim coveralls and shorts with D-ring web belts. Adjustable undershirts, long-sleeved union suits, side-buttoned shirts with banded collars, and fold-over cuffs on kneesocks accentuated maturity. Shoe stores fitted boys with buckled, fringed, and tasseled boots and shoes, sold with matching caps.

In the 1930s, American, British, and Australian boys wore rubber boots with felt linings and canvas slouch hats or felt berets to accompany stirrup pants and crushed velveteen double-breasted coats. High-tops in two-tone leather offered lace-up vamps, a rounded toe, diamond punch work, and less trim at the ankles. Short-sleeved shirts exhibited the front plackets and fold-back collars of adult men's attire. Corduroy and cotton pique extended the life of play shorts and pants. Short summer playsuits added piped bands and matching neckerchiefs for style.

Postwar Trends

From 1946 to the 1960s, boys' outfits in the United States and Europe ventured toward collegiate styles with two-tone varsity and V-neck sweaters, striped T-shirts, baseball uniforms, and notched-collar gabardine or twill jackets with billed Arctic caps. In the Alps, lederhosen with a drop-front flap and leather suspenders survived rough play and hiking. Males emulated the military with anchors and red, white, and blue braid on jackets, riding pants, and neckerchiefs. Playtime called for canvas athletic shoes with traction treads and colorful laces.

U.S. television introduced fantasy dressing with Davy Crockett coonskin caps, Howdy Doody Western jeans and plaid shirts, and Mouseketeer skullcaps with ears. Felt cowboy hats, fiberboard helmets, T-shirts in cotton terry cloth, and ribbed knit briefs introduced adult-style leisure wear to pair with cotton pants held up by elastic suspenders.

In the 1960s and 1970s, American boys preferred long-sleeved pullovers or patchwork cowboy shirts, authentic snap-waist denim bell bottoms, and standard Wranglers with contrasting top stitching to wear with nylon-topped plastic zip-up boots and imitation Vietnam combat boots. Mock neck sweaters with patch pockets on the chest came in a variety of patterns and colors.

Mothers applauded Sears Toughskins, children's denim playwear in regular and slim cuts. Made from cotton, nylon, and polyester yarns, the jeans offered reinforced knees to protect the garments from wear. Play attire consisted of polyester/cotton blends in paisleys, polka dots, and checks for shirts, button-down plaid flannel shirts and flannel-lined jeans for winter, and seersucker for hot weather. Dressier pants in Great Britain sported permanent cuffs and creases for wear with gold-button blazers. Nylon windbreakers bore team names and emblems.

As a result of globalization in the final decade of the twentieth century, two-piece sweat suits and cotton/polyester cargo pants, worn over turtlenecks or raglan-sleeve T-shirts, placed the adult silhouette on boys worldwide. One-piece bathing suits of nylon/Lycra came in the same sporty stripes as polo shirts. Nylon sneakers with Velcro® straps introduced a fitted shoe that did not require the child to tie a bow. Variable closures also accommodated different thicknesses of socks, from thin anklets and tights to thicker tennis socks and cabled kneesocks.

Oshkosh introduced a slimmer fit in elastic-waist pants for wearing over adult-type Jockey briefs and teaming with sherpa-lined jeans jackets, plaid flannel loggers' shirts, camouflage sweatshirts, sports jerseys, hoodies, and football-shaped fleece slippers. Lycra bathing suits in abstract

prints echoed the designs of beach towels and umbrellas. For snowy days, elongated toboggans (stocking caps) with colorful pompoms complemented boots and jackets. Pajamas, robes, and underwear featured comic-book superheroes Spiderman, Batman, the Hulk, and Angry Birds, among other pop culture icons.

See also: Baby Clothes; Children's Clothing, Girls.

Further Reading

Cook, Daniel Thomas. *The Commodification of Childhood: The Children's Clothing Industry and the Rise of the Child Consumer.* Durham, NC: Duke University Press, 2004.

Marshall, Noreen. *Dictionary of Children's Clothes: 1700s to Present.* New York: Victoria and Albert Museum, 2008.

Paoletti, Jo B. *Pink and Blue: Telling the Boys from the Girls in America.* Bloomington: Indiana University Press, 2012.

Children's Clothing, Girls

Global fashion for girls has fluctuated over time from imitations of women's wear to adaptations of boys' apparel. After 2700 B.C.E., Hmong girls in southeastern China studied stitchery from age six in preparation for making wedding bodices, skirts, sashes, and tasseled headdress in time for marriage at age 14. In medieval China, girls wore a *dou dou* (apron) until age three; asymmetric patchwork jackets for girls tied on the side over trousers. Islamic needlework, tatting, and crochet graced girls' caps, cuffs, and bodices with fertility symbols, numerology, and blessings.

Mexican girls wore tunics embroidered with beneficent spiders. Afghan girls wore ankle-length dresses with trousers over sandals. In Turkey and India, stitchery protected disabled children with magic squares and grids. Thirteenth-century Scandinavian families tucked bearskin lap robes and throws over girls and women to protect them from frostbite and windburn.

During the Renaissance in Europe, French girls acquired the whaleboned girdling and wide skirts of adult women. In Ecuador, sundresses displayed hand embroidery in primary colors on stylized flower shapes. In seventeenth-century China, girls slipped padded overshoes over decorative slippers. In 1660, French staymakers shaped wood splits, reeds, or baleen into vertical ribbing to apply to girls' undergarments. Parents approved stiff corsetry for their daughters as posture support and preparation for womanhood.

Just for Girls

In the mid-eighteenth century, European and North American girls' fashions deviated from adult laced stays for correct posture under panniered gowns to attire made specifically for youth. Girls donned drop-waist dresses and tied velveteen ribbons at the neck. In 1781 at the London Foundling Hospital, young girls wore short coats, aprons, and washable cotton rompers sewn by older children at the hospital.

Nineteenth-century proselytizing by Christians and Muslims forced Malay girls to cover their torsos with a bodice. In 1803, the Padri movement in western Sumatra expounded Muslim revivalism along with the wearing of white clothing for girls as a symbol of chastity. In Melaka, Malaysia, during the 1820s, Nyonya girls dressed in sarongs or long dresses garnished with brooches. Unfinished calico and muslin from India reached global colonies via the British East India Company for use in smocks and petticoats. Givers of birthday presents favored coral beads that seamen dredged up on the shores of the Mediterranean Sea. The orange necklace, choker, cameo, or bracelet reputedly protected the wearer from rickets, stomach cramps, fever, smallpox, and typhus.

For pioneer families on the Oregon Trail after 1836, the recycling of canvas wagon covers yielded weathered fabric for dresses, sunbonnets, and aprons. Yarn unraveled from old sweaters supplied material for knit caps and mittens. In log cabins and sod huts across the North American heartland, girls learned to sew their own clothes and bonnets and make patchwork gifts and wardrobes for dolls from scraps and animal pelts. By weighting hems, mothers protected their daughters' legs from prairie gales and blizzards.

In the mid-1860s, velvet Alice bands modeled on British artist John Tenniel's illustrations from *Alice's Adventures in Wonderland* (1865) held hair off the face. Sashed pinafores favoring shades of pink

covered dresses during play as a protection from spills and tears. Throughout the British colonies, the addition to bonnets of face and neck ruffles and neck drapes, quilted or woven straw crowns, and bills in silk faille enhanced femininity while protecting delicate skin from the sun and wind.

In preparation for womanhood in Westernized societies, parents dressed little girls in linen pantalettes with scallop trim, cloth and whalebone corsets, and wire hoop skirts. Style-conscious mothers completed the ensemble with the habiliments of the fashionable adult pictured in *Godey's Lady's Book*. Gathering along the bodice of the high-waisted Empire dress, slip, or pinafore, cap sleeves, and complementary linen undershirt eased the fit for mobility and comfort.

Patterned calicos, plaid velvet, piqué, and black silk produced long bustled overdresses and aprons for the stylish girl. For outdoor wear, high-button shoes, unheeled moccasins with high backs and low vamp, and buckled Mary Janes in pastel colors offered adult styles with rounded toes, cutouts, and soft linings. In Japan, girls wore inexpensive straw *waraji* (sandals) in dry weather and geta (clogs) in rain and mud.

On the Iberian Peninsula, designers accented European girls' wool capes, boleros, brocaded polonaises (puffed tunics), and yoked bodices with soutache braids, insets, frog closures, beading, silk linings, tatting, and quilting. Turtleneck sweaters under chambray jumpers and dolman-style capes increased choices in layered dressing for outdoors. More elegant dressing called for ermine stoles, angora muff and collar sets, and beaver fur coats with silk linings, common sights in Scandinavia and Russia.

In North America, flattop bonnets featured woven straw, satin ribbon, and rosette trim in styles imitating adult female hats. Ear flaps added upper body warmth, as did wool knit collars. Elegant satin or suede slippers emulated the ankle ties of ballet toe shoes, a British trend. Slip-on Albert shoes with colonial toe buckles or leather bows, low-heeled boots with kid or fabric tops, and Mary Janes in patent leather over silk stockings offered adult comfort and decor.

Early Twentieth Century

In the first decades of the 1900s, girls in industrialized nations dressed in fake fur coats over silk georgette, seersucker, Battenberg lace, or batiste dropwaist gowns, two-piece dresses with machine-lace appliqué, peplum overblouses, sheer camisoles and pinafores, aprons, and A-line slips without hoops or bustles. Surplice necklines, knife pleats, and shawl collars along with wide pleated fan-topped hats replicated comfortable afternoon ensembles for adult women. A trend toward sculpted collars and banded hems on dresses continued the evolution of little girls' fashions away from frills.

For play in urban America, Australia, and Europe, girls moved freely in muslin middy blouses and baggy linen knickers, two-piece bathing suits, and lace-up gaiter boots or white canvas shoes, a jaunty style copied from boys' fashions. Ensembles featured chambray skirts over wool bloomers, two-strap sandals, knitted mohair tams and berets, beaver fur hats, and double-breasted melton cloth coats. White kid gloves and satin ballet slippers with kid soles enhanced the girlishness of female apparel.

In the 1920s, Filipina girls made attire from abaca, a fiber extracted by machine from hemp. In the United States, meanwhile, girls of the Jazz Age wore heeled canvas oxfords, high-top lace-up boots, round-toed button-sided boots, web belts, and gaiter boots that emulated feminist modes. Two-tone rayon or voile dresses, chambray jumpers with buttoned straps, smocked calico blouses with matching gauze aprons, garters, bloomers, buckram cloche hats, and floral nighties expressed budding femininity. For play, one-piece bathing suits, linen knickers with knit drawers, and Peter Pan collar shirts encouraged freedom in the outdoors. Fake fur cloches with braided bands covered heads in snowy weather.

In the 1930s, girlish taste, epitomized by the movies of Shirley Temple, received input from style-savvy department store clerks. Parents encouraged self-conscious dressing and vanity by choosing the chemise dress in sheer cotton, smocked two-tone dresses and self-sash sleeveless dresses for every day, and the wool crepe dress and cape or dotted swiss dress with a cardigan sweater

for dress-up. Formal dresses came with tulle headpieces consisting of rosettes and ribbons on wire frames. Play outfits coordinated sleeveless gym suits with sandals and chamois-edged snowsuits with hoods or felted wool cloches.

Era of Convenience and Mass Media

After World War II, girls' fashions in the United States and Japan echoed the military theme of boys' styles in sailor dresses with acetate trim around the collar and Hollywood-style boy-leg bathing suits and fringed cowgirl skirts, vests, and separate cuffs and Western hats. School outfits in the United States and Great Britain combined blouses with plaid skirts and suspenders. Leggings accompanied cheviot (sheepskin) coats with fur collars. Anklet socks complemented oxfords or two-strap shoes with metal studs around the vamp to accompany sheer sundresses and pinafores. At bedtime, crepe kimonos covered nightgowns, some printed with cartoon characters.

In the mid-twentieth century, one-piece snowsuits, modeled after U.S. Air Force and NASA styles, zipped across the shoulders and from the neck to the left stirrup. Sweaters for girls topped the neck seam with a hood, drawstring, and tassels. Fruit appliqué and bias tape edgings decorated denim tops. Elastic-waist corduroy pants, shortalls, and jeans pulled on easily below T-shirts featuring Disney cartoon characters.

U.S. and European girls' wardrobes contained dress-up attire made from organdy, chiffon, and taffeta tied at the waist with grosgrain ribbon. Denim play clothes sported embroidered animals, moon and stars, and rainbows. Jeans and Wrangler shorts with bandanna print peasant blouses and ponchos imitated hippie wear. Globally, Ethiopian-style cornrowing appealed to children emulating African styles.

At century's end, designs for American girls dressed up corduroy jeans, hip huggers, and overalls with floral prints and adorned nightgowns with Smurfs, Strawberry Shortcake, and popular cartoon figures screen-printed on the front. Skirts bore appliqués in primary colors to wear with colorful tights, suede sneakers, and T-shirts. Sneakers and perennial Mary Janes continued to dominate the shoe market in man-made acrylics and patent leather. For nighttime, fake fur slippers took the shapes of koalas, dogs, and cats.

In the early 2000s, immodest girls' clothes worldwide alarmed parents and educators. Stylish outfits paired one-shoulder tanks with mock-cheerleader miniskirts. Skinny jeans, jeggings (a cross between jeans and leggings), and bikinis introduced tweens to provocative dressing. Schools combated immodesty by instituting uniforms.

See also: Baby Clothes; Children's Clothing, Boys.

Further Reading

Cook, Daniel Thomas. *The Commodification of Childhood: The Children's Clothing Industry and the Rise of the Child Consumer.* Durham, NC: Duke University Press, 2004.

Marshall, Noreen. *Dictionary of Children's Clothes: 1700s to Present.* New York: Victoria and Albert Museum, 2008.

Paoletti, Jo B. *Pink and Blue: Telling the Boys from the Girls in America.* Bloomington: Indiana University Press, 2012.

Chinese Clothing

In a nation comprising 56 ethnicities, Chinese attire has historically displayed native technology and regional elegance. In 3000 B.C.E., Gansu folk styles of north-central China consisted of a long poncho cinched at the waist with rope. Jewelry made from bones, shells, turquoise, jade, and ivory complemented sashes. Ornaments dressed hair and beards that citizens never cut.

Early Dynasties

Traditional Han Chinese style, called Hanfu, dated to the Shang dynasty after 1600 B.C.E., when clothes evolved symmetry of design and harmony of color and pattern. Knee-length tunics with curved hems paired with long sashed skirts or split-crotch pants, which dictated methods of dressing, kneeling, and sitting to conceal the privates. To denote social hierarchy, designers awarded the imperial family and upper class ankle-length sleeves, ample cloaks, ornate embellishments, and tall phoenix crowns, all of the finest silks. Both genders wore loose wrapped tops over pants for leisure.

In the Western Zhou dynasty after 1046 B.C.E., laws established dress codes for courtiers, brides, soldiers, ancestor worshippers, and mourners. Only the emperor robed himself in yellow. The gentry chose from black, green, red, and white. Chinese women popularized wigs to give fullness and adornment to the head. Males adopted wigs as indications of dignity and prominence. Mummies from this era at Taklamakan wore two-tone plaids identifying clan membership.

By 770 B.C.E., matriarchal clans of the Spring and Autumn period liberalized dress codes. Felt or straw slippers and high-top leather boots with treaded soles suited the needs of most Chinese. In the Warring States period after 475 B.C.E., women abandoned traditional braids and coiled their hair into buns.

Civilian box-toed and turned-up-toed shoes as seen in the terra-cotta army statues buried with Emperor Qin Shi Huangdi in 210 B.C.E. reflected the footwear of men. Western Han rulers after 206 C.E. encouraged simple dress based on the seasons. By 220, the migrations of people from distant regions to central China encouraged blended and assimilated styles, including the Bai octagonal head scarf, Hani turban, Dai silver ornamentation, and Lisu pleated skirt.

Migrations from the north brought Mongol influences. By 280, the Chinese had adopted Hun felt for shaping into headbands and girdles and, later, into druggets, body drapes fastened across the torso with bindings. After 618, the beginning of the Tang dynasty, the Chinese empress Lady Dou wore a ceremonial hairpiece to which she attached ornaments. Wig coverage extended from the hairline to frame the features of locals and missionary priests posted to China.

During the Tang dynasty in the southwest, Chinese men popularized a broad-toed closed pump with single strap similar to the Mary Jane. Women's shoes featured phoenix designs that coordinated with jackets, skirts, and trousers. From 618, Korean minorities in China wore the one-piece wood clog for wet weather; for indoor wear, they wore the short boot, a felt or soft cloth shoe attached to a flat sole.

The south-central Chinese of Guizhou Province

The silk elegance of Chinese women's shoes from the nineteenth century belies the painful and crippling tradition of foot binding. The practice stunted growth from early childhood to keep women's feet "dainty." Short, arched shoes enhanced the tiny image. *(SSPL/Getty Images)*

adapted traditional costumes with the batiking of lotus and peony patterns and geometric designs on bleached cloth made of hemp or cotton. Using a thin bronze knife to edge sharp outlines, minority Miao crafters applied indigo to freehand clouds, dragons, and serpents with beeswax or worm wax in deep blue and white.

The Bound Foot

Into the early Middle Ages, Chinese women displayed attractive feet in form-fitting uppers with soft padded soles and toes pointed no more than 1 inch (2.5 centimeters). Around 950, however, the epitome of male dominance emerged with the binding, folding under, and breaking of little girls' toes to warp the arch and shorten the foot. The concept of foot binding grew in the families of high court officials out of the Confucian ideal of the sedentary wife, mother, and needleworker.

With gauze swaddling and the careful tying of loops and laces, the mother forced her daughter's feet into the prescribed shape and size, 3 inches (7.6 centimeters) long. Little girls learned to cope with pain that readied them for childbirth. As the arch took on a tight U shape, dusting with medicated powder softened ligaments, concealed odors from constrained tissue, and sped healing from injury to softened ligaments. As the child grew, constant binding reshaped the sole into

the eroticized adult image called *jinlian* (golden lilies).

Wealthy females gave up mobility and self-direction to indulge the male fantasy of the tiny-footed woman. The process yielded a horrific deformation of the lower limbs with "lotus feet," a romanticized symbol of fertility that women topped with leggings in order to conceal distorted anklebones. Heel inserts under the sole, high heels, external tabs and heel straps, and tasseling enhanced the optical illusion of a tiny arched foot. The downward curve mimicked the carp, emblem of the treasured bride. The creation of the small foot bestowed admiration and status to the adult female for her shuffling gait or hobbling on the knees.

Custom arched slippers featured thin hemp or padded soles and high silk vamps embroidered with flowers and bound along the center seam from toe to throat in ornate braid. Wood clogs bore intricate vine and flower motifs lacquered to shield them from wear. Overshoes with layers of quilted cotton protected delicate shoes; straw versions strapped to the ankle to give traction for walking. Other models featured pegged treads for wet weather and felt snowshoes waterproofed with tar.

Despite Manchu laws criminalizing foot binding after the founding of the Qing dynasty in 1644 and the condemnation of Christian missionaries, the mutilation of women's feet continued until the establishment of Mao Zedong's Communist regime in 1949.

Breaks with Tradition

After 1644, when European women cultivated the long, slim foot silhouette, Manchu emperors banned traditional Chinese styles. Gentlewomen elevated their shoes with high-heel platforms. In the 1840s, at the height of Western influence, Chinese men favored an unfitted boot, broad at the upturned toe, to wear with Mandarin jackets. The conical red silk hat with sable brim distinguished Qing dynasty apparel until the early 1900s. After 1912, women in the Republic of China bound their breasts with vests. China's interaction with Westerners introduced the felt cap, Henley boater, and homburg, styles unknown in Asia before the 1910s.

Among the Hoklo and Tanka fisherfolk of Hong Kong, cotton or hemp baby carriers bore lucky symbols appliquéd on a patchwork pouch along with bells to protect infants from harm. At the child's birth, friends contributed red yarn for the making of "hundred families tassels" worn by infants to secure their fortune. Mothers strengthened the child's luck with red cords tied around ankles and wrists.

In 1927, at the time when Chinese mothers were abandoning breast binding, they added to the infant wardrobe a navel cover to secure the abdomen from abrasion within a hemp carrier. Families spread a cloth lattice support for an infant's head while lying in adult arms.

In the 1950s, in contrast to American fads, Chinese boys and girls continued to wear the long, side-fastening tunic embroidered with lucky symbols and a surcoat for New Year's gatherings and formal occasions. Infant hats in animal shapes bulging eyes and oversized fangs symbolically provided children with protection and ears attuned to danger. Appliquéd segmented collars with five or six lobes featured lucky red tones and tiger shapes. Quilted or padded wind hats with pompoms for boys added traditional neck flaps to protect from drafts. Girls wore plain satin or silk earmuffs that cloaked the ears. Fur from protective animals edged the oval shapes. Under the rule of Mao Zedong in 1966, the Miao painted cotton baby carriers and hats with Communist slogans, such as "Red flower at sunrise" and "Long Live the Cultural Revolution," and rising suns and bat and cat motifs, emphasizing the luck of nocturnal hunters.

In 1978, during the early post-Mao era, China emerged from drab colors and rigid Mao jackets to adopt the high heels, jeans, plaids, disco shirts, sneakers, permed hair, and sunglasses of Western attire. In Zhengzhou in 2003, activist Wang Letian, father of the Hanfu movement, revived folk dressing by appearing in a traditional belted robe and skirt. Community discussions increased public enthusiasm for the national costume, which Western styles subsumed. Citizens chose Hanfu outfits for school and work, coming-of-age ceremonies, holidays, and weddings.

Fabric innovations in synthetics offered new materials such as Velcro® and high-impact plastics for garments, shoes, and millinery. Industrial investment made China the world's largest apparel manufacturer. In the 2010s, panne velvet required treating with sodium hydrogen sulfate to dissolve cellulose pile shaping a motif, a favorite material for making the slim-fitting cheongsam (Chinese dress) with side slits.

See also: Ethnic and National Dress; Orientalism; Slippers; Tunics and Togas.

Further Reading

Finnane, Antonia. *Changing Clothes in China: Fashion, History, Nation.* New York: Columbia University Press, 2008.

Garrett, Valery. *Chinese Dress: From the Qing Dynasty to the Present.* North Clarendon, VT: Tuttle, 2007.

Hua, Mei. *Chinese Clothing.* New York: Cambridge University Press, 2011.

Tsui, Christine. *China Fashion: Conversations with Designers.* New York: Bloomsbury, 2010.

Circus Costumes

An element of surprise and spectacle in live performance, circus costumes have set the tone of animal and clown acts, aerial artistry, and ensemble processions since at least ancient Egypt. The earliest known appearance of street mimes occurred in 2270 B.C.E. under Pharaoh Pepi II. The grotesquerie of the mime influenced the evolution of the Greek god Typhon, the comic with the waggling tongue. Similar frivolity at Mohenjo-daro, present-day Pakistan, from 2500 B.C.E. depicted a troupe of dwarfs dancing to the tap of drums around their necks.

The Ancient Circus

After 700 B.C.E., exaggerated tunics, capes, and props marked Corinthian, Doric, and Spartan clowns, who displayed oversized swords and padded phalluses as sources of derision. After the Jugurthine War in 94 B.C.E., the Roman statesman Lucius Cornelius Sulla entertained the citizenry with a hunt for Mauretanian lions led by North Africans in native dress. Charioteers in Rome's Circus Maximus raced horses under four explicit colors—green, gray, orange, and white. For the costumes of circus performers, weavers mixed extracts of alum, woad, madder, broom, pomegranate seed, and Egyptian acacia for unusual tints.

The invasion of Rome by Alaric and the Visigoths in 410 destroyed the imperial economy, including the importation of dyestuffs from Africa and Asia. For the next millennium, circuses and animal acts traveled to the outer rim of the Roman Empire with a ragtag collection of garments and spangles acquired at flea markets. Circus acts in Constantinople's Hippodrome featured charioteers in racing green, red, white, or blue as well as pantomime dances, wild beast shows, pole vaulters, and theatrical hunts featuring mock armor and shields.

Theodora, the wife of the Emperor Justinian, grew up in a circus family. She, her sisters, and their widowed mother performed in flower garlands. Theodora starred in a bird act in which she stripped most of her clothes and allowed geese to peck barley from her torso. Because of ecclesiastical strictures against nudity by Byzantine clergy, only circus performers and dancers displayed bare arms and lower legs.

Farther east, India maintained the prominence of vivid costumes for Vidushaka, the stock comic in *kutiyattam,* classical Sanskrit drama. Dressed in vivid black, red, and white with torn boots and a fantastic headdress, and carrying a crooked stick, he colored his face green above a paper frame about the jaws, the source of classic wisdom. His buffoonery prepared the audience for a series of outlandish lapses and eccentricities that satirized human frailties, especially gluttony.

Revival

More peaceful times in Europe during the 1200s restored dyeing to the fashion arts, a revival explained by commentary in Geoffrey Chaucer's *Canterbury Tales* (1385). Circus costumes added flair to contortion, sleight of hand, storytelling, and puppetry. For Punch and Judy acts in the 1500s, seamstresses sewed miniature costumes from scraps of red velvet for Punch's tasseled cap and suit and a yellow muslin mobcap and apron for Judy, the perennial housewife.

Renaissance jesters chose yellow and green to color jackets, hoods, and hose and elicited applause by tumbling in costumes edged in bells. The Italian version of the madcap, known as Arlecchino, sported patchwork or motley for his improvisational *lazzi* (skits). The British version depicted the fool as an unschooled rustic dressed in plowman's attire and battered boots and cap. In North America during the 1660s, following the austere rule of Puritans, farceurs and quipsters added fluffy mustaches and wigs to their court costumes to enhance zany repartee.

In clown regalia for circuses, a stark white base grounded eye, nose, mouth, and neck makeup in red and black. London-born mime Joseph "Joey" Grimaldi painted his complexion for the role of Pierrot, a comic servant invented by the playwright Molière in 1673. Reputedly the inventor of the whiteface clown, Grimaldi covered his face and neck in chalky white and reddened his lips and two triangles on his cheeks to accompany a baggy white suit, neck ruff, red-striped hose, slippers, and a blue Mohawk ruff on his head. Stylized greasepaint around his eyes and mouth projected the grimaces and shocks of his playacting, an influence of New York clown George "Humpty Dumpty" Fox.

Three-Ring Circus

Circus as a pop culture art form dates to 1763, when English soldier Philip Astley showcased horse training, juggling, tumbling, and rope dancing acts throughout Europe. The clown, Mr. Merryman, played by John Ducrow, sported a baggy blue playsuit, red-and-white-striped hose and sleeves, white ruff, tufts of hair, and cheeks and lips enhanced with red. Clad in powdered queue, black coat, white jabot, and knee boots, Astley created the persona of the ringmaster, who summoned animals with a crack of his whip.

Jacob Bates, a contemporary, took equestrian acts to Germany, Russia, and North America, where horsemen appeared in plush riding habits. In 1782, trick rider Charles Hughes gave the name "circus" to the show that entertained Russian empress Catherine the Great in St. Petersburg. Other late eighteenth-century entrepreneurs assembled acts and costumes to delight patrons in Philadelphia, Montreal, Havana, and Mexico City.

In Paris in 1800, Laurent Franconi's military-style horse tricks coordinated gold-edged satin horse blankets and matching red military jacket with gold braid and riding crop. Acrobat Jules Léotard inspired a multipurpose outfit in the 1850s made from red-and-gold-fringed buskins, collar, and kilt over a skintight white knit body stocking named "leotard" in his honor. For La Course aux Trapèzes at the Cirque Napoléon, Léotard jumped from bar to bar in stretchy comfort topped by the flame-stitched costume. London-born high-wire artist Selina Dolaro feminized the stretchy bodysuit with plaid bloomers and high-heeled buskins.

Extravagant color marked the style and effect of the bumbling French *auguste* (trickster clown). Face paint in pearl powder, carmine from cochineal and alumina, powdered vegetable rouge, and Chinese blacking caused no harm to the comic's skin, but applications of bismuth, arsenic, white lead, and cinnabar (sulphur of mercury) poisoned the body, caused palsy, and wrinkled the skin.

In 1840, "Yankee Dan" Rice, a forerunner of Uncle Sam, Americanized circus costuming with a stovepipe hat, blue leotard, and red and white tights. In 1866, French trick rider Louis Soul-lier promoted ethnic costuming with perch-pole, juggling, hoop-diving, and plate-spinning acts featuring Chinese troupers. Costumers of Japanese circuses limited male acrobats, gymnasts, and animal tamers to solid colors. More vivid presenters sparked visual thrills with short, flouncy skirts and umbrellas on female riders, matching suspendered pants on Tweedledum and Tweedledee, sashes and lace-up boots on strongmen, and striped jester suits and caps on amputees.

Getups and Greasepaint

According to *De Witt's How to Manage Amateur Theatricals* (1880), greasepaint and lining sticks came on the market in tones suited to Italian, Gypsy (Roma), Chinese, Moorish, African, and East and North American Indian complexions. By 1900, clowns used paint, outsized props, rubber skullcaps, and wigs to accessorize stereotypical costumes of the bindle stiff, keystone cop, dwarf, and man in women's attire. Props ranged from ragged bindle and nightstick to the oversized female pocketbook and veiled hat.

In 1919, Ringling Brothers cut costs by leaving up to employees and sideshow freaks the fabrics and trappings of gilded headdresses, tutus, belly pads, firemen's uniforms, and baggy drawers that would hold up to hard wear while fostering sight gags and pratfalls. The full effect of ragged clothes, sprigs of hair, and face paint projected a happy, quizzical, or sad emotion, the standard expression of hobo clown Emmett Kelly. After 1923, Kelly turned his tragic figure of Weary Willie into a circus classic.

Managers highlighted the exotic capes and feathers of elephant riders, form-fitting tights of musclemen, animal skin sarongs and grass skirts of Africans, and the allure of bosom-revealing bodices edged in sequins, iridescent bangles, and marabou, and the body paint of the semi-naked "statue girl," the specialty of Hungarian performer Tiny Kline. In her memoir, Kline explained the purpose of bare-midriff costumes and long, beaded fringe. In "cooch" shows, flashy beads accentuated the shimmies of shoulders, breasts, and hips and the toss of matching garters. Aerialist Lillian Leitzel of Breslau, Germany, twirled from a swivel ring to display a costume of silver and pink so light that it looked like flesh.

As circus acts gravitated away from skin shows, the Russian circus in 1927 tapped the grace and strength of ballet by training gymnasts. Costumers and choreographers refined variety acts that whirled feathered capes and skirts appliquéd in beads, fringe, and satin. An American known for his exaggerated face paint and rhinestone nose, Felix Adler performed in the clown alley of Ringling Brothers Barnum and Bailey Circus, at the White House, and in the film *The Greatest Show on Earth* (1952). Adler's skills presaged face painting and acrylic modifications, an extension of makeup colors to emulate animals and fantasy figures.

In the late 1900s, the availability of Velcro®, Spandex, lamé, and traction soles increased the flexibility and safety of gaudy performance wardrobes for Australia's Circus Oz, the Canadian Cirque du Soleil, and Circus China's martial arts displays and acrobatics. Stilt walkers cloaked themselves in flashy synthetic fabrics, leopard prints, metallic bustiers, and vizards topped with rhinestone crowns, such as that worn by Ringling aerialist Dolly Jacobs. Elephant riders evoked the reds, pinks, and golds of India in body briefers that matched animal regalia. Canadian mime Richard Pochinko adapted the Amerindian *heyoka* act to clown repertory by substituting full-face masks for greasepaint.

See also: Motley; Patchwork.

Further Reading

Culhane, John. *The American Circus: An Illustrated History.* New York: Henry Holt, 1990.

Kline, Tiny. *Circus Queen & Tinker Bell: The Memoir of Tiny Kline.* Urbana: University of Illinois Press, 2008.

Neirick, Miriam. *When Pigs Could Fly and Bears Could Dance: A History of the Soviet Circus.* Madison: University of Wisconsin Press, 2012.

Claiborne, Liz (1929–2007)

Successful American businesswoman and trendsetter Liz Claiborne turned her moderately priced career clothing company into the nation's largest apparel distributor. Liz Claiborne Inc. became the first company founded by a woman to make the Fortune 500 list of largest U.S. corporations, and Claiborne herself became the first woman to serve as chair and CEO of a Fortune 500 company.

Born Anne Elisabeth Jane "Liz" Claiborne in Brussels, Belgium, on March 31, 1929, she was a scion of prestigious Louisianans. Her mother, Louise Carol Fenner Claiborne, instructed her in sewing and impeccable grooming. The family moved back to New Orleans when Claiborne was 10. She entered ninth grade at a boarding school called St. Timothy's in Catonsville, Maryland.

Her father, Omer Villere Claiborne, a financier with the Morgan Guaranty Trust Company, rescued her from a stereotypical education by sending her to Europe. In her teens, she studied color and proportion at the Fine Arts School and Painter's Studio in Brussels and the Nice Academy in France. Learning pattern making at night, she designed a woman's coat in 1948 that won the Jacques Heim competition for *Harper's Bazaar*.

At age 20, Claiborne began modeling and sketching sportswear for designer Tina Leser in New York City. In Milwaukee, she created preppy garments for Ben Reig, Juniorite, Dan Keller, and Rhea Manufacturing. A working wife and mother in 1954, she raised a son and two stepchildren while freelancing as head of the junior dress division of Jonathan Logan. The company's unwillingness to adapt to realistic ensembles for the 1970s inspired Claiborne to individualize her own styles for the American marketplace.

To provide alternatives to unattractive business suits, the designer and her husband, textile manufacturer Arthur Ortenberg, launched Liz Claiborne Inc. in 1976, and the company was an immediate financial success. By marketing no-iron sportswear for the middle-class professional lifestyle, the firm sold $2 million in goods during the first year. Claiborne's imaginative 9-to-5 wardrobe expanded choices in regular, petite, and tall separates—cowl-neck sweaters, ponchos, safari jackets, culottes, chinos and trousers, sarong skirts, rayon-silk blazers, chambray jumpsuits, and polyester crepe chemises.

In 1980, Claiborne became the first female fashion designer to earn Ernst & Young's prestigious Entrepreneur of the Year award. The introduction of Liz Claiborne Accessories that same year preceded the advance of the firm among Fortune 500 companies. By 1988, her separates, sold at Bloomingdale's, Dillard's, and Saks, dominated one-third of the American leisure market at the rate of $1.4 billion annually.

Key to Claiborne's weathering of shifts in fashion, a computerized inventory strategy returned data on each of her practical mix-and-match pieces sold under the Ellen Tracy, Russ, Lizwear, Lucky Brand, Lizsport, and Juicy Couture labels. Body scans at Cornell University determined the waist, hip, and inseam measurements of typical shoppers. For firsthand understanding of consumers, the designer posed as a clerk in department stores to hear comments and complaints.

In retirement at age 60, Claiborne employed 8,000 people who continued to build her line of scarves, contour belts, gloves, totes, and hats as well as flats and pumps, faux tortoise sunglasses, costume jewelry, and menswear. Upon her death at New York Presbyterian Hospital from abdominal cancer on June 26, 2007, she was admired in international business circles for succeeding in a male-dominated fashion world.

Her honors include election to the National Business Hall of Fame, a citation from the Council of Fashion Designers of America, a *Working Woman* "Women Who Have Changed the World" listing, a Woolknit Association Award, and a PhD from the Rhode Island School of Design. The original Liz Claiborne brand was sold to J.C. Penney in October 2011, and Liz Claiborne Inc. was officially renamed Fifth & Pacific Companies, Inc., on May 15, 2012.

See also: Fashion Design; Ready-to-Wear.

Further Reading

Chazen, Jerome A. *My Life at Liz Claiborne: How We Broke the Rules and Built the Largest Fashion Company in the World.* Bloomington, IN: AuthorHouse, 2011.

Fifth & Pacific Companies. http://fifthandpacific.com

Ortenberg, Art. *Liz Claiborne: The Legend, the Woman.* Lanham, MD: Taylor Trade, 2010.

Clan Attire

Since prehistory, co-descendants of kinship groups have displayed shared ancestry with body adornment and clan apparel crafted from traditional colors and patterns. Clan identification appears in the Old Testament in Numbers 2:2, regarding the separate encampments of Hebrew families in the Sinai. In the ancient world, textile motifs, amulets, and dynastic body markings—tooth ablation, scarification, tattoos of ancestral spirits, tribal body painting and piercing, coated hairstyles—identified affinity to a clan or sept, a branch of the family tree.

Clothing styles provided family members with differentiation from other clans. Examples include the pointed headdress of unwed Lolo and Shan women in Hsin-kai-tzu, China, the red petticoats and blue cloaks of clanswomen in Claddagh, Ireland, and the Gujjar turban and the sash tie and cock of the hat among Aziz and Burkoz clan members in Persia. Tartan garments, an ancient art form, marked apparel in Bhutan, Japan, Spain, Ireland, Austria, Wales, and central Africa.

In Kazakhstan around 2000 B.C.E., weavers shrouded mummies in black, blue, and yellow plaid. The oldest and humblest pattern, the Falkirk tartan (shepherd's check), originated with the Picts around 235 C.E. Weavers alternated natural yarns—brown or black with cream or white—in equal amounts over a herringbone weave. Among central Australian Aborigines, the feathered headdress worn by emu clan members for rituals established the clan totem as a source of guidance and strength.

Scots Plaid

From as early as 1578, Scottish clans provided armigers (members) with surnames, a shared family tree, and blood connection to a chief, which they displayed in kinship attire at clan gatherings, weddings, and funerals. Until the Battle of Culloden on April 16, 1746, and the suppression of Jacobite plots to place Charles Edward Stuart (Bonnie Prince Charlie) on the English throne, Scots wore tartans, one-piece wraparound garments that constituted the entire costume. As a gesture of clan solidarity, followers of the chief wore a tartan cloth or great wrap, a long garment gathered into folds and belted around the waist. However, clans displayed a variety of colors and patterns rather than a single uniform as group identification. Their woolen plaids (shoulder capes) prefigured the clan kilt, an untailored, multifunctional garment woven in homes and dyed from natural vegetable colors.

In 1581, historian George Buchanan admired woolens of purple and indigo, an imported dye from Holland. A subsequent eyewitness account from 1594 described Gaelic mercenaries from the Hebrides Islands dressed in plaids, calf-length cloaks fastened with girdles in the style of the belted plaid, the Scots national costume. Contemporaneous with the evolution of the kilt, the Balmoral bonnet, a round, flat-topped cap, repeated traditional colors in the felted or woven wool band.

Paintings from the seventeenth century corroborate earlier descriptions of male clan attire based on a 4-yard (3.7-meter) length of wool or linsey-woolsey. In 1618 at Braemar, a village in Aberdeenshire, poet John Taylor described hunting attire—a warm plaid mantle over the shoulders repeating the pattern of a tartan jerkin (tight jacket). Plaited straw or tufted garters secured the stockings.

Women established their own clan patterns, usually on a light background. *A Description of the Western Isles of Scotland* (1703), a travelogue by Martin Martin of Skye, characterized women's *earasaid* (also *arisaid* or *arisad*), a pleated cream or white plaid mantle or robe striped in black, blue, and red most common in the Hebrides Islands. Covering the body from the neck down, the 6-yard (5.5-meter) garment fastened with a buckle on the sternum and a leather belt around the waist. A linen head scarf and red sleeves adorned with gold lace and fine circular brooches completed the outfit.

Men's plaids, bearing the blues, golds, greens, oranges, reds, and yellows of individual districts, covered the left arm, draped the torso, and returned to the left arm. A leather belt secured pleating to

the knee in a shape known as the great kilt. An alternate pairing, the kilt worn with the fly plaid (tartan scarf), featured a lighter shoulder dressing that fell straight to the knee without encircling the shoulder.

Evolving Clan Dress

The eighteenth century brought change to the standard Highland plaid. As early as 1707, lowlanders emulated Highland clans by adopting their own plaids. In the 1720s, an adaptation by Quaker industrialist Thomas Rawlinson popularized the little kilt for the convenience of charcoal and iron foundrymen and lumbermen at factories in Glengarie and Lochaber. By cutting the plaid in half,

Scotsmen since the sixteenth century have donned wool plaids (shoulder capes) and kilts in a tartan (criss-cross pattern) featuring colors unique to specific clans. The British banned tartan from 1746 to 1782 to quell fighting between warrior clans. *(Antony Jones/UK Press via Getty Images)*

laborers discarded the top portion and wore only the kilt for indoor tasks.

The British well understood the value of the plaid to Scots clans. To suppress a revolt against the rule of William and Mary, the British Act of Proscription of 1746 attempted to destroy clan unity by placing a ban on plaids. To crush the feudal authority of chiefs, Parliament annulled inherited offices and threatened six months in prison or deportment to a British colony for infractions of the dress code. When a vote repealed the law in 1782, clan plaids surged in popularity.

At Bannockburn from 1770, lowland weaver William Wilson's factory made tartans sold throughout Europe, India, and the Western Hemisphere. Because he sought samples of tartans for pattern books with name and number identification, historians claim that Wilson linked individual designs with specific clans. The collection, perpetuated by his three sons, included the designs for more than 250 setts, or woven squares, notably Aberdeen and Dundee district tartans, priest tartans of blue or lavender with black for the clergy, and MacDonald and MacGregor clan tartans.

Tartans and Identity

The state visit of King George IV to Scotland in 1822 prompted Highlanders to make tartans their national dress. Led by poet Walter Scott, hosts to the king exhibited pride in their pageantry by wearing partially tailored kilts. Historians surmise that wearers may have attached loops to the plaid and threaded the length on a corded drawstring, a simple solution to the problem of forming pleats with one hand while enfolding the torso in cloth with the other. Regimental uniforms refashioned the plain round hummel bonnet into the glengarry, a thin back-to-front cap with pleated crown usually knitted and felted by a family member.

The systematic naming of tartans began after 1848, when Queen Victoria commissioned Prince Albert to refurbish Balmoral Castle, where Royal Stewart and Hunting Stewart plaids set the tone. The royal family dressed in tartans, a costume that fired local enthusiasm for clan apparel. The standard male morning dress included a gray or black kilt jacket, white shirt, and tartan vest or sack coat

(suit jacket) over the kilt, a Norse wraparound skirt with fringed aprons (end panels) lapped in front, left over right, and buckled at the right hip.

Over the kilt, the leather sporran adorned with tassels, animal heads, regimental horsehair, or a Celtic knot served as a pocket. To indicate peaceful intent, the right garter held in place a seventeenth-century antler-hilted single-edged dagger, a weapon the wearer could conceal in the armpit against criminal threats. Victoria's enthusiasm for clan attire took an unusual turn in 1880, when she presented Sultan Abu Bakr of Johor with his own tartan, a product of Thomas Gordon & Sons of Glasgow.

See also: British Clothing and Fashion; Color Trends; Ethnic and National Dress; Livery and Heraldry; Prehistoric Clothing; Symbolic Colors, Patterns, and Motifs.

Further Reading

Coe, Kathryn. *The Ancestress Hypothesis: Visual Art as Adaptation.* New Brunswick, NJ: Rutgers University Press, 2003.

Milne, Norman. *Scottish Culture and Traditions.* London: Paragon, 2010.

Schoeser, Mary. *World Textiles: A Concise History.* New York: Thames & Hudson, 2003.

Cloaks and Capes

From prehistory, short capes and long cloaks have provided a convenient shield against wind, cold, and damp. After 38,000 B.C.E., Australian Aborigines pieced mammal and bird pelts into unstructured cloaks suited to the needs of nomads. Around 6000 B.C.E., prehistoric intertwining of hammered cedar bark, raffia, palm fronds, and yucca fiber produced rain capes with a weave that shed rain. North African varieties from 4000 B.C.E. legitimized the dignity and status of priests wrapped in ceremonial leopard or panther skins adorned with foxtails. Asians and Europeans invented felt cloaks by layering and pounding animal hair into a matted material, such as the tent-shaped mantle or rain cape that Middle Eastern travelers pulled around them and over the head for a hooded cloak.

Cro-Magnon clothes makers stitched hides and rabbit pelts into cloaks and ponchos, such as those that ancient Germanic tribes laced around themselves with vines, roots, and babiche. After 12,000 B.C.E., the Ahrensburgian culture of Sweden, ancestors of the migratory Sami (Lapp) reindeer herders, increased the warmth of sealskin capes by lining them with fur. The Anasazi of the Great Basin of North America and the Yanomami of Brazil whipstitched fur tufts, horn, colored stones, and eagle, crane, egret, and turkey feathers to flat materials, such as elk hides, to shield body paint.

In 6000 B.C.E. east of the Tigris River, Ninevites pounded goat hair and sheep fleece into felt for shawls and belted capes. Shepherds and temple attendants received allotments of raw wool to shape into rectangular body wraps. After 4000 B.C.E., Egyptian priests enveloped themselves in leopard or panther pelts, and ritual cloaks empowered against harmful spirits. Farther west in the area of Tunisia, Algeria, and Morocco in 3400 B.C.E., courtiers established status with patchwork cloaks. In 2500 B.C.E. at Ur, Sumerian soldiers under Prince Eannatum of Lagash introduced armored cloaks and helmets to protect the neck and body from projectiles. In the area of Libya around 2300 B.C.E., the leather cloak over one shoulder supplied its wearers with a wind cover and sunscreen for their naked torsos.

National Dress

Capes suited various styles of ethnic dress. In the traditional clothing style of China after 1600 B.C.E., called Hanfu, full silk cloaks complemented knee-length tunics, long skirts, or loose pants. Military uniforms from around 1390 B.C.E. found in Vejle, Denmark, enfolded wraparound kilts with cowhide rain capes. After 1000 B.C.E., Assyrian military uniforms gave up standard shawls and kilts for leather field cloaks worn over belted short-sleeved tunics.

Greek hikers clasped at the shoulder the semicircular Macedonian *chlamys* (short mantle) over the chiton. On stage, Corinthian, Doric, and Spartan comics used voluminous chlamys lengths as a place to hide notes and stolen money-bags. For the field, Roman soldiers draped their uniforms and armor with a hip-length short cape or a loose knee-length rain cloak, which they fastened at

the shoulder with a thorn or brooch. For supplies, quartermasters designated linen factories in Western Europe and Iberia to produce wool cloaks for northern regiments. After 27 B.C.E., dress regulations allowed only the Roman emperor, consul, or dictator to display the red cloak of office.

At Persepolis by the second century B.C.E., the Parthians gave up the Hellenistic chiton and mantle and reclaimed the *qaba* (cloak), a more fitted method of dressing with buttons down the side. From Kohrasan and Kabul between 224 and 651 C.E., Sassanid drapers exported leather capes and fleece cloaks by sea along Indian Ocean trade routes to China, Mongolia, and Russia and to Rome in the West. Cameleers popularized the coat and warm calf wrappings under a felt rain cape. In Algeria and Tunisia, Christian Donatists impressed local Muslims by adopting the coarse Numidian wool cloak.

In the North American Great Basin from 500 C.E., Pueblo, Hopi, and Zuni weavers fashioned everyday cotton mantas (blanket capes) and striped serapes (shoulder wraps) from colorful yarn. In the mid-500s, when Byzantines began abandoning the toga, wearers draped the tunic in a short mantle or cloak of varying lengths for warmth and dignity. Throughout the Catholic world in the 600s, abbesses decorated ritual cowls and ankle-length copes for priests. Greek friars and monks turned sheep fleece into everyday *melotes* (cloaks) naturally waterproofed with lanolin.

After the spread of Islam to Libya, Algeria, and Tunisia, Muslims adopted the burnoosc (hooded cloak), a derivative of the Roman *paenula* (traveler's cloak). In Arabia, Bahrain, Kuwait, Oman, and Yemen after 610, the Prophet Muhammad forced his 13 wives to mask the entire face, leaving only an eye slit or two eyeholes. Along with the abaya (sleeved cloak) or the chador (full-body cloak), veiling virtually hid females from the outside world. Men adhered to *tiraz,* the stitching of Koranic verses on the ritual *rida'* (cloak).

For desert travel, eighth-century Berber dress relied on the hooded burnoose and djellaba (tunic). By the tenth century, Byzantine dress codes limited the *scaramangion* (sports coat) to imperial males, who paired it with a short scarlet cloak to ward off chilly or inclement weather. A parallel custom of the man's cape found favor among the Maasai runners of Central Africa, who outlined leather mantles with beaded chevrons. During the Ottoman control of Algiers and Tunis, Arab dealers sold short cloaks of *catifa* (wool velvet).

Thirteenth-century outdoorsmen and female laborers in Holland, the South Pacific, Zimbabwe, and Southeast Asia wrapped themselves in hooded capes. Pieceworkers made expansive garments, such as the gored felt circlets worn by shepherds and the wool cloaks of Persian Sufi dervishes, who limited their head wear to semicircular patchwork cloaks. At the Fourth Lateran Council of 1215, Pope Innocent III decreed that Jews, like Muslims, should set themselves apart from Christians by wearing the Jewish round cloak.

The Maori of New Zealand marked the departure from the earthly self by smearing clay over the torsos of the dead and concealing their flesh with *kahu kiwi* (royal cloaks) of flax edged in moa, honeyeater, bush pigeon, parrot, kiwi, and seabird feathers. Farther south, indigenous Australians sewed capes out of indigenous crocodile, opossum, and kangaroo hides, a source of strong, supple protective apparel.

Fashion

In the fourteenth century, dapper Gallic horsemen donned semicircular cloaks buckled at the right shoulder over the uniform. The *tablion,* a trapezoidal chest panel, denoted rank. In like fashion, in the Eastern Pacific, Polynesian islanders designated nobility with capes and helmets shaped from interwoven plumes. The feathered shoulder drapings impressed Captain James Cook and other global voyagers with their grandeur and tropical colors.

The wool ruana, a knee-length rectangular blanket slit up the front to drape over the neck and shoulders, kept Andeans warm in winter. Farther north in Mexico, Aztec court cloaks featured tie-dyed iconography. In the mid-fifteenth century at Tenochtitlan (now Mexico City), the Aztec emperor Montezuma I exacted an annual tax of 200,000 embroidered cotton mantas. From the Totonac, Montezuma collected an annual tribute of 2,560 cloaks, either quilted, striped, or richly tinted.

During the early Renaissance, Spanish conquistadores discovered that Amazonian natives used resins from rubber trees for waterproofing wool cloaks. After 1562, colonial Mexicans added the rectangular rebozo to women's dress as an adaptable elbow-length cape or blanket. In Europe, felt gabardine, a tightly woven, ribbed fabric, produced a cheap, water-resistant riding cloak or rain cape. Used clothing dealers in Florence specialized in secondhand fur capes and satin-lined cloaks.

Persians under the Muslim rule of the Safavids after 1501 decreed the wearing of the full-body veil or latticed panel over drawstring harem pants for women, topped by a velvet or silk brocade cape. During the 1600s, the European male doublet and cloak gave way to coat, vest, and breeches, but capes maintained prominence in women's outfits. After 1610, the security force surrounding France's Louis XIII (r. 1610–1643) topped waist-length pelerines (short capes) in light blue with red-and-white plumed hats and jackboots. The downfall of the Bourbon dynasty by the French Revolution of 1789 forced citizens to abandon colorful coats and breeches and adopt sober black and charcoal coats and tweed capes.

On the American frontier, mantas, wolf- and rabbit-pelt wraps, and buffalo blankets doubled as warm capes and hoods as well as bedrolls. The Alaskan Tlingit interwove yellow cedar bark with dog or coyote hair, duck down, and the wool of the white mountain goat to make capes, which they beautified with flannel appliqué, thin pelt linings, and abalone or dentalium shell buttons. South American kidskin furnished riders with rain wraps. An oilskin slicker shielded the body against hail or snow.

Throughout the Napoleonic era (1799–1815), women popularized the Polish Witzchoura mantle, a fur-edged cloak with open sleeves. In 1818, English reformer Robert Peel promoted a Dublin patrol of "Peelers," Irish urban police who sported red cloaks for ease of identification. The invention of satin *velouté* around 1837 provided a rich, workable cape fabric for the knee-length Rigoletto mantle, a caped cloak edged in fur. Light, warm satin merino, a plush textile marketed after 1846, suited the lining of the camail, a collared, waist-length cloak, and the loose sleeves and gathered yoke of the quilted mantle, theater cape, or Algerian burnoose.

As of the mid-1800s, caped surtouts, overcoats with suede or velvet collars, signaled the rank and prominence of English businessmen and politicians. In the late 1860s, London department stores featured the caped mantelet or pelerine as models of womanly wardrobe refinement. Sewing patterns featured the velvet sack cape, hooded cloak, capelet, and fur muff in varied sizes. In Bulgaria, women dressed for the outdoors in slippers and long *ferrajis* (cloaks), which covered embroidered bodices worn atop aprons and trousers.

In the 1870s, the man's Balmoral mantle or double-caped Inverness topcoat over a tuxedo or genteel black and gray business suit coat rounded out the well-appointed business or evening wardrobe, piper's uniform, or doorman's all-weather uniform. The double-breasted ulster with patch pockets, cape, and half-belt in Donegal (herringbone) tweed provided roomy comfort for country walks such as those described in Arthur Conan Doyle's Sherlock Holmes mysteries. The female ulsterette featured more colorful lining, contrasting topstitching, and a suede or velvet collar.

From the late 1880s to 1914, the Belle Époque demonstrated lush French haute couture featuring opera capes in alternating weaves of cut velvet and silk satin trimmed in silk fringe and tassels. Little girls wore less extravagant wool capes and polonaises (puffed tunics). Socialism in the 1890s inspired men's outsized cloaks, a Bohemian favorite. Matronly prenatal garments called wrappers hid the pregnant shape. After 1911, *Woman's Home Companion*'s patterns featured a raglan-sleeve maternity cape.

Burberry extended dramatic cloaking with topcoats and tweed capes. In the 1930s, girls' clothing emulated the couture of child movie star Shirley Temple, who appeared on-screen in a matching crepe dress and cape. For jungle fighting during World War II, the U.S. Army issued a waterproof poncho with drawcord hood that doubled as rain cape, tent, or groundsheet. The

design remains popular for outdoor wear and as standard issue military equipment. In the 1980s, Japanese fabric engineers experimented with sheer rain cloaks made in a kite shape.

Today, Ndebele matrons in South Africa retain the beaded cloak for dancing. Similarly, Zulu women display their married status by wearing a cloak and beaded bag with a wrap skirt. Among Maasai herders, men wear a belted cowhide cloak or a cape knotted over one shoulder. The Dida of the Ivory Coast decorate cloaks with tie-dyed geometrics.

In Eritrea and Sudan, Bedouin and Beja chiefs and imams retain the *bisht* (cloak) as evidence of status and dignity. The Berber of the Maghreb wear the djellaba, a loose cloak and hood of cotton or wool that shields wearers from cold in the mountains of Algeria and Morocco. A shoulder-length version, the *ddil,* pairs with a silk scarf pinned with a brooch. In Morocco, King Mohammed VI compromises by wearing Western suits for business and a white robe, cloak, and turban for religious events.

See also: Blankets; Rainwear.

Further Reading

Beaujot, Ariel. *Victorian Fashion Accessories.* New York: Bloomsbury, 2012.

Gale, Colin, and Jasbir Kaur. *Fashion and Textiles: An Overview.* New York: Bloomsbury, 2004.

Netherton, Robin, and Gale R. Owen-Crocker, eds. *Medieval Clothing and Textiles.* Vol. 4. Woodbridge, UK: Boydell & Brewer, 2008.

Club and Organizational Attire

Club apparel indicates the adherence of members to customs and credos espoused by the organization. After 206 B.C.E., the Hung Society in China identified male members with a triangular seal, white coat and pants, grass sandals, lopped queue, and red cream smeared around the eyes. Their distinctive appearance earned them the name "Red Eyebrows," the ominous face paint presaging political activism against the emperor.

In contrast to the Chinese expression of aggression, American Indian men's clubs—Sioux warrior societies and Pueblo kiva brotherhoods—adopted the red fighter's blanket or the Kachina clown's cross-dressing as emblems of cultural solidarity. Similarly unified, West African secret societies in Guinea, Liberia, Ivory Coast, and Sierra Leone required masking during initiation ceremonies. The Poro men's society and Sande women's organization superintended scarification, the marking of neck, chest, and back in recognition of coming of age and official membership in these communities.

With the debut of working men's clubs in nineteenth-century industrial areas of England, Wales, Ireland, and Australia, similarity of dress promoted camaraderie and shared rites and projects. As a stimulus to courtesy and harmony among islanders and sailors of different ethnicities, from the 1840s in Australia, the Working Men's Club promoted starched shirts and club ties and pins. In New South Wales, the Cronulla club badge featured a gold-framed lozenge with two concentric circles centered with a red shell and seabird with upstretched wings.

The Freemasons, the most storied men's organization, flourished throughout Europe, the Ottoman Empire, Australia, and the Americas. Based on thirteenth-century English workers' fraternities, Masons in London formed the first grand lodge on June 24, 1717. Members conferred the apron as a unifying symbol of a brotherhood of laborers. Colors varied, as with the red frill and tassels on the U-shaped Swedish model and the red passion cross against a black satin background on the reverse side of the Scottish version.

From sheep's pelt and lambskin to linen models, the development of Masonic membership attire after 1731 passed through hand painting, blue-edged rosettes, tassels, fringe, and embroidery. The formation of an American brotherhood emphasized red, white, and blue on the fringed apron. Group mysticism promoted a complex array of work-related and spiritual symbols—eye of God, sword, compass, level, gauge, Bible, steps, beehive, and sun.

Spread across Great Britain, Australia, Canada, and the United States, the symbols of the Knights

Templar, named for Malta-based pilgrims of the First Crusade (1096–1099), deviated from standard shapes. A Minnesota chapter honored inductees with a triangular apron centered with crossed swords pointing downward on the flap, above a skull and crossbones. For ritual, members donned a hooded white cloak lined in red satin, featuring the red Maltese cross spreading four equal arms over the heart.

In the nineteenth century, benevolent and altruistic organizations favored less symbolism in attire and accessories. In 1819, Thomas Wilkey formed the International Order of Odd Fellows in Baltimore under a three-link chain pin centering the letters FLT for "friendship, love, and truth." In 1836, the Ancient Order of Hibernians (AOH) grew from a Pennsylvania marching unit in New York's St. Patrick's Day parade. The men, miners from Schuylkill County, promoted camaraderie among American males of like ethnicity and religion. A Celtic Catholic constituency begun by Rory O'Moore in County Kildare in 1565 and blessed by Pope Urban VIII in 1642, the fraternity joined Irish male immigrants under a green, white, and orange sash and a nationalistic badge picturing 10 shamrocks and an Irish harp in a crest topped with the letters AOH.

Efforts at Equality

With the growth of U.S. immigration, on October 13, 1843, Henry Jones of New York's Lower East Side convened the first B'nai B'rith (children of the covenant) league, a group of German Jewish males. As international chapters opened in Romania, Israel, and Sri Lanka, men gathered under the seven-armed menorah to combat anti-Semitism and bigotry. In contrast to the spiritual Jewish men's fraternity, the Knights of Pythias under founder Justus Henry Rathbone allied in Washington, D.C., on February 19, 1864, with a display of long swords marked with FCB, for "friendship, charity, benevolence."

The creation of the Elks Club in 1868 affiliated white males under the "11 O'clock" Badge, a red, white, and blue circle picturing an antlered elk's head and clock above the letters BPOE (Benevolent and Protective Order of Elks). The clock hands and numbers in Roman numerals reminded members of mortality and their limited opportunities to do good works.

Following emancipation from slavery, black men recognized the value of fraternal associations offering charity, recreation, youth guidance, and old age and burial insurance. By organizing black chapters of Masons and Elks, club members initiated an era of social segregation under similar symbols and badges. On September 28, 1898, the formation of the Improved Benevolent Protective Order of the Elks of the World in Cincinnati, Ohio, by former slaves introduced a sedate headdress—a white fez and tassel above a jeweled collar with the lodge insignia on a pendant.

The Shriners, an adjunct of Freemasonry organized by actor William J. Conlin in Manhattan on August 13, 1870, gained media attention for appearing in parades and at fund-raisers for children's hospitals wearing the cylindrical red fez. Officials—potentates, rabbans (teachers), prophets, and guides—sported the black-tasseled fez with the Shrine insignia, a scimitar above an inverted crescent and star. Initiates dressed in white tunics and skullcaps.

Pageantry called for Arab patrols and band units clownishly garbed in fezzes, cummerbunds, loose trousers, and white spats. The outfit epitomized the Middle Eastern source of the group's name, the Ancient Arabic Order of the Nobles of the Mystic Shrine. In the Yukon and British Columbia, members topped the cummerbund and trousers with a white straight-collared jacket embroidered with gold braid.

On March 29, 1882, at St. Mary's Church in New Haven, Connecticut, Catholic priest Michael J. McGivney initiated the Knights of Columbus, a men's service league dedicated to education and charity. The "K of C" insignia featured a cluster of four equilateral triangles under a shield marked by a sword, anchor, and Roman fasces, an ax mounted on a bundle of rods as a symbol of strength in unity. Gold dominated the color symbolism, with red, white, and blue as background tones.

In 1900, the formation of service clubs and volunteer associations resulted in national and international federations, beginning in 1905 with the Rotary Club in Chicago, the National Exchange Club in Detroit in 1911, and the Kiwanis Club of Detroit in 1915. Contemporary with Kiwanis, the Rosicrucians allied in New York under a cross centered with a rose, the universal symbol of the Virgin Mary. Significant to Rosicrucian memorabilia, the black-edged collar of Napoleon bore olive branches surrounding an equilateral triangle, a symbol of the Christian trinity. The Rosicrucians' pendant created a vertical hierarchy, beginning with a five-pointed crown and red rose over a red cross and the mother pelican pulling flesh from her breast to feed three nestlings.

Subsequent men's leagues—the Lions Club International in 1917 in Chicago and the Optimist Club in 1919 in Lexington, Kentucky—established crests, which appeared on pins and association jewelry. Rotarians chose the 13-spoke wagon wheel, altered in 1923 to the six-spoke gear wheel. The Lions framed the L between roaring lion heads facing left and right. Freighted with less symbolism, the Kiwanis badge featured the letter K and the words "Kiwanis International" within a circle with braided edge. Optimist International, an association of Optimist Clubs worldwide, fashioned a logo without myth or legend by simply framing an O superimposed on an I within an octagonal frame.

In Ismailia, Egypt, Imam Hasan al-Banna initiated the Society of the Muslim Brothers, or Muslim Brotherhood, in March 1928. A small Islamic fraternity, the brotherhood morphed into a violent fundamentalist action coalition across the Middle East. Members wore signifiers marked by a green circle and crossed swords pointed upward around a copy of the Koran covered in red. Below in Arabic, the motto "Make Ready" declared a commitment to jihad.

Scouting Uniforms

On August 1, 1907, at Brownsea Island in southern England, British general Robert Baden-Powell, a hero of the Boer War, founded the Boy Scouts. He introduced a military theme that equalized races and social classes with uniforms. In February 1910, he rendered scouting gender equal by organizing the Girl Guides, an anti-Victorian source of education and physical training and forerunner of the Girl Scouts.

Based on regulation army attire, regulation Boy Scout uniforms in the 1920s featured a wool choke-collar coat and high-crowned campaign hat over knickers and leggings, all in khaki. Scout leaders wore the belted Norfolk jacket over knickers or trousers.

Over the course of a century, scouting outfitters have allowed for considerable choice and variety, notably a red beret, baseball cap, navy blue outfits for Cub Scouts, Sea Scout caps, and convertible cargo pants that zip down to shorts. Throughout the 1950s, Explorer scouts distinguished their rank with spruce-green shirts over pants. In 1965, U.S. scouting regalia changed to a permanent press fabric in light green. The right shoulder displayed the American flag and the scouting logo. For formal ceremonies, members displayed their patches, medals, bars, and ribbons on a merit badge sash. For global representation, the World Scout Crest encircled a fleur-de-lis with a plaited rope and square knot at bottom, which represented service and brotherhood.

After decades of tan uniform shirts with epaulets and buttoned pocket flaps designed by Oscar de la Renta, the Centennial Scout Uniform in August 2008 featured changes in the familiar khaki. Olive shorts or trousers secured with a green webbed belt coordinated with green socks. Nationalistic color coding included an orange neckerchief for Ivory Coast scouts, blue-and-white-striped neckerchiefs in Greece, green epaulets in Canada, sky-blue shirts in El Salvador, gray shirts in Malaysia, and red berets on Arabian scouts. Female troop leaders paired the standard-issue shirt with their choice of culottes, shorts, slacks, or skirt.

The parallel growth of American Girl Scouts, established on March 12, 1912, by Juliette Gordon Low, called for a standard tunic, vest, sash, pants, and skirt to create a sense of belonging and female empowerment. The base color altered from navy and khaki in 1914 to brown with an insignia tab for Brownie Scouts in the primary grades and forest green for girls eight and older. Low contributed a stirring four-lobed emblem with "GS" prominent

above an American eagle with wings outspread. Globally, variances identified nationality, as with red pullovers in Barbados, green pleated skirts in Nepal, bright blue sweaters with shamrock insignia in Portugal, and white tunics, pants, and head scarves in Pakistan. The World Flag contrasted a trio of yellow blocks and a white corner symbolizing peace.

See also: Badges and Insignias; Symbolic Colors, Patterns, and Motifs.

Further Reading

Axelrod, Alan. *The International Encyclopedia of Fraternal Orders and Secret Societies.* New York: Facts on File, 1997.
Barrett, David V. *A Brief History of Secret Societies: An Unbiased History of Our Desire for Secret Knowledge.* New York: Carroll & Graf, 2007.
Cherrington, Ruth. *Not Just Beer and Bingo: A Social History of Working Men's Clubs.* Bloomington, IN: AuthorHouse, 2012.

Coats and Jackets

The Western-style coat or jacket remains a wardrobe staple in much of the world. Introduced in ancient Persia to pair with loose pants, the fitted men's jacket ended centuries of dependence on tunics and capes or cloaks. The Greeks scorned the body-hugging Phrygian jacket with sleeves and declared it awkward and less dignified than the chiton. Romans adopted the fitted shift after 200 C.E., but continued to issue cloaks to legionaries.

Coats and jackets flourished in Asian fashion into the 1200s. From Khorasan and Kabul between 224 to 651 C.E., East Asian cameleers paired contoured Afghan coats with leg wrappings for warmth. In the eighth century, the Japanese *happi* (short coat) consisted of a fitted bodice above a flared peplum. After his coronation in 800, Charlemagne preferred the contoured jacket made of otter or marten skins.

By the 900s, imperial dress codes at Constantinople reserved the *scaramangion* (sports coat) for male courtiers. In the same era, Abbasids universalized the open-front coat, which revealed lavishly embroidered sashes. In south-central Iran during the 1300s, felt overcoats from Tabriz found eager buyers among herders and cameleers.

Medieval Refinements and Styling

During the Renaissance, European designers chose emerald, jade, lapis, topaz, amethyst, and ruby velvet for knee-length men's coats and lined them with silk. Boys reached a coming-of-age plateau upon short coating, the presentation of their first button-up high-neck jackets. In the French duchy of Burgundy in 1476, Charles the Bold flaunted a flashy satin version of the jacket. The Muslim rule of the Safavids after 1501 revived the fur-lined coat with frog closures, an ornamental corded detail from prehistoric China that projected affluence and pomp.

After 1509, English weavers refined Sicilienne, wool corded with silk, for jerkins and fitted satin truss coats worn over doublets to add flair to the outfit. From serge and sheep's gray, a black and gray-beige homespun, tailors made pea coats, popular jackets with sailors for their durability. During Japan's golden age, after 1560, consumers valued silk and gold yarns gracing the silk and damask patchwork *dofuku* (coat), a loose, buttonless style common to the privileged mercantile and warrior classes.

During the 1600s, European fashions dropped the doublet in favor of the trio of coat, waistcoat, and breeches and, for at-home leisure, the smoking jacket of silk velvet, made from luxury fabrics imported from Asia. English clothiers specialized in wool or cashmere greatcoats and over-frock coats for outer layers.

Introduced in England during the reign of Charles II (1660–1685), the justacorps (a knee-length fitted coat with ample skirt worn with full lace jabot and lacy cuffs revealed by turn-back cuffs) created demand for lush damasks and heavy brocades. Italian tailors turned lavish wine and gold combinations into justacorps. Under Russian reformer Peter the Great after 1682, a modernized army uniformed its recruits in the German frock coat, vest, and pants and French footwear.

Lined with padded satin, men's embroidered jackets in 1750 followed the contours of the chest and back more closely than the justacorps of the previous century. Women emulated male styles by topping riding habits with man-tailored three-quarter Brunswicks and frock coats with generous peplums. For everyday outfits, the female caraco featured a tight-waisted bodice open down the front to display an embroidered stomacher.

Mainstay of World Fashion

The British frock coat influenced men's attire throughout the empire. Around 1725, Agaja, the king of Dahomey, impressed his guests by changing jackets during a state dinner. His display began with a red velvet coat trimmed in gilt and advanced to a plain black dress coat before giving way to an oversized housecoat of silver brocade.

In England and the United States after the 1750s, young dandies followed trends toward the macaroni coat, when the stylish forced themselves into ridiculously tight jackets. When the British outfitted the Indian navy at Bombay, they gave detailed instructions for quality blue cloth for a nine-button jacket with black velvet lapels and cuffs and pocket flaps lined in white silk.

The onslaught of the French Revolution of 1789 ended the demand for vivid, feminized men's attire and popularized black and charcoal jackets, the apparel of the serious patriot. The Napoleonic era (1799–1815) returned elegance to the man's high-collared frock coat, the unisex waist-length spencer, and the women's sleeveless pelisse (straight overdress or coat) and braided redingote (long unlined coat). Dapper styles encouraged the cutting of men's knee-length, double-breasted frock coats from silk and wool twill, both appropriate fabrics for weddings.

The cut of a man's coat established his place in society. The Petersham frock coat displayed a velvet collar, cuffs, and lapel and large hip pockets slanting toward the side seam. During the English Regency era (1811–1820), the severe three-piece suit defined the sober male while the mundane box coat identified the working coachman.

In the mid-1800s, men's attire underwent a fine tuning. Philip Stanhope, the earl of Chesterfield, introduced the straight-bodied Chesterfield, a black or charcoal fly front topcoat with a velvet

With the opening of China to Western influence and a market economy in the late 1970s and early 1980s, the drab blue and green tunics of the Mao Zedong era gave way to European-style suit jackets and sports coats. *(Jeff Hacker)*

collar. Prince Albert set the Victorian tone of the formal frock coat with notched, 3-inch (7.6-centimeter) velvet collar. He appeared in silk-faced jackets with bow ties and caped surtouts with suede collars, a model of business attire.

In the 1860s, Figaro or Zouave jackets and angle-fronted coats folded away from the front to furnish an unobstructed view of the waistcoat. For lounging, the Leicester jacket offered set-to-the-collar raglan sleeves. Women followed a more body-defining silhouette in the basque, a nipped-in jacket detailed with a wide front yoke, butterfly sleeves, and a broad hemline that accommodated hoopskirts.

In North America, Indians favored winter blanket coats paired with leggings. In the trans-Mississippi West, frontier guides Kit Carson and Jim Beckwourth cut, stitched, and fringed three deer hides into the bodice and sleeves of a standard long coat. After the Civil War, army, telegraph, and railroad scouts and Pony Express riders found Plains buckskins with skin buttons comfortable and adaptable for riding and tracking.

Modernization

Details improved the warmth and durability of jackets and coats. Levi Strauss, inventor of denim jeans, augmented outdoor attire by marketing blanket-lined jackets. In the 1870s, Englishmen added weather protection to the suit coat or tuxedo with the Balmoral mantle or double-caped Inverness topcoat. For rural jaunts, they favored the double-breasted ulster in Donegal (herringbone) tweed.

The women's ulsterette supplied more style with contrasting top stitching, a colorful lining, and a suede or velvet collar. A dust coat of cozy cheviot or Melton cloth protected women's summer outfits. In June 1873, *Harper's Bazaar* advertised made-to-measure patterns for ladies' maternity tea jackets and men's morning coats, cutaways suited to horseback riding. Irish writer and fashion trendsetter Oscar Wilde modernized the male silhouette with a frock coat featuring a breast pocket and foulard pocket square to complement his tie.

Globally, the jacket supplied fit, comfort, and style throughout the late 1800s, including the indigo coat favored by Japanese peasants. Around 1900, tailors slimmed down the fit with linen and waxed cotton for split-back dusters, unisex auto coats, and men's summer jackets, and with serge for evening tails. Heavier wardrobe additions included the army-style overcoat and the naval reefer, a sturdy, all-round jacket for casual wear adorned with brass buttons, a favorite of farmers and dockworkers.

The influx of Western coats in colonial Africa replaced ceremonial apparel. The spread of Western styles created a brisk trade in used coats and jackets, particularly among cosmopolitan youth. Winston Churchill agreed with Christian missionaries that African chiefs should avoid emulating the English khaki jacket and should revive stately dress by returning to ceremonial robes. In Kenya, Chief Mumia agreed and accepted a dark embroidered cloak to replace British hand-me-downs. Ganda, Luo, and Luyia chiefs followed Mumia's example only for state occasions.

Uniforms, Symbols, and Fashion Trends

During the rise of communism, Soviet, Maoist, and Korean padded work coats became an unchanging uniform for proletarians. Under capitalism in the 1930s, American and British men indulged in variety—the four-pocket safari and hacking jacket, the leather motorcycle jacket with snaps and zippers, and the thick wool duffel or convoy coat with toggle closures. Women and girls favored the car or motoring coat, a hip-length wool or quilted travel garment popular during the 1940s. After World War II, men retained navy pea coats for everyday wear; women opted for fur-lined coats in celebration of the end of rationing. The boutiques of the 1950s marketed women's bolero jackets, quilted silk mandarin coats, unisex slickers, pea coats, trench coats, and smoking jackets.

In the 1960s, women topped long skirts with maxi coats, a tubular silhouette fitted with three or four buttons and left open from waist to hem. Urban men enjoyed the brief popularity of the Nehru jacket, a button-up coat lacking lapels, which gave respite from the staid two- and three-button sport jacket. In 1968, tony New York haberdashers imported French and Italian styles in unvented suit coats and overcoats, both of which flattered the slender male. In Tanzania, Kenya, Uganda, and the Comoros Islands, men created a bicontinental look by adding a blazer or sport coat to the ankle-length *kanzu* (tunic), a standard in East Africa.

As women swelled the workforce in industrialized countries, they embraced the dress suit or pantsuit, a tailored work uniform usually paired with white or pastel shirts. Men retained the wool, suede, or corduroy sport jacket, an office standard often detailed with leather elbow patches. In 1999, Tencel replaced quilted nylon in ready-to-wear with a sleeker material for football and bomber jackets and hooded parkas or cagouls. In the twenty-first century, Thinsulate insulated toggle coats for high-risk sports, including car racing, orienteering, and mountain climbing. In 2012, women revived the peplum jacket, a retro style suited to slim waists.

See also: Business Attire; Denim and Jeans; Uniforms, Military.

Further Reading

Alto, Marta, Susan Neall, and Pati Palmer. *Jackets for Real People: Tailoring Made Easy.* Portland, OR: Palmer/Pletsch, 2006.

Lagerfeld, Karl, and Carine Roitfeld. *The Little Black Jacket: Chanel's Classic Revisited.* London: Steidl, 2012.

Shannon, Brent Alan. *The Cut of His Coat: Men, Dress, and Consumer Culture in Britain, 1860–1914.* Athens: Ohio University Press, 2006.

Soyer, Daniel, ed. *A Coat of Many Colors: Immigration, Globalization, and Reform in New York City's Garment Industry.* New York: Fordham University Press, 2005.

Cobblery

Unlike shoemaking, cobblery historically has filled a need for repairs and modifications to leather shoes, purses, and garments. According to temple mosaics, adjustments of shoe comfort date to Egypt around 2750 B.C.E. By 400 B.C.E., Hippocrates recommended shoe inserts, padding, and orthotics to correct deformed feet and ankles. Throughout the Roman Empire and as far north in Britain as Hadrian's Wall, towns and forts provided steady work for the cobbler applying flanges and inserts, modifying ill-fitting boots, and repairing shoes, bags, helmets, and leather armor. The work was labor-intensive and poorly paid.

Around 50 C.E., Egyptian Copts developed the turnshoe, a one-piece shoe stitched on the flesh side and turned to the grain side. For travelers on foot, innkeepers offered matted or felted animal hair to pad shoes and boots. When the turnshoe reached Britain, Irish and Scots cobblers made more comfortable repairs with tarred thread. They applied wool inside sandals to relieve strain and completed their work with tallow, nails, and blacking. Celts preferred the moccasin, a one-piece footbag requiring resewing at the heel and toe with a tunnel stitch for durability and waterproofing.

In the 270s, Crispin and Crispianus, Christian cobblers at Noviodunum (Soissons, France), dedicated their craft to poor Gauls. In the Middle Ages, the devout celebrated October 25 in honor of the two saints, whom the emperor Maximianus decapitated on October 25, 286, in Belgium. Pilgrims found cobbleries at hotels and abbeys, including Cluny, France, and Santiago de Compostela, Spain, where shoe repairers enabled walkers to continue their journeys to Christian shrines.

Cobblers positioned straddle benches fitted with a last or an elevated work surface within easy reach of the awl, bend and moon knives, pincers and nippers, mallets, files, hobnails and rivets, scissors, lapstone, and needles threaded with thongs. Vats held leather in a mulling (softening) soak for cutting into soles, vamps, toe caps, and lacings, the essentials of civilian and military footwear. Fashionable netting in women's shoes and handbags required patching and replacement, as did the scuffed leather covering wood heels. Pattens, the elevated platforms for walking on muddy streets, demanded frequent replacement of straps.

The Trade

In Suzhou, China, the leather repairman carried a basket of tools and materials through the streets in hopes of employment, which paid only 75 percent of a blacksmith's wage. In Arabia and at Goa, India, the cobbler supplemented his sandal repair business by making bags. By the 1100s, cobblery provided steady work for the leather crafter in cities and castles, where landowners valued quality shoes and mentioned them in their wills as family legacies.

In Körmend, Hungary, known for some 40 crafts, Jewish cobblers gained prominence for skilled leather repair and the use of technologically advanced hand-cranked machines. In 1410, Henry IV identified cobbling in London as a repair business separate from cordwaining (shoemaking). Denied a part in shoe manufacture, the cobbler added nonslip treads for fishers and dockworkers and monitored orthotics, such as insulating and cushioning brogans for laborers. Around 1625, a royal cobbler inserted brass supports in the boots of Charles I of England, a victim of rickets.

Colonial American history records the arrival of the first cobbler, Thomas Brand, a passenger on the *Lyon's Whelp,* to Salem, Massachusetts, in July 1629. In the Massachusetts Colony in 1675, at a time when imported English shoes cost $1.33 per pair, the cobbler's restitching and re-soling extended wear. The itinerant cobbler, called a "cat whipper," arrived each fall and boarded at individual homes while repairing the family's shoes in preparation for winter. For patching, he trimmed and applied the hides of farm animals slaughtered during the year. To reattach wood soles to leather vamps, he either repegged or used the cat-whipping stitch, which double-sewed from opposite directions with two lengths of waxed twine. To extend wear, he added hobnails, colorful patches, and iron heelpieces.

The Artisan's Shop

By 1750, one-man shoe shops began replacing the routes of traveling cobblers. Apprentices specialized in single chores, such as pegging, binding, and "bottoming" (re-soling). Into the Revolutionary War era, when the fashionable ordered shoes from France, a respected colonial cobbler could earn 70 cents per day. On plantations in the South, each household relied on slave cobblers, who made and repaired slave footwear, belts, and bags. The planter earned cash returns from skilled cobblers by leasing them to other plantations. A famous slave-era cobbler, Anna Murray, escaped north from Maryland with her husband, Frederick Douglass, and set up a shoe repair shop in New Bedford, Massachusetts, that served runaways on the Underground Railroad. Her skill provided crucial assistance to slaves traveling on foot from the South as far north as Quebec.

Despite the unionizing of cobblers into the Daughters of St. Crispin in 1860 and the Order of the Knights of St. Crispin in 1870, cobblery paid limited returns in the nineteenth century as mechanized shoemaking reduced prices for footwear. Cheaper footwear encouraged the abandonment of worn leather goods rather than repair or upgrade. Many cobblers worked out of their homes in poor lighting and suffered the scorn of more polished artisans. In winter, out-of-work fishers increased the competition for small leather repair jobs on brogans and women's shoes, such as the application of metal supports to halt the wearing down of heels caused by weak ankles or a limping gait.

In New York in 1805, cobblers received 25 cents for ornamental straps and binding, 50 cents for foxing (replacing the vamp) or applying cork soles, and 75 cents for stitching or strapping the tops of boots. In 1832, daily earnings in Massachusetts ranged from 33 to 46 cents per day for men, 30 cents for apprentices, and 14 cents for women. Better wages and higher standards in Philadelphia derived from immigrant German cobblers, who imported European methods and tools as well as restyling techniques.

Machine Repair

After the Emancipation Proclamation of 1863, cobblery became a specialty for former slaves, who could take classes in leather craft. Freedmen's schools taught shoe repair, such as the classes offered at Booker T. Washington's Tuskegee Institute in Mason County, Alabama, and at the National Training School for Women and Girls in Washington, D.C. Black-owned cobbleries, such as those serving Beaufort, South Carolina, and Nashville, Tennessee, attested to a viable industry for freedmen in shoe repair, heel plating, tongue replacement, lifts and taps, and stretching.

After the patenting of vulcanization in 1898, cobblers added to their chores the replacement of rubber heels and soles as well as stretching and applying fiber soles, bunion protectors, and arch supports for flat feet and weak arches. Glass cases demonstrated the restyling of old shoes and displayed before-and-after models of repairs that extended the life of brogans and boots. On-site repairs encouraged shoppers to examine new leather goods, such as matching gaiters, handbags, wallets, and laces.

In 1910, cobbler's supplies added minimal costs, with taps at 25 cents per pound, Cuban heels at 3 cents per pair, leather scraps for 3.5 cents per pound, and calfskin for a penny an ounce. Repair charges ranged from 25 cents for new heels to 75 cents for soles, with Goodyear welt soles bringing $1. Peripheral sales in buttonhooks, wax, creams and polishes, blacking, lacing and eyelets, flexible arch supports, buttoned ankle supports, celluloid tops, buckles, and bows ensured a more lucrative business.

Modern Trends

During World War I, conscientious objectors could satisfy their military obligations by working in shoe repair. By the 1920s, poverty drove Jewish cobblers from Lithuania, Poland, Ukraine, and Russia to the urban centers of Western Europe, Britain, and North America. The destruction of cobbleries in Europe during World War II generated a new wave of leatherworkers to migrate to North America, where they opened Old World repair shops.

For twine, leatherworkers inserted hog bristle and waxed hemp or linen fiber and rolled the length into a consistent thickness for stitching split uppers. The final repair began with hammering pegs into awl holes and brushing polish over scuffs. Women's shoes received new wood heels and strokes of a rasp to smooth stitching and wood tacks.

By the mid-1900s, cheap imported leather goods, man-made fabrics, canvas, and plastic made most shoes expendable, further depleting the cobbler's clientele. The economic downturn of 2008 and succeeding years returned cobblers to work extending the life of shoes and masking scuff marks with buff cloths and polish. Repair shops also offered the addition or removal of ornamentation, gel lifts, waterproofing, and the replacement of inner soles, Velcro®, and zippers.

See also: Boots; Leather and Suede; Shoes, Men's; Shoes, Women's.

Further Reading

Bergstein, Rachelle. *Women from the Ankle Down: The Story of Shoes and How They Define Us.* New York: HarperCollins, 2012.

DeMello, Margo. *Feet and Footwear: A Cultural Encyclopedia.* New York: Macmillan, 2009.

Leno, John Bedford. *The Art of Boot and Shoemaking: A Practical Handbook Including Measurement, Last-Fitting, Cutting-Out, Closing, and Making.* Reprint, 1865. Eastford, CT: Martino, 2010.

Swann, June. *Shoemaking.* Princes Risborough, UK: Shire, 2003.

Collars

An adornment of the neck, the collar frames the face while providing both dignity and completion to apparel. From 3150 B.C.E., the royal collar identified Egyptian sovereigns. During the Middle Kingdom after 1938 B.C.E., the Lady Senebtisi of El-Lisht south of Cairo wore a copper collar. In 1323 B.C.E., the tomb of Egyptian boy king Tutankhamen in the Valley of the Kings contained a woven tunic with tapestry collar.

Byzantine women ornamented themselves Egyptian-style in spiked, segmented metal collars positioned below the clavicle and over the upper arm. From 383 C.E. to the high tenth century, the ruler's ensemble in Constantinople featured a collar on the *dalmatica* (wide-sleeved tunic), another emulation of Egyptian apparel. After 527, the empress Theodora made a jeweled, shoulder-length collar a part of her imperial parure, a set of matching jewelry.

Medieval attire centered on the chemise or smock, a loose variant of the tunic. The drawstring neckline, which formed a box-pleated ruffle, preceded the turndown neckline and the separate linen or cambric collar. As clothing construction became more sophisticated and more fitted to the individual body, the collar presented a complicated sewing project. Across Europe, collars attached to a partlet extending to mid-sternum or tied separately above the bodice. In contrast, the spread of Islam by missionaries in North Africa after 625 initiated males to standard Arab dress, the long collarless silk tunic adorned only with neckline embroidery.

Around 1300, courtiers from southern Russia adopted tight bodices with collars embroidered around the edge with colored or metallic thread. Peasant women of Archangel and Novgorod preserved decorative yokes and collars with matching cuffs, which they passed to their daughters as female legacies. Some collars opened at the throat. Others fastened in back or at the side to give the appearance of a full circle.

Early Embellishment

Medieval portraiture depicted the pleated ruffs and lace collars worn throughout Europe as evidence of vanity and social rank. With raw cotton from the colonies, court seamstresses fashioned collars and cuffs, which they shaped with hot goffering irons and fluting sticks or tongs into starched masterworks assembled into a row of figure eights. A prime example from the Tudor era, Queen Elizabeth I posed for court portraits in 1563, 1575, and 1588—once in a lace or filigreed collar and twice in ruffs elevated on frames. In 1578, Elizabeth's sister-in-law, Mary, Queen of Scots, adorned her robes with cutwork linen collars stiffened with whale baleen and trimmed to complement her caps.

Renaissance men also accessorized their doublets with piccadillies—broad collars that lapped over sleeve caps—and ruffs like the ones worn by Sir Francis Drake for a miniature painted in 1581 and by Sir Walter Raleigh for a 1614 engraving. By the 1590s, ruffs extended from the back of the head to the extremes of shoulders and mid-chest into a millstone collar tilted downward.

In the late 1500s and early 1600s, collars included fluted starched cotton or muslin ruffs, lace yokes, neck cloths, and falling bands, with batiste or lawn rectangles tied to the collars or bare necks of formally dressed judges, ministers, cathedral choristers, and college deans. Men attached bags to the collars of formal apparel to contain the powder that whitened the queues of their wigs. While the Dutch and Spanish clung to the Elizabethan ruff and scalloped Van Dyke collar, English and French females abandoned the ruff for plunging necklines outlined by flat lace collars, status symbols among the advancing gentry.

In the eighteenth century, colonial men favored collarless jackets and shirts topped with ruffles that extended into the gap of the waistcoat. By mid-century in the Western Hemisphere and Australia, collars on men's jackets and shirts replaced ruffles, especially in the more sedate New England colonies. In 1760, the advent of chemical bleaching whitened shirtfronts, frills, collars, and cuffs without the laborious scrubbing of grime with a laundry brush.

By the late 1700s, women set off the bodice with attachable fichus (scarves knotted over the breasts), long filigree neck cloths, flounces, and collared or ruffled yokes that covered the sternum. The fashion savvy folded the square neckerchief into a small scarf, a linen or batiste fill-in for a revealing neckline.

The priestly cassock vest revealed a detachable clerical collar that encircled the throat, a seamless look adopted by seminarians. In Montreal, the Grey Nuns, outfitted by founder Marguerite d'Youville, extended the black wimple into a collar covering the chest.

Choosing and Maintaining the Collar

Late in the eighteenth century, European sewing circles collected fabric and trim in patch bags for mending or replacing worn collars and cuffs on men's shirts and nightclothes. In 1797, launderers attacked ground-in dirt and grease in collars on corrugated wood washboards and whitened neck surfaces with commercial sodium hypochlorite bleach. By 1833, the grooved zinc, copper, tin, or iron washboards intensified the effect of hand scrubbing, but shortened the life of collar and cuffs.

In South Africa, the full beaded collar represented opposition to colonialism. In the 1820s, as Nguni refugees pressed south into Xhosa territory, the immigrants maintained their cultural identity by wearing distinctive ceremonial collars. Thus, the Mfengu and Thembu promoted tribalism by displaying evidence of northern ancestry.

In the early 1800s, Western shawl-collared maternity apparel cloaked expanding bosoms. The Napoleonic era (1799–1815) encouraged the elegance of men's high-collared frock coats with collarless vests and women's habits fitted with double or triple collars. The starched detachable wing collar for men, invented in 1827 in Troy, New York, buttoned to the neckband with a pair of metal studs, one in front and another at back. The separate collar provided clothiers with a popular item for business and formal apparel that ended the problem of the collar wearing out before the shirt.

Victorian chinoiserie and hand-crocheted collars made in Ireland encircled women's stand-up necklines. In the mid-1800s, *Godey's Lady's Book* and *Peterson's Magazine* issued patterns for cross-stitching, monogramming, knitting, or crocheting detachable cambric shawl collars that pinned at the neck. A neat white collar enhanced the image of the professional female social worker, innkeeper, nurse, and secretary as efficient and well-groomed.

In the mid-1800s, Englishmen emulated Prince Albert's frock coat and, for weddings and receptions, adorned the notched velvet collar with a boutonniere. Caped surtouts with suede collars established the rank and prominence of businessmen and politicians. Philip Stanhope, the earl of Chesterfield, modeled an overcoat—which came to be called a Chesterfield—that featured a notched velvet collar. Haberdashers offered colored silk ties, ascots, dickeys, shirtfronts, and detachable patent collars in wing or butterfly style.

Tailors personalized men's suits with impeccable collars and ties, elements of good grooming that suited the wearer's style and the shape of the neck and face. Bone, horn, baleen, mother of pearl, brass, steel, or sterling silver stays stiffened collar points, such as the horizontal wings of the Gladstone collar, which contained stitched compartments to secure the stays. In their leisure, businessmen removed stays and abrasive starched collars and repaired to the den in smoking jackets or morning coats that featured a soft rolled velvet collar.

Elegant female dressing in the mid-nineteenth century called for angora muff-and-collar sets and fur evening wraps, as well as lace collars for little girls. In the 1860s, formal equestrienne apparel favored stand-up collars. After 1870, neck garnishes ranged from the cravat bow tie to the lace fichu with tulle. The man's Shakespeare vest emphasized a turndown collar over notched lapels. Boys' suits featured the Buster Brown collar, a wide, flat neck frame worn with a ruffle or bow tie. Boarding schools added stiff buttoned collars to their dress codes.

Modern American Collars

In the 1880s, Italian and German-Jewish female laborers produced collars for the American garment industry. Contractors assigned pocket and collar jobs in-house and imported beaded, embroidered, or knitted collars and chokers from Europe. Outdoorsmen purchased rainwear and hunting attire fitted with storm collars and cuffs. Into the 1900s, men turned the plain imperial collar into a brief Edwardian fashion trend while women favored the high-neck collar centered with a brooch or cameo. Girls dressed in surplice necklines and shawl collars for afternoon. In Freetown, Sierra Leone, in 1887, West Indian reformer Edward Wilmot Blyden, the "Father of Pan-Africanism" and author of *African Life and Customs* (1908), promoted the collarless tribal dashiki (tunic) rather than British suits and ridiculed the inappropriate starched collar, vest, and necktie in a tropical climate.

American collars acquired class-related distinctions, with blue collars symbolizing factory laborers, pink collars denoting typically female jobs, and white collars as the acme of the business and professional hierarchy. In the early 1900s, the white collar and striped or colored men's shirt produced a common combination. For a debonair fit of collar and tie knot, well-appointed men's apparel called for the collar tab, barbell, or pin—a means of pulling the collar points neatly toward the chest—a spiffy look associated with screen dancer Fred Astaire.

For women, *Vogue* featured discussions of bishop sleeves and celluloid collars and cuffs. For snowy weather, Burberry advertised shawl-collared ski suits. Girls wore shirts with Peter Pan collars. In the 1920s, boys played in side-buttoned shirts with banded collars. With the invention of dry cleaning, cleaners pre-treated neck grime on shirt collars. In Paris, exotic dancer Josephine Baker revived the slave collar as a trendy adornment for her stage presentations. The Great Depression resurrected the recycling of scraps into quilted yokes and collars, which extended the life of garments.

During World War II, U.S. flight crews stayed warm in jackets fitted with mouton collars. Although rationing limited haute couture, French designer Jeanne Lanvin meted out drapery material as linings for collars, which she overlaid with ribbon and lace or quilting. In 1944, *Harper's Bazaar* advertised Simplicity patterns for a combination bra and collar.

Girls' postwar fashions featured braided sailor collars halfway down the back of middies or dresses, and fur collars for sweaters and coats. After 1946, boys wore notched-collared gabardine or twill jackets similar to those favored by their fathers. The Elvis craze of the 1950s created a fad for pink-and-black fashions with turned-up collars. In contrast to teen trends, Paris couturier Pierre Balmain swathed an afternoon dress with a drape that converted from a head wrap to a loose collar.

In the 1960s, Western men popularized the Nehru jacket, a button-up coat fitted with a high circular Mandarin collar worn without lapels or neckties. Women popularized the V-neck blouse or dress with Chelsea collar descending into long points. In the film *Doctor Zhivago* (1965), actor Omar Sharif modeled banded Cossack collars and hooded parkas with ring collars, which enjoyed a brief fashion resurgence.

Throughout Africa, clergymen denoted their authority by wearing clerical dress with a Roman collar. Among Protestant and evangelical ministers, the visual representation of orthodoxy empowered wearers within social settings and shielded them from overt racism on public transportation. During opposition to apartheid in the 1970s, clerical dress enabled Archbishop Desmond Tutu to protest disenfranchisement of blacks in Soweto, South Africa.

On casual Fridays in the 1990s, business and professional men freed the neck from collars and ties by wearing round-necked shirts. Women's winter jackets featured the cutaway collar, a sloped tailoring that left room for scarves and turtleneck sweaters. Mohair and wool coats from the collections of Japanese fabric engineer Issey Miyake incorporated collars that converted to a variety of fits and shapes. Among Chinese scholars, the dignified *shangfu* (court robe) with a round collar continues to denote authority. In 2013, women's evening jewelry featured the retro rhinestone or sequined evening collar, worn either as a necklace or as an accessory for a blouse or sweater.

See also: Accessories; Sleeves and Cuffs; Ties and Cravats.

Further Reading

Kinsey, Mindy, ed. *Necklines & Collars: A Directory of Design Details and Techniques.* East Petersburg, PA: Fox Chapel, 2011.

Stamper, Anita A., and Jill Condra. *Clothing Through American History: The Civil War Through the Gilded Age, 1861–1899.* Santa Barbara, CA: Greenwood, 2011.

Color Trends

Stylistic eras capture the subliminal effects of shifting color trends, such as the pink and black of the Elvis years, the black nail polish and lipstick of Goth subculture, and the orange and pink Mohawk hairstyles of punk rockers.

Color Coding in History

In the sixth century B.C.E., Persians based their fashions on lapis blue, turquoise, olive green, and brown. Their contemporaries in Greece displayed little interest in dyeing. Colors of the chiton (standard knee- or full-length garment) reflected social prominence, usually white or natural hues for gentry and gray or brown for the working class. Roman magistrates distinguished themselves in reddish-purple *mullei calcei* (mullet-colored shoes), the hue of royalty.

After 27 B.C.E., only the Roman emperor, consul, or dictator could wear the red cloak of office, an honor bestowed in a public ceremony on the Capitoline Hill. Candidates for public office appeared in the *toga candida* (gleaming toga), a symbol of blamelessness whitened with chalk. Priests and augurs adopted yellow to depict a sacred office. Mourners left their faces unshaven and displayed sorrow in gray or black garments made from the wool of black sheep.

Around the late 700s C.E., Byzantine social coding reserved black as the appropriate tone of monasticism. Shoes bore status colors—red for nobles, blue for courtiers, and green for the imperial valet. Imperial robes in deep monochrome reds, purples, and greens contrasted Republican Rome's insistence on natural and white togas, the male citizen's uniform.

Medieval stylists emphasized light yellow, berettino (pale blue), bice or bisset (brownish gray), bleche (bleached white), moster develers (gray), porreye (leek green), and aureate (gold). Shifts to deeper tones in the fifteenth century popularized peacock and *feu d'enfer* (hellfire red) for purflings (edgings). By the Renaissance, the splash of red, aurora (orange), azure (sky blue), beasar (light blue), and murrey (purple) under slashes and on parti-color hose of luxury lovers outshone the somber black of clerics and Puritans. The contrast incited loud debates about the implications of riotous shades, which conservatives interpreted as frivolous and promiscuous.

In Tudor England, the stereotypical colors of courtier dress reflected the value of individuals to the king or queen. Young men dressed in light shades such as ash white, marble gray, marigold, arnatto (orange), peach, primrose (pale yellow), and arsadine (arsenic yellow) with pearl hose to imply quick decision making and buoyance of wit. More reserved elders retreated into fur-lined puke (russet-black) damask jackets and shoe black to characterize their earnest loyalty and stability of reason. After 1644, a rigid control of color in Chinese garments followed the regulations of the Qing dynasty court, balancing hues with social status.

Eighteenth-century stage attire featured gauzy pastels in cerulean, slate blue, pistachio, apricot, apple green, columbine (lavender gray), ambergris (copper green), and citron. In 1702, the introduction of the complex Prussian blue synthesized from iron salt and potash offered a sophisticated contrast to black-green, mulberry (reddish purple), musk (cinnamon), raspberry red, and "blankers," the white of shirts and undergarments. In mid-century, French royalty popularized maroon (brownish red) velvet embroidered in gold and robes of *bleu de roi* (royal blue), a variant from centuries of wine red.

The downfall of the Bourbon dynasty in 1792 during the French Revolution dramatically reduced color and glamour in fabrics that had tended toward lemon yellow, marshmallow (reddish lilac), ochre (brownish yellow), porcelain blue, and lastery (red). Men gravitated toward sobriety in black and charcoal frock coats and tweed capes. For at-home attire, they saved bright embroidery in beryl (sea green), langouste (lobster orange), pea green, paroquet (parrot green), or bitumen (light brown) for dressing gowns and smoking caps.

Under the influence of the French empress Eugenie during the Napoleonic era (1799–1815), women's gowns tended toward shades of ivory, nutmeg gray, leghorn yellow, lilac, maiden's blush (rose), and lavender-blue. Victorian tastes in gold, lichen (black-green), iodine green, wine, and invisible blue (midnight blue) attested to the depths of fabric dyes for women's attire. The sobriety of men's black and gray suits and vests opposite impeccable white shirts established an anticolor mind-set attached to male wardrobe. In 1856, William Henry Perkin's synthesis of mauveine from quinine preceded the addition of chic aniline tints of fuchsia, violet, and magenta for suits and coats paired with putty-colored kid gloves.

Mid-century globalism introduced cross-cultural color trends. The London International Exhibition of 1862 launched a demand for paisleys and Asian patterns in shawls and dresses featuring dark claret, malachite (emerald), mandarin (orangey yellow), Ophelia (pinkish mauve), and maize. Because of Queen Victoria's connection with Balmoral Castle, Scots plaids from the north gained popularity throughout Great Britain.

In 1890, *Good Housekeeping* recommended *blé d'or* (wheaten gold) and an American combination—black lace over Parma violet, a romanticized name for heliotrope. *Ridleys' Fashion Magazine,* a New York City quarterly, rebuked stylists for embedding sentiment in tints, as with fickle green, prudish brown, and pink shame. Editors at *Science* magazine complained in 1892 of the nebulous description in "crushed strawberry" and "elephant's breath."

Stimulated by two trendsetters, writer Oscar Wilde and actor Ellen Terry, the late nineteenth-century fad for aesthetic ascots and tea gowns influenced fabric manufacturers. Color marketing invigorated displays in department stores, notably Hamilton's and the Liberty of London department store, a shopping mecca for imported goods on Regent Street. It was during the same era that color choices for English infants and toddlers settled on pink for girls and blue for boys.

The late nineteenth-century penchant for debutante balls in England, Latin America, Australia, and the United States prompted demand for black tuxedos for men. Young girls of marriageable age presented themselves before society in frothy white or eggshell gowns, pearls, long white gloves, and white ostrich feathers.

Modern Merchandising

Turn-of-the century print media spurred the popularity of dust shades for motoring coats and veiled hats, the iridescent shades popularized by stained glass artist Louis Comfort Tiffany, and trendy mother-of-pearl gray, moss rose green, ashes of roses, and prune apparel of the Edwardian era. Children's clothes featured the navy-on-white sailor middy and navy tam or bonnet. Campus choices favored argyle diamonds in pullovers and socks. The light blue, pink, and slate green gowns for women during World War I expressed naiveté, while men's suits retained sober gray, brown, and navy. A short-lived curiosity about the Egyptian garments recovered from the tomb of Tutankhamen in 1922 initiated a surge of clothing in natural linen.

Jolted into radical pursuits and extreme haircuts, American and European women in the Jazz Age elevated silver, red, green, and designer Elsa Schiaparelli's shocking pink as the appropriate tints for the flapper chemise. Women accessorized with dyed-to-march T-strap shoes, brown-and-white spectator pumps, and the solid-color cloche. Lingerie took on the erotic pairing of red and black, symbolic of energy and seduction. Yachters and tennis players embraced cream slacks, white V-neck sweaters, and buff canvas tennis shoes as the sportsman's wardrobe.

Cubist painters Georges Braque and Pablo Picasso inspired bold color blocking in dresses, blouses, sweaters, two-toned pumps, and handbags. The contrast of light against dark caught on with teens, who popularized saddle shoes in white against either brown or black. In 1926, designer Coco Chanel designated the "little black dress" as a neutral wardrobe staple. Singers Maria Callas and Edith Piaf and film stars Marlene Dietrich, Clara Bow, and Audrey Hepburn adopted black as an expression of style and sophistication.

In Germany, the rise of Nazism during the 1930s turned the dull brown and black of jackboots into the iconic tones of virulent militarism. North American color trends favored plaids and ginghams as well as youthful blue denim, fashions reflecting American intent to remain neutral in the late 1930s. The French counterculture produced the Zazous, young men dressed in garish checkered lumber jackets, multicolored scarves, and white socks as a protest of European fascism. Simultaneously, urban males elevated the zoot suit, an eye-catching 1940s combination of tapered pants and long jackets with fedoras in flashy red, plum, aqua, and yellow, colors previously absent from men's wardrobes.

Post–World War II travels by Americans amused Europeans with the dominance of black for evening wear and red, white, and blue in sportswear, caps, and socks. From the opposite perspective, Americans puzzled over the black, gray, and brown that adult Europeans favored for shoes, skirts, sweaters, suits, and shawls. Gradually, American color trends crept into European department stores, introducing a globalism that influenced Japanese styles as well.

Media and Technology

Twentieth-century trends thrived on media exploitation, as with turquoise jackets and gloves in the 1950s and funky tie-dyed T-shirts and madras plaid Bermuda shorts and sport shirts in the late 1960s. Snow togs from the Winter Olympics popularized sleek jumpsuits in silver over white boots as emblems of coordination and speed. The next decade debuted disco glitz, with metallic and plastic sheen coating purples and reds in unitards and parkas made from acrylic fabrics. The techno trend also added gloss to bathing suits in bronze and silver. Jogging suits tended toward racing stripes in crayon colors that matched running shoes. For the classroom and office, solid colors simplified the coordination of blazers, stretchy tops, thigh-length sweaters, and tailored shirts.

Monochromatic fashions in the 1980s influenced mauve shoes, metallic jackets, black leather athletic shoes, and purple rock-and-roll garb. For sportswear, children and adults imitated army camouflage, an offshoot of military dress dating to the Korean War. At the same time, a prevalent myth stereotyped a preference for lavender as an indicator of homosexuality. The Rastafarian and reggae modes touched up leisure outfits with crocheted T-shirts and caps in red, black, green, and yellow, the traditional colors of Africa.

Designers perennially shocked consumers with notable shifts, from A-line dresses in neutral beige and taupe to chartreuse, neon orange, or electric red miniskirts, T-shirts, and patent leather boots. Late in the twentieth century, the business concept of casual Fridays revived khaki slacks and single-color knit shirts for men. Campus wear abandoned the preppy trend and instituted individual looks in a variety of slacks, shorts, T-shirts, windbreakers, and sandal or athletic shoe combinations.

To regulate student attire, school boards introduced dress codes, which suppressed gang colors and slogan shirts by requiring khaki or navy slacks, pinafores, blazers, and skirts and white or blue button-up shirts and blouses. By 2010, one-quarter of American public school systems required standardized dress, which included belts and dress shoes as a backlash against droopy pants and flip-flops. Disgruntled parents sought litigation by the American Civil Liberties Union to allow students to express idiosyncrasies through choice of fabrics and colors.

See also: Batiking; Dyeing; Sumptuary Laws; Symbolic Colors, Patterns, and Motifs; Tie-Dye.

Further Reading

Benney, Lona, Fran Black, and Marisa Bulzone, eds. *The Color of Fashion.* New York: Stewart, Tabori & Chang, 1992.

Craik, Jennifer. *Fashion: The Key Concepts.* New York: Bloomsbury, 2009.

Eiseman, Leatrice, and Keith Recker. *Pantone: The 20th Century in Color.* San Francisco: Chronicle, 2011.

Coming-of-Age Attire

In cultures throughout the world, the acceptance of youth into adult society rewards initiates with clothing and rituals acknowledging maturity. During the ritual transition to adulthood, ethnic communities modify the child's hairstyle and/or wardrobe to encourage full participation in society, the military, and family life, as with the beaded aprons worn by South African maidens, the masking of youth in West Africa, and the ox-hide capes and aprons worn by the Bantwane brides of Botswana. Other maturation ceremonies include the first haircut of the school-age boy in Poland and the capping of twenty-year-old men in China.

In early Rome, discarding the leather or gold *bulla* (locket) preceded an offering of the protective necklace to the family gods. On March 17, freeborn boys became citizens at age 14 by shedding the *toga praetexta,* the purple-edged white tunic of childhood. In the year leading up to the transition, boys practiced dignified dressing by keeping the left arm immobilized inside the tunic. Newly garbed in the white *toga virilis* (toga of manhood), they registered with the military, developed pro-

fessional careers, and fulfilled marital obligations to childhood fiancées.

In a gendered ritual, Roman girls ceased the dressing of dolls and dedicated their toys and girlish hairnet, linen *supparus* (underwear), and *strophium* (breast band) to the goddess Fortuna Virginalis. Twelve-year-old girls learned to spin, weave, and sew by making the *vitta* (womanly fillet) and *tunica recta* (upright tunic), a yellow garment symbolizing both virginity and readiness to manage a household. Belted before a young woman's marriage, the adult *stola* (overdress) and *palla* (short wrap) epitomized the correct behavior and wholesome attitude of a new wife. After she presented her *lunula* (crescent locket) at the household altar, the husband received her into matrimony by removing her *flammeum* (red veil) and unknotting the waist tie, gestures evocative of sexual deflowering.

From the first century C.E., Judeo-Christian communities observed confirmation as a holy act. To demonstrate purity and innocence, confirmands typically wore white robes during a ministerial blessing. Girls encircled their heads with bands of white flowers. For a first Christian communion at age 16, initiates into religious faith dressed in white and knelt before priests, who wore the red robes of epiphany, the coming of the Holy Spirit to Christ's apostles. For the bar mitzvah, Jewish boys appeared before the congregation in tefillin, leather cubes containing verses of scripture written on parchment.

In Japan since 714, the introduction of a 12-year-old boy or girl to the Shinto shrine at a *genpuku* (maturation) ceremony coincided with the taking of an adult name and clothing and a mature hairstyle. For *seiji no hi* (coming of age) on the second Monday in January, 20-year-old girls sported womanly makeup and hairstyles, *zori* (thong sandals), evening purses, and long-sleeved kimonos and obis. Modern dress standards involve topping the ensembles with waist-length fur collars.

From 965, during the rule of King Gwangjong, Korean rites of passage awarded flowers to the honoree, who dressed in *hanbok,* traditional adult garments. At the *Gwan rye* ritual on the third Monday in May, 15-year-old boys received the bamboo and horsehair *gat,* a wide-brimmed black hat; a high cylindrical crown covered the topknot and tied under the chin with long strings. Girls announced their womanhood by coiling their hair at the nape, pinning the length with a *binyeo* (hairpin), and wearing a *jokduri* (ceremonial cap), a black silk Mongolian crown decorated with tassels, embroidery, and costume jewelry.

Rites of Passage in the Modern Era

During the Renaissance, European children wore dresses or sacks (gowns) until the age of toilet training. At an early rite of passage, short coating presented male toddlers with their first short coats—button-up high-neck jackets fitted with leading strings or ribbons for guiding their first steps. The breeching ritual introduced three-year-old boys to men's knickerbockers, pantaloon and skeleton suits, daggers at the belt, and masculine haircuts parted

at the side. A third stage in coming of age occurred during the first official year of schooling, when the six-year-old adopted long pants.

In Britain, presentation at the royal court, a custom that flourished until 1958, demanded the height of debutante evening dress with a train in white, cream, or ivory. Girls of highest lineage took precedence in the order of presentation. Each aristocratic presentee to royalty accessorized her gown with such items as gloves, pearls or family jewels, fans, veils, and a feathered headdress and bobbed in full court curtsy. During the reign of George III and Charlotte of Mecklenburg after 1760, standard debutante attire called for hooped skirts and ostrich plumes. Seamstresses often recycled the coming-out gown into wedding attire.

Into the 1800s, European girls maintained shoulder-length curls or braids until their mid-teens, when they put their hair up to indicate the staid womanhood that followed girlish flirta-

Young South Koreans take part in the annual May rite of passage called *Gwan rye,* dating to the tenth century. Girls gather their hair in a bun and wear a silk crown as a symbol of womanhood. Boys don a black hat made of bamboo and horsehair called a *gat. (Jung Yeon-Je/ AFP/Getty Images)*

tion. British debutantes wore the obligatory tulle headdress and triad of feathers at court presentation during the Victorian and Edwardian eras. In Savannah, Georgia, from 1817, aristocratic white girls made their social debut at the Christmas Cotillion, America's oldest imitation of European court presentation.

In New Orleans, mulatta debutante balls prevented the exploitation of free black girls. As described in Isabel Allende's historical novel *Island Beneath the Sea* (2010), a coming-out ball following the Louisiana Purchase of 1803 presented mixed-blood maidens at the height of their sexual appeal. The training of biracial city girls in etiquette, dance, corsetry, makeup, and refined couture enabled them to negotiate affairs with potential lovers from a position of power.

Among Native Americans, traditional celebration of maturation ceremonies honored age-old rites of passage, as with the dressing of a Pueblo girl at menarche in an ochre-stained buckskin dress and warming her body with heated rocks. The Shasta of Northern California supplied a similar skin dress and moccasins, belt, cloak, headband, and anklets as rewards for womanhood. The California Karok painted the girl's face before a night dance. In Arizona, Yuma girls at first menstruation washed their hair daily and coated it in mud.

In Northern California, the Maidu performed similar clothing and body painting ceremonies to initiate teen females. The Tututni of southern Oregon dressed the pubescent girl in a deerskin head covering and attached a tiny basket to the neck containing sharp instruments for a ritual bloodletting. Apache coming-of-age rituals in Arizona and New Mexico welcomed the female into adulthood with an eagle feather hair ornament, a protective abalone fetish on the forehead, and a beaded necklace conferring womanly authority.

Naked South Seas youth adopted the lavalava (loincloth), tattooing, shell necklaces, leaf anklets and bracelets, flower garlands, and bark dance skirts, a wardrobe transformation described in anthropologist Margaret Mead's *Coming of Age in Samoa* (1928). Similarly, in Borneo, a pubescent Iban boy marked adulthood by donning his first *sirat* (loincloth). Boys in Papua New Guinea re-ceived a conical hat edged in leaves that extended to the hips. In Bali, maturity ritual involved the filing of the canine teeth, emblematic of the acceptance of adult demeanor.

Contemporary Coming of Age

Today, physical grooming dominates the coming-of-age transition. Threading, an Asian form of hair removal on maidens, begins with the twisting of string for sliding over hair on the nubile body. Iranian women depilate the face, armpits, and pubic areas of a virgin bride before her wedding. In Buddhist culture, novices in their late teens abandon rich dressing for robes, such as the red habits worn in Kashmir, yellow in Thailand, red in Burma, and gray in Vietnam.

Hindu youths between the ages of eight and 12 accept manhood at the *upanayana,* a ceremony involving the draping of the circular *yajnopavita* (sacred thread) from the left shoulder to the waist. A subsequent ritual, *keshanta* (shaving), at age 16 readies the young man for male grooming. Girls celebrate *ritushuddhi* (menarche) by retreating from family life for three days and abandoning sewing.

American sweet sixteen parties extol transition for teenage girls. A male family member or godfather presents high-heel shoes to the honoree, who removes girlish slippers to don women's footwear; a female family member positions a tiara on the birthday girl's head. In the Philippines, women celebrate a debut at age 18 by dressing in formal apparel and carrying 18 roses to a cotillion, or debutante ball.

In Latin America, the *quinceañera* (fifteenth birthday festivity), derived from Aztec, French, and Spanish ritual, celebrates female coming of age with womanly makeup and nail painting, high-heel shoes, and elegant evening gowns, customary dress. Young men in tuxedos join the dining and dancing. In Ecuador, the birthday girl receives gifts of jewelry and a tiara. In Mexico, birthday jewelry consists of a rosary or religious pendant honoring the Virgin of Guadalupe.

See also: Body Painting; Courtship Attire; Flowers; Jewish Religious Attire; Ritual Garments; Teen Trends; Wedding Dress.

Further Reading

Adams, J. Michael, and Angelo Carfagna. *Coming of Age in a Globalized World: The Next Generation.* Bloomfield, CT: Kumarian, 2006.

Gennep, Arnold van. *The Rites of Passage.* Reprint. New York: Routledge, 2010.

Markstrom, Carol A. *Empowerment of North American Indian Girls: Ritual Expressions at Puberty.* Lincoln: University of Nebraska Press, 2008.

Corsets and Girdles

Waistline shaping for men and women has ignited intense controversies over the endangerment of health for the sake of fashion. In the late Middle Ages, corsetry originated in England with the kirtle, a gown restrained at the midline with looped fasteners. The kirtle proportioned bust, waist, and hips, a shape denounced in 1257 by Pope Alexander IV.

In the 1350s, the French midriff support created the illusion of proportion by whittling the waist while boosting the bust. Arab, Dutch, Frankish, Hun, Viking, and Welsh fashions highlighted the female form in laced bodice, slim waist, and profuse linen petticoats. In the 1500s, French and English body binders earned the name *corps à la baleine* (whale bodies), though some took their shape from wood or reed inserts in women's farthingales and men's court doublets. The inflexibility of the female waist in these garments caused problems with walking, sitting, dancing, and physical exercise, increasing the risk of fainting.

Made obligatory by high society, the laced bodice and triangular torso shaper separated self-controlled women from "loose" females, a euphemism for the uncorseted streetwalker. Contributing to a discreet fit, the invention of the wire hook and eye in 1697 secured the curvaceous silhouette. In the 1700s, stays altered with dress fashion to accommodate new styles and fabrics, including the Austrian and Bavarian vest-corset, a deep-cut laced bodice for folk dancers. In the September 1785 issue of *The Lancet,* philosopher Jean-Jacques Rousseau addressed the physical handicaps of girdling and their effects on normal motion and breathing.

In the mid-eighteenth century, Belgian bal-lerina Marie Camargo and French choreographer Marie Sallé featured natural female bodies in muslin stage costumes devoid of boning and cinching. The influence of bendable bodies in haute couture resulted in fewer busks and shorter corset bars, which shrank by half to 6 inches (15 centimeters). Meanwhile, Creole girls in New Orleans boosted their appeal in the slimmers corset that allowed freedom to dance and walk with swaying hips.

In the early nineteenth century, when French Empress Joséphine de Beauharnais reduced boned foundation garments, Beau Brummell in England influenced men's stays, a stomacher braced with whalebone to restrain the paunch. Couturier Charles Frederick Worth advocated similar female shaping with padded bustle and bamboo and rattan corset lining. By the 1840s, corsets contained steel and hardened leather as well as cording. Ends that fastened in front with humped hooks and eyes and in back with lacing produced an artificial hourglass figure in women as well as little girls.

During the reign of England's Queen Victoria from 1837 to 1901, lacing reduced the wasp waist; its S-bend shape held the torso upright while thrusting the hips out behind, a silhouette modeled by actors Sarah Bernhardt and Lillie Langtry. In the 1850s, William F. Thomas & Company in London shortened the production time for corsets by purchasing sewing machines capable of stitching flattening devices into cloth. In Tangiers and Bangkok, Asian women mused over a garment that supposedly "trained" the figure by distorting normal female curves.

In the 1860s, American and British consumers flattened the rounded abdomen with the busk board, a corset reinforced with oak planks, ivory, or whalebone and covered in baronette and sateen weaves of cotton and rayon. *Ladies Quarterly of Broadway Fashions* advertised Butterick's 1866 patterns for corsets in 13 sizes, which seamstresses laced with plaited strings available at department stores. Charles Dana Gibson's drawings of "Gibson Girls" featured slim women laced into corseted swimsuits and faggoted bust bodices.

Gay Nineties girlie photos pictured camisoles laced back and front over leather or white coutil waspies (waist cinches), with punitive straps and

plastic boning to generate the pouter pigeon bosom. Empress Elizabeth of Austria, wife of Franz Joseph I, set the equestrienne style in buttoned bodice over a leather split-busk corset. A young Laura Ingalls Wilder, later the author of the Little House on the Prairie series of children's books, rankled at having to sleep in a body shaper, a crime against girls bemoaned in *The Gentlewoman* magazine.

Although *Vogue* editor Josephine Redding reviled body binding after 1892 as slavery to fashion, the tiny middle prevailed. Sears, Roebuck, Montgomery Ward, and Eaton catalogs advocated "healthy corsetry" molded from coraline (boning made from ixtle plant fibers) bound with elasticized cotton. According to the *American Journal of Nursing* and *Corset and Underwear Review,* embroidered corset covers, maternity waist supports, and flexible riding corsets remained mainstays of female fashion into the Edwardian era. Department stores drew consumers by advertising trained corsetieres to ensure an elegant profile.

Early in the 1900s, French couturier Paul Poiret advised women to abandon the rigid corset and embrace a simpler, less tortured waistless dress revealing natural curves. Designer Lucy Duff-Gordon repudiated the strain and unnatural shape of the waist cinch by offering sheer lingerie as an alternative. During World War I, working women had no choice but to abandon body restriction during their labors. Polish Jewish immigrants contributed a silent protest by wearing no boning under their dresses.

As corsetry lost appeal in the 1910s, couturiers Jeanne Lanvin, Madeleine Vionnet, Coco Chanel, and Jean Patou began to hype the natural body as youthful and sexually appealing. In the 1930s, Hollywood vamp Mae West popularized the boned corselette over natural waist and hips. British rationing of metal and rubber during World War II limited the availability of stretchy corset materials.

After the war, manufacturers joined bra to girdle to form the body shaper, an all-in-one foundation garment. Frederick's of Hollywood and designer Jean Paul Gaultier redirected undergarments from "unmentionables" to lace corset exhibition; the garment shifted from a suppression of womanhood to an element of seduction and womanly empowerment. By the

1950s, the Lycra power net girdle replaced boned undergarments as a means of controlling jiggle in the hips.

Second-wave feminism in the 1960s ended the dominance of figure control in women's ready-to-wear as natural-style clothing replaced the manipulated silhouettes of the past. In the first decades of the twenty-first century, corsets survive as titillating retro lingerie and in stage performances by entertainers such as Selena Gomez and Madonna.

See also: Bodices; Bohemian Style and Fashion; Brassieres; Dress Reform; Gendered Dressing; Whalebone.

Further Reading

Kortsch, Christine Bayles. *Dress Culture in Late Victorian Women's Fiction: Literacy, Textiles, and Activism.* Burlington, VT: Ashgate, 2009.

Seleshanko, Kristina. *Bound & Determined: A Visual History of Corsets, 1850–1960.* Mineola, NY: Dover, 2012.

Steele, Valerie, ed. *The Corset: A Cultural History.* New Haven, CT: Yale University Press, 2004.

Cosmetics

The cleansing and grooming of features and skin tone with natural or synthetic cosmetics constitutes an ancient and global phenomenon. Beautification in China began in 3000 B.C.E. with gelatinous or waxen nail polish available in red, black, or metallic shades. Kohl (antimony or lampblack) eye color lined the eyelids and darkened eyelashes and brows. A similar application of face colorants along the cheekbones brightened the faces of Harappan women in the Indus Valley.

Across much of Asia, facial therapists practiced threading, an epilation of the forehead carried out by dragging a twisted string over tiny hairs to smooth the complexion, often before a wedding or festival. To enhance appeal and display sexual maturity, Sumerian women abraded their complexions with pumice, scraped with razors to exfoliate, and applied crushed gemstones around the eyes to accentuate prominent features. Cockleshells served as storage pots for palm and lip rouge. At Ur in 3600 B.C.E., the Akkadian queen Puabi (or Shub-ad) reddened her lips with crushed ochre

and lead carbonate and stored beauty treatments in a lapis, silver, and seashell box.

In North Africa around 2000 B.C.E., priests superintended the distillation of balsam and cedar soil into body fragrances. By 1480 B.C.E., dressing table flacons of alabaster and obsidian stored perfumed unguents and bath oils and henna colorants pearlized with fish scales, used to glorify social status. Emollients to lighten skin tone and combat wrinkles—honey, frankincense, castor oil, and moringa oil—assumed places alongside pots of resinous hairdressings and facials of egg albumen. Lip stain made from fucus (brown seaweed), crushed beetles, red ochre, iodine, and bromine mannite (sea minerals dissolved in apple cider) offered hues from orange and magenta to blue-black.

History identifies some women by their expertise with facial beautifiers. Kohl or malachite eyeliner became the defining cosmetic featured on the bust of Nefertiti sculpted by Thutmose around 1350 B.C.E. at Amarna, Egypt. In the mid-ninth century B.C.E., Jezebel, a Phoenician princess and queen of Israel, paganized the idea of makeup by painting herself brazenly and worshipping idols. A subsequent biblical figure, Esther, the putative wife of Persian king Xerxes I (also known as Ahasuerus) in the mid-fifth century B.C.E., reversed the stereotype of the femme fatale by beautifying herself to rescue the Jews from genocide.

Although Lycurgus outlawed cosmetics in Sparta around 750 B.C.E., Greek and Roman females treated the complexion with olive oil and dyed their hair blonde. Trendsetting women whitened their skin with chalk or lead carbonate paste and painted on artificial blue veins; men preferred tin oxide and starch creamed into animal fat. Minoan women on Crete and Thera flaunted reddish-purple lips from applications of natural colorants—seaweed, red wine sediment, and mulberry juice.

By 400 B.C.E., hair dye and face powder contributed commodities to trade. Ornate cosmetics boxes followed upper-class Mediterranean women to their graves. Slave marketers obtained high prices for the trained *ornatrix* (cosmetologist) and her *cosmatae* (beauty specialists). For military triumphs, Roman heroes covered their faces in costly vermilion (cinnabar), a toxic red dye.

Roman occupation of Britannia introduced women to the use of the bronze mortar and pestle for pulverizing mineral pigment or dried bladderwrack (seaweed) into *fucus vesiculosus* (foundation). Around 50 B.C.E., Cleopatra preferred carmine, an aluminum salt made from cochineal scale insects and their eggs. Vials of her favorite makeup may have followed her to the tomb for self-adornment in the afterlife. Around 175 C.E., Galen of Pergamum, a Greco-Roman physician, invented *cera alba* (white beeswax), an herbal pore cleanser and moisturizer blended with rose water and olive oil. The collapse of the Roman Empire in 476 suppressed European cosmetics along with personal hygiene.

Medieval Beauty Treatments

In fifth-century China, women promoted facial beauty and welcomed the synthesis of vermilion from mercury and sulfur into mercury sulfide pigment. Late in the seventh century, Japanese women evolved a battery of facial treatments beginning with a wax or oil base and texturized rice paste sponged over plucked eyebrows and the nape of the neck and chest. After painting on false eyebrows with charcoal, they finished the look with red or white parts of the safflower plant. By crushing blossom parts, beautifiers created colorants for brushing on eyes, brows, nose, and mouth and set the treatment with fine rice powder. For contrast, they blackened their teeth with iron filings.

In Germanic and Anglo-Saxon enclaves around 700, women popularized orange lip rouge, rosewater, and honey-based cosmetics. By the 800s, wealthy women invested in crystal beauty table containers imported from Constantinople. In Italy, red lip rouge and blusher heightened the attraction of upper-class women. Irish women, on the outskirts of major trade routes, relied on herbal colorants and whitened their hair with limewater and teeth with crushed mint.

Under the rule of Islam, Middle Eastern cosmetics remained acceptable unless applied as a disguise, source of seduction, or toxin. Around 1000 C.E., the *Kitab al-Tasrif* (*The Method of Medicine*)

categorized cosmetics and scented oils as pharmaceuticals. The author, Iberian encyclopedist al-Zahrawi, an Arab surgeon and pharmacologist living in Moorish Iberia, invented molded lipstick and rub-on perfume made from ambergris and musk.

In 1099, European warriors returning from the First Crusade brought fragrance and face paint from the Middle East. Trotula's *De Ornatu Mulierum* (*Women's Cosmetics,* ca. 1210), a best-selling compendium on gynecology and beauty treatments, originated in Salerno from Arabic sources and remained in print throughout the Renaissance. In contrast to Middle Eastern doctrines, the leaders of Christendom during the high Middle Ages condemned Byzantine makeup as a tool of Satan and disparaged the impious alchemist as a perverter of nature. Women evaded the interdiction by imitating the colors of the lily and rose, symbols of the Virgin Mary.

Renaissance Makeup

As Christianity lost its hold over human ornamentation during the Renaissance, France and the city-state of Venice led European markets in the distribution of cosmetics and perfumes to women unconcerned with church pressures. After 1461, Edward IV of England condoned cosmetics for male and female courtiers. By the 1500s, Iberian and Italian trendsetters excelled at contrasting light skin with rosy colorants. However, only noblewomen, actresses, and prostitutes in London, Milan, Paris, and Venice wore a full range of complexion products and set foundation with egg white, which hardened into a mask.

Despite puritanical sermons objecting to blatant vanity, European women developed regimens to redden the lips, whiten teeth, and lighten the skin to a pallor suggesting youth and elitism. Urban rumors declared lipstick a magical potion capable of warding off lethal disease. Experimenters dabbled in bizarre beauty treatments of dog fat, pig and alligator organs, and wolf's blood blended with the consumer's urine and created face peels from mercury, which they followed with a wash of ass's milk.

Plant juices or fish glue blended with beeswax

and white wine produced lipsticks for the ordinary woman. Alum, talcum, and tin ash blended with green figs or vinegar served as whiteners of freckled cheeks, on which women drew fake blue veins. Plucking yielded a higher hairline and shaped brows.

For sparkling eyes, women resorted to drops of belladonna (atropine) pressed from nightshade berries, a source of toxic alkaloids. Rhubarb steeped in white wine brightened faded blonde locks. Butter and venison suet restored chapped skin.

After 1558, Elizabeth I of England popularized the use of two toxins in face creams—arsenic and Venetian ceruse, a lead carbonate base dissolved in vinegar. While concealing smallpox scars, the base coordinated with her white ruff and golden-red hair to create the ideal of Elizabethan beauty. The queen rolled colorants into ground alabaster or plaster of Paris for a lip pencil and followed personal recipes for lip gloss blended from gum arabic (acacia sap), cochineal, egg albumen, and fig milk. Elizabeth also created a demand for mirrors as wall decor and encouraged her ladies-in-waiting to reapply white makeup rather than cleansing their faces to begin afresh. In France, the accession of Henry III in 1573 created a similar climate of facial improvement.

Evolving Cosmetology

Under James I after 1607, Englishwomen tended to enlarge the lower lip with cherry red for its allure. The wealthy indulged in bear grease, a more expensive emollient than the pig fat used by peasants. Male courtiers boldly asserted effeminacy with cosmetics, perhaps betokening the king's unconcealed homosexuality.

In the half-century following 1620, both French and English flirts stuffed their cheeks with fiber plumpers and glued felt or velvet *mouches* (patches) to the head and upper body. Patching, initially a concealment of scars and blemishes, spurred pundits to interpret the shapes and locations as amorous code or political emblems. With his poem "Wishes to His Supposed Mistress" (1646), poet Richard Cranshaw dubbed these women "made up," a term he coined for "cosmetically modified."

After the restoration of Charles II of England in 1660, men and women applied red lip stain and thick foundation to emulate a tan. Into the 1700s, cosmetic applications were available to all classes and valuable to survivors of smallpox and syphilis. In France, chemists excelled at the creation of new colorants for hair, nails, eyes, and lips. After 1715, Louis XV legitimized the use of lead-based foundation for men. In obvious scorn of French aesthetics, the British Parliament in 1770 declared lipstick a tool of sorceresses.

European cosmetics merchants developed a wide consumer base. In the 1780s, bold French-women bought some 2 million pots of rouge annually, usually red lip and cheek colorants blended from vermilion mixed with iodine or brick dust. Prior to the French Revolution of 1789, the colorant offended outsiders, who marveled at extreme face paints available in some two dozen brands. For the next six decades, sober French patriots preferred natural skin tones to the gaudy look that had accompanied extravagant sybarites to the guillotine.

In the early 1800s, Englishwomen bought recipe books that described home cosmetics preparations involving crushed elderberries in fireplace ash to darken eyelashes, tamarisk bark to whiten teeth, oatmeal to soften hands, hair dye from barberry bark and rhubarb, and almond oil and cucumber juice for clarifying skin. They revived their complexions with brisk walking, riding, and swimming and perfumed themselves with light toilet water blended from gardenias, lavender, or roses. A thorough facial preparation included lanolin and zinc oxide foundation, fine talcum, pearly bismuth powder, lip salve, and rouge applied with fabric or paper sheets permeated with pigmented powder.

The British experience in Egypt, Turkey, and India introduced the application to eyelashes of burned cork or black soot emulsified in oil, a forerunner of cream mascara invented in 1844 by French perfumer Eugène Rimmel. By 1850, savvy women avoided lead carbonate and China red vermilion, both of which were known poisons. Instead, they ate chalk and revitalized pale faces by chewing their lips and pinching their cheeks.

In 1872, Western makeup reached Japan, where consumers bought Shiseido beauty treatments marketed in drugstores by naval pharmacist Arinobu Fukuhara. In South Africa, Christian nuns discouraged application of the customary red ochre body paint displayed on Xhosa women at rituals and the white ochre painted on newborns.

Into the Belle Époque, makeup followed trends of ballerinas and actors Lillian Russell, Lillie Langtry, and Sarah Bernhardt, who endorsed commercial cosmetics. For stage appearances, they brushed on lip rouge made from wax, oil, and carmine dye. Electrolysis, a depilatory technique invented in 1875 by ophthalmologist Charles Michel, destroyed unwanted hair at the root.

In 1883, theatrical cosmetologist Alexandre Napoléon Bourjois, the inventor of greasepaint, formulated pastel base and dry blush. The next year, French cosmetics from Guerlain introduced *rouge baiser* (lipstick) synthesized from beeswax, castor oil, and deer tallow and wrapped in silk paper.

In the United States, during the declining days of the Jim Crow era, Anthony Overton introduced cosmetic products for African Americans in the F.W. Woolworth's chain store. A contemporary, Annie Turnbo Malone, developed Poro cosmetics, which she marketed in the Caribbean, Africa, and North and South America. In Denver, Pittsburgh, and Indianapolis, America's first black female millionaire, Madame C.J. Walker, compounded competitive hair relaxers, hot comb oils, and skin treatments for black women. During the Jazz Age, her products flourished in Harlem as elements of ethnic pride.

Selling and Regulating Makeup

By the end of the nineteenth century, more American women were purchasing pots of lip rouge, which Sears, Roebuck advertised in its catalogs as "Blush of Roses" for 65 cents. On June 30, 1906, the Pure Food and Drug Act outlawed toxic metals in cosmetics. The demands of film close-ups led to the invention of false eyelashes, a gauze crescent layered with human hairs first photographed for cinema by D.W. Griffith for *Intolerance* (1916). After World War I, women worldwide sampled the makeup advertised in women's magazines and sold in department store beauty bars and hair salons. In 1917, chemist Thomas Lyle Williams marketed Maybelline mascara, which he mixed from coal and petrolatum.

Early cinema created a fad for the glamorous facial features of Mary Pickford, Jean Harlow, and Lillian Gish. In the 1920s, cosmetic advertising and the invention of the Kurlash eyelash curler along with the discovery of eyeliner in the tomb of Tutankhamen increased attention to the eyes. Female enfranchisement inspired women to assert their independence with more pronounced facial color, white powder, smoky eye shadow, and a bow-shaped mouth. Black women emulated white film stars by purchasing skin bleaches under the names Black-No-More, Cocotone Skin Whitener, and Fair-Plex Ointment. In 1922, Puig, a Barcelona firm headed by Antonio Puig Castelló, marketed the first Spanish lipstick, called Milady.

Fashion-conscious women vivified the face with mascara, red lipstick, and tanned skin, an enhancement that received global approval for all classes. A massage with cold cream, an emulsion of animal fat or almond oil with water, softened and moisturized the skin while removing residue from wrinkles and pores. In 1931, Almay's hypoallergenic makeup, a fragrance-free Revlon spinoff, targeted sensitive skin for color enhancement and toning with natural cucumber, meadowsweet, moringa oil, aloe, milk thistle, rosehips, and licorice. The following year, Lawrence Gelb entered market competition for delicate beauties by inventing less caustic Clairol hair dye.

Pharmacies and department store chains specialized in beauty and hair treatments by Elizabeth Arden, Helena Rubinstein, and L'Oréal. Avon's door-to-door vendors encouraged consumers to undergo pore cleansing and massage and to sample scents, creams, and lipsticks in shades of pink, crimson, and lilac. One experimental lash dye, Lash Lure, contained toxic aniline dye, which blinded some users and killed others. The Federal Food, Drug, and Cosmetic Act of 1938 limited impure and dangerous substances in hair and skin care products.

Industrialized Cosmetics

At the end of the Great Depression, new beauty products flooded the world market, beginning in 1938 with Volupté compacts, art deco atomizers, and lip liner pencil, made in Elizabeth, New Jersey, and advertised in *Mademoiselle* and *Vogue*. The company's hussy red outsold lady pink by more than 83 percent. Polish cosmetologist Max Factor of Hollywood introduced pancake makeup in 12 shades, waterproof mascara, lip gloss, false eyelashes, and nail cream. In 1938, he mixed chalk or kaolin with talcum, magnesium stearate, zinc oxide, titanium dioxide, and pigment into Erace concealer, a thick foundation that masked acne, bruising, broken veins, and circles under the eyes.

During World War II, the brightening of the face with lip color and complexion powder and the use of Richard Hudnut and Toni home permanents enabled U.S. female noncombatants to maintain cheer. In contrast, many women in Argentina, Cuba, and Mexico remained too poor to buy even toothpaste. In the postwar era, advertising for Cover Girl glorified the youthful consumer who enhanced her skin, eyes, nails, and lips. Cosmetics firms promoted facial softening by adding cocoa butter and petrolatum to creams and lotions.

In the mid-1900s throughout Western Europe, Mexico, Japan, and Argentina, Revlon marketed complementary shades of eye shadow, lip and nail color, and matte base makeup texturized with silica. In 1949, chemist Hazel Bishop improved twist tubes of lip color by inventing an indelible skin stain guaranteed smudge-proof, "kissable," and long lasting. Following the product introduction, company profits boomed to 20 times its original earnings.

In Argentina in 1953, guidelines for shaving cream, talcum powder, and hair dye regulated flammability, antimicrobial ingredients, and irritants. In 1956, while Marilyn Monroe's film *Bus Stop* promoted bleached hair, Helena Rubinstein contributed cream mascara available in a tube and applied with a brush. The product sold particularly well after Elizabeth Taylor popularized Egyptian eye enhancement in the film *Cleopatra* (1963). Teens sported false eyelashes as elements of flirtation.

Second-wave feminism in the 1960s introduced the "natural" look—a rejection of ponytails, lacquered bouffant hairdos, winged eyeglasses, shimmering titanium makeup, and frosted nail enamel of the 1950s. Late in the decade, teen trends popularized pearly pink lips, silver and blue lipstick, flavored lip gloss, and two-tone eye shadow, all elements of women's "Cinderella complex," a need to dress to please men. Actor Julie Christie and models Twiggy and Jean Shrimpton brought the 1960s to a close with lined eye sockets and hollow cheeks. Holiday looks tended toward mica-tinged lipstick and metallic glitter for hair and face.

The evolving naturalized makeup of the 1970s incorporated a range of skin tones in sheer emulsions, which smoothed on without emphasizing lines and imperfections. Maybelline, which marketed Great Lash mascara in 1971, rose to a 33 percent share of U.S. eye makeup sales. Olay boosted sales in the United States, Brazil, Mexico, France, and Italy from $7 million to $117 million. In contrast to global advertising used to promote other products, Japanese flaw-vanishing cream and pomade from Shiseido and cosmetics from Kosé in Hong Kong remained localized, spreading no farther than Taiwan and Singapore.

In Brazil, Natura cosmetics, founded by Luiz da Cunha Seabra, competed with more familiar lines by advertising toiletries, cosmetics, and skin cleaners made from sustainable sources for women and babies. The business grew at a rate of 40 percent each year. Natura skin care solutions flourished in Argentina, Chile, and Portugal. A competitor, Caipirinha, fought back with media claims of natural oil and Amazonian cupuacu butter in high concentrations.

Afro-Caribbean products identified 36 gradations for the complexion and lips, ranging from ebony and mahogany to light tan. In Chicago in 1974, John Harold Johnson debuted Fashion Fair Cosmetics, which catered to African American women with coppery malachite suited to a dark complexion. With the emergence of the African look in world fashion capitals, demand for darker cosmetics increased the profits of Josepha of Martinique, who set up distribution in the Latin Quarter of Paris. Clients popularized her mudpacks, lip tints, tribal eye colors, and pomades for cornrowing hair, which she marketed under such names as Baobab, Tafia, Bambera, and Dankali.

Silvery white highlighter exaggerated the eyes much as lip liner and brushed fill-ins emphasized the lips. Detergent shampoos cleansed the scalp and hair. Pomade, conditioners, and brilliantines restored gloss and body to men's and women's hair and beards depleted by daily cleansing, hydrogen peroxide bleaches, blow-drying, Afro perming, hair straightening, and permanent waves.

The 1980s introduced concern for aging and unhealthful beauty regimens. For instant youth, professional women and men spiked their hair with mousse and bronzed the skin with artificial tan tones. The British brand Lush, sold by mail order and in boutiques in Singapore, Japan, Australia, and South America, catered to the eco-friendly market by advertising fresh ingredients and fewer preservatives. In the late twentieth century, a top layer of lip gels and stains in brown and frosted tones produced by bismuth oxychloride enhanced the texture of waxy red lipsticks. Advertising mentioned shea butter, aloe vera, and vitamin E to promote the wholesome and beneficial side of makeup.

Regulation outside the United States, as demanded by customers in Canada, Brazil, India, and Thailand, began with rigorous testing. The cosmetic and sunscreen standards set in South Africa in 1993 and in Russia and Brazil in the late 1990s ensured purity and safety of ingredients. Spray-on fixatives increased the time that makeup remained in place. By 1997, chemical peels and dermabrasion lightened scars, while laser treatment removed tattoos, skin blemishes, and hair. In South Korea, the demand for whitening creams topped consumers' lists.

In the 2000s, when U.S. consumer spending on cosmetics topped $20 billion, marketers in Israel, Iran, Saudi Arabia, and the United Arab Emirates reached Middle Eastern consumers with products that cleansed and pampered hair and skin. In Yemen, consumers gave up black-masked eyes and turmeric face powder for cosmopolitan makeup. Likewise, Turkish, Lithuanian, Polish, Hungarian, Russian, and Ukrainian women promoted German imports of face and eye makeup.

Globally, regularly scheduled eyebrow and facial waxings, manicures, pedicures, and skin treatments increased as urbanites improved their looks and battled the effects of air pollution. Cosmetic brands featured fruit and vegetable ingredients, from cucumber, mint, and banana to goat milk and açaí and dewberries. In January 2008, the U.S. Food and Drug Administration (FDA) recalled kumkum, a lead-based saffron makeup from India for the forehead and hairline sold in Asian stores. The following year, the FDA required cosmetic labeling identifying carmine, a red dye that can cause lethal allergic reactions.

By 2010, cosmetic sales worldwide reached an estimated $330 billion. In 2012, vendors of all-natural cosmetics stressed their reliance on beeswax, castor oil, and jojoba oil rather than harsh metals and pore-clogging thickeners. Cosmetic surgery tourism lured customers to Malaysia, Dominican Republic, Mexico, Philippines, Argentina, Brazil, Costa Rica, South Africa, Poland, and Thailand. In Florence, Italy, the Santa Maria Novella line introduced papaya gel and balsa cream to support skin care and shrink scars after plastic surgery. Today, DNA testing enables young, sexually active, and aging consumers to personalize anti-aging creams and makeup to individual genetic needs.

See also: Body Painting; Nail Art.

Further Reading

Barel, Andre O., Marc Paye, and Howard I. Maibach, eds. *Handbook of Cosmetic Science and Technology.* New York: Taylor & Francis, 2005.

Corson, Richard. *Fashions in Makeup: From Ancient to Modern Times.* London: Peter Owen, 2004.

Hernandez, Gabriela. *Classic Beauty: The History of Makeup.* Atglen, PA: Schiffer, 2011.

Jones, Geoffrey. *Beauty Imagined: A History of the Global Beauty Industry.* New York: Oxford University Press, 2010.

Costume Design, Film

Cinematography changed the thinking of viewers about the styles, materials, and accessories of current and historical attire. Hollywood spawned unique costumes for characters, from the feathered green cap of Douglas Fairbanks as Robin Hood in 1922 and the turbans of Turkish pashas in the films of Rudolf Valentino in the mid-1920s to the female Kikuyu dress in *Out of Africa* (1987) and the intergalactic travel attire of the Starship *Enterprise* crew in the TV and film franchise *Star Trek*. Large casts involved mass wardrobes, such as the leopard-skin headbands and battle kilts featured in *Zulu* (1965) and thirteen-century B.C.E. armor in the film *Troy* (2004). Some film characters acquired lasting identity by virtue of their costumes, as with Scarlett O'Hara's dress made from velvet portieres and gold drapery cords in *Gone with the Wind* (1939).

Stars impacted haute couture with identifiable combinations, such as the little-girl looks of Judy Garland in *The Wizard of Oz* (1939) and carnival outfits for *Carousel* (1956). In the 1930s, Mae West's Gay Nineties revival required five-inch heels, boas, plumes, rhinestones, boned bodices, and no corsetry. Two costume versions, one loose for sitting and one skin-tight for standing, enhanced the actor's reputation for sex appeal and fashion savvy, which caught the eye of designers in Europe and the United States. In imitation of the plumed netted hats of Mae West, designs on the street paired feathers with long veils.

Jean Harlow's white satin bias slip-dress in *Dinner at Eight* (1933) became the first of many cinema outfits suited to an actor's best features. To heighten an aristocratic air in *Conquest* (1937), a 90-inch (2.3-meter) length of silk with satin fringe swathed Greta Garbo over a high Empire gown. Ensembles matched the actor and part, as with Martha Ray's black silk and silver toreador outfit for *Tropic Holiday* (1938), Maureen O'Hara's "gypsy" costumes for *The Hunchback of Notre Dame* (1939), and Claude Rains's Vichy French uniform in *Casablanca* (1942).

Clothes Make the Actor

The complementing of action and personality turned Claudette Colbert, one of the nation's 10 best-dressed women of the 1930s, into a vamp in Cecil B. DeMille's spectacular biopic *Cleopatra* (1934). Highlights ranged from spangles, winged headpieces, and dark wig and eye shadow to the body-conscious corded waist, which illustrated with an X the queen's allure. Although anachronistic and unsuited to a desert climate, fluid velvets, slinky satins, and ruching from the glamorous European and American fashions of the 1930s emphasized Colbert's shapely legs framed by an art deco throne and royal crest.

Moviegoers and department stores copied halter-top gowns and the satin crepe sarong sewn onto Dorothy Lamour for *Jungle Princess* (1936) and the man-tailored jackets and slacks of Katharine Hepburn in *Woman of the Year* (1942). To conceal Joan Crawford's broad hips, costumers stressed broad shoulders with padding, fur stoles, jeweled turbans, and ruffled sleeves in *I Live My Life* (1935). The long, thin lines focused attention on a single- or two-tone garment over the inverted triangle torso, a nipped-in waist, and knee-length skirt or toreador pants to the ankle, all tapering to discreet high heels. Accessories featured sashes and organza wraps with envelope bags and mid-length white gloves, all of which boosted department store sales of film knockoffs.

Hollywood contributed to the wig mystique with character-changing hair and beard styles. Vigorous acting threatened fragile hairpieces, such as Alec Guinness's Saudi styles in *Lawrence of Arabia* (1963) and Cate Blanchett's red coif in *Elizabeth* (1998). Some headdresses required duplicates to maintain character appearance. To meet the demand, Ern and Perc Westmore opened a Hollywood salon on Sunset Boulevard in 1935, when the clientele included Clara Bow, Marlene Dietrich, Carole Lombard, Myrna Loy, Lana Turner, and Rita Hayworth. The Westmore family, masters of Hollywood makeup, shaped notions about fantasy figures with the hair and skin of Frankenstein's monster and the Mummy.

Unlikely folk fad items had their beginnings in film scenarios, such as Roddy McDowall's Welsh flat-bill cap in *How Green Was My Valley* (1941). Depictions of Latina dress in *Masquerade in Mexico* (1945) popularized the *camisa* (peasant blouse), *rebozo* (shawl), and poncho. Chiaroscuro incorporated light and dark aspects of villainy and corrupt values for William Bendix, Marlon Brando, Alan Ladd, Veronica Lake, Fred MacMurray, Edward G. Robinson, and Barbara Stanwyck in major film noir—*This Gun for Hire* (1942), *The Blue Dahlia* (1946), and *A Streetcar Named Desire* (1947), all initiators of the "noir" look. For Hollywood's influence on costume authenticity, the Academy Awards recognized costume design with its own Oscar beginning in 1949.

As a lightweight alternative to cambric-based wigs, the Max Factor makeup company began marketing toupees sewn on flesh-hued lace, the style favored by actors Charles Boyer, George Burns, James Stewart, Bing Crosby, Fred Astaire, Gene Kelly, Sean Connery, John Wayne, Burt Reynolds, and Rob Reiner. In 1956, during the filming of *The King and I*, Yul Brynner broke the pattern of

concealing hair loss by shaving his head. American wig styles emulated Bette Davis's shoulder-length style in *All About Eve* (1950) and Leslie Caron's updo in *Gigi* (1958). In addition to custom-made toupees and wiglets, additional aids to hair aesthetics include hair weaves and extensions.

From 1956 to 1987, Scots wig mistress Nina Lawson cleaned and styled period hairpieces and wigs for Metropolitan Opera stars and the TV movie *Manon Lescaut* (1980). Bouffant wigs, as depicted in the film *Grease* (1978), gained popular favor. Using models from *Opera News*, Lawson built the Metropolitan's inventory to 1,400 wigs purchased in Europe. Her personalized hair systems with tulle fronts accommodated singers Roberta Peters, Beverly Sills, Luciano Pavarotti, Maria Callas, Renata Tebaldi, and Plácido Domingo. For

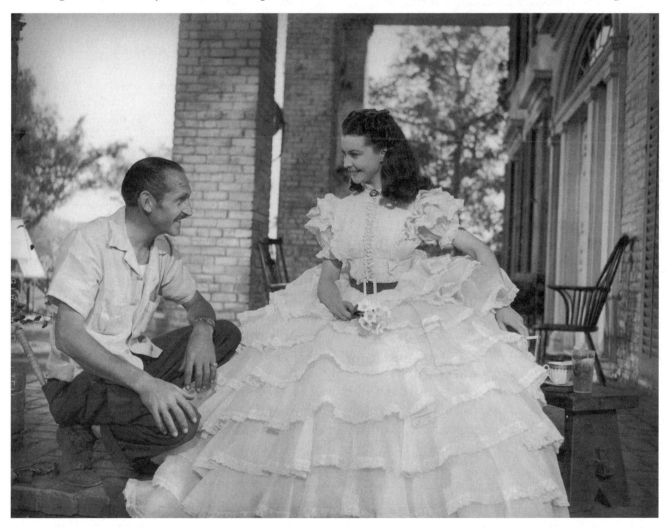

Costume designer Walter Plunkett (left) puts final touches on the antebellum ball gown of Scarlett O'Hara, played by Vivien Leigh, in the 1939 film classic *Gone With the Wind*. Plunkett designed more than 5,000 clothing items for the production. *(John Kobal Foundation/Getty Images)*

screen adaptations of Giacomo Puccini's *Madame Butterfly*, Lawson padded the loops of 20 wigs, steamed them with a steam iron, and lacquered the surface. The finished hairpieces resembled Japanese geisha wigs used in 1904 at Nagasaki, where stylists dressed them with camellia oil and wax.

Craft and Concept

Modest films required at least 60 outfits per picture, creating work for wardrobe mistresses, jewelers, patterners and cutters, and seamstresses. The job called for creativity amid shortages of imported silk, velvet, duchesse satin, and gold lamé during World War II, when remodeling of outfits required substitution of synthetic materials from Hollywood warehouses. During lengthy shoots, costume clerks maintained clean copies of garments and repaired frazzled pieces that could be reused, such as the Japanese military uniforms in *The Bridge on the River Kwai* (1958) and the slave attire in *Gladiator* (2001).

Oscars honored the sophisticated "Sabrina" look, a boat-neck sheath and pillbox hat edged in bugle beads worn in 1954 by Audrey Hepburn. The demand for realism reduced the need for an expensive wardrobe for lead actor Shirley Booth in *Come Back, Little Sheba* (1952) and for Shirley MacLaine and Jack Lemmon in *The Apartment* (1960). To maintain the rustic Western ambience of *Shane* (1953), Alan Ladd's buckskin contrasted with Jack Palance's black boots, the emblem of the villain. For *War of the Worlds* (1953), metal armbands and cuffs accompanied a futuristic bodysuit, studded belt, and headpiece consisting of silvery concentric rings and antennae, a fictional foundation for subsequent sci-fi thrillers such as *Star Wars* (1977) and *Aliens* (1986).

Cinema wardrobe influenced not only viewer perception of the past but also self-concepts of fashion. Historical headdresses and tunics in *Ben-Hur* (1959) and *The Ten Commandments* (1956) introduced filmgoers to scholarly research into fabric, weave, and leather and metalwork, notably Yul Brynner's Egyptian headdress, gold collar, and cape for characterization of the young Moses.

From Alfred Hitchcock's screen triumphs featuring contemporary dress, pattern publishers marketed patterns for a boxy suit with surplice blouse, sundress with bolero jacket, marabou-edged A-line gown, slip-dress with tie-front shrug, and peasant dress and stole. For the beginning seamstress, home versions tended toward few pieces and easy construction.

Twenty-first-century history films maintained quality replication of clothing styles and conditions, as in Washington, D.C., costumes in *Lincoln* (2013) and tattered peasant attire for *Les Misérables* (2013).

See also: Beaton, Cecil; Costume Design, Theater; Head, Edith.

Further Reading

Landis, Deborah Nadoolman. *Costume Design.* New York: Taylor & Francis, 2003.

———. *Dressed: A Century of Hollywood Costume Design.* New York: Collins Design, 2007.

Leese, Elizabeth. *Costume Design in the Movies: An Illustrated Guide to the Work of 157 Great Designers.* New York: Dover, 1991.

Munich, Adrienne. *Fashion in Film.* Bloomington: Indiana University Press, 2011.

Costume Design, Theater

Stage wardrobe enhances the playwright's intent to dramatize the human condition. Primitive theatricals applied feathers, body paint, animal pelts, and masks to mime the intersection of people with nature. Performances directed sorcery toward acts of bravery and stressed the role of courage in supplying tribes with food and raw materials from the hunt.

Classical theater developed the sleeved tunic as a base for portrayal of archetypal characters and emotions. Gods appeared in long gowns dyed saffron and pocked with glitter and gems. Goddess portrayers attached gold embellishments to purple chitons. Kings' tunics trailed behind them in a show of majesty. Buffoons stripped the tunic of dignity by wearing it short and tight over flesh-toned leggings and the red leather phallus, a relic of fertility rites.

Greek and Roman actors developed the open-toed *kothornos* half-boot or buskin, a cork or wood-soled shoe with plaited leather covering the ankle. The boot as well as the elevated *onkos* (headdress) and fillets gave height and dignity to the cast of the tragedies of Aeschylus, Euripides, and Sophocles. Actors enlarged gestures and responses by wearing gloves and cork or linen masks fitted with megaphones.

The technique of varying the importance of characters by the height of their buskins, size of gloves, and exaggerated expression on masks survived in the Etruscan and Roman fashion world in Carnival and processional apparel of the kind still in use in Brazil, the Caribbean, and Venice. Under control of the Catholic Church, medieval troupes depicted the clash of good and evil in morality plays and hagiography. Actors wore contrasting masks and priestly vestments evolved from Byzantine church ceremony.

For scriptural caricature, angels and saints simpered in gilded head coverings, albs, and disc halos. Demons glowered satanic intent in bird and monster masks, furry leggings, horns, and forked tails. Villainous roles such as Pharaoh, Haman, Judas, Herod, and Pontius Pilate required costume details suggesting duplicity and connivance.

Secular Theater

As Elizabethan theater wrested the stage from the church, actors mimicked ancient dress with Greek and Roman drapery, the specialty of British designer and architect Inigo Jones. In token of the divine right of kings, togas represented political power and royal piety. Dissolute female characters overdressed in bustiers, diaphanous yellow skirts, and scarlet petticoats. Male characters displayed crowns, tall hats, and velvet caps as indicators of status and wealth.

Derived from Etruscan drama, the commedia dell'arte of the 1500s lopped the full mask to a half-mask over the eyes that left the face and mouth free for hyperbolized improvisation and *lazzi* (tricks). Variations on diamond patchwork for the Arlecchino character and saggy red drawers for Pantalone identified stock personalities. The French playwright Molière advanced stage symbolism by introducing masked players and gradually dropping face coverings to reveal stark features, an acknowledgment of complex personalities.

Court fêtes and theater under Louis XIV developed wardrobe to extremes of classic attire for tragedy, and wigs, plumes, lace, ribbon, copper embroidery, brocade, velvet, and satin for comedy. Stylistic detail reached a height in the *Carrousel de Louis XIV* (1662), a spectacle ballet for which costumes sparkled under torchlight. Patronage underwrote the high cost of costumes or donated ornate outfits, which overbalanced stage scenes as visual extravaganza.

The excesses and questionable taste of court performances led English Puritans to close theaters for three decades. At Drury Lane Theater, actor David Garrick directed stage wardrobe during the mid-1700s toward historical accuracy, including Scots kilts for Macbeth and ermine for Richard III. The first professional actresses, La Clairon and Marie Justine Favart in France, replaced panniered skirts with classic dress of Greek and Roman matrons.

Commercial Theater

In the style of Renaissance Italy, preparation for U.S. minstrel shows and rodeos typically began with the whitening of the face. For minstrel characters, Jim Crow, a Caucasian performer, wore blackface with oversized white lips and brandished a top hat. He projected satiric humor and vernacular sass toward white masters. Thomas Dartmouth Rice popularized blackface in 1828 with the song "Jump Jim Crow." Ruggero Leoncavallo's opera *Pagliacci* (1892) added clown paint to singers' makeup. The replacement of candles with electric arc lighting increased audience delight in theatrical wardrobe.

In the mid-1800s, actors Sarah Bernhardt and Eugénie Doch, stars of *La Dame aux Camélias* (1852), set cosmopolitan style in swansdown and feather adornment. Fashion commentators described swansdown as a sinuous and seductive plume in boas, hats, stoles, victorines or tippets, and the folding fan, a necessary item for flirtatious roles. The femme fatale's sultane (Turkish dress) and turban flaunted a seabird plume from the tropical purple gallinule or rail—an iridescent blue-green marsh bird—the epitome of orientalism.

Couturier emulation of Ellen Terry, Isadora Duncan, Eleanora Duse, and the Ballets Russes transferred to North America the free-spirited styles of the entertainment world. Canadian women demanded the importation of feathers for use in provincial millinery. By 1891, Ontario's census identified 2,472 milliners, who copied European stage fashions for New World apparel.

Edwardian stage costuming into the 1910s continued to experiment with plumage, notably in the Merry Widow hat, a black straw picture hat with deep crown covered in feathers or stuffed birds, named in 1907 for a Franz Lehár operetta. The extravagant brim shaded the head and shoulders like a parasol. Authenticity dimmed in importance from the experiment of West End Theatre around 1913 with resetting Greek and Elizabethan dramas in contemporary dress.

Mid-1900 touring companies restored costuming exoticism and razzle-dazzle to the Golden Age of Broadway musicals—*Annie Get Your Gun* (1946), *Guys and Dolls* (1950), *My Fair Lady* (1956), *Camelot* (1960), *The King and I* (1951), *Hello, Dolly!* (1964), and *South Pacific* (1949). A long run of Broadway hits energized stage wardrobe with square-dance outfits for *Oklahoma!* (1943), hippie style in *Hair* (1968), raffish dance couture for *A Chorus Line* (1975), and a fun presentation of drag in *La Cage aux Folles* (1983). Large-scale puppetry contributed ruched animal costumes for *The Lion King* (1997) and *War Horse* (2011) as well as African headdresses and World War I uniforms.

See also: Body Painting; Costume Design, Film; Erté; Jones, Robert Edmond.

Further Reading

Archer, Stephen M., Cynthia M. Gendrich, and Woodrow B. Hood. *Theatre: Its Art and Craft.* Lanham, MD: Rowman & Littlefield, 2010.

Barranger, Milly S. *Theatre: A Way of Seeing.* Belmont, CA: Cengage Learning, 2006.

Pecktal, Lynn. *Costume Design: Techniques of Modern Masters.* New York: Back Stage, 1999.

Schweitzer, Marlis. *When Broadway Was the Runway: Theater, Fashion, and American Culture.* Philadelphia: University of Pennsylvania Press, 2009.

Costume Parties

An amusement common to the Western world, fancy dress balls and masquerades employ wigs and costumes to shift the persona from the everyday to the historic, fanciful, or exotic. In the Middle Ages, peasants and landowners interacted at masquerades in the same social mix as slave and master at the Roman Saturnalia. While maintaining anonymity, women and men traded gender roles for ironic play.

The Carnival of Venice dated to a Venetian sea victory over Aquileia, celebrated on December 26, 1162. In related events from the Christian calendar, citizens welcomed saints' days and Lent at Piazza San Marco with a promenade of allegorical mummery, feathered costumes, tricorn hats, false beards, and capes. Traditional participants chose either the expressionless leather or porcelain *bauta* (full mask) or Colombina (half-mask or vizard) on a stick, the playful disguise featured in stage and film productions of *Much Ado About Nothing*.

Masking and pageantry, entertainments of the 1400s, commemorated celebrity couples such as the biblical Adam and Eve, mythological Venus and Adonis, and Titania and Oberon, queen and king of the fairies. Venetian mask makers formed a guild in 1436 to protect their original designs in papier-mâché or plaster, including the hairy savage, the transvestite, ragged peasants, and the flirtatious egg thrower in a rabbit disguise.

The choice of a bird mask by French physician Charles de Lorme in the early 1600s while treating plague victims provided maskers a grotesque face covering consisting of empty eye sockets and a long curved beak over a long black wimple and mantle. The growing middle class in Europe enjoyed music, dance, *ciarlatani* (tricksters), and ribaldry as emblems of rising social status. Puritanic forces launched antimasquerade efforts to end foreign influences and the promiscuity of costuming.

Swiss impresario John James Heidegger scandalized Londoners in 1717 by instituting masquerade balls at the Haymarket Theater. Royalty and commoners bought tickets at White's coffeehouse and mingled in a Carnivalesque atmosphere devoid of rigid etiquette. In 1746, Venetian opera singer

Theresa Cornelys promoted the Haymarket balls. Subsequent *ridottos* (costume balls) in London's Ranelagh Gardens and Vauxhall tended toward imitation of excessive French royal attire, high-heeled shoes, and powdered wigs. In the American colonies, less risqué activities involved guessing games about the identity of maskers.

Throughout Europe, pranksters chose the guise of masked stilt walker, boatman on the Grand Canal, Arab blanket masker, lustful *magnifico* (swaggerer), she-devil with horns, and veiled visage of the *servetta muta* (the silent maid), who held her oval black velvet mask by a stem fitted between the teeth. Lighter wax cloth masks concealed the *larva* (ghost). Disguised partiers, some decked in one-piece head coverings with peepholes, cruised red light districts, taverns, and casinos with impunity.

In the 1800s, Europeans injected whimsy into balls with historical and fantasy costumes. In Paris around 1810, l'École des Beaux Arts began a dress-up extravaganza dedicated to beauty, nudity, and gender bending. To honor the arts and foster creativity, celebrities donned panther pelts, velvet fruit, monster headdresses, and insect antennae.

Twentieth-century costume balls raised money for the arts, museums, and charities by proposing a single theme, such as the Roaring Twenties, space creatures, and Mardi Gras. Cities such as Venice, Mobile, New Orleans, and Rio de Janeiro promoted traditional masking and costumes as draws for tourism. In 1930, France celebrated the colonization of Algiers with a theme party in which guests dressed as *chasseurs d'afrique* (African hunters) and Zouaves (North African infantry) from the previous century.

In the latter part of the twentieth and early twenty-first centuries, imported costumes, masks, and wigs reduced to an affordable level for most people the cost of gorilla, cancan, mermaid, and pirate costumes. Popular costumes allowed individuals to satirize ninja warriors, Sonny and Cher, and President Richard Nixon. Parodies of themed attire offered sets of Old West, *M*A*S*H*, Lady Gaga, Rambo, Elvis, and *Star Wars* garments complete with Colt pistols, scalpels, metallic bras, camo, spangled jumpsuits, and ray guns for improvised clowning. Oscar celebrations welcomed

wearers of costumes from *The Great Gatsby, Grease, The Lord of the Rings,* and *Harry Potter,* among other hits.

See also: Disguise and Spy Wear; Halloween Costumes; Mardi Gras and Carnival Costumes.

Further Reading

Jowers, Sidney, and John Cavanagh. *Theatrical Costume, Masks, Make-up and Wigs: A Biography and Iconography.* New York: Routledge, 2000.

Kuss, Malena. *Music in Latin America and the Caribbean.* Vol. 2. *Performing the Caribbean Experience.* Austin: University of Texas Press, 2007.

Watts, Linda S. *Encyclopedia of American Folklore.* New York: Facts on File, 2006.

Cotton and Cotton Products

An airy, washable fiber evolved from the *Gossypium malavaceae* family of mallows, cotton provides soft, absorbent cloth for outerwear, hosiery, night wear, and underclothes for babies and adults.

Ancient Weaving

Around 4700 B.C.E., Chinese needleworkers embroidered cotton robes and slippers with mythic dragon and phoenix designs. After 1700 B.C.E., both the Chinese and Aztec reinforced chest armor by padding quilted jackets with cotton fiber. On the Indian subcontinent, compilers of the Rig-Veda (ca. 1200 B.C.E.) chose cotton weaving as a metaphor for order in the universe and spread their cloth artistry along Hindu mission paths. In the early thirteenth century B.C.E., the Olmec, Mexico's first significant civilization, who resided in the areas of present-day Veracruz and Tabasco, combed native cottons for weaving breechcloths. On the other side of the world, Egyptian cotton earned fame before 1000 B.C.E., when priests made wide-sleeved robes out of the soft fiber.

After the establishment of the Achaemenid Empire in 550 B.C.E., Persian dressmakers painted, adorned, and pleated elegant cotton robes. Cotton face shields masked the priests of Zoroaster for ritual tending of the sacred fire. According to the

Greek historian Herodotus, for the second Persian War in April 480 B.C.E., Xerxes dressed several hundred thousand soldiers in cotton, the largest outlay for military uniforms in world history.

Around 327 B.C.E., the troops of Alexander the Great abandoned Macedonian woolens in favor of soft cotton tunics, loincloths, and saddlecloths from the Indus Valley, where alluvial soils produced an ample crop. A quarter-century later in Nazca, Peru, the Paraca netted mantles, voile, and cordage. Perusals of graves attested to sophisticated textile artistry in winding sheets, snoods, headbands, knitted fringe, and caps made from a blend of camelid hair with cotton, which grew in a variety of natural shades from brown and tan to mauve and pale green. In the Roman colonies of North Africa, cotton tunics replaced traditional African dress with an unbelted, flowing garment suited to desert wear.

Medieval Garments

Medieval clothiers almost everywhere retained cotton as a primary source of garments, such as the shrouds of Malian saints in Timbuktu and the soft cotton string and rags that Persian knitters turned into house shoes. In the American Southwest from 500 C.E., the Pueblo, Hopi, and Zuni hand spun and loomed traditional cotton mantas (capes), serapes (shoulder wraps), blankets, adult kilts, and baby swaddling.

By the eighth century, Chinese ships from Denzhou ferried cotton across the Yellow Sea to Korea and Japan. The medieval journey of cottonseed involved Arab sailors in the spread of cotton culture to Sicily and, after 912, to Córdoba in Muslim Spain. In the mid-fourteenth century, Chinese in the Lower Yangtze (Chang Jiang) basin profited from cotton planting. Textile processors of Guizhou Province bleached imported cottons and patterned them with wax for batiking to produce an elite textile reserved for the rich and powerful.

The mythic *Travels of Sir John Mandeville* (1357) rhapsodized on a fluff gathered from an imaginary animal, the delicate baby "vegetable lambs" of Scythia. In reality, cotton plants grew abundantly in China and Persia by the end of the thirteenth century, according to *The Travels of Marco Polo* (ca. 1300), a memoir packed with cultural and agronomic facts. In Hong Kong, the Hoklo and Tanka swaddled babies in patchwork made from cotton pieces. In North Africa, Moors furled impeccable white cotton into turbans. As far west as southeastern Europe, cotton fabric dominated the Slavic peasant tradition of tunics, narrow pants, and cloth caps.

In the Western Hemisphere, Tarahumara weavers in Mesoamerica turned the thread of native *Gossypium hirsutum* into fringed blankets and coverlets woven from long and short staple fibers. At Tenochtitlan (Mexico City) after 1440, the Emperor Montezuma I demanded an annual payment of 200,000 embroidered cotton mantas to nobles from the Aztec, who relied on raw fiber from Cuernavaca. From the Totonac, Montezuma exacted an annual tax of 2,560 cloaks, either quilted, striped, or richly tinted.

Before the Spanish conquistador Hernán Cortés arrived at coastal Mexico in February 1519, he ordered Cuban Indian women at Havana to stuff cotton into armor to shield soldiers from Aztec arrows. Among the priests of Tlaxcala, Cortés admired the awnings and sleeveless ritual robes fringed with cotton. The people pledged fabric to bribe Cortés to free them from Aztec control. At the court of Montezuma II in November 1519, Cortés received embroidered white cottons in tribute but carried out a genocidal plot to kill the emperor and 100,000 of his people.

In North America from 1607, cotton planting at Jamestown provided fiber for suits and dresses. Cotton spread as a viable cash crop across the Carolinas in 1664, Georgia in 1734, and as far west as Texas in 1821. New World entrepreneurs withdrew funds from Old World fleets and invested in cotton from Virginia, transported to Europe by deep-draft vessels. With raw cotton from the colonies, European court dress made use of light handkerchiefs and collars and cuffs fluted with hot goffering irons and tongs.

Modern Fashions and Innovations

Cotton has clothed much of Earth's human population. Natural dyes from Brazil, Honduras, Mexico, and Jamaica enlarged the European choices of hosiery colors and tinting for busks, made from striped twill lined with cotton sateen. In Persia, parents lined infant hats with soft cotton padding. Chinese women and children chose quilted overshoes to cover ornate slippers. In India and other British colonies near the equator, the invention of cotton seersucker produced a woven material that promoted ventilation.

In the Pacific, Dayak males of Borneo preferred unbleached cotton yarn and fringe for decorating loincloths. At Kazembe in present-day Zambia, cotton fabric robes, leopard skins, and feather headdress marked the investiture of royalty. Fabric bribes maintained peace among authorities clamoring to profit on cotton commodities. In 1740, textile gifts to vassals secured the loyalty of Zambian peasants to the warrior-king Ng'anga Bilonda of the Luba-Lunda Kingdom.

In 1742, Gaston-Laurent Coeurdoux, a noted Jesuit missionary and linguist at Coromandel, India, instructed Europeans on Indian textile production. The kalamkari method, a secret since 3000 B.C.E., involved treating fibers with blood, milk, urine, or dung. Artisans dyed cotton with carved wood blocks or sketched designs with bamboo pens filled with jagri ink, fermented from iron and molasses, to create permanent patterns.

In mid-eighteenth-century England, cottons began gaining respect among the elite. Equestrienne habits of cotton nankeen replaced the more courtly velvet. On the European continent, gauze and muslin for thin dresses and Indian paisley shawls adorned with polychromatic tambour embroidery established the style of the Napoleonic era (1799–1815). In the 1830s, knitters in Balbriggan, Ireland, turned quality cotton yarn into hosiery. Glovers provided servants, footmen, coachmen, and police with thin, washable Berlin gloves.

In New England and Canada, meanwhile, knitters chose cotton yarn for gloves and hose. In the American South, cotton plantations anchored the economy of the region, where a field hand could pick up to 300 pounds (136 kilograms) per day. The need for black press gangs raised the value of enslaved field hands as well as the mules that turned antebellum presses to shape loads into bales of varying weight and size. Thus, bondage and cotton fused into a single issue of American human rights.

Frontier dealers relied on cotton fabrics. On the Plains of North America, wranglers chose cotton bandannas to wipe themselves clean of sweat and dust. Westering women labored over balls of cotton crochet yarn; a relief from tedium, the craft produced stretchy collars, mitts, and caps. Cotton wadding padded the hems of skirts to improve drape.

The revival of indigo and madder by English designer William Morris intensified the patterns of cotton goods, turning paisley into a Victorian era fad. In Russia, Novgorod peasants supplanted hemp and flax for blouses and skirts with cotton calico. In the United States, one-piece boilersuits served as work garments for factory workers and cotton socks padded the feet beneath high-button shoes. Into the Belle Époque, European women wore striped twill bustle petticoats and batiste chemises bordered with *broderie anglaise* and paired cotton hosiery with kid bedroom slippers.

In Zanzibar, cotton fabric became a banner of liberation. After 1870, Swahili women of Africa's southeast coast robed themselves in bright cotton rectangles called *kangas*. By draping the lower body, the torso, and the head in cotton pieces, they emulated Muslim fashions. Manufacturers in Kenya, Egypt, and Tanzania as well as East Asia supplied the devout of East Africa with traditional designs and prints containing holy proverbs.

Twentieth-century innovations with cotton included men's round-necked T-shirts and women's elasticized net bust bodices, batiste underarm shields and pantalettes, and lace brassieres tied with ribbons. Canadians in Ontario buried their dead with cotton wool laid over the eyes and stuffed into body orifices, and a cotton kerchief on the head tied under the chin. Both the Axis and Allied armies during World War I clothed soldiers in inch-thick cotton body armor to protect them from shell fragments or shrapnel. By 1916, cotton production in the United States more than doubled from 15.9 million acres (6.4 million hectares) to 35.0 million acres (14.2 million hectares).

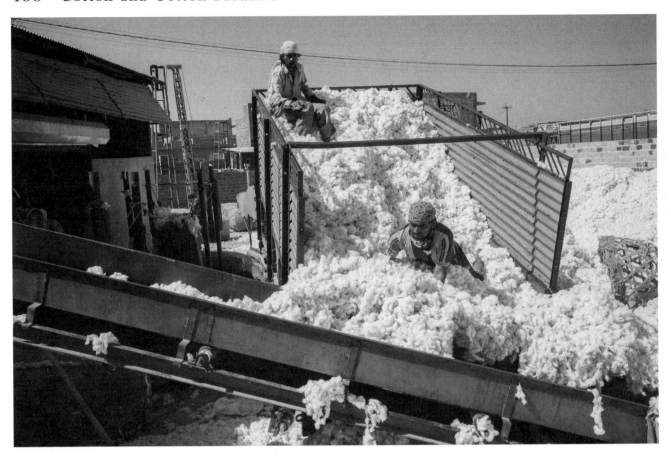

Workers load raw cotton at a processing plant in Rajasthan, northern India. Cotton in raw and woven form has been a primary national trade commodity for millennia. India remains the world's second-largest exporter of cotton, after the United States. *(Sanjit Das/Bloomberg via Getty Images)*

Into the 1920s, practical American women bought washable aprons, teddies, and smocks, gauze infant diapers, cotton terry cloth bibs, and rolled hose made of lisle and mercerized cotton, a product of mill villages in the Carolinas. Russian traditionalists purchased cotton yard goods printed at local factories rather than in India. The late 1930s increased the demand among American and English women for cotton anklet hosiery knitted from three-ply yarn, and among American women for cotton intimate garments and cotton corduroy and pique for children's play clothes.

During World War II, soldiers again shielded soft flesh from strafing with cotton vests and aprons over khaki-colored chino uniforms. For civilians, cotton canvas replaced rationed leather for family shoes while rayon and silk gave place to cotton mesh for stockings. Bobby-soxers popularized cotton anklet socks reinforced with nylon, a man-made fabric synthesized in 1935 by Wallace Carothers, a DuPont chemist.

Because of the competition from polyester double knit, cotton processors improved the wrinkle resistance of finished fabrics. After the synthesis of spandex in 1959, marketers of athletic bindings, cargo pants, sport knits, and dance tights continued to use cotton fibers for softness and body ventilation in stretchy fabrics. In the 1960s, teens made a uniform of preppy shorts and shirts in madras, a lightweight plaid dyed in handmade substances that bled and faded with laundering and use. In the same period, men adopted the Nehru jacket, a button-up jacket reflecting Indian male formal wear that featured a high circular collar rather than notched lapels. In 1969, the *Apollo 9* space launch required soft, absorbent cotton and nylon long underwear for astronauts.

In 2012, fashion designer Rina Dhaka encouraged Indian women to return to cotton saris. By preferring cotton above silk, consumers could boost profits for Maharashtra farmers. The shift would revive the spirit of Mohandas Gandhi, who protested the wage of seven cents a day for Indian pickers and fought British imperialism by refusing to purchase goods woven in Lancashire.

See also: African Clothing, Sub-Saharan; Batiking; Calico; Cotton Trade; Fibers, Natural; Textile Manufacturing; Weaving.

Further Reading

Lemire, Beverly. *Cotton.* New York: Bloomsbury, 2011.
Messier, Marion W. *The History of Cotton: South Carolina Cotton Museum.* Virginia Beach, VA: Donning, 2005.
Yafa, Stephen. *Cotton: The Biography of a Revolutionary Fiber.* New York: Penguin, 2005.

Cotton Trade

A global staple for adult and children's garments, cotton goods have long remained a constant among world textile commodities. From 8000 B.C.E., the plant's 49 species flourished in the tropics and subtropics around the world. In Mesopotamia, Peru, Nubia, Nigeria, and Mesoamerica, gatherers of fiber from prickly bolls prized it for cordage, yarn, and thread for weaving and netting. Around 800 B.C.E., Indians turned short-staple Asiatic cottons into a cottage industry.

After 705 B.C.E., the Assyrian king Sennacherib encouraged the planting of Egyptian and Sudanese cotton to expand Mesopotamian textile markets through the Levant. In the summer of 325 B.C.E., the return of Alexander the Great's troops from the Indus Valley introduced the Mediterranean world to soft, comfortable cotton tunics. The cultural exchange promoted an east-west trade that is still in existence.

Ancient and Medieval Exchange

In the mid-400s B.C.E., Nubian weavers at Meroé profited from exporting West African cotton. From the fourth century B.C.E., Bengali women wove wispy muslins as tightly as 1,800 threads per inch. The Greeks favored fine muslin from Bengal for sheer clothing worn in hot climates, particularly the colonies in Sicily. Rome shouldered the high cost of importing Indian cotton, a source of legionary uniforms during the Gallic Wars (58–50 B.C.E.) and for canvas to shade Roman theaters and the Forum. Roman women favored semitransparent gauze garments woven from the cottons that a fleet of 120 ships imported from Malabar, India, each year to Oceles on the Arabian Gulf.

From 37 B.C.E., caravans brought cotton from China and India over the Silk Road to weavers of luxury goods in Italy. By 100 C.E., cotton marketing burgeoned along Arabian shipping routes and in the Amazon River basin, where *Gossypium barbadense* (wild cotton) provided fiber for lamp wicks, sashes, bags, fishing nets, and hunting pouches. In 130, trade in *kutun* (cotton) fabrics between India and Arabia exploited the value of soft cellulose fibers over wool and flax.

After the invention of the treadle loom at Tarsus in southern Turkey in 298, peasant weavers around the Mediterranean Rim bought cotton yarn for the manufacture of work clothes and aprons. In the 600s, Arabs distributed Indian cottons along the Silk Road as far west as Constantinople and Venice. By the eleventh century, West Africans cleared land for cotton growing and wove textiles for trade.

In 1096, the First Crusade promoted a cotton industry in the crusader states and boosted trade with Asia and Italy's city-states. By the 1100s, cotton weaving flourished from Sicily across Europe. Barcelona textile mills established Spain's cotton manufacturing center. Around 1200, Korean merchants began competing with Chinese cotton dealers. At Timbuktu, Mali, in February 1353, Moroccan travel writer Ibn Battuta observed a brisk traffic in Byzantine cottons and African indigo cloth. In Mexico after 1440, Montezuma I forbade the people of Tlaxcala to trade in cotton, which the Aztec emperor demanded as an annual tribute.

By the Renaissance, demand for cotton textiles from Gujarat, Coromandel, and Bengal surpassed the demand for silks. Cotton undergirded trade between India and Indonesia, Japan, Arabia, Egypt, West Africa, Congo, and Ethiopia, where coastal dealers exchanged beads and glass for cloth. Indian manufacturers shipped cottons marked with traditional grids to Thailand; Southeast Asians preferred sawtooth borders on hip wrappers. At Gao on the Niger River after 1493, the progressive Songhai king Askia the Great promoted trade in glazed cottons from Tera in exchange for luxury silk and woolens imported through North African ports. In Armenia, Christian artisans marked fabric for altar cloths. Imported cotton stockings, soled cashambles, and stirrup hose increased the comfort of footwear in England.

Global Expansion

Mesoamericans thrived on cotton shirts, sleeping mats, priestly robes, and armor, all produced by slave labor. On October 12, 1492, in the Bahamas, Christopher Columbus marveled at the extra-long staple of sea island cotton, a wild "dooryard" fiber later called pima cotton. Upon his arrival on July 30, 1502, to the island of Guanaja off the coast of Honduras in the western Caribbean, he encountered Jicaque or Paya traders dressed in dyed cotton shirts and loincloths, evidence of a sophisticated Mesoamerican textile industry.

Spanish adventurers admired the commodities of the Maya enclaves of Yucatán, visited in March 1512 by explorer Francisco Hernández de Córdoba of Castile and coveted by colonizer Diego Velázquez. As early as 1519, Spanish conquistadores in Mesoamerica began plotting ways of turning local cotton, cassia, lumber, and sugar into sources of revenue. By 1556, Spaniards in Florida became the first Europeans to introduce cotton cultivation in New Spain. After 1650, Barbados became the first New World colony to ship cotton to Europe.

Because of the demand for exotic textiles worldwide, cotton goods replaced rice and spices in value among the Mughal textile manufacturers of India and outranked ivory from central Africa. Shippers maintained constant traffic from the Bight of Benin in Asante cotton robes of *adinkra* stamped with bark dye and in Hausan *adire alabere,* a tie-dyed commodity that passed through warehouses in the Gold Coast and Senegal. The commercial ventures of Portuguese navigator Vasco da Gama in the late fifteenth century introduced colorful cottons from states along the Indian Ocean to Portugal for trade throughout Europe. Haida, Kwakiutl, and Kutenai of the western Canadian coast and tribes along the Ohio and Mississippi river valleys bought cotton blankets from French traders.

Across Africa, buyers spent fortunes on *capotin* (checked or striped fabric), *canequin* (black or indigo calico), *zuarte* (indigo cloth), *cutonia* (cotton and silk striped cloth), *ardian* (blue cloth), and *samatere* (white cloth). Caravans passed the goods from Zanzibar west by northwest over circuitous routes to Kazembe (Zambia). Farmers experimented with cottonseed and gradually increased their sophistication with the use of cotton for food and fiber.

To control valuable Indian cottons and other commodities, following the Battle Plassey on June 23, 1757, the East India Company, led by Robert Clive, seized the cotton fields in Bengal between Calcutta and the Indian Ocean. British textile mills profited from cheap labor and high-quality fibers, which they turned into trade goods. In 1775, American colonists emulated the British factory system as a means of shucking off East India Company control of imported garments.

Industrialized Textiles

At the beginning of the 1830s, global mechanization elevated cotton to a major source of income. The consumption of cotton textiles, which rose from an estimated 1,339 tons in 1750 to 125,000 tons in 1831, drew workers from farms to milling regions, such as Lanarkshire, Scotland, and Cheshire, England. Competing with British textiles, both Belgium and New England contributed to the centrality of cotton to the Industrial Revolution.

In the 1840s, cotton kimonos with obi sashes imported from Japan to England supplanted women's dressing gowns. Cotton lace mitts and parasol covers with picot scallops enhanced afternoon outfits. Men's banyans (dressing gowns), nightcaps, and coat and vest linings featured cottons dyed and painted in Coromandel and imported by either the Dutch or the English. For drawers, weavers turned cotton into soft, absorbent flannel or cambric. The advance of transportation by rail and through the

Suez Canal reduced the price of cottons imported to sub-Saharan Africa, depressing the market for traditional kente and *bògòlanfini* (mud cloth).

By the 1900s in northern China, low-priced cottons in Western designs began replacing traditional silks. Simultaneously, the application of rayon outpaced that of cotton in Libya and Sudan. Commerce foundered during the Great Depression of the 1930s, when tribe members of the South African Transkei abandoned imported cotton goods for animal pelts. The Maasai rejected Western garb favored by Christian proselytizers by returning to bare buttocks and a red toga tossed over one shoulder.

In the 2000s, a retreat from synthetics and the revival of practical cotton and nylon blends for briefs and kneesocks increased the market share for such brands as Hanes, Playtex, Maidenform, Warner's, Fruit of the Loom, and Jockey. In Indonesia in 2012, designer Suraj Melwani applied the deluxe pima fibers commonly used in women's sleepwear to men's T-shirts. The result, called *sifr*, extended premium cottons into the manufacture of socks, boxer shorts, polo shirts, hoodies, and scarves.

See also: African Clothing, Sub-Saharan; Cotton and Cotton Products; Textile Trade.

Further Reading

Riello, Giorgio, and Prasannan Parthasarathi. *The Spinning World: A Global History of Cotton Textiles, 1200–1850.* New York: Oxford University Press, 2009.

Roche, Julian. *The International Cotton Trade.* Sawston, UK: Woodhead, 1994.

Yafa, Stephen. *Big Cotton: How A Humble Fiber Created Fortunes, Wrecked Civilizations, and Put America on the Map.* New York: Viking, 2005.

Courtship Attire

Readying the young for mating has historically focused on hair, skin, garments, and accessories. In the pre-Christian era, flowers epitomized the delicacy and chastity of maidenhood, as with the wildflower wreath marking a girl's attendance at the Slavic summer solstice. From the first century C.E., Judeo-Christians decked young females with circlets of white flowers, a singular adornment similar to the Egyptian chaplet of ivy, narcissus, lotus, and pomegranate blossoms.

Native Adornments

In Polynesia, young men abandoned childhood nudity and knotted leaf swags on the lavalava (loincloth) to symbolize readiness for courtship. In New Zealand and Hawaii from the 700s, the twining of leaves, fern, moss, and feathers into leis as hatbands added fragrance to graceful male apparel. Koreans presented flowers to young men to acknowledge readiness for mating. On Tonga and Samoa and in the part of the Indus Valley that is now Pakistan, young women expressed their interest in romance with whole blossoms tucked behind the ear or coiled in the hair.

In the 900s, the Viking male displayed an heirloom sword throughout courtship. The maiden wore a *kransen,* a red wreath indicating propriety and social status. Upon preparing for marriage, the girl and her attendants washed in a sauna and rinsed in herbal water scented with flower oil. The bride-to-be topped her braids with a *hustrulinet,* a white linen headcloth attached to a metallic fillet tied with silk cords. In the fourteenth century, German and Scandinavian girls draped their bosoms with May Day garlands, a colorful enticement to male peers.

Gifts and Signs Around the World

Courtship in Renaissance Europe promoted apparel messages, including the red silk hose worn by young German males in Augsburg in 1526. The English encouraged gifts between couples, beginning with flowers in curvilinear C and S shapes, from which men chose boutonnieres. A youth could present a ring, gloves, purse, belt, hat, neckerchief, gown, petticoat, garters, hose, slippers, buttons and sewing supplies, satin, or lace as an appropriate fairing (love token). Maidens extended parts of their attire as gifts, usually a handkerchief, garter, or detachable sleeve. During wooing, the girl often socialized with her beloved while combing weekly fairs for flattering garments and accessories.

In Argentina, Bolivia, Chile, and Peru, men and women dressed provocatively for the *cueca*, a courtship dance set to guitar music. Males flaunted the cowboy's poncho, tight pants, and boots. Women waved handkerchiefs overhead while lifting flounced skirts to reveal petticoats and ankles. A variant, the Basque *aurresku*, displayed male chain dancing, with each man thrusting his shoulders back to display full-sleeved shirts beneath short bolero vests.

As described in Jane Austen's social novels, Regency England favored the riding outfit as evidence of marriageability. Men outlined the torso in linen shirts with stocks (cravats) over tight breeches and thigh-high boots. A double-breasted, long-tailed riding jacket revealed the mature chest and arms. Women chose similar high-fashion equestrienne jackets, waistcoats, and riding skirts that enhanced female curves.

In mid-eighteenth-century Europe, girls approached potential courtship in low-necked French dresses layered over corsets and voluminous petticoats. A stomacher or fitted bodice emphasized the bosom, which a modest girl covered in a muslin neck cloth lapped over the sternum. Evening clothes encouraged a display of bare arms and shoulders. Young men evidenced their social status and sobriety with the selection of an adult jacket or surtout.

In colonial Pennsylvania and New England, families permitted bundling, the sharing of a bed on which a board separated the couple. The pair supposedly cuddled in cloth sacks tied at the neck, but the 30 percent pregnancy rate of brides suggested more intimate contact. In other colonies, men decked themselves in heritage garments—the Mexican guayabera shirt, Hawaiian flower shirt, Indian Nehru jacket, Spanish embroidered shirt, or African dashiki tunic—while women chose romantic flowers, such as the Spanish orange blossom.

During the Victorian era, the debutante already possessed an appealing posture from years of wearing tight-laced corsets. A fair complexion required wide-brimmed hats and lemon or buttermilk bleaching creams massaged into the elbows, shoulder, and nails. For sparkling, fragrant hair, girls shared recipes consisting primarily of citrus juice, rainwater, and rosemary.

Essential to courtship ensembles for men, the top hat, cravat, and spats attested to fashion savvy. A watch and chain suggested maturity. Nubile girls carefully matched hat with dress and handkerchief and jacket with belt and shoes. Both fan and parasol kept female hands engaged with items of flirtation until the male presented her an engagement ring, a circular emblem without beginning or end.

In the mid-nineteenth century, plantation slaves in the Caribbean and American South treasured beads and ribbon, discarded petticoats and slippers, and dressy attire suitable for church attendance, corn shucking, or juba, a slave dance based on the traditions of the Yoruba, Nipe, Tiv, and Akan of West Africa. Single girls oiled their skin, wrapped their hair in a fresh *tignon* (turban), and defeated agricultural and kitchen odors with crumpled basil, honeysuckle, rose petals, or gardenia rubbed on the torso and clothing.

Planters took pride in house parties where staff appeared clean and neatly dressed. Bondsmen wore plantation-made vested suits, jackets, shirts, and breeches tied at wrist and knee. A cocked hat indicated interest in women. Girls recycled gauze handkerchiefs, curtains, and ribbons discarded by the mistress to adorn cast-off veiled gowns and chemises for their weddings.

Surveys of Melanesian social customs in the 1920s disclosed minimal clothing patterns integral to wooing. On the Trobriand Islands of the South Pacific, males took care to conceal their genitals. At age 14, boys carefully arranged the phallic leaf but revealed the rest of the body without shame. Melanesian females wore gala clothing, shell armlets, and betel nut makeup for village dances. Girls displayed fiber skirts as elements of modesty and tradition, a parallel of woven grass or leather waistbands worn by Ghanaian women.

Contemporary Courtship

Habits of attire, taste, and grooming continue to influence would-be mates worldwide, as with the beaded tab bag necklace that a Zulu girl sends to a potential mate in South Africa. The man responds by dressing in Western attire and a red and white cloth, a Zulu tradition.

Parents observe courteous dressing as well as cleanliness and grooming as evidence of sincerity and worthy background, such as the neatness of a Khmer girl in group games at Cambodian festivals and the rural Chilean man's choice of the poncho, chaps, cowboy boots with spurs, and straw hat. Lacking more tangible proof of readiness for matrimony, both parties and their relatives survey clothing choices to determine careful selection rather than eccentricity or flashy trendiness.

A safe choice among Filipino youths consists of red shirts or skirts on Valentine's Day, a parallel to the red sari worn by an unwed Hindu woman. The Khmer male indicates his commitment to a bride-to-be by carrying the girl's scarf. Among the Cham of Cambodia, national dress in batik sarongs with shirts or blouses and scarves or turbans symbolizes obedience to social tradition. Similarly, Vietnamese girls wear the standard leaf hat with *ao dai,* a white tunic over tight black pantaloons.

In Laos, Myanmar, and Thailand, Akha and Hmong youths sport freshly embroidered and beaded black jackets, skirts, aprons, boots, turbans, and courting bags holding musical instruments. Contributing color, they attach metal buttons and coins, braided yarn, and tassels as well as embroidery. On Women's New Year, potential brides add silver headdress, buckles, necklaces, earrings, and bracelets that flash with light during dancing. In Myanmar, Karen ritual encourages courtship during funerals. Females grace the trousseau with bright colors but remain outfitted in white ankle-length tunics stitched with virginal red. Shawls rattle tassels made of beetle wings. Men comb long hair to the side and clasp it with metal pins.

Malaysian men bombard their beloveds with garments—shawls, scarves, shoes, rings, handbags. Women respond with gifts of handmade velvet caps, shirts, and slippers.

See also: Coming-of-Age Attire; Flowers; Wedding Dress.

Further Reading

Phegley, Jennifer. *Courtship and Marriage in Victorian England.* Santa Barbara, CA: ABC-CLIO, 2012.

Rothman, Ellen. *Hands and Hearts: A History of Courtship in America.* Cambridge, MA: Harvard University Press, 1987.

Sears, James T. *The Greenwood Encyclopedia of Love, Courtship, and Sexuality Through History.* Westport, CT: Greenwood, 2007.

Couturiers

The artisans who outfit royalty and the privileged class, couturiers apply original pattern making and custom fitting to unique garments.

In the mid-1800s, French-born British designer Charles Frederick Worth studied ensembles and headdress in portraiture. For advertisement, he applied individualized styling to Marie-Augustine Vernet, his wife and first customer, who strolled in public to entice potential clients.

At London's Great Exhibition on May 1, 1851, Worth introduced the concept of investment dressing by private female clients seeking one-of-a-kind luxury attire. He proposed catering to the body and the occasion, from afternoon strolls and loungewear to costume parties and presentations at court. From his sketch board, seasonal designs passed to the pattern room and on to 20 seamstresses for cutting and tailoring to the buyer's body measurements. For well-dressed clients, his atelier offered redesign and refitting.

In 1868, Worth resurrected the medieval guild concept in the Chambre Syndicale de la Couture Parisienne (Syndicated Chamber of Parisian Dress Design). The regulatory commission protected couturiers from pattern piracy and label enfranchisement. Members of the collective superintended the semi-annual runway shows before the Paris media. Models presented ensembles for afternoon, evening, and weddings as well as accessories and jewelry.

At the height of high fashion, French couturiers put their stamp on period innovations, notably translucent gowns in pastel colors by Jacques Doucet. The antique lace and ribbons introduced in 1895 by the Callot sisters—Marie, Marthe, Regina, and Joséphine—reprised trim from the early Industrial Revolution. Paul Poiret, a designer at the House of Worth, unveiled modernity in his practical dress, harem pants, and the kimono coat, a Japanese shape he made for Elena Bariatinsky, a Russian princess.

In the early 1900s, Paris couturier Madeleine Chéruit promoted the opulence of the previous century, which publisher Lucien Vogel featured in the style magazine *La Gazette du Bon Ton.* London designer Lucy Duff-Gordon liberated women with the slit skirt and streamlined lingerie. French milliner Jeanne Lanvin extended haute couture to children's fashion in 1909. Madeleine Vionnet experimented with bias cuts to reveal the female form in motion, an inspiration to dancer Isadora Duncan. Elsa Schiaparelli contributed practical knits and sportswear displaying unusual buttons and zippers.

In 1926, Coco Chanel popularized a fashion phenomenon, the "little black dress," which expanded from haute couture to an everywoman's closet staple. Alix Grès introduced cutouts and draped silk jersey culottes for discriminating tastes. For the refined flapper, Irish couturier Edward Molyneux melded classic drape with chemise lines trimmed in beading, burnout, and appliqué and topped with a feathered chubby (short buttonless coat).

After World War II, French couturiers Christian Dior, Jean Patou, Jacques Fath, Lucien Lelong, and Robert Piguet set the parameters for haute couture, which served a declining clientele largely consisting of movie stars and the nouveau riche. Designers collaborated on the fashion doll, a miniature exhibition of the country's unique designs and fabrics, including fur cuffs, corduroy jackets, cork-soled wedges with glass inlays, and the velvet toque. The traveling display of broad-shouldered coats, low necklines, and balloon skirts revived French couture. By the mid-1900s, Paris artisans met competition from fashion houses in London, Milan, New York, and Tokyo.

In 1953, French designer Hubert de Givenchy began dismantling the notion of made-to-order couture by democratizing luxury lines. His instincts about profit and loss presaged a report in 1957 that haute couture reaped returns as low as 2 percent. Givenchy's contemporaries, Pierre Cardin and Cristóbal Balenciaga, promoted *prêt-à-porter* (ready-to-wear) by licensing the bubble dress and

sack silhouette. Industrial manufacture preceded distribution in department stores.

Failing returns lured designers Jean-Paul Gaultier and Thierry Mugler from haute couture into ready-to-wear. Late twentieth-century retreats from exclusive apparel involved Ralph Lauren, Calvin Klein, Roy Halston, and Giorgio Armani in the everyman/everywoman look of denim, turtlenecks, pantsuits, and leather jackets. In the twenty-first century, still dedicated to Worth's notion of one-of-a-kind styles, Valentino Garavani, Julien Fournié, and other couturiers carry on the tradition of exclusive garments for their clients.

See also: Dolls, Fashion; Fashion Design; Haute Couture; Labels; Worth, Charles Frederick.

Further Reading

English, Bonnie. *Fashion: The 50 Most Influential Fashion Designers of All Time.* Hauppauge, NY: Barron's, 2010.

Palmer, Alexandra. *Couture & Commerce: The Transatlantic Fashion Trade in the 1950s.* Vancouver: UBC Press, 2001.

Taylor, Lou. *The Study of Dress History.* Manchester, UK; New York: Manchester University Press, 2002.

Watson, Linda. *Vogue Fashion: Over 100 Years of Style by Decade and Designer.* Richmond Hill, ON: Firefly, 2008.

Cross-Dressing

For reasons of celebration, entertainment, disguise, status, or gender identification, men and women cross-dress in the attire common to the opposite sex. Gender transference requires skill at hairstyling and makeup and knowledge of clothing and mannerisms, according to the method of fifth-century Lebanese monk Marina the Ascetic. For costume balls, masking and makeup enhance the illusion of gender shift, the ploy of twentieth-century Beijing opera star and spy Shi Pei Pu.

Clandestine transdressers may choose to wear female intimate garments and stockings under normal male attire. More blatant gender bending confuses the issue of strict sex roles by stressing the androgyny of the tuxedo, ambiguous facial makeup, and the double-gendered social behaviors of the Oglala Lakota or Winnebago berdache. Successful examples include Indian women posing as Hindu noblemen as a form of satire, athletes concealing gender as an athletic advantage, or an unshaven man garbed in a woman's dress for Halloween or Mardi Gras.

World mythology includes a number of divinities and humans—Hercules, Odin, Athena, Hagbard, Bapiya—who concealed their gender under inappropriate attire. Misaligned apparel cost Epipole of Carystus death by stoning for donning armor and accompanying the Greek army during the Trojan War (ca. 1200 B.C.E.). Loss of male identity became the punishment of the Greek Tiresias and the Hindu Arjuna, whose transgendering forced them to dress as women. Legend pictured the females Fa Mulan of fourth-century China, Pope Joan of ninth-century Europe, and nineteenth-century Swiss explorer and writer Isabelle Eberhardt, in Arab Sufist cloak, as heroines who could achieve their aims only by dressing as men.

History has glimpsed the regendering of notables through wardrobe and hairstyle, including Alexander the Great, camouflaged as the huntress Artemis in 324 B.C.E. A flagrant voluptuary and practitioner of Persian transvestism, Elagabalus, Rome's cross-dressing emperor, earned a charge of *impudicitia* (shamelessness) in 218 B.C.E. for wearing boots adorned with cameos. Fourteenth-century Breton privateer Jeanne de Clisson and Flemish raider Joanna "la Flamme" of Flanders are less well known for their exploits.

Elizabethan stage troupes hired boys to play the parts of women, such as Shakespeare's Portia, Ophelia, and Rosalind, a role that shifts the actor back to shepherd's attire in a double gender switch. Kabuki troupes featured Japanese females in every role at Edo from 1608 until the banning of women from the stage in 1629. After two decades of all-boy troupes, professional kabuki filled stage companies with adult males, boosting the career of character actor Ichikawa Kodanji IV, who excelled in warrior dress, in the kimono of the female ghost, and with the hand fan and parasol of the courtesan.

Intrigue dogged the lives of four eighteenth-century transdressers—French opera singer Julie d'Aubigny, pirates Anne Bonny and Mary Read, and Bonnie Prince Charlie, the Stuart pretender.

D'Aubigny, clad in tight fencing jacket and breeches, dueled against men. The two buccaneers pled pregnancy in 1721 to avoid the gallows. The Stuart prince's flight by boat from the Isle of Skye in 1746 required his dressing as Betty Burke, an Irish lady's maid.

The closure of combat to women produced noteworthy females willing to don uniforms and conceal their gender, the choice of Italian mercenary Onorata Rodiani in 1423 and French cavalry leader Joan of Arc in 1429. Earning a living in the field suited the talents of Spanish conquistador Catalina de Erauaso in 1536, Finnish horse soldier Brita Olofsdotter in 1569, Swedish artillery soldier Ulrika Eleonora Stalhammar in 1713, English dragoon Ann Mills in 1740, English marine Hannah Snell Summs in 1747, Burgundian spy Charlotte d'Eon de Beaumont in 1756, Continental infantryman Deborah Sampson in 1778, and English front-line sapper Dorothy Lawrence in 1917.

Military historians list three females in pants who won military citations—Russian hussar Nadezhda Durova in 1806, Polish battle hero Joanna Zubr in 1809, and Mary Edwards Walker, an abolitionist and Union Army surgeon throughout the American Civil War. With more stagecraft, Union soldier Sarah Emma Edmonds dressed as a man to join a Union infantry regiment and serve as a field nurse; she later dyed her skin and took on the guise of a black laundress to gather intelligence behind Confederate lines.

Among civilians in the 1860s, stagecoach driver Charlotte Darkey Parkhurst maintained her disguise as "Charlie" over a decade of driving six-horse teams from Los Gatos to Santa Cruz, California. In Siam, Welsh governess Anna Leonowens condoned the disguise of a harem girl as a Buddhist monk to reunite her with a lover. In November 1868 at Sandy Flat in New South Wales, Australia, womanly disguise concealed Ned Kelly's gang of outlaws, who revived an Irish trope of male brigands in dresses.

Entertainers and mimics have exploited transdressing in circus and vaudeville acts and stage parody. In September 1974, male dancers in New York City formed a drag ballet corps, Les Ballets Trockadero de Monte Carlo. Dressed in leotard tops, tutus or waltz-length chiffon skirts, tights, and toe shoes, accomplished "Trocks" parody the romantic clichés of stage dance with comic performances of *Swan Lake, Giselle, The Nutcracker, Sleeping Beauty,* and *Les Sylphides.*

An interview in the April 7, 2013, edition of *The New York Times* revealed a prejudicial aspect of cross-dressing. In Queens, New York, the transgender community protested a high rate of police suspicion and harassment based on dress. Of 300 residents in the Jackson Heights area, 28 percent of straight citizens reported police questioning regarding loitering with intent to sell sex. For bisexual, gay, lesbian, and transgender individuals, the percentage was 54, an indication that dressing up on the street nearly doubled the possibility of implication by officers in criminality.

See also: Disguise and Spy Wear; Gendered Dressing; Unisex Clothing.

Further Reading

Ackroyd, Peter. *Dressing Up: Transvestism and Drag: The History of an Obsession.* New York: Simon & Schuster, 1979.

Garber, Marjorie B. *Vested Interests: Cross-Dressing and Cultural Anxiety.* New York: Routledge, 1992.

Krimmer, Elisabeth. *In the Company of Men: Cross-Dressed Women Around 1800.* Detroit, MI: Wayne State University Press, 2004.

Kuefler, Mathew. *The Manly Eunuch: Masculinity, Gender Ambiguity, and Christian Ideology in Late Antiquity.* Chicago: University of Chicago Press, 2001.

Crowns and Tiaras

A symbolic head adornment and badge of supremacy, the crown epitomizes the power and rightful rule of a monarch, the glory of a deity or saint, the distinction of a leader, or the achievement of sports heroes. Through the literary workings of synecdoche, the "crown" became so familiar an identification of royalty that it replaced other terms.

For centuries after 1917 B.C.E., Assyrian rulers shaped the *aga* (tiara or half coronet) from interwoven feathers supporting bullhorns, a symbol marking the Babylonian Crown of Anu, god of heaven. Among Hebrews from 1600 B.C.E., the Jewish high priest wore a three-stage miter topped with a turban. In Ethiopia, the royal gold cylinder fit over the pharaoh's turban, as with the headdress of Shabaka between 721 and 706 B.C.E.

The Mycenaeans crowned maternal goddesses Rhea and Cybele with the *polos,* a high metal ring. In sixth-century Greece, worshippers adorned the statues of Dionysus, Apollo, Zeus, Hades, and Herakles with the *korone* (wreath) woven of vines or the *stemma* (chaplet or corolla) of flowers like that worn by the goddess Flora. On the Acropolis and elsewhere, the devout reserved the embossed crested helmet for Athene, goddess of war and wisdom.

Divine Right of Kings

The fifth-century B.C.E. tyrants of Syracusa, Dionysius I and II, tied gold wreaths around their turbans as evidence of divine approval of their violent reigns. In the fourth century B.C.E., Persian royal regalia consisted of towering miters (headdresses) ornamented with lappets (flaps) for princes and the king's fillet (cloth or leather headband) or metal *taj* (diadem) topped with a tall, conical wool or linen tiara, such as that of Achaemenid monarch Darius III after 336 B.C.E. Ties on the side of Darius's diadem trailed to the shoulder.

After 330 B.C.E., Darius's conqueror, Alexander the Great, appeared on coins in the horned diadem, evidence of semidivine authority from the cult of the horned god Ammon. Following Alexander's death in 323 B.C.E., several of his successors—Ptolemy I in Egypt, Lysimachus in Thrace, Antigonus I of Babylon, and Seleucus I of Persia—adopted the plain diadem as evidence of royal power. Other successors in Sparta and Sicily refused to deck themselves with symbolic claims of divine right.

In Rome, chaplets (wreaths) represented earthly honors. Dignitaries received coronas of laurel, myrtle, or olive leaves; the combat hero sported a *corona civica* made from oak leaves and dotted with acorns. Gold coronas, symbolizing rank, awaited naval heroes and the first legionaries to breach the walls at siege sites.

In 44 B.C.E., because Romans rejected the concept of hereditary dynasties, they disapproved of a diadem that Mark Anthony presented to the dictator Julius Caesar. Caesar donated the diadem to the Temple of Zeus and chose for himself a modest laurel wreath, which covered his bald spot. In winter 37 B.C.E., mobs raged at the diadem that crowned Mark Anthony as consort to Queen Cleopatra VII after their marriage at Antioch, Syria.

Over time, Roman opinions softened toward kingly regalia and rights of succession. From 284 C.E., Roman emperors wore the emblematic imperial diadem, which had originated in Persia with Ardasir I after 224. Between 253 and 260, Emperor Valerian II added tall sunbeams to his diadem. Under Diocletian after 285, the Roman diadem became standard imperial regalia.

Symbols of Power

In the British Isles, Celtic kings wielded bronze and iron scepters paired with bronze or gold diadems, such as the bronze crown buried in present-day Kent around 200 B.C.E. Royal headdress also became the insignia of Roman potentates in Britannia over the next 250 years. Following the Anglo-Saxon conquest in 449, England's heptarchy from Hengist to Aethelstan evolved the jeweled helmet into a diadem or crown.

After 527, the Byzantine emperor Justinian I combined the royal diadem with a Christian *stephanos* (crown), a hierarchical symbol of the emperor's power over the Eastern Roman Empire and of the rule of Christ over Justinian. Subsequent Byzantine monarchs added ermine linings, arches, pearl pendants, and chains in imitation of Greek diadem ribbons. To the north and east, seventh-century Visigoth crowns lavished gold bases with a mass of precious gemstones and filigreed pendants.

On Christmas Day, 800, at St. Peter's Cathedral in Rome, Pope Leo III crowned Charlemagne as emperor of Rome with a cap-like diadem featuring alternating gold plaques decorated with emeralds and sapphires and enameling picturing Jesus, David, Solomon, and Hezekiah as models of piety and wisdom. Other heads of state wore circlets marked with royal crests, such as the uraeus (asp) and sun rays on the Egyptian crown, the bone wheel on the Tibetan crown, pearl and silk lappets on the Arabian caliph's felt-and-gold fillet, fleur-de-lis and arch on the Czech Crown of Saint Wenceslas, the tall spired Great Crown of Victory of Thailand, the feathered crown of Aztec king Montezuma II, gold lace and lotus blossom on the Russian Cap of Monomakh, and allegorical enameling of the Danish Crown of Christian IV. At the Vatican, the peaked miter and double keys to the kingdom marked Pope Constantine with sacral elements that connected him to St. Peter, the first pope. The weighty headgear took prominence in religious ritual under Pope Nicholas I after 858.

The Imperial State Crown, a glittering symbol of British monarchical sovereignty, is carried into Parliament and worn by the king or queen for the opening of the annual legislative session. The crown includes more than 3,000 precious gems. *(Suzanne Plunkett—WPA Pool/Getty Images)*

The Passing of Rule

At a turning point in European history, William I of Normandy marked his conquest of England in October 1066 with a plain crenellated circlet, a shape replicated along the battlements of medieval forts. In 1076, Dmitar Zvonimir of Croatia received the unique Hungarian crown, marked by long pendilia (dangling ornaments) at the sides, yet various artistic representations of his sovereignty vary the shape and height of his headdress. In twelfth-century Morocco, female aristocrats retained their tiaras while devout Muslim women adopted modest veils. In 1306, Robert I the Bruce came to the Scots throne at Scone wearing a plain corona over a warrior's helmet, a suitable distinction for a freedom fighter. For utilitarian reasons, some crowns, such as that of Sancho IV of Castile, were hinged to simplify the fitting of the circlet on the next head of state.

The sovereign's crown began expanding in application and meaning during the early Renaissance from the unique distinction of the sultan's *taj* (crown) with its embroidered panel and the Turkish emperor's striped silk turban with jeweled aigrette (feathered tuft) to less momentous honors. A variety of Greek Orthodox priests, Bavarian abbesses, Russian brides, French noblewomen, Venetian doges, and royal mistresses wore coronets and miters. In 1576, Rudolf II came to the Austrian throne bearing a massive circle and miter above a red velvet inner cushion for comfort.

The restoration of England's Charles II in 1660 involved a procession of viscounts carrying gold circlets topped with pearls, emblems of blamelessness in the execution of the previous king, Charles I. At his coronation on April 23, 1661, Charles II received new regalia in the form of St. Edward's Crown, which replaced precious state jewelry melted down or sold by Puritan zealot Oliver Cromwell, head of the British Commonwealth after 1649. Also in this period, images of the crown began appearing on princely buttons, crests, signet rings, and furnishings as a royal cypher.

Crowns as Treasure

From the seventeenth century, the parure, a suite of matching ceremonial jewelry—bandeau, belt clasp, bracelet, brooch, comb, diadem, earrings, necklace, pins, rings, tiara—embodied dynastic status and power. As treasure, such items ensured the monetary basis of a dynasty as well as the traditions and rituals undergirding the act of coronation. In 1510, Milanese artisan Cristoforo Caradosso Foppa worked gold ore to shape the three-tiered tiara of Pope Julius II, who spent 2 million ducats (about $4 million) on the world's largest emerald and other gems for its bejeweling. Because Napoleon claimed indemnity from the papacy to the French under the Peace of Tolentino in 1797, Pope Pius VI melted down the tiara for coins.

In the nineteenth century, Queen Victoria invested royal crowns with jewels from the British Empire, notably the Second Star of Africa on the Imperial State Crown and the First Star of Africa on the Sovereign's Sceptre. On the platinum crown, she displayed the 186-carat Koh-i-Noor diamond from India, worn in the regalia of Hindu, Mughal, Iranian, Afghan, and Sikh monarchs over the previous four centuries. For state occasions from 1870 until her burial on February 4, 1901, Victoria wore a lightweight diamond crown.

Subsequent royal nuptials called for public display of jeweled headdress, notably the tiara centered with the pink Noor-ol-Ain diamond that Farah Diba wore for her union with Reza Shah Pahlavi of Iran on December 21, 1959. An anomalous wedding between Wallis Warfield Simpson and David Windsor, the former Edward VIII of England, involved the presentation of a platinum and diamond tiara, which royal advisers forbade. For her marriage to Crown Prince Charles of England on July 29, 1981, Lady Diana Spencer added to her wedding ensemble the Spencer diamond tiara, a feminine scrolled headpiece mounted on silver.

Today, state crowns and regalia survive as tourist attractions at national museums and other repositories, such as the Tower of London, Vienna's Imperial Treasury, the Kremlin in Moscow, the Royal Mausoleum of Hawaii, and the National Palace of Kuala Lumpur. The Iranian crown jewels, including the red velvet Kiani Crown, remain on display at the Central Bank of Iran. South Koreans exhibit the mesh golden inner cap of the Silla

Crown and other state treasures at the Haeinsa temple in the Gaya Mountains.

See also: Accessories; Feathers; Headdress, Formal; Jewels and Jewelry; Pageantry; Royal Attire; Wedding Dress.

Further Reading

Munn, Geoffrey C. *Tiaras: A History of Splendour.* Woodbridge, UK: Antique Collectors' Club, 2001.

———. *Tiaras: Past and Present.* London: V&A; New York: Harry N. Abrams, 2008.

Scarisbrick, Diana, Christophe Vachaudez, and Jan Walgrave. *Royal Jewels: From Charlemagne to the Romanovs.* New York: Vendome, 2008.

Customs, Lore, and Myth

Apparel lore permeates mystic folk literature with the mundane and magical qualities of textiles, clothing, shoes, and jewelry.

Ancient Webbing and Weaving

Perhaps as old as Minoan oral literature of 3600 B.C.E., Greek Titan mythology pictured time and human longevity as the works of Clotho (the spinner), Lachesis (the apportioner), and Atropos (the inevitable). The sisters, called the Moirai (Fates), were the daughters of almighty Zeus and Themis (divine law). Like Frigga, the spinner of clouds and guardian of wives in the Norse Edda, the Greek Clotho spooled out a mortal thread from her spindle for Lachesis, the hand of destiny, to measure. Atropos snipped the apportioned filament with scissors, the metaphorical stroke of death. The fibers represented the enculturation of women with belief systems that supported intelligence and spirituality.

Neith, the Egyptian version of the yarn maker and ruler of cosmic order, overturned the Greek myth of the doom-laden apportioner and executioner by applying a beneficent meaning. In the paradigm of thread work, Neith became the creator of bandages and winding cloths and the shielder of the dead. The image of tension between threads loomed at right angles vivified the struggle for life among the sick and perishing. Similarly compassionate to the mortal state, Amaterasu, the mythic

Japanese loom mistress of the Heavenly Grotto, and the Nommo spirits of the Dogon people of Mali powered primeval looms as sources of the netting that held together Earth, heaven, oceans, and humankind.

Perhaps evolved from Lydian mythology or a Mediterranean allegory of competing textile centers from 3000 to 1400 B.C.E., Greek and Cretan mythos developed multiple concepts of spinning, knotting, and dyeing as equivalents of human industry. Arachne, the weaver, learned to loom thread in her father's dye works, which tinted plain cloth Tyrian purple. The aggrandized color connected Arachne with royalty and pretension.

Greek weaving lore bore in its philosophy the possibility of destruction. Arachne fell into the sin of hubris (pride) by declaring her skill innate rather than a gift of Athena, goddess of wisdom and fiber work. Athena punished Arachne by destroying her shuttle and the tapestry in her loom and reducing the arrogant weaver to a spider. Arachne thus became a mindless artisan forever exuding thread in meaningless segments. Attempting hanging to end her humiliation, the doomed weaver dangled from a thread until Athena granted her the power to fashion webs.

The concept of netting and mending suffused Appalachian, Irish, and Hungarian wonder tales with ways of eluding fearful conditions, particularly falling from precipices or drowning at sea during fishing expeditions. In contrast, the Chinese legend of sericulture directed woman's work toward economic benefit. Dating to the reign of Emperor Huangdi along the Yellow River in 2600 B.C.E., the protohistory of silk dramatized Queen Leizu's contribution to textile manufacture as divine inspiration, a cultic gift enshrined at Kamo, Miwa, and Izushi. For Queen Leizu and her people, the weaving of silk elevated the Chinese fabric trade, producing an historic commodity still profitable in the twenty-first century.

Interlacing the Elements

In 2000 B.C.E., Maya lore of the Yucatán, Belize, Guatemala, and Honduras elevated female invention to tribal masterstroke. Maya origin myths set Ixchel, a lunar and rain deity, to the tasks of conception, midwifery, and weaving. A parallel image pictured the Slavonic Moist Mother Earth as the spinner of waters over soil, the cyclic renewer of nature. Both views of female powers incorporated liquid and interwoven tissue as emblems of birth, a proto-scientific reverencing of the amnion, chorion, umbilicus, and placenta, a matrix that nurtures the unborn much as a woven nest sustains neophyte birds.

After 100 B.C.E., Teotihuacan myth of central Mexico pictured the supreme goddess as Spider Woman, the putative source of the Keresan Pueblo Spider Grandmother in the petroglyphs of Arizona and New Mexico. Navajo and Hopi lore imagined the skilled fingers knotting a web of wild cotton and hemp, sprinkling the mesh with dewdrops, and spanning the sky with it, turning the twinkling water spots into constellations. Under orders from Spider Grandmother, Pueblo parents rubbed the fingers of baby daughters with spiderwebs to ready them for making clothing and blankets, a cyclic renewal of female skills.

According to *Hellenos Periegesis* (*Description of Greece*, ca. 150 C.E.) by the Greek travel writer Pausanias, webwork served early Mediterranean history as a metaphor for collaboration. In 588 B.C.E. in the northwestern Peloponnesus, the fabric workers of Elis settled through peacemaking some 40 years of intrigue under the tyrant Damophon of Pisa. As a metaphoric gesture to Hera, the goddess of women and marriage, female delegates from 16 cities wove a robe for the Olympian statue of the goddess. The image of weaving as woman's work symbolized the organization and harmony of a local federation that freed the Eleans of hostility.

Among the Inca of Cuzco, present-day Peru, after 1200 C.E., *acllas,* or sun virgins, remained celibate as part of their dedication to female domesticity and submission to the gods. From ages 4 to 14, the virgins wove priestly vestments until their burial alive in honor of the sun deity. The fabric symbolized Andean kinship with the emperor and with the sacred in nature. Thus, the myths of the acllas strengthened tradition by linking the making of clothes with a higher purpose.

Fairy Tale Weavers

Textiles in oral lore, such as the Swahili tale "The Cloth of the Serpent Pembe Mirui," Hans Christian Andersen's "The Emperor's New Clothes," Russian Baba Yaga loom stories, and the Japanese tale "The Crane Wife," represented cultural expansion and resilience. Germanic and Middle Eastern tale-telling implied that domestication through the fabric arts could build character traits that overpowered the connivance of witches and ogres and the ferocity of males, the theme of the Armenian story of Arevhat. In the shrewd oral lore describing the fight against evil, spinning and weaving empowered female characters to break curses and spells, the focus of a suite of Grimm brothers' fairy tales—"Rumpelstiltskin," "Rapunzel," "The Six Swans," "Briar Rose," and "Twelve Brothers."

In the Grimms' didactic story "Spindle, Shuttle, and Needle," the transformation of these three female tools into messengers to a handsome prince rescued a virtuous spinner from drudgery while supplying the prince with a competent wife. The double-edged solution to mutual problems, as found in the Chinese myth of the Weaving Maiden and the Armenian tale "Clever Anaeet," embodied the folk notion of uniquely male and female contributions to the family. Storytellers turned the repetitive motion of spinning flax into yarn and weaving threads into robes and blankets into the cultural sustenance of oral narrative, a text interwoven with new and old verbal threads. The humble but reliable female therapy against chaos and catastrophe appeared repeatedly in legends of Jewish women weaving curtains for Jerusalem's Temple on the Mount, medieval illuminations and tapestry, Renaissance portraiture, and the colonial American myth of Betsy Ross, the flag maker.

Modern fiction incorporates the customs and lore of the fabric arts as elements of connection and recreation—the solaces of Hester Prynne, the outcast seamstress in Nathaniel Hawthorne's *The Scarlet Letter* (1850); of frontierswoman Caroline Ingalls in the *Little House* series (1930s–1940s); and of a dynasty of shawl makers in Sandra Cisneros's *Caramelo* (2003). In Alice Walker's parable *The Color Purple* (1982), Celie stitches pants for

Nettie, the sister living among the Olinka in West Africa, and relieves suppressed anger against the abusive Mr. Albert by opening a sewing boutique in Memphis, Tennessee. Unlike the Greek myth of Philomela and the veil, illustrated with scenes of her rape, Celie chooses a creative alternative to blame and vengeance and transforms herself into a self-empowered entrepreneur.

Also gynocentric in theme, the story of Penelope, the abandoned wife in Homer's *Odyssey* (ca. 800 B.C.E.), turned the weaving and unraveling of the obligatory winding sheet for her father-in-law Laertes into a ruse to forestall suitors. In connivance against would-be usurpers of queen and throne, Penelope and her handmaidens perpetrated an act of female resistance to patriarchy. In her novel *Penelopiad* (2005), Canadian author Margaret Atwood's modern version of unraveling celebrates sisterhood, a convergence of female initiative to save Penelope and her 12 maids from male-imposed paralysis. To counter the glorification of the wandering Odysseus, Atwood's retelling of the epic elevates Penelope the weaver and un-weaver to a strategist on a par with her famed deceiver husband.

See also: Amerindian Clothing, Pre-Columbian; Divinities; Gendered Dressing; Greek Clothing, Ancient; Noble, Princely, and Chivalric Attire; Ritual Garments; Royal Attire; Symbolic Colors, Patterns, and Motifs.

Further Reading

Bahun-Radunovic, Sanja, and V.G. Julie Rajan, eds. *Myth and Violence in the Contemporary Female Text: New Cassandras.* Burlington, VT: Ashgate, 2011.

Como, Michael. *Weaving and Binding: Immigrant Gods and Female Immortals in Ancient Japan.* Honolulu: University of Hawaii Press, 2009.

Kruger, Kathryn Sullivan. *Weaving the Word: The Metaphorics of Weaving and Female Textual Production.* Danvers, MA: Rosemont, 2001.

Dance Costumes

For dance performances, costumes have traditionally highlighted the energy, drama, and passion of choreography. According to evidence from 33,000 B.C.E., found in Canada, Turkey, Czech Republic, Siberia, and France, costuming set dancers apart from viewers by transforming them into divine beings or icons of nature. Individualized styles turned feathers into visual prayers among Australia's Aborigines, painted skulls into sacred props among the Aztec of Mesoamerica, and bone whistles, clappers, bells, and rattles into rhythmic instruments among the Pueblo tribes of the Great Basin.

After 1570 B.C.E., the Egyptian *bedleh,* or female belly dance costume, consisted of kilts and aprons that freed the midriff for undulation. As the dance formalized, the dancer coordinated a crop top with a translucent skirt or harem pants, which fastened around the ankles. Ponytails, layers of clinking coin necklaces, sheer hand and headscarves, finger cymbals, and wispy veils reflected light against whole body whirls. Egyptian men and women accessorized with armlets and collars of bright stones set in metal. The Turkish version of the belly dance decked the male partner in a plumed turban, skimpy vest or bare chest, and loose trousers.

In the Iron Age after 1200 B.C.E., the Celtic jig, ring sets, and sword and step dance developed in Ireland under the influence of Druidism and waves of migrants. For professional country dances in later eras, Highlanders paired short fitted dresses with headbands and shawls for women. The male contingent wore a plain kilt or tight pants, sash, and vest with a *brat* (cloak), which enhanced drama and sweep. Unique black footwear called gillies secured tongueless lace-up slippers at the ankle, over thin hose.

Traditional Dance

In the South Seas and Africa, dancing required no shoes. For Fijian story-dance, around 800 B.C.E., Lapitan seafarers from Indonesia redirected emphasis from the lower body to a seated narrative featuring flower collars and hand and shoulder gestures accentuated by shell bracelets. Tribal designations took the form of body paint, tattoos, and piercings with thorns or animal fangs. After 200 B.C.E., Tahitian, Cook Island, and Hawaiian dancers stitched grass, ti leaves, and barkcloth into skirts worn below oiled chests. Dance troupes incorporated natural motifs with leaf belts, flower leis, and garlands of greenery for ankles, heads, and wrists.

For the Midimu ritual, aboriginal Makonde dancers of southern Tanzania and Mozambique filed their teeth and cloaked long pants and shirt with string netting, bells, and a cloth helmet reaching to the shoulders. From the 400s C.E., the Sotho of South Africa propitiated rain by gyrating and leaping in black ostrich plumes and a blanket cloak. After 700, Fono dancers from the Ivory Coast created costumes from raffia fringes and skirts, bead necklaces, whisks, and mud or wood masks detailed with horns, feathers, bones, teeth, and shells. Stilts covered in fabric elongated the legs into a fantasy beast. Similarly nature-based, a loose confederacy of north Nigerian troupes from 948 performed the Agaba (lion dance) in coarse suits stitched with rustling seeds and brass bells.

From 1250, religious dance emphasized song rather than costume, as with Balkan line dances, ring sets performed in Bologna, the *estampie* of Catalonia, and Danish chain dances. In contrast, Kathakali dance drama in Kerala, India, in the late 1500s showcased costumes and massive headdresses. Companies used makeup to highlight facial, hand,

and body posturing set to percussive and vocal music.

In pantomimes of martial arts and Sanskrit scripture and ritual, Southwestern Indian theatricals perpetuated classic tales and myths and recounted cosmic and historical events. The dancer wore a short-sleeved bodice over an ankle-length flounced skirt. Character actors padded overcoats and wrappers into bulbous shapes and starched neck cloths and skirts to vivify impersonations. Alluring accessories—crowns, long wigs, tassels, forearm covers, beads from neck to hip, shawls, and Turkish slippers—emphasized the dynamics of story-dance.

In Malayan and Tibetan style, stark coloration identified Kathakali characters by social status, gender, and profession. For portrayal of Indian noblemen, actors colored their faces green. Demon portrayers added red streaks and beards to the green base. Gods displayed beards whitened with rice paste. Woodsmen and hermits appeared in black. Amazons wore yellow.

European Staged Dance

After Italian composer Balthasar de Beaujoyeulx outfitted French dancers for *Le Ballet-Comique* at the French court of Catherine de' Medici in 1581, dance companies created ballet skirts and low-heeled slippers that suited female needs. Male court performers typically topped stockings and shoes with brocade coats that flared into skirts, a stylized version of Roman armor. At London's Covent Garden during the late Renaissance, stage designer Inigo Jones stitched allegorical and mythic confections for performers in masques, intermezzi, and *tableaux vivants* (living pictures), as with the armbands and military kilt and boots in the 1609 performance of *Virtu, Bellerophon and the Chimaera*.

In the 1720s and 1730s, dance costumes became more spectacular and less restrictive as head, arm, leg, and torso movements acquired complexity and athleticism. Contributing to the separation between street clothes and stage costumes, principal ballerina Marie Camargo of Belgium and French choreographer Marie Sallé introduced ethereal muslin dresses without the period corset and panniers. In the mid-1700s, Louis XV restored propriety by decreeing that dancers at the Paris Opéra wear the *maillot* (tights) with *caleçon* (underpants).

Late in the century, stretchy leg coverings promoted naturalistic stage techniques for story ballet that physicalized characters. The rise of *ballet d'action* altered the importance of costume from decoration to an element of impressionism. For

A Kathakali dancer from the southern Indian state of Kerala performs in the traditional medieval style. Kathakali dance drama marked a break in world religious dance with its emphasis on costume, headdress, and makeup rather than song. *(AP Photo/ Bikas Das)*

Jean-Georges Noverre's opera *Diane et Endymion* in 1791, dancer Victoire Saulnier debuted the filmy tunic, a radical shift from full skirts to a columnar dress over maillot and caleçon that revealed her form in motion. In 1796, French prima ballerina Rose Parisot galvanized London viewers in a costume for *Le Triomphe de l'Amour* that revealed all of her legs in jetés (leaps) and *grands battements* (waist-high leg lifts).

Nineteenth-century dancewear continued to stray from everyday fashions to professional costumes. In 1832, choreographer Filippo Taglioni invented the mid-calf muslin skirt for his daughter, dancer Marie Taglioni, in the romantic title role of *La Sylphide.* Subsequent stage wardrobe added the spaghetti-strap or strapless bodice over tulle skirts that revealed female musculature.

Dance Shoes

In the American South at house parties at Oak Alley Plantation in New Orleans and Monmouth Plantation in Natchez, Mississippi, the kid dance slipper enabled women to glide over the floor in a sarabande or galop. Soft soles secured the feet in motion to balance layered crinolines and swaying hoop skirts.

Influenced by Marie Taglioni, the pointe shoe evolved from leather and wood to a satin cover over kidskin or cardboard arch and a layered toe box blocked from paper, canvas, or burlap and securely glued. An Italian cobbler, Salvatore Capezio of Lucano, worked near the Metropolitan Opera House in New York in 1887 and extended his business by repairing ballet slippers and toe shoes, the beginning of the Capezio dance shoe industry. His most famous patron, Russian star Anna Pavlova, ordered Capezio pointe shoes in 1910 for her repertory company.

America's premier stage couple, Vernon and Irene Castle, popularized modern face-to-face dance after their debut in 1911. Setting fashion trends with suave costuming, they performed social dance in fashionable tuxedos and elegant gowns worn with street shoes. With Vernon and as a solo performer, Irene modeled handkerchief hems and low-heeled pumps, a comfortable shoe that gained popularity during World War I.

During the Great Depression, movie star Ginger Rogers flashed high-heeled pumps and single-strap shoes in her performances with Fred Astaire in *Top Hat* (1935) and *Shall We Dance* (1937). Later in the decade, American women emulated her one-strap dancing slippers for evenings at supper clubs. From 1935 to 1940, Shirley Temple epitomized innocence and propriety in Mary Jane tap shoes with anklets and kneesocks, a look carried over on costumed dolls. In *The Wizard of Oz* (1939), Judy Garland wowed young girls with glittery red pumps. One of the film's most memorable props, the ruby slippers prefaced a trend in rhinestone evening shoes for adult women.

Modern Innovations

In 1950, Russian-born costumer Barbara Karinska solved a staging problem for the corps de ballet. In place of the flat, wired tutu, she devised a powder puff version of six or seven self-supporting net layers that remained fluffed, a contribution to George Balanchine's production of *Symphony in C.* Another design, the knee-length chiffon costume for Balanchine's *Allegro Brillante* (1956), set a standard for its ladylike grace.

Dance wear continued changing and developing into the late twentieth century with adoption of the unitard, sports bra, battery-powered, light-up leotards, and synthetic Spandex, invented in 1959. A tight fit improved the warm-up of muscles to prevent injury. Gel-toed pointe shoes prevented toe damage from long-term balance of body weight.

Costuming for the Ballet Folklórico de México turned jewel-toned bias gowns and black toreador pants into a signature look for extravagant corps de ballet production numbers. Alvin Ailey lead dancer Judith Jamison adopted the long, body-hugging bias dress for her solo "Cry" in May 1979. For *Grand,* performed by the Sydney Dance Company in 2011, Australian designer Akira Isogawa pioneered translucent stage garments made from Modal, pliant rayon extracted from beechwood.

See also: African Clothing, Sub-Saharan; Mardi Gras and Carnival Costumes; Pacific Island Clothing; Petticoats; Skirts; Slippers.

Further Reading

Carter, Alexandra. *Rethinking Dance History: A Reader.* New York: Routledge, 2004.

Kassing, Gayle. *History of Dance: An Interactive Arts Approach.* Champaign, IL: Human Kinetics, 2007.

Morris, Mary Burke. *The Costume Book: The Non-Professional's Guide to Professional Results.* Atglen, PA: Schiffer, 2002.

Russell, Douglas A. *Costume History and Style.* Englewood Cliffs, NJ: Prentice-Hall, 1983.

de la Renta, Oscar (1932–)

Internationally known American couturier Oscar de la Renta built his reputation on glamorous, expensive, ready-to-wear feminine fashions.

A native of Santo Domingo, Dominican Republic, he was born Óscar Aristides Ortiz de la Renta Fiallo on July 22, 1932. The only son of the seven children of María Antonia Fiallo and Óscar Avelino de la Renta, a Puerto Rican insurance magnate, the designer acquired an appreciation for female taste from his six sisters. In 1950, he trained in art in Santo Domingo before studying abstract painting at the Academía de San Fernando in Madrid, Spain.

Immersion in tropical foliage and Iberian flamenco influenced de la Renta's love of opulent patterns and drama in motion. After apprenticing with Cristóbal Balenciaga at his Eisa boutique in Madrid, de la Renta joined the Paris staff of Jeanne Lanvin, where he sketched jewels, hand stitchery, and elegant fabrics. On July 9, 1956, his poufy two-layered evening gown graced the cover of *Life* magazine on debutante Beatrice Anna Cabot Lodge.

At age 31, de la Renta took the advice of Diana Vreeland, the editor of *Vogue,* and moved to the United States. In New York City, he improved profitability for cosmetician Elizabeth Arden and Jane Derby, a designer for mature women, before debuting his own label in 1965. His vision, influenced by the savvy of his wife, French *Vogue* editor Françoise de Langlade, focused on ready-to-wear evening gowns and wedding attire.

Vogue featured Raquel Welch in his black silk jumpsuit in March 1969 and Ali MacGraw in de la Renta fashions a year later. His revival of maxi skirts in 1970 provoked protest from devotees of minis, which he continued to exhibit in *Ebony* magazine. Actor and singer Liza Minnelli championed his evening dresses, which displayed floating crepe de chine and chiffon skirts. Home sewers popularized his Vogue patterns, which featured women's garments for sun, shopping, dinner, and office.

De la Renta ventured into bohemian ensembles, modeled by actor Lesley Warren, in 1971, and followed with uniforms for Boy Scouts and Girl Scouts and ensembles for the Barbie doll. He dressed such celebrities as dancer Twyla Tharp and the American Ballet Theatre, social luminaries Brooke Astor and Anne Ford, broadcast journalist Barbara Walters, newspaper publisher Katharine Graham, singers Dionne Warwick and Cher, actors Kim Basinger and Shirley MacLaine, and models Brooke Shields, Cindy Crawford, and Marisa Berenson. His innovations with quilting, nuanced torso-skimming, and bold color combinations earned him two Coty awards, a Tiberius honorarium, and, in 1973, entry into the Coty Hall of Fame.

The designer gained notoriety for influencing the public image of presidents' wives. For Jacqueline Kennedy, Nancy Reagan, Laura Bush, and Michelle Obama, de la Renta helped ease the transition from political wife to first lady. To reshape the public perception of Hillary Clinton, he put her in pastels as a switch from somber black suits.

For the fashion-conscious bride, he engulfed the torso in a bubble mini-gown of pink satin and tulle veil, leaving the shoulders and legs unadorned. To meet the demand of career women, he produced more day wear and separates for the office and classroom, grossing $450 million in 1991.

In 1992, de la Renta began a nine-year collaboration with Pierre Balmain in Paris and introduced the ready-to-wear line Ivoire. During his tenure, he reprised Gypsy couture and Russian ball gowns trimmed in fur. In 2001, he departed France to profit from the ready-to-wear boom in the Americas. He also introduced a line of boots, shoes, belts, handbags, swimsuits, sleepwear, furs, eyeglasses, and jewelry, modeled by Lauren Hutton. At age 70, he focused on practical machine-made designs rather than hand-sewn couture fashions. He stressed female strength by pairing denim with cashmere, a charmeuse gown with a neck ring, chenille arabesques on a bolero jacket, and oversized metal collars with silk tulle ballerina skirts.

De la Renta fine-tuned his vision in spring 2005 by showing a bouffant pink taffeta skirt with a T-shirt, one of the fun touches that marked his whimsical styles. In 2006, he dressed film star Diane Lane to receive an Academy Award and also specialized in wedding shoes, bags, veils, and beaded and embroidered dresses. His flowing deep blue silk organza dress for Oprah Winfrey's 2010 appearance at the Metropolitan Opera employed under-the-bust beading to outline a plunging decolletage.

The verve and ingenuity of de la Renta took wing in 2012, when he topped cubist fabrics à la Pablo Picasso with black paper hats emulating gaucho styles. That same year, he launched a line of boys' and girls' clothing from infants to early teens featuring bright floral dresses, ballerina flats, and boys in preppy navy blazers, white shorts, and striped shirts keyed to the colors of shoelaces. For 2013, he pared down the female silhouette to a modest A-line below the hip and showcased the shape of knee and calf in flirty, checkered tights.

See also: Fashion Design.

Further Reading

Darraj, Susan Muaddi. *Oscar de la Renta.* New York: Facts on File, 2010.

Mower, Sarah, and Anna Wintour. *Oscar: The Style, Inspiration and Life of Oscar de la Renta.* New York: Assouline, 2002.

Oscar de la Renta. www.oscardelarenta.com

Denim and Jeans

A versatile fabric for leisure and work clothes from the late 1500s, denim earned a global reputation for egalitarianism, value, utility, and sociability. According to the *London Encyclopaedia* (1829), denim took its name from *serge de Nîmes,* referring to cotton fabric from a city in southern France that manufactured heavy twills, or serge. The choice of indigo dye derived from a unique, widely available colorant that required no mordant or fixative.

From the late Renaissance, raw (unwashed) denim straight from the loom acquired a reputation among working-class men for strength and endurance, especially in port cities of the Mediterranean. Cutting pant legs along the woven selvage for sewing produced an inner leg seam that resisted raveling. Heavy wear faded the garment at stress points, particularly the seat and knees, revealing a unique glimpse of the owner's lifestyle. Despite extended use, denim pants could last for more than 1,000 wearings per pair.

Jeans earned their name from the French for Genoa, the source of a heavy corded fabric, a popular sailors' uniform. French laborers favored work blues and dungarees made of indigo cotton twill. By 1810, a factory in Berkshire, England, established itself as a maker of denim. Cincinnati, Ohio, entered the denim manufacturing competition before 1815.

Denim outfitted the American West from Washington to Colorado. The unique cut and stitchery got their start in 1870 in San Francisco from a collaboration of Bavarian Jewish merchant Morris Loeb "Levi" Strauss with Jacob Davis, a Latvian tailor who purchased fabric from Strauss. Their breakthrough innovation was the use of copper rivets to reinforce the pants at stress points, which earned Strauss and Davis a U.S. patent for their pants design in 1873. Levi Strauss & Co. went on to merchandise a full line of men's wear, including boot-cut pants, carpenter's pants, jackets, overalls, and vests in denim. Levi's 501 model, introduced in the 1890s, went on to become the best-selling clothing item in the world.

To compete for the workingman's dollar, other companies imitated the popular Levi's jeans. In 1889, Lee pants, manufactured in Salina, Kansas, anchored the world's largest clothing company. Embroidered on the pocket with the Lazy S logo, work wear by industrialist Henry David Lee included denim dungarees, jumpsuits, and jackets. Lee pants took a new direction in the 1920s with the zipper fly.

In 1935, Levi's introduced Lady Levi's in *Vogue* magazine, a signal for relaxed standards in women's leisure wear. Social analysts marked this era as the beginning of a decline in formal etiquette, a loss of class consciousness, and a tendency toward public discourtesy and truculence by jeans wearers.

During World War II, the jeans culture migrated east toward the Atlantic Coast. In natural indigo, sulfur dye, or synthetic dye, denim pants served factory workers in the postwar era, when Wrangler first entered the denim market with serviceable play clothes and the denim snap shirt. For individualizing styles, jeans came to stores in plain weave and straight-cut, tapered, boot-cut, flared, or skinny with pegged ankles.

In the 1970s, jeans with polo shirts, T-shirts, and running shoes consolidated the pop culture image with a comfortable, socially acceptable uniform. Stonewashing, invented in Alberta, Canada, softened stiff denim and faded the indigo dye by pummeling new garments in a rotating drum with stones or pumice. Men's fashions embraced black jeans with knit shirts and blazers and denim sports coats with khaki pants.

During the globalization of fashion in the 1980s, jeans consumers took varied paths. Consumers popularized expensive designer jeans, pedal pushers, denim jumpsuits, knit-waist jeans with drawstrings, denim print jeggings (a cross between jeans and leggings), and zipper-sided jeans. Levi's 501s marketed a straight cut through the seat, thigh, and leg and an authentic five-pocket design with button tab waist and fly. Politicians with the standing of Ronald Reagan signaled sympathy with the commoner by dressing down in jeans and chambray shirts for press-the-flesh sessions and chats with workers.

In the 1990s, for commercial ready-to-wear, Lee, Levi's, and Wrangler manufactured vintage dark, heavyweight jeans with cuffed hems. In 1993, Lands' End featured denim as the "World's Friendliest Fabric." The statement acknowledged the welcome of denim to maternity wear, teen fads, and relaxed office wear on "dress down" Fridays.

Jeans retained their former flexibility and staying power because they signaled shifts in social values and behaviors that both complemented and countered each other. The highest number of denim purchases and wearings belonged to Germany, Brazil, Colombia, and Russia. Americans and Europeans bought curvy jeans in cuts that flattered all body types. Fashion hard-liners returned to raw denim, the unwashed look that survived for months, allowing the wearer to distress them naturally. In 2011, widespread silicosis among workers in Bangladesh and Turkey from high-velocity water and silica blasting of denim generated a backlash from Benetton, Burberry, Esprit, Gucci, and Levi's, all of whom banned the process.

See also: American Western Clothing; Leisure Wear; Strauss, Levi.

Further Reading

Kyi, Tanya Lloyd. *The Blue Jean Book: The Story Behind the Seams.* Toronto: Annick, 2005.

Marsh, Graham, and Paul Trynka. *Denim: From Cowboys to Catwalks: A Visual History of the World's Most Legendary Fabric.* London: Aurum, 2005.

Miller, Daniel, and Sophie Woodward, eds. *Global Denim.* New York: Bloomsbury, 2011.

Sullivan, James. *Jeans: A Cultural History of an American Icon.* New York: Gotham, 2007.

Department Stores

A merchandising strategy of the early nineteenth century, the department store democratized retailing with a one-stop emporium offering quality goods and service to the consumer. From the beginning, firms such as David Jones in Sydney, Australia, Le Bon Marché in Paris, and Kendals in Manchester, England, improved on dressmaker shops, dry goods stores, and haberdashers by offering a comprehensive line of clothing and coordinating hosiery, hats, gloves, costume jewelry, and umbrellas. After 1823, many of the fashions at A.T. Stewart's Marble Palace on Manhattan's "Ladies Mile" came from company mills in New York, New England, Belfast, Ireland, and Nottingham, England.

Merchandisers focused on the interests of their clientele and combed European and Asian markets for quality calico, velvet, lace, leather, and furs. In 1826, the opening of Lord & Taylor in Manhattan courted the home seamstress with orderly arrays of bolts of serge and dimity and sewing notions. By 1841, Jordan Marsh in Boston appealed to affluent customers with upscale linen and silk goods.

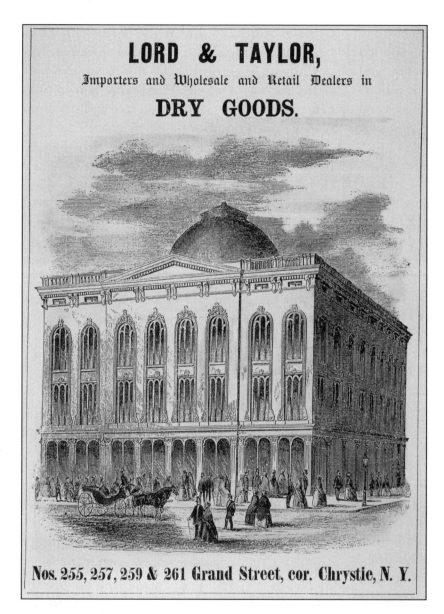

LORD & TAYLOR,

Importers and Wholesale and Retail Dealers in

DRY GOODS.

Nos. 255, 257, 259 & 261 Grand Street, cor. Chrystie, N. Y.

America's oldest upscale department store chain, Lord & Taylor opened in 1826 in lower Manhattan. In 1853, it moved into a larger, custom-designed building (pictured here) at Grand and Chrystie streets. Today, it operates nearly 50 stores. *(The Granger Collection, NYC—All rights reserved)*

J. Bacon & Sons in Louisville, Kentucky, arranged apparel under 63 department headings clearly marked by signs, simplifying the location of shoes, lingerie, and men's socks and belts. A competitor, Levy Brothers, catered to men and children as well as women, who made up 90 percent of department store shoppers. In Atlanta two years after the end of the Civil War, Rich's Department Store revived the city's economy as well as its flair for stylish clothes.

Accommodating Early Patrons

Unlike boutiques, department stores enabled consumers to assemble an outfit in one commercial establishment and designate garments for altera-

tion. In 1846, the Marble Palace added women's apparel to stocks of silk, lace, and embroidered accessories. Farther into the Industrial Revolution, large emporiums—Abraham & Straus, B. Altman, and McCreary's in New York; Meier & Frank in Portland, Oregon; and Lipman Wolfe & Company in Sacramento, California, and Virginia City, Nevada—grouped dresses and suits on racks near multi-view mirrors. Staff welcomed middle-class consumers who had the disposable income and leisure time for trying on apparel in comfortable surroundings.

To satisfy the demands of the fashion-conscious, single buyers superintended the stocking of each department, a system that influenced the management of Falabella in Santiago, Chile's oldest department chain, and Magasin du Nord in Copenhagen, Denmark. In 1858, Macy's imported kid gloves and purses, lingerie, and feathers and artificial flowers for trimming hats. Merchandisers arranged shawls and cloaks by fabric and size and offered men's ties, hosiery, and handkerchiefs for sale at one price.

The rise of print merchandising in newspapers and magazines increased consumer awareness of variety and availability as well as the economy of shopping at clearance sales. Stores enticed new patrons with a no-questions return policy and the convenience of bargain basements and home delivery by horse-drawn van.

By catering to gender-based tastes in the late 1860s, urban merchants—Hamilton's, Harrods, and Liberty in London; Wanamaker's in Philadelphia; Zion's Cooperative Mercantile in Salt Lake City; Goldwater's in San Francisco; and Marshall Field in Chicago—emphasized the interests of families and hired polite staff to satisfy wardrobe and jewelry needs. In 1872, Bloomingdale's in Manhattan introduced ever-changing European trends for men and women. The replacement of gas lamps with electric lighting and mechanical cash registers increased the professionalism of transactions.

Entrepreneurs enlarged their outreach by introducing mail order, the strategy of Jelmoli in Zurich, Switzerland. Other firms opened branches, as with the GUM emporiums throughout Russia and Hudson's, a chain store that debuted in Detroit in 1881 and expanded to eight cities in the Midwest. Because of increased demand for apparel, companies such as the May Company and I. Magnin in San Francisco bought in bulk, thus promoting mass production of ready-to-wear. The offer of layaway plans and short-term credit furthered the appeal of shopping to the middle class, especially during the Christmas season.

Knockoffs and Discounts

In the early 1900s, the sale of knockoff ready-to-wear introduced low-price chic patterned after the wardrobe of the wealthy. To satisfy the needs of shoppers, Le Bon Marché employed 4,500 staff members by 1912. The Chinese exploited the marketing-chain model in 1915 by opening

Oriental Stores Ltd. in Yangon (Rangoon), Thailand. Meanwhile, steamships stocked emporiums in Chinese, Southeast Asian, and Australian port cities, such as Anthony Hordern & Son in Sydney, with colonial fashions and lace and silk from Guangzhou (Canton).

In Taiwan, Sun Yat-sen, founder of the Republic of China, identified the department store as a useful agency for modernization. In Chile, Gath y Chaves, the "Harrod's of Buenos Aires," offered five o'clock tea as evidence of its European modernism. On Nanking Road in Shanghai, China, Sun Sun Ltd. guaranteed high quality and customer service, an essential for the middle-class clothing shopper. Wing On in Tokyo, Japan, opened branches at subway stations and stayed open until 2 A.M.

After World War I, Western consumers took fashion cues from Gucci leather goods in department store windows, indoor modeling of knitwear by Elsa Schiaparelli, and expertise in displaying ready-to-wear by such future fashion stars as Ralph Lauren and Giorgio Armani. In 1926, during the golden age of department stores, clothing merchants competed against variety retailers and the mail-order conglomerates J.C. Penney's, Montgomery Ward, and Sears, Roebuck.

The Great Depression forced merchants to accommodate pinched budgets. Bainbridge's in Newcastle, England, introduced an installment plan that encouraged weekly payments. By the end of World War II, savvy store managers courted freer spending on the family wardrobe with customer service and the niceties demanded by female shoppers, who purchased 60 percent of menswear.

Suburban shopping further altered merchandising by anchoring malls with such big-name chains as Nordstrom and Neiman Marcus in the United States, Printemps in France, Jiuguang in China, Breuninger in Germany, Falabella in Chile, and La Rinascente in Italy. Entrepreneur John Harold Johnson promoted Fashion Fair cosmetics for dark skin at department store chains in Canada, the Caribbean, and France and at Kingsway, West Africa's first department store, which opened in Lagos in 1947.

By the 1950s, department store merchandising with high apparel turnover ended the great Ottoman *souks* (bazaars) of Beirut, Istanbul, Izmir, Cairo, and Thessalonica. Hagkaup in Reykjavik, Iceland, further challenged traditional modes in 1967 by creating a hypermarket selling clothing, electronics, and foods. In China in the mid-1980s, the economic revolution ended the rationing of cotton cloth and offered buyers apparel in synthetic fiber, silk, down, and leather. As department stores courted teens, the 1990s brought youthful buyers to malls with booteries and T-shirt and denim shops.

In the 2000s, discounted couture by such notable designers as Jason Wu, Marc Jacobs, and Vera Wang boosted sales at T.J. Maxx and Loehmann's and the hypermarkets Target and Walmart, which sold clothing and groceries in the Americas, Africa, Europe, India, and China. By 2010, discounted goods accounted for 87 percent of retail sales, a dominance that hastened the end of the department store boom. Nonetheless, chains such as South Korea's Lotte, Galeries Lafayette and Géant in France, and David Jones in Australia continued to scout new locations in China, Russia, Vietnam, Qatar, Morocco, Saudi Arabia, Bahrain, Uruguay, Kuwait, and Indonesia.

See also: Catalogs, Clothing and Fashion; Knockoff Fashions; Mail Order; Ready-to-Wear; Retail Trade.

Further Reading

Barmash, Isadore. *Macy's for Sale.* Washington, DC: Beard, 2003.

Hendrickson, Robert. *The Grand Emporiums: The Illustrated History of America's Great Department Stores.* New York: Stein and Day, 1979.

Whitaker, Jan. *Service and Style: How the American Department Store Fashioned the Middle Class.* New York: St. Martin's, 2006.

Whitten, David O. *The Birth of Big Business in the United States, 1860–1914.* Westport, CT: Greenwood, 2006.

Design

See Fashion Design

Dior, Christian (1905–1957)

The famed French couturier Christian Dior revolutionized women's apparel with a revival of the billowing skirt and hourglass figure. His "New Look" concept in women's clothes design reestablished Paris as the center of world fashion after World War II.

A native of Granville on the Normandy coast of France, he was born on January 21, 1905, to Marie-Madeleine Juliette Martin and Alexandre Louis Maurice Dior, a wealthy manufacturer of fertilizer. Growing up in Paris, in addition to decorating the house and laying out a garden, he created Carnival costumes for his siblings and began peddling his clothing sketches for a few cents each.

After uninspiring studies at Lycée Gerson and l'École des Sciences Politiques, Dior at age 23 opened Galerie Jacques Bonjean to sell the modern art of Pablo Picasso and Georges Braque. At age 30, Dior served as a sapper for the engineering corps of the French army in Provençe until the surrender of France to the Nazis. In 1940, after recovering from tuberculosis on the Spanish island of Ibiza, he joined the fashion house of Swiss designer Robert Piguet in Paris as a sketch artist; as an original designer, Dior gained attention for his Café Anglais dress, a houndstooth afternoon ensemble featuring a petticoat trim at the hem.

Pursuing his career in couture during the occupation of Paris, Dior sketched hats for Madame Agnès, costumed actors for a production of *School for Scandal,* and contributed original ideas to Coco Chanel and Hermès at Cannes. In 1941, Dior designed for Lucien Lelong's Paris salon the ensembles featured in issues of *Le Figaro.* French collaborators and the wives of SS officers became Dior's steady clients.

Finally on December 16, 1946, after years of poverty and rationing, Dior opened his own fashion house, Christian Dior Limited, on the posh Avenue Montaigne in downtown Paris. On February 12, 1947, he initiated his first collection, a luxury line that *Harper's Bazaar* editor Carmel Snow classed as the "New Look." His emphasis on female curves, inspired by the lines created by Jeanne Lanvin, required starched fabric, boned basques, padded hips, flared petticoats, and waist cinches.

The clamor of American department chains for Dior's dresses and classic suits boosted the French economy and earned the designer an award from the Neiman Marcus store. Although his ballerina-length skirts, using some 20 yards (18.3 meters) of fabric, met with hostility from competitor Coco Chanel, he succeeded in transforming feminine style with a bustier, slim-waisted silhouette. In a tribute to French elegance, he paired opera gloves and hand fans with sleeveless velvet bodices, plunging necklines, and voluminous organdy skirts.

Rita Hayworth modeled a Dior dress in the film *Gilda* (1946), and dancer Leslie Carol wore his costumes in the ballet *Thirteen Dances* (1947). In 1948, French *Vogue* praised Dior's iconic look, which retrieved from wartime austerity the nation's tradition of extravagant beading, brocades, and embroidery, elements enhancing his cashmere sweaters, fur-lined coats, and broad, crownless hats.

Dior's celebrity spread across the Western world. His strapless evening gowns and peplum jackets won headlines in April 1950 following a show at London's Savoy Hotel and a private showing for the queen of England and her daughters. Displayed at his boutique on Fifth Avenue in New York City, Dior's feminine wardrobe appealed to such knowledgeable clientele as socialite Wallis Warfield Simpson and dancer Margot Fonteyn. Actor Marlene Dietrich wore Dior dresses in the films *Stage Fright* (1950) and *No Highway in the Sky* (1951). England's Princess Margaret wore a one-shoulder silk organza Dior gown for her twenty-first birthday.

Dior's apparel sold in the 1950s at the English department store chain Marks & Spencer, Ohrbach's in New York City, a Mayfair boutique in London, and Marshall Field in Chicago. His stockings, furs, ties, and dresses, representing the height of a golden era of couture, became prime targets of fashion piracy. He achieved fame from photography by Richard Avedon and Cecil Beaton's overview in *The Glass of Fashion* (1954).

Dior apparel, designed in part by assistant Yves St. Laurent in 1955, accounted for half of France's fashion exports at the time. Consumers favored the luxury look of Dior beaded knits, sleek tulip dresses, low-heeled satin pumps, and brocade high-heeled sandals. He increased his presence in Hollywood with Olivia de Havilland's wedding dress for *The Ambassador's Daughter* (1955) and Ava Gardner's wardrobe for *The Little Hut* (1956), an island romance featuring grass skirts, halter tops, and swimsuits, as well as cocktail sheaths and evening gowns.

Increased notoriety and overwork exacerbated Dior's existing heart condition. His death from a heart attack in Montecatini, Italy, on October 23, 1957, brought to an end his rise in haute couture but not the influence of his stylistic vision. In 1990, the Dior house received a Fashion Industry Foundation honorarium. Into the 2000s, retro copies of Dior's garments introduced the New Look to a younger generation of women eager to abandon modernist geometrics and adopt the more feminine styles of the mid-twentieth century.

See also: Fashion Design; French Clothing and Fashion; Saint Laurent, Yves.

Further Reading
De Rethy, Esmeralda, and Jean-Louis Perreau. *Christian Dior: The Glory Years, 1947–1957.* New York: Vendome, 2002.
Dior. www.dior.com
Martin, Richard, and Harold Koda. *Christian Dior.* New York: Metropolitan Museum of Art, 2000.
Pochna, Marie France. *Dior.* New York: Assouline, 2004.

Disguise and Spy Wear

A disguise facilitates the social interaction of criminals, spies, celebrities, impersonators, and people disfigured by birth defect, disease, or accident. For entertainment, the disguise motif creates mystery and suspense in costume balls, Halloween celebrations, spy novels, and films. As a popular performance form, the impersonation of stars revives favorite outfits and mannerisms as a form of honor.

Historical examples of feigned identity characterize the need for anonymity or a change of persona for unique reasons. After 220 B.C.E., Hannibal, the Carthaginian general, pursued daily disguise with wigs, which he regularly discarded to maintain anonymity in public. For Joan of Arc, disguise in men's clothing enabled her to pass through enemy lands in northern France to reach the court of Charles VII. In armor on April 29, 1429, she rode with the royal forces to victory over Henry V's insurgents at the siege of Orléans.

Subterfuge influenced the outbreak of the American Revolution. On December 16, 1773, to counter an English tax on tea, Paul Revere, Samuel Adams, and 100 to 150 Sons of Liberty dressed in Mohawk blankets and headdress. After abettors Sarah Bradlee Fulton and Ann Dunlap Bradlee applied body paint blended from red ochre and lampblack, the raiders successfully thwarted the unloading of 342 crates of tea by tossing them into Boston Harbor. Washed clean of disguises, the men and boys receded into the crowd, out of the range of vengeful redcoats.

In the eighteenth century, masquerade balls in London, Paris, Vienna, St. Petersburg, and Venice allowed guests to elude social strictures and mingle, flirt, drink, and dance without revealing their identity. Some chose the mock livery of the Lord of Misrule or such mythological and historical costumes as the lion skin worn by Hercules and Greek gown and veil of Helen of Troy. Others opted to conceal themselves under crusading knights and dragons in mummer's plays, peasant women's dresses and aprons worn by English Molly dancers, or a cowl and domino, a mask covering only the eyes.

Other instances of human disguise expressed the need to overcome shortcomings or repression. French Impressionist artists Gustave Caillebotte, Edgar Degas, Édouard Manet, and Pierre-Auguste Renoir depicted stylish women who lacked independence hiding their curiosities and interests behind wide bonnets, veils, gloves, and parasols, fashionable camouflage of the true self. Also during the late nineteenth century, the American emphasis on youthful appearance encouraged balding men to purchase head coverings. The Manhattan custom wig maker and disguise artist William Hepner advertised hair shorn from French children

and maintained the largest number of styles and colors in the nation.

In Britain after 1940, devices of the Special Operations Executive (SOE) enabled operatives to undermine the invading Germans and assist anti-Nazi resistance through infiltration, misinformation, and sabotage. British, Irish, French, American, Canadian, Dutch, Polish, Russian, Slavic, Arab, Italian, and Scandinavian agents of "Churchill's Secret Army" applied oversized footprints to shoes and wore facial hair and sideburns, neutral wardrobe, and a variety of spectacles, sunglasses, and refugee clothes and hats. The outfits fabricated spurious identities of secret agents assigned to missions throughout Europe, Africa, and Asia. When adopting false personas, agents implemented behavioral changes to alter their gestures, hair part, gait, eye contact, cleanliness, and even eating and breathing.

Detailed SOE manuals emphasized the simple adoption of snow camouflage, peroxide, untidy hair, unclean nails, scuffed boots, padded jackets, and the obvious display of rings, watches, keys, luggage, newspapers, lunch pails, gum, and tobacco products and lighters or matches. Elevating the crown of a hat, hoisting and rebelting trousers, and carrying an umbrella increased the impression of height. Padded torsos and loosened belts contributed a paunch. Plucking reshaped eyebrows. Collodian wax created instant scars and concealed cleft chins. Contact lenses created the illusion of cataracts or blindness. Mapacreme, walnut hulls, potassium permanganate, rust, soot, and carotene yellowed or browned the skin, much as iodine discolored teeth. Padding reshaped nostrils, cheeks, and gum lines. Plastic surgery, dental treatment, and overlaid tattooing made permanent alterations. In event of discovery during normal operations or when undertaking suicide missions, operatives carried cyanide pills masked as coat or collar buttons.

During Cold War espionage, disguise officers at the U.S. Central Intelligence Agency in McLean, Virginia, perfected shoe lifts, eye color alteration, affected speech, stooped posture, and latex and silicone body sculpting of fake ears and modified teeth and jawlines. Facial artists created wrinkles, warts, and scars and matched wigs to an altered skin tone. A tobacco pipe clenched in the teeth conducted sound for surveillance while falsifying a personal habit. A belt, keys, necktie, collar stud, ID bracelet, or hatband concealed encrypted messages.

Government cosmetologists enabled infiltrators during the Vietnam War to alter ethnic appearance and national identity in seconds and pass through roadblocks undetected. An example from the 1980s involved dressing an agent in seductive dress, blue glasses, flashy makeup, and blonde curls to ready her for a Friday night mission at a nightclub. To turn an agent into the nerdy Mr. Orkin for court testimony in 1998, specialists authenticated his alias with physical details. They reshaped his hairline and dressed him in a lumpy blue suit, white shirt, and shabby glasses held together with tape.

In the 2000s, U.S. rescue operations involved commandos outfitted as peddlers, refugees, and beggars for the storming of buildings holding defectors and kidnap victims. Examples in 2012 involved a male pilgrim dressed as a woman who entered Saudi Arabia illegally to join a hajj pilgrimage to Mecca. A similar illicit use of deceptive apparel enabled gangs in police uniforms to attack Muslim worshippers in Kaduna, Nigeria. In both instances, authorities heightened efforts to winnow out frauds from the populace.

North American crime rates rose in Fort Worth, Texas; Miami, Florida; Fresno, California; and Snellville, Georgia, in October 2012 from felons' use of hardhats, safety vests, power company and highway patrol uniforms, and cowboy hats and bandannas as camouflage. As a result of the 2011 Stanley Cup Riot in Vancouver, the Canadian House of Commons passed a bill outlawing disguises and masks as a means of committing a crime or rioting. Civil libertarians protested that masking during civil disorder is a way for nonviolent observers to protect their identity.

See also: Body Painting; Cross-Dressing; Halloween Costumes, Masks and Masking; Veils and Veiling.

Further Reading

Nunly, John W., and Cara McCarty. *Masks: Faces of Culture.* New York: Harry N. Abrams, 1999.

Sample, John. *Methods of Disguise.* 2nd ed. Port Townsend, WA: Breakout Productions, 2000.

Wallace, Robert, H. Keith Melton, and Henry R. Schlesinger. *Spycraft: The Secret History of the CIA's Spytechs from Communism to Al-Qaeda.* New York: Dutton, 2008.

Divinities

From prehistory, visual representation of deities presented the divine in heroic nudity or dressed in anthropomorphic apparel. Egyptian art pictured deities attired in ancient regalia and antique hairstyles. At Catal Höyük in south-central Anatolia, the Neolithic matriarchal society depicted a bulbous naked female goddess. In the same region at Lapana, the Hittites veiled the seated image of Iyaya, a parallel fertility goddess.

Farther east, in Mesopotamia, reverence twice a day involved temple attendants in washing, dressing in resplendent feathered kilt, and adorning with cylindrical crown holy icons of Marduk, the Babylonian sun god. From 4000 B.C.E., artisans at the Eanna temple compound at Uruk on the Euphrates River kept icon wardrobes clean and repaired. The use of gold, agate, turquoise, carnelian, and lapis lazuli in temple gifts illustrated the sincerity of offerings and the power of sacred amulets.

Images of the Sumerian mother goddess Asherah wore gifts of new turbans and shawls woven by female devotees and adorned with tassels over her ankle-length skirt, kilt, and robe. After the annual clothing ceremony for Nanaya, the deity of beauty and sensuality, her image sported ropes of gold barrel beads, chains, quilled headdresses, and breast ornaments allotted from royal treasuries. Ishtar, a goddess of physical passion, modeled sequins, lion belt, crescent breastplate, torque, fibula, earrings, sun disk, and tiara marked in front with a rosette. Introduced by Amorites after 2000 B.C.E., Nabu, the god of wisdom and destiny, wore a purple wool mantle and silver shoes.

In India from 1700 B.C.E., ritual statues of Shiva the Transformer, the supreme Hindu deity, pictured his bare chest adorned with a snake and strings of beads. On his plaited hair, he displayed a crescent moon. A thong consisted of a cloth rectangle tied with four waist strings. His wife Parvati, the benevolent goddess of love and power, wore a simple white drape for modesty.

Additional Hindu apparel emblems included red saris for the joy of weddings, leafy green for peace, and the white dress and lotus of Saraswati, goddess of knowledge, for purity. Saffron and turmeric dye energized a memorable ensemble to signify the wisdom and competence of Krishna, a divine being. Disciples changed his attire and jewelry for each season of the year and awarded him perfume and flowers.

Kali, the mother goddess, raised her eight arms to flaunt bows, arrows, spears, snakes, and daggers and wore a girdle of amputated hands and a breastplate of skulls as evidence of her might. Attendants acquired blessings through daily clothing, embracing, fanning, and food service to Kali.

Classical Images

From the 700s B.C.E., classical Greek sculpture identified deities with iconic props—Zeus's loincloth and thunderbolt, Demeter's crown of grain heads, Hermes's winged helmet and sandals, the trident of Poseidon, shawl of Artemis, wings and cloak of the infant Eros, and helmet and aegis (breastplate) of Athena. Diadems accompanying Hera's matronly dress and scarf and the single undraped breast of the victory goddess Nike set the divinities apart from portrait sculpture and bas-reliefs of real women. Following the ritual bathing of Nike, votive gifts of jewels, flower wreaths, star and rosette ornaments, and drapery arrayed the cult statue in procession.

From 566 B.C.E., every four years in anticipation of the Great Panathenaia on August 14, selected Greek maidens set up looms on the Acropolis and wove a new peplos (robe) for the statue of Athena, featuring a single black stripe. As depicted on the Parthenon frieze, weavers presented the finished garment to the goddess in mid-May and stored it in her treasury. The refurbishment of Athena's wardrobe occurred in mid-June. Her discarded garments required burial in the sacred precincts.

Supplicants obtained divine blessing with gifts from their own collection of wool cloaks, leather belts, silk headbands and ribbons, and linen tunics, most of them women's offerings. Around 350 B.C.E., Praxiteles of Athens sculpted Aphrodite nude before her bath while she clutches a tunic. The pose set a standard for subsequent nude depictions of Dionysus and Apollo.

During the Hellenistic period, after 323 B.C.E., artists experimented with variety and innovation expressing *humanitas* (civilization). The natural female drapery of previous centuries shifted to a pair of contemporary chitons, the layered apparel swathed over the Winged Victory of Samothrace and on secularized visions of Aphrodite. The more transparent overdress made from Egyptian linen or the silk of Kos manifested regional prosperity. Additional opulence from fringed selvages, ceremonial plaits or tassels, and ornate hairstyles set female divinities apart from the more muscular, determined poses of Eros and Dionysus.

Egyptian worshippers identified their pantheon with Nubian wigs and distinctive headdresses. The size and loft of the sun disk and tall cow horns of Isis, the maternal deity at the temple at Abydos, and the double feathered crown of her son Horus, the hawk-headed war god, betokened grandeur and godly power. Temple ritual at Dendera in Upper Egypt around 305 B.C.E. required the daily cleansing and redressing of cultic images. Suitable appearance included renewed application of eye makeup and perfume and anointing with oil.

Christian Divinity

Early Christian statue dress expressed particular elements of the church year. After 200 C.E., celebrants of the fifth Sunday of Lent swathed statues with purple cloth as an indication of the Easter passion according to John 8:59. Following the example of Constantine and his mother Helena, Christians smartened their apparel with pectoral pendants, visual evidence of religiosity bearing images of Christ and the Virgin Mary, relics, symbols, and scriptural phrases.

Byzantine aesthetics initiated a luminous vision of deities. The earlier depictions of white robes and loincloths gave place to deep blue and red tunics and gold-braided mantles set against the golden tesserae of wall and ceiling mosaics. The most respected examples illustrated walls and altars in Cyprus and, after 360, barrel vaults and ceiling medallions of the Hagia Sophia basilica in Constantinople. After 450, early Christian art blazoned the tomb of Galla Placidia, daughter of the emperor Theodosius I, in present-day Ravenna, Italy. For authenticity, the mosaicists retreated from Byzantine pomp to the white robes of the Good Shepherd and seraphic drapings of angels.

As a result of the Crusades, reliquaries ensconced for veneration the body parts and garments of saints and deities, such as the embroidered wardrobe and jeweled crown of the Madonna in the Basilica of Our Lady of the Pillar in Zaragoza, Spain. Throughout European art, apparel for holy figures remained spare, as with the loincloths that engirthed the martyred St. Hippolytus and the crucified Christ of Giotto di Bondone. Images of the infant Jesus depicted him swaddled, a model for child care among the devout. According to Clara Erskine Waters's *A Handbook of Legendary and Mythological Art* (1874), the Madonna wore a simple white cloak over a loose tunic, typically rendered in blue for constancy and adorned with gold braid.

During the Renaissance, artists retained classical drapery on simulations of the divine but replaced realistic attire with transparent folds, as with the spare garments in Giulio Romano's painting *Jupiter and Olympia,* Andrea Mantegna's *Parnassus,* and Michelangelo da Caravaggio's *Bacchus.* Ethereal to the point of invisibility, the gauzy tunics and mantles symbolized emotional states denied to mortals, as in Gerard van Honthorst's *Orpheus,* Antoine Coypel's *Baptism of Christ,* and Michele Tosini's *Archangel Raphael.* Enwrapped in allegorical enlightenment, epiphany, and spiritual ecstasy, figures glowed with a transcendent soul state, as in Fra Bartolomeo's *Deposition,* Giuliano Bugiardini's *Saint Sebastian,* and Giovanni Bernini's *Ecstasy of Saint Teresa of Avila.*

Colors created a religious atmosphere in medieval art—purple headscarves evoked Lenten self-denial, red cloaks represented martyrdom or royalty, white gowns complemented holy festivities, and black veils and handkerchiefs represented sorrow. Flowers symbolized worthy qualities, as with rose wreaths for beneficence and jubilance, violet nosegays for innocence and a pure heart, and handheld lilies for blamelessness. Circlets of myrtle expressed hope for life and health, as on a celebratory headdress depicted in Lorenzo Lotto's *Venus and Cupid.*

From 1530 to the 1800s, Catholic chapels and nunneries in France collected dressy garments for clothing icons of the Virgin and the saints. Gift apparel included the voluminous veil by which Saint Veronica wiped Jesus's face and the 70 outfits worn by the Infant Jesus of Prague. The contributions of expensive gowns and wedding attire met with the approval of Pope Clement VII (1478–1534), a worldly prelate endowed with Medici tastes.

In more recent times, gifts to divinities continued to express adoration, notably, gold lamé robes spangled with gems and a massive haloed crown for Our Lady of Charity at a chapel in El Cobre, Cuba. In 1608 at the Bay of Nipe, she arrived in the white dress of an islander; though she came by sea, her garments remained dry. In 1916, Pope Benedict XV proclaimed her the island's patron saint.

For national holidays, pilgrims have dressed the 16-inch (41-centimeter) image of Our Lady of Charity in traditional blue and white and the infant Jesus in red, the colors of the Cuban flag. On January 24, 1998, following a procession to Santiago, Pope John Paul II placed a gold crown on the statue. On March 27, 2012, Pope Benedict XVI made a subsequent papal visit and prayed before the ornate statue for hope and renewal for Cubans.

See also: Customs, Lore, and Myth; Greek Clothing, Ancient; Jewels and Jewelry; Symbolic Colors, Patterns, and Motifs.

Further Reading

Holland, Glenn. *Gods in the Desert: Religions of the Ancient Near East.* Lanham, MD: Rowman & Littlefield, 2009.

James, Sharon L., and Sheila Dillon, eds. *A Companion to Women in the Ancient World.* Malden, MA: Blackwell, 2012.

Pleij, Herman. *Colors Demonic and Divine: Shades of Meaning in the Middle Ages and After.* Trans. Diane Webb. New York: Columbia University Press, 2002.

Dolls, Fashion

Fashion designers have long used model dolls to display miniature exemplars of wardrobe creations and trends. The concept, which debuted in 1391, enabled Robert de Varennes, the tailor for Charles VI of France, to send wardrobe ideas from Queen Isabeau of Bavaria to Queen Anne of Bohemia, the wife of England's Richard II. In 1496, Anne of Brittany, wife of Charles VIII of France, dispatched a life-size doll and chic wardrobe to Isabella d'Este, a trendsetter of the Italian Renaissance.

Known as Pandoras, model dolls became standard sales ambassadors for couturiers in England, Germany, Italy, and Spain. Dressmakers copied fashion silhouettes as well as underclothing, bustles and hoops, furs, hairstyles, and appliquéd and embroidered details. Couriers secured doll safety during wartime with special visas for *les grand courriers de la mode* (grand style messengers).

Around 1686, Louis XIV of France commissioned engravings and life-size *poupées de mode* (model dolls) from Burgundy and dispatched them from Versailles as promoters of French waistcoats, breeches, hats, and shoes in European courts. A likeness of Madame de Pompadour, the mistress of Louis XV, possessed a wardrobe of formal wear, negligees, and varied wig styles. In the 1780s, Marie Antoinette commissioned modiste Rose Bertin to dress porcelain, wax, and wood "fashion babies" in panniers and hoop skirts as gifts to the queen's family in Austria. After the French Revolution of 1789, Bertin opened a shop in London employing refugee French embroiderers, coiffeurs, and lace makers and continued supplying fashion dolls to courtiers from London to Constantinople, Moscow, and St. Petersburg, Russia.

As fashion regained its edge, model dolls returned to use as publicity. Made of porcelain with cloth or leather torsos and glass eyes, French fashion dolls of the 1850s enjoyed three decades of popularity among children of the wealthy. In-house seamstresses disassembled outfits and made paper patterns to reflect the measurements of the household. Germany toy makers seized the doll market in the 1880s.

In the Americas, elegant alabaster and china "lady dolls" from England and France posed in nightdresses, formal wear, and appropriate hats, accessories, and high-heeled boots for outfits. The miniatures illustrated quality fabric and needlework and encouraged play that replicated social ritual and manners. At a time when the average worker earned $4.50 per month, the wealthy paid $30 for a single doll ensemble. Nineteenth-century French luggage designer Louis Vuitton made trunks for fashion dolls and their wardrobes. As a source of advertising, fashion dolls competed with the first fashion magazines.

To reestablish French couture after World War II, the Chambre Syndicale de la Couture of Paris in 1945, led by designer Robert Ricci and director Jean Cocteau, guided the creation of a miniature fashion show. They dispatched the Théâtre de la Mode, a doll show of 13 sets and 237 dolls correctly detailed to 1 millimeter (0.04 inches). The suite traveled from Barcelona to London, Stockholm, Copenhagen, Vienna and, finally, on May 1, 1946, New York.

In 1952, Reinhard Beüthien, a cartoonist for the *Bild-Zeitung* newspaper in Hamburg, Germany, created Lilli, a baby-faced media figure that appeared over her comments about dating and wardrobe. Within a year, plastic Lilli dolls projected the self-confidence of the 1950s clotheshorse in beach outfits, pajamas, office attire, and dirndls, the national costume of Alpine women.

In the United States, Ruth Handler, a founder of the Mattel toy company, copied the fashion doll concept and, at $3 each, marketed the wasp-waisted Barbie in 1959, the beginning of a toy craze for hedonistic style. Joined in 1961 by boyfriend Ken, Barbie, at the proportion of one-sixth adult size, modeled a broad spectrum of fashion—Givenchy harem skirts, Farrah Fawcett halter dresses, hoodies, and maillots—as well as cheerleading, stewardess, firefighter, and astronaut uniforms. Ken, over the years, wore military camouflage, leisure suits, tennis togs, metrosexual vests and earrings, and cowboy and sports gear, some available in Simplicity patterns.

Mattel rounded out a growing wardrobe of Ken and Barbie clothes with Hispanic Teresa in camisas, bell-bottoms, and boho chic, and African

American Christie in Egyptian collar necklaces, animal prints, and caftans. During the fiftieth anniversary of Barbie in 2009, designers Calvin Klein, Tommy Hilfiger, Norma Kamali, Diane von Fürstenberg, and Vera Wang originated haute couture for the famed doll. Following the death of singer Karen Carpenter from anorexia nervosa in 1983, feminists denounced the stylized body image of Barbie and her playmates for promoting extreme weight loss.

In 2001, the introduction of Bratz, a hip fashion doll from MGA Entertainment, added a line of stylized model toys to modish commercialism. Unlike Barbie, Bratz girls and boys modeled teen styles in short shorts, boots, jean jackets, and caps, all appearing in *Bratz: The Movie* (2007). In 2007, the American Psychological Association charged MGA Entertainment with sexualizing girls in stiletto sandals, boas, fishnet hose, halter tops, and miniskirts. In September 2012, the company launched a video game encouraging young fashion designers to outfit Bratz dolls with trendy clothes.

See also: Advertising; Fashion Design.

Further Reading

Charles-Roux, Edmond, Herbert R. Lottman, Stanley Garfinkel, and Nadine Gasc. *Théâtre de la Mode: Fashion Dolls: The Survival of Haute Couture.* Portland, OR: Palmer/Pletsch, 2002.

Peers, Juliette. *The Fashion Doll: From Bébé Jumeau to Barbie.* New York: Bloomsbury, 2004.

Tarnowska, Maree. *Fashion Dolls.* Cumberland, MD: Hobby House, 1986.

Dress Codes and Conventions

The issuance of official regulations concerning appearance tends to focus on socially appropriate apparel as well as hygiene and physical safety. Dress codes have set royalty apart with the wearing of crowns, gold jewelry, purple capes, and feathers, the trappings of Hawaiian and Maori monarchs and the sixteenth-century Aztec king Montezuma II in Tenochtitlan. Among the Maya of Mesoamerica, outstanding warriors distinguished their status by donning a bodysuit consisting of the head, pelt, and tail of a jaguar. On the Pacific Northwest coast of North America, Chilkat, Haida, and Tsimshian chiefs wrapped themselves in elaborate blanket robes held together with bone pins.

Classical World

In late Republican Rome, when citizens became a *gens togata* (togaed people), patriotism demanded respect for the state uniform. Under official scrutiny, matrons wore the *stola* (overdress), and men dignified their wardrobes with the *toga virilis* (man's toga). The passage of 14-year-old Roman males from the purple-hemmed boyhood *toga praetexta* to a man's garment and signet ring preceded circumspect dressing for religious festivals, theaters, law courts, and the Curia (Senate). Those who were refused full citizenship—slaves, felons, aliens, adulterers—lived apart in a mishmash of apparel and headdress.

Patricians further distanced themselves from plebeians in rank and economic status by wearing equestrian *calcei* (sandals) and white shoes for consuls. At the beginning of the Roman Empire in 27 B.C.E., the emperor stood out in the *toga picta* (figured toga) and purple cape, a color limited to aristocrats and military heroes. Ancient historians judged rulers by their respect for dress codes—Marcus Aurelius in 161 C.E. for choosing the unadorned white toga, and Elagabalus, an 18-year-old transvestite whom the security guard assassinated in 222 for cross-dressing in the attire of a Syrian woman.

Apparel by Class

Medieval dress codes of the 1100s designated the elite by reserving luxury apparel, furs, lacing, heeled shoes, and accessories for the aristocracy. Enforcement wavered following the Black Death of the mid-fourteenth century, when survivors sorted through the wardrobes of the landed gentry and claimed braid, silks, pearls, and grand trains as inherited goods.

From the time of Anthony the Great, the founder of monasticism in fourth-century Egypt,

Christian prelates required modest attire for nuns and laywomen and humiliating badges, bells, and hats for Jews and Muslims. In North Africa and Muslim Spain under the Umayyads from 661 to 750, Islamic laws made Christians and Jews a suspect class and required them to dress in mismatched red and black shoes and tie bells around their necks. In Tunisia, rigid customs obliged men to wear the heavy cotton or camlet *barrakan* (mantle) and women to adopt the white rectangular *safsari,* a body veil adapted from Berbers.

To ensure obedience to Arab strictures, Moroccan officials at Rabat periodically issued decrees reinstating the Islamic male's blue headscarf, dark cap and robe, and black slippers. After 1121, the Almohads at Tinmei in the Atlas Mountains increased regimentation by forcing non-Muslims to wear sleeves stretching to the feet and ridiculous caps reaching below the ears. In Iran and Iraq, Christians and Jews who breached dress codes could suffer the death penalty. Enforcement fell less stringently in Baghdad, Syria, and not at all in the Levant.

In India, Hindus observed strict dress at temples—saris for women and bare chest and *mundu* (hip wrap) for men. Brahmans presented their daughters for marriage in head-to-foot coverings, an extension of purdah. Women displayed married status by lining the part of the hair with red powder. Male Sikhs marked their religiosity with turbans. Farther north, in the Himalayas, Buddhist monks accepted gifts of clothing but cut garments into pieces and sewed them into patchwork to fulfill vows of poverty.

During the European settlement of the New World, religious groups imposed dress codes on community members. Across Manitoba, Saskatchewan, and Ontario, submissive Mennonite women from Germany, Russia, and Switzerland covered their uncut hair with gauze caps and wore no makeup. Female wardrobes consisted of plain caped dresses and black hose with lace-up, closed-toed shoes. Under less regimentation, Mennonite males wore ordinary work clothes and black hats and suits on Sundays. Liberal standards favoring men allowed them to court outsiders and marry outside of the faith. Emerging rights movements among Mennonite women repudiated the implication that women required standardized dress because they lacked the moral fiber of churchmen and fell easily into sin and shame.

Standardizing Modern Attire

The rise of professionalism in the mid-1800s introduced uniforms for nurses, police, teachers, priests, and judges. Females in hospitals covered blue or gray shifts with white pinafores and fastened their hair to the back of the head. Worldwide, law enforcement officers identified their authority with blue, black, or khaki uniforms marked with badges, rank insignias, and a cudgel, nightstick, or revolver.

Academics attended class in scholarly robes and caps, much as judges and priests identified themselves in black attire. During the forced cultural indoctrination of Native American children at Canadian and U.S. boarding schools, braid cutting and burning of moccasins and medicine bags, amulets, and headbands forced the student body into cultural genocide. At the Carlisle Indian School in Pennsylvania, during the 39-year experiment begun in 1879, some 17 percent of the 12,000 native students from 140 tribes fled the campus rather than conform to the dress code of white Christians.

In the United States in the late 1980s, disparities in educational outcomes in parochial, private, and public schools suggested that uniforms make a difference in student attitude and achievement. By 1988, based on centuries of dress codes in British schools, eight U.S. public schools in the area of the Delmarva Peninsula on the East Coast had initiated dress codes. Late twentieth-century public and governmental controversy raised issues of fascist dress codes—the uniformed Hitler Youth of the late 1930s, Mao suits in 1949, and Bolshevik regulations under Josef Stalin during the early 1950s. Neither side convinced the other that American pupil discipline improved under a mandatory code.

At the suggestion of President Bill Clinton in his State of the Union Address on January 23, 1996, some inner-city school systems standardized dress to curb gangs, violence, and vandalism.

Academics and parents pondered the value of diversity to democratic classrooms and the need for social control by deemphasizing individualized dress. At issue, message T-shirts, low-cleavage blouses, pants worn below the waist, flip-flops, and Goth makeup and nail polish raised questions of propriety.

After the shooting deaths of 15 people at Columbine High in Littleton, Colorado, on April 20, 1999, nervous school boards prepared to challenge the American Civil Liberties Union on issues of the students' First Amendment right to choose their classroom attire. On March 28, 2013, 100 students received two-day suspensions from a Mobile, Alabama, high school for willful breach of the standard dress code of green, orange, or white shirts and khaki pants. That same week in Meridian, Mississippi, the trend in arbitrary regimentation began to flag when school authorities prepared to dismantle a dress code that disproportionately targeted minority pupils.

See also: Academic Garb; Badges and Insignias; Burka; Business Attire; School Attire; Sumptuary Laws; Tunics and Togas; Uniforms, Occupational; Veils and Veiling.

Further Reading

Brunsma, David L. *The School Uniform Movement and What It Tells Us About American Education: A Symbolic Crusade.* Lanham, MD: Scarecrow Education, 2004.

Stillman, Yedida Kalfon. *Arab Dress, A Short History: From the Dawn of Islam to Modern Times.* Ed. Norman A. Stillman. Boston: Brill, 2003.

Dress Reform

The reshaping of personal and professional wardrobes illustrates revised thinking about how to clothe the body with comfort and dignity. In 1682, Russian reformer Peter the Great surveyed military dress in Germany and France and equipped his army with modernized uniforms. In place of the Byzantine caftan, black cap, and untrimmed beard, he designed a roomy frock coat and tricorn hat. In 1700, he extended his reform by redressing regiments in Belarus and the Ukraine with garments suited to action rather than parade dress.

In Victorian England, dress reform influenced the British Empire to rethink male appearance. After 1837, ensembles for men abandoned class-based outfits from the previous century. In place of extravagant costumes, wigs, and plumes, tailors and haberdashers sold plain business and formal wear consisting of impeccable white shirts, tailored coats, vests, and pants. The look set the tone of menswear into the twenty-first century.

Women's dress reform followed a political and economic arc toward full citizenship for females. With the launching of the women's rights movement in Seneca Falls, New York, in 1848 and the organization of the National Dress Reform Association in 1856, protesters in the United States, England, and Australia followed the example of polemicists Libby Smith and Elizabeth Cady Stanton and actor Fanny Kemble. Rebels replaced burdensome skirts with pantalettes, harem pants, divided skirts, and Turkish trousers.

The New Woman—a title applied to nurse Clara Barton, author Harriet Beecher Stowe, surgeon Mary Edwards Walker, temperance leader Frances E. Willard, and others in the late nineteenth century—demanded functional, hygienic apparel for business, shopping, walking, bicycling, and housework. The movement gained support in France, Germany, and Sweden. During exercise, schoolgirls wore gymnasium dress, a liberating uniform introduced by physical culturist Dio Lewis. Gynecologist Alice Bunker Stockham led a revolt against laced corsets, especially the pregnancy corset, which endangered both mother and fetus by displacing organs. In lieu of inflexible boned underwear, women adopted the woven union suit and the emancipation bodice, a sleeveless shirt that attached to a petticoat or drawers.

Backed by Horace Greeley's editorials in the *New York Tribune,* nineteenth-century women's dress reform precipitated modernization in other venues. In France after the fall of Napoleon III in 1870, women gave up imitations of the Empress Eugénie's elegant ensembles and accessories and established unadorned jackets, shirtwaists, and skirts as appropriate for the active woman. In 1887, another champion of appropriate dress, Edward Wilmot Blyden, as founder of the Dress Reform Society, reshaped the silhouette of natives of Sierra Leone in a Pan-African look that supplanted British business attire with the collarless dashiki, a cool cotton tunic suited to a hot climate and tribal customs. In 1894, in place of the *dopo* (robe) and traditional headdress, social reform in Korea outlined utilitarian dress for courtiers, soldiers, and students.

The reform of women's dress continued into the twentieth century, vexing mainstream society in diverse locations. Canadian hygienist Lelia A. Davis addressed the subject in *Woman's Dress, a Question of the Day* (1894), which labeled waist constriction and heavy skirts a "disgrace of civilization." A sports enthusiast, swimmer-diver Annette Kellerman of Australia defied fussy bathing cover-ups and recommended the unitard as appropriate swimwear. In her book *The Body Beautiful* (1912), she advised women to reject the corset and promoted bathing exercises and underwater ballet in streamlined bodysuits. Suffragists in Great Britain, Australia, New Zealand, and the United States followed the example of feminists Nellie McClung, Alice Paul, and Emmeline Pankhurst by jettisoning veiled hats and frills for no-nonsense skirted suits and dresses.

Dress reform influenced thinking for institutional wear in orphanages, workhouses, and jails. Prison reformers in the 1920s indicated a shift in penal philosophy from punishment of inmates in striped work suits to rehabilitation in khaki work shirts and pants, tennis shoes, and baseball caps similar in style to normal working apparel.

Periodic shifts in material and style also reflected social exigencies, as with the rationing of leather, silk, and nylon during World War II. When husbands left home for the military, women revamped their shirts and pants into work uniforms suited to farms and factories. In the 1940s, *Vogue* magazine featured the reduction of women's purses to envelope bags and clutches, a reform based on patriotism and compliance with rationing regulations.

During the Black is Beautiful movement of the 1960s, Harlem poet and reformer LeRoi Jones (Amiri Baraka) initiated distinctly anticolonial attire that reflected African American tastes. Trendsetters Bobby Seale, Huey Newton, and Marvin

Gaye modeled Yoruban braids or full Afros, black berets, *kufis* (round caps), circle beards, and African medallions. Women looked to the Afro-American styles of poet Maya Angelou, radical Angela Davis, and singer Tina Turner for revivals of big hair, hoop earrings, turbans, Ghanaian dress, and glass kiffa beads.

In England, Wales, and Australia, judicial attire underwent sweeping reform in the 2000s. By abandoning out-of-date robes, gloves, and wigs in favor of simpler, less dramatic designs, court officials presented a more businesslike presence in the courtroom based on reason rather than pomp. In place of wing collars and ermine scarves, judges donned plain robes with stand-up collars, cuffs, and pockets.

See also: Brassieres; Business Attire; Corsets and Girdles; Dress Codes and Conventions; Feminist Styles and Fashions; Rationing; Swimwear; Veils and Veiling.

Further Reading

Cunningham, Patricia A. *Reforming Women's Fashion, 1850–1920: Politics, Health and Art.* Kent, OH: Kent State University Press, 2003.

Fischer, Gayle V. *Pantaloons and Power: A Nineteenth-Century Dress Reform in the United States.* Kent, OH: Kent State University Press, 2001.

Hamilton, Neil A. *Rebels and Renegades: A Chronology of Social and Political Dissent in the United States.* New York: Routledge, 2002.

Dresses and Dressmaking

Contoured dress design for both men and women, an early medieval innovation, revolutionized centuries of couture based on the T-shaped tunic and draped toga, *palla, parieu,* and sari. Following the First Crusade, fusion fashions in the early 1100s initiated the Byzantine *bliaut,* the original fitted garment laced up the back. Originally a unisex design, it emphasized the broad masculine chest and narrow torso as well as the feminine curves of breasts, waist, and hips.

Dressmaking introduced medieval women to a craft and business conducted entirely by females. Specialists possessing knowledge of the function and shape of the body during childhood, puberty, adulthood, and pregnancy fostered demand for their skills in bodice design, millinery, and footwear. Late fourteenth-century dresses paired with flats and slippers made in matching fabric.

Because of the dress's contour, artists featured its outlines in sculpture, portraiture, and tapestry. The dress developed into the British kirtle and evening gown, introduced to the Burgundy court after 1419 by Philip the Good. Made from silk or wool crepe, the late medieval European dress exhibited dramatic pointed sleeves stretching to the ankles. Seamstresses attended clients at home and cut and customized fabric for special occasions, such as lengthy travel or introduction at royal court.

Elizabethan enhancements included court trains and high starched collars, lace cuffs, and ruffs over wheel-shaped farthingales. Eighteenth-century stylists added sweep with the *robe à la française,* a sack-back gown covered from neck to hem in unpressed pleats that hid flaws in the female figure, such as swayback, scoliosis, and hunchback. In 1781 at the London Foundling Home, the creation of the baby gown fitted the bodice with ties down the back.

More feminine developments stressed the hourglass shape, beginning with high-waisted Empire designs of the Napoleonic era (1799–1815) in France, leg-of-mutton sleeves on taffeta afternoon wear, and the calico frocks of frontierswomen. England's Queen Victoria chose bouffant crinolines and caged hoop skirts for mourning apparel in 1861. In 1869, designer Charles Frederick Worth diminished the expanse of fabric with the bustle, often paired with a fringed apron for outlining the lower torso.

Edwardian dress style suited a broader spectrum of needs and activities, such as lawn tennis and horse jumping. For girls, the sleeveless gymslip or pinafore freed the body for exercise. Erté's art deco sketches enticed the adventurer to try harem dresses and medieval bliauts. Caribbean women flaunted liberation from bondage in the pairing of the French Creole *tignon* (turban) with the elegant body draping of Ghanaian dress.

By 1900, quality dressmaking in gowns, office apparel, and swim dresses competed with the skills of men's tailors. In 1909, *Harper's Bazaar* pictured dainty afternoon frocks with matching lawn or linen parasols. Policewomen and Red Cross nurses worked in uniform dresses sewn from easily washed fabrics. In Russia, the sumptuous low-cut court dress retained its lavish presence on Czarina Alexandra, who died from executioners' bullets on July 17, 1918, punishment for extravagant spending on gowns while peasants starved.

Modernist couturier Coco Chanel continued paring down female shapes in 1926 with a cocktail style known as the "little black dress," a slender, unadorned sheath easily accessorized with jewelry, shawls, and long gloves. By 1927, Simplicity patterns offered the home seamstress options for leisure and wrap dresses as well as haltered beach dresses and evening and bridesmaid apparel. Mexican artist Frida Kahlo displayed a skin-revealing sundress with oversized beads and a bun of hair at the nape. In 1935, Elsa Schiaparelli's application of the zipper to the side or back of the dress improved contouring for the strapless gown, a common costume in glamorous Hollywood films starring Barbara Stanwyck and Jean Harlow.

In the post–World War II era, ready-to-wear gave consumers broad choices in dresses. Women's departments in Neiman Marcus, Lord & Taylor, and other department stores supplied consumers with the alteration services of dressmakers. Three-way mirrors produced multiple views for the study of balance and movement. Upscale tailoring began with full body measurements in flat shoes and high heels. Dressmakers and their apprentices kept data for regular customers on muslin patterns or full-torso dressmaking forms.

In the 1950s, housewives and girls adopted the shirtdress, a button-front style that Christian Dior tailored with the functional collar, placket, and sleeve detailing of men's shirts. Pierre Cardin altered the straight skirt for the flounced cocktail ensemble and bubble dress, introduced in 1954. In the 1960s, hippies engineered Bohemian looks from the T-dress and tie-top sundress to the maxi dress, often made from machine-pleated gauzy fabric. Yves Saint Laurent refined the boho look with multi-ethnic "gypsy" dresses. Meanwhile, London clothier Mary Quant applied the short skirt to the minidress, signature apparel of the mod sixties.

Diane von Furstenberg liberated the tight bodice in 1972 with the jersey wrap dress, a surplice neckline over straight or full skirt introduced in the 1930s by Manhattan couturier Claire McCardell. Design in the twenty-first century continued tweaking the basic dress with side slits, disco shapewear in Lurex, mermaid skirts, handkerchief and lettuce hems, and one-shoulder bodices. Synthetic, knit, and sheer fabrics gave dressmakers new methods of revealing natural female curves. Specialty designs such as Vera Wang's Olympic skating dresses and Issa London's one-of-a-kind designs for royal bride Kate Middleton gained media attention for flawless tailoring.

See also: Bodices; Byzantine Clothing; Collars; Dress Reform; Skirts.

Further Reading

Anawalt, Patricia Rieff. *The Worldwide History of Dress.* New York: Thames & Hudson, 2007.

Design Museum. *Fifty Dresses That Changed the World.* London: Conran, 2009.

Krohn, Katherine. *Calico Dresses and Buffalo Robes: American West Fashions from the 1840s to the 1890s.* Minneapolis, MN: Twenty-First Century Books, 2012.

McKean, Erin. *The Hundred Dresses: The Most Iconic Styles of Our Time.* New York: Bloomsbury, 2013.

Netherton, Robin, and Gale R. Owen-Crocker, ed. *Medieval Clothing and Textiles.* Woodbridge, UK: Boydell, 2008.

Dry Cleaning

The cleansing of garments with chemical solvents spares fabrics and ornamentation the rigor of soap, water, and washing machines. Absorbent earth cleaners date to 1600 B.C.E., when they provided work by Mycenaean dry cleaners, who pummeled dirty garments with their feet. Greek cataloging from Pylos and Thebes named Pekitas as the royal dry cleaner.

At the Roman *fullonica* (laundry), fullers developed means of whitening and deodorizing woolen togas with fuller's earth (aluminum silicate clay) and ammonia, which pedestrians donated in the form of urine. The kneading of laundry with the calcium bentonite or magnesium oxide in clay extracted grease, lanolin, oil, paint, and tar, along with moisture. The process concluded with the raising of wool nap with a hedgehog pelt.

The application of petrochemicals included camphor oil, benzene, gasoline, naphtha, chloroform, glycol ether, and turpentine, first used in 1690 to remove rosin. In 1849, French dye master and tailor Jean-Baptiste Jolly-Bellin discovered the value of petrochemicals in ridding table linens of stains. Using camphene as a universal solvent for laundry, the Jolly-Bellin company in Paris offered *nettoyage à sec* (dry cleaning) of dirty garments by hand and drying by evaporation. In 1898, Virginia-born dyer and chemist Ernest Christian Klipstein imported Carbona (carbon tetrachloride), a German spot cleaner that he later manufactured in Charleston, West Virginia.

In 1924, William J. Stoddard, an inventor in Atlanta, Georgia, introduced mineral spirits, a distillate of paraffin, as a nonflammable dry cleaning solution for acetate, rayon, silk, suede, and leather. The solution replaced raw white gasoline, the main dry cleaning agent in the early 1900s. The Stoddard method remained in use over two decades, employing rotating perforated tubs that agitated clothing in about 200 gallons (760 liters) of solution with small additions of anhydrous (waterless) detergent.

Professional cleaners began each batch by inspecting collars for identification, removing items from pockets and cuffs, and pretreating stains. Baffles pummeled loads weighing up to 100 pounds (45 kilograms). After rinsing with clean solvent and drying, the processor steamed, pressed, and folded garments.

Because of the danger of explosion, fire, or nerve, liver, or kidney damage from touching or breathing mineral spirits, chemical engineers in 1948 introduced perchloroethylene ("perc") as a fabric cleaner. Coin-operated machines introduced by Whirlpool in 1960 proved unappealing to customers. Because of perc's link with leukemia, esophageal cancer, infertility, and miscarriages, between 1985 and 2006, use of perc in the dry cleaning industry fell by more than 90 percent. In June 1989, amendments to the U.S. Clean Water Act condemned perc as a groundwater pollutant.

Chemists began searching for less hazardous, less contaminating systems. One possibility, GreenEarth Cleaning with liquid silicone, introduced in 1999, doubled the price of dry cleaning. Less toxic to the environment, liquid carbon dioxide in pressurized chambers, a system begun in 1999 in Wilmington, North Carolina, produced no sludge or hazardous exhaust or waste. DrySolv, a bromide cleanser, gained limited use in 2006. And in 2010, Soumi Banerjee and Pieter Mulder won an AkzoNobel incentive award for their development of an environmentally safe application of carbon dioxide to dry cleaning.

See also: Ironing; Laundry.

Dyeing

The coloring of fabrics and yarns enables individuals to choose shades that suit character, mood, and occasion. As early as 36,000 B.C.E., flax workers east of the Black Sea added tints to fibers. Patagonians blended bone marrow with pulverized minerals.

Sources of color from nature increased the study and categorization of minerals, insects, fungi, flowers, berries, pods, leaves, and roots. After 8000 B.C.E., Neolithic dyers in Provence and Assyria collected the *Kermes vermilio,* a scale insect, to extract the red dye kermes. The vibrant red known as vermilion, or China red, also colored the grave shrouds of Scandinavians. The use of red ochre and indigo at Çatal Höyük, Turkey, after 7500 B.C.E. indicated stylistic concern for color contrasts. Similar preparation of dyestuffs in Asia and Europe resulted in lac dye in India for silk and wool and in China for leather, and the Slavic production of red from the scale insect *Porphyrophora polonica,* a valuable trade commodity.

At Abydos, Egypt, the stitchery of flax fabrics after 5500 B.C.E. required fine threads, some dyed blue with indigo (*Indigofera tinctoria*) or imported Assyrian woad (*Isatis tinctoria*) and some dyed with madder (*Rubia tinctorum*), which colors fibers brick red. Around 4000 B.C.E., the cultivation of henna (*Lawsonia inermis)* and sumac (*Rhus coriaria*) yielded a reddish-brown colorant for hair, skin, wool, and leather. Egyptian dye masters at Athribis pioneered the addition of metallic salt mordants to secure henna in mummy wrappings. From local colorfast yarns, weavers produced polychrome linen by intermingling henna red with yellow extracted from curcuma (*Curcuma longa*) from Arabia and Libya and indigo imported from Yemen.

Other cultures extracted dyes from plants and insects. At Mohenjo-daro, in present-day Pakistan, after 3000 B.C.E., hermits colored garments red with madder and betel nut (*Chavica betle*), a brownish-red colorant in use as far east as Malaysia. Around 2200 B.C.E., the Chinese dye works created black and red fabric as a gift for the Emperor Yu. Later Chinese formula compendia detailed the blending of vivid colors from powdered safflower, rice and wood ash, dried plums, and ground shells.

Professional Dyeing

On the Greek island of Santorini around 1600 B.C.E., the collection of stigmas from the crocus (*Crocus sativus*) yielded yellow and yellow-orange dyes for processing at Sidon and Tyre. Around 1500 B.C.E., Minoans exploited Tyrian purple-red dye from a vein in the head of the murex sea snail (*Murex brandaris*). Introduced in Phoenicia in 1440 B.C.E., the vivid hue added panache to the earth-tone clothing of aristocrats and royalty. A similar trade item, the purple-blue from another mollusk, the *Hexaplex trunculus,* required the collection of up to 12,000 sea snails to yield 1 gram (0.04 ounces) of dye valued for Jewish ritual robes.

Before 500 B.C.E., Persian conquest in Kashmir contributed saffron-yellow dye to trade goods already stocked with yellow weld (*Reseda luteola*). The Medo-Persian influence inspired the addition of yellow to blue and red for tinting shoes. At the death of Siddhartha Gautama in 483 B.C.E. in northeastern India, the demand for yellow dye increased after Buddhist disciples adopted saffron as the colorant for ritual mantles and robes. Two millennia ago, in the Sahara Desert, the Tuareg dyed men's turbans with dry indigo because of lack of water for solution. The leaching of indigo to the skin colored their faces blue.

Roman dyers suspended fleeces and hanks of

yarn from wood poles into vats of local madder root and indigo imported from India. Fullers (launderers) also offered a re-dyeing service for faded garments. In the forum, shops sold both colored fabrics on the bolt and ready-to-wear fashioned by *vestiarii* (clothiers). In *Ars amatoria* (*The Art of Love,* 2 C.E.), the Roman poet Ovid advised women on choosing wardrobe hues that complemented their skin. He mentioned pink, light gray, myrtle green, amethyst, cerulean, aquamarine, saffron orange, almond, chestnut brown, gold, and yellow.

Roman affection for color fueled Mediterranean trade that focused on Egyptian luxury goods and silks from China, Cos, and Assyria. From Cyprus and Verona came copper oxides, the source of an earthy Appian green. In addition to the spectacle of circus and stage costumes, colored attire took on religious significance in the *flammeum* (red veil) worn over the saffron-yellow slip-shaped *tunica talaris* (ankle-length tunic) with a knotted belt for bridal attire and the habits of vestal virgins.

Patriotic uses of dye ranged from the violet-purple imported from Tyre for tunic borders and the Tyrian purple or garnet reserved for the emperor Alexander Severus and his entourage after 225. For maximum depth on magistrate's robes, dyers offered *dibapha* (double-dyed) Tyrian cloth. Counterfeiters replicated royal purple with blends of indigo and kermes or madder.

Marketing Colors

Both German and British fabric processors formed medieval guilds to protect their secret formulas, such as the use of copperas (ferrous sulfate) to make ebon (black), one of the five mother colors. A blend of blue woad with yellow weld produced the olive hints in Lincoln or Kendal green for wool, a relief from the tedium of medieval dun (brownish gray) and fallow (yellow). From the 900s, Islamic silk factories maintained stocks of blue, green, and red, the dominant shades of patterned silk. In 1204, after the burning and pillage of Constantinople by Latins at the end of the Fourth Crusade, dyers lost the formula for the murex plum that had colored the royal robes of Justinian I. Purple murex dye remained a mystery until its rediscovery in 1833 by Venetian chemist Bartolomeo Bizio.

Professional dyestuffs advanced late medieval colorants, such as emerald, porreye (leek green) from Douai and Ghent, and litmus, a blue dye that Valencian alchemist Arnaldus de Villa Nova extracted from the *Roccella tinctoria* lichen in 1300. In 1327, Edward III boosted the English textile industry by welcoming immigrant dye masters from Holland and Iberia, who reclaimed ancient formulas. By 1429, Italian commercial fabric makers could refer to the Aquileian manual *Mariegola dell'Arte de Tentori* (*Training in the Dyer's Art*) for technical instruction. A subsequent work, Giovanni Ventura Rosetti's *Plictho de Larte de Tentori* (*Instruction in the Art of Dyeing,* 1540), itemized formulas in use by the Venetian Dyers Guild for silk, hides, feathers, and wool.

Renaissance designers of luxury *camore* (gowns), quilted hem bands, neck ribbons, undersleeves, breeches, waistcoats, mantles, and silk-lined knee-length coats chose velvet dyed in jewel tones—emerald, jade, lapis, topaz, amethyst, and ruby, the favorite of Pope Paul II. Crane- (ash gray) and dove- (lavender gray) colored linings offset the rich drake's neck (iridescent green) in the wardrobe of Elizabeth I.

From the New World came chica (*Arrabidaea chica*), an orangey red that South American natives used to paint their skin. European explorers discovered American Indian sources of colorants, such as the purples the Choctaw achieved with berries of bryony (*Bryonia alba*), the deep brown of walnut (*Juglans nigra*) that the Cherokee applied to hides, and the red alder bark, green hemlock, or yellow lichen with which the Salish dyed blankets and robes.

For trade from Mexico, the Spanish profited from cochineal carmine, a valuable dye from Oaxaca. The Aztec collected the cochineal parasite (*Dactylopius coccus*) from cactus plants for dyeing the state robes of Montezuma II. Because the color remained bright and fade-proof, trade in cochineal red quickly outpaced that in kermes. The color created such a demand that Dutch and French pirates smuggled infested cacti to Caribbean islands and east to Africa, the Canary Islands, and the Mediterranean to found new dye works.

Two lesser sources of red hues, logwood

(*Haematoxylum campechianum*) from the Yucatán, Honduras, and Jamaica, and brazilwood (*Caesalpinia echinata*) from the Amazon Basin, increased the range of dyes for cotton and wool beyond maroon, a color extracted from European chestnuts. Through changes in formulas, dyers used logwood to produce a formal black suitable for European funereal dress. The trade in dyestuffs by the East India Company increased competition for exotic goods in blue, black, and dark green. Around 1625 in Frankfurt, German dealers sold indigo in cakes or balls imported from Dominique at 220 guilders per hundredweight (112 pounds, or 51 kilograms), more than nine times the price of oak gall dye and 31 times the cost of madder.

Modern Trends

In the early seventeenth century, British shoemakers colored the sole of brogues with India red, an earth tone produced from rust (iron oxide). To identify new shades, English clergyman Henry Peacham's *Compleat Gentleman* (1622) applied such unusual terms as "turkie" (red) and "gran-gran" (mixed shades). In 1630, Dutch chemist Cornelius Drebbel's treatment of cochineal with an acidic tin solution brightened red dye into the original Venetian scarlet, the color of British army coats and the robes of Catholic cardinals. The discovery signified the advance of natural dyeing into a chemical process, which Irish chemist Robert Boyle summarized in *Experimenta et Considerationes de Coloribus* (*Experiments and Studies of Colors,* 1665).

While Persia and Smyrna continued to supply familiar citron, crimson, and purple in 1747, colonial Georgia and South Carolina stimulated the indigo market with newly discovered wild plants. Eighteenth-century fashions popularized Saxon blue, a blend of indigo with sulphuric acid, and Saxon green, a mix of indigo with fustic (*Maclura tinctoria*). Scots physician Cuthbert Gordon experimented in 1758 with the addition of cudbear (*Roccella tinctoria*), a boiled lichen, to produce blue-purple tints for silk and wool. In the 1760s at Philadelphia, the processing of fancy goat and sheep leather with red and yellow dyes enabled colonial designers to imitate fine Moroccan, Spanish, and Turkish footwear and handbag styles.

The experiments of English inventor Edward Bancroft in 1775 introduced quercitron, a bright yellow extracted from the bark of the North American black oak (*Quercus velutina*). An Arab tincture of alkanet (*Alkanna tinctoria*), imported from southern Turkey, added chartreuse to color choices. In summer 1775, the appearance of Marie Antoinette in puce created a run on French dye works to supply those wanting to dress like the queen.

In 1856, English chemist William Henry Perkin introduced synthetic dyes by oxidizing aniline (coal tar) from soft coal into a lilac-lavender shade called mauveine. London manufacturers applied the inexpensive colorant to silk, which Queen Victoria promoted by wearing a mauve gown to the Royal Exhibition. A rush of synthetic colorants between 1858 and 1900 added magenta, Bismarck brown, methyl blue, malachite green, Vidal black, and Congo red. Color master William Morris revived natural dyes at his Staffordshire factory, where he reintroduced indigo and madder for dyeing cotton, wool, silk, and embroidery yarn.

Improved dyeing and tanning after 1900 increased variety in footwear choices with sporty canvas and leather styles for croquet and tennis. The outbreak of World War I curtailed England's control of fabric markets. Shortages caused by the Allied blockade and the seizure of German factories in North America impeded U.S. dyers, who imported 90 percent of colorants from Germany. The most popular, turkey red, brightened men's hatbands and ties and women's dresses and skirts.

Dyeing Technology

In 1914, Du Pont moved heavily into organic dye research at Deepwater, New Jersey, to accommodate the coloring of rayon and cellulose. Postwar trade barriers after 1921 buoyed American profits by suppressing German and Swiss chemical firms while the hiring of German-trained chemists transferred European skills to North American laboratories. By the 1930s, colorfast materials synthesized by Du Pont increased the life of everyday garments and nylon hosiery.

Subsequent trade disruption in the 1940s

forced apparel compromises. The shortage of aniline dyes caused the shift of brown Girl Scout uniforms to green and the revival of lichen dyes for yarn. Dominance of the dye market by I.G. Farben in Frankfurt, Germany, into the mid-1940s preceded the branching of the chemical operations. A new division, BASF at Ludwigshafen, marketed methylene blue for antimicrobial and protective fabrics and eosin red for bright cotton, silk, and wool.

After decades of the dyeing industry's success with petroleum-based dyes, oil shortages and price increases returned chemists to the search for cheaper, more sustainable dyestuffs. In 1968, dye pioneer Miriam Cohen Rice, an artist in Mendocino, California, experimented with mushroom pigments and produced a lemon yellow, the first all-fungal dye. Her success with burgundy, rose, and purple preceded a manual, *Mushrooms for Color* (1980) and *Mushrooms for Dyes, Paper, Pigments & Myco-Stix* (2007), and further fungal studies at the International Mushroom Dye Institute. In the early 2010s, the revival of natural dyes from colonial American history resulted in the tinting of retro petticoats, skirts, men's shirts, and wool and other fibers with herbs, vegetables, berry juice, and weak tea.

See also: Batiking; Color Trends; Silk and Sericulture; Tie-Dye; Wool and Wool Products.

Further Reading

Cannon, John, and Margaret Cannon. *Dye Plants and Dyeing.* Portland, OR: Royal Botanic Gardens, 2003.

Kassinger, Ruth G. *Dyes: From Sea Snails to Synthetics.* Brookfield, CT: Twenty-First Century, 2003.

Kirby, Jo. *Dyes in History and Archaeology.* Vol. 19. London: Archetype, 2007.

Eastern European Clothing

Apparel in Eastern Europe typically features functional garments graced with folk details and motifs. As early as 38,000 B.C.E., residents of Potok Cave in present-day Karavanke, Slovenia, improved on skin wrappers and parkas by evolving needle-and-thread technology. By lacing and sewing oddments of fur and hide with horse hair, veins, catgut, leather thongs, or sinew from the backbone of mammals, crafters weatherproofed apparel that standardized dress in coming centuries.

Migratory Goths, Dacians, Roxolans, and Scythians wrapped their legs and feet in thick woolen bands. Found in Smolensk east of Belarus, crude bark sandals and drugget (wool felt) leggings created a look of coarse hardiness. Herders in the area of Hungary created a distinctive uniform in the *suba,* an ankle-length wool cape and rain shield tanned on the outside and lined with unclipped sheepskin. Women appliquéd the surface with leather strips and flower shapes alongside colorful embroidery.

Medieval wool processing dominated Eastern European styles. Over centuries of refinement, Czechs, Hungarians, Polish, Slovaks, and Ukrainians adopted the collarless, sleeveless *bunda* (hairy coat) for work and travel. Made from up to 15 skins of long-fleeced sheep, the Bosnian version featured seaming with colorful leather cording and silk stitchery. For extra warmth in Carpathian snows, Transylvanians wore the fleece on the inside and added a black lambskin cape.

National Costume

During the economic expansion under the Frankish king Charlemagne in 800 C.E., Persian imports influenced Eastern and Central European dress, notably the *sziir* or *szür,* a mantle with hanging sleeves favored by shepherds and Magyar insurgents. A leather strap and buckle fastened the mantle loosely around the shoulders. Folds at the wrists served as pockets. A collar hanging to the back waist displayed elegant embroidery in black and red, emblems of soil and blood colored by Armenian dyes.

Czech and Slovak women dressed for Sundays and festivals in a unified outfit composed of a high circular headdress, white headcloth, puff-sleeved blouse with collar, square-neck vest, short gathered skirt, and short black boots. Adornment with cutwork and lace contributed ethnic and tribal touches. Under anti-Semitic edicts dispensed at Rome by the Fourth Lateran Council on November 11, 1215, Catholic majorities required color insignias denoting ethnicity that made Jews and Saracens (Muslims) stand out from other citizens. Additional decrees banished non-Christians from the streets during Holy Week.

While urbanity crept into Western European styles, agrarian aesthetics dominated Bulgarian, Hungarian, Romanian, Siberian, and Ukrainian crafts. Herders tanned hides into side-laced military boots, carpentry belts, merchants' pouches, and torso shields for butchers and blacksmiths. To the basic overcoat, designers added linen undershirts, dense wool or sheepskin vests, and leather jackets individualized with braiding, couching, and cording.

Renaissance styles rescued medieval attire from primitive materials. Crafters glorified the bride and groom with garnished satins and silks and added chamois, eel skin, and kidskin gloves, wallets, underarm dress shields, and hats and plaited hatbands to everyday wear. In the 1490s, male toddlers wore the bell-shaped *ungarina,* a Hungarian coming-of-age dress of luxurious material heavily braided and closed with frogs in regional style.

Religious and Ethnic Prejudice

Under Hapsburg dominance in the fourteenth and fifteenth centuries, Slovenian men adopted leather leggings. Traditional costume shifted under the Ottoman Turks after their conquest of Serbia in 1389, Bulgaria in 1396, Bosnia in 1463, Albania in 1478, Herzegovina in 1482, Montenegro in 1498, and Hungary in 1541. Bulgarians abandoned traditional attire in favor of the Turkish fez and *shalwar kameez,* loose trousers with tight ankles for men and women.

Bosnian women yielded to the Muslim concept of female modesty by wearing the head and face drape. Albanian and Croatian costumes incorporated the felt hat with Islamic designs for men and lace and cutwork chemises over horsehair-stuffed trousers for women. Montenegrin and Serbian Christians defied Islamic usurpation by sewing bolero vests and weaving linen belts and sashes in traditional red and black.

From the early 1500s, Polish, Ukrainian, and Hungarian-Jewish noblemen and hussars (cavalry) embraced the *zupan,* a silk, damask, or brocade caftan that supplied mittens at the ends of sleeves. The poor imitated upscale men's wardrobes by fashioning the zupan from hemp. Elegant cuffs and linings and the contrasting *kontusz* (outer robe) increased the demand for handwork, such as that made in workshops by Jewish seamstresses.

By 1550, the addition of the *delia* (loose coat) with its double rows of metal buttons and gold braid added to the eminence of male attire. Moldavian and Romanian embroidery preserved fertility symbols on trim for men's knee-length boots and women's drawstring blouses and frog fasteners for jackets. Until the Hapsburg empress Maria Theresa outlawed Romany clothing in 1767, elements of Roma (Gypsy) allure heightened Romanian preference for red fabric turbans, multiple necklaces of beads and coins, low-cut blouses, waists bound with shawls, and hand-worked borders.

Independent Ukrainian peasants retained the woman's *sarafan* (jumper) and kerchief for modesty as well as girdles and sashed hosiery for men. Young girls proclaimed their unmarried status by wearing crowns or diadems until their capping at nuptial ceremonies, a blessing on the couple and their progeny. For gala wedding celebrations, Lithuanian Jews restricted themselves to modest dress.

Baltic fashions featured pre-Christian protective rhombuses and agricultural motifs on knitted gloves. Bordered shawls and skirts, green wreaths, and headdresses tinkling with metal coins identified Albanian, Estonian, Latvian, and Lithuanian dance troupes. Christian needleworkers created the one-piece binder called a whittle (baby shawl) used for swaddling infants. Bavarian lederhosen (leather short breeches) with shoulder straps offered durable leather outdoor wear for children and work wear for laborers and farmers.

Political and Industrial Influence

After January 4, 1700, when Russia's reformist czar Peter the Great forced European attire on Belarus and the Ukraine, he targeted for extinction the Byzantine black cap, caftan, and long beard. Nonetheless, peasant women retained their folk chemises and wool aprons denoting motherhood and housewifery. Hungarian men flaunted tall Turkish hats with side plumes.

Polish women expressed Galician and Silesian taste for gauzy white aprons with zigzag hems. Macedonian women adopted oversized belts and double aprons and flaunted red and black fringe to ward off the evil eye. Albanian women trimmed the fringe to indicate divorce and availability on the marriage market.

The rise of fabric manufacture and shoemaking in Silesia, Moravia, and Bohemia in 1775 introduced irreversible industrialization and urbanization. With city factories boosting the cash economy of Warsaw between 1760 and 1792, the population increased by 400 percent. At Prague

A lithograph from the 1890s depicts miscellaneous Eastern and Central European folk costumes (left to right): a Georgian couple, Iranian man, Albanian man, Icelandic woman, Russian woman, Romanian woman, and Polish couple. *(The Granger Collection, NYC—All rights reserved)*

and among the Magyar nobility of Hungary, demand rose for ready-made garments. The rise of capitalism after the Napoleonic Wars of 1814 elevated standards of living to include cosmetics and more changes of clothes.

In the mid-1800s, Slovak males popularized the rolled brim felt hat with a low crown and the *kosárky,* a cluster of plumes and rooster tail feathers angled toward the shoulder. Albanian rebels abandoned Turkish pants for the *foustanella,* a short kilt similar to those worn by Greek security guards. Bulgarian costume stressed layered fabrics and textures in a variety of stripes and plaids.

The emergence of haute couture in Western Europe encouraged Eastern Europeans to romanticize traditional attire as a gesture to folklore and defiance of suppressors. Jewish emigration from 1880 to 1910 drew from textile and clothing experts, who set up new businesses in the Americas. In late December 1916, orthodox Jews in Poland

who refused to assimilate suffered exile from public areas for dressing in black attire (men) and using uncorseted dresses and wigs (women). To avoid persecution and pogroms, those emigrating from the countryside to Cracow, Minsk, Zagreb, Prague, Kiev, and Bucharest outfitted themselves in urban attire.

The Modern Consumer

After World War I, urbanites of Eastern Europe began buying ready-to-wear. As a result, rural citizens chafed at class differentiation and social inequities inflicted by city dwellers. During the economic depression of the 1930s, however, as factory wages declined, falling prices for apparel enabled smallholders to buy more clothes.

In December 1942, Roma in Ochakov, Romania, suffered a lack of food, firewood, medicine, clothing, and shoes and resorted to theft from Russians to survive the winter. In mid-February

1944, the Nazis deported Moldovan Roma from Transnistria north to the Chelmno death camp in Poland and sent Russians from Chechnya east to Kazakhstan with only the clothes on their backs. The brutal resettlement cost 60 percent of deportee lives from inadequate winter clothing and shoes. By May 1944, removal of Tatars from the Crimea to Uzbekistan cost 110,000 lives because of a lack of adequate apparel for 110-degree Fahrenheit (43-degree Celsius) desert heat. In 1949, the rescue of Armenian displaced persons from shelters in Italy and Germany required international donations of clothing and shoes, especially for orphans.

When communism failed to produce quality garments and shoes for the Eastern European market during the Cold War, underground hand-sewing businesses and well-preserved heirloom costumes sustained farm families. In 1962, Bulgarian city dwellers complained of ill-chosen pinks and greens and selections of only three sizes from Soviet factories. Into the 1970s, rural exploiters profited from the private production of jewelry, apparel, and shoes.

In the 1980s, Bulgaria promoted mono-ethnicism by outlawing the dress of Roma and Turks. Victimization continued in 2002 against Roma children in Ukraine who lacked school uniforms because of unemployment in the Transcarpathian region. Adult Roma in Mukachevo, Ukraine, suffered from cold on December 17, 2002, when police held them in outdoor custody without adequate winter wear. In late February 2013, British convoys delivered clothing to the poor in Romania and Ukraine.

See also: Ethnic and National Dress; Jewish Religious Attire; Medieval European Clothing.

Further Reading

Bideleux, Robert, and Ian Jeffries. *A History of Eastern Europe: Crisis and Change.* New York: Routledge, 2007.

Bren, Paulina, and Mary Neuburger. *Communism Unwrapped: Consumption in Cold War Eastern Europe.* Jefferson, NC: McFarland, 2012.

Rubitzsch, Gunter. *Off the Wall: Fashion from East Germany, 1964 to 1980.* New York: Bloomsbury, 2005.

Weyrauch, Walter Otto. *Gypsy Law: Romani Legal Traditions and Culture.* Berkeley: University of California Press, 2001.

Eco-fashion

Sustainable apparel enables consumers to build their wardrobes while supporting environmental guardianship and minimizing waste. Early forms of dressing with whole animal hides and woven rectangles made full use of natural resources. The Polynesian barkcloth pareu, Indian sari, Japanese kimono, Greek chiton, and Roman *palla* (short wrap) generated no waste.

Around 2000 B.C.E. in Chamba, Kashmir, Kutch, and the Punjab, Indian needleworkers repaired loincloths, shawls, tunics, and veils with bright scraps cut into images of Hindu deities. Out of reverence for Mother Earth, American Indians sliced babiche from rabbit skins and stitched the thongs into hats and baby carriers. They made footwear, breechcloths, and capes from biodegradable sisal, seal fur strips, and animal hides, which caused no harm to nature. Byzantine recyclers purchased used apparel and cut out emblems and trims for reuse on linen and wool. Scythian and Slavic sewers rejected tailored European styles by maintaining full lengths of linen and wool.

Medieval fashion employed nettle fabric, a rival of silk that grew on substandard soil without fertilizer. Dacian and Hun sewers pieced trousers and vests from wool oddments. Slavic women stitched bell skirts from bands of homespun requiring no cutting. In nineteenth-century Japan, the patchwork *happi* coat found a use for scraps of indigo cloth. On the Australian frontier, women developed patching to an art by appliquéing scraps over rips.

The Responsible Shopper

In the mid-1800s, values-based consumerism in Europe, Australia, and the Americas began influencing the thinking of clothiers about such social blights as child labor and sweatshops, subjects of the novels of Charles Dickens. Conservationists objected to turning animal parts into fashion commodities, as with fox furs and muff purses. As the Industrial Revolution increased the chemical complexity of textile processing and toxic dyes, finishing mills became major contaminators of air, soil, and water. In 1866, Prussian biologist Ernst Heinrich Haeckel coined the term "ecology" to emphasize the interrelation of the environment with living creatures and agricultural products.

In Great Britain, Russia, and North America, the rise of feather adornment for women's hats and hairstyles generated antiplumage initiatives. On May 25, 1900, the U.S. Congress passed the Lacey Act, which protected wild birds from commercial use, a shielding of species dubbed the Audubon Plumage Law. Nonetheless, trafficking in the scarlet ibis from Guyana, the rhea from Patagonia, the emu in Tasmania, New Guinean cassowaries, ostriches from Zimbabwe, and Brazilian macaws for apparel ornamentation continued to flourish. Feather smuggling also involved the plumage of the harpy eagle, toucan, and roseate spoonbill.

The late twentieth century introduced conscience into eco-chic and energy-efficient produc-tion, forcing couturiers to produce minimalist designs and to find trendy uses for waste pieces. In the 1980s, Belgian deconstructionist Martin Margiela introduced repurposed leather and made swimwear from plastic bags, blouses from gloves, sweaters from socks, vests from mirror tiles, and coats from wigs.

Fashions featuring pelts from animal farms came under the scrutiny of People for the Ethi-cal Treatment of Animals, or PETA, an animal rights group headquartered in Norfolk, Virginia, that combats and exposes corporate consumerism that involves the torture of fur-bearing mammals. Led by Ingrid Newkirk, some 300 volunteers in 1981 began protesting fur farming with acts of civil disobedience at department stores. Demon-strators carried anticruelty banners proclaiming "Cruelty-Free Silk" and "Animals Are Not Ours to Wear."

Models at the first Eco Chio fashion show in Jakarta, Indonesia, in 2008 present original creations made of organic or recycled material. The sustainable clothing movement values clean, energy-efficient production as well as the use of natural or repurposed materials. *(AP Photo/Achmad Ibrahim)*

The global backlash against trapping, caging, and slaughtering mammals for their pelts targeted Chinese dog and cat fur farms, the world's largest exporters of pelts. Joining the crusade to save animals, designers Calvin Klein, Stella McCartney, Rei Kawakubo, and others promoted fair trade craft items. In defense of fur as clothing, furriers organized their own ad campaign proclaiming pelt farming to be eco-friendly and economically vital to the Inuit, who have hunted wildlife for millennia.

Designers began claiming green practices as their trademark. Xuly-Bët's patchwork accessories and Charmoné's faux leather shoes earned renown for responsible manufacture. Ethical fashion featured sustainable bamboo and banana fabrics, vegetal leather coated with Amazonian latex, hypoallergenic hemp and ramie, and natural-color cottons for infant clothes, kimonos, and saris.

In London in the 1990s, Earthwear sanctioned recycled clothing materials by repurposing worn denim for new designs and appliqué of otherwise useless cloth and leather scraps into fun apparel and Halloween costumes. The reclamation of rayon, organic cotton, car and bus upholstery, and polyethylene terephthalate (PET) water and cola bottles and polyester gave new value to avant-garde T-shirts, eyeglass cases, and handbags. The upcycling of old tires, billboards, cassette tapes, and seatbelts into jackets, shoulder bags and clutches, jewelry, watchbands, belts, buttons, messenger totes, and sandals helped reduce the dumping of 25 percent of waste vinyl in landfills.

Fabric from Wood

Surveys of the impact of apparel manufacture on the environment charged cotton farmers with promoting the use of 25 percent of the world's biocides and some 8,000 chemical processors. The British product Lyocell or Tencel, a rayon fabric first marketed in 1991, regenerated cellulose dissolved from waste paper and tree-farmed beech and eucalyptus trunks grown on substandard soil. Blended into cotton denim, Tencel reduced the waste from cultivation and irrigation of cotton by 20 percent. The resulting bleached garment material mimicked the look and feel of denim, ramie, linen, chino, terry cloth, leather, silk, and suede.

With the addition of plastic zippers, Tencel apparel became 100 percent recyclable. Tencel outerwear supplied thermal insulation and protection from ultraviolet rays.

For maternity clothes, baby night wear, play clothes, yoga and cycling gear, and hospital and restaurant uniforms, the durable, antibacterial botanic Tencel offered 50 percent more absorbency than cotton and higher retention of dye for color brilliance. Smooth Tencel fibers retained skin moisture and elasticity and prevented chafing from hosiery, corduroy, and jersey knits. In 2013, Dawn Ellams, a Scots student at Heriot-Watt University in Edinburgh, invented sustainable denim jeans made from Tencel with no cotton additives.

In 2009, the United Nations fostered awareness of sustainable fashion by declaring the International Year of Natural Fibers, such as the Modal rayon made from beechwood that Australian designer Akira Isogawa introduced to dance companies. Contributions to sustainable couture increased the popularity of Gucci's bio-plastic shoes, Hatley PVC- and phthalate-free rainwear for children, men's sweaters and suits made of vintage fabrics by Preloved, Harricana's recycled coyote and raccoon ski mittens and hats, and Manolo Blahnik's fish skin and cork wedges.

Fair trade exporters from developing world markets introduced batik linings from Malaysia, tagua nut jewelry from Ecuador and Bolivia, jute bags from India, organic alpaca yarns from Peru, açaí palm hats from Belize, crocheted wool necklaces from Morocco, and upscale palm fiber bags and sandals from the Caribbean. In late February 2013, 30 percent of discarded garments from U.K. charities reached Eastern Europe to supply those in need. Professional dancers in Watchung, New Jersey, recycled used and unused dancewear to send to impoverished dancers in Cuba.

See also: Fibers, Natural.

Further Reading

Black, Sandy. *Eco-chic: The Fashion Paradox.* London: Black Dog, 2008.

Brown, Sass. *Eco Fashion.* London: Laurence King, 2010.

Fletcher, Kate. *Sustainable Fashion and Textiles: Design Journeys.* Sterling, VA: Earthscan, 2008.

Education, Fashion

Design schools as well as practical association with the clothing business prepare students to enter the field of fashion design and marketing. Until the nineteenth century, apprenticeships in sketching and fabric choice readied youth for the profession. Just as African girls learned to paint mud cloth in the 1100s at San in what is now southeastern Mali, male Chinese and Japanese leatherworkers studied at cobbleries. In eighteenth-century France, itinerant wig makers alternated sessions at training centers in Rouen, Nantes, Orléans, and Versailles. Likewise, British and French loom boys of the late 1700s assisted weavers before attempting their own fabric designs.

In the 1830s, Charles Frederick Worth, the founder of couture and branded fashions, educated himself at the London National Gallery and in the portrait gallery of the Louvre in Paris. A contemporary, bag maker Louis Vuitton, acquired his skills from a trunk maker. A decade later, coat tailor Thomas Burberry worked in his teens for a draper and dressmaker. Similarly, bag crafter Guccio Gucci learned leather grading at sites in Florence and Rome. Couturier Giorgio Armani, his education delayed by World War I, developed wardrobe skills by dressing windows and selling menswear at La Rinascente department store in Milan.

Style Training in the 1900s

Some twentieth-century designers learned through apprenticing, the choice of British cult designer Mary Quant, Italian-born structuralist Pierre Cardin, and French couturier Coco Chanel, who worked as a seamstress and modiste (hat and dress designer) and sold stockings in a boutique. Basque tailor Cristóbal Balenciaga studied tailoring at his mother's shop before his teens and later trained under color specialist Emanuel Ungaro. Others, including film costumer Edith Head, took art courses at various universities. Those who struggled with career choice prepared in a separate field before selecting fashion, the shift made by Gianni Versace from architectural drafting, by Vera Wang after studying French and art history at the Sorbonne, and by Elsa Schiaparelli after earning a degree in philosophy from the University of Rome.

Geoffrey Beene combined a university education with window dressing for I. Magnin in Los Angeles. In similar fashion, milliner Roy Halston, who observed designer Lilly Daché creating hats in New York City, built department store displays and took night courses at the School of the Art Institute of Chicago (SAIC). Begun in 1866 as the Chicago Academy of Design, the facility, America's second-largest art school, combined with major art collections and libraries a curriculum in technology, theory, fashion design, film, architecture, painting, photography, print, sculpture, and visual studies. A more recent graduate of SAIC, Cynthia Rowley, won the 1994 Perry Ellis Award for New Talent.

Oleg Cassini began his education at the Accademia di Belle Arti di Firenze under Giorgio de Chirico, the set designer and costumer for the Ballets Russes. Established in Florence by the fifteenth-century merchant-prince Cosimo de' Medici, the academy incorporated in its staff Michelangelo and Benvenuto Cellini, two of the master artists of the 1500s. In 1614, the faculty admitted Artemisia Gentileschi, the rare female instructor. In the twenty-first century, the Accademia's three-year program focuses on technical experimentation and innovation suited to future fashion markets. Coursework incorporates spatial and sensual orientation, textiles, patterning, and accessories.

The Russian-born French designer Erté studied art at the Académie Julian and l'École des Beaux-Arts in Paris, a bastion of classical antiquity and its influence on subsequent art periods. Hubert de Givenchy combined training at the same alma mater with work alongside two masters, Christian Dior, a self-taught couturier, and Pierre Balmain, also a graduate of l'École des Beaux-Arts. Established by the Italian-born French cardinal and chief minister Jules Mazarin in 1648, the school focused on painting, sculpture, and architecture. A demanding curriculum prepared notable illustrators and artists as well as Lombard couturier Valentino Garavani, who created apparel for Jacqueline Kennedy Onassis, Elizabeth Taylor, Grace Kelly, and Audrey Hepburn.

Preceding an apprenticeship under Christian Dior, Yves Saint Laurent achieved superstardom from coursework at l'École de la Chambre Syndicale de la Couture Parisienne (The School of the Syndicated Chamber of Parisian Dress Design). Among trendsetters in Western glamour, Saint Laurent joined other designers in the standardization of French style. Subsequent curriculum covered basic techniques established in 1868 by Charles Frederick Worth. Modern applications include mastery of computer-aided design (CAD), an outgrowth of the electronic age of fashion design.

Course Basics

In 1939, couturier Bill Blass learned dressmaking at the Parsons School of Design in Greenwich Village, New York City. Founded in 1896 by painter William Merritt Chase, the institution expanded from the fine arts into graphics, advertising, decor, and fashion. A prime U.S. training ground in design, the campus offers studio courses in theory and fashion history as well as standard industrial technology and an annual fashion show. Notable alumni include Jason Wu, Tom Ford, Marc Jacobs, Donna Karan, and Claire McCardell, who made a name for herself in costume illustration and bias structure.

Calvin Klein received training at the Fashion Institute of Technology (FIT) in New York City, one of the world's top five fashion training centers. Opened in 1944, FIT offers the basics—advanced sewing techniques, display and exhibiting, sketching, textiles, and accessories—as well as photography and fragrance marketing. Venezuelan designer Carolina Herrera, an alumna, learned relaxed women's wear at FIT. Another graduate, Michael Kors, developed his early projects into classic women's sportswear that earned him the 2010 Geoffrey Beene Lifetime Achievement Award.

Japanese designer Issey Miyake completed a graphics degree from Tama Art University and studied at l'Ecole de la Chambre Syndicale de la Couture Parisienne. At Tama, established in Tokyo, Japan, in 1953, Miyake took an interest in patterns, visual concepts, ultra-modern fibers,

and the social relevance of textiles. Coursework in weaving and dyeing provided the technical groundwork for self-expression in couture and production of ready-to-wear.

An accounting of world fashion colleges suggests a variety of professional possibilities, such as a concentration on cosmetics at London's Studio Bercot, purchasing and brand management at Shanghai's Raffles University, hand crafting at Suzhou Institute of Silk Science, makeup and cosmetology at Tokyo's Mode Gakuen in Japan, and fashion illustration at the Copenhagen Academy of Fashion Design in Denmark. Australia's Melbourne School of Fashion schedules classes in bespoke bridal wear and millinery. The Academy of Art University in San Francisco offers courses in designing knitwear and fashion journalism and marketing. London's University of the Arts, the alma mater of Alexander McQueen and Stella McCartney, offers honors degrees in menswear, women's wear, and jewelry design.

See also: Couturiers.

Further Reading

Cabrera, Alfredo. *101 Things I Learned in Fashion School.* New York: Grand Central, 2010.

Faerm, Steven. *Fashion Design Course: Principles, Practice, and Techniques: A Practical Guide for Aspiring Fashion Designers.* Hauppauge, NY: Barron's, 2010.

Freese, Susan M. *Fashion.* North Mankato, MN: Abdo, 2011.

Jones, Sue Jenkyn. *Fashion Design.* London: Laurence King, 2005.

Edwardian Styles and Fashions

The Edwardian period in British history, from 1901 to 1910, retained some of the elegance of the Victorian era while introducing erotic lingerie and women's career and leisure apparel. King Edward VII and his popular Danish queen, Alexandra, set the model for a sumptuous display in dress and decorum among the bon ton (fashionable). Royalty established appropriate styles for court appearances and official mourning, which required black for men, women, and children. Alexandra

The feminine ideal of the Gibson Girl, the pen-and-ink vision of illustrator Charles Dana Gibson in the 1890s and early 1900s, emphasized a cool, refined beauty, the latest in fashionable (and slender) attire, and a signature mound of pinned-up hair. *(Elias Goldensky/George Eastman House/Getty Images)*

had dignified mourning dress tailored by Redfern & Sons in London and by Jacques Doucet in Paris. New World imitators ordered stylish women's wear from the National Cloak & Suit Company in New York City.

For impeccable outfits, furs, mitts and gloves, hats, and shoes for formal occasions, men and women in Europe and the Americas searched style guides in *The Lady's Realm* and *La Gazette du Bon Ton* and fashion plates in *Vanity Fair*. Women bought partially made bodices, sailor collars, and Nottingham lace insets and hired dressmakers to fit them into custom outfits for such outings as the Ascot Races, sailing jaunts on the Great Lakes and Suez Canal, and parties at Marlborough House in London, the Château Frontenac in Quebec, the Taj Mahal in Bombay, and the Waldorf-Astoria Hotel in New York City. For the individual touch, the chic invested in accessories such as waistline jewels, fans, handkerchiefs, and stiff dog collars, a jewelry item Queen Alexandra introduced to cover a surgical scar on her throat.

Unlike frivolous female peacocks, men emphasized neatly groomed short hair, curled mustaches, and rounded beards. Cutaway coats and knife creases in trousers and cuffs added stature to topcoats and business suits. Pocket watches on chains supplied a muted glimpse of gold. The fashionable paired lounge coats with bowlers and dinner jackets and frock coats with top hats, the epitome of the Edwardian male silhouette.

The pomp of men's shirts with the imperial collar paralleled the female high neck centered with a velvet ribbon, brooch, or cameo. Women created a flurry of demand for virginal white as well as gold and silver lamé, a weighty fabric that demanded erect carriage and swan-like movements and dance steps. They favored Queen Alexandra's "sweet pea colors" for bias-cut tea gowns, frothy chiffon trains, and off-the-shoulder styles or surplice or décolleté necklines by Italian couturier Mariano Fortuny.

Popular accessories ranged from the locket, matching mother-of-pearl combs, parasols, and braided hair bracelet to the muff purse. In addition to elegant opera cloaks and capes, women draped fox furs around the shoulders. The Merry Widow hat, a grand black straw headpiece swathed with undulating plumes, topped poufy charwoman hairdos, the favored style of the Gibson Girl, first drawn by American illustrator Charles Dana Gibson in the 1890s.

Female underwear gained respect for defining femininity and sensual appeal. The laced corset and hip pads forced the female body into a sinuous, full-bosomed hourglass shape, especially for riding sidesaddle in the park. In Chicago, New York, London, and Paris, lingerie shops extended the range of intimate wear with trousseau negligees, gowns, open-crotch drawers, and ribbed silk or lisle hosiery. Married shoppers bought lingerie dresses, petticoats, and kimono jackets for lounging at home during pregnancy and recuperation from childbirth.

For work as innkeepers, secretaries, bank tellers, nursing supervisors, shopkeepers, and milliners, career couture influenced women to emulate men with the boned collar, tie, and vest triad accompanying wool suits. Bonnets and floor-length trumpet or yoked skirts carried dampness from bad weather and chapped the neck and ankles. Blouses, known as shirtwaists, tended toward the low neckline and puffed sleeve cap. Belts, sashes, and bib-front aprons emphasized attractive proportions. As the Edwardian style lost favor, narrowed skirts edged up the ankle to show laced leather boots.

In Great Britain, New Zealand, and Australia, the feminist concept of the New Woman liberated reformers such as Emmeline Pankhurst and Nellie McClung to march in parades and rallies in London and Winnipeg, always in refined outfits. The role of females in society and government shifted leisured gentility to suffrage and activities outside the home such as horseback riding, lawn tennis, cycling, golf, sailing, and croquet. During long family trips to health spas in Davos-Platz, Switzerland, and Wiesbaden, Germany, women chose veiled hats, goggles, and travel dusters to protect tailored jackets and gored umbrella skirts with frou-frou taffeta or moiré petticoats from the grime of carriages and trains. The domed trunk with hanging rods and drawers secured garments during long sea voyages to Hong Kong, Burma, Barbados, and other colonial vacation spots.

For beach strolling, trekking, birding, and skeet shooting, men favored soft, closely woven tweeds, the epitome of informality and comfort. They wore the double-breasted ulster with patch pockets over the flannel blazer or Norfolk jacket, newmarket vest, knickerbockers, and flat caps or boater hats. Leather or canvas gaiters or spats protected brogans and ankle boots for golfing in Gleneagles, Scotland, and billiards at the Raffles Hotel in Singapore.

While performers Sarah Bernhardt, Isadora Duncan, and Lillian Russell modeled cloaks and gowns for dressmakers for free, one-third of English society incurred debt to pay for a similar life of dining, dancing, and conspicuous costumes and rituals for each event. It is not surprising that penny markets, dealerships in secondhand clothing, flourished in Budapest, Hungary, and Vilnius, Lithuania; at Boston, New York, and San Francisco in North America; and at Houndsditch, London, Leeds, Liverpool, Yorkshire, Lancashire, and Manchester in England. Colonial consumers snapped up used Edwardian fashions at market stalls among the Fulani in Nigeria and Zambia; in Mombasa, Kenya; and in Mexico, Nicaragua, Guatemala, and Costa Rica.

See also: Art Nouveau and Art Deco Fashion; British Clothing and Fashion; Formal Attire, Female; Formal Attire, Male; Leisure Wear.

Further Reading

Affleck, Diane L. Fagan, and Karen J. Herbaugh. *Textiles for Victorian and Edwardian Clothing, 1880–1920.* Arlington, VA: Q Graphics, 2004.

Grimble, Frances. *The Edwardian Modiste: 85 Authentic Patterns with Instructions, Fashion Plates, and Period Sewing Techniques.* San Francisco: Lavolta, 1997.

Harris, Kristina. *Victorian & Edwardian Fashions for Women, 1840–1919.* Atglen, PA: Schiffer, 2002.

Elderly, Clothing for the

Consumers in late adulthood have typically selected cosmetics, hairstyles, and clothing that suit changing lifestyles and aging bodies. Over much of history, the oldest members of society have accommodated changes in mobility and agility by donning shawls, wraps, rainproof ponchos and caps, and blankets, while dressing aging feet in slip-on sandals, mukluks, or clogs.

Ancient Times to the Modern Era

From ancient times, Egyptians combated aging with cosmetics. They rinsed hair with henna (*Lawsonia inermis*) and re-tinted graying roots. The mixing of aloe vera or chickpeas with skin-toned colorants enabled the elderly to conceal scars or lighten the dark pigments of solar lentigo (liver spots), normal markers incurred from sun exposure.

Chinese seniors of the Han era after 206 B.C.E., especially males, preferred the ankle-length *paofu* (long gown) as a cover-up. Either quilted or padded, the casual gown supplied warmth and shielding of the legs for modesty. Wide sleeves tied around the wrists. Tomb paintings pictured the female paofu with festoons around the hem.

In the early Middle Ages, aging and retirement placed specific wardrobe demands on the elderly, such as black garb for Catalonian and Sardinian widows, sun hats to shield the skin, and yoked smocks in workhouses and poorhouses to cover kyphosis, known as dowager's hump. At the monasteries of Kosmosoteira in Greece, Reichenau on the Swiss-German border, Fulda and Corvey abbeys in Germany, and St. Gall, Switzerland, monks supplied retirees and widows with heated lodging, shoes, and hose. Robes and mantles of wool and linen served in cold and warm seasons. For amputees and paralytics, silk undershirts, bed jackets, and nightshirts offered a loose fit for sleep and lounging. Ambulatory residents sat fireside and repaired tatters and rips.

In the late 1300s, older European and Asian women avoided overdressing and presented themselves in simple, respectable apparel and coifs (fitted caps). Elderly men preferred a loose, front-opening gown with trailing back hem. In the 1600s, the calico dressing gown acquired the English name of banyan and, in Japanese, *kosode*.

Functional changes in dress for the elderly eased the privations and difficulties of aging. As early as the 1400s, for example, the pince-nez secured glasses on the nose with a spring clip. As the trend toward powdered wigs ended, European and American seniors continued to wear them to cover gray or thinning hair and to warm the head. Adjustable braces, or cloth suspender straps, invented in 1787, fastened with hooks and eyes.

Tailors cut raglan and dolman sleeves to enhance range of motion, stitched seams flat, and attached deep patch pockets on outerwear to hold medicines, handkerchiefs, ear trumpets, and glasses. During the decline in dependence on woolens in Scotland near the end of the eighteenth century, elderly men chose cotton shirts and hose. Older women wore print cotton gowns, muslin aprons, and cotton stockings. Lorgnettes fitted a handle to spectacles in the early 1800s, enabling readers with impaired vision to decipher small print.

To protect fragile bones, old people in Europe tied hip pads around the waist. For workers, linen or cotton bib-and-brace overalls placed less stress on the waistline and featured adjustable straps for accommodating shirts or sweaters. In the sunny climates of Australia, South Africa, and the North American frontier, bonnets with deep visors protected eyes and skin. In New England, women embraced age by wearing dark-colored clothing and white morning caps. In China, women's embroidered shoes and ankle wraps displayed bound feet.

Worldwide, older citizens honored traditional attire that modernization endangered, including hammered barkcloth wraps in Polynesia, brilliant tiered skirts among the Seminole women of southern Florida, and unisex bark strip or grass skirts among the Chumash of west-central California. Among the pastoral Ovambo of northern Namibia after 1870, proud elderly women ignored the anti-nativist teachings of Finnish missionaries and, in Onyanka tribal style, decked their bodies in hide, bark, roots, copper beads, protective amulets, and nickel earrings.

Softer, Gentler Attire and Technological Innovations

In the early 1900s, the application of synthetic, no-iron fabrics to age-appropriate clothing made garments silkier against fragile skin, simpler to launder and hang dry, and warmer for impaired circulation in ambient temperatures. Flat seaming prevented pressure sores. Sock pullers, reaching devices, and long shoe horns aided the less limber with dressing the feet.

Other elements of comfort and safety upgraded

lives. Low-compression, nonskid bariatric socks protected patients from friction and compression. Polar fleece, velour, flannel, corduroy, seersucker, and French terry cloth pull-on slacks, shorts, and cardigans and acrylic and thermal socks offered comfort and extra warmth to easily chilled torsos and extremities. With wide-tab zippers and snaps on the waists, backs, and cuffs making clothes easier to fasten, stroke and dementia victims and persons in wheelchairs were able to maintain their dignity and independence while enjoying self-confidence and a sense of style.

The invention of low-heeled orthopedic shoes supplied foot and ankle support as well as stretchy contouring, a wide toe box, removable insoles, and soft linings to cushion plantar fasciitis, bunions, and corns. In the 1920s, knitted and stretchy turbans in bright colors suited wearers of all ages by cloaking thinning hair and alopecia. Smokers chose long cigarette holders as a means of distancing themselves from fire and ashes.

Numerous wardrobe innovations in the 1930s improved the lives of seniors. Shower shields of anticling nylon mesh fastened around the neck during medical treatment and grooming. Back snaps decreased pressure on the spine. Snap-crotch underwear, incontinence briefs, and pants with 22-inch (56-centimeter) side and bilateral zippers simplified personal care and toileting to involve less stooping and bending.

At mid-century, designers offered older women the Circassian bodice to cover the chest with surplice-style folds reaching from shoulder to waist. For adaptation to imbalance, tremors, weakness, and the lost finger dexterity common to Parkinson's disease, multiple sclerosis, and cerebral palsy, stores stocked hobo bags, slip-on shoes, and zip-front dresses, T-shirts, model coats, and pullover gowns. Less demanding garments prevented falls during dressing and chair exercises. Capes gave caregivers easy access to IVs, catheters, ostomy appliances, and feeding tubes.

In the mid-1960s, while pop culture devalued mature women by promoting the miniskirt, manufacturers targeted mature shoppers with crinkly boho skirts, dashikis (tunics), Hawaiian shirts, wrap tops, muumuus, swim dresses, and smocks to cover expanded waists. Wrap skirts, stretch pants, pantsuits, culottes, suede boots, and wedge sandals suited gardening, volunteering, and golf. Unisex back flaps on pants eased the difficulty of dressing people who were unable to bear weight on their feet.

In the late 1960s, consumers with rheumatic conditions found Velcro® closures handy for securing robes, blouses, drop-front pants, and foot snugglers and slippers. Adjustable hook and loop strips varied the fit over edema or swollen joints. Washable seamless shoes with pressure closures and nonskid soles promoted self-assurance in patients with diminished hand strength and an unsteady gait. Pants with generous stretchy waistbands assisted the incontinent and users of walkers with quick access to the toilet or to adult disposable diapers, invented in 1969.

The mid-1970s introduced battery-heated oversized gloves and socks, scarves, and jackets to accommodate seniors living in cold climates. Polypropylene and microfibers shielded the body from wetness and maintained body heat in aching joints. Among the Inuit, lightweight Neoprene replaced sealskin. To reduce bulk in cold weather, the elderly layered thermal underwear and liners to protect frail bodies from chill.

In 2006, news outlets reported that 19 percent of Americans needed adaptive clothing for special needs. Aging women reshaped sagging bosoms with molded plastic bras and silicone gel cups. Lingerie designers facilitated the replacement of breasts lost to mastectomy by fitting recovering women with silicone gel prostheses. For women with limited dexterity, arthritis bras fastened in front with hooks and eyes.

Unisex lap robes, molded or pleated face masks, and hand, arm, and leg protectors increased the comfort of the frail and the peace of mind of residential, nursing home, and hospice care. Jumpsuits, sweat suits, overlapping shirts, and one-piece rompers and sleepers supplied nonbinding apparel to the chairbound and bedbound. Open-back gowns and jumpers helped physical therapists and caregivers tend to clients' personal needs and medication. Shower robes quickly warmed the body after shampooing and bathing.

Waterproof bibs and aprons assisted paralytics who had difficulty managing utensils and swallowing. Grab loops and oversized buttons aided the arthritic in pulling on pants and fastening sweaters without painful tugging. Flame-proof fabrics lessened the chance of burning deaths from cooking or smoking, 80 percent of which affected the elderly because of impaired reaction time and weak grasp.

See also: Eyeglasses; Protective and Orthotic Clothing.

Further Reading

Schwarz, Shelley Peterman. *Dressing Tips and Clothing Resources for Making Life Easier.* Verona, WI: Attainment, 2000.

Twigg, Julia. *Fashion and Age: Dress, the Body, and Later Life.* London: Bristol Classical, 2013.

Elizabethan Styles and Fashions

During the reign of England's Elizabeth I from 1558 to 1603, the queen and her court set the tone for fabric choices, clothing designs, and grooming. Elizabeth's daily attire included cambric, lawn, and gauze camisoles and French hoods. A snowy mask of alum, white lead, or arsenic powder and egg white contrasted her 80 red wigs, emphasizing the virtue of the "virgin queen." Puritans condemned her display of cloth of gold, sable, and ermine, which only the queen's family wore.

To frame her face for royal portraiture in 1563, 1575, and 1588, Elizabeth dressed in the Tudor mode, with linen ruffles and a grand lace or filigreed collar tied at the neck. She promoted the hand knitting of stockings, a cottage industry that flourished in London, Norfolk, Aberdeen, and the Shetland Islands. In 1578, her cousin, Mary, Queen of Scots, extended Battenburg linen collars on whalebone props to pair with the white atifet, a heart-shaped cap that tied under the chin.

Whalebone bound the queen and her ladies-in-waiting in gowns that expanded in diameter over farthingales and porte-trains, petticoats that supported a trailing overskirt. A whalebone busk that attached to the midriff with busk points gave the illusion of a flat stomach. Women wound po-nytails and mushroom hairdos in frills and covered their ears with ribbon rosettes. They shielded their faces and necks from sun with a tasseled scarf or the boned *bongrace* (forehead visor) and concealed pregnancy under aprons. Corsets and triangular torso shapers epitomized self-control within the aristocracy even if they hampered the stride.

The Elizabethan era elevated male fashions to heights of color and panache. The queen's Yeomen of the Guard sported high-crowned flat caps flanked by feathers. Guest knights from Germany and Switzerland flattered the queen by branding satin caps in her honor. The palace staff curled their hair with hot irons, secured locks with gum or wax, and starched their beards. They identified their rank with a color code—ash, slate gray, orangey-yellow, apricot, and pale yellow worn over pearly stockings, the shades of the quick-witted, decisive young courtier. Older males chose russet-black damask for coats and blacking on boots to symbolize gravitas and reliable counsel. For fur trim, they chose fox, lynx, leopard, wolf, marten, lambskin, or otter.

Court hunters and cavalry officers folded down the collar of thigh-high riding boots bound with drawstrings. Tudor males framed their own faces in feathered caps, ruffs, and piccadillies (broad collars), which extended over cap sleeves, a favorite of naval hero Sir Francis Drake. By the 1590s, the fluted starched cotton or muslin ruff reached beyond shoulders and tilted down below the underarms.

Tudor social climbers favored Venetian heeled slippers and protective cork chopines (overshoes). More reserved courtiers chose powdered wigs, winged sleeves, and wool robes lined in black silk, a serious color appropriate to the Reformation. In contrast to asceticism, feathers from exotic birds added to embroidered heraldry and crests. Plumed fans with jeweled tortoiseshell handles tied at the female midline.

Quilting, hair or linen canvas, stiffeners, interlining, and wool felt reshaped natural curves into geometric extremes. The period under-doublet with eyelets and detachable buttons in emerald, jade, lapis, topaz, amethyst, and ruby required shoulder-to-hip plumping. The padding turned the male upper body into a jewel-toned mound that Germans called "goose stomach."

The peasecod doublet featured fullness over the waist and parti-color stockings. Cotton wool filled out sleeves and exaggerated the codpiece, a triangular gusset introduced by Elizabeth's father, Henry VIII, that doubled as a coin purse. From the waist down, knee-length pumpkin breeches in velvet or wool buckled to the upper calf over trunk hose, which required additional filler.

For women, Renaissance dressmakers padded the lower edges of *camore* (gowns) with velvet to warm the ankles and feet. By slashing sleeves, tailors showcased stuffing and *fenestrelle* (windows) to undersleeves lined in red, orange, blue, or purple. The trendy cushioned trunk sleeve ballooned over the arm from top to mid-forearm and contoured into a tightly bound wrist. As a balance to stuffed bodices and breast shaping, the bum roll, filled with batting, encircled the midline to pad female hips.

By 1594, English whaling fleets scoured Cape Breton for baleen to support the elegant ruffs, collars, stomachers, girdling, and farthingales that gave Elizabethan fashion its dramatic presence. In the last years of the Elizabethan Age, neck styles reached extremes with the lace yoke, neck cloth, and falling band, a batiste or lawn rectangle tied at the neck of professional garb for college dignitaries, judges, ministers, and liturgical choristers. In the Stuart era that began with Elizabeth's death on March 24, 1603, English and French women

Queen Elizabeth I of England and Ireland donned a full lace or filigree collar to sit for a series of formal portraits. Ornamentation, elegance, and sumptuous materials defined aristocratic English style during the late sixteenth century. *(The Granger Collection, NYC—All rights reserved)*

relieved the neck of cloying styles by making deep cuts in necklines edged with flat lace collars.

See also: British Clothing and Fashion; Collars; Lace and Tatting; Sumptuary Laws.

Further Reading

Elgin, Kathy. *Elizabethan England.* Costume and Fashion Source Books. New York: Facts on File, 2005.

Jones, Ann Rosalind, and Peter Stallybrass. *Renaissance Clothing and the Materials of Memory.* New York: Cambridge University Press, 2000.

Elle

The world's leading fashion journal, *Elle* established its priority with the selection of a French title meaning "she." Debuting on October 1, 1945, at a low point in French fashion marketing, the magazine reflected the survival instincts of its founder, Hélène Gordon-Lazareff.

A Russian refugee of the Bolshevik Revolution of 1917, she had fled home at age eight. Trained in ethnography at the Sorbonne in Paris, she entered the media in the 1930s as a journalist for *France-Soir.* In flight again after the Nazi occupation of Paris in June 1940, Gordon-Lazareff and her husband, Pierre Lazareff, wrote for the U.S. media in New York. She left *Harper's Bazaar* and *Vogue* to work on the women's page of *The New York Times.* Upon the liberation of Paris in August 1944, she returned to Paris and began formulating a fashion magazine.

On November 21, 1947, Gordon-Lazareff introduced *Elle,* a weekly, at a time when French fashion moguls were regrouping to reclaim their prominence among world clothing designers. A beacon of democracy and pop culture, *Elle* appealed to the female consumer with color photos of American models, coupons, and up-to-the-minute news about style, all elements of comfort after an era of combat and rationing. Inventive advice on how to stay warm during a shortage of gas for heating and how to reclaim old sweaters acknowledged Western Europe's plight without sinking into despair.

With a decline in the publisher's health in 1946, Swiss-Turkish journalist Françoise Giroud,

a dynamic fiction writer for *Paris-Soir,* took over as editor of *Elle.* To jolt France out of its postwar malaise, Giroud wrote provocative essays on cleanliness and the upkeep of underwear and declared that the war had liberated women from the need to dress up like dolls. As liberated members of the workforce, females were encouraged to select clothes and accessories that amused them and suited their everyday needs, such as the trio of afternoon dresses by Cristóbal Balenciaga, Pierre Balmain, and Christian Dior on the cover on April 1, 1948.

In competition with *Claudine* and *Marie-Claire, Elle* funded a radio program, ideal housewife contest, and downtown kiosk in Paris. As emblems of a new spirit of femininity and poise, style consultants promoted Dior's midi skirts with nipped-in waists and dresses complementing slender necks and long legs. Giroud proclaimed French couture a parallel of other arts for coordinating clever ideas with an historic sense of taste and resistance to coercion. While she admired American women for popularizing clean hair and comfortable, fun ready-to-wear, she opined in November 1952 that French women expressed a more elegant essence by nurturing cultivation and coquetry.

In 1955, *Elle* recognized the era of the female teen consumer and her appetite for self-fulfillment. Fashions projected the look of the working mother and citizen, a mature woman capable of controlling a lifestyle set on multiple fronts. On the cover on February 21, 1955, a Dior-style beauty in a wide pleated skirt and sheer blouse enjoys a drink from a modern refrigerator, an icon of the female life freed from drudgery and penury.

By the 1960s, some 800,000 women remained loyal readers of *Elle.* Admirers of the imaginative poses photographed by Swiss art director Peter Knapp reassessed beauty in terms of the innocence of model Jean Shrimpton and the self-assurance of actor Charlotte Rampling. The photographer's innovative layouts applauded the unconfined female body in minidress and tights, a combination that also drew male readers. Knapp promoted the liberating feel of ribbed knits by André Courrèges, who mixed haute couture with street panache.

The magazine passed to U.S. ownership in

1981 and began issuing 25 foreign editions featuring the era's status dressing. In October 1985, fashion news presented the dynamics of Valentino lambskin gloves, Malaysian Mary Janes, and Gitano sports skirts, stretch pants, leggings, and backpacks. Color shoots of that era stressed Azzedine Alaïa's clingy tops, Norma Kamali's and Anne Klein's contributions to professional power dressing, and color-blocked dresses and layered separates modeled by Elle Macpherson and Isabelle Adjani.

In 2001, a teen spin-off, *Elle Girl,* targeted the independent schoolgirl with suggestions for autumn wardrobe development and accessories suited to a limited budget. Available in 60 countries, *Elle* in the 2010s appealed to the young-to-middle-aged single college graduate of above-average means. Articles advised on easily maintained haircuts and skin regimens, contrasting fabrics, high-fashion wedding ensembles, the flowing styles by Singapore-born couturier Prabal Gurung, and the casual elegance of models Jennifer Aniston and Britney Spears.

See also: Models and Modeling; Photography, Fashion.

Further Reading

Demachy, Jean, and Francois Baudot. *Elle Style: The 1980s.* New York: Filipacchi, 2003.
Elle. www.elle.com
Weiner, Susan. *Enfants Terribles: Youth & Femininity in the Mass Media in France, 1945–1968.* Baltimore, MD: Johns Hopkins University Press, 2001.

Embroidery

An embellishment for garments worldwide, embroidery combines natural and man-made thread and yarn to produce a textured or three-dimensional design. Evident in clothing from as early as around 2400 B.C.E. in Assyria, 2000 B.C.E. in India, in China after 1558 B.C.E., and among Hebrew needleworkers after 1400 B.C.E., stitched designs, glyphs, and monograms adorned ceremonial garments as well as hats, shirts, capes, and stockings. A tunic recovered from the island of Euboea northeast of Athens dating to 1000 B.C.E. displayed decorative weaving and embroidery in stylized patterns adapted from local flora and fauna. Art needlework added sewn-on accents—appliqués, beads, bells, crystals, fringe, glass, lace, metal shapes, pearls, pompoms, quills, ribbon, rosettes, sequins, tassels, vellum, wire—to enhance beauty and symbolism.

The earliest embroidered goods had specific domestic uses, such as the Afghan triangles over the breast of women's blouses in Baluch and the interlace or herringbone stitch on linens, aprons, and shirts for Kandahar men. Beyond the mundane chores of quilting, lining, repairing, and darning, traditional embroidery from 300 B.C.E. created patterns with chain stitches, a method employed in embellishing silk gauze grave goods in Hubei, China, and in traditional white-on-white *chikan* embroidery in India.

Goldwork, invented in the first century C.E., required investment in gold, silver, pewter, or copper thread for stitching with silk to a robe, regalia, livery, or uniform, such as the geometric collars of the Sami of Sweden and the monastery vestments produced in Austria, Germany, and Switzerland. From 225, Persian men and women embroidered linen trousers, headbands, and cumberbunds with parallel floral borders, an imported Mongolian decoration for festivals that charmed the Syrian queen Zenobia.

Folk Embroidery

English stitchery guilds formalized the output of *opus Anglicanum* (English work), expensive handwork based on Anglo-Saxon models after the accession of Knute, a Danish king, to the throne of England in 1016. Opus Anglicanum decorated linen costumes, head coverings, and vestments with backstitch, a source of fine detail. The addition of angels, stars, eagles, virgins, and martyrs, a process known as "powdering," required less needlework skill.

When worked in one- or two-ply wool yarn, embroidery produced crewelwork, a free style invented around 1000 for production on canvas secured on a hoop or frame. The skill, cultivated by ladies of leisure, received royal promotion by Queen Edith of Wessex for the robes of Edward the Confessor after 1045 and by Queen Margaret of Scotland, wife of Malcolm III, in 1070 for ladies of the court making handbags and tunics. For stretch in fitted garments, embroiderers developed smocking, a gathering of fabric with long running stitches of linen thread into tubes or unpressed pleats.

The French of Provence evolved a popular fifteenth-century method, *broderie de Marseille,* the stitching of whole cloth layers into quilted fabric. Creative variations produced artistic results, such as featherstitch, which paired designs on opposite sides of a vertical line, creating mirror images right and left. The French knot involved twisting the thread two or three times around the needle before pulling it through the base, thus creating eyes for birds and sepals for flowers. Barbing required a contrasting thread sewn over top of the basic stitch. The Spanish Basque stitch or picot anchored a loop below each stitch.

In Italy, Casalguidi stitchery applied the satin stitch on top of a thick yarn to pad shapes in high relief. Counted-thread silk embroidery involved the fill-in of a geometric or floral background on even-weave fabric, leaving the detail unstitched. When completed in black or red thread on chemises, sleeves, handkerchiefs, collars, and cuffs, it carried the name blackwork or scarletwork. The Holbein stitch, a two-sided decoration, emulated the backstitch but completed the line on both sides of the material, an adornment for blackwork and Assisi embroidery.

Artistic Stitchery

During the Renaissance, world needlework advanced with the zigzag borders sewn by the nomadic Rabari of Kutch in western India. To learn stitches and knots, young girls made samplers, a practical educational tool kept in the sewing basket for reference. The stitchery of the Punjab and Iran adorned leather shoes with turned-up toes that curled back into decorative points. A more detailed form, *bagh,* covered the entire foundation material.

In Agra and Lahore, India, Akbar the Great, the third Mughal emperor, maintained workshops where seamstresses produced designs on fine fabrics for costumes and linens. In Europe,

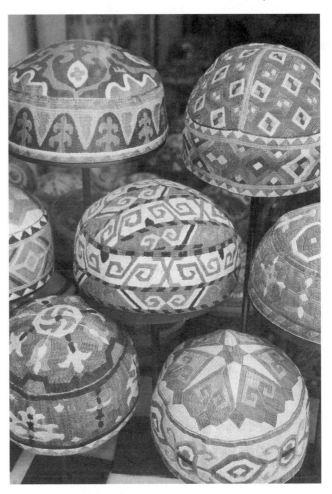

Traditional Turkish hats for men epitomize the mastery of folk embroidery in cultures everywhere. The design may represent the owner's age, economic status, or standing in the community. A woman's embroidery skills affirm her own status and respect. *(Martin Child/ Robert Harding World Imagery/Getty Images)*

Catherine de' Medici so valued needlework that she arrived in France for her wedding to Henry II in 1533 with Venetian pattern designer Frederico de Vinciolo, who collected models of unicorns, peacocks, griffons, and stags in the volume *Les Singuliers et Nouveaux Pourtraicts* (*Unique and New Portraits,* 1587).

Tudor England produced history's first grand era of embroidered attire and badges. For Henry VIII, Anne Boleyn, and Elizabeth I, French petit point, worked over the intersection of a warp-and-weft thread, heightened the visual effect and majesty of court garments, particularly capes, gloves, garters, and boot hose. Skullcaps and petticoats of cambric and lawn featured delicate borders of flowers, grain stalks, and stars. Mary, Queen of Scots, retained Pierre Oudry and Charles Plouvart as her personal needleworkers, plus three staff embroiderers who replicated the French lily, the English acorn, and the Scots thistle as national symbols.

Vibrant silk and gold threads on velvet heightened the luxuriance of attire and increased its worth, both as a symbol of royalty and as a trade commodity, such as the patchwork silk kimonos favored by Japanese warlord Uesugi Kenshin. Stumpwork increased texture by stitching wire to the foundation material for greater three-dimensional effect. The application of sixteenth-century Hungarian point or bargello outlined arches, diamonds, medallions, or flames in wool needlepoint on canvas or other foundation fabric for bandoleros, handbags, and quilts.

Italian needleworkers also revived the ancient Persian art of Hardanger, a white monochrome embroidery involving counted threads and drawn or pulled threads. The method yielded a compact lacy surface also known as needleweaving. After Hardanger work traveled to Great Britain and Scandinavia aboard trading vessels, Danes, Dutch, Norwegians, and Scots valued the geometric shapes for blouses and aprons in their national costumes.

The seventeenth century produced artistic variances in embroidery, such as Russian *kaitag,* which reclaimed Ottoman designs for cradle cloths, shrouds, and wedding dresses. Punjabi, Pakistani, and Irani needleworkers enhanced *zardozi,* a royal embellishment in silver and gold thread with metal stars and wires.

In 1603, the court of James I of England encouraged fanciful scrollery, leaves, animals, the tree of life, and thistles in needlework known as Jacobean embroidery, a style based on Asian *suzani.* In 1628, Louis XIII of France restricted superfluous finery, claiming gold embroidery, ribbon, and metallic thread as the embellishment of nobles and royalty alone.

To the east, seventeenth-century Muslim art elevated embroidery for the court and home. Workers at Cairo, Damascus, and Istanbul sold tunics, robes, handkerchiefs, scarves, uniforms, slippers, and shoes made to order for individual clients to indicate prominence and classic taste.

In the North American colonies, New England women at dame schools and Ursuline sisters at convents in Quebec taught girls religious faith, citizenship, and independence by assigning needlework projects that incorporated wise sayings and scripture as well as family trees. In addition to rural styles, women purchased fine needlepoint and whitework from Boston, which elevated standards for color, material, and motif. Novelist Nathaniel Hawthorne captured the pride of the embroiderer in the character of Hester Prynne, protagonist of *The Scarlet Letter* (1850), in which a fallen woman in the Massachusetts Colony earns a living for herself and her daughter by embroidering and monogramming collars, cuffs, gloves, and shrouds.

Industrial Embroidery

Automated needlework in the 1900s simulated tufted candlewicking, smocking, trapunto, hemstitch and buttonhole, matelassé, damask, or satin stitch, the standard fill-in for outlined figures such as ribbons, petals, vines, and leaves expressed with running stitches. For shading, the embroiderer used brick stitches to insert deeper or lighter hues of the same color in half stitches. A more difficult stitchery, *broderie Anglaise* (English embroidery) or cutwork involved lacy patterns in buttonhole stitch and the trimming of centers with sharp scissors.

Embroidery skills served a variety of practical purposes. In 1825, Quaker teacher Johanna Carter formed a workshop in Montmellick, Ireland, to teach girls a salable skill by embroidering white oak leaves, fern, blackberries, ivy, and shamrocks on white cotton cloth in thick matte cotton yarn for fringed, scalloped, and knotted nightdresses, bags, and handkerchiefs. For patching and tears, Japanese *sashiko,* a reinforcing running stitch, developed into a decorative contrast of red thread against indigo cloth. In the 1840s, Berlin wool work applied worsted (or twisted) wool needlepoint to canvas in contrasting colors to give a three-dimensional look to purses and slippers.

In England, two types of needleworkers influenced style and method. For some 3 million female outworkers, commercial and custom stitchery provided a livelihood or supplemented other income. For hobbyists, embroidery resulted in a satisfying domestic achievement for costume and exhibit. Described in *The Englishwoman's Domestic Magazine,* the Berlin style in wool work attracted women who had the leisure and funds to explore new fashions in embroidery. In the 1880s, the fad for crazy quilts encouraged embroiders to connect scraps of varied fabrics to appliqué, bind, and piece lengths to tunics, skirts, sashes, and vests.

In the mid-twentieth century, François Lesage at Michonet supplied embroidery to designer Cristóbal Balenciaga. Lesage remained up to date with new fabrics and technology, including hot melt adhesives, catalytic evaporation, holograms, and embroidery employing resins, metal, rock crystal, feathers, shells, cellophane, and thermoplastic film.

See also: Appliqué; Lace and Tatting; Monogramming.

Further Reading

Brick, Cindy, and Nancy Kirk. *Crazy Quilts: History, Techniques, Embroidery Motifs.* St. Paul, MN: Voyageur, 2011.

Cluckie, Linda. *The Rise and Fall of Art Needlework: Its Socio-Economic and Cultural Aspects.* Bury St. Edmunds, UK: Arena, 2008.

Leslie, Catherine Amoroso. *Needlework Through History: An Encyclopedia.* Westport, CT: Greenwood, 2007.

Synge, Lanto. *Art of Embroidery: A History of Art and Design.* Woodbridge, UK: Antique Collectors' Club, 2000.

Equestrian Attire

Since the taming of the horse around 4500 B.C.E., riders have outfitted themselves in ensembles that combined durability, comfort, and protection. After 2330 B.C.E., Assyrian charioteers encased their lower legs with knee-high boots. Equestrian tunics for Arabians and Sumerians remained short to accommodate a sword belt. On forays into China after 1200 B.C.E., Turkish Huns chose tight felt jackets and tall boots for cross-country travel and bow hunting.

Early Riding Garb

For Greek riders after 500 B.C.E., the short tunic fastened only on the left shoulder for travel, crafts, fishing, and punting. Late in the Roman Empire, the increase in foreign mercenaries introduced the Coptic shirt-like tunic with woven roundels. Two-part Germanic dress—the *dalmatica* (wide-sleeved tunic) and *braccae* (trousers)—became the common riding outfit for men living in northwestern Europe and along the Danube.

In the Middle Ages, central Asian nomads stitched soft-skin ankle boots for riding. Both men and women rode astride for sport, pleasure, and travel. In northwest India and present-day Pakistan, riders evolved bias-cut flared *salwar* pants, with leather-reinforced seats and tight calves and ankles, worn with upturned Mojari slippers. Farther north, Mongolian men adapted heeled riding shoes for speed and competitive equitation.

Around 590 in the Sassanian Empire, Queen Shirin, riding her horse Gulgun (Rosie), played *chaugan* (polo) in loose robes in competition against King Khosrau II Parviz and his Persian nobles. For horseback processions in Constantinople, Byzantine males shielded their garments with the *scaramangion,* a lightweight Persian-style sports coat reaching to the mid-thigh.

By the 900s, royal statutes prohibited the coat for use by Byzantine commoners. Only imperial males appeared in scaramangia for parades, often under scarlet short cloaks for brisk or wet weather. After the cordwainers' (shoemakers') guild organized shoe crafting in 1000, buyers could choose from buckled galoshes or overshoes and thigh-high strapped or buckled heuse riding boots, a boon to the hunter and traveler. The cavalry of Genghis Khan completed riding attire with peaked hats surrounded by thick fur ruffs.

Around 1350, horsemen and servants wore a short almuce (fur hood) to warm the body while freeing the arms and shoulders for pleasure riding and hunting. Taboos against women on horseback spread false notions that riding threatened virginity, conception, and childbirth. Invalidating that gender myth, Geoffrey Chaucer's *Prologue to the Canterbury Tales* (1385) pictured the Wife of Bath in a spurred riding costume that included a whip. In 1392, Anne of Bohemia, the first wife of Richard II, introduced a compromise—the sidesaddle, an awkward seat that allowed women to drape their legs and long riding skirts to one side.

In the 1400s, the Armenian, Georgian, and Ottoman or Seljuk Turk caftan opened down the front to facilitate horseback maneuvers. To feminize Burgundian riding ensembles, Countess Isabelle de Croye embroidered a kerchief with her colors, blue and silver, which also marked her plumed riding cap. In the 1500s, heels and soles for shoes set the style of the flat-soled, shin-high *borzacchino* (riding boot), which designers tapered at the toe to slip into stirrups.

Fashionable Riders

In the mid-sixteenth century, Western designers introduced the formal female riding habit. Essential to hand and wrist protection, gloves of chamois, doe, kid, stag, or suede took on primary importance in equestrienne outfits. Women protected their skin with long cuffs, sometimes perfumed, and loosened rings from constriction through slashes in the finger tubes.

In the 1600s, European soldiers introduced to civilians thick-soled riding boots with collared tops that could be worn up or down. For hawking, mounted men and women chose elbow-length gauntlets with wide cuffs to protect the forearm from sharp talons. Horsemen in the 1640s favored jackboots, which tanners hardened with boiling water and a brush of pitch. Dressier bucket-top jackboots featured decorative buttons, spurs, and lacings over reinforced soft leather. Riders protected costly footwear with gambados, a waterproof covering. Sherryvallies, or over-breeches, buttoned from hip to knee to shield fine breeches from road dust and the odor of horses. For Comanche and Hawaiian women, riding demanded loose tunics with leggings or chaps to protect the legs from thorns.

Queen Henrietta Maria, wife of Charles II of England, and Catherine the Great of Russia popularized the riding habit in court portraits and among ladies-in-waiting. For riding sidesaddle, women chose man-tailored suits with necktie and shirt, plumed cavalier hats with veils, gloves and crops, whalebone whips, and calf-length boots laced up the front with tapered Italian heels. Soutache and military braid edged coats that folded back to display damask waistcoats. During the shooting and horse-racing fads of the mid-1700s, men wore jockey boots or half-boots. Women's habits lost their courtly embellishments and developed plain tailoring from functional cotton nankeen or wool rather than velvet.

The Hessian heeled boot worn by German Hussar mercenaries during the American Revolution preceded the Wellington riding and hunting boot; at a V-shaped notch at the knee, a gold tassel adorned the all-black leather below men's pantaloons. The Russian military abandoned powdered wigs and braided queues in the 1780s. On horseback, riders controlled hair from blowing by fastening with a buckle or tying the Ramillies wig with a large bow to the pigtail at the nape and a smaller bow below it. Spanish riders wore high-collared riding boots and mid-thigh length coats with tails that turned back at the vent to reveal leather lining. Women chose knee-length half-boots for riding and driving and pulled them on with hooks. Slipper stirrups with stitched toe caps and velvet linings provided comfort for ladies and children in the saddle.

From 1804 to 1810, the Napoleonic Empire restored powdered wigs for horsemen, who completed their outfits with high-collared frock coats and a top hat. Women applied the fashionable Empire line to habits with double or triple collars or topped petticoats with redingotes trimmed in military braid.

Late in the Regency period (1811–1837), a voluminous riding habit for women, featuring a frilled blouse and balloon sleeves and topped with a tasseled tam, seized the fashion world. A short spencer (riding jacket) displayed a neck ruff and ample bow. At the beginning of the Victorian era, a slimmer sleeve replaced puffed shapes. Tailored jackets acquired peplums that emphasized the slim waist above stirrup pants. The veiled hat tilted toward the face at a rakish angle.

Civilian men tended to own two types of footwear, sewn shoes for dress and pegged boots for work, hunting, and horseback riding. For British colonials in India, sportsmen preferred cloth boots to leather because of their elasticity.

In the 1860s, elegant British equestriennes favored stand-up collars and leather gauntlets, soft wrist-length gloves that arrived on the market in colors to match plaid double-breasted outfits featuring open-sided apron skirts over riding pants and ample peplums. Hats swathed in chiffon softened the masculinity of high crowns over neat chignons, which controlled long hair during brisk canters. Lace collars, feathered snap-brim hats, and scalloped boots completed a similar ensemble for girls. Skirts covered the entire leg and stirrup for maximum propriety in the saddle.

In the 1880s, manufacturing techniques forced skilled makers of riding and paddock boots out of business. Empress Elizabeth of Austria, wife of Franz Joseph I, promoted riding and hunting as exercise, popularizing the tightly buttoned boned bodice over a leather split-busk corset and skirts with an apron drape that enhanced the hourglass figure.

By the Belle Époque (late 1871–1914), the Englishwoman's riding jacket took on a chic hip length and leg-of-mutton sleeves, which emphasized correct posture during rides in Hyde Park. Edwardian-era riding outfits maintained the long lines of the 1890s over a flexible riding corset. A Melton cloth skirt unbuttoned for ease of mounting and dismounting. French equestriennes preferred the short-tail jacket to the English button tails.

In the 1890s, Pratap Singh, a British Indian military officer, introduced jodhpurs to the English, who added goatskin or sheepskin half-chaps. Irishwomen wore safety skirts that wrapped in the back or leather-seated breeches. Knee pockets on riding skirts gave access to handkerchiefs.

In 1872, Isabella Bird, a member of the Long Rider Guild and traveler of Australia, Japan, Hawaii, North America, Persia, and Tibet, adopted a unisex outfit consisting of vest, duster, breeches, and heeled boots for riding "man-fashion." In Miles City, Montana, English photographer Evelyn Cameron risked local outrage and arrest in 1895 by riding into town astride in a split skirt. Two years later, six female rodeo contestants in Havre, Montana, created comfortable attire out of pants, tops, and the high-heeled boots favored by cowboys and bicyclists.

Twentieth-century English hunting attire for men took on elements of a uniform with top hats, short crops, red split-tail jackets, and buff pants worn with smartly polished black boots. During the demise of the sidesaddle, designers of women's habits in New York and Washington, D.C., developed velvet collars, diagonal buttoning, box-pleated peplums, and princess lines to soften man-tailored jackets. Colors replicated men's apparel with red jackets and black top hats veiled in buff or gray to match buttoned riding skirts and gloves.

In 1910, long rider and sharpshooter Nan Aspinwall galloped from San Francisco to New York in split skirts, a functional garb she defended with her six-gun. In the 1920s, female riders adopted plain, single-button jackets in summer-weight gabardine, breeches with gaiters, and bowler hats. The cutaway coat introduced in the 1930s retained female elegance and dignity for dressage and jumping.

In the 1950s, Queen Elizabeth II maintained a military air, riding in a black skirt and red blazer, trimmed with gold piping, braided sash, and long buttoned cuffs, and complemented by a cockaded bonnet. Into the 2000s, equestrian ensembles retained a tight fit in short jackets, form-fitting breeches, and helmets.

See also: American Western Clothing; Boots.

Further Reading

Cumming, Valerie, C.W. Cunnington, and P.E. Cunnington. *The Dictionary of Fashion History.* New York: Bloomsbury, 2010.

Marshall, Amelia Sue, and Terry L. Tobey. *Oakland's Equestrian Heritage.* Charleston, SC: Arcadia, 2008.

Slaughter, Jane R. *The Woman Equestrian.* Terre Haute, IN: Wish, 2003.

Erté (1892–1990)

A Russo-Gallic influence on twentieth-century costume, jewelry, magazine illustration, and theatrical design, Erté earned renown as the "Father of Art Deco."

A native of St. Petersburg, Russia, he was born Romain de Tirtoff on November 23, 1892, to a prestigious military family. At age five, he designed a gown for his mother, Natalia Mikhailova. The State Hermitage Museum in his native city displayed Egyptian, Greek, Hindu, Byzantine, Chinese, Arabian, and Persian miniatures that he viewed as a boy, influencing his extravagant style. At age 15, while living in Paris, he came under the spell of radical illustrator Aubrey Beardsley and considered a career in dance after viewing impresario Sergei Diaghilev's Ballet Russe. To separate his artistry from the naval career of his father, fleet admiral Pyotr Ivanovich Tirtoff, the designer turned the French pronunciation of his initials into Erté.

Until age 20, Erté studied art at the Académie Julian and the École des Beaux-Arts in Paris and dedicated himself to the cult of beauty. He mastered flowing, practical dress and kimono design under couturier Paul Poiret of the House of Worth and published sketches of curvilinear females in the Russian magazine *Damsky Mir* and the slick Parisian magazine *La Gazette du Bon Ton.* Under the influence of the art nouveau of Gustav Klimt, Alphonse Mucha, and René Lalique, Erté developed expertise at draping eyelet lace, cording, tricot, moiré, silk jersey, satin, chiffon, chinchilla, chamois, lamé, and velvet decked with medallions, guipure (cut-out) lace, and glyphs drawn from classic art.

Erté's unified outfits reflected a vivid imagination and a flair for playacting with clothes. Flamboyant details—Chinese buttons, tasseled picture hats, oversized ruffs, faille bags, fur linings, suede bootlets—set the female form as the centerpiece of the fashion world.

His exotic drawings of sinuous, elongated female forms stressed headdresses and wigs, panniers, trains, draped sleeves, dark eye makeup, and body decor—veils, rings and armlets, fans, tassels, stoles, and parasols—as well as artificial wings and fish and tiger tails. For inspiration, he studied gypsies, harem girls, odalisques, the Three Graces, angels, vamps, and equestriennes and posed female shapes as models of indifference, sadness, mystery, mysticism, and jealousy. His palette favored gilded garments in bold blues, black, purples, and flame red to depict signs of the zodiac, the four seasons, letters of the alphabet, and the Seven Deadly Sins. Romanticized costumes for tartar chiefs, Prince Charming, Scaramouche, Moses, Pierrot, Arlecchino, and King Balthasar retained the bold shades of his female garments as well as paisleys and feathers on turbans and flowing sleeves, cloaks, masks, and trains.

At age 23, Erté established his style in costumes for the Casino de Paris and the Bal Tabarin and sketches for *Cosmopolitan, Harper's Bazaar, Illustrated London News, Ladies' Home Journal,* and *Vogue.* His cover art exemplified art deco lines in furs, feathers, harem dresses, negligees, muffs, snoods, wimples, and beads at once fanciful and historic. He produced period ensembles for the classic characters Aphrodite, Hera, Medea, Cleopatra, Juliet, Madame Butterfly, and Delilah and costumes for dancer Mata Hari, ballerina Anna Pavlova, and actors Lillian Gish and Sarah Bernhardt.

Erté's style reached the masses in oriental stage settings and character dress. In 1923, he began costuming dancers for the Ziegfeld Follies and contributed designs to the Folies Bergère, George White's Scandals, the Chicago Opera Company, Radio City Music Hall, and the films *Ben-Hur* (1925), *The Mystic* (1925), and *Dance Madness* (1926). His collective costuming assembled characters in coordinated groupings, a stylistic unity obvious in the horse race scene in *My Fair Lady* (1964). Erté's unique female fashion enjoyed a revival in the 1960s with dramatic androgyny. Shortly before his death in Paris on April 21, 1990, from kidney disease, he published *My Life, My Art: An Autobiography* (1989).

French critic Roland Barthes honored Erté as an inventor of the modern woman. By stylizing the robust womanly physique and hair in high gloss, Erté abstracted and celebrated the princess silhouette, a model of femininity and self-willed figuration emerging from the suffrage movement. His rhapsodic designs continued to shape fashion and theatrical costuming in France, Great Britain, Japan, and the United States. Erté's art has survived as well in paper dolls and coloring books, graphics and stationery, and museum exhibits in London, Paris, Tokyo, New York, and Washington, D.C.

See also: Art Nouveau and Art Deco Fashion; Costume Design, Theater; Orientalism.

Further Reading

Fischer, Lucy. *Designing Women: Cinema, Art Deco, and the Female Form.* New York: Columbia University Press, 2003.

Spencer, Charles. *Erté.* New York: Three Rivers Press, 1986.

Tibbetts, Jean. *Erté.* London, UK: Grange, 1997.

Vassiliev, Alexandre. *Beauty in Exile: The Artists, Models, and Nobility Who Fled the Russian Revolution and Influenced the World of Fashion.* New York: Harry N. Abrams, 2000.

Esquire

An American magazine published by Hearst Corporation and devoted to men's grooming, style, and lifestyle, *Esquire* has offered wardrobe insights to the affluent since the Great Depression. Designed in 1932 by media mogul Arnold Gingrich, the deluxe quarterly began on October 15, 1933, under a courtesy title or honorific introduced in the 1300s. *Esquire*'s first 5,000 copies sold out immediately, disseminating the disclaimer that it had no intention of becoming a "primer for fops." Marketers created opportunities for male cover models and body builders Eugen Sandow, Bernarr Macfadden, and Tony Sansone.

The focus of "Eskie" reflected male tastes, such as checked pants and vests in 1934, blue dungarees and trout-fishing boots in 1935, the double-breasted striped suit in 1937, the homburg hat and Windsor knot in 1942, and the Eisenhower jacket in 1945. Subsequent photography pictured the corduroy sport jacket, silk shantung dinner jacket, kneesocks, monogrammed shirts, and fur-collared trench coat. Under graphic designer George Lois in *Esquire*'s heyday during the 1960s and 1970s, pop culture figured in brief takes on the Nehru collar, Mao suits, and the mod styles of British rock bands. No-no's for the refined male—the ascot, wedgies, boxer shorts, unshined shoes, and bold plaid suits—separated sophisticates from rubes.

In addition to "Vargas Girl" pin-ups (painted by Alberto Vargas), magazine text has included male-dominant fiction by Ernest Hemingway, Raymond Carver, Tim O'Brien, and Norman Mailer and the cartoons of Ben Shahn. Cover art has featured a variety of male culture icons, from Robert De Niro, Bill Clinton, Clint Eastwood, and Arnold Schwarzenegger in suits and ties to George Clooney in rolled cuffs, Woody Harrelson in a porkpie hat, and Bruce Willis, Daniel Craig, and Tom Cruise in black T-shirts. Articles have covered leisurewear for golf and sailing, suits for graduate classes, the suave black turtleneck, and the best- and worst-dressed men at the Academy Awards.

Publication of a hardcover compendium, *Esquire's Encyclopedia of 20th Century Men's Fashions* (1974), brought together overviews from years of magazine surveys. Under David M. Granger's editorial control since 1997, *Esquire* began publishing the *Big Black Book*, a single-issue men's style guide issued twice annually, in spring/summer and fall/winter. Pitched to the "successful man," the *Big Black Book* offers a seasonal manual on clothes, accessories, dating, travel, cocktails, and living well.

Esquire regularly warns the American adult male against sophomoric choices and behaviors best left at the fraternity house. Other features—Dubious Achievement Award, Sexiest Woman Alive, parodies of notables, illustrations by Roberto Parada—contribute to *Esquire*'s popularity. In 2011, the glossy received the National Magazine Award for features, profiles, and leisure interests. In 2012, *Esquire* had a circulation of nearly 711,000.

Recent commentary, such as a history of the bikini, took on a bemused air in reporting on women's revealing swimwear, from the Rudi Gernreich monokini and Farah Fawcett in an unzipped one-piece to Sacha Baron Cohen in a mankini. Maverick styles—deconstructed jackets, suede wing tips, desert boots, white jeans—set the fashion risk-taker apart from conservatives in their tried and true.

See also: Formal Attire, Male; Leisure Wear.

Further Reading

Editors of *Esquire* Magazine. *Esquire, The Handbook of Style: A Man's Guide to Looking Good.* New York: Hearst, 2009.

Esquire. www.esquire.com

McNeil, Peter, and Vicki Karaminas, eds. *The Men's Fashion Reader.* New York: Bloomsbury, 2009.

Ethnic and National Dress

The racial and tribal designation of apparel as national dress epitomizes the need of humankind for garments, hairstyles, and accessories that signify place and group solidarity. From 500 B.C.E., Greek and Roman citizens clung to the wool Doric chiton and toga over a tunic as the uniform of male citizens. When Roman imperialism swept through North Africa, men in the Atlas Mountains of Algeria, Morocco, and Tunisia adapted the Roman traveler's cloak into a national unfitted mantle, the djellaba or burnoose, a parallel of the West African *boubou* (loose gown).

By 300 B.C.E., Korean folk costume introduced the high waistline of the unisex *hanbok,* a short jacket worn over trousers or a wraparound skirt. Padding in winter ensured warmth without altering the silhouette. The feet stayed comfortable in *beoseon,* anklet hose filled with fiber and tied above the anklebones. By 960 C.E., Chinese clothiers profited from national dress in similar padded jackets and pants stuffed with raw silk threads. Women feminized the unisex look with jeweled hair ornaments and embellished sashes.

Medieval styles and materials expressed localized culture, particularly the *szür* or *szür* (mantle) of the Magyars, Malaysian batik, and the bronze, copper, and tin neck rings and earrings popular among Ukrainians. Czech and Slovakian formal apparel for women involved a full ensemble consisting of a tall circular headdress above a white headcloth, collared blouse, vest, short skirt, and black boots. Stitchery identified the ethnic background of clothiers, as with the appliquéd elm barkcloth of the Ainu, native Japanese hunter-gatherers. According to Arab fashion writer Abu Muhammad al-Washsha, author of *Kitab al-zarf wa'l-zurafa'* (*Book on Elegance and Elegant People,* ca. 930), gold and silver stitchery and silk roundels turned Syria's linen cloaks into works of art.

For texture on pants, wrap skirts, and aprons, Romanian needleworkers applied couching by stitching diagonally over yarn. The *bokhara* couching of the Sogdiana (Iranians) created a similar effect by holding yarn in place with small cross-stitches on turbans and caftans. In Lower Saxony and Switzerland around 1250, monochrome Romanesque wedding attire, bags, infant garments, and handkerchiefs in *opus teutonicum* (German work) displayed white linen thread on white linen, sometimes accented in blue or brown, a contrast to the vivid colors of Iberian couching in gold cording. Late in the century, Italians developed trapunto, embroidered channels stuffed with padding along stand-up collars and cuffs.

Asian innovations turned domestic garments into keepsakes. In the late 1300s, embroiderers in Korea developed stitchery that elevated the hanbok to high art. A needlework tradition of Central Asia and the Caucasus employed *suzani,* an embroidery technique of couching cotton or silk on slippers, skirts, ritual attire, and lap robes. Caravans transported the elegant needlework from Georgian, Turkish, and Armenian clothiers over the Silk Road to Eastern Europe.

Symbolic Expression

By the 1400s, artistic needlework acquired ethnic and religious distinctions, as with the outlining of scriptural phrases on the hem of a nun's veil in Catholic lands. In Arabia, Bahrain, Kuwait, Oman, and Yemen, women routinely embellished the *niqab* (veil or mask), a traditional face cover reaching to the waist, with silk embroidery and border art. At Batavia and Singapore, Balinese women wore the customary East Asian *kebaya,* a wrap skirt paired with round-necked tunic and wrist-length sleeves.

The sixteenth-century sea trade introduced Hardanger, a monochromatic white stitchery invented in classical Persia. Carried by Italian sailors to Scandinavia and Great Britain, the embroidery found eager buyers. As a result of adaptation to local themes, Hardanger edging adorned the aprons and blouses of traditional Dutch, Danish, Norwegian, and Scots national dress. In Mexico, similar bicultural commerce in fabric and ribbon introduced mestizas and indigenous Mexicans to beribboned *china poblana* skirts and petticoats. After independence, women plaited their hair and looped braids to their ears with patriotic green, red, and white ties.

In rural Denmark after 1627, men, women,

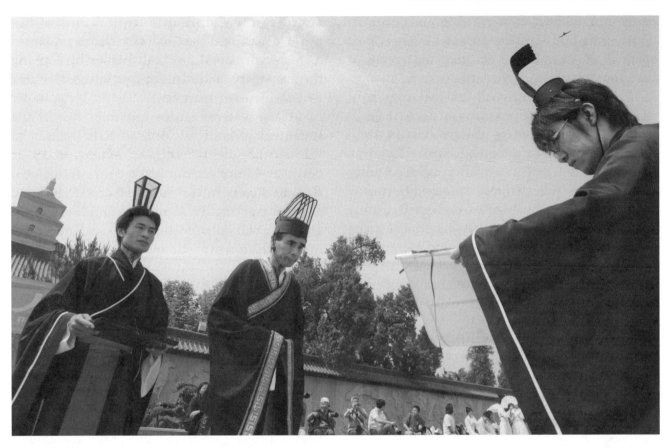

Young men in medieval Han Chinese costume participate in a coming-of-age ceremony in 2009. The event promoted the Hanfu cultural revival, a movement to reintroduce traditional Han style, banned under the Manchu Qing dynasty in 1644 *(China Photos/Getty Images)*

and babies exhibited a damask pattern on the *nattrøje,* a cropped, square-necked undershirt or jacket for any time of day. Knitters applied stockinette stitches at the hem to create a contoured silhouette. Because of comfortable underarm gussets, the nattrøje fit under a bodice or vest as a part of the Danish national costume.

A Tibetan lama, Shabdrung Ngawang Namgyal, the unifier of Bhutan after 1637, codified the *Driglam Namzha* (system of rules), which established a Bhutanese dress standard called *gho.* Men fastened their cotton or wool knee-length robes with a cloth belt. For visits to temples, worshippers crossed the torso from left shoulder to right hip with a white sash or silk scarf. Women topped their tunics with a jacket and silk rectangular scarf or, for formal occasions, an embroidered shoulder sash.

In Spain, men wore bolero jackets with sombreros. Ladies of quality cloaked head and ensemble in the black silk mantilla. Reaching to the hem, the dramatic veil accentuated the national costume and proclaimed reverence for Catholicism. At Valencia in the 1700s, Spanish women not only retained the black veil of their national costume but stretched it over a *peineta* (comb) or atifet (wire frame) to arch above both sides of the skull into a prominent headdress. With less pomp, Welsh women donned fringed flannel shawls topped with black hats.

Nationalism and Politics

Nineteenth-century European nationalism promoted the adoption and display of preindustrial folk dress, as with Scots tartans, blousy Breton knee breeches, Argentine combs, and Celtic symbols stitched on Irish garments. In the Tyrol, Bavarian and Austrian seamstresses made dirndl skirts and engineered Alpine sweaters with a vining stitch that marked female folk costume. By the late 1850s, needleworkers in Greenland incorporated the Icelandic and Norwegian round-yoked sweater into the island's national attire. The circular shoulder design reached across the chest and down the upper arm. In 1883, Cretan and Greek women adapted waistbands and embroidered aprons as coverings for ornate petticoats.

Colonization threatened national self-image through the revision of everyday attire in far-flung locations. French control of Cambodia in 1863 raised opposition to the unisex *sampot* (culotte), which implied gender equality among indigenous Khmer. When Britain colonized Burma on January 1, 1886, authorities inveighed against unisex dressing in long skirts, functional attire that equalized native Pyu, Mon, and Pali women with men. The visual contrast between national dress on citizens and Western uniforms on British authorities stated without words the transfer of power to Europeans.

Globally, power dressing involved the choice of significant apparel as a political statement. In the 1920s, Filipina suffragists chose the butterfly-sleeved *terno* (blouse) and *pañuelo* (full skirt) as a nonthreatening costume for demanding the vote. Korean feminists adopted the same strategy of dressing in the traditional hanbok to secure support for women's rights.

The manipulation of national costume failed for Germany's Nazi Party, which attempted a visual gender separation by posing hyper-masculine uniformed soldiers alongside wives romanticized in the stereotypical peasant braids and dirndl skirts. In mainland China after 1945, Jiang Ching, the wife of Mao Zedong, fashioned a national silhouette that purportedly revived a costume from the Tang dynasty of 618. A similar ploy in India linked sympathy for the poor with *khadi,* the homespun cloth used for making flags, and the dhoti, a soft cotton hip wrap. Astute opponents raised protests against corrupt politicians and their manipulation of the electorate.

Global Market

With the globalization of the clothing industry beginning in the late 1960s, tribal ensembles lost majority appeal, especially in the youth market. American couturier Geoffrey Beene softened the male silhouette with jerseys and pullovers paired with denim jeans, a look adopted by U.S. soldiers

on leave in foreign lands. Men in Tanzania, Kenya, Uganda, and the Comoros Islands promoted a cross-continental cultural merger by topping the customary ankle-length *kanzu* (tunic) with a British blazer or sport coat.

Asians teetered on the question of dress as a statement of political ideals. At the request of Filipino president Ferdinand Marcos in 1971, designer Pierre Cardin altered the traditional *Barong Tagalog* (tunic shirt). His modernization entailed tapering the torso, widening the sleeves, removing cuff links, opening the front, and replacing white-on-white stitchery with more colorful embroidery.

In 1978, post-Mao China abandoned the drab Mao jacket and pants, unofficial uniform of the proletarian revolution. As the Communist regime embraced free-market economics and opened the nation to foreign influences, Chinese teens adopted Western ideals of comfort and style in denim and disco colors. In 1989, freedom fighter Aung San Suu Kyi, leader of the pro-democracy movement in Burma, began 21 years of house arrest in the traditional tubular sarong, expressing symbolic support for peasant freedoms. To signal hope to supporters, she adorned her hair with fresh flowers.

As television and film broadcast Western styles worldwide, local and media defenders of folk custom blamed blue jeans, message T-shirts, and running shoes for eroding centuries-old costume and decorum. Because of their ubiquity and tight fit, jeans earned the disapproval of conservative Muslims, especially for married women. Nonetheless, denim remains the most common unisex attire worldwide, not least because of its comfort. Designers have further vitiated traditional national dress by modernizing customary ensembles, as with Sydney native Michael Lo Sordo's refashioning of the Australian outback look and Vietnamese couturier Duc Hung's garnishing of the *ao dai* (tunic dress) with beading and sheer panels.

See also: Clan Attire; Globalization; Ritual Garments; Symbolic Colors, Patterns, and Motifs.

Further Reading

Geoffrey-Schneiter, Berenice. *Ethnic Style: History and Fashion.* New York: Assouline, 2001.

Kennett, Frances. *Ethnic Dress: A Comprehensive Guide to the Folk Costume of the World.* New York: Facts on File, 1995.

Parker, Mary S. *The Folkwear Book of Ethnic Clothing: Easy Ways to Sew & Embellish Fabulous Garments from Around the World.* New York: Lark, 2002.

Roces, Mina, and Louise P. Edwards, eds. *The Politics of Dress in Asia and the Americas.* Portland, OR: Sussex Academic, 2007.

Eton Style

A standard of unisex dress and comportment named for the independent boarding school near Windsor in south-central England, Eton style defined the grooming of elite English male scholars from the end of the fifteenth century. From its founding in 1440 by King Henry VI, Eton College schooled royal and aristocratic teens. It later employed Aldous Huxley as a French teacher and educated Prime Minister William Pitt, novelist George Orwell, poet Percy Bysshe Shelley, chemist Robert Boyle, economist John Maynard Keynes, King Rama VII of Siam, and William and Harry, the sons of Prince Charles and Diana, Princess of Wales. Fashion trendsetter Beau Brummell earned credit for passing on the Eton dress code to adult males in the early 1800s and, eventually, adult females.

Eighteenth-century Eton gained a reputation for elite male dress in blue or red morning dress coat cut just over the hip line. The youngest Etonians appeared in wide cambric turn-down collars, short nankeen pants, and white stockings with low shoes. Carefully plotted, the Eton jacket exhibited tight uncuffed sleeves seamed to the thumb and complemented a single-breasted vest, detachable fold-down collar, and cashmere pinstriped pants, called "spongebags" for duplicating the pattern on a traveler's shaving kit.

Gradually, the appendages of the swallowtail coat disappeared as the Eton jacket became a morning coat. Yellow trousers became baggier, more like workmen's pants. Cuffless sleeves and a vest topped gray pants. In 1798, schoolchildren adopted the short Eton coat with hemline cut straight across over white canvas or duck knee pants strapped to the insteps of tasseled Hessian boots.

In 1810, members of the Eton Society set themselves apart from the rest of the school population with stick-up collars, double-breasted vests—colored by day and white at night—with patent leather shoes and a furled umbrella. The dress code required that students turn down their collars over greatcoats. Summer wear added blazers and panama hats. In 1820, the student body adopted black as the preferred color of the jacket and tie over trousers rather than knickers.

During the Victorian age, the British emulated Eton's dress code for school uniforms and boys' dress outfits. Most required wide cravats, stiff white collars with broad points, and a lined Eton jacket with braid, flap pockets, and wide lapels left unbuttoned over the vest. Tailors reported that the Eton style adapted to all shapes and sizes of boys over a period of one year's growth. A cropped hairstyle created a boyish air of innocence and rigor.

In the 1880s, English and American women favored the Eton jacket, a popular tailored coat that remained in vogue into the 1910s. The American fashion monthly *Delineator* pictured a trim, boyish coat with lapels open and extended to the waist, or in a feminine version, fastened with 10 tiny buttons. Four waistline darts followed the contour of the torso. Tab trim and braided details on lapels and cuffs lent a military air.

Twentieth-century Eton inculcated habits of neatness and hygiene, from a knotted striped tie to shined shoes. In 1914, Prince Henry, son of King George V and Queen Mary, attended class in a regulation jacket, vest, tie, and white shirt over flannel trousers and high-gloss lace-up shoes. His silk top hat, scorned as a "chimney pot," derived from the cone hats of 1600 and beaver hats of the 1800s.

In the 1920s, the severely masculine "Eton crop" hairstyle became the fad with *la maschietta* (the European tomboy or flapper). A trendsetter in Paris, African American dancer Josephine Baker chose the head-hugging shingled or bobbed haircut with fishhooks (spit curls) as a statement of rebellion against American racism. After World War II, the straw boater replaced Eton's black topper.

At Eton today, King's Scholars model gentlemanly dress in tailcoat and black gown with surplice. From a starched white stock collar, students graduate to bow tie and winged collar, a holdover from clerical and academic band collars of the late Middle Ages. Star students in the sixth form earn silver vest buttons. House captains distinguish themselves in mottled gray vests. Etonians appear in top hat and cane only for formal dress-up.

See also: Brummell, Beau; School Attire.

Further Reading

Danziger, Danny. *Eton Voices: Interviews.* New York: Viking, 1989.

Kelly, Ian. *Beau Brummell: The Ultimate Dandy.* London: Hodder & Stoughton, 2005.

Eyeglasses

The addition of fashionable eyeglasses to facial adornment supplies refraction to correct vision, protection from debris, a shield against intense light, and high style to the face. As early as the twenty-third century B.C.E., the Chinese emperor Yao used polished crystal for stargazing. Additional archaeological finds at Knossos, Cyprus, Ephesus, Anatolia, Nineveh, Tyre, and Troy attest to the ancient use of rock crystals as short-focus enhancers of vision.

Dating to 500 B.C.E. in Assyria and Egypt, corrective crystals magnified viewing material, an idea the Roman dramatist Seneca advanced with a water globe. After 54 C.E., the Roman emperor Nero viewed sporting events through a concave emerald, the forerunner of the reading stone, a glass magnifier placed over reading material. The emperor may have found the green color soothing during a sunny day of watching gladiators in the arena.

Medieval vision correction owed its theory to the "Father of Modern Optics," Alhazen, an Iraqi scientist trained at Basra and Baghdad and practicing primarily in Cairo. He introduced the principles of magnification and refraction in the encyclopedic *Kitab al-Manazir* (*Book of Optics,* 1021). Following the translation of Alhazen's concepts into Latin, English scientist and philosopher Roger Bacon in 1267 developed convex lenses into magnifying glasses for people with myopia (nearsightedness).

Scientific theory undergirded medieval advances in utilitarian invention, including applications of optic laws. Venetian opticians developed reading glasses in a frame that the user held to the eyes. In the 1100s, Chinese opticians introduced smoked quartz panes as sunglasses.

First Spectacles

A Dominican monk, Giordano da Pisa, invented *occhiali* (eyeglasses) in Tuscany in 1286 and passed the concept on to optician Alessandro della Spina, an altruistic monk at St. Catherine's Monastery in Pisa. Within 15 years, an optical guild marketed convex eyeglasses made by Venetian glass blowers as a benefit to the needy and elderly. At Treviso, Italian frescoes by Tommaso da Modena from the 1350s depicted Dominican monastery copyists in glasses hinged at the center with a pincer.

A late medieval invention, the pince-nez, a unisex form of nose-pinching spectacles, squeezed lenses against the nose bridge and combated far-sightedness. Placement remained secure from the pressure of a hinge or spring clip and cork-padded stabilizers attached to frames of wood, baleen, or steel. When not in use, the spectacles dangled from a neck chain or ribbon tied to a lapel or brooch.

In the mid-fifteenth century, with the rise in print material and geometric perspective in art, demand for eyewear increased. From 1462, the Milanese factories operated by Francesco and Galeazzo Maria Sforza profited from the sale of spectacles. In June 1466, the company ordered 200 pairs of glasses ranked by the wearers' ages to suit diminishing eyesight up to age 70.

At Florence, Medici courtiers, whose hereditary nearsightedness earned remarks in historical biographies, gave eyewear as gifts. A parallel Dutch industry supplied glasses to the English. Crystal lenses in silver or gold frames suited the budgets of ministers, aristocrats, and scholars; laborers bought the cheapest grades of glass in less expensive frames.

After Pope Leo X announced his nearsightedness in 1513, he wore concave glasses for hunting trips, with quartz lenses mounted in leather, bone, or metal frames. Portuguese colonists in Brazil and Spaniards in Argentina exported sea-green beryl and transparent pebble and quartz crystals to Europe and Russia.

Scratch-resistant South American refractors set eyewear trends in Holland, Germany, France, and Iberia during the sixteenth century. Meanwhile, European missionaries introduced eyewear in China, where people chose amber lenses to treat conjunctivitis. The yellow-orange spectacles found favor with hunters and marksmen, who preferred amber for improving vision in fog and mist.

In 1604, German astronomer Johannes Kepler attacked the problem of myopia (nearsightedness) and theorized how a concave lens increases visual acuity. By 1629, England launched its first optics lab in competition with the German spectacles industry. Opticians profited from increasing readership of the first newspaper, the *London Gazette,* in 1665 as well as from the merchandising of tinted lenses, spectacles with springy slit bridges, and pocket spyglasses, miniature telescopes invented by the Dutch. Nuremberg-style spectacles with copper wire frames injected style into accessorized eyewear. Vain users hid their glasses in the hinges of fans and the knobs of walking canes.

Innovation and Style

In eighteenth-century Europe, English optician George Adams debuted the lorgnette, binocular spectacles on an ornate metal, tortoise shell, or mother-of-pearl handle. A forerunner of achromatic (clear) opera glasses, the lorgnette became a tool for the pretentious. The wire-edged "eye ring" or monocle, popularized in Rome by Prussian antiquities collector Philipp von Stosch in the 1720s, tied to the neck with silk ribbon. A faddish accessory in Germany, Austria, and Russia, the threaded monocle dangled down the chest until the user looped it over one ear and straightened the focus in the eye socket. Known as a "quizzer," or quizzing glass, for its use in close inspections, the monocle retained its position in the eye orbit with the aid of a metal spring.

A subsequent advance, *binocles-ciseaux* (scissors glasses), mounted on a Y-shaped stem, supplied binocular distance correction in both round and oval lenses. Around 1727 in Soho, London, optician Edward Scarlett, royal glasses maker for George

II, hinged the first temple pieces that passed from frame to ears. Spiral finials held eyewear in place behind the ear. The French avoided such utilitarian eyewear as bulky, but the Spanish created a glasses fad as a boost to social prominence.

For more complex refraction, perhaps as early as the 1730s, colonial polymath Benjamin Franklin devised bifocals to relieve the need for two pairs of glasses. To combat myopia and hypermetropia (farsightedness), he topped concave with convex refraction in one lens. By the 1790s, American artist Benjamin West profited from Franklin's clever merger of lenses. Late eighteenth-century advances added a second pair of lenses above the brows. The user of super-orbital eyewear could fold down the top lenses for added magnification during meticulous tasks, such as dentistry, engraving, sewing, and watch repair.

Nineteenth-century design applied industrial skills to eyeglass manufacture and solved the problem of fastening pince-nez cords around the head under wigs. The production of flint (leaded) optical glass in 1807 by the Swiss firm of Pierre Louis Guinaud & Sons advanced homogeneity by removing the waviness of soda glass. In 1824, British engineer John Isaac Hawkins advanced Franklin's bifocals to trifocals. Lens specialist George Biddell Airy in 1825 completed work at Trinity College, Cambridge, on correcting astigmatism with cylindrical lenses.

German technology dominated optic breakthroughs. At Philadelphia in 1836, German American inventor Isaac Schnaitman engineered the grinding of distance and reading lenses into double-focus spectacles. Around 1849, German American optician John Jacob Bausch shaped durable frames from vulcanite (hard rubber). Late in the century, French eye surgeon Louis de Wecker strengthened bifocals by fusing lenses. Optics specialist Moritz von Rohr first stabilized vision with spherical lenses developed at Zeiss laboratories in Jena, Germany.

By the early 1900s, the stigma of "four-eyes" eased as injection-molded bioplastic frames became fashionable. The elevation of Theodore Roosevelt to the presidency of the United States in 1901 placed in constant public view a vigorous leader who wore rimless pince-nez. World war ended the appeal of the monocle, which the Allies connected with German eyewear. Thereafter, tortoiseshell and celluloid added style to glasses frames. In 1929 at Woolworths, entrepreneur Sam Foster began marketing Foster Grant sunglasses, the start of a fashion trend.

Since 1938, comic books have linked the horn-rimmed eyewear of Clark Kent with his alternate persona as Superman. Media photographers stressed the prominence of aviator glasses to General Douglas MacArthur, horn-rimmed browline glasses to Malcolm X, the cat-eye look on Marilyn Monroe, Ray-Bans on Dan Aykroyd and John Belushi, and bug-eye shapes to Sophia Loren.

Eyeglass manufacture improved in the mid-twentieth century with the creation of polymer-reinforced glass to reduce breakage and, in 1953, polycarbonate lenses in shatter-resistant safety glasses. The first seamless union of graduated lenses, the work of Irving Rips in 1955 in Torrance, California, reduced the social stigma of obvious multiple grinds in a single lens. Called progressive or varifocal lenses, Rips's invention enabled wearers to focus the eyes and turn the head more normally for improved acuity. The varifocal lens lessened headaches, nausea, and eye fatigue.

In the 1960s, Roger Araujo, a glass engineer for Corning, created photochromic lenses. By bonding polymer film to the eyeglass surface, he reduced the effects of ultraviolet glare, a hardship for the eyes causing squinting and frowning. As transition lens darkened in outdoor light, the photosensitive coating filtered light and sharpened vision. Adaptive glasses became the lens of choice for golfers, race car drivers, and water sports enthusiasts.

In May 2013, Google Glass appended a high-tech side screen to glass frames. Initially priced at $1,500, Google Glass provided the user with access to online newspapers and social networking.

See also: Accessories; Protective and Orthotic Clothing.

Further Reading

Corson, Richard. *Fashions in Eyeglasses: From the Fourteenth Century to the Present Day.* 3rd ed. London: Peter Owen, 2011.

Ilardi, Vincent. *Renaissance Vision from Spectacles to Telescopes.* Philadelphia: American Philosophical Society, 2007.

Segrave, Kerry. *Vision Aids in America: A Social History of Eyewear and Sight Correction.* Jefferson, NC: McFarland, 2011.

Fans, Hand

A natural means of ventilation and self-cooling, the hand fan can also accentuate the personal ensemble. Egyptian fans appeared in a bas-relief from 3200 B.C.E., picturing the Scorpion King and Queen Shesh. Around 2366 B.C.E., Egyptian tomb art honoring Vizier Mereruka of Saqqara connected tall feathered fans with political power. A pair of ostrich fans accompanied King Tutankhamen to the grave in 1352 B.C.E.

After 1350 B.C.E., Assyrians attached horse-hair or vegetable fiber to wood handles to make fly whisks. At Nimrud on the Tigris River after 745 B.C.E., Mesopotamian artistry combined the purpose of the fan and the ritual scepter by gilding the frame and adding heraldic ciphers. To the southeast, in India, fans varied from yak tails to small wood squares or elliptical leaves mounted like flags to the side of the handle, a tool of midwives for cooling the faces of women in childbirth.

During the Roman Republic, matrons adorned dressy outfits with peacock-feathered fans, a female accessory also popular in Greece around 30 B.C.E. Common materials included plantain and lotus leaves and branches of acacia and myrtle. Tomb sculpture at Cumbria in Roman England pictured a *flabellum* (cockade fan), a full circle of pleated material on a handle.

The Asian Fan

In China from 100 B.C.E., both men and women wafted fans of palm or straw leaves or pheasant or peacock feathers, which cooled the face while shielding the eyes. Bamboo montures (frames) and handles kept the crescent, leaf-shaped, or oval fan light but rigid. When not in use, the fan remained tucked under sleeves out of sight. After 220 C.E., gauze and gilding over fine-grained white palm leaves covered fan ribs in Guangdong Province.

The Japanese emulated the technology with rigid silk fans and folding paper and slatted cypress wood fans in the 600s, when inventors joined the ribs with a pin or rivet and then connected them with ribbon or thread to anchor their radiation. The concept passed to Korea, where housewives fluttered fans in the kitchen to encourage flames in the stove. Uses extended to troop commanders, sumo referees, musicians, and Noh players. Monks and priests turned fans into amulets or charms.

After the 690s, Chinese fan painting developed into a decorative art that began with the scraping of the frame to thin it. A century later, mourners included woven bamboo fans in grave goods in the feudal Chu state in southeastern China. Some featured bamboo threads, paper cuts, and oil paper in lunar shapes covered in designs of bells, lanterns, crab apples, gourds, plum and peach blossoms, sunflowers, narcissus, and hearts.

Japanese samurai adapted the war fan from wood, brass, bronze, or iron and lacquered leaves. The shapes, painted on opposite sides with sun and moon, directed signals and provided a harmless-looking dueling weapon for *tessenjutsu* (martial arts). Japanese geishas and Korean court dancers incorporated fan gestures and flirtations in stage performances. Japanese street acrobats and storytellers enhanced their acts with the motions of oversized fans. Aristocrats attached fans to their belts with a clip and used open fans in a court toss game.

In the ninth century, Japanese sumptuary laws limited excessive decoration of cypress strip fans with tassels. After 960, handmade paper, vellum, and silk fans featured artistic paintings, printed scenes, and mottos, verse from poetry competitions, or scriptural sutras in calligraphy. In 1074 and 1124, Japanese and Korean envoys brought fans to China as gifts to the emperor. In Burma, monks used fans as sun shields and fanned their faces to deflect their eyes from the sight of women. In the late 1300s, members of the Ming aristocracy displayed the clan coat of arms on elegant fabric fans attached to sticks of bone, ivory, mica, mother-of-pearl, sandalwood, or tortoise shell.

Medieval Craft and Fashion

In the twelfth century, crusaders brought fans from the Middle East back to Europe. In the 1400s, Italian ladies chose fans of peacock plumes for their luxurious sweep and vivid colors. The Portuguese introduced Asian fan technology to Iberia, where fans became integral props in flamenco dancing. Varied fan leaves featured glittery mica and kid leather with cutout patterns.

Upon her arrival from Italy in 1533 to marry Henry II of France, Catherine de' Medici carried ornate fans as part of her dowry. Sixteenth-century fan makers flourished in England, France, and Holland, where customers bought paper lanterns, parasols, and fans as examples of Asian culture and crafts. In 1550, women's feather fans attached at the waist by a ribbon tied to the jeweled handle. By the 1600s, embroidered and painted fans were popular lovers' gifts and souvenirs.

Queen Elizabeth I owned a variety of feathered, jeweled, and radial folding fans with pompoms. Gradually in the 1630s, the feminine feather fan shrank to one lone feather or a folding fan with ivory or tortoiseshell ribs. After 1675, Chinese court staff elevated long, exquisite fans formed of the tail feathers of birds grouped in elegant patterns as status symbols for royalty and their concubines.

As Protestants emigrated from France in 1685, fan makers established their workshops in more countries. By the 1700s, when accessories attained fashion prominence, elaborate parchment and silk fans bore artistic designs. The East India Company imported lacquer sticks from Amoy and Canton and marketed Chinese folding versions. Automated varieties animated with a wind-up key added a curio to fashion.

Spanish women use folding fans for protection from the sun during the Catholic procession of Corpus Christi. Elaborately painted or lace hand fans are a common accessory in Spanish folk costume and flamenco dancing. *(© Miguel Sotomayor/Flickr/Getty Images)*

Modern Designs

In 1709, British fan makers established their own guild, which fashioned leaves from calico, lace, paper, or chicken or lambskin. The *Spectator* and *Tatler* poked fun at women's addiction to fans. In 1760, a mold made of walnut wood simplified the folding of leaves. The precision work passed to machines in 1859, when Alphonse Baude of Oise, France, mechanized the process.

Late eighteenth-century fan makers employed the broadening V of the brisé fan, made entirely of sticks, and added loops, ribbon, and tassels to the frame. During the Napoleonic era (1799–1815), fans retreated in size to dainty embroidered hand accessories. Victorian fans grew in proportion with hoop skirts from 8- to 20-inch (20- to 51-centimeter) spans and displayed the European fascination with chinoiserie.

Women clipped fans to their sashes and attached pencils for writing memos or messages. Popular uses of fan surfaces included presentation of dance steps, riddles and games, political campaigns, dance and theater programs, menus, maps, season's fashions, and calendars. In the Belle Époque, impressionist painters Edgar Degas, Antoine Watteau, Paul Gauguin, Claude Monet, and Camille Pissarro added their artistry to fans.

In 1914, the House of Worth in Paris exploited the beauty and grandeur of feathers with the feather fan as an accessory for evening gowns. For decades, sandalwood fans were a specialty of factories in Suzhou, China, where artists inscribed images of the Twin Pagodas and the Jade Belt on paper-thin covers. At the Chicago World's Fair of 1933–1934 and in the film *Bolero* (1934), burlesque dancer Sally Rand upended the use of fans to hide shyness, creating the illusion of nude dancing behind a pair of fans made of ostrich feathers 4 feet (1.2 meters) long.

See also: Accessories; Chinese Clothing; Japanese Clothing and Fashion; Korean Clothing and Fashion; Spanish and Portuguese Clothing.

Further Reading

Beaujot, Ariel. *Victorian Fashion Accessories.* New York: Bloomsbury, 2012.

Frédéric, Louis. *Japan Encyclopedia.* Trans. Kathë Roth. Cambridge, MA: Harvard University Press, 2002.

Qian, Gonglin. *Chinese Fans: Artistry and Aesthetics.* San Francisco: Long River, 2004.

Farming Attire

Historically, agrarian and herding apparel has satisfied the working needs and physical comfort of rural peasants. The settling of Mesopotamian nomads on farms after 8000 B.C.E. introduced flax as a viable crop and a source of soft fiber for hip wraps, tunics, headbands, and head wraps. By 6000 B.C.E., Assyrian farmers at Nineveh east of the Tigris River added felted goat hair to materials for loincloths and kilts.

North African farmers of the Maghreb crossbred wild flax around 5000 B.C.E. to supply the linen for simple sleeveless pullovers for men and women. Moroccan farmers covered the head, body, and limbs in softly draped fabrics, the same type worn by Berber herders of Tunisia, Libya, and Mauretania. In Egypt, plowmen along the Nile limited garments to a hip wrap tied at the waist.

In Latin America from 4000 B.C.E., straw hats protected Central American farmers from sunstroke. Around 500 B.C.E., the Zapotec of Oaxaca limited work wear to wrapped kilts and breechcloths. The Nahua of Mexico, El Salvador, Guatemala, Nicaragua, and Panama paired deerhide moccasins with breechcloths and sleeveless bodices for hot, sweaty tilling and reaping. On the Bering Sea, Aleut cultivators and fox farmers on Attu Island and the Pribilofs stitched utilitarian work pants, parkas, and boots from sealskin.

For barnyards and sowing fields at Mount Kenya and Kilimanjaro, fifth-century B.C.E. plainsmen purchased rawhide and leather garments from cattlemen. Low-country West Africans relied on apparel plaited from palm leaves. Around 100 C.E., Central Africans wove their plowing and hoeing outfits from raffia.

First-century farmers in Madagascar advanced to looming jute and flax into field wear. By the year 500, south of Egypt, Nubians tamed flax stalks to supply linen fiber for lightweight work shirts. In the Middle East after 750, Abbasid field workers and camel drivers dressed in cool caftans and tied on leather soles by wrapping cording around the ankles.

Comfort

Farmers made moderate changes to work apparel in the late Middle Ages. In south-central Mexico after 1250, the Toltec added style to loincloths with complex knotting. Fifteenth-century English farmers and laborers layered loose smocks over knit ganseys (shirts) and turtlenecks bought from hand-crafters on Guernsey and Jersey. To soften wool for adding stretch to knits, yarn specialists applied whale oil to fleece. Late in the fifteenth century, unspun lopi fiber from sheep of the Faroe Islands and Iceland increased the warmth of pullovers for blustery, cold-weather labor.

In 1519, Aztec cotton and grain harvesters and sheep shearers dressed in tie-waisted pants and tunics or loose *camisas* (blouses), long skirts, and aprons. Sombreros shielded workers from overheating, the cause of death for Arawak, Carib, Ciboney, Galibi, and Taíno work gangs throughout the Caribbean. Bandannas secured around the face warded off sweat, dust, debris, and the soot and smoke of burning swiddens, plots cultivated by slash-and-burn tactics.

Into the sixteenth century, leaving feet bare remained more common than protecting them with agave or maguey fiber sandals and leather huaraches or moccasins, the footwear of the Pueblo of Arizona and New Mexico. For pulling farm carts with dray animals, workers usually sat astride the lead beast. During produce deliveries through the desert, riders protected their legs from cactus spines with rawhide chaps laced over drawstring breeches. Leather caps over stirrups protected the toes.

Europeans developed a specialty in wood footwear for the farm and barnyard. French peasants imitated the thick Dutch urban *klomp* (clog) with the slimmer Belgian and French *sabot,* a one-piece safety clog used during plowing. Carved wood also covered the whole foot for herding chores and market gardening. The full-fronted shape protected the feet from thorns and animal dung.

For dairy chores, workers shielded leather shoes by pulling on wood pattens (overshoes) with hide straps. Wood heels and toes, like those on the Japanese geta and Korean *namaksin,* elevated the foot out of barnyard runoff and muck. In northern Spain, the Cantabrian version, the *albarca,* featured three legs (a heel at the rear and two at the front) to prevent slipping.

In New World colonies, the first settlers purchased moccasins from the native peoples. Cobbleries made winter boots to sell to rural women and work brogans to fit their husbands. In New France, Canadian women shaped *bavolettes* (sunbonnets) out of linen and pulled the back flap over the neck to prevent sunburn. Acadian men harvested grain in knee breeches veed at the back waist to accommodate bending.

Diversity

In China, agriculture required wrap jackets sashed at the waist over short pants and bare feet. In Southeast Asia, Vietnamese rice farmers chose Mandarin hats and cotton shirts and shorts over bare feet for wading into rice paddies. The Japanese recycled scrap fabric and leather into everyday patchwork jumpers and coats, which easily washed clean of the gore of pig or pond fish slaughter.

On Saint Eustatius and Saint Martin in the 1630s, indigenous Caribbeans tended Dutch fields virtually naked, while overlords sported sweaters knitted by farm wives in Gotland. In the British Virgin Islands, Saba, Saint Croix, and Guyana from 1660, enslaved sugarcane growers received little clothing from their owners. In the 1730s, the Caquetío of Venezuela, Curaçao, Bonaire, and Aruba preferred nudity for outdoor work. In Zambia, rural families imported cottonseed from Zanzibar and learned to weave cotton fibers into clothing.

Eighteenth-century Bavarian workers popularized sturdy leather lederhosen (short leather breeches with shoulder straps), a field uniform worn by children and adults. In the same spirit of utility, workers in Bombay, India, turned raw calico or sailcloth into dungarees, the forerunner of overalls. In the North American colonies, farm women tended kitchen gardens, herb beds, and flocks in shapeless gowns pleated across the back yoke to ease restriction on the arms and shoulders.

Men adopted the bib-and-brace overall, or boiler-suit, in the 1790s.

On large North American plantations, domestic servants wore livery. In contrast to pampered house slaves, field hands sewed inferior yard goods into unisex head wraps and caps, drop-shoulder shirts, and pants tied at the midriff with rope. Cotton duck picking sacks and canvas planting and canning aprons supplied deep receptacles to hold seeds, vegetables and fruit, herbs, kindling, chicken feed, and eggs. Slaves stitched their own shoes from cowhide and lined the bottoms with cardboard.

Twentieth-century rural America depended on mail order from Montgomery Ward in Chicago and the Timothy Eaton catalog from Winnipeg for military overcoats and reefers, one-piece ticking overalls, "hooverettes" (wrap aprons), cloth caps, and sewing notions to turn muslin grain sacks into everyday attire. In the 1910s, laborers adopted crewneck T-shirts from U.S. Navy issue and purchased them by the half-dozen from the Sears, Roebuck catalog for $1.44 or on credit from the general store. Flannel for underwear and gingham for women's dresses and children's outfits cost 10 cents per yard from peddlers, who sometimes accepted milk, butter, eggs, and dried beans in payment.

After Russia entered World War I, army brides constrained by rationing refashioned their husbands' farm shirts and baggy pants, which they held up with suspenders. To make boots fit, farmwives padded the soles and toes with felt. The recycling of menswear reduced rural women to few changes of clothing, a situation that made laundry imperative when weather allowed.

Low price, flexible knit, and ease of laundering and repairing kept jersey knit tops in style throughout the Great Depression. Worn overalls, stockings, and jackets bore patches made from discarded garments and flour sacks. Black, Mexican, American Indian, Japanese, and white migrant workers in the United States made do with cast-off denims and gifts from Quaker interracial relief programs. In lieu of shoes, child cultivators and pickers bound their feet in rags. The rest of the ragbag provided patches and strips for rag rugs.

Korea and Maoist China issued unisex padded work jackets, pants, gloves, and shoes to rural people. After 1916, Park Chung Hee's dictatorship in Korea suspended support for rural peasants, leaving them strapped for clothes and footwear. The failures of communism to provide standardized Soviet apparel and footwear for Eastern Europeans in the 1960s returned Siberian potato growers to hand sewing and reviving clothing legacies from previous generations, usually woefully out of date. The dearth of work clothes in Cuba and Honduras in 1964 forced indigent smallholders to bargain for used apparel, sandals, and rubber boots for mucking out stalls and chicken houses.

Current agricultural attire meets the demands of high-tech methods, such as the spiked shoes used by cacao and fruit harvesters and the padded Tyvek coveralls with zip or Velcro® closures used by farm workers exposed to biohazardous dust. For tending beehives, scrubbing farrowing parlors with disinfectant, or spraying orchards with fertilizer and insecticide, farmers cover their faces in disposable masks and turbans. For the use of heavy machinery, especially diesel-powered tractors, drivers wear earplugs and safety glasses.

See also: American Western Clothing.

Further Reading
Evans, Susan Toby, and David L. Webster, eds. *Archaeology of Ancient Mexico and Central America: An Encyclopedia.* New York: Garland, 2001.
Hewitt, Nancy A., ed. *A Companion to American Women's History.* Malden, MA: Blackwell, 2002.
Rogonzinski, Jan. *A Brief History of the Caribbean: From the Arawak and Carib to the Present.* New York: Plume, 2000.

Fashion Design

A profession dedicated to the aesthetic appeal of garments and accessories, fashion design reflects elements of socioeconomic status, technological advancement, and gendered expression of self-image.

Introduced by Paris designer Charles Frederick Worth and London tailor Henry Poole in the mid-1800s, the role of couturier extended the task of the dressmaker and clothier by applying the restraint of court style to individual outfits for work, travel, hunting, and horseback riding. In-house teams presented clients with sketches or sample bespoke apparel and offered choices of materials and ornamentation to personalize the silhouette, such as a watch, fob, and chain to accompany a sober-colored three-piece business suit, a pristine cravat and collar, and gaiters for footwear. After taking meticulous measurements, the designer completed the order and delivered it to the purchaser, sparing both team and client extensive fittings.

In the early 1900s, French fashion promoters such as Paul Poiret, Jacques Doucet, and Jeanne Paquin advertised drawings and photos of art deco, impressionist, and oriental ready-to-wear for adaptation by dressmakers and tailors. Factories produced ready-to-wear knockoffs for sale in department stores as far away as Madrid and Buenos Aires. Practical day wear, nightclothes, underwear, shoes, and hats broadened the range of design from military uniforms and tea gowns to everyday styles for beachwear, motoring, playing golf or tennis, and walking. Men popularized overcoats with military epaulets, nautical reefers (pea coats), creased trousers, motoring dusters, and boxer shorts. Designers offered seasonal changes on live models at runway shows.

Fashion designers favored the day suit for married and professional women and the off-the-rack single-breasted jacket and slacks for men. French designer Caroline Reboux popularized the veiled theater hat, toques, berets, cloches, and Gainsborough hats from her shops in Paris and London. Burberry mastered the trench coat, an outgrowth of World War I that remained trendy with civilian men and women. For the average consumer, Madeleine Vionnet specialized in bias cuts, handkerchief hems, cowl necks, and Grecian drape, complex styles frequently pirated by dressmakers and pattern makers. English textile specialist William Morris added historical touches to tie and blouse fabrics, notably, romantic Asian paisleys and medieval woodcut designs.

Celebrity Dressing

The shift in clientele during the 1920s and 1930s from royalty to movie stars and the nouveau riche introduced film, sporting events, the ballet, and society columns as major fashion venues. Menswear featured sports-weight woolens suited to a variety of activities, a lifestyle shift modeled by Edward VIII. Egyptian archaeology reprised tunics and sandals from the fourteenth century B.C.E. In Spain, Mariano Fortuny reprised classical flow by turning permanently pleated silk into a Greek column dress adorned with Venetian glass beads.

Designer Coco Chanel profited from dressing Gloria Swanson for the screen and by popularizing stretchy jersey and the "little black dress," the workhorse of the female wardrobe. Chanel's rival, Elsa Schiaparelli, promoted knits and skiwear decked with Dada and surreal art by Jean Cocteau and Salvador Dalí as well as film costumes for Zsa Zsa Gabor and Mae West. Manhattan designer Claire McCardell, a down-to-earth creator of comfortable apparel, introduced the "American look" in affordable, mass-produced leisure wear—ballet slippers, sundresses, shifts, wrap dresses—available at Lord & Taylor.

During World War II, European designers made do with rationed wool and cotton by narrowing belts, shortening and slimming skirts, replacing silk with nylon, and making shoes out of canvas rather than leather. Factory laborers adapted to denim work wear. Chicago milliner Charles James, America's first couturier, refined the understructure of garments for all-season capes and coats. Lilly Daché turned snoods and turbans into fashion art. Practical American dressmaker Vera Maxwell debuted wraparound dresses and Ultrasuede in collarless jackets in earth tones. A contemporary, Anne Klein, directed her energies toward sportswear, an American staple.

Clothiers in Chicago, Detroit, and Memphis outfitted men in two-toned shoes, oversized jackets, long chains, and pegged pants, the flashy zoot suit of the late 1940s. The influence of jeans, Hawaiian flower prints, and skiwear applied washable, wrinkle-free textiles to leisure wear. In 1947, women admired the feminine flare mastered by Christian Dior, whose "new look" favored the busty, slim-waisted woman. Dior set the example of displaying a global label visible on items as diverse as perfume, swimsuits, and Scots cashmere sweaters.

Designs for the Individual

The idiosyncratic style of the 1950s democratized luxury. Fashion commentary set apart the color-blocked chemise of Cristóbal Balenciaga, the sarong sheaths of Pierre Balmain, the Hollywood screen costumes of Edith Head and Gilbert Adrian, and the youthful patterns of Hubert de Givenchy, Jean Patou, and Lucienne Day.

By the 1960s, independent style ended domination by a single look or Savile Row outfitter. In place of static ensembles, Mary Quant introduced the miniskirt, Pierre Cardin launched unisex shirts and tunics, Yves Saint Laurent put women in tuxedos, Guy Laroche upped the wattage of colors, and André Courrèges reached into the future for space age geometrics.

Design in the final decades of the twentieth century freed artistry to repackage the female body, as exemplified by Rudi Gernreich's sheer stretch bra, Paco Rabanne's aluminum paillette (sequin) creations, Oleg Cassini's boxy jackets, Onia Rykiel's fake furs, and Emilio Pucci's psychedelic colors. The 1970s paired these innovations with unisex motorcycle trends, abstract prints, and denim, the dominant fabric statement of a youthful society. Rock stars premiered their glam stage costuming in fashionable men's vests, tunics, jeans, camouflage, T-shirts, and army boots. Laura Ashley contributed the crocheted shawl over country girl floral dresses. Roy Halston dressed the 1970s woman in sleek, impeccable glamour.

Fashion design in the 1980s revived the exhibitionism of the Bourbon dynasty with spandex, bustles, Lycra bustiers, and leather. Women's business attire reflected the tailoring and shoulder padding of men's power suits. Christian Lacroix extracted theatrical detail from historic design with flounces and lacy stockings. Venezuelan couturier Carolina Herrera specialized in romantic evening gowns. Tokyo-born textile specialist Rei Kawakubo contributed unconstructed antifashion, an ascetic 1980s touch in black, gray, and white. Donna Karan stressed the modules of a "seven easy pieces" wardrobe.

Minimalism held firm in the 1990s, as avantgarde designers Helmut Lang, Dolce & Gabbana, and Gianni Versace abandoned froufrou for stark outlines and ethnic touches from the Indian sari and Persian caftan. Investment dressing favored Jil Sander's office pantsuit, Gucci bags, Yoji Yamamoto's evening dresses, and the classicism of Prada leather goods and sportswear. Recycled and distressed denim marked the customized looks of clothes by Belgian designer Martin Margiela.

The 2000s brought antimodernism to the fore as designers looked back to retro classics by Chanel and Dior and jeans and T-shirts by Karl Lagerfeld. Vivienne Westwood resurrected 1970s punk style with high platform shoes, distressed leather, chains, and dog collars. Computer-aided design (CAD) produced abstract prints and brought Photoshop precision to florals, as in the designs of Duncan Cheetham. In a gesture toward traditional wedding attire, Sarah Burton provided the English royal bride Kate Middleton with an elegantly trained lace-top gown and illusion veil, a design copied around the world. Favoring the ordinary consumer, innovators Stella McCartney and Jaclyn Smith offered low- to mid-price apparel at Target and Kmart.

See also: Couturiers; Dolls, Fashion; Fashion Plates; Haute Couture; Labels; Ready-to-Wear; Worth, Charles Frederick.

Further Reading

Bye, Elizabeth. *Fashion Design.* New York: Bloomsbury, 2010.
Hopkins, John. *Menswear.* La Vergne, TN: Ava, 2011.
Loschek, Ingrid. *When Clothes Become Fashion: Design and Innovation Systems.* New York: Bloomsbury, 2009.

Fashion Photography

- -

See Photography, Fashion

Fashion Plates

- -

A minor art form based on costume portraits of monarchs, jousters, and diplomats from the 1500s, the fashion plate amplified Western wardrobe consciousness with a depiction of styles and materials sold by milliners, seamstresses, bootmakers, and tailors.

In 1517, to exemplify appropriate court attire, Slovenian ambassador Siegmund von Herberstein

The fashion plate, featured in a number of Belle Époque mass-circulation magazines in Europe and the United States, was the primary medium for popularizing women's and men's clothing styles before the advent of photography. *(Stock Montage/Getty Images)*

of Vienna, a forerunner of the fashion artist, recorded in sketches the brocaded robes and greatcoats that he wore on missions to Maximilian I, Charles V, Vasily III, and Ferdinand I.

Renaissance curiosity about style created a need for the detailed fashion plate. In the 1520s and 1530s, German painter Hans Holbein surveyed the attire, wigs, color schemes, and fabrics worn by sitters for portraits. Venetian engraver Fernando Bertelli's *Trachtenbuch* (*Costume Book,* 1563) and Venetian fashion commentator Cesare Vecellio's costume drawings for *De gli Habiti Antichi, et Moderni di Diverse Parti del Mondo* (*On Ancient and Modern Costume in Different Parts of the World,* 1590) surveyed high fashion. The illustrations generated disapproval among conservatives for their promotion of conceit and pride with

lacings, slashed sleeves, petticoats, farthingales, plaits, ruffs, lace collars, and stiffened hemlines throughout England, France, Iberia, and Italy.

Bavarian *Hofkleiderbücher* (court attire manuals) from 1551 and 1588 illustrated formal apparel as well as the posture of dignified men and women as courtiers, dukes, security guards, suppliants, cavalry officers, falconers, and liveried messengers. The rise of Puritanism resulted in proposals for simpler apparel in French printmaker Jacques Callot's *La Noblesse* and French etcher and watercolorist Abraham Bosse's *Galerie du Palais* (1636), both stylized records of shifting tastes. In the 1630s and 1640s, Wenceslas Hollar etched fashion portraits featuring the female hood, vizard (half-mask), and fur coat.

Print media extended the range of fashion plates, beginning in 1672 with French publicist

Jean Donneau de Visé's magazine *Mercure Galant.* Picture piracy increased the circulation in Amsterdam, London, and Paris of drawings by Antoine Hérisset, François Octavien, Bernard Picart, and Jean de St. Jean. From 1770, illustrations and sketches of stylized models in the latest silhouettes circulated in *The Lady's Magazine,* for which dressmakers provided coloration. The British fashion magazine remained in business until 1837 to define Empire and Georgian period fashions, including fringed shawls, curled feathers, and gauze ribbon. The features of its stylized models promoted the image of the female as passive representative of the fashion industry.

Mass reproduction of hand-tinted engravings and woodcuts advanced to chromo-lithography, which drew attention to individuals and their socioeconomic status. In France, a pioneering effort by publishers Jacques Esnauts and Michel Rapilly in *La Galerie des Modes* in 1778 presented chic garments and hairstyles on human forms. A competitor in Germany, *Journal des Luxus und der Moden,* thrived from 1786 to 1826. In 1794, the London fashion world presented sketch artist Nicolaus Heideloff's hand-tinted plates in *Gallery of Fashion,* a source of detail on Empire dresses, light curls, hair bands, and turbans.

In 1797, French artist Pierre de La Mésangère drew and tinted clothing illustrations for the weekly *Journal des Dames et Des Modes* that pictured Parisian women dressed in modish outfits and engaged in contemporary activities. Into the nineteenth century, issues of *The Lady's Monthly Museum, Le Beau Monde,* and *La Belle Assemblée* enticed followers of fashion with illustrated news of cravat ties and advice on ensembles of whalebone, horsehair crinoline, muffs, hats, and mitts. Drape and fabric wholesalers circulated broadside images alongside fashion plates of ready-made apparel, hats, and shoes.

After the introduction of Philadelphia-based *Godey's Lady's Book* in June 1830, copies of French engravings influenced American costume, as well as the ideal of the delicate female hand and hourglass figure. In 1839, technology outpaced the plates with detail fashion photography. In 1860, Firmin Didot, editor of the French fashion weekly *La Mode Illustrée,* issued the first fashion plates intended to instruct seamstresses on how to duplicate garments. For maximum display of apparel in genteel settings, artists pictured side views of models at the piano or harp.

By the late 1860s, fashion followers imitated ensembles pictured in such publications as *France Mode, Graham's Magazine, The Queen,* and *Peterson's Magazine.* All fashion plates tended toward interchangeable figures in stiff mannequin poses and gestures. Illustrator Jules David signed some 2,600 fashion plates for *The Englishwoman's Domestic Magazine.* Commentary included advice on children's outfits and the prominence of navy, plum, and scarlet in dresses and coats. Heightened publicity shaped the taste of the bon ton and fostered the ready-to-wear market.

Into the Edwardian period, pochoir (stenciled) fashion plates brushed with color over a copper or zinc template continued to promote the designs of French couturier Paul Poiret. With the expertise of sketch artists Paul Iribe and Georges Lepape, Poiret introduced kimono jackets, Magyar sleeves, turbans, Turkish tunics over harem skirts, and silk brocades in his fashion album, *Les Robes de Paul Poiret* (*The Dresses of Paul Poiret,* 1908). Erté's sinuous art deco drawings for *Harper's Bazaar* in the 1910s and 1920s, and illustrations by Tom Keogh for *French Vogue* and Bernard Blossac for French magazines in the 1940s, redirected the fashion plate.

In the 1980s, *La Mode en Peinture* magazine presented artist Tony Viramontes's stylized versions of ensembles by Valentino and Yves Saint Laurent. Ruben Alterio provided similar abstract crayon and watercolor sketches in 1997 for *Mirabella,* an American fashion magazine that influenced the tastes of a half-million readers.

See also: Dolls, Fashion; *Godey's Lady's Book;* Photography, Fashion.

Further Reading

Beetham, Margaret, and Kay Boardman. *Victorian Women's Magazines: An Anthology.* New York: Manchester University Press, 2001.

Blackman, Cally. *100 Years of Fashion Illustration.* London: Laurence King, 2007.

Davis, Mary E. *Classic Chic: Music, Fashion, and Modernism.* Berkeley: University of California Press, 2006.

Fasteners

From prehistory, clothing fasteners have developed from vines and hide strips to intricate devices and clasps that add flair and contour to attire. Archaeological digs at Crete, Egypt, Nineveh, Tyre, and Troy have turned up glass and crystal spheres used as buttons, sash ornaments, and badges. Lacing, the most primitive garment closure, dates to hunter-gatherers around 5000 B.C.E. The thorn threaded with sinew supplied the first closure technology to pierce a garment.

From 2800 B.C.E. at Mohenjo-daro in the Indus Valley and from 2000 B.C.E. in China and Egypt, people closed apparel with midriff chains, brooches, and buckles pierced with holes for needle-and-thread attachment. They stitched ornamental shell buttons to belts and apparel by sewing the shanks on one side and connecting the buttons with loops on the opposite edge. The Chinese pioneered the pressure snap fastener, which they applied to horse harnesses, and the paired belt buckle, created in bronze by the nomadic Xiongnu of Central Asia. A hook on one side engaged an aperture on the other.

Early Native Americans formed lacing from rawhide and babiche made from rabbit skin. In the Amazonian forest, tribes dressed their apparel with wood, bone, and stone sewn into place. Arctic peoples valued walrus ivory for toggles, and baleen and soapstone for adornments carved like seals or halibut and incised with a bow drill. In the Society Islands, buttons of barkcloth sufficed as a closure for belts and cloaks.

Accessory Fasteners

Clothiers improved fasteners as a means of supplying a snug fit to loose jackets and coats. In the 1300s B.C.E. in Mycenae, Greek clothiers created a common tunic or cloak fastener, the hinged fibula (safety pin). In spiral and bow shapes, the fibula became a lucrative trade item in Macedonia, Crete, Cyprus, Magna Graecia, and the Balkans. Roman women used tortoiseshell buttons or a bronze fibula at the shoulder or chest to secure the *palla* (short wrap). Artisans carved lava from Mount Vesuvius into portrait rounds or ovals. Imperial legionaries fastened their helmets with a chin strap and bronze buckle, the first plate or hinged frame fastener to secure two ends with an adjustable clasp and prong.

For purses, jackets, and cavalry harnesses, Byzantine and Saxon designers made the buckle fashionable with elegant filigree and engraving. An English version from the early 600s C.E., the gold buckle included in grave goods of a ship burial at Sutton Hoo disguised the clasp as jewelry. For active wear, Scots males overlapped the plaid and secured it at the upper right thigh with a bone or wood poniard similar to the German *spina* (pin). Topping the weighted pin, animal shapes, oak leaves and acorns, thistles, jewels, and clan symbols added appropriate touches to folk costume. The Tara Brooch, crafted of gilded silver in the early 700s, applied Celtic metallurgy to the penannular (pin and ring) fastener, a circle pierced by a long removable skewer.

Secure fastening enhanced the revelation of the human torso via contoured garments. At the end of the First Crusade in 1099, soldiers brought home as souvenirs Turkish and Mongolian buttoned garments from Palestine. The alignment of buttons with buttonholes first closed shirts and jackets in Germany in the mid-1200s. Buttons gained permanent application throughout Europe in bone, horn, hoof, leather, pearl, and shell. Around 1340, Charles de Blois of Brittany flaunted a snug-fitting coat with buttons from elbow to wrist. By the 1400s, the Byzantines revamped the Roman *stola* (overdress) with buttons from neck to hem. In the late Middle Ages, buttons of precious metals inlaid with gems advertised wealth and status.

Artistry

Renaissance fasteners stressed the artistry of form rather than function, particularly for royalty and courtiers. In a forerunner of cuff links, men fastened wristbands with cuff strings passed through small holes. The wealthy flaunted a variety of buttons— *ajouré* (pierced), diamante (jeweled), *verre églomisé* (mirrored), and Florentine mosaic shapes in *pietra dura* (hard stone). In Nuremberg, the spherical toggle button closed a cloak with a thin chain, a metallic adornment that added flash to woolens and furs.

Seventeenth-century tin-glazed ceramic buttons, glass and ivory knobs, and hollow cache buttons for smuggling preceded the silvered bone uniform buttons that King Louis XIV decreed for the French army. After 1615, the wearer of the Japanese kimono or *kosode* (robe) attached a separate *inro* (pocket) to the sash with a netsuke, a knob or toggle sculpted from boxwood, walnuts, agate, ivory, walrus teeth or tusks, horns, clay, or cane. In 1649, England's Charles I went to the chopping block wearing a knit silk Henley tunic fastened with 13 crocheted buttons.

French artisan and cabinetmaker André Charles Boulle perfected the crafting of fasteners from tortoiseshell and ebony. In 1697, the first wire hook and eye, an improvement on the medieval crocheted button and loop, discreetly cinched breeches and doublets. The technology became the mainstay of corsetry for its thin profile.

Early fasteners met competition around 1700 from the English Dorset thread or twist button. The flat webbed cartwheel began as a brass wire ring oversewn with soft cotton thread. Variations centered each circle with embroidery around a glass paste or spangle center, a luxury that brought scrutiny under sumptuary laws.

A sedate coat button in France involved the covering of wood cores with silk cording. In 1730, an Alsatian jeweler to Louis XV named Georg Friedrich Strass, the "Father of the Rhinestone," turned paste into faceted glass buttons backed with foil. In Philadelphia in 1750, merchant Hans Caspar Wistar enriched himself by manufacturing brass buttons, a standard adornment of colonial apparel.

By the 1770s, the cost of fasteners accounted for as much as 80 percent of tailoring bills. Metal buttons imported from France graced the jackets and sleeves of the Continental Army. Common buttons of horn and metal came under regulation in England and Wales, where laws banned the sale of Dorset twist buttons. The wealthy chose from Wedgwood stoneware, or the habitat button, a glass casing for a bit of fern or an insect.

Glass buttons and garter buckles hand-painted by portraitist Jean-Baptiste Isabey achieved a cachet that earned him appointment as Napoleon's chief designer. Wire filigree or fretwork buttons involved the soldering of coils and granules into works of art. In the 1820s, George IV of England wore shirts secured with mother-of-pearl buttons, the next trend in fasteners. Meanwhile, Korean artisans gilded cloisonné (enameled metal) spheres into jacket garnishing. In Africa and Australia, the scarcity of brass buttons made them collectors' items and trading currency.

Practical Solutions

After American inventor Charles Goodyear vulcanized gum rubber with sulfur in January 1839, rubber buttons supplied military needs, ranging from pea coats to patterned tunic decor featuring cameos, Greek key motifs, anchors, artillery, and ornate stars and swirls. Birmingham, England, became a punching, stamping, soldering, gilding, and pressing center for fasteners from copper, silver, and tortoiseshell. In the 1840s, knitters of the Lusekofte spotted frock in southern Norway fastened the neck with pewter clasps, the sweater's trademark garnish.

After 1841, British jewelers John Aston and Humphrey Jeffries devised the three-fold linen button. The two inventors encased a pasteboard foundation with linen and locked the layers into place with a metal circlet. The fabric covering and shank eased the discomfort of shifts and drawers.

Humped hooks and eyes offered a more secure closure for corsets and bustiers at minimal cost. In 1864, vegetable ivory buttons synthesized from the Corozo palm reduced the need for expensive elephant tusks. For manipulating starched collars and cuffs, men preferred metal studs and cuff links, some inlaid with onyx, pearl, or gemstones. Late Victorian styles featured ferrotype or daguerreotype, a photograph transferred to a polished surface of iron or silver.

The Industrial Revolution popularized inexpensive fasteners, such as German inventor Heribert Bauer's two-part brass socket snap. The simple device held men's pants in place with an S-shaped internal spring on the base that grasped a knob on the upper section. In 1895, brothers Howard and

John Longlear of Detroit, Michigan, began making a semiautomatic two-point fastener for grommeting buttons into place on shoes. From century's end until the early 1930s, the trend in shoe buttons overtook old-style lacing as the fastener of choice for men, women, and children.

The early twentieth century supplied ready-to-wear clothing with a variety of closures—hooks and eyes, tie clips, snaps, the Charvet twisted braid cuff link, and the flat shirt button with four holes. The Bakelite (celluloid) buckle and button could imitate jasper, horn, ivory, and tortoiseshell at minimal cost. In 1913, Swedish engineer Gideon Sundback refined a toothed fastener into the first slide or hookless fastener. In use by the U.S. military, zippers secured duffel bags and garments for the doughboys of World War I. For civilians, the rationing of metal forced clothing manufacturers to shape buckles from wood adorned with glass disks.

American entrepreneur Benjamin Franklin Goodrich applied zipper technology to waterproof galoshes and, in 1925, coined the onomatopoetic term "zip" for the sound the device made. As a curiosity for purses and sportswear, Gallo-German designer Émile-Maurice Hermès in the 1930s applied the zipper to chic couture. In Paris, Coco Chanel added a masculine touch to women's blouses with cuff links. Haberdashers stocked men's short collars equipped with small buttonholes through which slender pins or bars connected both sides.

In the second half of the 1900s, snaps on Western shirts, nylon buckles, D rings, and plastic buttons molded and filled with glass on women's and children's apparel lowered the price of adornments. Elegant buckles and mother-of-pearl, shell, and ivory buttons lost popularity in the 1970s after depleting trochus sea snails from Australia and Tahitia, pearl oyster shells from Burma and Taiwan, hawksbill turtles off the Chinese shores, butter clams from the Aleutian Islands, and African elephants and hippopotami. The hiatus gave nature an opportunity to recover from the harvesting of deep divers, shore scavengers, and safari hunters.

As Velcro® and stretch fabrics snugged garments to the torso, buckles, hooks and eyes, and buttons lost their purpose in many garments. Fashion houses marketed brass snaps on fly-front jeans, retro Western pearl snaps and buckles, and tiny cloth-covered globes for wedding dresses as marks of history and tradition.

See also: Lacing; Needle and Thread; Ribbons and Embellishments; Sumptuary Laws; Velcro.

Further Reading

Edwards, Nina. *On the Button: The Significance of an Ordinary Item.* New York: I.B. Tauris, 2011.

Friedel, Robert D. *Zipper: An Exploration in Novelty.* New York: W.W. Norton, 1994.

Hughes, Elizabeth, and Marion Lester. *The Big Book of Buttons.* Haworth, NJ: St. Johann, 2010.

Read, Brian. *Hooked-Clasps and Eyes: A Classification and Catalogue of Sharp- or Blunt-Hooked Clasps and Miscellaneous Hooks, Eyes, Loops, Rings and Toggles.* Langport, UK: Portcullis, 2008.

Feathers

Feathers have attained a number of costume uses as religious, ethnic, military, and fashion linings and trimmings. Feathered bird skins provided prehistoric nomads with garments as warm as fur but lighter in weight and less likely to absorb rain. Among the Yanomami of Brazil, bird feather bracelets complemented body paint in black, gray, red, and purple.

In Assyria, Babylonia, Arabia, and Egypt, the feather—clothing of the goddesses Ishtar, Allat, and Maat—symbolized justice because of the even distribution of fiber on each side of the shaft. In Egypt, the sacred ibis feather cooled the priest of Isis, crowned the head of the god Thoth, adorned shamanic regalia, and served as a protective. For their beauty, feathers influenced worship and symbolism, as with the owl in Athens, quetzal in Central America, peacock in China, crane in Japan, swan among Hindus, bird of paradise in New Guinea, kiwi in New Zealand, and gamecock and ostrich in Mesopotamia and Iran. The demand for Arabian ostrich plumage in Syria as a gift to royalty led to the bird's extinction.

In Britain, the brimless Scots bonnet combined

three feathers with a rosette to decorate a twilled plaid sarcenet (fine silk). For padded coats and hats, designers chose eiderdown and goose down, a fluffy substance that resisted compaction while insulating the body with air pockets. The domestic use of eiderdown and the feathers of seabirds in vests and jackets enriched breeders and hunters in Greenland, Iceland, Norway, and Siberia.

Renaissance Fashion

In the fifteenth century, Venetians reduced the size of feathered skullcaps to reveal a flow of curled hair. In contrast, the Turkish emperor at Trebizond chose a hat of marten skin bounded by gold cords and crane feathers. In 1400, soldiers of Henry IV limited crests to feathers for the decoration of the morion, a helmet topped by a curved peak. Beginning in 1413, the reign of England's Henry V saw an increase in feather and plume embellishments for helmets and for civilian hats set at a jaunty angle with gold-spangled feathers that curled at the ear. Under Edward IV from 1461 to 1471, men-at-arms adorned helmets with feathers.

The 1470s saw the embellishment of army uniforms and those of the Order of the Garter with swan, ostrich, and peacock plumage, either clipped, curled, jeweled, or straight. In 1475 at Neuss, Germany, Charles the Bold, the duke of Burgundy, lost to the spoils of combat a cloth-of-gold hat set with pearls, sapphires, and rubies adorning two feathers, one red and one white. Scavengers dismembered the hat and sold the feathers and jewels separately as war prizes.

A model from 1480 pictures the attachment of a heron's feather to a fur hat with a jeweled cross, a common adornment that Richard III limited to bachelors. During the reign of Henry VII, while the French reduced plumage, Englishmen's beaver hats sported a clutch of ostrich plumes in black, white, and red to coordinate with red hose. A variation involved dyeing half a white ostrich plume black to adorn a broad-brimmed beaver hat and complement striped or parti-color stockings.

Toward the end of the 1400s, frivolous Flemish and Italian caps acquired feathers in the shape of a bird wing or tail. In 1497, the French gallant displayed a cocked hat and plume some 25 inches (64 centimeters) long. In the early 1500s, ostrich feathers supplied down for felting into *estrich* or *estridge,* a French fabric as soft as fine woolens to replace beaver in hats. The Scots Balmoral bonnet, a round, flat-topped cap, repeated plaid colors in its jaunty black ostrich feather and red pompom.

In 1520, when feathered berets dominated men's fashions, Henry VIII appeared in a chic velvet bonnet topped with jewels and black plumes. On a more colorful note, Henry's contemporary, Francis I of France, sported a surcoat lined in heron's plumes. Around 1550, feather muffs snuggled women's hands. Demand for feathers as luxury items during the Elizabethan Age increased investment in English and French goods. As a token of honor to Elizabeth I, the Yeomen of the Guard sported caps with side feathers. Visiting German and Swiss knights doffed satin caps before the queen to flourish their plumes.

1600s and 1700s

Baroque styles of the 1600s added exotic plumage to dapper hats, including feathers of guinea hens and African storks, status symbols that earned the scorn of Puritans. European paintings of Ottoman sultans pictured them in stereotypical oriental attire with black heron feathers at front center of the turban, an identifying embellishment of Murad IV, the sultan at Constantinople.

In portraiture around 1647, Rembrandt depicted the dignitary or military man who sports a feather on his hat, and the prince of Orange, similarly adorned with a single feather. Symbolically, Rembrandt painted a contemplative philosopher and poet with a beret topped with a cluster of colored feathers, emblems of inspiration and good humor. In 1657, portrait artist Frans van Mieris captured the dash of the era with a satin hat topped with feathers to dramatize a satin-lined velvet doublet and white shirt. In 1690, makers of women's fontange wigs completed the elaborate coiffure with ribbon and feathers.

In the 1700s, millinery plume fads—the feather knot, feathered pelerine (a narrow cape), and upright feathered headdress—in Europe and North America initiated wild bird domestication to feminize massive Gainsborough hats. To profit from fashion, poachers endangered egrets, ostriches, and peacocks, especially sources of the "Amazon plume," a curled ostrich feather from the wing, and the double fluff feather, a costly material traded at Aleppo, Syria.

As the market for plumes increased, feather commerce became the most competitive in the fashion industry. After the French Revolution of 1789, however, men abandoned plumage and adopted tall beaver hats with plain bands. In Canada, provincial governors traded wigs and feathers for the hat, an emblem of New World equality.

Expanding Market

The Napoleonic era (1799–1815) brought renewed emphasis on feathering with the adornment of beaver bonnets. At the height of the court of Louis XVI and Marie Antoinette in France, tall wigs decked with feathers or a triad of plumes increased the visibility of aristocratic women but limited the types of carriages they could enter without dislodging their headdresses. For men, the Egyptian hat featured a tuft of heron feathers and lace trim attached to a puffed handkerchief cap.

Nineteenth-century Frenchwomen favored marabou, the downy tail and underwing feathers of the stork. After 1833, fashion introduced the plaid silk Graham turban, a bonnet garnished with black feathers. Slovakian headgear of the 1830s joined the ostrich plume to cock's feathers for a downward thrust. In 1855, the pleated alma cloak for women exhibited white ostrich trim and a triple tassel of black and gold on the hood, a luxurious evening wrap featured in *Peterson's Magazine*.

Milliners reduced the feathered hat to the diadem or fanchon bonnet, a strip of ruching or tulle adorned with a tuft and tied at the throat with a satin ribbon. To shape the rounded boa, feather workers trimmed the barbs, inserted swansdown, and fluffed the remaining shafts into a dramatic, fluttery, 8-foot (2.4-meter) neckpiece that framed a milk-white complexion.

Anti-Plumage Movement

In 1883, South African taxes on birds and eggs impeded the export of ostriches to farms in Alge-

ria, Argentina, Australia, and North America. A feather glut in the 1880s dropped the price from £250 to £25 per feather. The 1890s produced improvements in the breeding of various kinds of birds with high-quality feathers, which milliners incorporated into flat-crowned Russian Oldenburg bonnets. Some creations featured entire bird bodies.

Between 1892 and 1912, the cost of South African ostrich plumes tripled, elevating the value of plumes from the species above those of osprey, emu, bird of paradise, cassowary, and rhea for adorning adult hats and baby bonnets. Despite protests from conservationists, from 1890 to 1929, France alone imported 50,000 tons of feathers from pheasants, penguins, hummingbirds, flamingos, partridges, and turkeys from clearinghouses operated in Aleppo, Alexandria, California, the Cape of Good Hope, and Tripoli.

The marketing of prime white feathers from African ostrich farms also spawned wild bird hunting in southern Sudan and the Sahel. Camel trains delivered plumage to Lagos. Other supplies came from Mediterranean plumage farms. In the London and New York fashion industries, Russian-Lithuanian Jewish *plumassieres* (feather workers) dominated plume processing and trade. A consignment of plumes that sank with the *Titanic* in 1912 cost investors £20,000.

By 1910, Canadian women popularized upswept coifs and ostrich plumes. With the onset of World War I–era austerity, hair took prominence over hats, causing the feather market to plunge and reducing dealers to selling feather dusters. In Canada, a do-it-yourself millinery craze in 1924 encouraged women to buy buckram foundations and add their own feathers or to refashion old hats in chic styles. In the early 2000s, the variety of hat trimmings ranged from the coque (rooster feathers), spadone (sword-like feather), and spiky goose biot (wing feather) to the peacock brush, marabou strip, strings of chicken hackles (neck feathers), and arrowhead quill, a lance shape fashioned from a turkey feather.

See also: Accessories; Hats, Men's; Ribbons and Embellishments.

Further Reading

Craik, Jennifer. *Fashion: The Key Concepts.* New York: Bloomsbury, 2009.

Gale, Colin, and Jasbir Kaur. *Fashion and Textiles: An Overview.* New York: Bloomsbury, 2004.

Havelin, Kate. *Buckskin Dresses and Pumpkin Breeches: Colonial Fashions from the 1580s to the 1670s.* Minneapolis, MN: Twenty-First Century Books, 2012.

Stein, Sarah Abrevaya. *Plumes: Ostrich Feathers, Jews, and a Lost World of Global Commerce.* New Haven, CT: Yale University Press, 2008.

Felt

- -

A light, flexible, matted fabric made from tangled hair, felt may be humankind's oldest clothing material. The felting process developed around 6000 B.C.E. across Asia and Europe from the layering, dampening, shrinkage, rubbing, pounding, and compacting of beaver fur and sheep, goat, and camel hair into a tough interlinking fiber. Grease or oil provided sizing before the felt maker began rolling, unrolling, and rerolling from the opposite direction, a process that took half a day.

A quicker method involved the stuffing of wool into leather skins or wrapping it about poles with tight bindings for dragging over rough ground by horse or camel to tangle the wool hairs. High humidity conditioned the fiber, causing a tighter conformation. Faster and less meticulous than weaving, felting produced a durable cold-weather fabric for socks and sweaters long before the invention of knitting. The prehistoric felting process influenced Chinese, Indian, and Greek apparel, but did not extend to Africa or the Americas.

A trade item introduced by Asian nomads during the Bronze Age, felt supplied a resilient fabric for hats, gloves, socks, slippers, and saddle blankets among Mongolian horsemen. The Chinese called Hun country the "land of felt," a term redolent with appreciation for artisans.

Felt appliqué spread to Central Asia by 300 B.C.E. among nomadic Uzbeks and Turks. Felt makers in Etruria, Pompeii, Greece, Persia, and India dampened wool fibers and worked them into perpendicular alignment to encourage the connection of natural scales on the hairs. Indians improved the nap and luster with a mowing knife.

Roman legionaries padded armor with felt inserts and layered metal chest guards over felt tunics. When the Roman army decamped from Britain in 450 C.E., Saxons seized England, bringing with them the conical felt military cap banded in metal and the domed shepherd's hat. During the same period, Vikings preferred felt for shoulder blankets. After 710, the Chinese presented a roll of felt as a state gift to the Japanese, who stored it in the imperial treasury.

During the 1100s, French crusader Renaud de Châtillon, the prince of Antioch, shaped a tiara of felt finished in gilt. In Fez, Morocco, men expressed their Arabic origins with a red felt cylinder topped by a black tassel—a hat that took the name of the city. French peasants popularized a brimless felt cap with a deep crown.

Wealthy men could afford lavish decoration for felt hats, which they trimmed with tufts, feathers, and lace. In Scotland, a round, flat-topped cap called the Balmoral bonnet, an element of Highland dress, repeated plaid colors in the wool band, which a family member wove or knitted and felted by hand.

The seventeenth century ushered in French demands for felt, including patches, bits of black felt cut into iconic shapes—moons, stars, hearts, and diamonds. In 1620, symbolic patches on women's faces represented passion when glued near the eye and flirtation when attached beside the lips or on the collarbone. Englishwomen emulated French patching and ringlets and unfurled pleated felt fans to draw attention to the eyes, while female Puritans chose white felt caps over buns as evidence of modesty. Around 1650, the creation of the felt carroting process involved mercuric nitrate and a hot water soak requiring no seams, glue, or stitchery in the conformation of hats.

In a rush of fashion consciousness, buyers with disposable income demanded beaver, hare, nutria, or rabbit fur shaped into felt for men's hats and leggings or women's swooping cavalier or Gainsborough hats, which featured long curling plumes. Men favored the cocked beaver felt hat and adorned the high crown with plumes, feathers, and brooches.

By the Industrial Revolution, felt conformed

by suction and pressured with rollers issued from factories by the bolt. In 1826, Turks of the Ottoman Empire displayed loyalty by wearing the felt fez, an egalitarian hat favored by Sultan Mahmud II as well as his underlings.

Around 1850, the hard bowler hat or derby, manufactured by Thomas and William Bowler of London, replaced earlier shapes for the British soldier, gamekeeper, and banker. Americans in the Far West adopted the bowler for ranching and railroad work. In England after the 1870s, the homburg took shape on a form with a front-to-back dent in the curved crown, a favorite of Edward VII. A European creation, the felt toreador hat of 1890 captured the insouciance of the bullfighter.

In the early 1900s, milliners relied on the felt basis for chic hats blocked into brims, skullcaps, and modish wings and spires. Men's fashions featured the felt fedora, homburg, and snap-brim trilby, while the men of the Niger Delta, and Aymara and Quechua women of Bolivia, seized on the derby as a cultural icon. The creation of trench warfare ended the flamboyant headgear of previous military pageantry and demanded a soft, comfortable shape, such as the khaki felt hat introduced during the Boer War. At the beginning of World War I in the United States and Europe, women's felt hats took on a military crispness and cocky slant.

Factories added thermal fusion to ensure a tight fiber and smooth surface. North American boys wore high rubber boots with felt linings. Fabric and trim shortages during the Great Depression encouraged experimentation with traditional felting and dyeing processes and revived the Tyrolean hat, an Austrian staple in forest green decorated with a feather cluster.

For the remainder of the 1900s, craft suppliers chose felt as material for contemporary art, such as Christmas stockings, car coats, Halloween costumes, handbags, and wall hangings. Into the 2000s, the revival of Sufi and Turk folk costume increased the demand for felt for ethnic jackets, vests, leggings, and hats.

See also: Hats, Men's; Hats, Women's; Prehistoric Clothing.

Further Reading

Houghton, Lizzie. *Felting Fashion: Creative and Inspirational Techniques for Feltmakers.* London: Batsford, 2009.

Jenkins, David, ed. *The Cambridge History of Western Textiles.* New York: Cambridge University Press, 2003.

Mullins, Willow. *Felt.* New York: Bloomsbury, 2009.

Feminist Styles and Fashions

The domination of women's appearance by androcentric couturiers and media met concerted challenges from suffragists and later waves of feminists. Preceding serious dress reform, the mid-eighteenth-century *bas bleu* (bluestockings), a group of women scholars and literati led by British social reformer Elizabeth Montagu, applied the thinking of male and female intellectuals to matters of wardrobe. Underlying their outlook was the belief that society judged males on actions and females on appearance. Stereotyped as "frumpy" at the time, the bluestockings popularized sensible tweeds and vests, practical purses, low-heeled shoes, and dresses devoid of burdensome panels and frilled petticoats.

Female journalists carried on the philosophy of the bluestockings. From 1837, Sarah Joseph Hale, the American editor of *Godey's Lady's Book,* championed healthful ideals in female wardrobe and hairstyles that echoed the feminist philosophy of author Catharine Beecher. By battling gender stereotyping and constrictive corsetry, Hale rejected trendy fashion that endangered women's comfort and freedom of movement. Magazine articles promoted sensible underwear for girls and women and beauty treatments based on natural products rather than bismuth, vermilion, lead carbonate, and zinc oxide.

The Edwardian era brought relief from Victorian formalism. In 1895, couturier Charles Frederick Worth adapted Englishmen's tailoring to women's ensembles. At the turn of the century, piqued by the example of the Gibson Girl, the lusty yet self-restrained ideal woman drawn by Charles Dana Gibson, women began abandoning the bustled and boned silhouette, revealing more leg, and smoking in public. Suffragists modeled comfortable footwear with Cuban heels, a blunt shape that secured balance on stairs and rough terrain. Those dedicated to full citizenship chose green, white, and violet jewelry—colors beginning with G, W, and V for "Give Women the Vote."

Suffrage and Fashion

During the suffrage movement, *Harper's Bazaar* reviewed the stereotype of the prim belle. In place of the ever-young style maven, magazine layouts depicted the New Woman in tailored skirt suits, coats, and dresses, symbols of ambition. Suffragists linked the fluttery plume on hats with female liberation. For the early feminist, the magazine promoted courses in home economics, fashion advertising, and newspaper illustration as well as viable careers in dressmaking, graphic arts, merchandising, and journalism.

In 1850 at Beaver Island, New York, Mormon reformer Elvira Field Strang sketched pantaloons, a design dubbed the "Mormon dress." *Godey's Lady's Book* denounced them as an outrage. Critics missed the point of comfortable apparel and linked dressing *à la turque* (Turkish-style) with the sexual savagery of Algerian and Levantine harem keepers. Disapproving men feared feminist styles as evidence of women's rejection of marital obedience.

In the September 1851 issue of *Harper's New Monthly Magazine,* a fashion adviser accepted pantaloons and suggested adding a vest for the convenience of first-wave feminists. Six American "Bloomer girls" strolled Piccadilly in London and lectured on the value of unfettered physical movement, drawing 700 male gawkers. Although the Mayfair Bloomer Ball on October 29, 1851, roused titters and sneers at London's Great Exhibition, Massachusetts physician Hannah Tracy Cutler launched split pant-skirts as a feminist coup.

Later in the Victorian era, pro-woman stylists embraced exercise as necessary to the health of all females. For the active girl and woman, feminist designers sketched leisure wear for wearing with canvas shoes during cycling, golf, sailing, croquet, lawn tennis, and horseback riding. As designers gave up the S-curve in the female silhouette, long

chemise styles and lingerie dresses presaged the flapper look of the late 1910s and 1920s.

Dress reformers found a champion in Coco Chanel, who introduced styles that defined the modern female. Key to the appeal of her fashion line, functional dresses, suits, and pocketbooks elevated the status of women by treating them as individuals rather than the sex objects and cardboard stereotypes that dominated early motion pictures. During the 1940s, defenders of female dignity decried the skimpily dressed pin-up that eroticized breasts and turned bikinis, sarongs, halters, high heels, and lingerie into hyper-feminine fantasy material. In London in the 1950s, couturier Mary Quant supplied perky looks in pantdresses, jumpers, smocks, and shorts that further freed females from traditional expectations.

Liberated Fashions

During the Women's Liberation Movement of the 1960s, second-wave feminist styles rejected corsets and girdles, tented maternity attire, ponytails, winged eyeglass frames, big hair, titanium makeup, and frosted nail polish. Feminists added comfortable shoes and all-business shoulder bags to their unfussy ensembles. Packagers of liberation ideals applied feminist slogans to aprons and T-shirts. Hippie females displayed disgruntlement with establishment standards by growing their hair long and wearing braless fishnet tops with jeans, head rags, hemp belts, and Birkenstocks. Second-wave apparel concerns sided with animal rights anti-fur campaigns and advocated eco-friendly rainwear and investment dressing in recyclable microfiber.

In the 1980s economic recession, feminists fought the image of women as dupes of couturiers and lowered their demands for chic style by reviving the plain dress pump and narrow belt. Reviewers of women's media and film raised alarms about bulimia and anorexia, often the sources of bone-thin, perky-breasted bodies among fashion-obsessed youth who chose Barbie dolls, James Bond's lovelies, and Twiggy as their icons. *Glamour* magazine courted feminist concurrence with style advice for college girls and awards for ambition and scholarship.

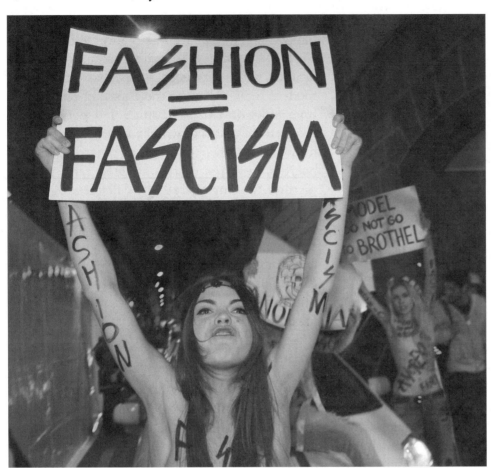

An activist with the Ukrainian-based feminist group FEMEN protests the use of anorexic models at the Milan (Italy) Womenswear Fashion Week in 2012. The organization staged topless international protests against the depiction of women as sex objects. *(Jacopo Raule/Getty Images)*

Ever vocal in the 2000s, feminist social critics supported antitanning campaigns and lambasted *Vogue* magazine for propagating beauty myths about waif-thin models. In assessing wardrobes for men and women, feminists charged manufacturers with making menswear sturdier than women's, and men's pockets more commodious. Another complaint focused on the higher prices for women's dry cleaning and grooming needs and for haircuts at unisex styling shops.

See also: Bloomer, Amelia; Dress Reform; Gendered Dressing; *Godey's Lady's Book.*

Further Reading

Beckingham, Carolyn. *Is Fashion a Woman's Right?* Portland, OR: Sussex Academic, 2005.

Scott, Linda M. *Fresh Lipstick: Redressing Fashion and Feminism.* New York: Palgrave Macmillan, 2005.

Tarrant, Shira, and Marjorie Jolles, eds. *Fashion Talks: Undressing the Power of Style.* Albany: State University of New York Press, 2012.

Wolf, Naomi. *The Beauty Myth: How Images of Beauty Are Used Against Women.* New York: Perennial, 2002.

Fibers, Natural

The manipulation of plant and animal fibers—seal sinew, fleece, cedar bark, linden and willow bast, esparto grass, palm, agave, kapok, cotton, ramie, flax, hemp, jute, sisal, nettle, coir—into apparel constituted a major advance in human invention. Initial fabric technology dates to 36,000 B.C.E. east of the Black Sea with the boiling, squeezing, and twirling of flax for linen, a cellulose fabric first woven in the Dzudzuana Cave, Georgia. Evidence from 10,000 B.C.E. found in Zagros, Anatolia, shows that herders turned goat fleece into yarn for capes and cloaks, a protein-based apparel trend that spread to Mesopotamia and Judea for application to socks and sweaters.

The Western Hemisphere evolved unique apparel from wild plants. In the Mesolithic era after 8000 B.C.E., inhabitants of the Guitarrero Cave west of Chimbote, Peru, twined or plaited cotton by alternating odd and even strands for bags and belts. Among Paleo-Indian tribes at the Windover archaeological site in Florida around 6000 B.C.E., weavers turned palm and palmetto leaves into burial shrouds. By 5500 B.C.E., indigenous Japanese wove elm bark and hemp into cloth, a skill that paralleled the Polynesian pounding of paper mulberry bark into fabric for capes.

In 5000 B.C.E., fiber technology broadened worldwide, providing an alternative to weighty hides and pelts through the processing of flax, palm, rushes, reeds, and papyrus. Swiss flax harvesters twisted fibers into linen thread. After the Egyptian development of sheep's fleece into blankets and ramie bast fiber into antimicrobial mummy shrouds, the processing methods spread to China, Nubia, and the Philippines.

Simultaneously, the Chinese developed spun silk, a durable natural fiber unwound from cocoon waste. The quality of tussah, which had its source in the cocoons of wild *Antheraea paphia* silkworms, depended on terroir, the complex interaction of geography, climate, and temperature on living organisms. Cotton came into use in China around 4700 B.C.E. with washable, cool fibers from the tropical or subtropical family of wild mallow (*Gossypium malavaceae*) shrubs.

Expanding Variety

While flax, hemp, cotton, wool, and silk acquired respect worldwide as trade goods, after 4300 B.C.E., the esparto grass (*Macrochloa tenacissima*) common to Iberia and northern Africa served the tunic makers and espadrille and bag plaiters of Cueva de los Murciélagos in southern Spain. By 4000 B.C.E., Egyptian clothiers relied on linen fabric for everyday kilts and tunics and for corpse wrappings. During the same era, yarn spinners in Sudan and subtropical Africa made a hemp-like yarn from kenaf (*Hibiscus cannabinus*) for coarse bags and tunics. In Borneo, hill-dwelling Dayaks formed long loincloths from the bark bast of the paper mulberry or ficus tree and graced the hip wraps with tiny feathers.

After 3500 B.C.E., the Valdivia of present-day Ecuador wove cotton for capes and mantles, sarongs, tabards, and wrapped skirts, while Andeans spun alpaca and llama hair into durable, cushiony wool thread for body wraps. Around 3000 B.C.E., later in the Neolithic era, the Harappa in the Indus

Valley turned cotton goods into women's saris and items for barter. By 2600 B.C.E., the more knowledgeable Chinese spinners were producing shimmering silk thread. The resulting court garments and trade goods marketed in Egypt, Syria, and Persia constituted the height of ancient textile arts.

Bronze Age clothiers developed specialized uses for individual fibers, as with the ritual leaf skirts and barkcloth beaten with mallets in Sumatra, the Philippines, and Bali as early as 2000 B.C.E. Archaeologists have identified fibers work from the first millennium B.C.E., notably the nettle (*Urtica diocia*) burial garments first loomed into fabric at what is now Voldtofte, Denmark, and the white cotton gauze and sheep's wool strap that bound a man mummified at Cherchen in the Tarim Basin of northwest China.

Among the Basketmaker and Pueblo tribes on the Colorado Plateau, the twining of sandals from yucca and human hair, and cotton yarn manufacture, began in 500 B.C.E. for use in bandoliers, aprons, belts, and headdress. Sophisticated dyeing and design marked scarves woven from alpaca and vicuña wool in Argentina, Bolivia, Peru, and Chile, as well as those made from goat and antelope fleece among Himalayan tribes around 300 B.C.E.

Processing Advances and Trade

Textile advancement took on new vigor during the Middle Ages, exemplified by the knotted elm barkcloth appliquéd for formal *attus* (tunics), the national costume of the Ainu hunter-gatherers of Japan. The Ainu turned seabird feathers, cattails (*Typha typhaceae*), nettle, abaca (*Musa textilis*), and wild rye into other woven and quilted apparel lighter and less brittle than barkcloth.

Globally, knitters chose short wool fibers from lambs for utilitarian stockings and sweaters. Skein yarn producers texturized superior fibers for hand knitting, as with the camel hair exported from Cyprus and Syria for cameline. Worsted spinning began with removal of short fibers during combing, then smoothing the finished yarn by twisting and winding it into fancy grades. Cashmere, a parallel of worsted sheep's wool, required the moisture of goat hair to soften strands.

In the last centuries of the medieval era, Japanese textile specialists on Ryukyu wove raw or boiled *basho* (banana fiber) into kimonos and work clothes and shared the technology with China in the 1300s. The Maori of New Zealand, meanwhile, used coir cording to weave bird feathers into tiaras and *kahu kiwi* (royal cloaks).

The 1600s introduced cross-cultural fiber exchange as adventurers in the Western Hemisphere and the Pacific and Indian oceans began studying native uses of Polynesian feathers and tapa barkcloth for cloaks, cedar bark for Kwakiutl capes in the Pacific Northwest, Pawnee deer hair sashes, basketry hats and raffia skirts among the California Pomo, Mexican henequen (*Agave fourcroydes*) netting, Inuit belting with seal sinew and gut, and Indian sisal for cording, hemp for bags and straps, and kapok for wadding in padded jackets. Conquistadores in Mexico observed Aztec repairing yucca sandals, and in Peru, viewed the weaving of fique (*Furcraea andina*) into purses and footwear and the twining of sisal or agave into toe-loop sandals. Frontier explorers of the Dakotas discovered the use of horsehair for fringing Lakota shirts.

By the 1800s, the application of chemistry to fabric finishing and dyes changed the sources and standards of the apparel industry. By laminating fibers with artificial waterproofing and extruding polymers into filament, the Industrial Revolution heightened consumer expectations of garments that outperformed historical staples. In the twentieth century, chemical application of silica, petrochemicals, and metal revitalized fashion with garments that met modern needs.

During the economic revolution in China in the 1980s, average consumers found adequate natural fiber goods increasingly available at department stores. In addition, buyers searched for natural silk, down, and leather apparel. The Green Movement of the 1990s and 2000s restored organic fibers to use as a means of supporting indigenous growers and herders producing sustainable fibers in such regions as Peru and Scandinavia and retaining traditional motifs of tribes in Malaysia and Oceania. At present, the Dida of the Ivory Coast express tribal membership by decorating cloaks, loincloths, and skirts with circles, ovals, dots, and rectangles. To make art cloth, they tie-dye raffia palm fiber into earth-toned plaits edged in knotting or fringe.

See also: Cotton and Cotton Products; Felt; Linen; Silk and Sericulture; Spinning, Textile; Textile Manufacturing; Wool and Wool Products; Yarn.

Further Reading

Jenkins, David, ed. *The Cambridge History of Western Textiles.* New York: Cambridge University Press, 2003.

McDonald, Fiona. *Textiles: A History.* Barnsley, UK: Remember When, 2011.

Schoeser, Mary. *World Textiles: A Concise History.* New York: Thames & Hudson, 2003.

Fibers, Synthetic

Clothing materials synthesized by inventors have improved the performance of woven and molded goods and lowered garment prices. From biblical times, royal courts displayed grandeur with cloth of gold, a refinement of silk with gold laminates. In India, weavers produced cloth of silver, a variant used for weaving priestly garments and kingly robes.

In the 600s C.E., Byzantine and Syrian yarn makers augmented the sheen and value of cotton and silk threads by wrapping them in gold. After the 800s, metallic fiber manufacture centered in Cyprus and farther west in Venice, Lucca, Genoa, and Sicily. Mediterranean traders supplied the world with glittering thread for embroidery, trim, and cord for military insignias on sleeves, collars, medals, buttons, and hat brims.

A heavier metallic cloth from Persia, samite (twilled silk) added gold foil to yarns for gilt material, which appealed to Vikings for burial wraps and, in the eleventh century, to Russians for gloves. Crusaders captured samite during raids on the Holy Lands. During his long reign over England in the thirteenth century, Henry III purchased cloth of gold and samite for the wardrobe of the royal family and for court livery. A show of metallic clothes inspired sumptuary laws, which forbade the lower classes from wearing regal fabrics.

Industrial Age Technologies

The creation of artificial silk from cellulose acetate began with the work of French chemist Paul Schüt-zenberger, who generated shiny filament from cotton and beech wood pulp in 1865, and from French industrialist Hilaire Bernigaud de Chardonnet, who invented viscose in 1889. Rather than alter the textile industry, cellulose acetate and viscose prefigured the injection molding of bio-plastic eyeglass frames in Italy at century's end. Around the same time, haute couture created a demand for lamé, a metallic fabric that added sparkle to evening gowns, shoes, and handbags.

In 1899, American inventor Humphrey O'Sullivan patented the rubber heel as a substitute for more expensive leather. Vulcanized rubber added waterproofing to heels and soles, and spring to the step. The formation of a rubber toe cap prevented the big toe from punching a hole in shoe material. Rubber heels accounted for 90 percent of men's selections and about 80 percent of women's footwear. Sailors found rubber-soled deck shoes an improvement over leather soles, which often slipped on climbs into the rigging or along the gunnels. In 1912, unvulcanized crepe rubber texturized with cashew nut shells formed the "tempered" sole, which replaced hard rubber for men's golf and leisure shoes.

During World War I, the adaptation of Celanese fabric to apparel introduced inexpensive trimming, top-stitching thread, lining, hosiery, and crochet yarn. After 1924, American clothing manufacturers began replacing silk yard goods and ribbon with acetate, a low-priced substitute that maintained a high sheen and held permanent pleats for skirts and dresses. Resilient acetate blends in taffeta, satin, and brocade weaves promoted luster while reducing wrinkles and fading in women's saris in India and Korean kimonos. Nylon, a DuPont thermoplastic with a silky sheen, helped protect soldiers as flak vests during World War II and satisfied women's need for low-cost hosiery. By 1945, nylon edged out cotton by controlling one-quarter of U.S. fabric manufacture.

The refinement of rayon fiber spinning in the 1940s yielded high-tenacity yarn from lignin (wood cellulose) or bamboo pulp. A renewable and biodegradable material, rayon imitated the texture and drape of linen, cotton, wool, and silk. Its ease of dyeing and cool feel against the skin generated demand for rayon shirts, jackets, lingerie, socks, and blankets in humid climates, particularly India. Simultaneously, in Germany, Bayer refined acrylon into Dralon, the equivalent of DuPont Orlon. In 1947, the addition of metallic yarns to U.S. fibers coincided with the popularity of haute couture and knockoff evening wear.

Synthetic Fad Attire

After 1950, the processing of synthetic fibers into fake fur supplied material for quick-drying winter apparel and skiwear at a low price; the same process made available easy-care Dacron nurse's uniforms. Designers Pierre Balmain and Christian Dior incorporated the light, waterproof fabrics in sportswear and advertised their warmth, fast drying, and minimal shrinkage.

In 1963, the introduction of Corfam artificial leather by DuPont reduced the prices and longevity of fashion goods, notably the faddish go-go boot. Designer André Courrèges promoted dance boots in acid-colored polyvinyl chloride (PVC) to create a Space Age image. Futuristic artificial leather vests and jackets topped polo sweaters, tight jeans, miniskirts, and biker boots.

The mass production of Vinylon, which chemist Lee Seung-ki developed from coal and limestone in Korea in 1939, produced a popular fabric for 1960s apparel. North Koreans applied the fiber to shoes and to stuffing for quilted jackets, but Vinylon never surpassed nylon in texture or value. During the same era, Italian chemists refined olefin polymers for use in CoolMax sportswear and for thermal jackets, gloves, boot linings, and hoods made from 3M's lightweight Thinsulate, a breathable, low-bulk replacement for duck and goose down.

In the United States, Orlon (acrylic polyester) seized the fashion world with a soft, woolly fiber that competed with cashmere for the manufacture of baby clothes, sweaters, scarves, socks, gloves, and hats. In Chelsea, England, in 1963, designer Mary Quant introduced youthful hot pants, miniskirts, and T-shirts in synthetics and wet-look rainwear in polyvinyl chloride, originating a new market for British fashion.

In the 1970s, the development of DuPont's para-aramid Kevlar for military body armor and police vests boosted the safety of wearers threatened by explosives and small arms fire. For ordinary consumers, the Kevlar market increased the tensile strength needed in protective chaps, sleeves, jacket padding, and gloves and the turnout gear of firefighters and rescue teams. Nike applied Kevlar advances to basketball shoes and laces, while Adidas used it in football boots.

The 1980s saw the incorporation of iridescent Lurex, metallic laminated nylon and polyester threads that boosted the appeal of sportswear and dance wear, such as the stainless steel–threaded mohair and realistic plastic skin bodice designed by fabric engineer Issey Miyake. Distributed from Paris and London, Lurex yarns added glitter to knitting, embroidery, and lace. Designers in New York, Milan, and Melbourne popularized Lurex among youthful consumers in metallic tones as well as red, violet, green, yellow, blue, and beige. Soft-glazed Lurex yielded sweater yarns for lightweight, body-hugging knits.

Gimp (stiffened) yarns made from wrapped viscose produced an antique effect suited to shawls and suits. Suncoco in Hong Kong advanced the metallic yarn industry by laminating acrylic and wool threads for fluffier yarns. In China, an end to the rationing of cotton fabric occurred in the mid-1980s, when distribution of synthetics boosted market share to 40 percent of dress goods. By 1987, Chinese department stores displayed a wide variety of qualities and styles in synthetic fibers at affordable prices.

After 1991 in the United States, Austria, and the United Kingdom, the manufacture of Tencel from eucalyptus wood heightened competition against cotton, ramie, and linen. More costly than cotton or rayon, Tencel, an imitator of silk, leather, and suede, suited the style and fit of chino and denim for play clothes and matched the feel and moisture uptake of knitting yarn and sports

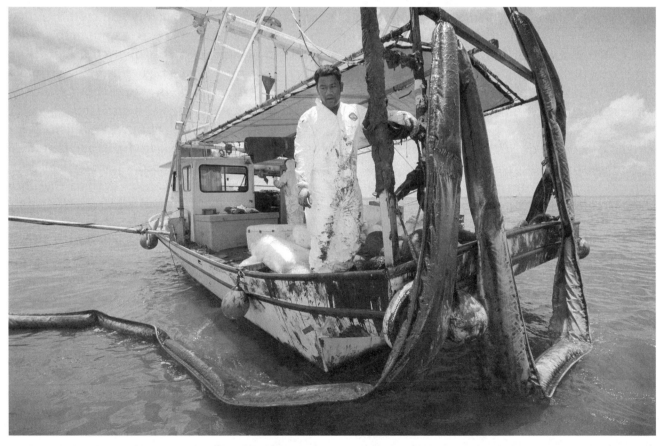

Workers in the Gulf of Mexico donned Tyvek hazmat suits for cleanup operations after the Deepwater Horizon oil spill in 2010. A waterproof polyethylene fiber, Tyvek is also used for laboratory coats, backpack material, and housing wrap. *(AP Photo/Charlie Neibergall)*

knits, as well as the sheen of dress shirts, blouses, and women's suits. The warmth of Tencel filament reduced the thickness of padded coats and skiwear while wicking away perspiration and maintaining body temperature. Additional selling points for Tencel included the durability of work clothes, softness for sensitive skin, and the bacteria shield necessary for medical uniforms and patient wear.

In the twenty-first century, the media has lauded the qualities of much synthetic attire, such as the Nomex flameproof suits and masks of race car drivers and the Thinsulate toggle coats, gloves, and boot insoles worn by the Canadian ski team and climbers of Mount Everest. Today, synthetic fibers solve apparel problems across the spectrum, from carbon thermal-resistant proximity suits for the oil industry and antiradiation garments for pregnant women to fiberglass sports helmets, Tyvek polyethylene laboratory coveralls and hazmat suits, and stainless steel work suits for butchers and astronauts. Polyethylene even solves the problems of cosmetic prosthetics with the formation of replacement ears and noses.

Fashion designers base flexible sportswear and dance and skating costumes on the elastomers in spandex and Lycra, both of which conform to reaching and stretching and protect the limbs of the disabled. In 2002, demand for China's synthetic yarns and fabrics and for India's synthetic garments remained high in unindustrialized areas of Benin, Nigeria, Ivory Coast, Togo, and South Africa. In Great Britain, a trend toward individual eyelash extensions derived from the manufacture of fake mink lashes made in Korea from silk or high-gloss Keraspecific Fibre, which imitates the look and feel of human hair when glued into place. Demand for more sustainable and biodegradable materials has increased the value of bamboo rayon, which requires no pesticides or fertilizer and half the irrigation of hardwoods.

See also: Microfiber; Nylon; Polyester; Rayon; Spandex; Textile Manufacturing.

Further Reading

Handley, Susannah. *Nylon: The Story of a Fashion Revolution.* Baltimore, MD: Johns Hopkins University Press, 1999.
McIntyre, J.E., ed. *Synthetic Fibres: Nylon, Polyester, Acrylic, Polyolefin.* Boca Raton, FL: CRC, 2005.
Smith, Matthew Boyd. *Polyester: The Indestructible Fashion.* Atglen, PA: Schiffer, 1998.

Flowers

An accessory to hair and body ornamentation, flowers and greenery provide fresh adornment that encompasses natural colors, shapes, and scents. In India from 1700 B.C.E., devotees of the divine being Krishna saluted him with seasonal attire, banyan leaves, blue water lilies, flax, and fragrant jasmine. Worship at Buddhist temples involved bouquets of henna flowers. Etruscan war heroes received U-shaped bay laurel (*Laurus nobilis*) crowns.

Ancient Adornments

Greek interest in flower adornment filled books describing types of blossoms and leaves and the accompanying decorum. At Delphi, champion athletes accepted *kotinos* (wreaths) twisted from branches growing on a sacred wild olive tree (*Olea oleaster*) behind the Temple of Zeus. Poets and playwrights received sprigs of laurel honoring the many-faceted god Apollo. Amid celebrants wearing laurel crowns, scholars accepted oak leaf (*Quercus*) crowns symbolizing the wisdom of Zeus.

After 776 B.C.E., Greek processions to the annual bathing of Nike, the victory goddess and symbol of the Olympic games, incorporated shoulder garlands as cult gifts. In the sixth century B.C.E., the devout capped the statues of Dionysus, Apollo, Zeus, Hades, and Herakles with wreaths of ivy (*Hedera helix*) or crowns of flowers like that worn by Helios, the harvest deity, and by Flora, the goddess of spring celebrated on May Day. Brides carried myrtle (*Myrtus communis*) wreaths and rooted a sprig to plant in the garden of their new homes.

On Roman holidays, priests sported the *corona spicea* (grain crown) or the *corona sacerdotalis* (priestly crown) woven of olive twigs. Merrymakers presented flower necklaces to the attendants at the Temple of Vesta and festooned statues and altars with the *corona longa* (flower swag). By order of the senate, garland thieves risked prison terms or execution.

Civic chaplets (wreath crowns) epitomized public acclamation, as with the grass crown of cereal grains, holly (*Ilex*), and flowers bestowed on Quintus Fabius Maximus, a commander who rescued Roman troops from defeat after the Battle of Cannae in 216 B.C.E. Following the legionary invasion of Britannia in 55 B.C.E., Julius Caesar surveyed the Druidic cult, which valued oak leaves and mistletoe for devotional crowns. For his victories, Caesar received the civic crown of oak leaves, an honorarium also bestowed on his nephew and successor, Augustus Caesar.

In the pre-Christian era, according to Slavic custom, Ukrainians decked young girls and maidens with the *vinok,* a wildflower wreath adorning the hair or maiden's cap during the summer solstice. From the first century C.E., Judeo-Christian communities reprised Roman wreath ceremonies by awarding white flowers, emblematic of innocence and purity, to female candidates for religious confirmation. Egyptians emulated Roman chaplets by interweaving ivy collars with narcissus, lotus buds, and pomegranate blossoms and, after the spread of Islam, by selling henna (*Lawsonia inermis*) bouquets at flower stalls under the sobriquet "Muhammad's blossoms."

Polynesian Rituals

From the Society Islands to New Zealand after the 700s C.E., flower garlands conveyed respect and affection for men, women, and children. Celebratory leis (flower loops) tied around the neck, wrist, or crown of a sun hat contained feathers, Spanish moss, fern fronds, and ti (*Cordyline fruticosa*) and maile (*Alyxia oliviformis*) leaves intertwined in a double helix with wiliwili (*Erythrina sandwicensis*) pods, carnations, orchids, heliotrope, bougainvillea, frangipani, and fragrant tuberoses, ginger, and jasmine. Polynesian youths entered coming-of-age rituals nude, then tied on the lavalava (loincloth) and garlands of leaves and blossoms.

Samoans shaped *sei,* clusters of blossoms pinned at the ear or in the hair. Tongans varied garland and loop arrangements with triangles and crescents. A more substantial garland for dancers,

the Hawaiian *kui* displayed flowers strung on a thread or length of raffia. The *humuhumu* (binding) began with a paper or felt backing and the overlapping of blossoms for stitching into necklaces, hatbands, and crowns.

Hawaiians draped the dead with blossoms and lianas and blessed a bride and groom with open garlands, which the couple tied into loops after taking their vows. Islanders honored divine icons and the *ali'i* (royal family) and their statues with multiple closed leis draped in front and back and garland streamers displayed across the shoulders. Citizens of the eight islands identified themselves with colors ranging from yellow for Oahu, purple for Kauai, and pink for Maui to the silver heliotrope of the sacred isle of Kaho'olawe.

Medieval and Modern Messages

Medieval flower adornment and the strewing of blossoms expressed welcome to visitors and congratulations to scholars and married couples. Examples include the jasmine garlands that Sindhi women on the Indus River coiled in their hair during festivals, miniature rosemary circlets presented to Polish couples, rue fillets on Lithuanian brides-to-be, and protective yarrow in the wreaths of Scots brides. From 965, during the rule of King Gwangjong, Korean rites of passage awarded flowers to youths as emblems of maturity. Men, too, enhanced holiday or feast ensembles with garlands, such as the laurel garland bestowed on the poet Petrarch in 1341. Vintners topped their heads with ivy circlets as a gesture of honor to grape vines during pruning.

In the late Middle Ages, German and Scandinavian maidens celebrated May Day by weaving daisy, lily, verbena, rosemary, and fennel into fillets, bracelets, and neck garlands and ground ivy (*Glechoma hederacea*) into swags to drape the breasts. In place of ropes of flowers and greenery, tussie-mussies or nosegays—small bud clusters wrapped in doilies and ribbons—offered alternatives for pinning to the hair or bodice or carrying in the hand. To preserve the sentiment and fragrance of head garlands, brides sometimes saved the petals for an aromatic sachet to sweeten chests of lingerie.

During the Renaissance, gifts of flowers in curvilinear C and S shapes introduced courtship rituals. Romantics elevated floriography (flower symbolism), which extolled single lilies for luminescence and purity of heart, rosebud garlands for beauty and celebration, and bouquets of violets and daisies for innocence and chastity. On January 6, 1540, at the fourth marriage of Henry VIII, Anne of Cleves adorned her hair with a rosemary bridal garland.

In the 1830s, flowered hair ornaments brightened Bohemian hairstyles. After 1837, Queen Victoria's subjects presented bouquets to her during public appearances. The Victorian Age established live corsages as a standard gift to mothers, grandmothers, and godmothers of the bride at weddings. Men communicated with women in the language of flowers but limited their own floral decoration to boutonnieres, which fastened to the buttonhole in the lapel.

The twentieth century promoted the growth of the floral business by telephone and Internet. Shops delivered to debutantes, prom dates, and graduates wrist corsages and orchids and tea roses in net or tulle tufts for pinning on gown, hair, or purse. Valentine's Day introduced the presentation of removable corsages fastened to candy boxes. For hospital patients, pillow corsages added a touched of beauty and fragrance to the sick room.

In the 1990s, retro departments at jewelry stores revitalized Victorian flower holders, tiny metal vases that fastened to dresses and wraps with pins. Twenty-first-century weddings revived naturalistic flower displays of the cascade and the arm bouquet, a loose gathering of blossoms sometimes contained in a basket.

See also: Accessories; Coming-of-Age Attire; Hairdressing; Holiday Costumes; Pageantry.

Further Reading

Fisher, Celia. *Flowers of the Renaissance.* London: Frances Lincoln Limited, 2011.

Lerner, Ernst. *Folklore and Symbolism of Flowers, Plants and Trees.* Mineola, NY: Dover, 2003.

Silvester, Hans. *Natural Fashion: Tribal Decoration from Africa.* New York: Thames & Hudson, 2008.

Watts, Donald. *Dictionary of Plant Lore.* Burlington, MA: Elsevier, 2007.

Formal Attire, Female

Special occasions have required meticulous dress, accessories, and grooming since early human history. From 2800 B.C.E., Indus Valley occasions called for the sari, an exquisite drape of fabric 12 to 27 feet (3.7 to 8.2 meters) long that enwrapped both earthly women and goddesses. Around 824 B.C.E., Queen Semiramis of Assyria returned from an expedition to India with 8,000 lush tiger pelts for use in throne garnishing and formal headdress.

In the early Middle Ages, Czech and Slovakian women arrayed themselves in a white head wrap under a tall circular headdress, while Chinese, India, Filipina, and Japanese women chose batiked waist sashes as evidence of official ensembles. Twelfth-century Chinese women adopted the *cheongsam* (long dress) for its elegant enhancement of the female body. Russian maidens garnished ordinary gowns with rabbit or squirrel fur, a costly hem lining, and completed the national costume with shiny black boots.

Around 1327, English widows formalized mourning with black habits and matching handkerchiefs, and with petticoats for funerals and graveside rites. After 1350, Indonesian, Thai, and Burmese women adorned themselves in the *kebaya* (blouse dress) of diaphanous silk or cotton embroidered with flowers. Furs so dominated fifteenth-century British formal dress that King James II of Scotland allowed female finery only on church holidays.

Late Renaissance dressing graced Spanish noblewomen in the mid-sixteenth century with the fur-lined velvet or taffeta *boemio* (demi-cloak), which reached between waist and hips, and once provided field dress for royal archers. Appreciating its flirty shape, settlers of the Spanish colonies carried the style to Latin America and the Caribbean. During the cold of winter, Russian women adorned evening wear with mittens and fur muffs, while Englishwomen adopted the chamois, doe, or suede glove as a formal hand dressing. After the 1670s, expensive Canadian furs fell out of fashion.

Eighteenth-century finery for Bhutanese women covered the obligatory jacket and tunic with an embroidered sash crossing the torso. In Valencia, Spanish noblewomen elongated their silhouette with a *peineta* (comb) or atifet (wire frame), a tall headdress topped with a black veil suitable for court or cathedral gatherings and events. Late in the century, Napoleonic fashion in gossamer Empire dresses required formal hand and arm warmers as accessories.

Victorian full dress reached heights of luxury and dignity. In 1852, couturier Charles Frederick Worth introduced haute couture, the creation of bespoke evening wear for women that included opera capes, feathered hats, and muffs reclaimed from the Napoleonic era (1799–1815). Stylists Jacques Doucet, Jeanne Paquin, and Paul Poiret advanced operatic glamour with oriental and art deco touches, notably the tasseled cowl on the luxurious pleated alma cloak made from velvet lined in satin and trimmed in ostrich feathers. Additional dependence on dazzling napped textiles wrapped the female torso in the velvet-lined mantelet closed at the throat with braided frogs.

The prominence of the tea gown in 1870 reduced the glamour of evening wear with the rise of glazed cottons, set-in cummerbunds, and Battenburg lace worn with lightweight tea jackets. For dressy horseback apparel, women fluted stand-up collars over jackets and tied lace fichus at the neck for draping the sternum. Female grooming standardized manicured oval nails to complement gloves buttoned at the wrist. Edwardian glamour derived from the theatrical flourishes of fashion plates, which featured the exotica of artists Antoni Gaudí, Alphonse Mucha, and Gustav Klimt and the filigree and gemstones of designers René Lalique and Louis Comfort Tiffany.

Late Belle Époque grandeur in the nineteenth century altered the female silhouette with bustles, fringed aprons, netted overlays, beading and ruching, and *gigot* (leg-of-mutton) sleeves above evening gloves. Russian designer Nadezhda Lamanova extended the French luxury look of ruffled tiers of duchesse satin and sequined trains in the formal wear she created for courtiers of Czar Nicholas II and Czarina Alexandra, the last of the Romanovs. Royal receptions and balls called for the height of tiaras and parures, treasures confiscated during the fall of the dynasty in 1917.

Opulent attire lost its dominance in the mid-1930s, when democratized couture replaced status-conscious fashion, especially among the young. For confirmation rituals, little girls in North America and Europe wore formal dresses with tulle headpieces. In China, young people chose unisex tunics and long coats that displayed propitious symbols for the New Year.

Swedish brides in the 1990s enhanced the shimmer of evening dresses and nuptial attire with microfiber organza and net. Today, still redolent with the stiff mannerisms of the past, Filipina debutantes continue to dress up for cotillions. Latina girls celebrate the *quinceañera* (fifteenth birthday) with opulent evening gowns and womanly makeup, tiaras, and high heels.

See also: Art Nouveau and Art Deco Fashion; Edwardian Styles and Fashions; Fur; Haute Couture; Satin; Silk and Sericulture; Velvet; Wedding Dress.

Further Reading

Dolin, Eric Jay. *Fur, Fortune, and Empire: The Epic History of the Fur Trade in America.* New York: W.W. Norton, 2010.

Jenkins, Jessica Kerwin. *Encyclopedia of the Exquisite: An Anecdotal History of Elegant Delights.* New York: Random House, 2010.

Metropolitan Museum of Art. *100 Dresses: The Costume Institute.* New York: Metropolitan Museum of Art, 2010.

Formal Attire, Male

Special masculine apparel has marked memorable life events and social gatherings from early history. Neolithic burial ritual after 12,000 B.C.E. marked Mesopotamian corpses with grand pendants and carved beads. After 6000 B.C.E. at Catal Höyük in south-central Anatolia, noble winding cloths, ochre dye, and plaster marked the corpse in splendor for the journey to the afterlife.

Among the Achaeans of Ancient Greece, dandies displayed the *chlamys* (cloak) and gold bands securing long hair. Mature Greek men modeled the himation (mantle), a unisex rectangular overgarment up to 12 feet (3.7 meters) long. After 715 B.C.E., Roman men and military officers blended formality with patriotism by draping themselves in the toga, a symbol of citizenship that the Emperor Augustus promoted after 27 B.C.E. The imperial army graced boots with animal paws and snouts as an integral part of parade dress. A formal woven robe set the tone for dinner parties.

Sixth-century C.E. Byzantium celebrated formal occasions with wait staff and guards dressed in imperial coats of arms and embroidered kilts. Upscale furriers from Genoa and Venice traveled to Constantinople to purchase astrakan, ermine, fox, marten, and sable, the favorite of the clergy for ceremonial stoles. Around 661, Islamic Arabs luxuriated in satin and silk robes over blousy pants, a compromise of formality with comfort.

Exquisite Materials

Late medieval formal dress focused on luxury, exemplified by the Dutch castor hat made from beaver or rabbit pelts and the English bag cap banded in fur. During the Renaissance, Bavarian males could consult a handbook, *Hofkleiderbücher* (*Court Attire Manual*), on types of formal attire suited to the status of honor guards, dukes, cavalry officers, and court messengers. Fifteenth-century dressing required formal academic regalia for officials and scholars that included the paneled scarf, cape and liripipe, hood, and corded bonnet or round cap.

For much of the Renaissance, accessories established status and dignity. The English set pulpit ministers apart from other males by outlining a uniform of black kirtle, habit, and cassock. Judges, college deans, and choristers enhanced plain robes with fluted ruffs, starched lace yokes, muslin neck cloths, and batiste or lawn falling bands reaching the bottom of the sternum. The contrast of white on black has remained dominant in men's formal attire to current times.

Late in the Renaissance, British dyers settled on logwood (*Haematoxylum campechianum*) from the Yucatán, Honduras, and Jamaica as the only true black tint for formal mourning apparel. To maintain black garments, wig bags prevented queues from spreading powder on the shoulders. Period style ornamented dressy equestrian outfits with a crop, an affectation that implied control of the horse but received little actual use. In China,

the *changshan* (long shirt) with mandarin collar equipped men for weddings and receptions.

In eighteenth-century southern Africa, traders to present-day Zimbabwe, Zambia, and Mozambique exploited the Zulu display of ceremonial leopard pelts at formal occasions honoring Shaka, an epic king. Around 1768, Nepalese males adopted the *daura* (tunic), *suruwal* (trousers), and *dhaki topi* (cap) as the most dignified silhouette for government receptions in Kathmandu. In 1794, during the Heian era in Japan, Shinto priests wore aristocratic apparel at temple services—a purple and red robe with a wood wand and peaked black hat, the formal headdress of samurai.

Suits and Uniforms

Eighteenth-century stately menswear for the British elevated military insignia and sashes, including the Scots kilt, tam, and formal plaid worn with short jacket and pointed vest. Noblemen favored extravagantly skirted frock coats, wigs, and plumes that accommodated riding to events on horseback. In British India, the standard *shalwar kameez* (long frock coat) provided the Muslim elite with an equivalent of the Englishman's dress coat. In 1736, the Prussian military chose a white Parisian cravat for formal parade dress. Into the Napoleonic era (1799–1815), the impeccable cravat with stickpin increased in prominence for formal occasions.

Style-conscious people in Europe and the Americas perused style guides in *The Lady's Realm* and *La Gazette du Bon Ton* and fashion plates in *Vanity Fair* for guidance to the best in contoured coats with well-appointed white tie, fur-collared mantles, gloves and mitts, top hats, and polished footwear. Men adopted meticulous grooming of short hair, curling mustaches, and clipped beards while emulating Prince Albert's wardrobe of dress frock coats with velvet lapels. To ensure proper appearance, haberdashers recommended the detachable wing collar and studs, a system invented in 1827.

Women's formal wear set a standard for public appearances by men. From the House of Worth after 1852, males purchased velvet formal wear to match the lush fabrics of female attire. European males replaced fitted overcoats with quilted mantles. At a family occasion in Denmark after

1863, King Christian IX sported a sedate black cutaway morning coat edged in braid along the notched lapels.

In the 1880s, the romantic female wardrobe required complementary menswear that included the lace or tulle fichu, trousers with piping down the leg, Bohemian cape, Balmoral cloak, and neatly trimmed beard. Urban silhouettes depicted men in dashing cravats or ascots with dress shirts and waistcoats, accoutrements eagerly mimicked by the American nouveau riche. Tuxedos topped by surtouts (overcoats) and Inverness capes required only the watch and chain, felt hat, and opera gloves as accessories.

Couture at the turn of the twentieth century favored men with military uniforms and tailored tuxedos featuring studs, notched velvet lapels, black tie, and cuff links. Pioneering fashion photographers Edward Steichen and Man Ray depicted elegant men in cutaway coats that revealed a trim waist. After 1910, George V of England clung to the traditional top hat, turned-up collar and cravat, knee-length frock coat with striped trousers, and cane. The Nehru jacket enjoyed a brief era of popularity in the 1960s, when men exchanged the lapels of the tuxedo for a button-up jacket with high circular collar.

A memorable array of men's formal dress accompanied the state funeral procession of President John F. Kennedy on November 25, 1963. Contrasting the dark jackets and ties of politicians and Washington officials, the shah of Iran, Lord Mountbatten, Ethiopian emperor Haile Selassie, and the Scots Black Watch arrived in braided uniforms displaying military honors. French president Charles de Gaulle contrasted exhibits of medals and sashes with a simple military suit adorned only with gold buttons and patch pockets.

To the present day, men in Kenya and Tanzania maintain the ankle-length *kanzu* (tunic) for dressy affairs and accessorize with a sport coat or *bisht* (cloak) and cap. Western formal attire, still based on the tuxedo, remains available from haberdashers who rent accessories, suits, footwear, canes, top hats, and capes for formal events. Middle Eastern celebrities alternate traditional robes and headdress with Western suit, shirt, and tie.

See also: Art Nouveau and Art Deco Fashion; Edwardian Styles and Fashions; Fur; Leisure Wear; Wedding Dress.

Further Reading

Beaujot, Ariel. *Victorian Fashion Accessories.* New York: Bloomsbury, 2012.

Flusser, Alan. *Dressing the Man: Mastering the Art of Permanent Fashion.* New York: HarperCollins, 2002.

Shannon, Brent Alan. *The Cut of His Coat: Men, Dress, and Consumer Culture in Britain, 1860–1914.* Athens: Ohio University Press, 2006.

French Clothing and Fashion

A nexus of international fashions, France has generated its own style from myriad influences. In the 200s B.C.E., early cobblers in Gaul cut laces for boots and offered shoe repairs and padding to travelers and pilgrims. By the late third century C.E., women were netting yarn into shoes and bags.

Frankish men in the Pyrenees added dash to plain apparel by rounding out blousy linen trousers with narrowed calves and attaching suede coin purses and pouches to belts for pockets. The Franks influenced the region's sense of formalism in 768, when Carloman chose the *casula* (choir gown) for priests and deacons. Charlemagne outfitted his army in 773 with mail armor and, after 800, set the tone of year-round comfort with his own fur-lined cloak, lambskin hunting coat, and high laced boots. His economic policies boosted imports of the Persian *sziir* or *szür,* a mantle with hanging sleeves.

Late medieval stitchery incorporated Arabic intarsia, geometric appliqués that added plants, animals, and coats of arms to shawls, mantles, and headdress. At the First Crusade in 1096, French officers graced shoulders with the red cross. While the cambric *cointoise* (caul) softened the female neckline, the midriff support, devised in 1350, shifted attention to a slim waist. Voyages to hot climates introduced soap makers to palm oil, which produced a softer laundry cleanser, a boon when people began changing clothes daily.

Royalty established wardrobe basics. After 1450, dressmakers tailored bodices to emphasize the female bust, a silhouette that suited the shape of Queen Marie d'Anjou. In Burgundy, Charles the Bold set the example of vivid coats by wearing a satin jacket. In 1496, Queen Anne of Brittany purchased life-size fashion dolls to instruct Isabella d'Este on French modes.

High Fashion

Bourbon tastes dominated the Renaissance as its most ornate, a source of hoods and doublets for portraiture, romantic eyewear of sea-green beryl and quartz crystal, quilted and petit point accessories, and skirts and slippers for the royal ballets organized by Catherine de' Medici. Accessories such as body binders, garters, ribbons, and feathered berets elevated ensembles for court appearances and accented children's couture with brocade and gilded stitchery. In 1520, the Italian square cap became a scholarly fad at the Sorbonne.

In the seventeenth century, dramatist Molière initiated stage masking to represent human duplicity in makeup and apparel. For the Gallic farmer, the revision of Dutch unisex wooden shoes as *sabots* supplied a functional one-piece clog for plowing and herding. Meanwhile, imported cotton prints channeled French fashion budgets to goods merchandised by the French East India Company and advertised in *Mercure Galant*. The light colors suited a trendy look in plunging necklines, popularized by the rising middle class. Coquettes back-combed their hairdos and garnished faces with cheek plumpers and *mouches* (patches), velvet scraps that covered blemishes. The extremes of Gallic high heels and powdered wigs created a breach with the English, who ridiculed the departure of French royalty from sensible dressing and hygiene.

At the court of Louis XIV in Versailles, details set formal wear apart from mundane attire. Prestigious courtiers favored glazed chintz, rhinestones, and metal and corded silk buttons. Males

During the reign of Louis XIV (1643–1715), the French court at Versailles set the trend in European dress. A fledgling fashion press marketed the latest court designs to the general public, opening the way for changing styles and fashion "seasons." *(DeA Picture Library/The Granger Collection, NYC—All rights reserved)*

maintained stature in powdered shoulder-length wigs and felt hats, which they topped with feathers. Chemists turned out stylish unisex colorants for lips, cheeks, eyelids, nails, and hair.

Social status in the 1740s established a schism. The aristocrat flaunted a pigtailed wig; his wife carried a towering jeweled headdress. French peasants, meanwhile, adopted the felt tricorn, a three-cocked brim around a raised crown dramatizing the prerevolutionary philosophy of *liberté, egalité, fraternité* (freedom, equality, brotherhood). The concept imbued world libertarians with egalitarian zeal and encouraged the sale of Gallic styles and footwear in North America and Russia.

French designs dominated wig making, lace, and costumes for ballet, relieving dancers of tight busks to free movement and improve breathing. Queen Marie Antoinette flaunted royal privilege by sporting wide felt hats, feathers, and ostrich plumes, affectations that cost her the Bourbon throne and her life. Following the French Revolution of 1789, survivors abandoned powdered wigs and cosmetics for more conservative dress. Sober Frenchmen adopted black and charcoal jackets, tall beaver hats with grosgrain bands and buckles, and small round felt hats that featured plumes impaled in red, white, and blue hatbands.

During the Napoleonic era (1799–1815), Continental Europeans emulated French court styles and added more choices of cosmetics and changes of apparel to their wardrobes. Empress Joséphine de Beauharnais reduced boning in women's waist cinches and introduced Empire styling to dresses, worn beneath an Indian shawl, sleeveless pelisse, or British redingote (long unlined coat). Men emulated the emperor's high-collar frock coat and short spencer made of silk or wool twill. After 1835, both men and women purchased gloves in standardized sizes, the innovation of a Grenoble glover.

The Belle Époque restored lush wardrobes to popularity, particularly the antique ribbons sold by the Callot Sisters, the translucent pastels popularized by Jacques Doucet, and the orientalism of designer Paul Poiret, who introduced kimonos and chemises. For formal entertaining and evenings out, women favored aprons, bustles, leg-of-mutton sleeves, short equestrienne jackets, and balletic bodices in taffeta and velvet. Designer René Lalique continued to satisfy the desire for beauty with filigree rings, bangles, and iridescent brooches picturing lianas, snakes, and butterflies. Department stores tempted consumers with art nouveau and art deco fabrics, swansdown and feathers, and lipsticks by Guerlain.

Coming Modernity

Still viable in Russia, Bourbon panache continued to invigorate royal couture for the Romanov court until its fall in 1917. In contrast to outdated couture, eccentric writer George Sand promoted feminist causes by rejecting skirts for slacks in public. Modiste Coco Chanel acknowledged the New Woman with travel suits, quilted jersey dresses, handbags, and hats, and the "little black dress" for a variety of evening events. Couturier Madeleine Vionnet impacted stage costuming with *déshabillés* (lingerie dresses) and bias cuts, the stock costume of improvisational dancer Isadora Duncan.

For tourists, Paris boutiques, the Printemps department store chain, and outdoor markets in Nice and Arles featured laces, lingerie, hosiery, and children's clothes. In the 1930s, Jeanne Lanvin marketed mother-daughter outfits and blended French opera dress with Middle Eastern touches to gowns and capes, a popular costume-party theme after the colonization of Algiers. By 1935, French manufacturers sold European quartermasters a one-piece helmet of polyethylene, a saver of lives during the coming world war.

After the Nazi occupation crushed Paris's chic design houses, fashion dolls dispatched to the United States, Iberia, and Scandinavia revived business in the 1940s and 1950s. Corsetiere Simone Pérèle replaced corsets with the bra, a feminist touch marketed in Paris. Globally, catalogs, such as La Redoute in Roubaix, increased demand for Caroline Reboux's hats and knockoff apparel imitating Christian Dior, Jean Patou, Jacques Fath, Lucien Lelong, and Robert Piguet.

A succession of twentieth-century celebrities has promoted the French flair, including singer Edith Piaff in knits, dancer Margot Fonteyn in Dior dresses, and actors Brigitte Bardot in tight designer jeans and Jeanne Moreau in suits and caped coats. The female models of Pierre Cardin made headlines in bubble hoods, kilts, and cat-suits, the men in zippered vests and unitards—styles that spread the French influence to Japan and Hong Kong. Spanish designer Cristóbal Balenciaga contributed seasonal balance to Air France stewardess uniforms in 1969.

See also: Belle Époque Fashion; Haute Couture; Mardi Gras and Carnival Costumes; Napoleonic Styles and Fashions.

Further Reading

DeJean, J.E. *The Essence of Style: How the French Invented High Fashion, Fine Food, Chic Cafés, Style, Sophistication, and Glamour.* New York: Free Press, 2005.

Holmes, Diana, and Carrie Tarr. *A "Belle Epoque"?: Women in French Society and Culture, 1890–1914.* New York: Berghahn, 2006.

Steele, Valerie. *Paris Fashion: A Cultural History.* 2nd ed. New York: Berg, 1998.

Stewart, Mary Lynn. *Dressing Modern Frenchwomen: Marketing Haute Couture, 1919–1939.* Baltimore, MD: Johns Hopkins University Press, 2008.

Weber, Caroline. *Queen of Fashion: What Marie Antoinette Wore to the Revolution.* New York: Henry Holt, 2006.

Fur

The pelts of land and sea mammals provided the first body coverings for humankind beginning in the Paleolithic era. The need for warmth and protection from harsh weather increased after 100,000 B.C.E., as the first *Homo sapiens* migrated north and northeast from Africa to Europe and Asia. The thickness and layering of pelts created an undercoat of down or ground hair on the thinnest examples and awn hair or a topcoat of guard hair on more luxurious, insulated skins, such as polar bear pelts.

Discerning clothing makers chose hides based on quality, texture, warmth, color, and exotic patterns and markings, such as white Arctic wolf for trim; long, soft Arctic fox belly fur in socks and around female chests to warm infants during breastfeeding; and the leopard pelts on the Zulu dancer's head, waist, and ankle dressing.

The most impressive combed fur garments denoted rank and ritual hierarchy and served as socioeconomic delineators as well as trade items for hunters and furriers and gifts to royalty. The earliest fur clothing took the form of shawls, wraps, and blankets, which wearers draped over their shoulders and tied into place with fibrous twine or leather thongs to ward off cold wind and rain or snow. Unfortunately, fur from animals sometimes carried fleas, which introduced epidemic contagion from typhus.

The invention of needle-and-thread technology around 38,000 B.C.E. enabled fashioners of garments to make a tidier, warmer coat and hood. Early couturiers tailored fur wardrobes to the first migrants into colder climes, where nomads hunted fox and reindeer. Siberian, Chinese, and Japanese potentates lined their garments and blankets with fur for warmth. Indigenous hunter-gatherers of Greenland, Japan, Russia and Siberia, Scandinavia, and northern North America valued bear, wolverine, and reindeer fur for insulation in socks and gloves. Fur also cushioned limbs and repelled water while hunters tracked their prey in winter as far north as the Arctic Circle.

Status

In the Nile Valley, skins from domesticated sheep provided ample pelts for shaping wraparound tunics. Clothing makers chose sheep fringe and lion tails for trimming mantles and state robes. In biblical times in North Africa, Palestine, and Arabia, furs adorned the Hebrew tabernacle and provided thinner pelts for kilts and fur collars. After 824 B.C.E., the Assyrian queen Semiramis appraised the success of a Babylonian campaign to India in terms of 8,000 tiger skins she carried home as trophies.

In the sixth century B.C.E., Greeks covered the standard chiton, or tunic, with whole animal pelts belted at the waist. They depicted the divine hero Hercules (Heracles or Herakles) in full lion skin, with the head as a hood, and honored the wine god Bacchus in panther skin, with paws and head symbolizing power. During journeys to the northeast around 450 B.C.E., the historian Herodotus admired ermine and sealskin, common furs of the Caspian peoples of Armenia, the ancient world's fur clearinghouse.

In North America about 250 B.C.E., the Apache and Sioux used buffalo pelts and deerskin for making cloaks. The Wampanoag of Massachusetts applied beaver, otter, or raccoon pelts to adult and children's wardrobes. The Nez Percé added otter collars to their buckskin shirts.

In the early days of Rome, soldiers wore the rain poncho, a simple pullover made of felted fur or leather. Throughout the Roman Empire after 27 B.C.E., officers decorated *cothurni* (combat boots) with the paws and snouts of smaller animals at the top as evidence of rank and power. For capes and tabards of animal pelts, Roman metalworkers fashioned brooches to hold garments in place at the shoulder.

In the Byzantine Empire, Constantinople achieved a reputation as a clothing center and fur market for Genoese and Venetian buyers of astrakhan (karakul, an aborted or young broadtail lamb), ermine, fox, marten, and sable. The highest outlays went for Russian sable, which women valued for softness and church prelates bought as symbols of godliness. For the lower classes, especially hunters, unclipped pelts provided material for fur garments, caps, and bags.

Practical Furs

Russian women made specific use of furs. Unmarried girls lengthened the hems of their tunics with 18 inches (46 centimeters) of rabbit or squirrel bellies, the softest and most flattering fur trim when stitched to fabrics. When seated in a draft, wearers of fur hems arranged the warm edgings around feet and ankles.

Romanesque costume featured fur in winter and summer and fur-lined tunics, gowns, leggings, and mantles for indoor wear in unheated castles and cathedrals. Feudal lords flaunted fine pelts as marks of status, particularly the black-spotted grey lynx pelt, a common lining or trimming. For prestige, Venetian doges edged fur capes in animal tails.

Italian designs influenced the cut and heft of Frankish clothes, which featured silk trimmed in genet (wildcat), hind (female red deer), lerion (dormouse), muskrat, otter, vair (squirrel), weasel, white rat, and wolf. In the 700s, the Franks developed a layered style that placed the tunic atop a fur pelisse (cloak) and over a chemise for three-layered warmth.

Imported Fashions

The Crusades, Christian military expeditions from the eleventh to the fourteenth century to capture the Holy Land, introduced knights to Persian lamb and other fine furs of Byzantium. Men in armor layered the rectangular basing cloak of *besshe* (squirrel fur) and the fur-edged surcoat with deep armholes to accommodate chain mail. The fur-edged semicircular cope, a unisex garment pinned on one shoulder, became fashionable and combined in winter with the fur-line *blanchet* (doublet) and a shoulder cape for warmth during travel. The Dutch added a separate topping, the castor hat, shaped from beaver or rabbit. In the household of England's King Henry III in 1217, Christmas livery established rank by the fur or cloth edging of their garments—vair for knights, rabbit for priests and chaplains, lamb for major servants, and plain cloth for the lowest staff members.

The Travels of Marco Polo (ca. 1300), a memoir by the Venetian trader in eastern Asia, piqued reader interest in Tatar fashion. The author cited examples of elegance, notably, the cloth-of-gold and silk *garnache* (tunic) with cape sleeves and lapels trimmed in ermine, fox, and sable and deep-crowned hats with earlaps, a Mongolian standard.

For the peerage, vair spotted with black lamb produced "miniver," the fur of choice for ranking earls and feudal lords. Young Englishmen popularized the bag cap, a turban-crowned tam adorned with a fur band. The Dutch added a new dimension in fur cloaks with the *houppelande,* a grand embroidered wrapper of velvet or silk trimmed in an ermine, marten, or sable collar that reached the ears. Commoners and serfs could afford only bird, cat, dog, lamb, moleskin, rabbit, sea mammal, or sheepskin pelts, the lowest in value.

Around 1350, European furriers emulated Asian styles with the almuce, a fur hood suitable for harsh weather. For court audiences, castellated or notched edges and long drooping angel sleeves on men or women revealed fur facings and linings.

Women cuffed long sleeves with fur and added folly bells as tinkly adornment.

After 1399, Henry IV of England enforced sumptuary laws to curtail underclass excesses in fur garments. During the rise of the fur-lined Italian *cioppa* and *pellanda* (overgowns) and the *zibellino,* a sable tippet, as a fashion accessory, Puritans in northwestern Europe and Bologna, Italy, suppressed expensive garments. In 1457, James II of Scotland reduced women's wearing of furs to holy days. Despite the trend toward economy, Anne of Brittany in 1491 displayed egregious wealth at her marriage to Maximilian I of Austria by wearing a wedding gown lined with 160 sable pelts.

The New World

The subarctic Kutchin people robed themselves in caribou hides with the fur turned inward to insulate the body. During the post-Columbian interchange between indigenous peoples and Europeans, the swapping of technology allotted pins, needles, scissors, knives, firearms, and kettles to Indians in exchange for mink, beaver, and otter pelts. Fur-lined moccasins, a common trade item, became an everyday shoe worn by natives and frontier settlers alike.

The rise in popularity of beaver or felted hats lured entrepreneurs into the fur trade in the upper Mississippi Valley and Canada, where deep winter pelts formed on small mammals, such as the American badger, a source of coarse, durable pelts. After 1550, Spanish ladies flaunted their wealth with the taffeta or velvet *boemio,* a formal demi-cloak lined in fur. The style migrated with colonists to the Caribbean, Mexico, and South America. The decline in European demand for high-fashion pelts after 1672 triggered a collapse in trade from the Canadian colonies, which undermined the French economy.

Specific fashion-driven demands turned the seventeenth century into the age of fur, a lucrative period for pelt graders and furriers. After 1627, the French *coureurs des bois* (woods runners) of New France dominated trade with the Huron, Ojibwa, and Iroquois from the Mississippi and Great Lakes regions along the Ottawa and St. Lawrence valleys. Dutch, Scots, and English fur dealers offered competition until 1670, when the Hudson's Bay Company established a monopoly on the pelt trade that it maintained for 320 years.

Fads

Because of a spike in world trade, eighteenth-century European fur styles stressed a blend of fashions, including the English busby, a tall military shako that remained popular for a half-century. The military inspired the short fur-lined pelisse popularized by Hussars as shoulder capes to top their uniforms, the forerunner of the fur-collared polonaise (greatcoat) adorned with silk frogs and fur-edged pockets. French uniforms acquired the fur *colback,* a cylindrical hat laced across the crown and topped with a plume.

Unlike the heelless, fur-edged mule, the Kampskatcha slipper, popular after 1786, added French low heels to Spanish uppers with Chinese upturned toes and fox fur linings. The banyan or nightgown, a loose fur-lined morning coat, provided warmth in the boudoir. The addition of a pelerine (elbow-length) cape displayed the lush combination of fur with velvet. For cold climates, seal fur gained popularity in the late 1700s. Farther south, the golden brown weasel pelt formed the lettice bonnet, which covered the ears. The Carolina beaver provided a thinner pelt for the Caroline hat, a less fashionable item worn by servants.

The nineteenth century revived interest in fur as a sport item with the fur-topped ankle-high Adelaide boot and the fur boa, tippet, or victorine, free-spirited accessories common to evening dress of the Gay Nineties. In 1894, Paris couturier Charles Frederick Worth added a fur collar and epaulettes to his velvet opera cloak. Girls' beaver fur derbies complemented fur muffs with matching tippets, which contained a padded tube pocketed to hold loose change and a card case for visits. Toques (wrapped velvet hats) featured astrakhan, an import to Western Europe from Uzbekistan and Turkmenistan.

In an era marred by high rates of tuberculosis, young women tucked "bosom friends" of fur into their coat bodices, which provided both warmth and protection during vigorous sports, such as

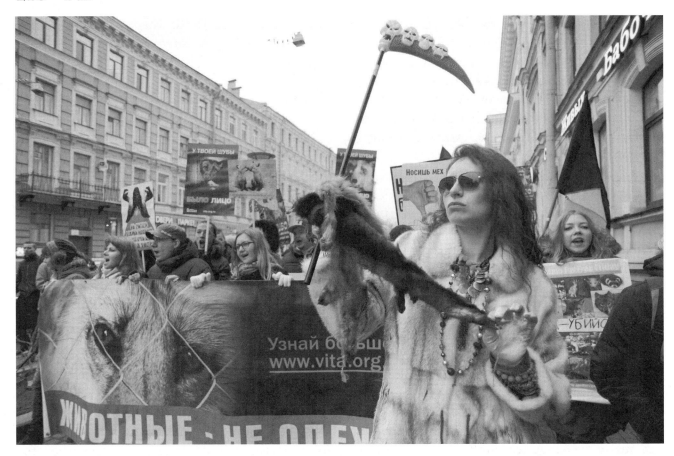

Animal rights activists protest in St. Petersburg, Russia, against the slaying of animals for fur. For centuries, Russia has been one of the world's largest traders in fox, sable, marten, lynx, mink, and other mammal furs prized for warm luxury attire. *(Olga Maltseva/AFP/Getty Images)*

sledding, hiking, and ice skating. The coatlet offered a fur bodice fastened with braided frogs and topped with a fanned collar. The late 1800s saw the rise of cheap raccoon and beaverette (dyed coney) for collars, cuffs, and trimming.

After the privations of World War I, high-fashion blue fox stoles, sheared chinchilla and nutria scarves, and mink and sable ankle-length coats in the 1920s returned furs to noble symbols of class distinction and privilege. Velvet baby shoes enhanced warmth with fur trim around the upper edge to match rabbit fur around knitted baby bonnets.

With the loss of family fortunes during the Great Depression, purchasers chose inexpensive fur boas for detail and warm raccoon coats for sports events. The World War II era produced a demand for angora, a soft, long-napped fiber from the angora goat or rabbit, the favorite of sweater girls. By the last decades of the twentieth century, however, threats to animal species and concerns over animal cruelty gave rise to anti-fur campaigns that challenged the status, prestige, and fashion appeal of natural fur garments.

See also: Arctic Attire; Hats, Men's; Hats, Women's; Needle and Thread; Prehistoric Clothing.

Further Reading

Dolin, Eric Jay. *Fur, Fortune, and Empire: The Epic History of the Fur Trade in America.* New York: W.W. Norton, 2010.

Gowans, Fred R. *Rocky Mountain Rendezvous: A History of the Fur Trade Rendezvous, 1825–1840.* Layton, UT: Gibbs Smith, 2005.

Isto, Sarah Crawford. *The Fur Farms of Alaska: Two Centuries of History and a Forgotten Stampede.* Fairbanks: University of Alaska Press, 2012.

Gap

A breakout chain retailer of youthful apparel for baby boomers and their children, the Gap profited from identifying trends in American pop culture and image and selling to teens in shopping malls.

In San Francisco in 1969, realtor Donald Fisher and modern art maven Doris Fisher invested $63,000 in a store that offered a broad range of Levi's jeans and Gap T-shirts arranged by size in wall cubbies. At the home store and a second store opened in San Jose in 1971, the company launched the sale of jeans and affordable khakis, chinos, corduroys, and pocket tees, along with records and tapes.

The conglomerate, which Doris Fisher named for the "generation gap," grew into a global chain selling windbreakers, tank tops, hoodies, sports bras, leggings, shorts, and recycled printed denim apparel and backpacks as well as maternity outfits. Advertisements linked Gap style with pop culture icons and models Whoopi Goldberg, Spike Lee, Lena Horne, LL Cool J, and Marilyn Monroe. Into the 1990s, trade analysis credited chief executive officer Millard S. "Mickey" Drexler with creating casual chic, the impetus to "casual" Fridays.

Gap stores achieved a reputation within a growing consumer base for quality and consistency. In April 1996, *Elle* magazine honored the Gap Corporation with compliments from designers Nino Cerruti, Carolina Herrera, and Giorgio Armani. In 1997, The Gap introduced online sales featuring GapFit for athletic bodies.

Within two years, the Gap had boosted its value by 24,000 percent—an overexpansion that saddled the company with long-term debt. Drexler's venture into brightly colored Gap brand low-rider pants and cropped T-shirts misjudged loyal Gap customers. The misstep preceded his ouster in May 2002 for misreading trends and boosting debt by $1.22 billion. The following autumn, his replacement, former Disney executive Paul S. Pressler, launched the Crazy Stripes campaign in sweaters, scarves, and hats, but failed at cost cutting, fashion research, and streamlining supply chains.

Reliance on child sweatshop labor in Saipan, Jordan, El Salvador, and India led to an undisclosed settlement of employee disputes in 2003 and a new company policy based on pro-labor ethics. In 2006, Gap stores promoted the sale of T-shirts from Lesotho, where profits uplifted disadvantaged workers. New designs, directed by Patrick Robinson, appealed to both genders in a range of economic and ethnic groups; however, a sales slump threatened the Gap, which lost market share in competition with J. Crew, The Limited, and Benetton and with the sale of Levi's products at Sears and J.C. Penney. In 2007, when the Fisher family owned 37 percent of Gap stock, company officials considered selling.

After Don Fisher's death on September 27, 2009, the company achieved sales of $16.27 billion. His sons Robert, William, and John managed 3,100 stores in the United States, Great Britain, Canada, France, Ireland, Israel, and Japan under company labels—Gap, Banana Republic, BabyGap, GapKids, GapBody, GapScents, Forth & Towne, Athleta, and Piperlime, an accessories and footwear emporium. The company's leading brand, Old Navy, discounted family apparel at 20–30 percent below retail, becoming the first retailer to top $1 billion in annual sales in less than four years.

Designer Patrick Robinson restored brand

fame in 2010 with Perfect Black Trousers but lost his post in May 2011 because of his failure to sell muted pastel shirts. The company committed a racial gaffe in 2012 with designer Mark McNairy's advertisement of a T-shirt emblazoned with the words "Manifest Destiny," a nineteenth-century slogan exonerating the United States for frontier land grabs and genocide of Native American tribes. An outcry on social media forced the company to pull the shirt from its store shelves. In 2013, Gap stores decreased in number by 21 percent but began infiltrating Brazilian, Croatian, Mexican, Puerto Rican, Korean, and Chinese retail markets.

See also: Retail Trade; Teen Trends.

Further Reading

Gap. www.gap.com

Nevaer, Louis E.V. *Into—and Out of—the Gap: A Cautionary Account of an American Retailer.* Westport, CT: Quorum, 2001.

Pasiuk, Laurie. *Vault Guide to the Top Retail Employers.* New York: Vault, 2005.

Gendered Dressing

From basic skin cloaks and blankets to unisex leggings, tunics, and pullover shirts, world fashion has evolved designs suited to the shape and tastes of both male and female. Living in clans and tribes, early humans developed means of signaling gender identity through the length and display of adult hairstyles. Field dress for active hunting and warfare and adaptable women's garments for pregnancy and breastfeeding further reduced androgyny, as with the surface manipulation of the *shamma* (body wrap) in Ethiopia to enhance sexual attraction.

Peruvian creation myths described primordial ancestors, the Ayar brothers, as appearing on earth fully garbed in gender-specific costume. Additional separation of the sexes derived from the style and application of Nuku Hivan tattoos in the Marquesas Islands, Nuba body paint in the Sudan, and the scarification of erotic patterns on the bodies of the Tiv of Nigeria. Conversely, the Japanese developed the kimono and the Koreans made the *hanbok* (square jacket) with no contouring for use by both men and women. Pacific islanders favored the New Guinean laplap (wrap skirt) and the Polynesian lavalava (loincloth or kilt), which left the upper body bare, for ritual and social events.

Around 1300 B.C.E., Assyrian dress codes introduced a form of female purdah requiring veiling and covered hair. Socialization taught girls how to maintain a womanly wardrobe and to adopt the grooming habits and gestures associated with long tunic skirts and headcloths. Social expectations reinforced gendered dress codes for Assyrian females.

Sexuality determined the clothing styles of Greeks, Etruscans, and Romans, who emphasized gendered dance and stage costumes to promote character identity. Classical mythology stressed the divide between male and female by the choice of astral symbols—the shield and spear of Aries/Mars for the bellicose male and the hand mirror of Aphrodite/Venus for the self-centered female. During the Roman Empire after 27 B.C.E., sumptuary regulations chastised women for vivid dyes and costume jewelry, two elements separating the female *palla* and *stola* from the ascetic male toga.

During the 700s C.E., Islamic androcentrism minimized public display of the female form with burkas and veiling. Far from Arabia in Morocco and Algeria, Maghrebi females managed veiling to suit their more liberal notions of femininity and a woman's right to wardrobe choice. Across northeastern Africa after 996 C.E., Caliph Al-Hakim halted the production and sale of shoes to women as a ploy to keep them sequestered.

Medieval law regulated sexual solicitation by publicizing gendered dress codes to set prostitutes apart from "decent" women. By the end of the First Crusade in 1099, Byzantine females began shaping the *bliaut* to accentuate the bosom, waist, and hips, contouring that rid clothing of T-shaped tunics. The Catholic hierarchy imposed a religious gendering of dress. In European convents, the Westminster code of 1127 banned women from wearing expensive pelts. Later church restrictions on jewelry and trailing headdress affected nuns but not priests or monks.

During the Renaissance, European males surpassed women in colored luxury fabrics, feathered hats, flashy shoes, and parti-color trunk hose. Men wore an oversized codpiece that doubled as a change purse. In England, the court of Elizabeth I favored damask with fur trim for men and distorted body shapes for women with farthingales and wheel petticoats that stressed a tiny waist.

The Stuart period in seventeenth-century England continued the trend toward gendered dressing with low necklines for women, but coats similar in cut to a man's doublet. Mid-eighteenth-century styles in France carried gendered extravagances to an extreme with pigtailed wigs for men and towering jeweled headdress for women. With the decapitations of the Bourbon king and queen Louis XVI and Marie Antoinette during the French Revolution, wardrobe shifted rapidly toward gendered but conservative garments.

Introduced by British trendsetter Beau Brummell, fashion in the Hanoverian era established a more sober wardrobe for men to complement the demure Empire style that women copied from France's Empress Joséphine. During the 1840s, at Hamilton's, Harrods, and Liberty in London, Wanamaker's in Philadelphia, Zion's Cooperative Mercantile in Salt Lake City, Goldwater's in San Francisco, and Marshall Field in Chicago, males differentiated their choices from female apparel by popularizing plain tailored white shirts, hip-length jackets, waistcoats, and ankle-length trousers. By century's end, men favored neatly trimmed beards and short hair along with creased trousers, cutaway coats, and suits. In marked contrast, women embraced the corset as the focus of the female wardrobe, followed in importance by petticoats and pantaloons.

Gender stereotypes began at birth with the grooming of infants. In the late nineteenth century, mothers in the West abandoned gender-neutral sacks and gowns and began choosing frilly pink outfits for daughters and masculine blue accoutrements for sons. Co-ed schools extended the gender identification with skirt uniforms for girls and pants for boys. In North America, religious groups, especially Quakers, Amish, and Mennonites, stressed spiritual expectations of men and women that paralleled home and farm duties, which society differentiated by gender.

The Edwardian notion of beauty amalgamated physical features with wardrobe selection and presentation. Glamour magazines positioned women's fashions and accessories, particularly hats and jewelry, to display femininity to best advantage. *Gentleman's Quarterly* (later *GQ*) took the opposite slant, featuring the well-outfitted male at work and play. The rise of female executives in the post–World War II era required reshaping of the male business suit, necktie, and oxfords to fit female needs in the workplace. Women who competed with men in business and the professions accepted restraint on girlish accessories as one of the compromises that allowed them to breach the glass ceiling, the invisible boundary impeding female advancement.

As gender stereotypes eroded in the 1970s, women had less difficulty finding medical, military, construction, and pilot's uniforms and shoes. Leisure wear—running shoes, shorts, T-shirts, and sportswear—featured unisex fabric and design that tailored garments to weather and outdoor conditions rather than gender. A 2010 campaign launched by *Ms.* magazine took dry cleaners, barbers, and toiletries merchants to task for charging more for women's purchases than men's.

See also: Bloomer, Amelia; Burka; Coming-of-Age Attire; Corsets and Girdles; Feminist Styles and Fashions; Sumptuary Laws; Unisex Clothing.

Further Reading

Crane, Diana. *Fashion and Its Social Agendas: Class, Gender, and Identity in Clothing.* Chicago: University of Chicago Press, 2000.

Levit, Nancy. *The Gender Line: Men, Women, and the Law.* New York: NYU Press, 2000.

Scranton, Philip, ed. *Beauty and Business: Commerce, Gender, and Culture in Modern America.* New York: Routledge, 2001.

Gimbel Brothers

A department store that grew into a chain and lasted a full century (1887–1987), Gimbels flourished in the American Northeast before advancing to branches in the West and South.

Adam Long Gimbel, a German Jewish immigrant from Rhein-Pfaltz, Bavaria, left dock work in New Orleans to become a pack peddler of ribbons and sewing notions. In 1842, at the Commercial House Hotel in Vincennes, Indiana, he established a two-and-a-half-story dry goods emporium called the Palace of Trade, which became the first department store in the Midwest. Rather than barter frontier style with whites and Native Americans, Adam advertised one-price retailing that democratized merchandising to all customers.

In 1843, he formed a partnership with younger brother Solomon Gimbel, called A. Gimbel & Bro., which sold shoes, cloaks, shawls, calico, flannel, velvet, muslin, silk, lace, ribbons, men's furnishings, and fur pelts. Adam Gimbel's sons—Benedict, Charles, Daniel, Ellis, Isaac, Jacob, and Louis—apprenticed as shipping clerks and buyers. Five of them relocated to Danville, Illinois, in 1881.

In 1887, Isaac and Jacob Gimbel tapped the retail promise of Milwaukee, Wisconsin, by opening a store with dedicated departments for handbags, jewelry, hosiery, cosmetics, and men's and women's clothing and shoes. By offering layaway, credit, charge plates, Friday bargains, and free delivery, manager Jacob Gimbel built both customer loyalty and volume. Louis Stanley Gimbel took control in 1894 and operated the Milwaukee emporium for 16 years. With an eye to the future, the two brothers began training Adam's eight grandsons to carry Gimbels into the twentieth century.

Following Adam Gimbel's retirement on March 17, 1894, sons Charles, Daniel, Ellis, and Jacob Gimbel opened a 5-acre (2-hectare) Philadelphia branch to robust crowds of women shoppers. The brothers developed modern merchandising by buying in bulk, selling at cut-rate prices, subletting military contracts, and delivering purchases in the first electric- and gas-powered wagons. To start the new year with basics, the January sale focused on underwear. On September 29, 1910, Bernard Feustman Gimbel, Isaac's son, opened a 28-acre (11-hectare) store on Herald Square in Manhattan and introduced the Promenade des Toilettes, a seasonal fashion show staged by Viennese designer Joseph Urban.

Perhaps because Bernard Gimbel kept the New York store dowdy to entice bargain hunters, brisk retailing in the 1910s built his fortune. Gimbels's rivalry with Macy's inspired bitter price wars carried out in newspaper advertisements and trade in such ready-to-wear items as ribbons, leather goods, Parisian millinery, and A. Steinhardt & Brothers fashion dolls. Ads hyped the $3.50 bathing dress as an improvement on baggy flannels. Gimbels increased competition by opening the nation's first bargain basement in 1912, which expanded to two levels.

Isaac Gimbel courted subway traffic with access through a company tunnel. The underground passage featured display windows lighted with purple, blue, green, and red to showcase Japanese kimonos. The company expanded its clientele with a 1915 holiday catalog featuring women's coats, petticoats in white and black, junior girls' apparel, and plumed hats. Ad copy declared the shirtwaist an American institution.

Tony ads pictured men and women modeling bowler hats, taffeta Easter bonnets, and Kuppenheimer suits in the $6.50 to $8.50 price range. Coordinated store displays in spring 1917 featured straw hats, golf caps, white oxfords, gaiters, and four-pocket jackets alongside golf clubs, tees, and balls. At the beginning of World War I, a custom shop supplied military officers with made-to-measure uniforms. A special on boys' suits offered one ensemble for $7.50 or two for $8.50. In January 1921, to supply the firm with underwear, Gimbels opened a Filipino factory in Manila, an early model of offshore clothing manufacture.

In 1923, company president Bernard Gimbel, backed by brother Frederic Adam Gimbel and Board Chairman Ellis Adam Gimbel, repositioned the chain in the clothing business with the addition of Saks 34th Street. That moderate-priced fashion mecca marketed cottons, chambrays, and pongee summer suits to the average consumer; an across-the-street bridge on the second floor level attached Saks to Gimbels headquarters. The company also made shrewd overseas investments, such as amber beads purchased at 76 cents and sold for $12.50, 16.4 times the original price. To speed carloads of apparel and shoes, Bernard employed telegraphy to factories and shippers.

Gimbels opened Saks Fifth Avenue, an upscale clothier and furrier, in 1924, with branches following in Chicago, Miami, and Palm Beach, Florida, over the next four years. Under the control of Bernard Gimbel's son, Lee Adam, and daughter-in-law, dress designer Sophie Haas Gimbel, Saks profited from the sale of sable coats, luxury hosiery, dinner dresses, and custom hats by milliner Tatiana du Plessix Liberman. In 1925, Gimbels added its Kaufman & Bauer location in Pittsburgh. Management increased sales by unitizing secondary goods around the shoe and dress departments and by establishing a Christmas letter service between children and Santa.

Throughout the late 1920s, Saks prospered at its Boston and San Francisco branches by competing against Filene's Basement, Marshall Field's, F. Simon, and Jordan's with such amenities as 26 escalators, subway stores, and multiple show windows. By 1930, the Gimbels-Saks conglomerate was the world's largest clothing chain. In 1941, *Life* magazine pictured the lavish evening couture of designer Sophie Gimbel—a bouffant satin damask evening gown graced with crystals and rhinestones, sold at the Salon Moderne, also the maker of Broadway costumes and culottes, an American fad.

On the other end of the consumer scene, Bernard Gimbel boasted full stocks of shoes and clothes for the whole family. In 1944, he earned the title of America's top merchant. His ads in *Boys' Life* featured campus trends in short raincoats, tweed sports coats, and fedoras. In 1947, the film *Miracle on 34th Street* boosted public awareness of chain-style merchandising.

Before Gimbels went out of business in 1987 under President Bruce Alva Gimbel, Bernard's son, store displays showcased leotards, bodysuits, swimwear, robes, drip-dry blouses, halter dresses, eyelet bridal wear, night wear, and matte nylon jersey gowns. Teens flocked to buy T-shirts garnished with skateboard and surfboard motifs by hot-iron transfer.

See also: Department Stores; Retail Trade.

Further Reading

Geenen, Paul H. *Schuster's & Gimbels: Milwaukee's Beloved Department Stores.* Charleston, SC: History, 2012.

Gimbel Brothers. *Gimbel's Illustrated 1915 Fashion Catalog.* New York: Dover, 1994.

Lisicky, Michael J. *Gimbels Has It!* Charleston, SC: History, 2011.

Givenchy, Hubert de (1927–)

Aristocratic fashion designer Hubert James Taffin de Givenchy added a genteel touch to French couture.

Born on February 21, 1927, in Beauvais to Béatrice Badin and Lucien de Givenchy, he is the grandson of Jules Jean Badin, a tapestry maker in Beauvais and Gobelins, and great-grandson of set makers for the Elysée Palace and the Paris Opera. After school, his maternal grandmother, Anne Marguerite Diéterlé, instructed him in a range of fabrics. Having chosen his life's work at age 10 at the 1937 Paris Exposition Universelle, he studied at the École des Beaux-Arts and apprenticed alongside Christian Dior and Pierre Balmain in Paris fashion houses, including those of Jacques Fath and Elsa Schiaparelli.

At age 25, Givenchy displayed his first collection, launching youthful separates from his fashion house, La Maison Givenchy, at the Parc Monceau. His business model for Givenchy Nouvelle Boutique helped to democratize luxury lines. His earliest silhouettes featured an ample 1950s skirt flowing from a slender waist that complemented a slender neck and sloping shoulders.

For supermodel Bettina Graziani, Givenchy created a classic, the Bettina blouse, with five eyelet-edged flounces on the forearm. With Cristóbal Balenciaga, he popularized the sack dress. Featured on the cover of *Life* magazine, he pioneered the leggy look, high-end Orlon fabrics, and ready-to-wear suited to street and air travel.

In 1953, Givenchy began making sculptured, ladylike apparel for actor Audrey Hepburn, designing the famed "little black dress" and a Bohemian cropped top and slender pedal pushers featured in *Sabrina* (1954). His silhouettes established Hepburn's elfin look, notably the high-bosomed, sleeveless, beltless costumes for *Funny*

Face (1957), *Love in the Afternoon* (1957), *Breakfast at Tiffany's* (1961), *Charade* (1963), *Paris When It Sizzles* (1964), *How to Steal a Million* (1966), and *Love Among Thieves* (1987). Hepburn reciprocated during the long collaboration by modeling Givenchy's designs.

A modernist trailblazer, Givenchy created wardrobes for opera star Maria Callas, actors Lauren Bacall and Grace Kelly, Wallis Warfield Simpson, Empress Farah Pahlavi of Iran, and Princess Caroline of Monaco. He decked his clients in bubble skirts, picture hats, bolero jackets, minimalist sportswear, cashmere coats, and a shawl-collared silk moiré ball gown. First Lady Jacqueline Kennedy wore a creamy silk Givenchy gown on a state visit to France in 1961; on November 24, 1963, she chose a black dress and veil of his design at the funeral for President John F. Kennedy. In 1963, Betsey Cushing Whitney modeled Givenchy's sleek princess dress in coral cotton lace embroidered in coral pieces and beads. In 1968, the designer created for Sunny Von Bülow a salmon silk dress edged at the neck, sleeves, and side slit in trembling feathers.

Givenchy introduced a men's line in 1973 that melded elegance with a refinement and masculinity that became his personal trademark. The designer sold his label to the Louis Vuitton Moët Hennessey conglomerate in 1988 and retired in 1995, leaving his couturier line to John Galliano and Alexander McQueen. In 2008, Christie's auction house auctioned Audrey Hepburn's "little black dress" from *Breakfast at Tiffany's* for $920,000.

See also: Fashion Design; French Clothing and Fashion.

Further Reading

Bye, Elizabeth. *Fashion Design.* New York: Bloomsbury, 2010.
Givenchy. www.givenchy.com
Polan, Brenda, and Roger Tredre. *The Great Fashion Designers.* New York: Bloomsbury, 2009.
Steele, Valerie, ed. *The Berg Companion to Fashion.* New York: Bloomsbury, 2010.

Glamour

A Condé Nast publication based in New York City, *Glamour* projects American style and pop culture to more than 2 million readers. An offshoot of *Hollywood Patterns,* the glossy monthly debuted in April 1939 as *Glamour of Hollywood,* selling for 15 cents per copy. In contrast to his reverence for elite *Vogue* readers, Nast intended for *Glamour* to inform a lower class of women, ages 18–49, of filmdom trends in clothing, hairstyles, accessories, and makeup. For early covers, the editor chose captivating shots of actors Vivien Leigh, Bette Davis, and Deanna Durbin.

Under the leadership of editor Alice Dickey Thompson, the early format influenced luxury consumers on what and where to buy to promote health, beauty, and charm. Thompson described the magazine's notion of "glamour" as the American girl's graciousness and vitality, a winning combination yielding happiness and success. Coverage extended to women's economic and career issues as well as articles on psychology and law. By March 1940, readers bought 200,000 copies; within another year, sales rose by 25 percent to 250,000.

In May 1941, the cover bore the title *Glamour,* subtitled *For Young Women—The Way to Fashion, Beauty, and Charm.* That July, covers began featuring unknown models rather than cinema stars. In 1941, the magazine hired Austrian-born graphics specialist Cipe Pineles, a feminist who became the first autonomous female art director of a mass-market publication. Pineles disliked the stodgy title "Glamour" and disdained Nast's condescension toward the working girl by developing tips on investment dressing and promoting individualism.

As World War II limited consumer spending on clothing and accessories, Pineles bolstered the magazine's fashion appeal by hiring the most talented artists and photographers of the day. In January 1942, she created a two-page spread of 35 miniature cartoons modeling resort wear—bathing suits and cover-ups, shorts sets, jumpsuits, pedal pushers with bolero, color block dress, and tunic dress. The following July, she published the arms of young women waving American flags, a gesture of support for females far from the war in Europe. A cover for January 1945 placed the confident working girl in a self-effacing pose with crossed ankles and handy umbrella.

In 1949, under second editor Elizabeth Penrose, another change to the subtitle—*for the girl with a job*—shifted *Glamour's* focus from complacent beauties and husband hunters to career women. When Kathleen Aston Casey took over as editor in 1954, she turned the magazine into a "fashion authority" and source on decor, food, travel, and amusement. August issues coordinated input from college girls. Careers dominated fashion layouts with visual tips for the smart, chic worker. Casey's focus in September, the selection of a versatile suit, acknowledged the importance of budgeting to the working girl. Another adjustment in September 1955 identified *Glamour* as *The Fashion Magazine for the Girl with a Job.* A final tweak in 1956 lopped the lengthy subtitle to *for young women.* In November 1959, the magazine was enlarged after absorbing *Charm,* a fashion magazine also directed by Pineles.

With one-quarter of editorial content devoted to wardrobe selection and chic ensembles, *Glamour* walked the high wire between feminism and vanity by making the smart young female feel valued by fashion designers as well as by the social network. A shift toward social consciousness in January 1968 under editor Ruth Whitney brought columns and features on pop culture, gender, and the cult of youth, as well as alerts to such bizarre fashion quirks as op art hosiery, go-go boots, and cartoonesque eye makeup. Writers ventured from beauty and style to commentary on birth control and the Vietnam War.

The staff achieved milestones in women's history with the first black model—Katiti Kironde—on the cover of an American fashion magazine in August 1968 and with commentary on women's frustrations with career obstacles. From 1981 to 1984, readers expressed their approval with a circulation bump of 15 percent. In 1992, *Glamour* earned a National Magazine Award for coverage of abortion issues, consent laws, lesbianism, sexually transmitted disease, smoking, diet and health, plastic surgery, and women's sports. In competition with *Cosmopolitan* and *Elle, Glamour* maintained its prominence for cool, sassy fashion and surveys of celebrities as well as coverage of standard dress sizes and misleading designer labels.

Glamour has made significant contributions to the feminist movement with its annual Top 10 College Women Competition. The staff winnowed the most promising college juniors out of a field of thousands of applicants from across the United States based on ambition, community service, and scholarship. Since 1989, the magazine has also hosted its annual Woman of the Year awards ceremony, citing notable contributors in the entertainment industry, media, and arts.

The British version of *Glamour,* launched in April 2001, celebrates National Glamour Week each September. Other foreign editions appear in France, Sweden, Italy, Germany, Spain, Russia, Greece, Poland, South Africa, Brazil, Hungary, Romania, Bulgaria, the Netherlands, Latin America, and Australia.

See also: Models and Modeling; Photography, Fashion.

Further Reading

Glamour. www.glamour.com

Heller, Steven, and Georgette Ballance, eds. *Graphic Design History.* New York: Skyhorse, 2001.

Sumner, David E. *The Magazine Century: American Magazines Since 1900.* New York: Peter Lang, 2010.

Globalization

The hybridity and ubiquity of contemporary world fashions have resulted from centuries of world trade and the advent of industrialization, mail-order merchandising, and Internet shopping.

By 138 B.C.E., the road projects of Han emperor Wu linked China to Parthia, Afghanistan, Turkestan, and Uzbekistan, encouraging the blending of Asian clothing designs. In the late thirteenth century, cotton, jute, and silk goods from India supplied markets in China and Southeast Asia. Curiosity about other nations generated business over the Silk Road, Portuguese trading routes to Africa and India, and the culture swap initiated by Christopher Columbus in 1492 between Spain and the New World.

Throughout the 1500s, exploration among Amerindians introduced outsiders to Eskimo anoraks, Yupik snow goggles, and Cree elk hide

World trends in luxury garments and sports shoes rely on low-cost labor in such developing nations as Vietnam, pictured here. Child labor and sweatshop conditions raise concerns for the social costs of dressing the style-conscious Western consumer. *(Hoang Dinh Nam/AFP/ Getty Images)*

moccasins. The importation of West African slaves to the Western Hemisphere further blended styles that brought the womanly *tignon* (turban) to Haiti and Ghanaian *pangi* cloth to coastal South America. Immigrants from China and India contributed to the mix of modes with silk slippers, kimonos, saris, and the dhoti, a comfortable kilt made of Indian calico.

The variety of transnational goods from Dutch and British importers introduced consumers to choices and name brands unlike the localized apparel available in village markets. In the mid-1800s, the development of department store chains the size of Macy's, Hudson's Bay, and Marks & Spencer broadened availability of seasonal goods and self-selection of investment outfits. During the same period, mail-order consumerism, introduced in Wales, linked much of the world with U.S., Canadian, and British merchandisers, who sold fashions gleaned from buyers shopping world markets.

Early twentieth-century films and subsequent television series educated consumers on the commodities sold by industrialized countries and began the homogenization of world styles. GIs stationed in German, Korean, and Vietnamese combat zones modeled U.S. leisure wear that bore the insouciance of American life. In reverse, through international exchange, traditional styles returned to immigrants in Europe and North America who yearned for sources of Tunisian caftans, Nigerian *boubous* (loose gowns), Spanish espadrilles, Mexican huaraches, Senegalese jewelry, Sri Lankan saris, and Ghanaian dashikis (tunics) and toques.

While France, Italy, Great Britain, the United States, and Japan spawned distinctive designs, manufacturers outsourced cutting and sewing to laborers in Mexico, Brazil, China, Bangladesh, Malaysia, Indonesia, the Philippines, Korea, Cambodia, and India. Clever entrepreneurs and sweatshop managers profited from knockoffs, producing the anomalies of fringed Sioux jackets made in Taipei and plastic *sabots* (clogs) injection-molded in China at a wage level suited to Asian labor standards.

Worldwide, adults began wearing denim jeans and work jackets with T-shirts and billed caps, a standardized silhouette. Children began seeking imported Nike athletic shoes and sweatshirts with team logos. Global sales of secondhand goods invited the eager imitator to assemble North American or European outfits picked from worn-out and discarded goods. Internet shopping made available folk textiles and artisanal sweaters, leather goods, cosmetics, and jewelry from smaller countries, including Malian mud cloth, Malaysian batik, Icelandic pullovers, German coin purses, Japanese skincare products, Asante kente cloth, Peruvian knits, and Turkish *tughras* (calligraphic monograms).

Constant communication between East and West has spawned a variety of social issues, as with the reclamation of the Korean *hanbok* and Malaysian batik and the Middle Eastern female rejection of the head scarf and black burka. In Iran after the Islamic Revolution of 1979, women adapted obligatory Muslim attire with colorful fabrics and patterns from foreign suppliers. In Afghanistan under the Taliban, women expressed themselves only in secret; daring girls and women concealed the nail enamel, hair dye, and makeup banned by conservative Muslims. In Dubai and Saudi Arabia, female consumers generated seasonal demand for German fashions.

In the early 2000s, *Elle* magazine supported the interest of Middle Easterners in global trends. In the years that followed, the spirit of multiculturalism embraced Brazilian flip-flops, Japanese eye shadow, and hammered metal collars from Istanbul. Beyond vanity and style shopping, consumers demanded fairness in the marketplace by protesting underage labor in Pakistan, child slavery in India and China, and sweatshop conditions in Puerto Rico and Burma.

See also: Mail Order; Merchandising; Sweatshops.

Further Reading

Anheier, Helmut K., and Yudhishthir Raj Isar, eds. *Cultures and Globalization: Cultural Expression, Creativity, and Innovation.* Thousand Oaks, CA: Sage, 2010.

Knox, Kristin. *Culture to Catwalk: How World Cultures Influence Fashion.* London: A. & C. Black, 2011.

Paulicelli, Eugenia, and Hazel Clark, eds. *The Fabric of Cultures: Fashion, Identity, and Globalization.* New York: Routledge, 2009.

Rabine, Leslie W. *The Global Circulation of African Fashion.* New York: Bloomsbury, 2002.

Gloves

Sold in haberdasheries, boutiques, and department stores, gloves have historically combined utility with warmth and beauty. After 38,000 B.C.E., indigenous hunter-gatherers of present-day Greenland, Japan, Russia and Siberia, Scandinavia, and northern North America employed needle-and-thread technology to turn bear, wolverine, and reindeer fur into bag-like hand and forearm covers. More sophisticated designs covered the thumb and four fingers individually to protect them from blisters, abrasions, and cuts from flint tools.

At Knossos after 1700 B.C.E., Minoan boxers protected their fists with leather bags that extended to the forearm. A trade item introduced by Bronze Age Asian nomads circa 1200 B.C.E., felt offered a soft but resilient material for gloves. Farther south, two pairs of woven linen gloves with wrist ties accompanied Tutankhamen to his tomb in the Valley of the Kings in 1323 B.C.E. Egyptian tanners provided materials for gloves, a common hand covering manufactured in Babylonia by Chaldeans. Before sleep, Egyptian women applied honey and emollients under silk hand wear to soften the skin. Persians outraged the Greeks with their effeminate accoutrements, which included umbrellas and gloves woven of hair.

Practical Uses

In the fifth century B.C.E., Greek actors enlarged gestures and responses by wearing gloves, while tanned leather hand wear improved the grip of Greek dockworkers. Boxers shaped hand covers from thongs bound over the fist. Roman epicures wore linen or silk gloves at the table to protect their hands from food stains and hot grease. During the Roman Empire, the imperial family wore *digitalia* (gloves) as well as *manicae,* winter glove sleeves or mufflers.

After 449 C.E., Anglo-Saxons valued gloves as court gifts. For two- and three-fingered split mittens and five-fingered gloves, the development of knitting offered a significant advance in elasticity and fit. By creating air pockets between hair scales, lightweight, flexible yarn absorbed moisture and retained body heat, making it the primary material for gloves. Stitchery embroidered the hand, fingers, and cuffs with couched ciphers and monograms.

Around 800, Charlemagne permitted hunting in royal preserves for monks seeking deerskin for gloves and belts. Perhaps from Vikings, hand covers took the Old Norse name *glofi.* Additional names included "hand shoes" and "sweet bags," a reference to the soaking of each pair in angelica or rose water or almond oil sprinkled with cloves. In the tenth century, gloves embellished with enamel and stones contributed majesty to the sheriff of London, judges, and prelates. Celebrants of the Catholic Mass offered the Eucharist to gloved worshippers.

Gloves held state significance at the coronation of England's Alfred the Great in 871 and Edward the Confessor in 1042. The treasury established the British glovers' guild to protect a growing industry. Following the Norman Conquest of 1066, monarchs and squires elevated their authority over captive Anglo-Saxons with gloves adorned with streamers.

Medieval Fashion

By the thirteenth century, women's linen or silk gloves had advanced from utility to decoration. At his crowning as Holy Roman Emperor in 1220, Frederick II wore heavily beaded gloves embroidered in gold and pearls. For the elite, Parisian glove makers promoted luxury by cutting patterns out of fur or delicate skins. To regulate social distinction, sumptuary laws enacted in Bologna in 1294 forbade expenditure on samite (twilled silk) gloves.

Hand wear achieved stature as a part of armor. Before the advent of firearms, the cloth, leather, and plate gauntlet, a wrist-to-hand covering resembling the glove, encased the sword arm of a knight or soldier. Around 1350, Edward, the Black Prince, wore gusseted gauntlets armed with knuckle spikes. Later models sported hinged wristlets, scaled forearm plates, and thumb guards.

In the mid-sixteenth century, when male aristocrats dressed in finery, Catherine de' Medici, the queen consort of France, set the tone for women's hand wear. Her daughter, Marguerite de Valois, introduced kidskin gloves to female court wear in Navarre. Ornate pairs featured tassels, ribbon trim, side tabs, tufting, and fringe around the cuff. Ladies had linen, lace, silk, and leather gloves dyed to match the colors of wine and stored their hand wear with fragrant sachets.

In cobbleries, the thinnest pelts provided sueded nap of the calf, deer, goat, or lamb for gloves. English glovers measured and cut patterns for bespoke, or custom-made, hand wear for hunting, archery, riding, and falconry. Perforations in a glove vented the hand, allowing perspiration to evaporate. Roman and Spanish women enhanced gloves with the scent of ambergris, civet, and musk oil or stored their hand wear in aromatic cedar or sandalwood boxes.

Royalty and Commerce

Embroiderers in Tudor England embellished the hand wear of Henry VIII and Anne Boleyn with petit point and monogrammed gloves with royal cyphers. In 1566, Elizabeth I added gold fringe and jewels to her gloves. The choice of chicken skin for material improved fit and dexterity while the queen played the virginal, a small harpsichord. Her promotion of English glovers made London a fashion center and hub of leather exports.

While Russian furriers continued to favor the warmth of muffs and mittens over five-fingered gloves, Western European designers accessorized the formal female riding habit with chamois, doe, stag, or suede gloves. For softness and mellow shades of ivory or ecru, glove makers chose the skins of milk-fed kids and buffed away blemishes with plush wheels. Long cuffs protected the hand and wrist from chafing and windburn. Straps enabled wearers to adjust the fit at the base of the thumb and across the back of the hand.

Around 1750, Irish tanners chose "slink" (unborn calf or lamb hides) for limerick gloves, a product later produced by the colonists of New Zealand. During the reign of George III, men and women soaked night gloves in unguents. Chicken-skin hand wear imparted delicacy to the skin and nails.

After 1802, Napoleon added 240 pairs of gloves to his accessories wardrobe, and women of the court emulated the Empress Joséphine's long gloves. The addition to formal attire supplied hand and arm warmers for women wearing thin gauze gowns and added a refined accessory to the flowing Empire line. In 1807, James Winter of Somerset, England, revolutionized leather stitchery by inventing the gloving donkey, which clamped small, slippery pattern pieces for consistent hand sewing.

In Regency England, ruching in women's opera gloves allowed for reducing the length by sliding the tube toward the wrist. Impeccable suede gloves contributed to the masculine fashion silhouette of trendsetter Beau Brummell. Under free-trade agreements after 1826, imported hand wear flooded the market and lowered prices for the multi-button English glove within range of the average budget. The popularity of gloves for varied occasions gave employment to women, who sewed the pieces cut by male patterners. Around 1835, French glover Xavier Jouvin of Grenoble standardized hand sizes.

Modern Styles

Fashions of the 1870s reclaimed the opera glove, adding buttons or snaps at the wrist slits, which allowed wearers to slip their hands out for drinking and eating. Actor Sarah Bernhardt introduced the glamorous elbow-length glove in stage roles requiring dramatic hand gestures. In the 1890s, actor Lillian Russell increased the length of fingerless kid opera gloves to the upper arm and wore them for bicycling. Into the Edwardian era, gloves continued to define the elegance and pomp of formal occasions.

Harley-Davidson's 1912 catalog, with 1,216 items in all, featured leather jackets and gloves for rider protection. The outfit influenced motorcy-

cling gear into current times, on the road, in films, and on television.

Around 1917, boys' flared-cuff mittens and gloves with wrist snaps added style to cold weather attire. White kid gloves and satin ballet slippers with kid soles enhanced the femininity of girls' attire.

Cabretta, an innovation in ski and racquetball wear in 1930, offered a durable glove material from Brazilian haired sheep. A rotating buffing wheel polished the finished garments to a glacé sheen. In the 1950s, opera gloves contributed to Christian Dior's sleeveless fashions. A triumph of 1957, opera-length gloves enhanced Cristóbal Balenciaga's semi-fitted sack.

See also: Accessories; Protective and Orthotic Clothing.

Further Reading

Cumming, Valerie, C.W. Cunnington, and P.E. Cunnington. *The Dictionary of Fashion History.* New York: Bloomsbury, 2010.

Jenkins, Jessica Kerwin. *Encyclopedia of the Exquisite: An Anecdotal History of Elegant Delights.* New York: Random House, 2010.

Tomshinsky, Ida. *Gloves: History and Present.* Bloomington, IN: Xlibris, 2011.

Godey's Lady's Book

An influential arbiter of female fashion sense and market achievement in America during the mid- to late 1800s, *Godey's Lady's Book,* the "queen of household magazines," impacted taste and clothing sales nationwide. Introduced in Philadelphia in June 1830, the magazine issued from Chestnut and Sixth streets under the direction of editor and publisher Louis Antoine Godey, who became rich on the charge of $2 per year per subscription. Based on English and French women's magazines, the popular trendsetter merged with *American Ladies' Magazine* in 1836 and quadrupled its distribution in 1839 to 40,000 subscriptions.

Patrons followed pragmatic suggestions on purchasing opera hoods, snoods, wedding and ball gowns, and frocks and accessorizing with the fichu, switch hairpiece, reticule, and sunbonnet. Basic dressing for women and girls—adjustable bustles, union suits, peignoirs and gowns, camisoles, and drawers—featured the best in embroidered lawn and linen with ribbon trim. From reports on European fads, Americans knitted and crocheted the Josephine shawl, a shoulder drape that added mystery to an ensemble.

Beginning in 1854, subscribers could obtain by mail unsized patterns from Madame Ellen Louise Demorest, a modiste (hat and dress designer) in New York City. In August 1857, a pattern for stays outlined tight waist measurements, the source of the hourglass figure that dominated mid-nineteenth-century fashion.

Editor Sarah Josepha Hale began 40 years of service to *Godey's Lady's Book* in 1837. In addition to Hale, Godey hired 150 freelance watercolorists to create engraved color fashion plates of family groupings of children and women fashionably clothed in the European mode.

Hale respected the female needleworker for individualizing her wardrobe with inexpensive materials. Crafters followed details on embroidering, crocheting, knitting, chenille work, and monogramming simple ruffs and gaiters, mitts (gloves without fingers), and socks, and infant wraps and toddler caps. Instructions featured patterns for making bathing dresses, cycling and equestrian attire, gymnastic outfits, chemises, and frocks as well as baby layettes, trousseau staples, and pincushions and accessories for the sewing box.

The magazine staff researched the history of clothing and added to contemporary dress sketches of classic, medieval, and Renaissance costuming. Columns followed the fashion savvy of France's Empress Eugenie and England's Queen Victoria and posted historic glimpses of Florence Nightingale, Abigail Adams, and Dolley Madison. Hints on the personal wardrobe suggested an assortment of yarns and silk threads for crafts, hairpins and coiffure adornment, jewelry, scarves, fans, and knitted flowers.

Issues of the magazine in 1855 pictured the English straw hat, the chemisette for lining a riding shirt, a Chantilly lace basque (chemise), and netted pocket for a pin-on watch. For boys, articles introduced the Milanese boater and gimp cap, an ornamental hat embroidered with cord or wire.

By 1860, *Godey's Lady's Book* had attained respect among women and girls for genteel attire and boasted a readership of 150,000. Smuggled issues penetrated the Southern port blockade after 1861, when the magazine expanded to double-page spreads. Issues featured patterns and body measurements for reproducing European slippers, cambric skirts and morning blouses, and ensembles of muslin, crepe de chine, and quilled ribbon in Zouave style.

In the post–Civil War era, Hale applauded Catharine Esther Beecher for formalizing home economics as a science and the role of women in dressmaking, millinery, and design. As canal barges, riverboats, stage lines, and the transcontinental railroad increased mail outreach, Irish housemaids, women on the frontier, and New England silk workers treasured magazine issues and emulated featured women's outfits with cheap yard goods. Dressmakers increased their lines with illustrated fashions, bringing self-confidence to the well-dressed woman in rural America.

The magazine applauded careers in fiber work, decor, and the fashion business, especially for widows and unmarried females supporting themselves. In addition to articles on the use of Elias Howe's sewing machine, its pages included suggestions on ways of personalizing readymade attire with creative monogramming and appliqué. Household tips enlightened the reader on keeping the personal wardrobe clean and in good repair.

In 1877, journalist Frank Andrew Munsey bought Godey's company and altered the title to *Godey's Magazine*. As women's opinions strayed from primness and refined attire, the first edition in January 1878 failed to maintain the interest of the "new woman." Munsey's fashion plates for 1880 stressed the slimmer female silhouette in double-breasted jackets, vests, slim walking skirts, and coats reminiscent of male dress, a shift in fashion indicating women's more businesslike appearance and the decline of frippery. Until the last issue in 1898, female readers gravitated away from *Godey's Magazine* to the more womanly ads and columns on popular apparel in *Atlantic* and *Harper's Bazaar*.

See also: Fashion Plates.

Further Reading

Johnston, Susan. *Fashion Paper Dolls from Godey's Lady's Book, 1840–1854 (Dover Victorian Paper Dolls)*. New York: Dover, 1977.

Piepmeier, Alison. *Out in Public: Configurations of Women's Bodies in Nineteenth-Century America*. Chapel Hill: University of North Carolina Press, 2004.

Sachsman, David B., S. Kittrell Rushing, and Roy Morris, Jr., eds. *Seeking a Voice: Images of Race and Gender in the 19th Century Press*. West Lafayette, IN: Purdue University Press, 2009.

Sun, Ming-Ju. *Godey's Fashions Paper Dolls 1860–1879 (Dover Victorian Paper Dolls)*. New York: Dover, 2004.

GQ

A glossy fashion monthly distributed in 19 countries, *Gentlemen's Quarterly* (*GQ*), the oldest magazine for men, follows trends in male dress, interests, and activities. Debuting in New York City in 1931 as *Apparel Arts,* the publication informed clothing dealers and haberdashers of fabrics and styles in men's garments and accessories. Page layout incorporated swatches and sketches of fashions from London's tony Savile Row.

In 1933, *Esquire* replaced *Apparel Arts* with a consumer magazine that dropped in price from $1.50 to $.50 per issue. Articles and advertising concentrated on suave styles from movie stars, most notably Gary Cooper. In 1939, a salute to technology featured the Jarman cedar-cured calfskin shoe that suppressed foot odor. A 1949 survey outlined for retailers the demographics of the college-age consumer, who spent $200 annually on his wardrobe.

Under the aegis of Esquire Inc., the publication shifted to quarterly issues in 1957 and guided the neophyte on choosing a suit for a job interview. Editor Dylan Jones explained the original purpose for advice to males, who lacked the fashion savvy of women. To maintain a serious tone, the magazine stopped distributing its girly calendars.

Within a year, the title changed to *Gentlemen's Quarterly* and the content addressed consumer interest in grooming and the male public image, which was mutating from the establishment "penguin" to the countercultural "peacock." Articles identified Botany 500 suits as prime tailoring and suggested colorful silk shirts as complements suited to the "fashion activist." A cover photo of actor Michael Caine set the standard for classic dressing. A 1968 issue suggested the Danté jewelry box for organizing valuables and exercise belts for toning muscles. A tip on trends reported that felt business hats looked outdated and that sophisticated slip-on shoes were replacing staid lace-ups.

In 1977, advice on purchasing jeans warned the shopper that Levi's 501s lacked shrinkage control. Skin-care tips promoted the use of Max Factor's Erace concealer on dark under-eye circles. Practical advice on shoes suggested a longer heel to improve balance and support the ankle. Articles on fads warned readers away from double knits and leisure suits. Photographs pictured attractive pairings of tweed pants with hooded sweaters and scarves and bomber jackets with casual pants.

After Condé Nast purchased *GQ* from Esquire Inc. in 1979, publisher Samuel Irving Newhouse, Jr., and editor Art Cooper joined a new wave of men's magazines. *GQ* extended the scope of content from the special interests of homosexuals to an evolving masculinity and lifestyle of straight men. Innovation earned Cooper a 1985 Editor of the Year award from *Adweek.* Piquing interest, iconic cover models exhibited mixed ethnicity and sexual orientation—actors Richard Gere in March 1980 and Dustin Hoffman in December 1988, politician Joe Kennedy in September 1988, and "style jocks" Joe Theismann in November 1983, Magic Johnson in March 1987, Greg Louganis in May 1988, and Michael Jordan in March 1989.

After 1984, *GQ* rejected some 245 pages of tasteless ads, a move that earned the magazine the top place in men's media in revenue, subscriptions, and newsstand sales. Fashion editor Marjorie "Nonnie" Moore refined the tone and casual look of fashion shoots, which introduced layered separates and affordable leisure wear. Unlike style advisers who remained in safe, predictable territory, she encouraged relaxation and confidence in the rising professional by combing the market for modern silhouettes, including those of Perry Ellis and Issey Miyake.

In 1994, Moore received a lifetime achievement honorarium from the Council of Fashion

Designers of America. She flourished in part for highlighting sensual photos of the cool consumer who chose "soccer chic" Zegna suits and Gucci leather over jock-style sweats and running shoes. In October 1994, *GQ* linked classic Italian tailoring with the Alfa Romeo and Fiat 500, Italy's classic cars. The aesthetic of narcissism, reflected in stark musculature and fitted wardrobe, extended vanity to the male-directed media.

In the early 2000s, *GQ* reached out to "metrosexuals," a neologism for eroticized and idealized urbanites. Trendsetters among the "new men," metrosexuals invested in quality menswear and trendy jeans, pantyhose, and watches as well as moisturizers and pedicures. In 2003, editor Jim Nelson, a former television news writer for CNN and purveyor of pop culture, began courting a younger male audience with an invigoration of content and photography that increased circulation by 24 percent. At the core of the twenty-first-century approach, Nelson promoted straightforward wardrobe advice to individualize male style. Covers featured athletes Mark Sanchez in September 2011 and Tim Tebow in September 2012 and actors Denzel Washington in October 2012 and Ben Affleck in December 2012. By June 2012, the magazine had reached a circulation of more than 963,000.

Contributing to *GQ*'s popularity, regular features enlighten readers to the basics of wardrobe planning. The Glenn O'Brien Style Archive answers apparel questions keyed to the educated, mostly single reader from ages 18 to 49. *GQ* Rules offer specifics of dress and grooming that ridicule antifashion rat tails, socks with flip-flops, Goth and pimp chic, pearl-snap shirts, concha belts, and plaid flannel.

The annual December issue awards the "*GQ* Men of the Year" designation to influential males, who have included actors Gary Oldman, Jeff Bridges, and Heath Ledger and cyclist Lance Armstrong. *GQ* photographs have also pictured worst-dressed men, including actors Al Pacino and Sean Combs, athlete Kobe Bryant, politician Paul Ryan, singer Elton John, and selected residents of Boulder, Colorado, and Nashville, Tennessee.

See also: Formal Attire, Male; Leisure Wear.

Further Reading
GQ. www.gq.com
Levin, Jo. *GQ Cool.* London: Pavilion, 2003.
McNeil, Peter, and Vicki Karaminas, eds. *The Men's Fashion Reader.* New York: Bloomsbury, 2009.

Greek Clothing, Ancient

Rather than form-fitting shapes cut to size, the attire of Greek men and women in the ancient world relied more heavily on loosely draped fabric. As early as the Aegean period in the Mediterranean, from circa 3000 B.C.E. to 1100 B.C.E., gold jewelry dominated the attire of Crete, Mycenae, and Thera in the form of earrings, tiaras, bracelets and armlets, and girdles or belts. Weaving, the typical woman's work, featured plain warp and woof of flax, goat and sheep hair, and hemp and netted openwork called sprang.

Cretan women at Knossos highlighted their eyes with kohl and wore ornamental fitted bodices with open cleavage and bare breasts over A-line tiered skirts resembling crinolines and adorned with tufted flounces. Men displayed less interest in fashion by wearing banded hair, tasseled loincloths and court kilts with rolled leather belts, and soft leather shoes. Hosts presented visitors with clothing as guest gifts, a central feature of ancient hospitality that supplied the visitor with creature comforts.

From 1600 to 1100 B.C.E., Mycenaean women displayed their breasts in tight-fitting bodices with peplums. Their tucked or flounced skirts appeared Asian in origin. Around 1200 B.C.E., Phrygian needleworkers enhanced tunics and stoles with dainty embroidery. Women's outfitting began with breast belt or breast band, a linen, wool, or leather wrapping worn under or across the breasts or over a chemise or inner tunic and braced over the shoulders for support.

From the Greek Heroic Age, just before and after 1000 B.C.E., the major female garment, the sleeveless peplos, consisted of a tube of sheer fabric extending from the feet to above the shoulders, where ties or fasteners held it in place. In the *Odyssey* (ca. 800 B.C.E.), Homer depicted a gift peplos and 12 pins for fastening it.

Only maidservants wore unpinned, long-sleeved tunics.

For high fashion, women favored a pairing of saffron over red as well as gray, green, indigo, madder, and violet for variety. They topped their outfits with an overdress, a thin, light-colored addition worn like a veil by women of rank. Transparent veils enhanced the flirtation of the *hetaira* (courtesan).

From the early 500s B.C.E., the beginning of the classical era, the Doric chiton dominated unisex fashions. The shaping of the chiton involved a tube of lightweight pleated linen or wool crepe that draped the body in graceful folds. The silhouette remained in service for over two millennia. The garment equaled the height of the wearer and

A bronze statue from Greece in the fourth century B.C.E. portrays the goddess Artemis in a light Ionic-style chiton (full-length sleeveless sheath) and *diplax* (double cloak). Torso banding prefigures the modern brassiere. *(DeA Picture Library/The Granger Collection, NYC—All rights reserved)*

sometimes trailed behind. The wearer folded the excess cloth inside out at the top from the shoulders to the hips and cinched the top portion at the waist or under the breasts with a *zonton* (girdle) of leather, netting, or fabric, creating the illusion of a belted top and skirt. For style, women double-belted their chitons, creating two soft folds at the waist.

Art depicted bearded men with clasped hair wearing the unbelted chiton, a standard sleeveless sheath of Phoenician design. The chiton fit under armor and weapons, which all males carried, even in peacetime. For vigorous action in Homeric times, men removed their shoulder wraps of goat, leopard, lion, or lynx skins or dressed in double aprons or bathing shorts for swimming. At the shoulder, the wearer buttoned the garment in place or secured it with bronze or iron clasps, buckles, or fibulae (safety pins), a common fastener invented in Mycenae in the 1300s B.C.E. and attached to shrouds. Homer depicted Odysseus's chiton as equipped with a metal tunnel to keep the pin from tearing his garment. The lower portion of the chiton could be worn open Spartan style or sewn closed in the more modest Attic and Corinthian style.

The Ionic style, a sheerer, more elaborate chiton of light, crinkly linen or silk gauze from Cos that was introduced after the end of the Persian Wars in 449 B.C.E., coincided with a pacifist movement. According to Herodotus, the Greek "Father of History," the new fashion supplanted Doric style after Athenian women stabbed a soldier to death with fibulae for surviving combat that killed all his comrades. To prevent future violence, a law prohibited the wearing of pins.

For men, the Ionic chiton, worn by priests, musicians, and charioteers, draped the upper body with one unfolded layer. The upper edge extended along the upper arms and fastened into slotted sleeves with buttons or matched brooches rather than stitches. The lower portion of the Ionic chiton either formed a tube or remained open on the left side.

Tassels and fringe added pizzazz to the Greek ensemble. The *chlamys* (cloak) served as formal garb for youths and dandies and for covering armor in the style of ancient animal pelts. In the luxurious style of Asia Minor, gold bands tied up Achaean men's long hair, fastened Thracian hair knots, or braided hair for athletics. Only slaves wore their hair short.

During shifts in style in the Hellenistic Age, the post-Alexandrian era (after 323 B.C.E.), Greek men took up shaving, a facial depilation that impacted male grooming in colonial Sicily and southern Italy. Women raised the belting of Ionic chitons to mid-chest in Empire style. They braided or embroidered the upper and lower hems of garments in intricate ivy and laurel designs, dentils, curvilinear detail, and Greek key or meander. After 200 B.C.E., the upper chiton acquired a chic pleated neckline.

The chic Greek woman constrained her hair in fillets (cords) or braids or topped upswept locks with a cloth sling tied at back, a metal headpiece attached to a goat hair net, or a headdress of yellow cotton, an expensive fiber grown in Elis. Later fashions called for nets, scarves, kerchiefs, or hair bags.

Cooler weather or formal occasions called for the addition of a himation (cloak), a rectangular over-garment up to 12 feet (3.7 meters) in length for both men and women. For either gender, the cloak fastened at left to leave the right arm free. Females wore an ampler himation embroidered at the borders. Like a stole or veil with weighted corners, the himation draped diagonally over the left or both shoulders, where brooches secured it. Some women preferred the *diplax,* a himation folded into double thickness.

See also: Hairdressing; Roman Clothing, Ancient; Tunics and Togas.

Further Reading

Gagarin, Michael, ed. *The Oxford Encyclopedia of Ancient Greece and Rome.* New York: Oxford University Press, 2010.

Llewellyn-Jones, Lloyd. *Women's Dress in the Ancient Greek World.* London: Swansea, 2002.

Salisbury, Joyce E. *Encyclopedia of Women in the Ancient World.* Santa Barbara, CA: ABC-CLIO, 2001.

Wilson, Nigel, ed. *Encyclopedia of Ancient Greece.* New York: Routledge, 2006.

Gucci, Guccio (1881–1953)

Italian leather craftsman and fashion designer Guccio Gucci founded a small family business in Florence, Italy, in 1921, and built it into an internationally recognized fashion brand and global consumer giant.

Born to the merchant class in Florence on March 26, 1881, Gucci emigrated to Paris and London as a young man to work at the Savoy Hotel. After World War I, he trained in leather grading at Ditta Franzi's leatherworks in Florence and Rome. Impressed by top-grade leather luggage, Gucci and his wife, Aida Calvelli, established a saddlery in 1921 that employed 60 leatherworkers. His Tuscan designs for leather harnesses and bags, based on horse bits and stirrups, gained popularity with jockeys. The product line grew with telescoping purses and bags and suitcases made of chamois and kidskin.

In 1938, the House of Gucci opened in Rome on the Via Condotti, where Gucci's sons Aldo and Vasco and daughter Grimalda joined the staff. The company distinguished itself with meticulous craftsmanship in handbags, belts, wallets, trunks, gloves, and shoes. During World War II, the rationing of leather forced Gucci to work in hemp, linen, jute, and cotton canvas, which bore the double G family crest above the diamante pattern. As the Allies demobilized, soldiers bought Gucci leather goods as souvenirs.

With Italy establishing itself as an international emporium of luxury goods after the war, Gucci adopted pigskin as the signature material in 1947. He designed "suiters" with hangers to accommodate the uniforms of military officers. Aldo Gucci added burnished cane handles to the sporty bamboo shoulder bag, a favorite with actor Grace Kelly. Another son, Rodolfo Gucci, who worked in film, introduced Bette Davis, Anna Magnani, Sophia Loren, and Katharine Hepburn to the family products.

The company developed a satellite business in Milan in 1951, when designers produced knits and silks for their commercial lines. A saddle girth design influenced the striped trademark, a symbol of postwar luxury. The company added a Manhattan location at the Savoy Plaza Hotel only weeks before Guccio Gucci's sudden death from heart attack in Rusper, England, on January 2, 1953.

The Gucci label gained film notoriety in

Viaggio in Italia (1953), in which actor Ingrid Bergman displayed a Gucci umbrella and bamboo bag. Jet-setters of the 1960s and 1970s turned the Gucci stiletto heel and loafers into status symbols. Celebrities such as Rock Hudson, Jacqueline Kennedy Onassis, Sammy Davis, Jr., Elizabeth Taylor, Ringo Starr, Audrey Hepburn, and Samuel Beckett popularized the Gucci shoulder bag, moccasins, Flora scarf and scarf dress, and unisex hobo bag. Red Skelton carried Gucci crocodile luggage with gold clasps. Maria Callas wore Gucci scarves, and Peter Sellers bought the attaché case. At a time when pirated knockoffs flooded the leather market, the Gucci Company expanded to Beverly Hills, Hong Kong, London, Palm Beach, Paris, and Tokyo and added a perfume line.

The development of Gucci's original designs increased with the debut of the Gucci Accessories Collection in 1979, pulling the company out of a slump. Workshops stocked ostrich skin from Indonesia, Scots cashmere, African crocodile, and boar hides from Poland. Stores offered calf, pigskin, and baby crocodile coats and boots ac-cessorized with silk foulards, snakehead buckles, sunglasses, and waterproof canvas and satin evening bags.

Gucci goods won acclaim at the company's first runway show in 1981 at the Sala Bianca in Florence. The company passed out of family control in 1988, when grandson Maurizio sold it to Bahrain-based Investcorp. It went public in 1995 with an initial public offering of stock that fetched $22 a share on the New York Stock Exchange. On the rebound, the House of Gucci won European Company of the Year honors in 1998. And in 2009, the company's eighty-eighth year, *BusinessWeek* ranked Gucci as number 41 on its list of top 100 brands worldwide.

See also: Fashion Design; Italian Clothing and Fashion.

Further Reading

Forden, Sara G. *The House of Gucci: A Sensational Story of Murder, Madness, Glamour, and Greed.* New York: HarperCollins, 2000.

Frisa, Maria Luisa. *Gucci.* New York: USA Rizzoli, 2011.

Gucci Online Boutique. www.gucci.com

Haberdashers

Retailers of men's clothing and accessories, haberdashers stock the accoutrements that accompany suits, jackets, and slacks. From *haberdashery,* a thirteenth-century Middle English word for small wares, the term *haberdashers* originally applied to sellers of spectacles and frames, mirrors, caps, and hats. In American English, the word became a general term for dealers in men's accessories or for sections in department stores that stock shirts, ties, hats, hosiery and garters, handkerchiefs and foulards, and underwear.

The haberdasher typically serves as a guide to trends in menswear and an adviser on selection of fabrics, patterns, and colors to build an individual wardrobe. Large establishments feature leather belts, caps, gloves, and bags. The experienced clothier recognizes quality textiles, leather, and stitchery and suggests additions for investment dressing for business and the professions.

Clothiers pride themselves on supplying the well-dressed man with a complete suit of clothes and accessories for every occasion, from walking and shooting to ballroom soirees and formal receptions. Larger haberdasheries also generally sell rainwear, canes, and fountain pens and other men's gift items and may rent tuxedos and formal accessories for weddings and formal occasions.

Historically, haberdashers sold a mishmash of merchandise. In 1431, a men's outfitter in Lynn, England, received a shipment of "fancy goods"— shoelaces, eyeglasses, and girlie calendars. In 1447, the profession became more structured after Henry VI of England chartered the Worshipful Company of Haberdashers to regulate hurrers, the makers of felt hats. In 1509, a Southampton wholesaler supplied English haberdashers with eyeglasses, brushes, and playing cards imported from Italy. In William Shakespeare's comedy *The Taming of the Shrew* (1591), the term *haberdasher* came closer to the current meaning in the outfitting of Petruchio with a new cap.

Haberdasheries flourished in seventeenth-century London as advisers on fit and the overall look of men's ensembles. The shops became gathering places for dandies, who stayed current with changing styles in feathered hats. According to records of businesses lost in a fire on the north end of London Bridge in February 1633, eight of the 43 owners were haberdashers dealing primarily in head wear. By the 1760s, English haberdashers publicized their offerings and prices in newspapers and, after 1770, in *Lady's Magazine.* Haberdasher John Hetherington of London launched a craze for the silk hat, which he invented in January 1797.

In 1851, a survey of the clothier's goods in a London "swag-shop" listed boots and laces, hosiery, silk purses, black handkerchiefs, braces, and caps, as well as shawls and nightcaps for girls and women. The compiler, journalist Henry Mayhew, concluded that the term *haberdasher* overlapped that of hosier, draper, glover, and shirtmaker by stocking a variety of apparel needs. As department stores supplanted smaller shops, managers placed the haberdasher's section close to the front to draw customers to inexpensive ties, handkerchiefs, and socks.

Men's clothiers maintained their edge by specializing, as with stores that catered to hunters, riders, and youth. In the Victorian era, military haberdashers concentrated on supplying army officers with tunics, vests, helmets, and cavalry boots. The knowledgeable outfitter kept current by reading *The Outfitter* and *Men's Wear,* prominent trade periodicals.

By 1900, more aggressive advertising promoted menswear, such as that of London outfitter E. Catesby & Sons. In the 1930s, haberdashers influenced correct dressing, especially in metropolitan areas, where males tended to wear a professional uniform deviating little from man to man. During World War II, clothiers supplied tropical shirts and drip-dry underwear for soldiers posted in the Pacific. Returning veterans made new demands on haberdashers for comfortable clothing.

Radical changes in American men's leisure wear after 1950 increased male consumerism, especially among urban homosexuals in the boutiques of such cities as Los Angeles and Palm Springs. In 1968, Le Mans Haberdashers on New York City's Upper West Side focused on outfitting African American entrepreneurs with Swiss silk or voile shirts, French suits and overcoats, and Italian shoes. In San Francisco, the Wild West Haberdashery provided Stetsons and cowboy gear. Advertising in magazines and newspapers extended the shop's trade to outdoorsmen in California and Oregon. In the 2000s, the Gentlemen's Haberdashery in Orange County, California, showcased stylish menswear modeled by business and community leaders.

See also: Accessories; Tailoring.

Further Reading

Jobling, Paul. *Man Appeal: Advertising, Modernism, and Menswear.* New York: Bloomsbury, 2005.

McNeil, Peter, and Vicki Karaminas, eds. *The Men's Fashion Reader.* New York: Bloomsbury, 2009.

Ugolini, Laura. *Men and Menswear: Sartorial Consumption in Britain, 1880–1939.* Burlington, VT: Ashgate, 2007.

Hairdressing

- -

As indicators of status, ethnicity, and personal preference, hairstyles place individual appearance conspicuously in the public domain. Archaeological evidence from Upper Paleolithic Beijing around 18,000 B.C.E. attests to the garnishing of East Asian hairstyles with bones and teeth, pebbles, shells, and stone amulet beads. By the third millennium B.C.E., carved beads and combs shaped the hairstyles of the Chinese national costume.

In north-central China after 3000 B.C.E., Gansu tradition featured bones and seashells as garnishes for the hair and beards. Because of the bother and discomfort of regular shaving, beards remained standard male facial dress until the 1400s.

Dressing, perfuming, and tinting hair likewise occupied the fashionable in Africa and the Middle East since ancient times. From 3200 B.C.E. at Ur (Iraq), Sumerian females arranged their plaits under scented netting. They topped their hairstyles with wax cones that melted, leaving perfume on the scalp. To the west after 3050 B.C.E., Egyptian women dyed their hair an orangey brown with henna (*Lawsonia inermis*) and sumac (*Rhus coriaria*) and garnished long locks with ribbon fillets (cords). Courtiers fought Saharan heat waves by shaving their heads and wearing blunt-cut wigs for ritual and state occasions.

Along the Fertile Crescent around 2270 B.C.E., Mesopotamian men grew long beards and hair, which they coiled at the nape. Women set their hair with bone pins and ties. During the expansion of the Assyrian Empire after 1300 B.C.E., both genders wore tight curls. Men squared the cut of their beards and dyed their eyebrows black. Women began covering their hair in scarves as a show of modesty, a custom that influenced Islamic veiling from the early seventh century C.E.

Gendered Styling

Minoan and Greek hairstyles featured banding as a simple control of loose strands, such as the flyaway long locks of Achaean athletes. Achaean women set their curls and braids in fabric slings, netting, and hair bags. Classic fillets bound hair, elongating the shape of the cranium as far back as the chignon, which ties gathered into a knot above the nape. The proportionate style adorned Greek statues of Aphrodite, including the Aphrodite of Melos (better known as the Venus de Milo), completed by an unknown artist after 130 B.C.E. in Melos (now called Milos).

Roman hairdressing revealed less idealism and more professional beauty care. For the wealthy, styling required the purchase of skilled slaves as personal coiffeurs. The setting of waves and curls in sulfurous mud worked like a permanent wave by shaping the protein in each strand. In 27 B.C.E., the Empress Livia flaunted her prominence with tight curls, wiglets, hair gems, and tiaras. Her husband, the Emperor Augustus, cropped his wavy hair short and, for ceremonial occasions, topped it with a diadem, a fashion introduced by his uncle, Julius Caesar, to hide a bald spot.

Asian and Pacific island coiffures identified gendered traits. Korean hairdressing from the first millennium B.C.E. featured unisex braids. Women knotted plaits at the neck with a horizontal wood or bamboo pin; men tied their braids into a topknot, a symbol of masculinity. From the 700s C.E. on Tonga and Samoa and in the part of the Indus Valley that is now Pakistan, young women announced marriageability by dressing their hair with blossoms, much as the Fulani of Guinea attached amber beads to the hair of nubile girls.

In ninth-century Christendom, monks shaved the pate, leaving the skull ringed with hair to the ears. The circular bald spot symbolized abandonment of worldly concerns. After 960, Chinese women feminized the unisex national costume by pinning jeweled ornaments in their hair. Twelfth-century Hindu matrons marked their married status with red powder dotted along the part of their hair. To limit ostentation in men's public appearance, the Nuremberg sumptuary laws of 1453 required German males to wear their hair in unparted tufts.

In sixteenth-century Mexico, women's hairdos began with plaits looped around the ears, a representation of female order and self-restraint. Northwestern natives and tribes of the Great Basin initiated trade in shell hair ornaments, which traveled as far as the North American Plains to garnish the grooming of brides. In 1570, Chinese hairstyles and accessories changed so often that historians referred to them as *shiyang* (the look of the moment).

English Tudor styles featured symmetry in linen headdress over neatly parted hair that women never cut. Thieves targeted children with long hair, especially blond or red, and sold their locks to wig makers. English sumptuary laws attempted to halt the rising merchant class from status hairdressing with colored powder and silk bands. In France, backcombing produced a frizzing effect for height. Women further elevated the look by fastening locks to rats (padded rolls) or atifets (wire frames).

In colonial Salem, Massachusetts, in 1629, Pastor Francis Higginson, New England's first Puritan minister, recorded the side-dressed locks of hair on the Wampanoag, who graced each with peacock feathers, red fabric, beads, chains, and ribbons. Persecution, fines, and executions controlled the personal choices of European settlers, notably their dressing and grooming for religious services. Judge Samuel Sewall's edict of 1679 banned curling, powdering wigs, and padding hair with wiglets as improprieties based on nefarious affectation and vanity.

Farther north among the conservative Christians of Manitoba, Saskatchewan, and Ontario, female Mennonite women emigrated from Germany, Russia, and Switzerland with uncut hair caught up in gauze caps. Their chaste covering of hair derived from New Testament commands that female Christians be sober, discreet, and subservient to males. In contrast to conservative European gendering, the Yanomami on the Orinoco River in Venezuela adopted a unisex style, with all members trimming their hair in a bowl shape.

Hairstyle and Personal Rights

In Great Britain and northwestern Europe, the Napoleonic era (1799–1815) introduced short hair for men and flowers and crocheted accessories for female hairdos. In contrast to self-styling as a fashion statement, short Victorian cuts for schoolboys indicated a concern for neatness and compliance with dress codes, such as those at Eton. Following the dictates of English femininity, girls retained long curls, which they rinsed in rainwater, perfumed with lemon juice and rosemary, and secured in Alice bands (named for Alice in Wonderland).

For much of the world, women's coiffure reflected status. In Spain, ladies bound strands with a carved *peinetón* (ornate comb) covered by a lace mantilla. All in all, the grandeur of the Spanish coif accorded respect and admiration to a noblewoman via her hairdressing. In the Western Hemisphere, slave women concealed their hair under a fresh *tignon* (turban), a common accessory on the streets of Havana and New Orleans.

After 230 years of Manchu custom, the issue of queues on male Chinese immigrants to California came to a crucial test in April 1876. Under the so-called Pigtail Ordinance, Sheriff Matthew Nunan, warden of the San Francisco County jail, lopped the braided pigtails of male Chinese prisoners to 1 inch (2.5 centimeters), ostensibly as a deterrent to lice and fleas. For disrespecting a symbol of Asian identity, Nunan faced a $10,000 lawsuit brought by inmate Ho Ah Kow. In June 1879, U.S. Supreme Court Justice Stephen Johnson Field—sitting in federal circuit court—found in favor of the plaintiff and declared the ordinance unconstitutional on grounds of discrimination.

For most white people in America and Europe, display of stylish hair modes set the tone of attractiveness as well as employability. Fashion plates in *La Mode Illustrée* during the late 1860s featured ringlets and a center part to set off gabardine and straw bonnets and satin headbands. Drawings in *Godey's Lady's Book* pictured hairpin adornment and switches (hairpieces) for plumping up short styles. Crocheted snoods protected the housekeeper's hairdo from dust.

Edwardian men groomed their short hair with antimacassar oil and shaped their mustaches and beards with wax. Late Edwardian hairstyles for women introduced the upswept charwoman, a mushroom-shaped arrangement suited to the plumed Merry Widow hat. In defiance of the businessman's adherence to ear-length cuts and sideburns, Bohemian men let unparted hair brush their shoulders and left their beards untrimmed. Similarly rebellious against gender stereotypes, female Bohemians favored luxuriant medieval styles dotted with fresh blossoms.

Turn-of-the-century coiffure in England, the Americas, and Russia popularized women's twists and buns garnished with feathers. Department stores such as Marks & Spencer, Macy's, and Gimbels appealed to fashionable women with hairpins, combs, and dresser sets containing implements for hair care.

To supply the needs of nonwhite women, Louisiana-born entrepreneur Madame C.J. Walker became North America's first black female millionaire by inventing a hot comb to straighten African American hair, along with styling lotions and gels to stem hair loss. Black grooming during the Jim Crow era in America reflected traditions in pomades and braiding, styles replicated in the Caribbean. In defiance of American racism during the 1920s, dancer Josephine Baker flaunted flapper-style bobbed hair with spit curls at each ear. Dancers in cocktail headbands and cloche hats over shingled boy cuts expressed their liberation from female confinement. Nightclub styles influenced the finger waves of women and conked (straightened) hair of black men in Harlem, Los Angeles, Detroit, Memphis, and Chicago.

During World War II, female factory laborers created a demand for the snood, a net hair smoother that controlled long locks to keep them from tangling in machine parts. Postwar guidance in *Glamour* and *Seventeen* encouraged trendy razoring and short clips for girls that revealed the ears and nape. Women's hairnets, made of nylon, elastic, and Tricel, stretched over the heads of workers in factories and cafés.

In the 1960s, counterculture rebellion provoked displays of long, untidy hair by hippie men and women as anti-establishment symbols. Models in the pages of *Elle, Hairdo, Harper's Bazaar, Journal,* and *Paris-Match* echoed the androgynous waif haircut of English trendsetter Twiggy and the affectations of adult women who altered their appearance at will with nylon wigs and hairpieces. Late twentieth-century styles in Afros, high-top fades, Jheri curls, Kenyan dreadlocks, and "big hair" received the attention of trendsetters writing for *Vogue* and *Jet.*

Hairdressing in the twenty-first century continues to illustrate the link between self-adornment and self-expression. In Orissa, India, fashionable Bondo women section their hair with strings of seed beads. At the birth of firstborn sons on the Horn of East Africa, Rendille tribeswomen celebrate by dyeing their hair ochre and setting it in a pompadour with lard and mud. American and European punk style features neon chartreuse, pink, and purple hair dye and streaking as models of a subculture ideology.

See also: African American Clothing and Fashion; Chinese Clothing; Gendered Dressing; Unisex Clothing; Veils and Veiling; Wigs.

Further Reading

Bryer, Robin. *The History of Hair: Fashion and Fantasy Down the Ages.* London: Philip Wilson, 2000.

Corson, Richard. *Fashions in Hair: The First Five Thousand Years.* 3rd ed. London: Peter Owen, 2000.

Fiell, Charlotte. *Hairstyles: Ancient to Present.* London: Fiell, 2010.

Sherrow, Victoria, ed. *Encyclopedia of Hair: A Cultural History.* Westport, CT: Greenwood, 2006.

Halloween Costumes

Unlike other Western holiday attire, Halloween costumes nurture imagination and individuality. Dating to Celtic culture in the first century C.E., Samhain, an early fall harvest festival, celebrated pagan folklore about goblins, *bogies* (ghosts), and brooms and corn shocks come to life. Despite the intervention of Christian missionaries St. Patrick in the early fifth century and St. Columcille in the sixth, the frolicking survived.

Because Pope Boniface IV adapted the holiday with Christian interpretation in 609, medieval merrymaking showcased animal hides, patchwork, and motley, the attire of the court jester. Renaissance disguises and soot-blackened faces and hands shielded the identity of celebrants from vengeful spirits set free from the netherworld on October 31. During the 1700s, costuming as pirates and witches concealed the identities of English youths petitioning for "soul cakes" and cider door to door.

Lighting and bonfires relieved the darkness of nighttime revelry. In Ireland and Scotland, firebrands and candles in hollow turnips lit the masker's path. Immigrants to North America found gourds and pumpkins easier to carve than turnips. By 1895, "guising" as devils, skeletons, and angels on lighted city streets became a traditional fall activity in Scotland and spread to Canada in 1911 and the United States in 1920.

Costuming for parades and trick-or-treating from the 1930s promoted the sale of felt for hats and vests by Spotlite Costumes of Manhattan, New York, and Ben Cooper, Inc., of Brooklyn. Cross-dressing satirized gendered vanities, as with women's quilted muscle shirts and unshaven males padded and costumed to look like women, a favorite disguise in the French Caribbean.

Halloween as we know it today is a festival of Scots-Irish origin, held on All Hallows Eve. Its rituals of costumes, pumpkins, and trick-or-treating came to the United States with the great wave of Scottish and Irish immigration in the mid-nineteenth century. *(Historic Photo Archive/Getty Image)*

Influenced by horror movies, caricatures in the late 1950s highlighted the gothic dress and postures of King Kong, Dracula, Wolf Man, Frankenstein's monster, and Igor, the humpbacked lab assistant. To collect coins for the United Nations International Children's Emergency Fund (UNICEF), children in the United States and Canada carried small orange boxes on their Halloween rounds.

Late twentieth-century Halloween fun involved fake teeth and noses, press-on tattoos, vacuum-formed plastic masks and armor, and fright wigs as well as dress-up hats and T-shirts for pet dogs. Comic book disguises based colors and styles on superheroes Captain Marvel, Superman, Spiderman, Zorro, and Wonder Woman. Such legendary figures as Cleopatra, Robin Hood, Uncle Sam, and Pocahontas supplied style cues for outfits and hairdos. Manufacturers acknowledged parental concerns over lighted candles by coating costume fabrics and Day-Glo masks with flame retardants.

In the 2000s, unisex Halloween costumes made from fake fur, oilcloth, leather scraps, and polyurethane depict toddlers as ladybugs, pumpkins, black cats, ducks, jack-o'-lanterns, and daisies. Shoppers at Disneyland survey a choice of fantasy masks and wigs; princess dresses with petticoats, tiaras, and sparkly slippers; ninja bodysuits and flashlights disguised as alien ray guns; and Tinker Bell fairy wands. Portrait masks of Michael Jackson, Barack Obama, and Madonna allow children to portray real figures or to choose the film personalities of Darth Vader, the Little Mermaid, Batman, Princess Leia, and Shrek. For costume parties, accessories include monster hands, fake blood, pitchforks, voice synthesizers, and headsmen's axes. Face and body painting eliminates investment in single-use headgear and masks and enhances the safety of children on dark streets by making them up as ghouls and zombies.

See also: Costume Parties; Disguise and Spy Wear; Holiday Costumes; Masks and Masking.

Further Reading

Bannatyne, Lesley Pratt. *Halloween Nation: Behind the Scenes of America's Fright Night.* Gretna, LA: Pelican, 2011.

Morton, Lisa. *The Halloween Encyclopedia.* Jefferson, NC: McFarland, 2011.

Rogers, Nicholas. *Halloween: From Pagan Ritual to Party Night.* New York: Oxford University Press, 2002.

Halston, Roy (1932–1990)

An internationally acclaimed minimalist, American fashion designer Roy Halston flourished during the rise of jet-setting and disco dancing in the 1960s and 1970s.

A native of Des Moines, Iowa, he was born Roy Halston Frowick on April 23, 1932, to accountant James Edward Frowick and homemaker Hallie May Holmes Frowick. His mother taught him millinery and alteration techniques. After one term at Indiana University, at age 20, he left for a job dressing department store windows and to take night courses at the School of the Art Institute of Chicago.

A feature in the *Chicago Daily News* introduced Halston to stardom. In 1957, under his middle name, he opened a millinery on Chicago's fashionable Michigan Avenue. After a year's apprenticeship in New York under designer Lilly Daché, he served Bergdorf Goodman as head milliner and clothing adviser to Jacqueline Kennedy. In 1960, the cover of *Harper's Bazaar* lauded his pillbox design, which earned a place in history on the head of Mrs. Kennedy at the presidential inauguration on January 20, 1961.

As a designer of sleek, glamorous ensembles on Madison Avenue, Halston in 1966 began outfitting women worldwide, including dancer Martha Graham, First Lady Betty Ford, publisher Katherine Graham, Princess Grace of Monaco, and actors Oprah Winfrey, Liza Minnelli, Lauren Bacall, and Elizabeth Taylor. His collections showcased purity of color and silhouette in a range of fabrics from matte jersey and Ultrasuede to cashmere. Innovative tailoring and materials turned his catwalk shows into social events. He made sunglasses, Greek column dresses, one-shoulder sheaths, jumpsuits, and shirtwaists for a variety of body types, from thin to hippy and overweight, and for the in crowd dancing at Le Cirque and Studio 54. On August 21, 1972,

Newsweek proclaimed Halston America's premier designer.

Halston's uniforms decked U.S. Olympic contenders in 1976 and outfitted Braniff International Airways stewardesses in 1977 and Girl Scouts the following year, when he also created cargo pants for the New York Police Department. In 1983, in a break with his dedication to jet-setters, Halston began merchandising his apparel through a first-of-its-kind licensing contract with J.C. Penney for eight annual collections and accessories. He died of AIDS and lung cancer on March 26, 1990.

See also: Fashion Design; Hats, Women's.

Further Reading

Bluttal, Steven, and Patricia Mears. *Halston.* Oxford, UK: Phaidon, 2011.

Gross, Elaine, and Fred Rottman. *Halston: An American Original.* New York: HarperCollins, 1999.

Halston. www.halston.com

Handbags

The combined purpose of handbags as carryalls, purses, and fashion statements has kept them prominent in apparel from prehistory to the present day. Across Africa and the Middle East, bundles and pouches served human nomads from as early as 38,000 B.C.E. By 30,000 B.C.E., Central Asian flax harvesters twisted stems into linen bags into which hunter-gatherers stowed birds, mollusks, mushrooms, and fruit.

Utility Across Civilizations

Around 8000 B.C.E., dwellers of the Guitarrero Cave west of present-day Chimbote, Peru, twined cotton strands into net bags and wove coca leaf and fique (*Furcraea andina*) into totes. Among the Shulaveri-Shomu culture of the Transcaucasus region, now southern Armenia, after 6000 B.C.E., netted cedar bark produced collapsible string sacks. After 4300 B.C.E., residents of Cueva de los Murciélagos in southern Spain plaited esparto grass (*Macrochloa tenacissima*) into bags. These carryalls paralleled coarse pouches made from kenaf in Sudan and subtropical Africa. Similar indigenous materials of the Inuit of northeastern Canada, Labrador, and Greenland produced seal flipper and caribou pelt pouches.

Bengali seamstresses of the second millennium B.C.E. embroidered *kantha* (rags) into sacks and wallets. Among the Maya of the southern Sierra Madre in 1500 B.C.E., agave and yucca supplied the stringy fiber for weaving totes. From 300 B.C.E., Uzbeks, Turks, and Siberians appliquéd felt ciphers, river pearls, and tassels onto camel bags.

Between 43 and 410 C.E., Roman legionaries wore out military bags, which cobblers as far north as Celtic Britain repaired by patching holes and replacing straps. By 100, men in the Amazon River basin knotted totes and hunting pouches from wild cotton. In France and Belgium in the late 200s, women's shoes and matching netted bags achieved favor among the fashionable. Byzantine women carried fabric purses graced with filigree and engraved buckles.

In Arabia and Goa, India, leatherworkers profited from the sale of personal water bags, a necessity in dry lands. At Sutton Hoo in Suffolk, England, grave goods from 500 include a purse and chatelaine, a key ring designating the matron of the family. Eighth-century Japanese girls marked *seiji no hi* (coming of age) with gifts of kimonos, obis, and evening bags.

Native Americans stored amulets, religious tokens, and supplies in medicine bags, buckskin pouches, parfleches (leather envelopes), and bandolier bags, such as the alligator hide pouches made by the swamp tribes of Florida and Georgia and the pouch featuring a clan emblem that Sauk war chief Black Hawk wore across his chest on a strap. Russian stitchery applied folk symbols that imparted luck and protection from harm. In England and Scotland after 1000, multicolored scenarios in crewelwork marked the purses of court ladies. Fourteenth-century money pouches from China featured the smooth seaming of silk.

During the Black Death of the mid-fourteenth century, people from China, the Crimea, and across Europe filled bags and purses with herbs and blossoms to ward off plague. In the early 1400s, leather dealers flouted papal bans on imported Islamic goods by selling handbags graced with gold leaf that Arab specialists applied with hot irons. Florentine marketers in the 1420s stocked specialty bags for peddlers, letter carriers, bird hunters, and hikers. Bags brocaded in Japan bore the *omamori* (talisman) that promised serenity and wealth. In the Congo, raffia and wood bark produced flexible bags for utilitarian purposes and travel.

High Fashion

Renaissance designers achieved the peak of stylish bags with the unisex Italian leather *borsa* (purse) and *scarsella* (coin pouch), the English sweet bag for carrying handkerchiefs, and the velvet purse from India and Spain. Late Renaissance trade brought knitted bags and gloves to England from Guernsey, the Orkneys, and the Shetland Islands. Youths gave purses to maidens as fairings (love tokens). In Eastern Europe, *punto unghero* (Hungarian point) or bargello outlined geometrics and flames on canvas bags.

During the 1700s, Middle Eastern tanners and leatherworkers profited from women's fashions in leather-bound purses and soft drawstring reticules. In the Western Hemisphere, bag pockets attached to the clothing of settlers as an expedient carryall for keys and small tools. Among the Black Watch regiment from Scotland in 1739, Highlanders accessorized their kilts with badger skin sporrans, pouches that served as pockets.

By 1745, mechanized matelassé, invented by English engineer Robert Elsden, quilted detachable pockets and purses. In colonial Philadelphia during the 1760s, leather processors imitated the dyed goat and sheep purses imported from Spain, Turkey, and Morocco. Cobblers purchased osnaburg and buckram from Ireland for fabric linings. The frivolities of the Napoleonic era (1799–1815) created a need for the cloth drawstring purse, a carrier of fragile dancing slippers to and from destinations.

Dutch styles in the 1820s featured the crocheted coin purse and handbag beaded to match collars and chokers. Berlin handwork applied twisted wool needlepoint to canvas bags and slippers. At Montmellick, Ireland, Quaker instructors taught girls to knot carryalls for sale. The importance of silk satin purses to the Victorian female

wardrobe created an underground market in stolen and used goods. In New York City, Macy's and Gimbels department stores grouped kid gloves and purses at specialty counters.

Late nineteenth-century styles matched napped fabric, metallic lamé, and wool plush handbags to ornate hats and evening pumps. For young girls, Edwardian muff purses met needs for hand warmers and card and change holders. At Canadian and U.S. boarding schools for Amerindian children, missionaries confiscated amulet pouches and medicine bags and burned them to strip the young of cultural ties to tribes.

Sophisticated merchandising in the early twentieth century drew Canadian shoppers to goat and alligators bags featured at Goodwin's in Montreal. In the 1920s, advertising and window dressing with rotating turntables increased profits in shoe and zippered handbag sets. Consumers popularized the faille purses designed by art deco master Erté and telescoping handbags with cane handles made by Tuscan designer Guccio Gucci. Purses styled by French couturier Coco Chanel featured quilted jersey or leather sides and chain handles. Hollywood stars of the 1930s modeled the envelope clutch paired with white gloves.

Postwar Styles

Rationing during World War II removed from the purse market exotic leathers and hardware and replaced them with hemp, mesh, canvas, and jute for drawstring pouches. Elsa Schiaparelli glamorized military olive drab and camouflage fabrics in stylish balloon handbags. The reform of women's finery in the 1940s, as featured in *Vogue*, reduced large purses to clutches and beaded evening bags, to which debutantes and prom goers pinned corsages.

Post–World War II nationalism in Central Africa returned to favor bags made from native kente cloth and mud cloth. In industrialized countries, manufacturers of synthetics marketed rayon faille for flat-sided purses and laminates for hard-sided and train case styles with Lucite handles. During the 1960s, feminists carried clean-lined shoulder bags as evidence of liberation from fussy purses.

Hippie fashions of the 1970s flaunted unisex

hobo bags without hardware and denim jeans bags with fly fronts and back pockets. Hobbyists appliquéd totes with felt and embroidered slouch sacks with rainbows, marijuana leaf shapes, and peace symbols. Imports from southern India introduced Banjara dowry bags garnished with chain stitching, tassels, and cowries. Haute couture produced alligator purses garnished with gold hardware, a specialty of designer Ralph Lauren and Marchioness in Hong Kong.

In the 1990s, boutiques such as Friedrichstrasse in Berlin filled their display windows with leather baguette bags, svelte pocketbooks, and coin purses by Guccio Gucci, Émile-Maurice Hermès, and Louis Vuitton. Earthwear outlets in London featured serviceable shoulder bags and envelope purses crafted from upcycled tape, seatbelts, vinyl car seats, and vehicle tires. Recycled goods fastened with snaps, magnets, and Velcro®.

Handbags continue to retain their utility and popularity as accessories and courtship gifts, as in the case of Berber painted leather totes, Italian envelope clutches and billfolds, vetiver grass carryalls from Dominica, studded Bohemian bags with bamboo handles, and Malaysian purses. In Laos, Myanmar, and Thailand, Akha and Hmong males carry musical instruments in courting bags when they approach attractive girls. Athletics stores feature unisex nylon fanny packs as convenient store-alls for keys, cash, ID, and cell phones.

The demand for totes and purses coordinated with high-fashion outfits boosts sales of retro cobra and python bags as well as Ultrasuede and Tencel clutches and the spherical bags of Issey Miyake. On street corners and the Internet, fashion pirates hawk knockoffs bearing Burberry, Louis Vuitton, Ralph Lauren, Ferragamo, Coach, Kate Spade, Very Vera, and Gucci labels. Fair trade stores offer jute totes from India and sling bags from Vietnam as a means of fostering sustainable fashions from the developing world.

See also: Accessories; Gucci, Guccio; Leather and Suede; Pockets; Vuitton, Louis.

Further Reading

Astrologo, Adrienne, and Nancy Schiffer. *High Fashion Handbags: Classic Vintage Designs.* Atglen, PA: Schiffer, 2007.
Clark, Judith. *Handbags: The Making of a Museum.* New Haven, CT: Yale University Press, 2012.
Cox, Caroline. *The Handbag: An Illustrated History.* New York: HarperCollins, 2007.

Handkerchiefs

Attesting to concern for personal hygiene and public health when carried in a pocket or handbag, the handkerchief provides a stylistic grace note and sign of gentility when displayed in a jacket pocket. Its use as an accessory goes back millennia.

The women of ancient Greece debuted the linen pocket square as a clothing adornment. In Scythia (modern Ukraine) from 500 B.C.E., brides carried hemp or linen handkerchiefs outlined in red stitchery. Roman men in the early empire identified the handkerchief as a *sudarium* (sweat cloth) and means of applying cologne; Roman women waved their handkerchiefs at the Colosseum in support of racing teams. Early Christians raised their pocket squares as a form of applause after a homily; priests acquired vestment "facials" (squares) edged in fringe and braid for use at the altar.

Around the mid-thirteenth century, *opus teutonicum* (German work) marked wedding handkerchiefs with white linen threads on white linen, symbols of purity and chastity. After 1377, King Richard II of England introduced the utilitarian handkerchief as a polite means of attending to a dripping nose or soiled lips. Children acquired their own "muckenders" as public displays of good manners.

Medieval herbalists advised knotting fragrant herbs and blossoms in handkerchiefs and pouches held to the mouth and nose to stave off plague. Late in the fourteenth century, European haberdashers added to the outfit of the civilized male foulards and handkerchiefs shaped in circles, triangles, and rectangles. Seamstresses offered monogramming as a personal garnish as well as identification of a lost pocket square.

During the Renaissance, Italian lace makers centered lawn handkerchiefs with rosette, star, and snowflake motifs in counted thread work and in monochromatic blackwork and scarletwork. A button on one corner, fastened within the pocket, kept the square centered and unmoving. As wooing gifts, European couples exchanged imported neckerchiefs, head rails, and tasseled handkerchiefs made from cambric and gauze from Bruges, Belgium, and Ghent and Ypres, Flanders.

Spanish handkerchief makers increased the size of the pocket square and added scent. Widows carried black rectangles trimmed in needle lace to denote sorrow. Sumptuary laws attempted to stem the use of pocket squares by peasants, who imitated the pretensions of aristocrats.

Queen Elizabeth I set the tone of court accessories by sporting dainty cambric, Holland cloth, and silk handkerchiefs. Items in her collection typically consisted of fabric measuring 4 inches by 4 inches (10 centimeters by 10 centimeters) and embroidered with love knots and edged in metallic gold lace. Men tied the squares over their wigs in inclement weather. Actors used foulards and pocket squares as stage props.

By the seventeenth century, colored fabrics began replacing white in handkerchiefs. At Cairo, Damascus, and Istanbul, Muslim stitchery adorned handkerchiefs with classic patterns matching those of scarves, tunics, and slippers. Late seventeenth-century print fabrics from Gujarat featured patterns that suited the tastes of customers in Arabia, Abyssinia, Turkey, Iran, East Africa, and Persia. Brides in India expected gifts of *rumals* (rectangles) intricately embroidered in *chamba,* a figurative art stitchery on unbleached *khaddar* cloth (homespun) from the Punjab.

The ubiquity of pocket squares and half handkerchiefs attested to their many uses, including the convenience of the snuff taker, eyeglass polisher, and sportsman. Eighteenth-century tailors stitched patch pockets on garments for the elderly to hold handkerchiefs and glasses. Handkerchiefs provided props for the Jewish *mitsve tants* (blessing dance), Russian *ulitsa* (street dance), and Greek *kalamatianos* (circle dance). In Argentina, Bolivia, Chile, and Peru, a dance gesture for the *cueca* involved the fluttering of handkerchiefs by women as they lifted skirt hems to reveal petticoats and lower legs.

In France during the Napoleonic era (1799–1815), the emperor promoted the sale of fashionable Valenciennes handkerchief lace made from the combined threads of 800 bobbins. Housewives folded small squares of it into triangles to drape around the head and knot at the chin. Men favored the silk "fogle" as an accessory to the business suit but saved the Madras square or bandanna for leisure time.

In Victorian wardrobes, muslin and silk charmeuse handkerchiefs imported by Greek, Spanish, Maltese, and Tuscan traders matched dresses, hats, and equestrienne outfits, which offered knee pockets for storage. Irish needleworkers sold organdy nuptial squares edged in Carrickmacross, a whitework appliqué of stylized blossoms and lianas on net to match wedding veils and wrap bridal bouquets. Patterns in *Godey's Lady's Book* illustrated how and where to apply italic monogramming of the bride's new initials.

Ensembles and accessories announced the maturity of marriageable females, who hooked a French fichu at the waistband or tucked a small square into the hemline pocket of the petticoat as a symbol of refinement. On colonial plantations in the Western Hemisphere, slave girls treasured discarded gauze handkerchiefs and scarves as additions to their dowries. Edwardian women considered lacy handkerchiefs as valuable elements of investment dressing. Recyclers stitched scalloped squares into quilts, doll dresses, and lap throws.

Penny bazaars profited from handkerchief sales, a point-of-purchase appeal that extended to department stores such as Marks & Spencer, Lord & Taylor, Gimbels, and Macy's. Buyers for Falabella in Santiago, Chile's oldest department-store chain, and Magasin du Nord in Copenhagen, Denmark, retained consumer interest with seasonal stock from India, Cambodia, Korea, Japan, Siam, China, and Afghanistan, including Lissue handkerchiefs for men and valentine squares for girlfriends. In 1914, innovator Mary Phelps "Polly" Jacob stitched together two silk squares to form the standard American bra.

Handkerchiefs in the twenty-first century still retain cultural significance, as with the cloth spread over the face of a Russian corpse before

burial or the waving of white squares to acknowledge courage in the Spanish bullring. Meanwhile, businessmen and well-dressed male celebrities on the cover of *GQ* maintain the pocket square as a finishing touch to suits.

See also: Accessories; Pockets.

Further Reading

Gustafson, Helen, and Jonathan Chester. *Hanky Panky: An Intimate History of the Handkerchief.* Berkeley, CA: Ten Speed, 2002.

Mihalick, Roseanna. *Collecting Handkerchiefs.* 2nd ed. Atglen, PA: Schiffer, 2007.

Harper's Bazaar

From its inception as a blue-chip weekly delineating clothing styles that appealed to East Coast socialites, *Harper's Bazaar* defined the tastes of upscale white cosmopolites. Designed by Fletcher Harper as a 16-page style-setting gazette with snob appeal, the magazine began publication on November 2, 1867, under the subtitle "Repository of Fashion, Pleasure, and Instruction." The first cover pictured four bonnets and two understated wedding gowns wrapped in illusion veils. Issued from Manhattan's Franklin Square at the annual rate of $4 for 52 issues, America's first beauty and fashion publication made New York City into "fashion city" and the "international community of dress."

Showcasing wardrobe news of the elite, Victorian fancy needlework, and fashion plates from Berlin, the magazine reflected the immersion of editor Mary Louise Booth, a skilled urban historian and French-English translator, in all things French, the global touchstone of style. Initial fashion trends—bonnets, headbands, chokers, parasols, bustles on hourglass figures—suited the dressing of sedate yet stylish women. The cover for October 3, 1868, pictured 15 hairstyles featuring the fleur-de-lis knot, braided chignon, and curled diadem. In June 1873, the magazine offered patterns for any outfit, tailored to the reader's measurements.

By 1877, circulation reached 80,000, reflecting the rapid expansion of American print jour-

nalism. On May 4, 1878, the cover featured three bridal outfits accessorized with bowed trains and full-length veils. Spreads on Paris mode featured the opulent court presentation gowns and cloaks designed by Charles Frederick Worth. An elegant dinner dress in 1894 appealed directly to the moneyed class with its oversized, embroidered satin sleeves and bust, a fringed sash to the hem, and feathered fan. At Easter 1896, cover art enhanced the stylized female figure in draped gown and lilies in pre-Raphaelite mode.

American Fashion Plate

In 1892, the cover sketch dispensed with frivolities to picture a street costume of brocade tunic by Worth edged in fur, sashed in dark satin, and topped by a plumed hat designed by Madame Marthe Virot of Paris. The turn of the twentieth century saw an emphasis on college women and fashions for children and young mothers. Illustrations pictured women as consumers and widows in shirred mourning dresses of crepe de chine and voile, embroidered satin appliqué on voile, and the classical and medieval underpinnings of draped fashions.

By 1901, *Harper's Bazaar* came out monthly, endorsing big-name couturiers and promoting stores selling their lines. At a dime per issue and one dollar for a year's subscription, the magazine in 1905 popularized etiquette books, investment dressing, and historical designs. Sketches by George Barbier, Edmund Dulac, and Gustav Michelson introduced fantasy, orientalism, and art deco lines to female costumes, which also flourished in *Harper's Bazaar UK,* established in 1929.

After 1918 and until 1930, the designer Erté published sketches of the punctilious, moneyed woman of fashion in stunningly chic day dresses with matching hats. One hat design from March 1918 offers instructions on overlaying a black straw hat with a white straw rectangle for latticing at the crown in a checkerboard pattern, the same black-on-white interweaving for a ribbon reticule, and the addition of a Turkish-style veil for the lower face to a toque (turban). Another do-it-yourself idea involved cutting a face hole in a rectangle of lace and tying it to the head with ribbon as a boudoir cap.

The Modern Magazine

In 1934 at the Hearst office on Madison Avenue, editor Carmel Snow and art director Alexey Brodovitch, a White Russian émigré to France in 1920, began revolutionizing the slick fashion magazine. In summer 1936, Snow encouraged haute couture columnist Diana Vreeland, a fashion authority, to compose "Why Don't You?"—a source of unusual styling tricks, such as the spacing of large faux diamonds in the hair and the wrapping of the shoulders in a colorful cashmere shawl in hotels and trains.

Until the onset of World War II, the magazine's layout appealed to high-toned as well as middle-brow female consumers. Brodovitch resolved to strip the magazine's pages of boredom with the drama he imparted to sets for the Ballet Russe in Paris. He edged in white space bold juxtapositions, vital cropped and deckle-edge photos, and innovative poster art.

For the postwar ready-to-wear consumer market, *Harper's Bazaar* stressed Christian Dior's 1947 fashion line, featuring a fitted white peplum jacket over a black full skirt and topped with a straw Mandarin hat. For the mass market, Brodovitch sought novelty poses of women in motion. He merged high fashion in single colors and portraits of body parts—hands, feet, lips, eyes—with current art by Salvador Dalí, Marc Chagall, Jean Cocteau, and Raoul Dufy.

Shifts in trends in 1980 introduced a youthful folkloric image stressed by editor Nonnie Moore and fashion photographer Oliviero Toscani. By 1990, Asian chic dominated the magazine's thrust, as with the Jean Paul Gaultier collection and accompanying jewelry and nose piercings featured in January 1994. In 1992, British style editor Liz Tilberis took the helm of *Harper's Bazaar* and creative director Fabien Baron revamped and revived the format.

In the 2000s, the work of former *Vogue* employee Kate Betts, the youngest editor of *Harper's Bazaar*, reflected a journalistic perception of trendsetting and whimsy in ordinary lives. Her failure

to establish a devoted readership for pop culture prompted the hiring of Glenda Bailey, former editor of *Marie Claire*. In 2007, *Harper's Bazaar* earned a Consumer Magazine of the Year award as well as honors from the Professional Publishers Association for Lucy Yeomans, editor of *Harper's Bazaar UK*.

In the foreword to *Harper's Bazaar: Fabulous at Every Age* (2009), Bailey states the magazine's creed that coordinating an outfit with panache and individuality outweighs factors of the wearer's age, size, and finances. The overview named long chains, boots, berets, metallic fabric, and minimal evening accessories as integral to a polished look on such successful public figures as model Iman, designer Diane von Furstenberg, and socialite Evelyn Lauder. Former Ford model Lizzette Kattan, the Honduran editor of *Harper's Bazaar Italy*, *Harper's Bazaar France*, and *Harper's Bazaar Uomo* (Harper's for men), promoted the fashions of Calvin Klein, Valentino, and Gianni Versace.

By the end of 2011, *Harper's Bazaar* maintained an annual readership of 735,212, in part for its salon and spa guides, advice on attire for public appearances, and tips on accessories and wardrobe development. Subsequent issues touting Kate Middleton, Nicole Kidman, Demi Moore, Keira Knightley, a reprise of Marilyn Monroe photos, 2012 summer Olympic styles, and the career of designer Karl Lagerfeld maintained readership at an all-time high. Top Pacific Coast editor Brana Wolf at *Harper's Bazaar Australia* exhibited élan in the role of fashion prophet by gleaning down-style trends and color moods from high-fashion runway shows and the Internet.

See also: Photography, Fashion.

Further Reading

Armstrong, Lisa. *Harper's Bazaar Fashion: Your Guide to Personal Style*. London: Aurum, 2010.

D'Souza, Nandini. *Harper's Bazaar: Fabulous at Every Age: Your Quick & Easy Guide to Fashion*. Ed. Jenny Barnett, with a foreword by Glenda Bailey. New York: Sterling, 2009.

Harper's Bazaar. www.harpersbazaar.com

Levin, Jenny. *Harper's Bazaar Great Style: The Best Ways to Update Your Look*. New York: Sterling, 2007.

Vreeland, Diana. *D.V.* New York: HarperCollins, 2011.

Hats, Men's

Civilian menswear historically has included diversified headgear suited to weather and activities as well as status and personal identity. From 1400 B.C.E., Asian traders satisfied clothiers with felt for hats, a handy replacement for palm branch rain shields and skin hoods. Kurdish felt hats exhibited individual style with beading and metal discs imported from India. Hebrew worship attire included both the turban and high-peaked hat. After 600 B.C.E., Greek men retained the woven straw *petasos* (sunshade) in open opposition to Persian umbrellas.

During the eighth century C.E., Zoroastrian Parsis escaped persecution by living among Hindus in India and distinguishing themselves with the *phenta,* a wicker frame covered with printed cotton. Late medieval winter wardrobes in Russia and Scandinavia contained fox fur head coverings that draped to the shoulders. The departure of crusaders from Castile and León in 1096 began with impressive cavalcades of mounted warriors in head wear marked by heraldic coats of arms, a garnish that enhanced the stature and authority of troops. Moroccan men displayed Arabism with the red felt fez, a cylinder graced with a black tassel. The Scots Balmoral bonnet exhibited a similar pride in tradition by modeling plaids on the band.

The peak-brimmed Byzantine hat with a high pyramidal dome gained respect after the accession of Emperor Andronicus I Comnenus in 1183. Middle Eastern Muslims kept their heads concealed under a cotton kaffiyeh, a cloth headdress pleated into a triangle and held in place by an *agal* (band). Orthodox clergy graced their headgear with the Greek letters chi and rho, an embroidered abbreviation of Christos. Late in the Middle Ages, the wide felt hat from Spain and the draped turban of Sikhs achieved global acceptance. Outdoor workers in Greece wore the Phrygian skullcap, a conical head covering similar in shape to the Mandarin hat.

Royalty declared power and influence with the headgear they wore. In Japan, the emperor topped his dramatic silk robes with a tall silk *kammuri* (black hat) fitted with a chin strap and topped with a dome. Under King Henry V beginning in 1413, English regimental helmets sported feathers and plumes that influenced civilians. English loyalists gilded the curled hat feather and angled it toward the ear.

Renaissance hatmakers applied technology to men's styles, as with the felting of ghost hair for hats in Mughal India, the chin straps on Iberian straw hats, plaited leather hatbands in Eastern Europe, and the embroidery of badges, beasts, swords, and anchors on British regimentals and livery. Andalusian men set the tone of the Spanish colonial era in soft felt styles. Court jesters dotted their hats with mirrors to ridicule the exhibitionism of period fops in rosettes, tassels, fringes, braids, and pompoms, and the buckled bands and rolled brims of the capotain or sugarloaf hat.

In the seventeenth century, baroque hats became more demonstrative of status, as with the jaunty Monmouth cocked hat, the schoolboy cone hat, and the brimless Scots bonnet identifying Highlanders. Persian mothers shielded baby boys with padded toddler hats. At the French court of Louis XIII, palace guards exaggerated their authority with red-and-white plumed hats. At the beheading of Charles I in 1649, English Puritans in high-crowned capotains or Geneva hats surveyed loyalists silently protesting by decking their hats in yew, rosemary, and rue, symbols of sorrow, remembrance, and regret. Protests in the fashion magazine *Mercure Galant* in the 1670s denounced luxury-loving French cavaliers for flaunting plumes on headgear that covered waist-length wigs.

Eighteenth-century men's hats varied in utility and exhibitionism, as with Mesoamerican straw coverings, Caribbean pirate tricorns, Texas "boss of the plains," and Argentine satinet mourning head wear garnished with black ribbons. After the French Revolution of 1789, pigtailed and powdered bouffant wigs gave way to the citizen's black tricorn and the cocked beaver dome with a plain band. The style-conscious purchased hat screws that forced the beaver felt back into shape after wetting.

During the Victorian era, beaver hats and semiformal homburgs for gentlemen, knob-topped

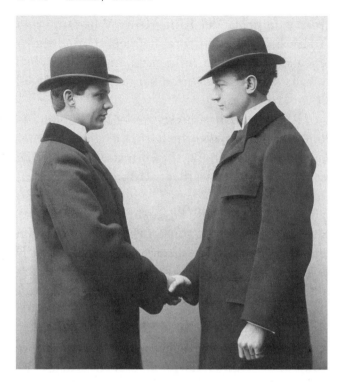

Designed in 1849, the bowler hat, or derby, was first popular with British bankers and workingmen and later with American cowboys and railroad workers. Twentieth-century comedians Charlie Chaplin and Laurel and Hardy gave it a comic aspect. *(The Granger Collection, NYC—All rights reserved)*

bollingers and chimney pots for vendors, and high domes with chin straps for bobbies marked the advance of males on the London street scene. Edwardian dress showcased the Utrecht velvet hat, a napped goat hair that held up in all weather. In North America, hard-domed bowlers, fedoras, flat-top boaters, cowboy hats, and the felt campaign hats of the Royal Canadian Mounted Police emphasized the democratization of dress styles in the New World.

Twentieth-century department stores and mail-order companies profited from the sale of nylon caps for baby boys, khaki bucket hats, hard-domed topis, upscale Dobbs men's head wear, high-top dress hats, boys' canvas outdoor tams, felt berets, and Harley-Davison caps with cycling goggles. Globalization made available panama hats from Ecuador, colorful *chullos* (knit toboggans) with pompoms and earflaps from Peru, and felt Stetsons and baseball caps from the United States. In Japan in 1939, stuffed wind hats and earmuffs warmed the heads of boys playing outdoors.

Rationing limited the availability of warm play clothes and sportswear. Exigencies in Italy forced the warehousing of fur, leather, and cloth hats until the end of World War II. American GIs found the garrison cap, a soft, folding hat creased from front to back, easy to maintain. At war's end, Malaysian and Pakistani court dress celebrated the end of British colonialism by reclaiming round Muslim caps.

In the twenty-first century, retro men's headgear raises the value of antique Bohemian leather, Russian Cossack hats of astrakhan, prison ward caps, Chinese toboggans, Australian slouch hats and boonies, Turkish fezzes, jockey caps, British deerstalkers, and Scots tweed golf caps. Travelers acquire patches to sew onto khaki field hats as a record of visits to world landmarks and Olympic events. Tourists value foreign additions to their wardrobes, especially the lantana straw cap from Nassau, sombrero from Baja California, Tyrolean fedora from Bavaria, and palm hat from Belize, St. Barts, and Trinidad.

See also: Accessories; Crowns and Tiaras; Feathers; Felt; Fur; Hats, Women's; Headdress, Formal; Headdress, Functional; Helmets, Military; Wigs.

Further Reading

Henderson, Debbie. *Hat Talk: Conversations with Hat Makers About Their Hats—the Fedora, Homburg, Straw, and Cap.* Yellow Springs, OH: Wild Goose, 2002.

———. *The Top Hat: An Illustrated History of Its Styling and Manufacture.* Yellow Springs, OH: Wild Goose, 2000.

Robinson, Fred Miller. *The Man in the Bowler Hat: His History and Iconography.* Chapel Hill: University of North Carolina Press, 1993.

Scott, William Ramsey. *Dressing Down: Modernism, Masculinity, and the Men's Leisurewear Industry in California, 1930–1960.* Ann Arbor, MI: ProQuest, 2008.

Hats, Women's

Unlike male headgear, women's hats have historically emphasized self-esteem, taste, and place in society rather than utilitarian purpose. In ancient Egypt, women blended the concept of hat and wig with the human or animal hair head covering shaped with a blunt cut and beaded for style. Ancient Greek and Roman and early medieval styles deviated from hats to veils and wimples. In the 1300s in Hungary, France, and Switzerland, the pointed *hennin* relieved the stark silhouette with a draped cambric *cointoise* (caul). By the late 1400s, tassels and turbans softened the look of female head wear.

In the French court of Catherine de' Medici in the 1550s, satin hats and headbands brightened ensembles by reflecting candlelight. In Tudor England, sumptuary laws forced commoners to reduce the trim of their linen, wool, and sheepskin head wear to velvet edging. In the New England colonies, female Puritans protested luxurious headgear by sewing white linen caps, a style adopted by the Amish and Mennonites for everyday modesty.

Stylish head wear reached a height in the seventeenth century. In about 1686, Louis XIV advanced the French fashion industry by commissioning illustrations and *poupées de mode* (fashion dolls) showcasing the best in millinery and wigs. The plumed Gainsborough hat of the 1700s lost status after the French Revolution of 1789, when overdressed women risked execution on the guillotine. The black hat of the Welsh women's national costume and the Italian Leghorn, a plaited straw sunshade, survived downsizing.

On the American frontier, the poke bonnet with neck drape shielded the outdoorswoman from wind and sun. Mobcaps protected the scalp from drafts during sleep. For more style, women chose the Gypsy hat, a wide-brimmed chip (palm leaf) hat with wide ties forcing the brim down the sides of ears. Long band ends fastened under the chin.

Nineteenth-century headgear in Turkey hybridized the European pillbox with the gauze veil. During the Victorian era in Europe, girls shielded their complexions by choosing wide-brimmed headgear for outdoor walks. For dressy hairstyles, ladies tied the Japanese straw plate or Dolly Varden straw hat to a chignon with ribbons. In the 1860s, shrinkage of the Continental bonnet and romantic picture hat reduced head wear to smaller pillboxes. Tiny styles sat on the crown and flaunted feathers, bows, jeweled hat pins, aigrets, and handmade flowers that demanded shading by parasols.

Edwardian trends in motoring costumes featured veiled hats over dusters. Travel luggage provided women with steamer trunks fitted with shelves and drawers to protect their hats, boudoir caps, berets, and shoes from crushing. Little girls emulated adults in woven straw sunshades, rosette-trimmed spring finery, skullcaps, and wool snow hats with fur earflaps matching muffs.

Early 1900s feminism shifted trends from the high-necked postures forced by Gainsborough and Merry Widow hats to practical outdoor head covering suited to walking, motoring, tennis, and golf. As evidence of patriotism, World War I–era fashions edged head wear toward military creases. After 1918, Canadians initiated home millinery as a way to restyle pre-wartime hats with feathers and ribbon.

For *La Gazette du Bon Ton* and *Harper's Bazaar*, fashion illustrator Erté promoted stylish velvet ensembles with matching toques and veils dotted with velvet cutouts. Flapper styles of the 1920s replaced romantic Merry Widow styles with the fitted buckram cloche pulled down on the forehead and dressy veiled head wear worn at a tilt. Wartime rationing reduced garnishes, including the rayon rosette, aigret, and netting. U.S. women in the Navy Nurse Corps sported sailor hats, while British Red Cross volunteers draped head and chest in nursing caps and long masks.

Postwar hobbyists and movie fans popularized the roll-up garden hat, the Mae West Merry Widow, and the soutache-edged cowgirl hat. French couturier Christian Dior revived femininity with broad-brimmed hats. In the 1960s, stylist Pierre Cardin reprised the helmet cap of the 1810s, a domed head covering formed of lace and ribbons. Silhouettes veered from bare-headed dressing to a revival of the Mandarin hat in the 1970s and dramatic shaped head wear in the 2000s.

See also: Accessories; Crowns and Tiaras; Felt; Fur; Hats, Men's; Headdress, Formal; Headdress, Functional; Velvet; Wigs.

Further Reading

Amphlett, Hilda. *Hats: A History of Fashion in Headwear.* Mineola, NY: Dover, 2006.

De Courtais, Georgine. *Women's Hats, Headdresses and Hairstyles: With 453 Illustrations, Medieval to Modern.* Mineola, NY: Dover, 2006.

Langley, Susan. *Vintage Hats & Bonnets, 1770–1970: Identification & Values.* 2nd ed. Paducah, KY: Collector, 2009.

Shephard, Norma. *1,000 Hats.* Atglen, PA: Schiffer, 2006.

Haute Couture

A French term for high fashion, haute couture supplies one-of-a-kind apparel for specific occasions, usually formal. Based on historic portraiture, block print, and scroll painting, the first bespoke styles in the mid-nineteenth century promoted the elegance of Western Europe with touches of exoticism from Asia and Africa. Contributing to the uniqueness of dresses, gowns, opera capes, and suits, ensembles featuring silver moiré, feathered muffs, pavé diamond parures, hand stitchery, couching, Belgian lace gussets, and ruching heightened the visual effect of romanticism.

In Paris from 1852, English-born couturier Charles Frederick Worth, the "Father of Haute Couture," flourished by reviving the Napoleonic glories of court attire favored by the Empress Joséphine de Beauharnais. Worth's wife, Marie Vernet, drew interest from aristocrats and royalty by modeling in conspicuous places his chic designs in luxury satin foulard and sultane manufactured in Lyon and Tulle. French stylists Jacques Doucet, Jeanne Paquin, and Paul Poiret contributed theatrical touches of orientalism, medievalism, and art nouveau to women's silhouettes, including lingerie and sleepwear.

The hedonism and affluence of the Belle Époque underwrote exorbitant fees for taffeta and cut velvet bustles and *gigot* (leg-of-mutton) sleeves edged in lace and fringe. *La femme parisienne* (the Parisian woman) set trends in impractical lamé shoes and handbags and Madeleine Vionnet's *déshabillés* (lingerie dresses). From the 1880s, menswear complemented the operatic style of women's evening dress with Balmoral mantles, Bohemian capes, and the fashionable beards lauded in *Town & Country.*

Couturiers courted European royalty and sketched wedding apparel and presentation attire vibrant with a splendor that perpetuated feudal notions of majesty and stateliness. In the last years of the nineteenth century, French touches on court trains and duchesse tiered skirts with netted overlays inspired Russian dressmaker Nadezhda Lamanova, who tailored attire for the Romanov court of Czar Nicholas II and Czarina Alexandra,

the nation's last dynasts. For the average consumer, opulent styles were too tightly fitted and smartly tailored for the everyday demands of walking, sitting, dining, and travel.

Contributing to the cachet of haute couture, fashion plates and sketches for *Vogue* and *Women's Wear Daily* created a demand for costly beading, pin tucking, spangles, and sequins. François Lesage supplied artistic embroidery, a specialty that set the height of style apart from the ordinary. Against the canvas of citified women in grandeur, men retreated to the tailored military uniform or the tuxedo, a smartly tailored suit touched up with velvet lapels and jeweled studs on the shirtfront.

In glamour shots of the 1930s, Hollywood screen stars Mae West and Jean Harlow modeled satin and velvet boned bodices with boas and picture hats and slip-dresses with fox stoles. Department stores bought prêt-à-porter (ready-to-wear) knockoffs of movie elegance, including the Empire gowns of Greta Garbo and slinky satins and foam lace worn by trendsetter Claudette Colbert. The availability of chic fashion for low budgets, cheap zippers and snaps, and sewing patterns from Vogue, Butterick, and McCall's began the demise of haute couture.

Rationing during World War II ended the first phase of one-of-a-kind ensembles. In the late 1940s and 1950s, the wealthy continued to seek status from haute couture by Jeanne Lanvin, Christian Dior, Yves Saint Laurent, and Elsa Schiaparelli and unique textiles by London costumer Cecil Beaton. The postwar glamour created by Jacques Fath, Lucien Lelong, and Robert Piguet appealed directly to moneyed Americans, the new boosters of haute couture who packed trunkfuls of ensembles for cruises on Cunard liners. The late-1950s addition of nylon to high fashion added sparkle and pizzazz to travel clothes, hosiery, and linings.

To develop a U.S. following, Spanish innovator Cristóbal Balenciaga restored the drama of flamenco and the portraiture of painters Diego Velázquez and Francisco Goya. Public appearances by American first lady Jacqueline Kennedy and Wallis Warfield Simpson, the duchess of Windsor, raised once more the image of the well-dressed social lion who flaunted modernist suits by Coco Chanel and bubble dresses by Pierre Cardin.

Into the 1960s, as Cardin, Balenciaga, and Hubert de Givenchy's ready-to-wear designs chipped away at the appeal of bespoke ensembles, André Courrèges, Oscar de la Renta, Mila Schön, and Emanuel Ungaro carried on the high-fashion tradition. *Harper's Bazaar* and *Vogue* touted the wedding attire and ombré silk chiffon evening apparel of American designer Geoffrey Beene. In Brussels, Milan, Rome, Vienna, Munich, and Paris, Beene's quirky futuristic touches further distanced haute couture from its lush beginnings. Jean Paul Gaultier and Thierry Mugler abandoned exclusive designs and prefaced the growing influence of Ralph Lauren, Calvin Klein, Roy Halston, and Giorgio Armani, the democratizers of fashion.

See also: Art Nouveau and Art Deco Fashion; Belle Époque Fashion; Couturiers; Fashion Design; French Clothing and Fashion; Models and Modeling; Orientalism; Worth, Charles Frederick.

Further Reading

Jacobs, Laura, and Victor Skrebneski. *The Art of Haute Couture.* New York: Abbeville, 1995.

Stewart, Mary Lynn. *Dressing Modern Frenchwomen: Marketing Haute Couture, 1919–1939.* Baltimore, MD: Johns Hopkins University Press, 2008.

Wilcox, Claire. *The Golden Age of Couture: Paris and London, 1947–1957.* London: V&A, 2007.

Zazzo, Anne, and Olivier Sillard. *Paris Haute Couture.* New York: Flammarion, 2013.

Head, Edith (1897–1981)

A master illusionist and taste-making costume designer for the film industry, Edith Claire Posener Head influenced viewer concepts of historic dress and soignée lines, accessories, and hairstyles.

The daughter of Anna E. Levy and haberdasher Max Posener, a Prussian immigrant, Head was born on October 28, 1897, in San Bernardino, California, of Austrian-Bavarian-Jewish heritage. During her mother's marriage to second husband Frank Spare, Spare's career in mining engineering took the family to Indian reservations and mining towns in the Southwest and Mexico, where Edith absorbed the desert light and shadows, influences

on her later designs for stage and film. She learned to sew as a child.

Head graduated from Los Angeles High School, earned a degree in art and French from the University of California at Berkeley (1919), and completed an MA in French and Spanish from Stanford University (1920). At age 23, she taught French and art at the Bishop's School in La Jolla and the Hollywood School for Girls, while studying art theory at night at Otis Art Institute and Chouinard Art College in Los Angeles. Her marriage to salesman Charles Head failed because of his alcoholism, but she retained the surname.

At age 27, Head joined the costume department at Paramount Pictures as a sketch artist of animal decor for *Peter Pan* (1924) and a designer of chaps, tassels, snoods, and riding gloves and skirts for silent movies starring Clara "The It Girl" Bow and Frances Farmer. The job involved pairing outfits with the script, selecting fabrics that would photograph well, stockpiling garment patterns in the body dimensions of each actor, and attending fittings for up to five films simultaneously. For *She Done Me Wrong* (1933), Head outfitted star Mae West in a torso-defining satin gown with trumpet skirt and feathered picture hat.

By 1938, Head had advanced to Paramount's lead designer, the first woman to attain that position and one of few women at a high level in the production hierarchy. Head's designs shaped the public images of Hollywood goddesses, tailoring suits with shoulder pads and slim skirts for Marlene Dietrich, no fewer than 25 gowns for Barbara Stanwyck's role in the high-fashion picture *The Lady Eve* (1941), and a revolutionary's togs and nun's habit for Ingrid Bergman in *For Whom the Bell Tolls* (1943) and *The Bells of St. Mary's* (1945), respectively. Head's costumes earned their own headlines, particularly the mink-lined dress covered in faux emeralds and rubies for Ginger Rogers in *Lady in the Dark* (1944), a costume too heavy for the dance scenes.

In a number of classic films, the designer muted costume trendiness and overdressing to focus on classic garments in muted solid colors suited to character and movement, the strategy that won acclaim for Ingrid Bergman in *Notorious*

(1946), Gloria Swanson in *Sunset Boulevard* (1950), and Doris Day in *The Man Who Knew Too Much* (1956). During her height of influence, from 1948 to 1966, Head earned 35 Oscar nominations and eight Academy Awards for Best Costume Design, setting a record for female film honoraria.

Head received her first nomination for Billy Wilder's Austrian-themed color musical, *The Emperor Waltz* (1948), for which she garbed singer Bing Crosby in a Tyrolean hat and lederhosen and Joan Fontaine in an upswept hairdo and poufy sleeves with parasol and picture hat topped with ostrich feathers. In 1949, Head won her first Academy Award for *The Heiress,* which swept

four Oscars and four additional nominations for transforming Olivia de Havilland from a poorly dressed rich girl into a seductress.

In both black-and-white and color scenarios, Head brought style to storytelling. For *All About Eve* (1950), she created lush gowns, shimmery stoles, and fur wraps for Bette Davis, Anne Baxter, Celeste Holm, and Marilyn Monroe, winning her the costume design Oscar. At the award ceremony the following year, Head claimed two statuettes— for Elizabeth Taylor's romantic wardrobe in the black-and-white *A Place in the Sun* (1951) and for the biblical color film *Samson and Delilah* (1949). Head's skill at minimizing faults resulted

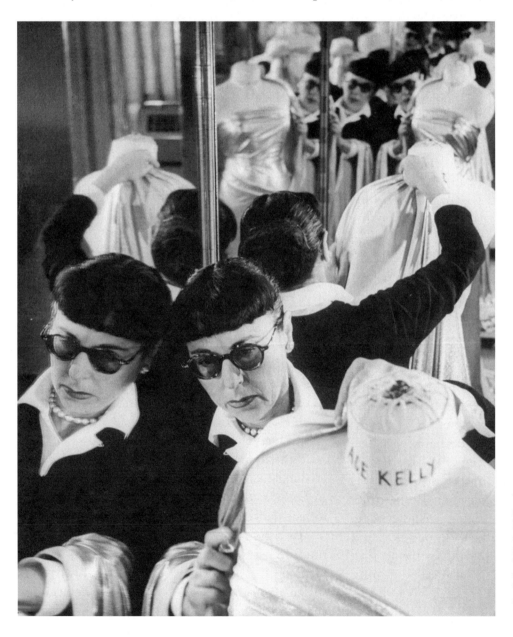

The grand dame of Hollywood costume design and the most honored woman in Academy Award history, Edith Head was nominated for 35 Oscars and won eight. "What a costume designer does," she once said, "is a cross between magic and camouflage." *(Allan Grant/Time Life Pictures/Getty Images)*

in Hollywood legends about the camouflaging of Loretta Young's long neck in stoles and the cloaking of Audrey Hepburn's skinny arms with long gloves.

As the designer gained celebrity, her accomplishments advanced from individualizing costume to establishing Hollywood as the fount of affordable world fashion. In addition, she designed uniforms for United Nations tour guides and Pan American Airlines flight crews. She followed with costumes for Eva Marie Saint, Barbara Stanwyck, and Zsa Zsa Gabor for public appearances on the red carpet, gala and fashion show outfits for Ann-Margret and Debbie Reynolds, and a going-away suit for Grace Kelly's wedding.

During a lengthy collaboration with director Alfred Hitchcock, Head invented the costume callboard, a visualization and harmonization of sets, lights, dance music, and camera angles. With her first book, *The Dress Doctor* (1959), she positioned herself among middle-class women who chose their wardrobes for psychological effect on them and the public. Head described personal dress as practical therapy and a source of happiness. At fashion shows and interviews for *American Film* and Canadian radio, she advised women on seasonal touches and investment dressing. Her articles for *Family Circle, Good Housekeeping, Modern Screen,* and *New Outlook* offered shopping advice for formal and informal occasions, including knockoffs of her flapper dress for Carroll Baker in *Harlow* (1965).

At age 70, Head faced a layoff from Paramount and began a 14-year association with Universal Pictures. Her final Oscar in 1974 rewarded period costumes for Paul Newman, Robert Shaw, and Robert Redford featured in *The Sting,* the first all-male star cast to earn an award for clothing design. In 1978, Head's career took an unusual side route to the Coast Guard, for which she designed the women's uniform, winner of a Meritorious Public Service Award. In her final project, she coordinated film clips from the 1940s with costumes for Steve Martin in *Dead Men Don't Wear Plaid* (1982).

Nearing age 84, Edith Head died of bone marrow disease on October 24, 1981. She had designed costumes for actors in 1,131 films made by six major studios. In 2003, a U.S. postal stamp depicted Head's contributions to American costume design as a historian, dressmaker of classic lines, and fashion pacesetter.

See also: Costume Design, Film.

Further Reading

Chierichetti, David. *Edith Head: The Life and Times of Hollywood's Celebrated Costume Designer.* New York: HarperCollins, 2002.

Ducey, Maxine Fleckner. "Elegance by Design: The Edith Head Collection in Wisconsin." *Wisconsin Magazine of History* (Winter 2001–2002): 18–27.

Jorgensen, Jay. *Edith Head: The Fifty-Year Career of Hollywood's Greatest Costume Designer.* New York: Lifetime Media, 2010.

Headdress, Formal

The envelopment of hair and head with elaborate styles has elevated folk costume from ancient times. At Abydos in the third millennium B.C.E., Egyptians distinguished their heads with Nubian wigs and contributed to the stature of Isis, the mother goddess, with towering cow horns and the disk of the sun god. In 400 B.C.E., reshaping the human form also involved feathers, shells, weaving, bird bodies, and lavish invention, as with the tall miters and ear lappets worn by Persian princes.

Color coding and shapes expressed social, governmental, and spiritual grandeur, making people seem larger than life, the purpose of feather warbonnets. On the lower Danube in the 300s B.C.E., Dacian royalty topped court ensembles with knobbed gold headgear painted with eyes to watch for the approach of evil. In Russia after 1000 C.E., rural women layered mother-of-pearl on the *kokoshnik* (headdress) for an iridescence that rounded out brightly colored holiday attire. Thirteenth-century circular headdress worn by Czech and Slovakian women on Sundays completed their folk ensemble.

As accessories, formal headdress drew attention in myriad ways. Albanian, Estonian, Latvian, and Lithuanian dancers attached metal coins to headdress to tinkle in time to body movements. Youths carrying sacred relics or holy icons in festival processions decorated their hair with flowers, a removable garnish they could strew to distribute color and fragrance. Among Croatians, formal triangular headgear displayed fantasy edging, a testimony to the imagination and skill of the seamstress. Amerindians impressed Europeans with the ingenuity of formal headdress made with claws, skins, and feathers. Explorers of the Pacific Northwest encountered Bella Coola and Kwakiutl who dressed their heads with representations of salmon and whales, religious symbols.

Formal headgear required an erect posture and graceful neck. In Ghana in 1701, Asante king Osei Kofi Tutu I ascended the throne amid a splendid court decked with plumes. Spanish noblewomen at Valencia added stature and grace with the *peineta* (comb) or atifet (wire frame) covered with black lace veils, hair toppings that elongated the silhouette.

By extension, posture and grace implied superiority. The choice of ribbons, pearls, and colored wigs by Marie Antoinette, the queen of France, enraged peasants and fueled the French Revolution of 1789. Riots and murders of the aristocracy led to the queen's execution on the guillotine, fitting punishment, many declared, for a woman whose expenditures on costly headdress coincided with starvation among the citizenry.

Nineteenth-century headdress expressed nationalism and ethnicity. In 1870, the Onyanka of Namibia signified pastoral ties with horns atop their plaits. Polish and Ukrainian altar dress honored the bride with a helmet of ruched ribbon in colors suited to season and holiday. For an overall look of celebration in China, Vietnam, Laos, and Thailand, the Miao favored the glitter of silver head adornment paired with collars and waist-length pendants.

Folk headdress influenced later styles. During the art deco craze, designer and fashion illustrator Erté restored exotic animal tails, tassels, and wings in place of ordinary hats and veils. Fashion magazines captured global head wear, such as that worn by Queen Tupou III of Tonga in 1953. Stage, television, and film representations cultivated admiration for historical headdress.

See also: Accessories; Crowns and Tiaras; Feathers; Mardi Gras and Carnival Costumes; Pageantry; Royal Attire.

Further Reading

Cutsem-Vanderstraete, Anne van, and Mauro Magliani. *Powerful Headdresses: Africa and Asia.* Milan, Italy: 5 Continents, 2010.

McDonald, Fiona. *Hats and Headdresses Through History.* Milwaukee, WI: Gareth Stevens, 2007.

Watts, Linda S. *Encyclopedia of American Folklore.* New York: Facts on File, 2006.

Headdress, Functional

Historically, a complete ensemble in global wardrobes involved covering the hair and head in a customary way to unify a group and set members apart from outsiders. From 5000 B.C.E., Australian Aborigines, Polynesian hunters, Tupinambá bird hunters of what is now Brazil, and north-central European tribes applied horns and feathers to the hair as indicators of social rank. From 3300 B.C.E., the Harappa of the Punjab and Maori and Lapita clans of the Pacific used headdress to indicate ethnicity and political advancement.

Functional headdress expressed the intent of individuals to alter their identity and appearance. Around 3000 B.C.E., Sumerian females perfumed their braids and added netting and pleated fabric for height. Egyptian strategies for cooling the body in the second millennium B.C.E. included shaving the head and dressing it with an animal fur or human hair wig threaded with beads and gold wire.

Materials for everyday headdress tended toward items and fibers found in nature. Among the Basketmaker and Pueblo Amerindians of the Colorado Plateau, the twining of wild cotton into yarn produced a hairdressing that flourished after 500 B.C.E. In Alaska, the Tlingit carved their headgear from cedar wood and personalized designs with tufts from coyotes, dogs, and mountain goats.

As a commodity, head covering in the Middle Ages increased the cost of daily wardrobes. French square headdress framed the features of Catherine of Valois in 1420, when she arrived in England. The new trend added to the stock of haberdashers, who profited from consumers emulating royalty.

When fads aroused jealousies and complaints, European sumptuary laws codified heights and materials that rid laywomen and nuns of displays of vanity and self-importance.

Female head garnishes dominated Tudor style, which featured linen drapes, colored powder, rats (padded rolls), and silk bands. In the same era, Mahratta women in southern India formed a tripartite head wrap from sheer scarves stitched with round plaques representing heavenly planets. Mid-eighteenth-century French female wig embellishment added jewels, birds, pearls, and sailing vessels to tall hair extensions completed with natural fragrances. In the mid-1800s, Paris designer Charles Frederick Worth completed his education in fashion by studying headdress on portraits at the Louvre museum.

Current customs retain traditional head adornment, as with the Dida application of tie-dyed geometric figures in brick red, brown-black, and yellow in Ivory Coast apparel. East of the Nile, Latooka males form a permanent head covering by weaving bark twine into their hair. Over time, the interweaving takes on a felted texture as much as 1.5 inches (3.8 centimeters) thick. By sewing a rim of cowrie shells to the hair with thread, beading strands, and topping the finished hairdo with polished copper and ostrich plumes, the individual completes a crested mitre.

See also: Accessories; Ethnic and National Dress; Hairdressing; Headdress, Formal.

Further Reading

Cutsem-Vanderstraete, Anne van, and Mauro Magliani. *Powerful Headdresses: Africa and Asia.* Milan, Italy: 5 Continents, 2010.

McDonald, Fiona. *Hats and Headdresses Through History.* Milwaukee, WI: Gareth Stevens, 2007.

Watts, Linda S. *Encyclopedia of American Folklore.* New York: Facts on File, 2006.

Helmets, Military

As skull and neck protection and, in some cases, a designation of military rank and authority, the helmet has covered heads in battle for three millennia. A high-topped Mycenaean skullcap of boar tusk scale armor from 1450 B.C.E. extended tabs in front of each ear that fastened under the chin, but left the ears unprotected. Around 900 B.C.E., Assyrian warriors in the world's first standing army warded off attacks by fist, blade, and arrow with leather and bronze headgear. Holes around the frame held leather ties that secured the lining.

After 800 B.C.E., Cretan soldiers extended a bronze dome to a neck band with ends that came close to meeting in front over the chin. In China, a complex helmet trim used sable and pearls to denote the imperial couple, stones and glass for army officers, and peacock feathers for princes and courtiers. Ornate Persian helmets decked a domed head covering with parabolic metal horns and a mail face and ear shield reaching the shoulders.

Early Greek soldiers provided their own helmets fashioned from boiled leather. Among Greek city-states arming for war in 700 B.C.E., Corinth devised a one-piece head covering hammered from a single sheet of bronze, excised at front to reveal the eyes, nose, and mouth; linen and leather liners glued with resin padded the interior. A century later, the bust of Pericles pictured him in a modified Corinthian helmet fitted with a full face covering cut out at the eyes and buttressed over the nose. The helmet weighed 5.5 pounds (2.5 kilograms).

Sparta stood out for its professionally clad army. Helmets extended a cheek guard capable of deflecting blows to the lower face and neck. In similar style, Greek and Trojan hoplites (citizen soldiers) shielded the head and face with a three-part helmet consisting of spherical skullcap, tall face guard incorporating nose and cheek shields, and an officer's crest marking rank in plumes or horsehair. In close combat, soldiers butted head to head or shoved their helmets into the adversary's chest.

Roman designers topped leather helmets with bear and feline pelts, a style that influenced the design of the first German head protectors. Throughout the Roman Empire, ironsmiths shaped head protection from a single iron sheet and repaired helmets smashed in battle. Legions stationed in Egypt adopted the crocodile skin helmet, an unusual application of hide to head protection.

The feared hoplite citizen-soldiers of ancient Sparta, who fought with spears and shields in phalanx formation, wore three-part bronze helmets (skullcap, face guard, and crest). Plumes or horsehair indicated an officer's rank. *(Universal History Archive/ Getty Images)*

For gladiators, a heavier, more confining helmet weighing 15.4 pounds (7 kilograms) topped the head with a skull protector and lobed bill above a grilled face guard that extended over the neck and upper shoulders.

In 310 C.E., Constantine I the Great, founder of Constantinople, displayed the chi-rho (XP), an abbreviation of Christos, on his helmet and shield as evidence of his conversion to Christianity. After 449, Anglo-Saxons at York marked bimetallic helmet quadrants with a crosspiece riveted or forge welded into place. By 550, the Vandals of Scandinavia adapted the standard dome with a protective grid and eyebrow shields on each side of the lengthy nasal (noseguard).

At the end of the first millennium, Vikings fashioned the iron *spangenhelm* (skull protector), a hemispheric or domed helmet fitted with a chin strap, internal leather suspension and sweat band, and noseguard. The Gjermundu helm, a Norwegian variation, riveted an eye and nose shield to the dome. Japanese samurai shaped headgear and neck shields from lacquered leather and Western-style plated metal.

Medieval Advancements

Western adaptations to the basic skullcap added a mail ventail (nape curtain), chin guard, and hinged earflaps, a burdening of the head that reached its height in the 1100s with shielding of the entire face. A two-piece Asiatic version used by the Bulgarian boyar from the early 1200s featured a full face mask with eye slits, ears, nose, and mouth.

In the 1300s, the lightweight sheet-iron bascinet (skullcap) with mail skirt gradually replaced heavy iron head covers. A hinged visor increased the versatility of the bascinet for use in phalanx formation or hand-to-hand combat. The addition of a front-to-back ridge over the cranium deflected sword blows.

Heraldry identified the knight in armor with a coat of arms. In 1400, soldiers of England's Henry IV topped with feathers the morion, a high-crested helmet marked by a curved peak. Beginning in 1413, the reign of Henry V saw the increase in plumage on military headgear as an indicator of rank. Under Edward IV from 1461 to 1471, feathered helmets identified men-at-arms, the royal security force.

In 1503, German engraver Albrecht Dürer sketched an ornate armet, or peaked jousting helmet, that featured a striated crown, ornamental rivets, and neck straps. The multiple pieces shaping the helmet totaled 12 pounds (5.4 kilograms). The armet with slotted visor, an Italian design that evolved from the 1450s, attached to a neck wrapper that placed the weight of the helmet on the shoulders rather than the head. A quilted arming cap under the helmet absorbed the impact of blows to the head from a hammer, mace, or jousting sword.

Modern Protection

After guns and cannon replaced the spear and arrows, advanced armed forces abandoned heavy metal helmets. Urban police in the late 1820s introduced domestic criteria for head protection. The cork or felt bobby helmet, based on the nineteenth-century German *Pickelhaube* (spiked helmet), protected the British or colonial constable on foot patrol with peaked headgear that featured a metal crest on the top, contoured brim, and double chin strap for stability in riots. Early motorists and pilots chose a leather skullcap with chin strap and separate goggles.

The onset of World War I introduced the French Adrian helmet, worn by firefighters, and the German steel helmet, the first of its kind. To enable radio operators to use earpieces, a 1918 model featured cutouts for the ears. When Germany rearmed in 1935, designers modified the helmet with lighter materials. French and Canadian crafters of the ballistic helmet shaped a one-piece helmet from fragmentation-resistant polyethylene, a shell-type skull cover weighing 3.1 pounds (1.4 kilograms).

A major advancement for U.S. infantry, Kevlar, a polymer fiber developed by DuPont chemist Stephanie Kwolek in 1964, increased protection without burdening the head with metal. Subsequent helmet designs mixed Kevlar and carbon fiber with polycarbonate or fiberglass, featured face shields of harder plastic, such as Lexan, and cushioned the head with expanded polystyrene foam.

During the Iraq War in the early 2000s, the advanced combat helmet, covered in camouflage, weighed 3.6 pounds (1.6 kilograms). It featured a harness that extended from the temporal zone around the chin and across the nape, a style emulated by NATO army headgear. To inform future helmet design, engineers added sensors that collected data on blast effects on head injuries.

See also: Armor; Protective and Orthotic Clothing; Uniforms, Military.

Further Reading

Attard, Robert. *Collecting Military Headgear: A Guide to 5000 Years of Helmet History.* Atglen, PA: Schiffer, 2004.

Ford, Roger, R.G. Grant, Adrian Gilbert, Philip Parker, and Richard Holmes. *Weapon: A Visual History of Arms and Armor.* New York: DK, 2010.

Parker, Geoffrey, ed. *The Cambridge Illustrated History of Warfare: The Triumph of the West.* New York: Cambridge University Press, 2008.

Hides

From prehistory, hides have shielded people from wind and weather and provided them with cloaks, shoes, bindings, baby carriers, aprons, and kilts. To maintain pliability, fleshers of rawhide scraped it of hair, fat, and tissue and stretched it in the sun or on pegs or frames over a smoky fire. Finishing required drying and bleaching the translucent hide, thinning with an adze or plane, rubbing with a stone, thinning again over a sinew or pole, and treating both sides with brains, fat, and liver to make mantles, footwear, and rain shields.

As early as 38,000 B.C.E., nomads cut hides into bindings to swaddle the feet and lower legs as a shield against thorns, rocks, and ice. Thin strips served the traveler as pocket string for securing bags and aided families securing grave bundles and mothers swaddling infants in hide sacks. Thongs also secured babies on the slatted frames of cradleboards to keep them safe during work and travel.

Legend connects hides with crucial events in history. In Homeric times around 800 B.C.E., Greek warriors wrapped their shoulders in goat, leopard, lion, or lynx skins with heads, tails, and paws still attached. Hesiod's *Works and Days* (ca. 700 B.C.E.) revealed that country folk and shepherds continued wearing traditional pelts and skins after urbanites switched to textiles.

Around 47 B.C.E., Roman soldiers following Julius Caesar into Gaul copied the Continental *Gallica* (mud shoe), a thick wood sole topped with a heavy pelt for warmth. In 43 C.E., Roman occupation forces moved into Britain to control commerce in hides. During their tenure, they educated Celtic hide workers in tanning and boot cobblery, a vital service for soldiers.

All-Purpose Material

The myriad uses of animal hide among Native Americans reflect the versatility of the material and its importance to everyday life and survival. Prehistoric native peoples selected untanned skins of antelope, bison, cattle, deer, elk, and Rocky Mountain goat as material for breechcloths, fetishes, medicine bags, bandoliers, straps, and parfleches (envelope bags), as well as robes for women, children, and warriors. In the Great Basin from 7000 B.C.E., the Anasazi hunted a half-ton elk for the skin. They softened hide robes and open-front jackets by tenderizing both sides with flaked scrapers. The Inuit valued hides as waterproof garments, which women softened by chewing on them. On the Great Lakes, the Santee Sioux turned hide bonnets into art with quilling, moose hair, and bindings. The Hopi shaped squash blossom hairstyles with lacings of hide.

For the northern Mandan and Canadian Cree and Ojibwa, the bison robe became a costume necessity. The white buffalo, varying in hue from ecru to gray, brought the highest price. For the Assiniboin and Gros Ventre, deer and antelope hide made the most serviceable shirts. Crow and Shoshone regalia based wearability on bighorn skins, which produced a long shirt or tunic adorned with the tail portion. The earliest models remained unsewn, with puncturing for decoration and drawstrings to secure the neck opening, a style worn by Sacagawea in the early 1800s during the Lewis and Clark expedition.

During processing, Naskapi, Creek, Washakie, Blackfoot, and Iroquois artisans painted or dyed buckskin with emblematic and historical detail and laced it into garments, belts for dance bustles, and medicine bags with thongs, sinew from animal spines, or babiche, a coil of pocket string sliced from rabbit hide. The method served subarctic tribes for snowshoes, Hidatsa and Teton Sioux women for leggings and garters, and Comanche, Dakota, and Cheyenne women for one-piece moccasin-leggings with the suede side turned inside in winter. The Omaha fitted infants with large-collared footwear pierced with a hole on one sole. The opening symbolized the child's vulnerability, which ended with the gift of new moccasins at puberty.

Smoked elk hides served Cree, Kootenai, Ojibwa, and Pawnee males for slipper-shaped moccasins and leggings stitched with buffalo, deer, or mountain lion sinew, fibrous tissue stripped from each side of the backbone. Female hide workers embroidered, fringed, or beaded the uppers over the toe. Winnebago moccasins featured appliqués and decorative stitchery and bindings around the ankle cuff or raised flaps, which protected the foot from sand and grit.

The Blackfoot and Ojibwa reputedly took their names from the style of moccasins made from a single U-shaped cut of leather, which yielded sole, upper, and tongue. Similar U-shaped moccasins served the Cree, Navajo, Crow, and Shoshone. The Arapaho varied the basic moc with an upper band. Apache shoemakers painted the tongue-like insert on the top of the vamp. Symbolic bow and arrow, horns, and a herd path with tracks recorded the hunter's success in shooting buffalo. Animal shapes—horses, rabbits, fish, lizards, snakes, horned toads—marked the slippers of an active outdoorsman. Other designs—the morning star, lightning, hills, tents, lakes, and snowbanks—signified blessings, dreams, peace, and abundance. A stripe depicted life.

For two-piece moccasins, the Ute and Arapaho placed stiffened rawhide on the soles for durability. The Ponca, Nez Percé, and Omaha used hide for sun visors and collared moccasins, a style that kept sand and dirt out of the vamp. After considerable wear, hide moccasins stretched and required reshaping and trimming to tighten the fit. The Shasta and Yavapai used leftover hides to trade for blankets.

Rawhide supplied the Sioux, Kansa, Crow, Cheyenne, and Arapaho of the Southern Plains with fringe for gloves, cuffs, armbands, shields, masks, saddle blankets, and feather fans. The Pawnee and Shoshone made hide armor, a hardened body or horse covering shaped from antelope skins glued together. Children fashioned doll clothing to resemble adult attire.

Practical Costume

As reported by French explorers in the 1750s, functional, foot-hugging moccasins, shaped in one piece from bison skin or parfleche (green hide) soaked in lye, required frequent restyling to restore the fit ruined by wetting and hard wear. Forest Indians increased their walking and running range in winter by fastening moccasins to wood-framed snowshoes with leather ties.

Cherokee moccasins featured a center seam and puckered toe. The Iroquois added a separate piece of leather as a covering of the center seam. Creek shoemakers used a two-piece construction to fasten the vamp to the sole, splicing in new threads without knots as they completed the seam. For a more decorative shoe, the Crow added a welt.

In the Southwest, the Comanche developed a mid-calf hide moccasin fringed up the ankle for use in desert sand and prairie grass. For fancy dancing, natives stitched on ribbons and metallic braid and added copper bells or brass or tin aglets (lace ends) or cones to leather strings to create a tinkling sound. Acquisition of steel awls, crescent knives, and needles in the 1850s increased native skill and speed at hide shaping.

Female Native Americans superintended the sewing of hides. At trading posts, women exchanged a single beaver skin for 24 needles or 12 ounces (340 grams) of beads. Timucua women in Florida limited their clothing to buckskin skirts. Plains women from the Mississippi River to the Continental Divide shaped two deerskins into the short-sleeved two-hide dress, which the Havasupai embellished with hoof tinklers. Chiricahua and Lipan Apache women wore two-piece buckskin dresses consisting of a long skirt and poncho. They sewed buckskin fringe to apparel, a practical addition that wicked away moisture and helped camouflage the wearers from their prey.

Among the Dutch and Swedes of West Jersey and Pennsylvania, primitive shoemaking resulted in buff leather moccasins similar to those worn by the local Indians. For hides, the settlers used bear, buffalo, elk, and wolf, which shoe finishers painted and embroidered at two shillings per pair for wearing with leather stockings. In the 1880s, depletion of buffalo herds ended the hide trade.

By the 1890s, woven cloth replaced hides, leaving only deerskin moccasins as models of hide clothing.

See also: Cobblery; Fur; Leather and Suede; Prehistoric Clothing.

Further Reading

Danver, Steven, ed. *Native Peoples of the World.* Armonk, NY: M.E. Sharpe, 2013.
Davenport, Gregory J. *Wilderness Living.* Mechanicsburg, PA: Stackpole, 2001.
Havelin, Kate. *Buckskin Dresses and Pumpkin Breeches: Colonial Fashions from the 1580s to the 1670s.* Minneapolis, MN: Twenty-First Century Books, 2012.
Johansen, Bruce E., and Barry M. Pritzker, eds. *Encyclopedia of American Indian History.* Santa Barbara, CA: ABC-CLIO, 2008.

Hippie and Mod Fashion

In the late 1950s and 1960s, Western countercultural styles enhanced the image of the youthful rebel. Mod fops from London's East End promoted labor-class chic in cycling getups, parkas and motoring jackets featuring collections of travel and flag patches and displays of the Union Jack. Hip

A British fashion model (left) poses in a dress by Swinging Sixties designer Alice Pollack, with a group of young hippies looking on. The boutiques, bars, and street scene of London's Carnaby Street were the epicenter of mod style in the mid- to late 1960s. *(Keystone-France/Gamma-Keystone via Getty Images)*

photographer Richard Avedon published glimpses of miniskirts, jumpsuits, A-line dresses with patch pockets, hot pants, and bright tights on Mary Quant, a model of mod whimsy and exhibitionism.

Throughout North America, celebrities set the mod tone and posture. Teens emulated Mick Jaggers's striped shirts, Twiggy's oversized earrings and mascara with little girl dresses and Mary Janes, and the winklepickers (pointed-toed shoes) of the Beatles. Models in bowl cuts strolled catwalks in plastic rainwear, bikinis, Pierre Cardin's geometric shift dresses, and polka-dotted helmets and dresses, a look promoted by Jean Shrimpton.

Unlike the fey mod, hippie style represented more blatant dress rebellion of the disaffected social dropout. Chief among hippie efforts to outrage adults, long, unkempt hairstyles, unisex braids, sideburns, Pan-African dreadlocks, and "big hair" flashed the anti-establishment message of noncompliance with social custom and minimal hygiene. The "long hairs" and "dreads" wandered public venues in scuffed boots, Jesus sandals (lace-ups), or barefoot. Bralessness, halter and crop tops, and denim slouch sacks displayed female disaffection for standard grooming and modesty.

For smug ridicule of pretense and consumer culture, hippies coined the slang "suit" to demean male capitalists who chose pinstriped suits, button-down shirts, rep ties, and wing-tip shoes as the conformist's business uniform. In place of "clothes as usual," the maverick hipster flaunted retro chic in shirts and jeans pieced from U.S. flags, travel patches on hats and sandals, Gypsy ankle bracelets, metal studs, and peace decals. Women reprised handcrafts with macramé edging and rainbows embroidered on ripped and raveled jean skirts, quilted hobo bags, and maxi skirts. In sympathy with the world's poor and American Indians, radicals vaunted back-to-the-land overalls, fringed vests, and customized T-shirts and chambrays.

Accessories sported insouciance in hoop earrings, granny glasses, camo jackets, cargo pants, lace-up boots, and combat and paratrooper footwear from army-navy overruns. Denim shoulder bags prefigured the nylon backpack, the carryall flaunted by grunge and punk aficionados. Into the 1970s, patches, tie-dye headbands, peace symbols, and marijuana leaf shapes silently promoted defiance. Leisure wear and patched outfits superseded standard attire for concerts, mall shopping, beachwear, and dining.

Fashion magazines connected barefoot wedding attire, tie-up shirts, hip huggers, peasant blouses, clogs, beads, and ponchos with underground, anarchist, and mod style exhibited by singers such as Cher, Paul McCartney, and Janis Joplin. Designer Yves Saint Laurent fought back against scruffy, psychedelic apparel by exemplifying female glamour with padded shoulders, plunging necklines, and fake fur jackets and vests.

A limited revival of mod and hippie chic in the 2000s popularized biker jackets, platform shoes, gauze skirts from India and Pakistan, "high hippie" paisley shawls, and natural fiber jeans and vests edged in top-stitching. At secondhand stores, retro hunters boosted the value of original Grateful Dead, Rolling Stones, and Woodstock tees and Hells Angels jackets. The annual Burning Man festival in the Nevada desert prompts nudity and body art celebrating hippie concepts of spontaneous creativity and personal freedom.

See also: Quant, Mary; Teen Trends; Tie-Dye.

Further Reading

Breward, Christopher, David Gilbert, and Jenny Lister, eds. *Swinging Sixties: Fashion in London and Beyond, 1955–1970.* London: Victoria & Albert Museum, 2006.

Issitt, Micah L. *Hippies: A Guide to an American Subculture.* Santa Barbara, CA: ABC-CLIO, 2009.

Lobenthal, Joel. *Radical Rags: Fashions of the Sixties.* New York: Abbeville, 1990.

Holiday Costumes

The celebration of religious feasts, saints' days, and thanksgivings has traditionally called for special clothing and masks. Ancient Egyptian processionals demanded splendid tunics for priests and sacred statues. In classical Rome, vestal virgins displayed gifts of daisy chains to complement the white wool *palla* (short wrap) and veil, the impetus for Christian nun's habits. Saturnalia, a late December family celebration, encouraged the swapping of toga or *stola* for tunic between master and slave for one day of reversed social positions.

Medieval agrarian holidays in Russia encouraged the stitching of headdresses, shawls, scarves, and bags with borders featuring plowed fields. Embroidery, braid, filigree, and charm belts protected peasants from harm. For European stage plays, characters represented allegorical figures as well as angels and devils. On Lazarus Day, the last Saturday of Lent, Bulgarian girls chose bridal finery and jingly coin belts and topped their hair with feather grass and flowers and danced the *bouenek* (handkerchief dance) to dispel evil.

During the Elizabethan Age, pro-business laws required the wearing of wool caps for Sundays and holidays, an obvious means of boosting sale of British textiles. For Purim, Jewish masqueraders took roles as Queen Esther, savior of her people, and other characters in the Book of Esther. In the costume exchange between South Americans and Spanish colonizers, Colombian and Peruvian mestizas acquired the *pollera,* a holiday circle skirt embroidered in festive colors.

Students at Oxford University in England costumed a chosen figure as the Lord of Misrule, master of ceremonies at Christmas festivals. On April 25, frolicking at the Christian Rogationtide required men to garb themselves in women's clothes and drape their heads in garlands. After 1605, English merrymakers concocted ludicrous masks and attire to commemorate the assassination plot of Guy Fawkes.

The Western Hemisphere boosted the appeal of holidays with body paint, masks, and garb. Pueblo Indians of the Great Basin hosted spring and summer performances of the Kachina clown society. Each player, masked as a particular spirit, carried wands and other props to contribute to comic antics. In 1916, Pope Benedict XV encouraged the holiday dressing of Our Lady of Charity at a chapel in El Cobre, Cuba. The statue received gold lamé robes and haloed crowns as well as red attire for the likeness of the infant Jesus.

In Mexico to the present day, celebration of the Day of the Dead on November 1 and 2 brings out skeleton costumes and skull masks. Chinese tra-

Celebrants in Costa Rica gather for the National Masquerade Day parade, an All Saints Day festival and ethnic celebration in which regional folk heroes come to life in costumes and giant puppets. *(Yuri Cortez/AFP/Getty Images)*

ditionalists retain jubilant segmented dragon costumes celebrating New Year and have reclaimed Hanfu dressing, the flowing robes of the Shang dynasty (after 1600 B.C.E.). Merchandisers take advantage of the need for holiday accessories and apparel for graduation, Kwanzaa, Easter, Christmas, Hanukkah, and Eid al-Fitr after Ramadan by advertising seasonal markdowns and sales.

See also: Costume Parties; Halloween Costumes; Mardi Gras and Carnival Costumes; Ritual Garments.

Further Reading

Barber, Elizabeth Wayland. *The Dancing Goddesses: Folklore, Archaeology, and the Origins of European Dance.* New York: W.W. Norton, 2013.

Fernald, Mary. *Historic Costumes and How to Make Them.* Mineola, NY: Dover, 2006.

Watts, Linda S. *Encyclopedia of American Folklore.* New York: Facts on File, 2006.

Hosiery, Men's

The history of men's hosiery chronicles the search for warm, comfortable, and fashionable leg wear. Greek *piloi* (socks) from 700 B.C.E. featured felted animal hair as suitable foot padding to ease the chafing of sandals and shoes. Egyptians and Romans varied stocking styles with footbags, looped sandal socks, and foot bindings, the quick-drying leg wear of infantrymen. For soldiers posted in Northern Europe and Britannia, the Roman *soccus* (sock) absorbed perspiration and protected the feet from frostbite.

As early as 57 B.C.E., the Korean national costume included *beoseon,* a quilted silk anklet sock; padding and ankle straps ensured warmth and a tight fit. At Constantinople, Byzantine clergy sported ritual silk hose under buskins (calf-high boots). Under *caligae,* thick soles laced over the lower leg, Byzantine shepherds wrapped the foot and upper leg in cloth strips, a rural version of stockings that also protected the shins and calves of Persian soldiers.

By the early Middle Ages, men added fabric stockings to leather and hide foot coverings. After 449 C.E., wealthy Anglo-Saxons coordinated soft shoes with leather hose fastened in place with strands of animal gut. Charlemagne avoided finery and reverted to the leg and foot bindings of the Roman legionary. Viking needleworkers loop-knotted socks by a Swedish method. During the Crusades in the eleventh century, fur linings contributed to the comfort and warmth of stockinette hose worn under chain mail.

Fashion Statement

Into the 1100s, stocking makers in Belgium, Flanders, and Italy bought needles from Spain and wool kersey yarn from England for knitting into hosiery. Fashionable courtiers tied to a belt one-piece leg-to-groin stockings or parti-color hose with legs in contrasting solid colors. Medieval Egyptian stylists created a toe-to-calf pattern completed with the insertion of a heel piece. The two-piece construction enabled the knitter to replace worn heels rather than discard the entire hose.

During the Joseon dynasty after 1392, Japanese men flaunted quilted silk slippers and winter socks. Seamstresses embroidered the tasseled toes with flower patterns. Samurai armored *tabis* (toe socks), a stocking knitted with a separation between the first two toes for wearing under thong sandals. After 1483, men revealed brilliant colors in cloth "nether stocks" or "lock-stocked hose" (tights) through slits in the sides of duck-bill shoes. Faddish males displayed their legs in knee-length hose topped with velvet fringe. For outdoor work, men layered visible stockings over base hosiery or stocking liners. From 1501 to 1722, Persian men emulated European hosiery by abandoning men's puttees in favor of stockings imported from Tus, an eastern supplier in Khorasan, Afghanistan.

In Tudor England, hosiery makers cut cloth on the bias for stretch and concealed side seams with "clocks," the industry name for details. To reduce sagging, in Calverton, Nottinghamshire, William Lee in 1589 mechanized knitting to yield a tighter stocking six times faster than hand knitting. Although Elizabeth I preferred hand-knit hosiery and shielded the cottage knitter from factory competition, the mechanization of knitting flourished into the 1620s at Derbyshire and Leicestershire. Machine-made hose increased the wearability of shoes by layering cotton, linen, or wool between the sole and foot.

In the early 1600s, Englishmen popularized stirrup hose for riding and Italian Mantua stockings with padding in the calves for masculine appeal. For indoor wear, they chose one-piece soled hose called cashambles, a knitted or mesh leg attached to whalebone or white leather bottoms. To adorn thigh-high riding and hunting footwear, haberdashers edged boot hose in fringe or lace. Highland Scots developed buckskin trews (leggings) for horseback riding and flaunted clan colors in the garters that held up tartan stockings displaying twined cables. The argyle diamond pattern remained an appealing motif into the 2000s.

White stockings dominated the look of the fashionable man in the eighteenth century. In the preindustrial era around 1760 in Lancashire, England, the flying shuttle mechanized James Hargreaves's spinning jenny, a moving carriage that stretched fibers as needles knitted them into hosiery. A row of yarn spindles could outpace the cottage knitter, thereby reducing stocking prices. Workers stretched finished tubes over leg-shaped boards to flatten seams and set a contoured shape. Reinforced heels and toes resisted holes and runs, especially in the thigh-high socks worn by children. The stout upper band rolled up over breeches, ending the need for buckles.

In the South American colonies, Peruvians learned to knit stocks from alpaca and llama yarn. To the north, children and slaves contributed hosiery to meet a constant need for new footwear. Among the Massachusetts settlers, leather stockings mimicked Lenni Lenape designs. At Monticello, Thomas Jefferson depended on slipper socks to ward off arthritis pain. Knitting societies exhibited patriotism by rejecting imported British footwear and making stockings of homespun yarn, supplying the Continental Army during the wretched winter of 1777, when barefoot men turned to foot rags for warmth.

Men's ankle-length socks came into vogue during the 1830s, replacing more restrictive hosiery. After 1837, knitting rooms in Balbriggan, Ireland, turned out high-quality lisle cotton stockings. Before and during the American Civil War, sewing societies made leg wear for infant and adult refugees on the Underground Railroad and for soldiers of the Confederate and Union armies. The yarn favored for leg wear varied from plain cotton or wool to cashmere and silk.

Commodity

Machine-knitted socks and hose presented a problem—lumpy seams extending from under the toes up the back of the calf. Women chose to knit men's socks with a pattern of stitches encircling the foot, a common addition to knickerbocker, golf, and bicycling outfits.

By the 1870s, industrial knitters emulated stitches in the round and applied the technology to fine silk hosiery. The popularity of factory-made stockings boosted the industry 175 percent in one decade from $4 million to $11 million, giving work primarily to female laborers. The 1897 Sears, Roebuck catalog featured a range of embroidered silk and ribbed half hose, lumbermen's wool socks, lisle and merino hose, even black socks with white bottoms for feet sensitive to dye.

In the 1900s, shoe stores courted trade in "ankle dress," patterned or striped hosiery and button-on ribbed stockings completing the look and fit of men's low brogans. The addition of the heelless half-sock to regular socks increased the absorbency and warmth of hunting and ski boots. Before World War I, boys wore over-the-knee socks with metal and rubber clasps that attached to sock suspenders. A burst of enthusiasm for silk hosiery in 1919 boosted factory production and curtailed enthusiasm for home knitting.

In 1938, the synthesis of nylon offered an artificial fiber to extend the flexibility and life of silk, wool, rayon, and cotton leg wear. The bobbed ankle sock in 1943 earned the following of teens, whom the media named bobby-soxers. The introduction of such materials as micromesh, silicone, and elastic further boosted durability and comfort.

The 1950s styles in hosiery introduced thermal socks and "mannyhose" for male athletes and divers as well as joggers, campers, hunters, riders, soldiers, and sufferers of diabetes, knee injury, and varicose veins. In Italy, hosier Emilio Cavallini popularized full-body stockings. By the 1980s, Datang, China, became the world's leading sock producer at the rate of 16 billion socks annually, the equivalent of two pairs for every person on Earth. In 2013, some men gave up flip-flops and slippers for toe socks with ankle straps and grips on the bottom, a nonslip element suited to lounging and workouts at home.

See also: Knitting and Crocheting; Shoes, Men's; Silk and Sericulture; Undergarments; Yarn.

Further Reading

Chapman, Stanley. *Hosiery and Knitwear: Four Centuries of Small-Scale Industry in Britain, ca. 1589–2000.* New York: Oxford University Press, 2002.

Cornell, Kari, ed. *Knitting Socks from Around the World.* Minneapolis, MN: Voyageur, 2011.

Strawn, Susan M. *Knitting America: A Glorious Heritage from Warm Socks to High Art.* Minneapolis, MN: Voyageur, 2007.

Hosiery, Women's

Historically, the appeal of women's leg wear has followed the rise in skirt lengths. In the 1100s, young Italian girls slip-knotted gauzy crepe thread on needles for knitting into lightweight stockings for women. Into the late Middle Ages, when hosiery lacked gender differentiation, wedding customs dictated that the bride should reveal her hosiery and toss a garter to male guests.

The Evolution

From the thirteenth century, stocking makers popularized the striped stocking with a rounded heel flap. Around 1400, garters held loose unisex leg tubes in place at the knee. In early Renaissance Europe, pattens (overshoes) fastened over soled hose with ties or straps, helping the housewife avoid water damage in the street or mop splashes in the kitchen.

In 1560, Queen Elizabeth I set the style in hand-knit women's stockings, which she preferred to bias fabric construction. English workhouses and knitting schools turned out more varieties than home needleworkers and prepared women

for the labor force in Yorkshire and the Midlands. In 1562, Eleonora of Toledo went to her grave in fancy silk stockings knitted with a filigree turn-down cuff, the handwork of a skilled professional. At century's end, knitted stockings enhanced the garment industry in London, Norfolk, Aberdeen, and the Shetland Islands. By 1618, London was exporting 175 million pairs of stockings annually.

At colonial Plymouth Plantation in 1624, knitters incorporated purled motifs and padded the heel cup with extra yarn. In Maryland, dancing slippers echoed the colors of ensembles along with knit silk or wool stockings and a set of decorated mules to protect leg wear from snags and rips. Needleworkers in Labrador and Newfoundland "thrummed" knit socks by incorporating unspun tufts of wool fleece for warmth. In Sussex in 1817, the first printed knitting patterns taught pupils at Worthing Girls' School to rib sock tops to increase flexibility and fit on the narrow ankles of little girls and women.

Before the American Civil War, hand knitters began replacing wool yarn with cotton, a more attractive look on the leg and foot when paired with high-button shoes. For evening wear, the insertion of a purled seam rib, embroidery, and lacy, shell, chain, and eyelet patterns in round-the-leg knitting appealed to style-conscious women. Linen tops and tapes or drawstrings secured hose while protecting delicate needlework. The term "silk stockings" identified privileged women.

In the 1890s, bed socks, heelless hospital foot-bags, and sleep socks warmed the feet, ankles, and calves of pregnant women and females sequestered with consumption. In 1891, Procter & Gamble targeted problems with delicate stockings by advertising Ivory Soap as a gentle cleanser for lingerie. In the less genteel settings of Paris cabarets, cancan dancers hiked skirts adorned with bows and lace over ruched black stockings.

The Jazz Age

During the 1920s, flappers flaunted rolled hose, a below-the-knee leg tube coiled around an elastic garter. To boost the sale of women's footwear, American merchandisers showcased stockings and sport socks with shoes, boots, sneakers, and matching handbags. Leg wear designs featured snake scales, blossoms, and peacock feathers. Advertising copy stressed the luster and strength of chemically mercerized (hardened) sea island cotton and lisle, a yarn spun in opposite directions before twining.

For absorbency, booteries recommended socks made of long-staple woolens over fabrics made with lamb's wool and high-grade worsteds in varied mixtures and tweeds, a common complement to two-toned oxfords. For luxury hosiery with open-toed pumps and dressy sandals, cashmere offered softness and cultivated silk provided contour and sheen. Additional choices ranged from wild tussah silk to artificial acetate and rayon, wood pulp derivatives that imitated the luster of silk.

As couturiers developed the chic tailoring of lush fabrics, runway models featured complementary leg wear. Media commentary noted the appropriate mating of the hemline and high heels and ankle-strapped shoes with the diamond-patterned silk or ribbed chiffon of tailored hosiery. Inspired by the clotheshorse tastes of Wallis Warfield Simpson, wife of Edward VIII, more expensive kid pumps featured pointed toes and a medium heel over dark silk stockings to slim the legs.

Available in 30 colors, stockings featured in newspaper ads bore whimsical names—bobolink, pigeon, meadowlark, champagne, zinc, cochin—as well as the more familiar ecru and nude, a generalized reference to the skin tone of Caucasian women. In July 1922, hosiery color charts took on romantic airs with new shades of camel, onyx, Parisian gray, and rose taupe. Store arrangements juxtaposed walking oxfords and cabretta sheepskin boots with wool kneesocks and support hose, the latter a necessity for the teacher and factory worker. Girls' preference for Mary Jane strap shoes popularized white anklet socks with embroidered or tatted edgings.

Women's hosiery in 1920s America varied in price from 25 cents to $10 per pair and encompassed silk and wool blends, clocked (detailed) styles, sandal and split foot, boot hose, lisle tops, mesh, French seamed, and seamless. Window displays, drawing on the flirtatious looks of Hollywood's dancing queens, complemented attractive buckle pumps with gray and silver sheer stockings

of Japanese silk that matched silk underwear. By 1929, more than 88 percent of women's stockings were sheer or opaque silk, which women purchased at the average rate of eight pairs per year.

The Nylon Revolution

In 1939, the demonstration of nylon stockings at the New York World's Fair revolutionized the hosiery market with a polymer substitute for silk invented by DuPont chemist Wallace Carothers. Lanolin treatment produced a velvety feel while retaining translucence. By 1940, DuPont had marketed 64 million pairs of women's nylons. In the United States, women could buy machine-made silk stockings for $1.35 and nylons for $2.95. Meanwhile, during nylon, silk, and wool rationing in England, women knitted short ladies' ankle socks from 9 cents' worth of three-ply cotton yarn.

When the Allied military commandeered silk and nylon for the manufacture of parachutes, tires, tow ropes, mosquito net, flak vests, and tents during World War II, *Life* magazine impressed on consumers the allure of gossamer thigh-high hose attached to garter belts. To spice up cocktail dresses, women emulated pin-up girl Betty Grable's leg wear with Max Factor's "liquid stockings" (tinted lotion) and a seam drawn up the back of the leg with eyebrow pencil. When nylons returned to the marketplace in September 1945, Macy's sold the first delivery of 50,000 pairs in six hours.

Hosiery makers built a following for elaborate silk patterns and fishnet styles, the choice of models and exotic dancers. The first seamless hose in 1950 derived from circular knit technology. A heat set reduced sagging and bunching by infixing human contours; micromesh stitching created a matte surface. The addition of spandex in 1959 increased comfort and extended the life of expensive hose and leggings.

Wave, diamond, and herringbone styles in the 1960s intensified demand for pantyhose under the miniskirts created by London designer Mary Quant. Simultaneously, pantsuits eliminated the need for long leg wear at the office. In knee-highs or trouser socks, women could save money while protecting themselves from vaginal yeast infections, a common result of long hours in constrictive waist-high nylon.

The exercise craze of the late 1970s triggered demands for matching and complementary leotards and tights for dance and yoga classes. The change in body awareness elevated leg wear from accessories to garments. Fishnet hose revived the matte black look in the 1980s and 1990s. Another style change in 2005 returned short leggings to use under hiked hemlines, hot pants, and long belted sweaters.

Wet-look leggings of the late 2000s derived from metallic yarn. In 2010, jeggings, the brainstorm of British designer Alexander McQueen, reduced the discomfort of skinny jeans by crossbreeding jeans with leggings woven of denim and stretchy fibers. Printed with pockets, zippers, snaps, and belt loops, jeggings offered the visual illusion of jeans without the bulk. In 2012, the women's hosiery market revived fads for titillating suspender stockings, stretch-lace hose, ultra-sheer body stockings, and sparkly and sequined tights.

See also: Hosiery, Men's; Knitting and Crocheting; Nylon; Shoes, Women's; Silk and Sericulture; Undergarments; Yarn.

Further Reading

Arwas, Victor. *The Stocking Book.* Guilford, CT: Skirt!, 2012.

Deutch, Yvonne. *A Glimpse of Stocking: A Short History of Stockings.* London: Michael O'Mara, 2002.

Jenkins, David, ed. *The Cambridge History of Western Textiles.* New York: Cambridge University Press, 2003.

Hunting and Fishing Attire

Globally, apparel for hunting and fishing have customarily stressed safety and comfort above style. As early as 42,000 B.C.E. from land, air, and sea, bush hunters and scavengers of sub-Saharan Africa stripped their prey of bone, sinew, fur, feathers, scales, gut skins, and hide. By recycling their kill, they protected their nude bodies with thong loincloths tied at the midriff with cording or sinew. Cupped pouches slung over the shoulder secured darts and arrows, which date to hunting gear found at the Stone Age Sibudu Cave in South Africa.

Prehistory

From 38,000 B.C.E., woven belts and gendered fur body coverings, carryalls, and forearm bands equipped nomad huntsmen for pursuing fox and reindeer and the river dweller for ice fishing and spear fishing. Around 30,000 B.C.E., linen hunting vests and bags accompanied Central Asian game birders into the wild. After 9000 B.C.E., Chinchorro fishers and hunters of the Atacama Desert in present-day Chile chose fringed grass skirts and kilts suited to intense heat.

Before the domestication of herding stock in prehistoric Africa, spear hunters draped themselves in pelt blankets and wraps tied with leather thongs or fibrous lianas and roots, a look paralleling the skin garments of Pipil-speaking pursuers of the Nicaraguan jungle. In Greenland, Japan, Russia and Siberia, Scandinavia, and northern North America, outdoor hand bags and footbags required lining with the pelts of wolverines, reindeer, and bear for comfort and warmth. In the humid climate of Borneo, Dayak outdoorsmen embroidered breechcloths with symbols attesting to field courage and skill.

After 5000 B.C.E., Paleo-Eskimo or Denbigh tundra dwellers crafted attire from skins to increase mobility along lakes, deer trails, and trout streams. Coursers adapted lacing technology to field dress. By threading sinew into a thorn, clothing makers tightened the fit of outdoor tunics, jackets, and footbags. After 3250 B.C.E., huntsmen at Guitarrero Cave west of Chimbote, Peru, satisfied tracking needs by plaiting, cording, or twining cotton fibers on looms for netted hunt pouches. Neolithic Korean trackers adorned themselves with animal fangs as evidence of manhood and shields against evil in the wild.

Around 3300 B.C.E., Ötzi the Iceman, whose remains were found high in the Italian Alps in 1991, exhibited skilled blending of animal pelts for gaming apparel. His outfit consisted of goatskin leggings and shirt, goat leather breechcloth, calf belt and pouch, chamois quiver, bearskin cap, and bear hide shoe soles. For warmth and comfort, he laced the leggings to the belt and stuffed his deer hide shoes with grass. His footwear anticipated later Alpine tucking of leggings into snowshoes.

Hunter and Horseman

In western China after 1200 B.C.E., Hun bow-hunters from the Levant dressed in felt jackets and tall boots for long gallops, a style emulated by Assyrian riders in the 600s B.C.E. By 500 B.C.E., leather became the chosen material for outdoorsmen and travelers. Greek fishermen lopped one strap off the short tunic to free the right arm for netting. The Melanesians of the South Pacific, North American Plains Indians, Yanomami of the Amazon Basin, Alaskan Eskimo, and Suri, Dahomey, and Maasai of Africa managed hunting and fishing expeditions with creels, game pouches, and nets, but without garments or shoes.

Around 44 B.C.E., Roman hunters adopted *cothurni* (calf-length boots) for mounted expeditions. In an improvement over raw seaming, thong stitching secured insole to sole. Leather banding from the vamp up the center seam and around the outer rim completed the look. A metal rivet or nail on the toe lengthened the life of the boot. From the Byzantine Empire north into Russia and Siberia as far as the Arctic Circle, huntsmen eschewed court finery embroidered with stylized animal hunts and wrapped themselves in the skins of their prey. Unclipped pelts became the raw material of tunics, parkas, caps, and bags.

From the Middle Ages, the aboriginal Ainu of Japan selected bast fibers of the elm tree to hammer into cloth, and tunics and loincloths padded with wild rye, cattails, and seabird feathers. European males turned survival tracking into gaming, a luxury sport that encouraged the purchase of hunting hounds and mounts as well as stylish trail fashions. In the 500s C.E., the Vikings of Norway, Sweden, and the Faroe, Orkney, and Shetland islands equipped themselves in wadmal (homespun wool fleece) garments topped with skin cloaks and paired with *glofi* (hand bags).

Ninth-century Frankish hunters purchased deer leather and suede pouches to attach to breech girdles. During Japan's Heian period after 894, huntsmen garnished the high-necked *kariginu* (hunting robe) with status symbols. In 1000, cordwainers (shoemakers) marketed hunting footwear ranging from buckled galoshes and overshoes to thigh-high heuse riding boots.

Twelfth-century Bamanan stalkers at San, Mali, turned handmade *bògòlanfini* (mud cloth) into camouflage shirts.

Thirteenth-century European pageantry gained crowd appeal with colors and coats of arms proclaiming noble dynasties. Welsh outriders topped the traditional tunic and pants outfit with Phrygian caps, symbolic of freedom from oppression. After 1350, European huntsmen and their squires favored the short almuce (fur hood) for warmth during lengthy horseback rides. The French camouflaged their clothing with branches. Florentine bird hunters stowed their kill in flexible leather pouches.

During the fifteenth century, the Tudor era in England injected fashion notes in hunting attire, including feathered caps and thigh-high riding boots with turn-down collars or tied at the top with drawstrings. English glovers custom-fit hunting gloves from thin napped pelts of lamb, deer, calf, and goat. For improved vision, Pope Leo X adapted period eyewear to hunting needs by wearing special concave glasses. Seagoing Greeks from Kos, Corfu, and Rhodes, and Irishmen from the mainland and Aran Islands fished in everyday "jumpers" (pullovers) and Fair Isle sweaters featuring home-style stitches and ribbing.

Materials and Styles

Sixteenth-century European explorers of the New World characterized Amerindian hunting attire as traditional, particularly the wild cotton pouches carried by huntsmen of the Amazon basin and the mouth shields worn by Mochica blowpipe hunters in what is now coastal Peru. In 1502 at Trujillo, Honduras, Christopher Columbus discovered the fishers of the Miskito Coast in straw sun hats. Apache moccasin makers in the Great basin painted the shoe tongue with events of successful expeditions. Outdoor symbols—rabbits, lightning, lakes, snowbanks—pictured the myriad scenes of the trail. In the Pacific Northwest, Chilkat, Haida, and Tsimshian fishers depicted fish fillets and mollusks on their woven blankets.

In the Brazilian rain forest, the Caiapó (or Kayapo) coated their bodies in black dye to conceal themselves from prey, a method paralleling the use of white clay paint by stalkers of Arnhem Land in northern Australia. Along the shores of the Great Lakes, Huron, Ojibwa, and Pawnee stalkers crawled on their bellies under buffalo heads and attached hides, a form of camouflage for tracking herds. Women followed up on successful hunts by removing antlers, skinning carcasses, and flensing hides to make capes, sleeveless tunics, hunting tools, and blankets to wear in temporary hunting camps as buffalo and whitetail deer followed seasonal migratory patterns.

In the early seventeenth century, thigh-high riding boots for the English gentleman featured complementary hosiery topped with lace and fringe. Scots Highlanders preferred rugged rawhide trews (leggings) and cabled tartan hosiery held in place by garters flaunting clan colors and argyle diamonds. Therapeutic whalebone sports corsets bolstered the spine during exercise, hunting, and riding. On the North American frontier, plainsmen smeared doeskin hunting shirts, breeches, and moccasins with buffalo fat for waterproofing. Trading posts updated the look with cavalry bib shirts, which flaunted two rows of horn or bone buttons.

Postcolonial hunters in North America abandoned the Hessian heeled boot in favor of black leather Wellingtons, which eased fit with pull-on straps and V-shaped notches at the knee. In England, French stag hunting dress flaunted the wig and cocked hat over a camlet frock coat, featuring braid and lace cravat with stock pin, and spurred boots. Buckskin breeches and roll-top jack boots increased knee flexibility. Double-breasted shadbelly (cutaway) coats replaced longer coattails for ease of mounting, riding, and running.

In the late Georgian era, after 1810, English hunters relieved the need to protect wigs by purchasing toupées made from the feathers of drakes and mallards. Colonial shooting, coursing, and stalking in Kenya, Burma, and India, and safaris in Africa, popularized the front- and back-billed topi (pith helmet) and jodhpurs fitted tightly at the ankles. Victorian era hunters chose the khaki Bombay bowler and pegged boots for riding to the subtropical hunt. In Japan, fishermen popularized the fitted indigo coat made from patchwork.

Hunting in Style

In the 1850s, Charles Frederick Worth, the "Father of Haute Couture," designed bespoke women's outfits for riding and hunting. Elegant stand-up collars on double-breasted jackets, chiffon-draped hats, and leather gauntlets enhanced femininity for female hunters. Young girls matched masculine flair with snap-brim hats with feathers, long skirts, and scalloped boots. Late in the decade, Empress Elizabeth of Austria, the wife of Franz Joseph I, modeled a chic boned bodice buttoned over a split-busk corset. She draped her skirts with aprons to draw attention to a wasp-waisted figure.

During the Edwardian era, outdoor displays of hunting and fishing togs marketed by Abercrombie & Fitch of New York and J. Barbour and Sons of South Shields, England, recommended lace-up boots for men and women, and waxed jackets for protection from wet weather during trophy hunting. Additional protection with storm collars and cuffs and pockets with drain holes kept hunters comfortable in the wild. By 1870, Thomas Burberry's gabardine field coats refined the look and weight of tracking clothes while supplying breathable, wind-proof surfaces. The customs of Malian hunters required field dress decked with amulets made from knotted rope, claws, shells, horns, and mirrors.

Early twentieth-century menswear featured beaver or twill top hats and red split-tail coats over buff pants and shiny black riding boots. Accessories ranged from military top hats and short crops to absorbent heelless half socks for comfort. Female hunters shopped specialty stores in New York and Washington, D.C., for velvet-collared jackets with nipped-in waists and peplums to pair with bowler hats with chin straps or hat guards, riding veils, tattersall waistcoats, short crops or crook-handled whips, fly whisks, and jodhpur boots.

After World War I, ready-to-wear targeted sportsmen with more choices in tracking gear and outdoor attire. Burberry marketed rainwear and Sears, Roebuck, flannel shirts and long underwear. The trend in specialty outfits came to an abrupt halt during the rationing accompanying World War II.

In the mid-twentieth century, men retained

army fatigues and green or brown camo caps to wear with red wool safety shirts for hunting. Patches on sleeves denoted training in safety courses. Blended polyester-cotton underwear warmed the bodies of elderly Tunumiit net-fishers of East Greenland. *Vogue* pictured women's corduroy hunting attire by Pierre Balmain with game pockets to hold grouse and rabbits.

The worldwide backlash against slaughter of mammals turned consumers against the fur industry. In the late 1960s, furriers responded to negative ad campaigns with support for the Inuit, for whom hunting provided food and materials for family clothing. L.L. Bean continued to dress hunters in jackets and heavy footwear and socks, which company catalogs offered in extra-long and extra-wide sizing. Norm Thompson Outfitters of Hillsboro, Oregon, popularized rugged outdoor sweaters for hikers and hunters.

In 1972, Canadian and Great Lakes hunters selected rough country climbing and hunting gear from the Hudson's Bay Company catalog, notably, the yellow or blaze-orange cap required by Wisconsin law. The stylish chose safari suits and bush jackets, designs influenced by colonial hunting gear from Burma, India, New Zealand, Tasmania, and Australia. Calvin Klein offered modish female hunters corduroy and gabardine hunting jackets paired with charmeuse blouses, a citified look featured in *Harper's Bazaar* and *Vogue*.

By 2008, the Yuketen plaid outdoor boot and the Ralph Lauren hunting lodge silhouette revived pheasant-feathered hats, plaid gaiters and vests, Navajo shoulder bags, distressed jackets, and blanket coats of past eras. In 2011, U.S. outdoorsmen could choose from 16,000 items in the L.L. Bean lineup, which featured waterproof waders, suspenders, and ragg sweaters for duck hunters.

See also: Arctic Attire; Catalogs, Clothing and Fashion; L.L. Bean; Prehistoric Clothing; Protective and Orthotic Clothing; Sports Attire, Recreational.

Further Reading

Allsen, Thomas T. *The Royal Hunt in Eurasian History.* Philadelphia: University of Pennsylvania Press, 2006.

Domnick, Sabine. *Cables, Diamonds, Herringbone: Secrets of Knitting Traditional Fishermen's Sweaters.* Camden, ME: Down East, 2007.

Sheehan, Larry, with Carol Sama Sheehan and Kathryn George. *The Sporting Life: A Passion for Hunting and Fishing.* New York: Clarkson Potter, 1992.

Indian and Pakistani Clothing

The traditional dress styles of India and Pakistan demonstrate old skills in weaving, tanning, dyeing, embroidery, quilting, and body painting. The most imaginative of henna decorators, early and contemporary Hindus have applied birds, paisleys, lotus blossoms, and vines to nuptial couples as blessings on their union. Evidence found at Mehrgarh, Pakistan, shows that Neolithic tanners had developed microbial fermentation to denude hides of tissue, fleece, and hair. Tamil reptile specialists in southern India added the skins of asps, kraits, and cobras to exotic leathers for shoes, bags, and belts.

From 3500 B.C.E., Indus Valley weavers turned sisal, ramie, and hemp into functional textiles. Appliqué, reverse appliqué, sprang (netted openwork), and embroidery on breechcloths, saris, tunics, veils, shawls, hats, and turbans began in 2000 B.C.E. with Hindu patterning in Chamba, Kashmir, Kutch, and the Punjab. Padding of caftans with short-staple *kutun* (cotton) around 800 B.C.E. increased the comfort of armored warriors.

Apparel from the Indian subcontinent and Ceylon appealed to consumers throughout southern Asia as far west as the Middle East. By 138 B.C.E., Chinese roadways over Parthia, Afghanistan, Turkestan, and Uzbekistan fostered hybridization of Asian clothing, blanket, and footwear styles. Hindus approved the backless silk slide from China rather than shoes made of the hides of sacred cows.

Stitchery supplied unique touches to apparel. Pictorial handwork by men and women featured sunbursts, paisley, peacocks, tiger claws, Hanuman (an ape-like deity), Ganesha (an elephant-headed deity), and the tree of life. In Bengal in northeastern India, the embroidery of *kantha,* a material quilted in flowers and leaf motifs from rags, recycled raveled thread for stitching soft materials into family apparel, wallets, handkerchiefs, purses, skirt borders, shawls, and bags. Professional embroiderers advanced *shisha,* the addition of coins, glass, mirror, or silver to embroidered garments such as the *choli,* a half blouse reaching to the bottom rib to complement a wrap skirt.

A similar skill in leather appliqué in Sindh, present-day Pakistan, involved stitchery in thick cording, metallic couching, or laid work, yarn held in place by tiny stitches at right angles on wedding blouses and vests. For major projects, Gujarati artisans embroidered intricate pieces of a large image on a solid foundation. In Bihari needlework from India's northeast, the appliqués consisted of a single motif sewn to the solid color base of the traditional sari. The *kurta* (men's tunic), cut from translucent textiles, complemented the dhoti (men's shorts), a voluminous garment made from nearly 5 yards (4.6 meters) of pleated cloth knotted in various styles.

In the first century B.C.E., Indian merchants exported to Arabia and the Mediterranean soft cottons, multihued brocades, and tabby silks, which varied everyday dressing in linen with textiles for bodices, petticoats, scarves, burkas, men's kilts, caps, and handkerchiefs. From factories in Surat, Indian families added to dowries the *patolo* (wedding dress) and red *chunri* (nuptial veil), a customary gift to the bride from a maternal uncle. For ceremonies and feasting, men wore the standard silk *pitámbar* (loincloth), which displayed a yellow background figured in red and gold.

A group of Indian women in the sacred Hindu city of Mathura exhibits the rich variety in color and pattern of the modern sari (Sanskrit for "strip of cloth"), the essential attire for women on the subcontinent for at least 4,000 years. *(Bill Bachmann/Perspectives/Getty Images)*

In the Punjab, cobblers crafted sturdy *paduka,* footwear for the street and for export. A raised platform featured a wood post and ball that the first two toes grasped for balance. For leisure footwear and horseback riding in the northwest, the leather *jutti* or *mojari* highlighted an Asian specialty, turned-up points that arched toward the ankle, a more gracious version of the woven *galesh,* a Persian slide with tilted points. For their comfort and subtle shape, unisex shoes from India gained popularity around Constantinople.

After 1556, leather slip-ons graced with gilt stitchery and pearls accessorized Mughal designs on velvet. Goat hair supplied fiber for felt hats and heavy capes. Pearls and aigrettes from gray herons graced royal turbans. Women's jewelry consisted of pendant earrings, the jade or jeweled *ta'wiz* (neck amulet), nose and septum rings set with

gemstones, and fan-shaped headdress modeled on Persian designs.

In 1608, a trend at Goa featured cotton pajamas as relaxing evening wear and costumes for Nautch dancing girls. In 1719, shipments of domestic *beteele* (muslin) from India supplied petticoats for European women's dresses. At the end of the eighteenth century, Napoleonic fashions turned the Kashmiri shawl with stitched border into the must-have accessory of the female wardrobe. Drawings of the Banjara Roma (or Gypsies) of western India and rajas from the south introduced romanticized notions of outdated costumes from past centuries featuring turbans, waist wraps, brocaded raja coats, and jingling anklets.

At the beginning of the Victorian era in the 1830s, factories at Coromandel satisfied tastes in calico and cotton pajamas, knee-length banyans (dressing gowns), and nightcaps, common exports for the British East India Company. Steam-powered looms in 1879 provided Indian clothiers with *sha* (gauze) and *tuan* (satin weave) silks from Suzhou, China. Finished goods sparked orientalist trends in England with imports of gauze tiered skirts, and fueled demand for crepe for mourning attire in the late 1800s, resist-dyed textiles from Gujarat, and wrinkle-free acetate saris in the late 1920s.

In the early 1980s, Pakistan's labor force began accepting outsourced apparel manufacture from industrialized countries. At present, India ranks second globally in the production of goods made from polyester cotton, including drawstring wraps, leisure wear, and stylish saris by couturier Rina Dhaka. Rural traditionalists perpetuate the tints of natural dyes on red wedding saris and head wraps as well as saffron and turmeric yellow temple dress. Globalization on the Internet makes native scarves, shirts, and saris available as contributions to the multicultural market.

See also: Appliqué; Ethnic and National Dress; Orientalism.

Further Reading

Gillow, John, and Nicholas Barnard. *Indian Textiles.* Rev. ed. New York: Thames & Hudson, 2008.

Kumar, Ritu. *Costumes and Textiles of Royal India.* Woodbridge, UK: Antique Collectors' Club, 2005.

Paine, Sheila. *Embroidery from India and Pakistan.* London: British Museum, 2001.

Rocca, Federico, ed. *Contemporary Indian Fashion.* Bologna, Italy: Damiani, 2009.

Ironing

The smoothing of fabric with steam or a hot implement reduces wrinkling while enhancing the garment's drape and flow. Egyptian flax workers soaked stems, then beat them with a flax batting staff, a method also in use in Japan and Korea to tame wrinkled linen. In the first century C.E., Roman women at Herculaneum and Pompeii spread damp folded tunics under the top board of a screw press, which could crease multiple layers of laundry in a single frame.

From 730, Chinese women worked in pairs, one holding the garment taut while the other filled a long-handled pan iron with hot sand or embers and guided it over the wrinkles. In northwestern Europe in the late 700s, Viking women smoothed apparel with heated stones or glass. In Wales, carved smoothing stones had handles for directing the flat edge over pleats and seams. Around 800, Norwegian women prized the whalebone smoothing board, on which they pressed clothing with heated rocks. A pumice polisher kept the bone surface even for smoothing night wear and skirts without snags.

In the mid-1400s, at washing stones along streams, British, Scandinavian, and Eastern European women brandished battledores to beat wrinkles from fabric. Ironworkers forged smoothing irons and flatirons to replace slickstones and bats. In Florence, Italy, ladies' maids freshened small pleats with a curved frilling iron, which rocked over an iron base.

Public laundries stretched damp blankets, capes, and evening wraps over frames and anchored the edges with tenterhooks. A calendering board allowed the rolling of lengths of simple apparel over drums for back-and-forth ironing. For the poor in Holland, Denmark, and Germany in the 1500s, a rolling pin or mangle board with handle increased friction on clothing wound on the pin or roller. In London, the addition of arum starch to lace collars, kerchiefs, and cuffs increased the need for heat applied directly to wet laundry.

For ruching, quilling, and pleating fine muslin dresses and bonnets, seventeenth-century irons consisted of glass, oak, or marble shaped like mushrooms. A self-heating chimney iron contained the mess and smell of charcoal inside the iron body and vent. A slug iron applied the heat of brick or metal slabs, which never reached a temperature high enough to scorch fabric.

A more complicated system, the box mangle held stones or sand that pressed on wet cloth as it passed over cylinders. The "mangling" action wrung out dampness and excess starch while flattening wrinkles. A mangle cloth prevented the mechanism from staining garments.

Nineteenth-century launderers gained speed and control of slacks and skirts by covering a fir or pine skirt board with a wool, baize, swanskin, or flannel pad overlaid with sheeting. In Ottumwa, Iowa, Mary Florence Potts's invention of a detachable handle in 1870 allowed the homemaker to heat a second metal iron to replace the one in use. As one iron cooled, the user removed the wood handle to slide into the frame of the hot base. To remove rust, the ironer scoured the cooled flat surface with sandpaper or emery and polished the bottom by rolling it over a candle.

At professional laundries, specialists smoothed the cuffs and linen fronts of men's shirts and the delicate embroidery of women's night wear, blouses, caps, and scarves on a bosom board. To prevent creasing, the launderer inserted a seam roll or tailor's ham as a pressing tool for silks and lined woolens. A fluting or goffering iron or crimping tongs pleated fancy trim and ruffs. For hats and puff sleeves, an egg iron reached into small corners and pleats. In 1887, the sleeve board of African American inventor Sarah Boone of New Haven, Connecticut, contoured long sleeves during ironing.

Although the electric iron came on the market in 1882, Charles T. Johnson-Vea and Ole Tverdahl of Stoughton, Wisconsin, around 1893 invented the two-part sad iron and insulated the steel base with asbestos to keep heat from burning the user's hand. An interchangeable "laundry set" included a presser, pointed flounce iron, polisher, and sleeve iron. A traveling asbestos iron sold for 35 cents.

Twentieth-century innovations introduced irons with glass, Lucite, or folding handles and heels on the frame for propping up the device to prevent scorching. Thermostats maintained low temperatures for silk, satin, taffeta, and acetate and high temperatures for cotton, linen, and ramie. To reduce the need for sprinkling and rolling laundry, Edward P. Schreyer invented the steam iron in 1941. Competitors tinkered with steam jets, water tanks, and home ironing machines while fabric makers applied formaldehyde to permanent-press cloth engineered by Ruth Benerito. Spray starch further simplified garment upkeep by ending the boiling, straining, and soaking steps preceding ironing. Subsequent refinements—automatic shutoff and handheld steamers—further advanced ironing from drudgery.

See also: Dry Cleaning; Laundry.

Italian Clothing and Fashion

Clothing and accessory styles from the Italian Peninsula have set global standards from ancient times to the present. After 37 B.C.E., weavers purchased cotton and silk arriving by caravan over the Silk Road. Early Christian art in Rome, Assisi, and Ravenna standardized the image of the Good Shepherd, Madonna, and angels with softly draped tunics and mantles and flowing hair.

Ninth-century noblewomen hand-loomed flax, nettle, cotton, and fleece for everyday attire but purchased their beauty-table accessories and red tints for lips and cheeks. Knitters outfitted families with hosiery fashioned of wool kersey yarn from England and Scotland. Italian men evolved a flashy style of stockings consisting of contrasting colors on each leg. Padding in Mantua stockings increased the illusion of muscular thighs.

The First Crusade in the late eleventh century launched a trend in military insignia and red crosses on helmets. Soldiers returning from the Holy Lands furthered the textile trade between Italian city-states and Asia, generating cotton-weaving centers in Sicily. Women slip-knotted gossamer crepe yarn into lightweight hose. Weavers turned *zetani* (satin) into a luxury fabric suitable for embassy gifts to visiting dignitaries.

Italian embroidery advanced in the thirteenth century with the adoption of Arabic intarsia, geometric appliqué that graced shawls, mantles, and hats with plants, animals, and family crests. Ribbons wrapped long curls and held flowers in hair arrangements. In the fourteenth century, the *cioppa* (flowing robe) supplied pendant pouches for pockets. Trapunto added embroidered channels and padding to collars and cuffs.

Later in the Middle Ages, Venetian costume books summarized the importance of Hardanger stitchery, slashed sleeves, lacing, ruffs, starched collars, and petticoats to aristocratic wardrobes. Dye masters published handbooks describing color mixing and the formulation of tanning treatments for hides. The patchwork of stage trickster Arlecchino added motley to festival and party costumes. Soldiers created a demand for quilted arming caps to line helmets.

Renaissance Italy shucked off the dreary church demands on wardrobe and profited from the sale of *camore* (gowns), peacock fans, perfumes, and egg-based foundation, a cosmetic regimen undergirding a porcelain complexion and blushing cheeks. Textile merchants fed the public demand for jewel-toned frock coats, stiffened hemlines, undersleeves, hair ribbons, and mantles and, in 1480, exported colored fabrics to Russia. Haberdashers sold eyeglasses and leather pouches to bird hunters and birettas to priests, shopkeepers, surgeons, and lawyers.

The sixteenth century gained admiration for refinements to dress and grooming, including the Neapolitan custom of massaging nails with oil and the choice of lavish costumes for Corpus Christi Day tableaux and floats. On the journey to France to marry Henry II in 1533, Catherine de' Medici packed elegant hand fans and brought along Frederico de Vinciola, a Venetian pattern designer who supplied her with needlework and lace.

Seventeenth-century designs blended French

strands of finery into Italian ensembles. Tailoring started a trend in the *justacorps,* a knee-length frock coat in burgundy and gold worn with an ample jabot and lace cuffs. For women, Venetian needle lace garnished necklines with lianas, fern fronds, and feathery designs.

Italian innovations from the 1800s included the Capezio ballet slipper and toe shoe and imperial workshops such as Torre del Greco south of Naples, where carvers turned coral and the shells of abalone, conch, and bullmouth helmet snails into cameos and intaglio jewelry. Late-century styles reshaped the female bodice with décolleté and surplice necklines by Mariano Fortuny. In 1902, military helmets displayed Italian fervor with rooster feathers bent toward the shoulder. After World War I, factories began turning cellulose from fir, pine, and poplar into viscose yarn.

Twentieth-century combat weakened the Italian economy and hampered clothing design. Stringent rationing in 1941 stripped haberdashers and apparel stores of shoes and leather goods, hats, furs, and textiles. Looms turned out monochromatic goods to dress Benito Mussolini's Black Shirts. Hand-knit sweaters began returning post–World War II exports to their former levels. Marketing of Continental styles by La Rinascente department stores made world couture available at reasonable prices, including envelope bags, Emilio Pucci's leisure wear, and the full-body stockings of Emilio Cavallini.

The Italian business suit set a global style for neatness and svelte contouring, which flattered small-framed males. In the late 1960s, Nino Cerruti and Giorgio Armani relieved men's business wear of stodginess by raising armholes and eliminating vents on suit jackets and improving the drape of overcoats. In the 1980s, Italian shoes, such as those by Salvatore Ferragamo, Pappagallo, and Giovanni Fabiani, once more dominated runways and department store displays.

In 2013, at Terni in southern Umbria, Italian textile manufacturers marketed Alcantara, a nylon microfiber popular in leisure wear. The luxury brand Fendi competed with the world's best in purses, watches, eyeglasses, boots, and women's leisure wear, its factories supplying luxury goods to branded retail outlets in the Americas, Asia, Australia, Africa, and the Middle East. For winter 2014, Dolce & Gabbana returned to the opulence of past eras for Byzantine beading, Renaissance tiaras, and the wide sleeves of Chinese Hanfu style.

See also: Medieval European Clothing; Roman Clothing, Ancient.

Further Reading

Sommers, Susan. *Italian Chic: The Italian Approach to Elegance.* New York: Villard, 1992.

Steele, Valerie. *Fashion, Italian Style.* New Haven, CT: Yale University Press, 2003.

White, Nicola. *Reconstructing Italian Fashion: America and the Development of the Italian Fashion Industry.* New York: Bloomsbury, 2000.

Jacquard, Joseph Marie (1752–1834)

French inventor Joseph Marie Jacquard studied repetitive damask and satin patterns and coded automatic programming for the weaver's loom by means of algorithms. His mechanical loom of 1804 was the first to successfully weave patterned fabrics, paving the way for the first fully automated loom and the modern textile industry. The system of punch cards he devised for producing patterns also provided a model for modern computer programming.

Born on July 7, 1752, in Lyon, France, to weavers Antoinette Rive and Jean Charles Jacquard, he had no formal education. In 1765, Jean-Marie Barret, the inventor's brother-in-law, taught him to read. At age 20, Jacquard inherited his father's drawloom business and involved himself in the silk trade. Business failures forced him into straw weaving, lime burning, knife making, bookbinding, and type founding.

At the loss of his fortune, Jacquard lived southwest of Lyon in Oullins with his wife, Claudine Boichon, on property from her dowry. Following a partisan raid on Lyon in June 1790, he served a stint in the revolutionary army alongside his teenage son, Jean Marie Jacquard, who died in combat.

Under patronage, the inventor devised the treadle loom in 1800 and, shortly thereafter, a loom for weaving fishing nets. The inventions won Jacquard a bronze medal at the 1801 National Exposition in Paris and the support of Lazare Carnot, France's minister of the interior.

The Jacquard Loom

In 1804, Jacquard patterned silk uniformly with a complex machine that followed the weaver's instructions by reading intricate figures punched on a perforated card. His device was based on a programming system of punched paper tape invented by Basile Bouchon in 1725, a cylinder of pierced cards devised by Jean-Baptiste Falcon in 1728, and mechanic Jacques de Vaucanson's ratcheted loom of 1750, which hooked warp threads and mechanized the task of the drawboy in manipulating the harness cords. The Jacquard loom greatly increased the weaver's productivity. He could now produce fine damask, brocade, and matelassé, using 300 to 900 weft threads on one warp. As a demonstration, Jacquard wove a self-portrait in black-and-white silk programmed on 10,000 perforated cards.

Amid increased foreign competition, the Emperor Napoleon and Empress Joséphine visited Lyon on April 12, 1805, to examine the Jacquard loom. State adoption of the system the following year earned the inventor a pension of 3,000 francs ($600) and royalties of 50 francs ($10) per loom sold over the next five years. Outraged at Jacquard for putting silk weavers out of work, Luddite mobs set fire to his model jigger (dyeing machine) and threw him into the Saône River. Despite such opposition, the efficiency of his invention led to general adoption within a few short years.

Jacquard died in Oullins on August 7, 1834. Six years later, the city of Lyon erected a statue of him at the site of his original model. The device influenced mathematician Charles Babbage to invent the programmable computer.

Fabric Technology

By 1812, Jacquard's loom streamlined the work of 11,000 French weavers in producing more defined fabric designs. The storage of patterns on cards allowed their reuse without new computations of thread and design and, ironically, increased incidence of industrial piracy through pattern theft. Newer machines added versatility and economy to the textile industry by lowering the cost of dobby, houndstooth, and herringbone weaves. By 1816, mills in Italy and Switzerland employed Jacquard's invention.

At Westminster in 1820, Francis Lambert patented the Jacquard loom for the weaving of gold and silver lace as well as cotton, wool, thread, and silk lace. The device revolutionized England's silk trade after its introduction at Spitalfields in 1823. David Smith immediately employed the Jacquard loom at Coventry to make figured ribbon in gauze, satin, and damask. Through industrial spying, London weaver Stephen Wilson applied the advanced technology to the weaving of shawls with 7,000 threads. The machine enabled linen manufacturers to increase the profitability of high-end clothing material and damask bed and table goods, which cost five times more than ordinary fabric.

By 1827, Jacquard looms operated at Taylor & Son in Halifax, Nova Scotia, the first programmed device in North America. By 1852, Guido Bonelli's electrification of the loom in Turin augmented capacity to more than 10,000 warp ends. In Vienna, at the International Exhibition of 1873, Norris & Company of Spitalfields loomed portrait damask consisting of 29,088 warp threads.

Still in use today, the modern Jacquard loom requires days of complex threading over thousands of warp ends to initiate weaving. In 2012, Thomas Ferguson Irish Linen of Banbridge, Ireland, increased the variety of apparel fabric available in flax and wool. The company employed Jacquard technology to custom weave fabric marked with family crests and coats of arms up to 10 feet (3 meters) wide.

See also: Looms; Weaving.

Further Reading

Epstein, Stephan R., and Maarten Roy Prak, eds. *Guilds, Innovation, and the European Economy, 1400–1800.* New York: Cambridge University Press, 2008.

Essinger, James. *Jacquard's Web: How a Hand-Loom Led to the Birth of the Information Age.* New York: Oxford University Press, 2007.

Jenkins, David, ed. *The Cambridge History of Western Textiles.* New York: Cambridge University Press, 2003.

Japanese Clothing and Fashion

Historically, apparel styles in Japan reflected an indigenous caste system, from the emperor's silk robes and slippers to Ainu hunter-gatherers in hammered barkcloth. The first island farmers cultivated hemp from 10,000 B.C.E. and wove the bast fibers into tunics and breechcloths. In the mid-5000s B.C.E., the Ainu blended hemp with elm bark for the *attu* (tunic), which they padded in winter with cattails, nettle, wild rye, and feathers.

After the perfection of the bow drill and needle-and-thread technology for stringing beads into necklaces, bracelets, and anklets, by 4500 B.C.E., traders carried Japanese bone, jade, and stone beads to Asian markets. Clan leaders lined their robes with fur as a declaration of status and added bear or wolverine pelts to gloves and socks for insulation. From 4000 B.C.E., adults kept swaddled infants safe and warm by tying them to the back or front of the mother's torso with fabric strips. After 2000 B.C.E., healers protected themselves from spells and evil by appliquéing bells and metal discs to their robes.

From 200 B.C.E., Japanese tastes imitated Chinese court styles in dress, shoes, and hairdos. The *fundoshi* (thong breechcloth) provided comfortable underwear and swimwear for men. Women whitened their faces, necks, and cheeks with rice paste applied to an oil or wax foundation and tinted cheeks and eyebrows with safflower and charcoal. A more utilitarian item, the collapsible oil paper umbrella, imported from China, opened on a central stem to reveal nature scenes and historical figures.

From the First Kimonos

After 600 C.E., Japanese clothiers introduced the proto-kimono, the upper part of a two-part outfit completed with long, blousy pants. Women combed their hair into a *kepatsu,* a boxy Chinese style finished with a thin ponytail at the nape. The elite displayed fashion accessories with flair, tying paper fans and rigid hand fans to belts in the Chinese style. Shinto priests adopted a ritual outfit consisting of a deep-sleeved silk robe and black skullcap.

In the 700s, during the Nara period, the Yoro Clothing Code instituted Chinese apparel as the obligatory silhouette, which wrapped from the left side to the right. The tight torso of the sleeveless *happi* (short tabard) contrasted a flared peplum, often made from Chinese cottons. Women added a stylized apron to their kimonos. Shoemakers curved the rectangular shape of men's shoes to suit women's feet. From China, traders imported wood hairstyling sticks, tortoiseshell combs, and metal pins graced with beads.

After 894, Heian artistry incorporated feminine sensibilities to fabric and color combinations in layering garments. With its open neck and corded wrists, the ramie or silk *hitatare* (short jacket) paired with the *hakama* (billowing culottes) for a light outfit or night wear. Women left their hair uncut and unbound in a long, straight fall. Batiked attire incorporated cherry blossoms and chrysanthemums on cummerbunds. Officials favored the over-robe, a linen or hemp tunic with wide sleeves garnished with the *kamon* or *mon* (round emblem), a common heraldic cipher. For leisure, the small-sleeved unisex *kosode* fit like a T-shirt.

In the Kamakura period from the 1180s, militarism defeated the previous centuries of sensitivity to texture and style and enforced utilitarianism. Clans adorned their warriors with tartans and the colors of leaders. Under feudalism, farmers recycled rice straw into hats and *zori* (thong sandals) to complement the unisex kimono. Wood-soled geta with double straps posed on two blocks, lifting feet out of the mud.

After the resumption of court decadence during the Muromachi period in 1392, men protected bare toes with home-quilted silk slippers

Like many other aspects of Japanese culture and tradition, clothes making in its most refined form—represented by this eighteenth-century gold silk kimono with dragon motif—rises to the level of artistic expression and spiritual contemplation. *(DeA Picture Library/ The Granger Collection, NYC—All rights reserved)*

and winter *tabi* (split-toe socks) for wearing with thong sandals. At home in the *genkan* (foyer), adults removed heavier shoes and put on *uwabaki* (slippers), clean, light-colored flats suitable for walking on *tatami* (grass mats) without damaging them. Women lengthened their robes and pulled panels over their heads for veiling.

Fifteenth-century brocade bags bore an *omamori* (talisman), a protector of the bearer from danger and an assurance of peace and prosperity in love and business. The introduction of cotton spinning and weaving gave rural women a domestic duty that grew into a cottage industry. The soft folds of cotton fabric supplied an intriguing shift from hemp homespun, which Japanese clothiers had woven since prehistory. The agrarian poor, who lacked the cash to buy new garments, recycled old cotton clothes into work pants, jackets, and vests.

During the Momoyama period, a time of unification and renaissance in the late sixteenth century, Japanese fashion accessorized creative combinations of color and texture for the sleeveless warrior robe and the *dofuku,* an ankle-length robe common to the wardrobes of monks, tea masters, and elderly males. An emerging commercial class flaunted the leisurely *dobuku* (over-jacket), an open coat made from damask and silk patchwork worn over loose trousers and garnished with velvet on narrow lapels.

After 1600, during the Edo period, women stressed waxed hairdos. The stylish shaved the hairline and garnished buns, knots, wings, and loops with sticks, combs, ribbons, and blossoms. Hairpieces gained favor with the wealthy and as costume elements of Kabuki and Noh theater. Around 1615, Japanese tailors sold separate pockets that attached to sashes with a *netsuke* (toggle). Advanced technology developed cut velvet, a valuable trade commodity and luxury fabric for the imperial court.

In the 1750s, during the sober Tokugawa period, official dress codes maintained vassals' subservience to lords by outlawing extravagant apparel. The strictures tightened to prevent the *chonin* (artisanal and merchant class) from adopting the opulent dress of the samurai. Details of Japanese dress codes forced farmers to wear wood clogs with cotton thongs or bamboo or straw sandals rather than the leather sandals of their social superiors. Rural females had to adorn their hair with bone or wood combs rather than the ivory combs, silk bands, or tortoiseshell combs of urban women.

Modern Multiculturalism

By the 1840s, exports of the Japanese national costume—handmade kimonos tied with obis—influenced English and North American leisure wear. Upon the opening of Japan to Western trade in 1854, Japanese consumers adopted elements of European attire, especially boots. After the introduction of the Singer sewing machine at Yokohama in 1860, Japanese dressmakers and tailors increased productivity by replacing embroidery with mechanized stitchery. Peasant consumers popularized the fitted fisherman's coat made from indigo cloth.

After 1870, the Industrial Revolution and Meiji Restoration inspired Japan's entrepreneurs to abandon feudalism and venture into sericulture and the cotton market. Students at government-sponsored schools began dressing in sailor suits, the required class uniform. In 1871, 60 students joined 48 administrators and scholars on the Iwakura Mission, a two-year diplomatic and industrial modernization tour that included manufacturing, weaving, and dyeing facilities in Western Europe and Scandinavia, Egypt, the Middle East, Vietnam, Hong Kong, and China.

Modernization also meant Westernizing the silhouette. The Roaring Twenties influenced Japanese women to emulate Americans by bobbing their hair. The decline of rayon in 1939 influenced Japanese industrialists to make foundation garments, baby shoes, and swimwear out of nylon.

In occupied Japan after 1945, the younger generation admired American officers in off-duty preppy ties, button-down shirts, and blazers. Western apparel began replacing traditional wrapped outfits and slip-on sandals for street use, home, weddings and funerals, and office. In 1985, Japanese factories revived nylon sportswear and added no-iron polyester to leisure attire.

In the twenty-first century, Japanese couture took on an international flair with touches of tradition, as with the flowing trousers in pantsuits by Chitose Abe. In April 2013, Kenzo and Miuccia Prada revived blossom designs with print fabrics outsourced to Chinese factories.

See also: Ethnic and National Dress; Livery and Heraldry; Miyake, Issey; Orientalism; Robes.

Further Reading
Dalby, Liza. *Kimono: Fashioning Culture.* New York: Vintage, 2001.

English, Bonnie. *Japanese Fashion Designers: The Work and Influence of Issey Miyake, Yohji Yamamoto and Rei Kawakubo.* New York: Berg, 2011.

Fukai, Akiko, Barbara Vinken, Susanna Frankel, and Hirfumi Korino. *Future Beauty: 30 Years of Japanese Fashion.* London: Merrell, 2013.

Slade, Toby. *Japanese Fashion: A Cultural History.* New York: Berg, 2009.

Jewels and Jewelry

A virtually endless variety of jewelry has enriched the human wardrobe from prehistory. Ancient burial objects featured amulets, solar discs, prayer beads, pendants, cameos, necklaces, armlets and anklets, friendship rings with precious stones, and jeweled hairpins—all adornments that readied the departed for the afterlife. As accessories, jeweled buttons, hairnets, ribbon ornaments, peacock fans, parasols, and purses enhanced female individuality and allure.

Jewelry making began with appreciation and veneration of nature, as evidenced by the fly-shaped pendants on Egyptian necklaces and simple shell pendants worn by the Neolithic Tuareg of the Sahara. A Mixtec hunter's success gave jaguar claws status when laced on a thong. In a humanizing gesture recapitulated in religion and myth everywhere, Hindu worshippers dressed statues of the divine being Krishna in seasonal apparel and jewelry. In the Andean region, the pre-Inca honored their dead with emerald beads.

Archaeological finds have reclaimed the artistry of past jewelry makers around the world—jade earrings from third-millennium B.C.E. China, Bhutanese and Tibetan *dzi* beads made from agate after 2000 B.C.E., and Olmec jadeite from Belize around 1600 B.C.E. Ancient Egyptian styles include cloisonné (vitreous enamel) inlaid with lapis lazuli and turquoise, such as a piece interred in 1397 B.C.E. with the remains of Senusret II and the royal collar and crown buried in 1323 B.C.E. with Tutankhamen. Intaglio surfacing, an innovation in jewel carving, developed in the Indus Valley as early as the 1300s B.C.E. Nubian gold crafting from 450 B.C.E. outfitted buyers in Meroë with gold finery.

Functional Adornments

Literal linchpins of Greek and Roman fashion, the brooch and fibula (safety pin) secured draped attire at the shoulder, a daily part of donning the Greek chiton or himation and the Roman tunic or toga. Roman girls wore a leather or metal *bulla,* a protective Etruscan-style locket containing amulets and suspended on a thong or chain. Boys received a ring with a phallic symbol for luck.

Young men acquired a signet ring, an iron, bronze, or gold band with figures or symbols carved on gemstones in low relief. The stone bore

an abbreviation of the owner's name and clan. By pressing the ring into warm wax, he could seal documents and scrolls with the pictographic equivalent of a signature. Signet rings passed through the male line as tokens of family and clan heritage.

Byzantine jewelry consisted of decorative chains, pendant earrings, and the intaglio ring, a flat gemstone or gold surface engraved with a design or figure in reverse relief, cameo style. In 325 C.E., the Emperor Constantine chose the Christian cross as a royal emblem. After 527, the Empress Theodora commissioned a full imperial parure, including a jeweled collar illustrated by her portrait on a mosaic in Ravenna, Italy. By the twelfth century, ornate buckles and chains contributed to the manly Byzantine costume.

Spanish conquistador Hernán Cortés's first glimpse of Maya adornment in 1519 revealed split tongues and lips, piercings, and labrets. Throughout the North American Great Basin, Great Lakes, and Mississippi Valley, Amerindian tribes traded protective fang and claw amulets, Cahokia hematites, and silver and turquoise bracelets, rings, and necklaces, which formed the basis of Navajo dowries. Rapid proselytizing introduced indigenous peoples of the Western Hemisphere to the Catholic rosary, an adornment similar in style to pagan pendants.

At the execution of England's King Charles I in 1649, Puritan zealot Oliver Cromwell melted state jewelry and sold the stones to finance the British Commonwealth. Upon the restoration of Charles II in 1661, royalists honored the returning king with buttons, rings, and crests featuring his likeness. Long after Puritan denunciation of finery, seventeenth-century embellishments included the lorgnette, eyeglasses on a handle that garnished both hands and eyes. More jewelry than refractors, lorgnettes became the forerunners of opera glasses, another device displayed like an accessory.

Commodities

Beginning in the 1830s, Victorian haberdashers outfitted businessmen with a limited array of gold jewelry—cuff links, a tie bar or tie pin for the cravat, and a pocket watch and fob linked across the waistcoat with an Albert chain, named for Queen Victoria's husband. Late nineteenth-century treasures included the filigreed and iridescent bangles and brooches of René Lalique, a designer of naturalistic *arts décoratifs*. At the other end of the economic spectrum, mail-order catalogs from Montgomery Ward and Sears, Roebuck in 1888 pictured watches, decorative fountain pens, and jewelry at bargain prices.

In the early twentieth century, the design of the wristwatch made timepieces less bulky and more functional. As civilians replaced their heirloom pocket watches with strap-on wrist models, the vest had less purpose in three-piece suits. Men's campus jewelry favored fraternity pins and monogrammed cigarette cases, a preface to the crests they would wear as adult members of the Masons and Lions, Rotary, and Optimist clubs.

Amid the cataclysmic social and economic changes wrought by World War I, beaded apparel and jewelry gained opprobrium as a privilege of the wealthy. In the 1920s, shimmying flappers favored hinged pendants that moved with the Charleston and black bottom. Coco Chanel, a feminist couturier of the 1930s, featured one-of-a-kind diamond jewelry set in platinum, a formal embellishment for her classic "little black dress." In Soviet Russia, Communist control of artisans forced the sale of handmade jewelry into the underground market.

Mid-century female accessories coordinated well with sack dresses. Hippie jewelry of the 1960s gave prominence to beads and peace symbols along with granny glasses, hoop earrings, Gypsy bangles, and tagua nut necklaces from Bolivia and Ecuador. In the 1980s, cable television merchandisers such as the Home Shopping Network and QVC aired a constant stream of advertisements for mail-order jewelry and accessories, usually consisting of imitation gems and rhinestones.

The early decades of the 2000s increased the investment value of retro jewelry, such as vintage screw-back earrings, amber or coral necklaces, and silver charm bracelets. Teenagers exchanged trendy pre-engagement and promise rings. Aficionados of antiques chose the rhinestone evening collar and sequined bag as accessories for twenty-first century formal wear.

See also: Accessories; Amulets; Beads and Beading; Body Piercing; Club and Organizational Attire; Crowns and Tiaras; Monogramming; Royal Attire.

Further Reading

DeMello, Margo. *Encyclopedia of Body Adornment.* Westport, CT: Greenwood, 2007.

Hesse, Rayner W. *Jewelrymaking Through History: An Encyclopedia.* Westport, CT: Greenwood, 2007.

Phillips, Clare. *Jewelry: From Antiquity to the Present.* New York: Thames & Hudson, 1996.

Tait, Hugh, ed. *7000 Years of Jewelry.* Richmond Hill, ON: Firefly, 2008.

Jewish Religious Attire

Jewish ritual dress codes have varied over time to satisfy dictates of period interpretation of scripture. Initially, Hebrews displayed unassuming apparel according to the dictates of Exodus 19:6, which pictured adherents as "a nation of priests and a holy people." Adaptations to ritual dress have included removing shoes before entering synagogues for thrice-daily prayers, tucking a red thread around the wrist or neck as protection against the evil eye, and wearing conical hats, turbans, and head cords. These variances reflected pre-Islamic Arabic influence.

In accordance with Deuteronomy 22:5, ancient Hebrew men wore linen robes styled uniquely for males. Observant males bound their garments with a gartel, a corded belt or tasseled sash, which separated the mind and heart from the rest of the body. Men never tattooed their skin or dyed their hair as women did. Women typically bathed in a mikvah (ritual bath) and wore a veil in the style of Rebecca before her marriage to Isaac in Genesis 24:65. Married women adopted long sleeves, high necklines, and scarves or wigs in accordance with the gendered demands of rabbinic times.

For morning prayer, males over age 13 obeyed Exodus 13:16 and Deuteronomy 11:18 by binding the forehead and upper left arm adjacent to the heart with *tefillin* (or phylacteries), cubical leather boxes containing fundamental scriptural verses written on parchment. The upper-arm strap extended around the forearm, palm, and fingers. Scriptural experts approved the boxes as evidence of God's presence among sober, humble adherents.

Since 1800 B.C.E., men have worn the cotton, wool, or silk tallit, a ritual prayer shawl striped with dark blue to epitomize reverence. (The Torah forbade blends of linen and wool.) During Hebrew bondage in pharaonic Egypt around 1520 B.C.E., the exclusion of Israelites from communal activities encouraged the development of uniquely modest attire. Such wardrobe customs as covering the head and torso set Jews apart from their more daring bare-chested enslavers and discouraged assimilation in faith, language, and appearance.

A detailed view of Aaron, the high priest of Israelites during the flight from Egypt, pictured him in a priestly turban. According to Exodus 28:31–35, he covered his undergarments and sleeveless floor-length tunic with an embroidered linen breastplate topped with four rows of 12 carved gemstones. Gold chains fastened the breastplate to an ephod (sleeveless apron). A twined linen sash and ornamented robe completed the ritual attire.

Readers of the Torah and cantors at the ark covered their heads and shoulders with the tallit. In obedience to Numbers 15:38, since 800 B.C.E., shawl makers tied the four corners with eight blue and white strands knotted five times into *tzitzit*

(fringes), symbolic representations of the legs of mammal skins. In Roman times, Jews wore the tallit, tefillin, and tunic in place of the toga, the obligatory uniform of male Roman citizens. Around 200 C.E., Jewish women distinguished themselves in Carthage by veiling their faces.

Adaptations

Medieval and Renaissance apparel displayed the fabrics and styles of the times, thus rooting out the traditions of an ancient desert people. Social boundaries established by Pope Innocent III at the Fourth Lateran Council of 1215 stipulated that Jews, like Muslims, should distinguish themselves from Christians by distinctive dress, including the Jewish round cloak. In Aragon in 1300 and Portugal in 1350, Jews had to wear red or white badges. In the 1400s, Jewish women emulated Islamic women in adopting the face veil and head covering to inhibit sexual allure, a violation of family honor. During the forced conversion of Iberian Jews in the fifteenth century, the devout wore ritual garments in secret.

In the sixteenth century, Algerian Muslims forced Jews to wear black sandals or shoes, a requirement that continued in Tunisia into the 1800s. Only wealthy Jews with connections at

For morning prayer recitation, Jewish adult males wear the tallit (striped ritual prayer shawl) and *tefillin,* or phylacteries (two small boxes containing scriptural text), attached to the forehead and left arm with leather straps. *(Photofusion/UIG via Getty Images)*

court could flout anti-Semitic dress codes. In Venice, a Jewish circumcision ensemble featured cotton needle fringe and pink velvet on taffeta gown, bonnet, hose, shoes, and cushion cover, an example of European extravagance violating Hebraic humility.

Rabbinic debate in the 1500s and 1600s questioned the observance of ancient customs regarding head coverings. For everyday wear, Jewish men traditionally capped the head with a cloth, leather, or knitted *kippah,* or yarmulke, as a reminder that God is always above humankind. Over the skullcap, orthodox males pulled the *tallit katan,* a rectangle opened in the middle with a hole for the head, and tied it around the waist. Gifts of tallits marked weddings and bar mitzvahs. Temples offered shawls for guests and visitors.

In the eleventh century, women began wearing the tallit. In Safed, Israel, in 1563, however, Rabbi Yosef Karo, compiler of the Code of Jewish Law, began restricting females from wearing standard male worship attire.

To separate devout from secular practice, Orthodox cantors and rabbis adopted the austere dress of Eastern Europe from the 1700s. In the 1800s, rabbinical students tended to grow their beards and hair long and, after marriage, to dress in black pants and coat with a white shirt over linen underwear. Rabbis and cantors favored the academic robes of university professors, a practice later replaced by conservative suits, vests, and ties. Hasidic rabbis added a black hat over the kippah.

Anti-Semitism worsened in the twentieth century, when non-Jews targeted Jewish clothing and appearance. In the 1900s, the Moroccan Jewish minority had no choice but to abandon ritual garments. In 1911, the playwright Shloyme Ansky and writer Isaac Leib Peretz surveyed Eastern European Jews in Volhynia, Poland, and Poldolia, Ukraine, to observe clothing, jewelry, and customs in the remnants of medieval and Renaissance Jewry. Their ethnographic study determined that Judaism had strayed from its cultural roots.

Modern Jewish Attire

Observant Jews today retain much of their ancient attitude toward humility, but most accept that ancient dress codes were meant as temporary guidelines. The Hebrew Israelites of West Africa deck themselves in African print tunics, tallit, and kippah. African women observe modesty with long dresses. In addition to the tallit, Ashkenazic (Germanic) married men attend evening prayers in a hand-stitched, pocketless *kittel* (tunic), a white linen garment replicating the priestly apparel of ancient times.

During a wedding ceremony, the kittel serves as a groom's garment symbolizing the beginning of a family. A tallit may cover the groom and his veiled bride as a ritual canopy. For the leader of the Seder (Passover dinner), the white tunic represents the flight from bondage into freedom. For communities wearing the kittel on Rosh Hashanah, the white tunic indicates the cleansing of sins.

As a *tachrich* (burial shroud), the kittel covers the face of the dead, and a sash secures the shroud. The white garments exemplify blamelessness and ensure the humility and equality of corpses that have undergone ritual purification. The tallit with one fringe removed wraps the corpse for burial as a symbol of the commandments. Hungarian Jews place the covered head on a pillow filled with soil from Israel, the traditional Hebrew homeland. Orthodox believers reject embalming, autopsies, and cremation as an affront to the body, the housing of the soul.

In duplication of the sorrow of the patriarch Jacob for his son Joseph and of David for King Saul, mourners display grief by rending a shirt, vest, or jacket that the wearer has cut on the left lapel over the heart. Non-Jewish customs have added the display of a torn black ribbon, armband, or tie and the covering of mirrors. Men cease to cut their nails, hair, and beards. Women avoid scent, hair coloring, and cosmetics.

See also: Coming-of-Age Attire; Priestly Attire; Ritual Garments.

Further Reading

Donnin, Hayim. *To Be a Jew: A Guide to Jewish Observance in Contemporary Life.* New York: Basic Books, 2001.

Katz, Steven T., ed. *The Cambridge History of Judaism.* Vol. 4. New York: Cambridge University Press, 2006.

Ochs, Vanessa L. *Inventing Jewish Ritual.* Philadelphia: Jewish Publication Society, 2007.

Jones, Robert Edmond (1887–1954)

Theatrical designer Robert Edmond Jones revolutionized American stagecraft in the first half of the twentieth century with expressionistic, mood-evoking sets, dramatic lighting, and costume designs integrated to enhance staging and the actor's craft.

A native of Milton, New Hampshire, Jones was born on December 12, 1887, to piano teacher Emma Jane Cowell and farmer Fred P. Jones. Acquiring a taste for language, music, and art from his maternal grandmother, he taught school to pay his tuition at Harvard, where he played violin with the university orchestra and sewed costumes for the drama club. From 1910 to 1912, he remained at his alma mater as an instructor of fine arts and developed skill at selecting colors and fabrics for theatrical costumes.

After small design jobs in New York City left him dismayed, Jones moved to Berlin in 1913 to apprentice under modernist stage master Max Reinhardt at the Deutsches Theater. Returning to the United States at the outbreak of World War I in Europe, Jones involved himself in improvisational directing and costume and set design in Massachusetts for the Provincetown Players, where he formed a professional relationship with dramatist Eugene O'Neill.

From age 28, Jones specialized in classic comedy and tragedy as well as musicals, opera, black folk plays, and Serge Diaghilev's Ballets Russes. Jones devised a gray set to contrast the comic checkerboard hat and tunic appliqué for Anatole France's adaptation of *The Man Who Married a Dumb Wife* (1915), a French folk farce. The following year, Jones marshaled a palette of pure color for the 300 costumes of 1,500 performers in the masque *Caliban,* which featured mimes in classic tunics, velvet boots, and oversized hats and ponchos draped with ribbons.

Jones excelled at integrating stage lighting, costume, props, and set for an impression that enhanced the overall atmosphere and tone. Notable in this regard was his assemblage of Gothic details for Vaslav Nijinsky's 1916 production of *Til Eulenspiegel,* a satiric folk ballet featuring tall medieval hats. Grotesque costumes blazed with color—lime-green tights and hot pink horned headdress over an orange robe with royal blue apron, floor-length red sleeves, and an orange jester's cap.

In 1920, the designer turned costume drama into a cohesive painting both alive and evocative in its scope. With the aid of his wife, voice coach Margaret Carrington, Jones showcased John Barrymore in *Richard III* as a monstrous king in an oversized robe. The scenic feast featured the tall veiled headdresses of Queen Elizabeth of York and her ladies-in-waiting. For *Macbeth* in 1921, Jones constructed huge abstract masks to complement an ominous set. In 1927 and 1928, he gained renown for his designs for the American Opera Company, which performed Goethe's *Faust* on Broadway at the Gallo Theater. The success of the Broadway comedy *See Naples and Die* (1929) depended on the effect of his costumes for Claudette Colbert.

Jones's mature work in the 1930s and 1940s included the Hollywood color film *Becky Sharp* (1934), in which the blue and green uniforms of the Napoleonic wars give way to officers in red, a symbol of wrath and blood. In 1932–1933, he contributed period costumes for actors Brian Aherne and Katharine Cornell in Thornton Wilder's adaptation of *Lucrece.* For the 1933 staging of Maxwell Anderson's *Mary of Scotland,* starring Helen Hayes and Helen Menken, the stage wardrobe established a contrast between the self-adulating Queen Elizabeth in a lace collar and pearls and Mary, garbed in black with a white cap and silver cross.

Jones is best remembered for angel robes and burlap garments and head rags for God and slaves in the Old Testament stage classic *The Green Pastures* (1930). The visual impact prefaced successes in the one-act ballet-legends *Pocahontas* and *Billy the Kid* (1939) and the debuts of Eugene O'Neill's *Mourning Becomes Electra* (1931), *Ah, Wilderness!* (1933), and *The Iceman Cometh* (1946). For a 1938 reprise of Anton Chekhov's *The Seagull,* Jones created color-blocked costumes for Sydney Greenstreet, Uta Hagen, Lynn Fontanne, and

Alfred Lunt. The designer's contribution to Marc Connelly's *Everywhere I Roam* (1938) involved a complex set of clothes for actors Anne Francis, Dean Jagger, and John Arthur Kennedy in a biographical play about Johnny Appleseed.

Jones received a nomination for the Donaldson Award for the tunics, doublet, and hose he designed for actors Uta Hagen and Paul Robeson in a 1943 revival of *Othello.* In 1946, the designer won the Donaldson Award for Mary Martin's stage wardrobe, featuring dominant Chinese red, in the musical *Lute Song,* a fourteenth-century folk drama. Jones died of cancer on November 26, 1954.

See also: Costume Design, Theater.

Further Reading

Black, Cheryl. *The Women of Provincetown, 1915–1922.* Tuscaloosa: University of Alabama Press, 2002.

Jones, Robert Edmond. *The Dramatic Imagination: Reflections and Speculations on the Art of the Theatre.* 1941. New York: Routledge, 2004.

Pendleton, Ralph. *The Theatre of Robert Edmond Jones.* Middletown, CT: Wesleyan University Press, 1958.

Klein, Calvin (1942–)

A perfectionist innovator in jewelry and no-frills sportswear, formal attire, and underwear, designer Calvin Richard Klein invigorated American fashion in the 1970s and beyond by supporting the active lifestyle of both women and men.

Born on November 19, 1942, in New York City to Austro-Hungarian immigrant grocers Flore "Flo" Stern and Leo Klein, he became a fashion trendsetter in kindergarten and operated his own sewing machine in boyhood. He learned basic tailoring from his seamstress grandmother, Molly Stern, and began sketching original women's dresses and suits in his early teens.

Klein studied at the Fashion Institute of Technology in New York City on scholarship but found the curriculum tedious. At age 20, after serving *Women's Wear Daily* as a copy boy, he apprenticed in tailoring with coat designer Dan Millstein, who introduced him to haute couture in Paris. By 1966, Klein was miserable at the task of sewing Dacron dresses and eager to start his own business.

With entrepreneur Barry K. Schwartz, on April 4, 1968, he put the Calvin Klein Limited label on six urban coats and three shifts at a small shop at the York Hotel in Manhattan. The company's first sale to Bonwit Teller launched a women's wear empire featuring gold lamé caftans, peasant tops, slim-ankled slacks, and Persian pants. Klein followed with ready-to-wear blazers and lingerie, a coatdress available in printed patterns, and, in 1970, high-waisted gaucho pants with nail-studded vests.

Klein's creation of skinny jeans in 1974 made him a household name among chic teens shopping at 12,000 stores nationwide. By 1975, his brand appeared in the *Prominent Designer Book* as

well as on the sleeves of T-shirts. Klein menswear featured hooded terry battle jackets over white pants. His choice of handkerchief linen in muted adobe, slate, and oatmeal befit evening gowns with matching shawls, which he detailed with faggoting and tucks.

Klein's jackets, culottes, hunting coats, and wrap skirts in gabardine and corduroy, blouses in challis and silk, and slip-dresses in crepe de chine, cashmere, and charmeuse flourished from features in newspapers, *Harper's Bazaar,* and *Vogue.* For men, he stressed relaxed, wearable leisure wear in knits.

In 1979, he exploited denim on dancer Twyla Tharp's troupe and on 15-year-old model Brooke Shields, whom Richard Avedon photographed in a seductive setting. Within a week, customers snapped up 40,000 pairs of Klein's designer jeans. The success of his jeans campaign made him America's first celebrity designer.

By selecting Kate Moss to model his briefs, Klein retained a natural look free of glamour and cosmetic surgery. He maintained concern for the consumer by promoting serge and Qiana jersey in place of silk, which the market overpriced. In July 1979, he jolted the fashion world by rejecting the Coty Award for promoting commercialism over creativity.

After debuting snazzy denim baby diapers in 1980 and women's briefs, bikinis, panties with flies, and boxer shorts in 1982, Klein created a market for unisex underwear. By 1983, as fashion turned to glitz, the designer advanced classy cashmere sweaters over wool flannel slacks, straight midi skirts, and flat-heeled suede boots. In France, China, and Qatar, the Klein label began appearing on hosiery, swimwear, sunglasses, shoes, and belts modeled by Christy Turlington and favored by first ladies Nancy Reagan and Rosalynn Carter and actors Goldie Hawn, Helen Hunt, Bianca Jagger, Gwyneth Paltrow, Sandra Bullock, and Julia Roberts. In the 1990s, Klein pushed the demise of the jacket and tie for men by legitimating the T-shirt as serious business wear.

The stagnation of jeans sales caused Klein to rekindle sensuality in his advertisements. Provocative billboard and media photos by Herb Ritts, Stephen Meisel, and Tiziano Magni of models Antonio Sabàto, Joel West, and Mark Wahlberg from July to November 1995 elicited criticism of Klein from President Bill Clinton, First Lady Hillary Clinton, and the Catholic League. A Justice Department investigation of child pornography yielded no formal charges, but bad publicity forced Klein to pull suggestive underwear ads from circulation.

A show of his menswear at Milan Fashion Week in 1998 began a decade of positive representation in the European mainstream. In 2001, he turned heads with a matte silk dress slit to the thighs over ankle boots and a sleeveless silk tissue shift with demi-hood.

In mid-December 2002, Klein retired and sold his business, which earned $6 billion per year. His honors include the 1980 Bath Museum of Costume Dress of the Year, three Council of Fashion Designs of America awards, three Coty American Fashion Critics citations, America's Best Designer of 1993, and an honorary PhD from his alma mater.

See also: Advertising; Fashion Design; Undergarments.

Further Reading

Calvin Klein. www.calvinklein.com

Cody, Matt W. *Calvin Klein*. New York: Facts on File, 2011.

Dakers, Diane. *Calvin Klein: Fashion Design Superstar*. New York: Crabtree, 2011.

Marsh, Lisa. *The House of Klein: Fashion, Controversy, and a Business Obsession*. Hoboken, NJ: John Wiley & Sons, 2003.

Knitting and Crocheting

Two ancient technologies, knitting and crocheting enabled a crafter to turn yarn into blankets, edgings, or garments without the use of a loom.

From 6500 B.C.E., varieties of yarn manipulation in Egypt, the Andes, and Judea preceded the aligning of rows or circles of interlocking loops through the interaction of two or more hand-operated needles or a single hook on a frame, a craft perfected by Yemenite sailors and North African Berber cameleers. Both knitting and crocheting advanced clothing with the creation of springy, contoured gloves, caps, and socks comprised of air pockets that absorbed perspiration while retaining body warmth.

After 300 B.C.E., the Paracas and Nazca peoples of southern Peru devised a single-needle circular netting of camelid hair and cotton for making edgings, hats, mantles, and shrouds. From 300 C.E., Chinese corpses went to their tombs with knitted braids. In the 600s, Egyptian Copts, trained by Arab knitters, applied a similar knotless craft to the knitting of sandal socks. A subsequent name for the technique, *nalebinding* or "Viking knitting," derives from the Danish for "needle binding," a method similar to a buttonhole stitch.

In 711, Arabian traders and Moorish artisans introduced silk netting in Iberia that showcased the crossed stocking stitch in silk and gold or silver thread. Christian knitters applied Arabic stitchery to altar gloves for Spain's Catholic worship. Late in the eighth century, Charlemagne, king of the Franks, preferred wool trousers over long linen drawers and knit hosiery, a flexible leg covering for horseback riding. Under the Abbasid dynasty in Persia, from 750 to 1250, crafters knitted cotton string or strips of rag into *giva*, humble, leather-bottomed house slippers.

Global Needlework

Medieval travelers carried knitting skills to distant lands. Middle Eastern knitting techniques reached England following the First Crusade (1097–1099). A popular war souvenir, the stretchy wool *jorab* (sock) worn with slippers in Azerbaijan offered relief from boots and leg armor. Into the 1100s, the Spanish forged metal needles for yarn workers in Belgium, Flanders, and Italy to turn English wool kersey into leg-to-groin stockings or parti-color hose.

Throughout the Middle Ages, convent knitters

provided the priestly gloves for ritual in white, gold, purple, or red silk, colors dictated by the liturgical calendar. Medieval Egyptian stylists at Fustat, the first Arab capital outside Cairo, looped a toe-to-calf shape to which they added a solid, easily replaced heel. They also varied colors by the intarsia process, which inlaid a new shade of yarn to create a pattern.

In the late medieval period, home crafters in Iberia, Belgium, Germany, Scandinavia, Holland, Switzerland, and France turned knitting into a cottage industry. By the late 1400s, French knitters had formed guilds to superintend the production of gloves, hosiery, snoods, and coifs, a head-to-shoulder protector. As the handicraft spread to Slovakia, Russia, and Hungary, institutional knitting by forced labor in orphanages, prisons, workhouses, and barracks put the idle to work. Knitters in Iceland and the Faroe Islands created patterns for mittens and the lopi sweater, a wool pullover with circular yoke that established an island folk tradition.

In 1589 in Nottinghamshire, England, William Lee invented a knitting machine to speed the work previously done by some 200,000 hand knitters. Crochet continued to thrive in schools for the poor throughout Great Britain and in Italian convents, earning the name "nun's lace." Nordic gloves achieved artistry among the Danes, who stitched rings on the fingers of knitted gloves. On the Shetland Islands, knitted hosiery promoted trade with Dutch sailors and Hanseatic merchants. Christian missionaries in India introduced yarn-working skills to a new populace. In Japan after 1603, Dutch, Portuguese, and Chinese sources passed stockinette methods to women in Nagasaki.

Evolving Needle Arts

Colonial American knitters specialized in stockings and gloves of silk, wool, or cotton. In 1759, the women of Germantown, Pennsylvania, knitted 60,000 pairs of stockings. In colonial towns and cities, children's footwear consisted of ribbed knit socks or thigh-high hosiery and soft kidskin shoes. Crocheting may have evolved in this era in the decorative arts of India, Persia, and Turkey

from chain lace or tambour embroidery, a looping technique involving a bone, wood, metal, or ivory hook.

Home crafts became a female means for the Daughters of Liberty to subvert the Stamp Act of 1765, which taxed imported goods. To clothe the Continental Army, knitting and sewing circles formed by Martha Custis Washington visited military camps to distribute hosiery and raise spirits. To supply yarn in the North American West, women raveled old sweaters, wound the yarn into a skein or ball, and used it for knitting and crocheting projects that relieved tedium and brightened wardrobes. Frontier needlecrafts protected children from the brutal winter cold of the Great Plains and added a touch of beauty to the edges of petticoats and cuffs.

Handicraft patterns first reached print in 1824 in the Dutch magazine *Pénelopé,* which debuted patterns for "shepherd's knitting," a Scots term for the crocheting of gaiters, hats, baby shoes, dickies, and belts out of wool or leather lacing. The income from Fair Isle sweaters, knitted lace, and fishermen's sweaters enabled impoverished Irish families to survive the 1845 potato famine and to afford passage to the United States, Canada, and Australia. Queen Victoria popularized Irish crochet and Shetland Island lace by wearing gifts of collars and delicate pelerines, the only adornment she added to her mourning wardrobe after the death of Prince Albert in 1861.

Scots and Irish knitting, tatting, netting, and crocheting took root among boarding school students learning the womanly arts. Latvian and Lithuanian immigrants to Australia and New Zealand bore with them the colors and forms of traditional yarn work, which schoolchildren produced for charity. In Central Africa, European immigrants taught local girls to knit chin straps to secure traditional headdress.

On the advice of domestic mavens Lydia Maria Child and Catharine Beecher, American women in the mid-1800s pursued a beneficial hobby that recycled used fiber. *Godey's Ladies' Book* and *Peterson's Magazine,* sources of patterns for the nubia (scarf), glove, slipper, collar, cap, fascinator (headscarf), beaded reticule, and stocking, promoted home knitting and crocheting as appropriate skills for refined ladies.

Yarn handicrafts supplied abolitionist charity fairs and closets that outfitted runaway slaves and warmed Union troops during the Civil War. Mary Anna Custis Lee, the wife of Confederate commander Robert E. Lee, knitted socks and scarves for rebel soldiers. Similarly, in Japan, the Samurai adopted Western military clothing and knitted their own gloves and *tabi* (socks).

World War I spiked the demand for navy and khaki socks, sweaters, balaclavas (head and neck covers), mufflers, and helmet liners, which volunteers produced for the Red Cross and 4-H clubs and at a 1918 fund-raiser sponsored by the New York City Navy League. After the armistice, women adorned themselves with the lacy crocheted edging they applied to underwear and handkerchiefs. Craft suppliers provided crochet handles with interchangeable hooks of amber or bone, a boon to Chinese knitters in Shanghai.

World War II mustered new knitting circles and introduced aluminum crochet hooks devoid of rationed nickel plating. Patterns costing 50 cents each derived from peasant craft centers in Peru, Mexico, Bavaria, Holland, Finland, and Iceland. Skilled needleworkers mastered the double-seed, cluster, wishbone cable, and trellis stiches of the intricate Aran Isle sweater or afghan from the west coast of Ireland and of Greek fishing sweaters from Kos, Corfu, and Rhodes. In Manitoba, depot master Willard McPhedrain established a fiber industry for poor immigrants and set up Mary Maximchuck, an outlet selling their bulky sweaters, slipper socks, bed socks, and caps.

Young mothers during the war produced infant soakers, garments replacing the elastic pants no longer available during the military monopoly on rubber. Teen girls popularized the twinset, a cardigan and short-sleeved sweater in wool, mohair, or Orlon worn as a pair. During the Korean War, American relief agencies promoted "Knit for Korea," an effort to provide warm winter garments for refugees and orphans. World travel inspired more yarn workers, who viewed handwork in progress in distant locales and exhibits at world's fairs.

In the 1960s, English crafter Kaffe Fassett established a career in knit patterns, which he published in *Vogue Knitting Magazine.* A college knitting fad introduced a new generation of women to domestic skills and to the crocheting of granny squares for handbags, afghans, "potholder vests," and shawls. Retirement homes spurred interest in knitting infant booties and caps from novelty fur, a means of reviving links between generations and restoring purpose in the lives of the elderly and handicapped. In Istanbul during the 1980s, consumers created a demand for hand-knit German sweaters. Low-priced imports discouraged Turkish knitters from pursuing handicrafts in traditional female circles, where women typically draped yarn on the back of the neck while walking with children or standing in the kitchen.

Into the 2000s, knitting provided pleasant therapy for male and female convalescents. Designs from Japanese fabric engineer Issey Miyake featured tie-dyed and ombré yarns that reveal variations of shades in the same color family. In 2004, the fad for clapotis introduced knitters to a wave pattern created on the bias to form an open-weave scarf or shawl that conformed to the contours of neck and shoulders. Global knitting and crochet societies continue to communicate by Internet exclusive patterns for unusual fibers and wire, some retrieved from traditional folk accessories and beaded jewelry.

See also: Gloves; Hosiery, Men's; Hosiery, Women's; Knitwear; Patterns; Sweaters; Wool and Wool Products; Yarn.

Further Reading

Kooler, Donna. *Donna Kooler's Encyclopedia of Crochet.* Little Rock, AR: Leisure Arts, 2009.

Leslie, Catherine Amoroso. *Needlework Through History: An Encyclopedia.* Westport, CT: Greenwood, 2007.

Wills, Kerry. *The Close-Knit Circle: American Knitters Today.* Westport, CT: Greenwood, 2007.

Knitwear

Knit fabrics relieve the bulk and strictures of hide, leather, felt, and woven apparel while supplying a source of warmth and evaporation of dampness. The advent of knit stitches introduced a comfortable stretch to garments as simple in shape as Copt sandal socks, Persian house shoes, Berber leggings, Scots clan caps, and infant sacks. More complex styles yielded medieval Baltic five-fingered gloves and bodysuits for adults, the forerunner of onesies for babies.

Since the 1500s, knitwear has been a standard part of everyday dress globally. Styles such as Irish fisherman's sweaters, Spanish hose, Arab macramé shawls, and Fair Isle yoke cardigans have filled a slot in fashion left unsatisfied by woven goods. In part at the promotion of Elizabeth I, guilds controlled the marketing of knitted goods from London, Cornwall, Guernsey, Jersey, and the Orkney and Shetland islands. In 1589, William Lee of Calverton, England, invented a knitting device to speed the production of hosiery. During the Industrial Revolution, machine knitting ended the demand for cottage crafts from Brittany and Norwich.

The utilitarian nature of seventeenth-century Nordic sweaters and wool guernsey or gansey pullovers from the Channel Islands appealed to the European military. From the early 1700s, British and French sailors preferred water-resistant socks and skull-contoured wool caps for cold nights on deck. Prussian soldiers fit knit caps into their pockets for wear under helmets during combat. At home, knits flourished in the female chenille scarf and the man's jelly bag, a silk tasseled nightcap worn by the elderly.

Global Knitwear

During the 1800s in *Punch* and *Spectator,* English clothiers advertised handmade pullovers and cardigans from Braemar, Coxmoore, and Shetland, marketers of luxury lambswool to the British royal family. Travelers introduced knitwear to Indonesia and the Philippines and lace knitting in the Shetland Islands. In the United States during the 1830s and 1840s, *Godey's Lady's Book* and *Peterson's Magazine* published patterns for hand-knit flowers, collars, gaiters, bead-knit evening bags, muffs, victorines, and baby layettes, home projects promoted by *Godey's* editor Sarah Josepha Hale.

In the mid-nineteenth century, an innovation by trapeze artist Jules Léotard eased the skin-tight wardrobe of circus performers at the Cirque Napoleon in Paris. Knit on circular needles, the full-body stocking earned the name "leotard," which became the standard torso garment of aerialists and dancers. The sale of contoured garments extended to rib-knit booties and undershirts for crib babies, soldiers' balaclavas during the Crimean War (1853–1856), and cuffs on snowsuits to ward off cold and damp at the neck, wrists, and ankles.

Early twentieth-century European catalogs listed Aran Island homespun apparel, Pringle cashmeres, banded cotton sweaters, open-seat drawers, and bias-cut knit couture, which freed the body for gardening, dance, lawn tennis, campus activities, and contact sports. According to a 1913 ad in *Cosmopolitan,* women's "porous" union suits from Avalon cost 50 cents. At the French seaside resorts of Deauville in 1913 and at Biarritz in 1916, designer Coco Chanel liberated women from constricting corsets and boned bodices by introducing crewneck *marinières* (sailor pullovers) and tricot jersey travel suits consisting of boxy jackets over pleated skirts. In 1927, Italian couturier Elsa Schiaparelli lightened skiwear with knit panels.

Advertising seized on the image of knits as healthful family essentials. Children played in knit drawers, sweaters, bonnets, berets, and tams. Milliners contributed the knit turban. In the 1930s, nylon and rayon yarns strengthened the gauge of knitted swimwear, men's leisure vests, women's snoods, and intimate wear and hosiery for adults and children. In 1934, Boy Scout stockings featured quality woolen knitwear to harmonize with olive uniforms.

Western fashion photography during World War II pictured men's Jockey briefs, women's knit earmuffs and chubbies (toppers), and sweater girls Jane Russell, Carole Landis, and Lana Turner in revealing garments shaped from clingy yarn. Post–World War II women's wear introduced sweater sets, string knit gloves, and formfitting suits for the office, a trend that returned Italian folk crafters to commercial production. Utilitarian coat sweaters appealed to older men, while men's and boys' Robert Bruce sports sweaters featured washable nylon and elasticized shoulders, a necessity for golfing and shooting.

During the postwar baby boom, knit creepers freed infants from stiffer fabrics and encouraged early crawling. Girls' knit T-shirts emulated male versions. The strapless knit swimsuit required an elasticized back and bust wiring to secure the top.

The Knit Industry

American and Western European teens in the 1950s reveled in the freedom of popcorn knit sweaters, Lastex T-shirts, locknit sports jerseys, watch caps, structured swimwear, and zippered catsuits, elements of a mix-and-match wardrobe that accommodated spur-of-the-moment activities. Emilio Pucci turned actor Marilyn Monroe into a "sweater girl" with his contoured knit shifts. Christian Dior advanced cashmere knits to beaded evening garments featured in *Vogue.* Designer Oleg Cassini outfitted screen stars Grace Kelly, Suzy Parker, and Nancy Kwan in knit suits and twinsets, the coed's favorite for displaying fraternity jewelry from beaus.

In January 1953, *Jet* magazine touted knit suits as the answer to the traveler's packing problems. Marks & Spencer marketed medium-priced men's stockinette ties and sleepwear shaped from polyester, Orlon, and viscose Marspun yarn. The addition of perky collars and leather buttons and belts punched up designs. For shape, Formfit in 1957 advertised a line of panties and girdles designed to be invisible under high-fashion knit fibers.

In 1960, Yves Saint Laurent defeated the coat-and-tie stereotype with the knit turtleneck and black leather jacket. Trends in the decade favored British model Twiggy in A-line knit skirts and teens in factory-knit cable kneesocks paired with matching mittens and caps for winter, a style invented by manufacturer William F. Paine of Godalming, Surrey, in 1907. Children and adults popularized ribbed knit undershirts and briefs as well as high-style Italian Ban-Lon sweaters by Leonardo Strassi. American designer Bill Blass revived the market for hand-knit raglan pullovers and V-neck sweaters paired with tweed jackets and casual slacks.

In the 1970s, couturier Gianni Versace and Mirsa of Milan sharpened the style of Tuscan bias-cut fabric, elevating knits to luxury weaves. U.S. designers Calvin Klein and Liz Claiborne favored less bulk in cowl-neck sweaters, which anchored women's pantsuits and added a gracefully draped collar to the lines of blazers. The exercise craze raised demand for tank tops, leg warmers, and compression shorts and tights for cycling, skating, yoga, Jazzercise, and aerobics.

In the 1980s, Lurex added glitz to yarn for knit disco dresses and crop tops available in metallic tones and bright colors. Late-century Tencel microfiber further varied texture, elasticity, and weight for intarsia suits, sports shirts, sports bras, and winter wear. Dress-down Fridays in the 1990s admitted to business attire the knit polo shirt for men and zippered cardigans and knit-waist pants for women. For beachwear and water sports, designer Anne Cole initiated the amphibious tankini for adults and children.

In the 2000s, Florida entrepreneur Sara Blakely profited from the debut of Spanx, footless pantyhose that spawned niche marketing in men's and women's "shapewear." To replace fur, Vera Wang chose slubbed yarn for shrugs to wear over evening dresses. Runway shows featured knit neck warmers, Canadian ruanas, unisex whole body zentai suits, and thigh-length sweaters with fur-lined hoods. Retro men's knits revived argyle sock and vest patterns and campus letter sweaters. In 2013, Lenzing, a global knitwear firm based in Austria, debuted MicroModal, a sustainable fiber made from birchwood pulp and added to cotton for soft, lustrous knits.

See also: Hosiery, Men's; Hosiery, Women's; Knitting and Crocheting; Sweaters; Wool and Wool Products.

Further Reading

Chapman, Stanley. *Hosiery and Knitwear: Four Centuries of Small-Scale Industry in Britain, ca. 1589–2000.* New York: Oxford University Press, 2002.

Conway, Henry, and Gail Downey. *Knit Couture: 20 Hand-Knit Designs from Runway to Reality.* New York: Macmillan, 2007.

Strawn, Susan M. *Knitting America: A Glorious Heritage from Warm Socks to High Art.* Minneapolis, MN: Voyageur, 2007.

Knockoff Fashions

The copying of styles and labels steals the creativity of clothing and robs designers and manufacturers of profits on innovative garments. Key to such exploitation, ill-paid laborers in India, Korea, Malaysia, and China toil at intricate stitchery that sells for top prices in Western markets.

In June 1870, 75 male Chinese strikebreakers whom industrialist Calvin T. Sampson shipped by steamer and train to North Adams, Massachusetts, turned print fabrics into copies of European fashions. Their pay, 8 cents per hour, cost factory owners less than half of wages paid to indigenous employees.

Because U.S. copyright laws omit fashions from legislation that protects literature, art, music, and cinema, knockoff marketers feed the frenzy for the latest in skinny jeans, running shoes, purses, and Navajo moccasins at a discount. Thus, clever clothing thieves can photograph a fashion show and replicate garments with cheaper fabric and inferior trim within weeks of their presentation without having to pay taxes or invest in advertising.

Only apparel sold under such registered brands as Prada, Aeropostale, American Eagle Outfitters, and Abercrombie receives the protection of U.S. laws against counterfeit. Under the Lanham Trademark Act of July 5, 1946, copiers of fashion labels on knockoffs perpetrate trademark infringement and false advertisement or fraud. Enforcement of the legislation in the 1960s helped Chelsea designer Mary Quant pursue imitators of her Wet Collection, rainwear made from polyvinyl chloride (PVC). In the 1970s, the satiny sheen of warp-knit nylon proved useful in production of counterfeit intimate wear.

A subsequent U.S. law, the Trademark Counterfeiting Act of October 10, 1984, criminalized the bootlegging of federally registered apparel or footwear, an ongoing practice that costs U.S. fashion houses Louis Vuitton, Gucci, Rolex, Omega, Levi Strauss, Tommy Hilfiger, and Tiffany billions of dollars in revenue every year. Because federal law applies only to the United States and its territories, knockoff specialists in other countries advertise their illicit goods with impunity and ship by mail directly to the American consumer, thereby bypassing border controls.

Under the 1984 regulation and additional acts in 1996 and 2007, complainants began seizing "fabulous fakes" and suing for treble damages to compensate for loss. U.S. Customs and Border Protection inspected carriers of imported goods and alerted manufacturers of suspect logos. In April 2010, customs agents confiscated $260 million in bogus clothing and accessories. Meanwhile, in 2006, Internet software called RegMarkMonitor began scrutinizing global trade to intercept fakes mailed from overseas suppliers and to penalize traffickers in phony merchandise.

Exploiters of fashion work quickly to market unlicensed replicas, as with Kate Middleton's Alexander McQueen wedding dress from April 2011, and First Lady Michelle Obama's Michael Kors jacquard dress worn on election night 2012. The speedy copying of must-have styles in countries offering low-cost labor makes haute couture available to the public at affordable prices. By flooding fashion outlets with replicas, style pirates hurry the demise of a trend and thereby prepare the way for new concepts.

Another diversion of profits results from gray marketing or parallel marketing, such as the transport of luxury jewelry and watches from a low-price market to a high-end locale, where the market price is higher. The major volume of gray market apparel comes from China, Malaysia, and India and passes through mass-market retailers such as Costco, Amazon, eBay, Kmart, and Alibaba. One fashion house, Christian Dior, devised a distribution scheme to equalize pricing worldwide and end the gray marketing of its apparel.

See also: Labels; Ready-to-Wear.

Further Reading

Jimenez, Guillermo C., ed. *Fashion Law: A Guide for Designers, Fashion Executives, and Attorneys.* New York: Fairchild, 2010.

Raustiala, Kal, and Christopher Sprigman. *The Knockoff Economy: How Imitation Sparks Innovation.* New York: Oxford University Press, 2012.

Thomas, Dana. *Deluxe: How Luxury Lost Its Luster.* New York: Penguin, 2007.

Korean Clothing and Fashion

The Korean wardrobe, one of the world's most conservative, for centuries has featured a loose jacket and pants for men and a bell-shaped silhouette for women. From 3000 B.C.E., Neolithic Koreans scraped animal pelts and stitched them into garments using bone needles threaded with fur or strands of hemp, which flourished in the north. Shells and stone formed the earliest amulets and accessories. Animal fangs strung on waist ties attested to the virility of male hunters and attached to children's clothes to protect them from evil.

Around 300 B.C.E., peasants developed a national costume from the combination of a women's shirt and full wraparound skirt tied over a petticoat and a men's shirt and billowing trousers. Both shirts tied at the upper right chest with bodice strings. Royal dynasties of Old Choson, ensconced in walled cities, displayed their pomp in robes, bronze buckles, and crowns. Emulating Chinese affectations, Korean priests dressed in ceremonial attire and directed prayers heavenward with wafts of hand fans.

As early as the Silla period after 57 B.C.E., Koreans in the southeast dressed in a forerunner of the traditional unisex *hanbok* (a square, bolero-style jacket and long skirt), which they padded for warmth. They adapted the loose shape from the attire of nomadic Manchurian horsemen, who needed nonbinding garments for their active lifestyle. Like Han Chinese fashions dating to 1600 B.C.E., Korean hemp kimonos wrapped at the waist with a tie. Complex jewelry, belts, crowns, and rings contrasted the simple, monochromatic outfits.

Folk Dress

For warmth and foot protection, the Korean national costume included the unisex *beoseon*, short socks padded with fiber lining and tied to the ankle. A unisex braid kept men's hair in a topknot and women's hair in a manageable nape ball or knot; a hairpin made of bamboo, coral, or jade secured the female style with one horizontal thrust from right to left. Mothers tied quilted infant carriers to their upper torso for warmth and stability. Upon the child's first birthday, parents provided the first hanbok and a cylindrical hat. For mourning, women dressed in hand-woven hemp for attending and shrouding the corpse in loose hempen folds.

Families stored their ceremonial garments, accessories, headdress, combs, mirrors, and sewing supplies in distinctive chests. Compartments, shelves, and drawers suited to each item preserved female legacies. The chest remained in the women's quarters as a symbol of the female role in outfitting the family.

Under King Gogukcheon and Queen U of Goguryeo after 179 C.E., Korean affluence impressed the Chinese Han. Through a series of tax levies, the elite were able to afford furs and silks and to garnish cylindrical caps and ceremonial crowns with precious metals. In 194, the king took pity on poor rural Koreans and, during planting season, advanced them grain and clothing from the public treasury at Goguryeo in north-central Korea.

Under King Beopheung of Silla after 514, citizen dress codes regulated the attire for a hierarchy of 17 castes and their horses. Color classification reserved purple for nobles, red for bureaucrats, and blue for commoners. During the seventh century, the interlocking *taegeuk* (great absolute) cipher, like the Chinese *taiji* (yin-yang), symbolized on slipper heels and taekwondo uniforms a cosmic balance of artistry and gendered powers.

Later in the 600s, folding and collapsible umbrella technology from China's Tang dynasty reached Korea, supplying a product for artisans to add to national commodities. In the eighth century, textile buyers clustered the shores of the Yellow Sea to purchase cotton yard goods from Chinese junks arriving from Denzhou. Under Manchurian influence of the Liao dynasty (Khitan Empire) in the early 900s, Koreans admired Khitan leather crafts and lamellar armor. Korean men added a Manchu robe and long jacket to their traditional dress.

While males gravitated toward hyper-masculine styles, Korean females retreated into delicacy and artisanal fabrics. Noblewomen dressed up for

A South Korean woman models a richly embroidered *hanbok*, the traditional national dress for both women and men. In a revival campaign launched in 1996 by the culture ministry, Koreans were urged to wear the hanbok on the first Saturday of every month. *(Linda Grove/Getty Images)*

rituals and weddings in an elaborate red gown fitted with long cylindrical sleeves embroidered with blossoms and lucky symbols. A detachable neckband protected bodices from wear.

A Textile Economy

Around 1123, according to Chinese encyclopedist Seo Geung, the Goryeo queen adorned state apparel with fashionable knots, multihued tassels, embroidered butterflies and tigers, and heirloom jade baubles and citron perfume cases tied to a waistband. In a break from imitating Chinese textiles, mid-twelfth-century weavers developed unique Korean sericulture. By 1200, Korean fabric merchants competed openly against Chinese dealers.

After Korean diplomat Mun Ik-jom hid cottonseed in his pipe to smuggle from Yuan (southeastern) China in 1363, eager fabric specialists invented a ginning device and spinning wheel. From cotton, Koreans developed a new textile industry as well as a source of fiber for padding. Prosperity enabled women to tie gold bells to their sashes with ribbon and to perfume ensembles with incense-filled sachets.

Under the rule of King Taejo of Joseon after July 1392, a budding technocracy reformed agriculture on the peninsula. The cotton economy produced military uniforms as well as goods for export to Japan and a form of currency. Aristocrats of the Yi dynasty forced commoners to become self-sufficient by growing cotton and hemp and making their own apparel. Nobles reserved for themselves the best ramie from Hansan and patterned silk graced at the hem with gold leaf, all designed and stitched by the Bureau of Royal Attire.

A surplus of cotton fabric during the fourteenth century yielded skirts and tunics paired with unisex trousers modeled on the Chinese attire of the Ming dynasty. Korean men topped the customary hanbok with a cylindrical black hat attached to a wide brim. Women adopted round silk caps garnished with ornaments or wore bulky wigs weighing up to about 9 pounds (4 kilograms). Yain raiders from the north supplemented their semi-agricultural economy with commodities stolen from Choson until Yi forces subdued them.

Fifteenth-century Korean dress introduced a unisex winter cap of quilted flannel open at the crown and decorated with ribbon, fur, braid, strings of beads, and a front tassel. The cap, which developed silk earflaps for warmth, became the traditional gift to baby girls on their first birthday. In the 1600s, knife makers supplied women with decorative blades for tucking into waistbands. More prominently, jade, cloisonné, gold, or silver *norigae* (pendants) attached to bodice ties.

Under King Yeongjo and Queen Jeongsun after 1724, Korea's cotton economy supported the nation with textiles for domestic boutiques and river trade and for export to China and Japan. The king's attire at lavish court ceremonies included grand dragon medallions on his state *dopo* (robe) and a tall crown. His neo-Confucianism imposed restraint on Korean wardrobes, beginning with the downsizing of men's hats. Women abandoned fur neckpieces; in place of wigs, they wore simple, unornamented silk caps.

Foreign Influence

Western attitudes infiltrated Korean wardrobe in 1870, when people began to wear imported European dresses and suits. Under a program of social reform in 1894, the government promoted utilitarian dress as a necessity of modernization. The Emperor Gojong gave up red robes and his pleated black crown for a Prussian military uniform with forearms covered in braid, an East-to-West transformation also adopted by Crown Prince Sunjong. Schools abandoned the red color code for students and instituted white shirts with black slacks.

At the height of the Industrial Revolution, Korean investors purchased *sha* (gauze) and *tuan* (satin weave) produced by steam power for use by clothiers. Increasing Japanese colonization after 1900 forced Koreans to rely on imported clothing, gloves, thread, and yarn. Grudgingly, Korean patriots adopted Japanese dress.

After World War I, Koreans invigorated their textile industry with influxes of capital and a nationalistic label. Military factories echoed Soviet uniform styles with padded coats and pants, shoes, snow hats, and mittens. Female fashions revealed a bare midriff between a Zouave jacket and petticoats above Turkish pants. In the 1930s, kimonos made from synthetic fibers relieved women of ironing chores.

Upon the Japanese surrender to Allied forces on August 15, 1945, Koreans dressed in traditional hanboks and proclaimed liberation in the streets. Rayon factories in Pyongyang flourished with the production of unisex trousers and slippers and natural-fiber kimonos. Cities across the peninsula welcomed European boutiques, including retailers of Louis Vuitton leather wallets, handbags, and luggage. In 1954, Korea's pioneer stylist, Nora Noh, arranged the nation's first fashion show at the Chosun Hotel in Seoul.

Following the devastation of the Korean War, the United States in 1956 aided South Korea's economy with gifts of flour, sugar, and cotton. After the fall of President Syngman Rhee in 1961, the dictatorship of Park Chung Hee suspended South Korean contributions to world fashion. While citizens suffered at home from low incomes and loss of self-sustaining farms, heightened industrialization yielded abundant ready-to-wear clothes, shoes, and wigs for export.

In the 1970s, a time of globalization for major European designers, South Koreans bought the accessories and perfumes of Yves Saint Laurent. Foreign influence reduced the traditional hanbok to a rare ceremonial dress of mostly rural folk. In the 1980s, South Korean factories competed at the production of Western wear by lowering overhead to 0.5 percent on the production of leather athletic shoes, Velcro®, and T-shirts.

In North Korea during the 1990s, when the distribution of blankets, sports clothes, shoes, and taekwondo uniforms as well as sewing machines failed to meet the needs of the population, socialist government managers responded to the nation's apparel failures by bureaucratizing the industry. By the end of the century, textile magnates profited from rising global demands for patterned and ombré ribbons for sashes and head wraps. For workers, Vinylon, a synthetic domestic textile made from anthracite and limestone, supplied the material for standard gray uniforms copied from Mao suits.

In 1996, a hanbok revival movement urged people across Korea to wear the national dress on the first Saturday of every month, much as the Japanese took renewed pride in displaying the kimono and Chinese tunics in Hanfu style. At the Orangerie in Paris in July 1996, South Korean designer Lee Young Hee presented hanbok fashions featuring Empire lines and bell skirts on evening gowns, afternoon dresses, and high-low cocktail apparel. In place of luxury fabrics, Korean factories began mass-producing inexpensive hanboks sold in department stores.

In the twenty-first century, amid ongoing economic mismanagement, North Koreans continued to receive socks, underwear, and winter clothes from international aid agencies or purchased ready-to-wear on the Chinese border from the black market. Ethnic Koreans living in Japan dispatched millions of dollars per year to impoverished North Korean relatives. The physical shortcomings of Vinylon, the fiber on which North Korea built its textile industry, proved to be a crippling economic setback for the nation in the early 2000s.

A further setback came in April 2013, during a surge in political tension with South Korea, when the Pyongyang regime barred the entry of plant managers and other workers from the south to a jointly run clothing manufacturer and other factories in the Kaesong Industrial Region along the border, forcing a cessation of output.

See also: Ethnic and National Dress; Orientalism.

Further Reading

Chung, Young Yang. *Silken Threads: A History of Embroidery in China, Korea, Japan, and Vietnam.* New York: Harry N. Abrams, 2005.

Lee, Kyung Ja, Na Young Hong, and Sook Hwan Chang. *Traditional Korean Costume.* Folkestone, UK: Brill/Global Oriental, 2005.

Yang, Sunny. *Hanbok: The Art of Korean Clothing.* Elizabeth, NJ: Hollym, 1997.

L.L. Bean

A niche brand of day wear and authentic sport clothing based in Freeport, Maine, L.L. Bean succeeds at retail, mail-order, and Internet sales under a money-back guarantee. Since 1912, the company has internationalized the logo of sportsman Leon Leonwood (or Linwood) Bean into the largest specialty mail-order house in the United States.

Bean learned everyday low-price retailing by working in the shoe store of his brother Otho. With the aid of a cobbler and the United States Rubber Company in Boston, Bean invented a rugged hunting boot by sewing a laced, 7.5-inch (19-centimeter) tan elk leather top to a waterproof rubber sole and vamp, which he field-tested in New England winters. Bean's initial four-page catalog focused on consumer service to the hunter, fisher, camper, and hiker by a staff of mostly retired hunting and fishing guides and game wardens. He retailed the boots by parcel post from the cellar of Otho's clothing shop to holders of out-of-state hunting licenses. Because the "Bean boot" satisfied only 10 of his first 100 customers, the designer returned the cost to 90 disgruntled purchasers. With a $400 loan from his brother, Bean fixed the problem of cracked soles and ripped uppers with triple stitching.

On Main Street in Freeport, Bean opened a store in 1917 and continued inventing sports gear, such as the safety hunting coat, which made hunters more visible to other hunters, for sale to outdoorsmen who visited the site. Catalog covers pictured men in realistic poses in the field and around campfires in knit caps and rumpled felt hats, canvas field jackets, laced boots and waders, and rain capes. Into the 1920s, Bean's all-wool socks, driving sweater, and boot dressing solved difficulties for the outdoorsman and wilderness motorist. In 1924, he introduced the duck hunter's field coat with sewn-in mittens and, four years later, the chamois shirt. His line increased with wading boots, hunting knives, and creels, but he rejected cushy eiderdown coats as wasteful.

Advancing ethical sales principles, Bean aimed to provide a needed service to hardy outdoorsmen and the consumer recreation market, such as his sheepskin innersoles to keep the feet dry and comfortable. At his third-floor factory, visitors could observe the production of moccasins, loafers, boots, and slippers through the soling, lining, and lacing stages. By 1937, Bean, dubbed the "Merchant of the Maine Woods," recorded $1 million in sales.

Bean aided the Pentagon during World War II in developing sturdy clothing for combat troops. In 1942, he issued *Hunting, Fishing, and Camping,* an introductory manual to outdoor sports. Chapter 12 listed the types of apparel necessary for deer hunting: moccasins and leather-top rubber boots, wool socks, union suit (one-piece long underwear), wool pants and coat with game pocket, red plaid shirt, reversible deer and duck cap, wool gloves with strips of leather on the fingers, and red bandannas for visibility, plus rain shirt, sweater, suspenders, and heavy belt. For camping, he added a sleeping bag and canvas knapsack. In 1954, Bean pioneered women's departments in his stores to cater to female customers.

In 1965, Bean's grandson, businessman and conservationist Leon A. Gorman, expanded the line by petitioning consumers for suggested additions to the catalog. From man-made fibers, Gorman touted the Hercules Olefin thermal sock at $2.50 a pair to replace two versions of discontinued cotton camp socks. At the death of the founder in 1967, Gorman began a 34-year run as company director, accelerating growth by 20 percent with database mailing and credit card service at an enlarged flagship store.

Gorman's appeal to buyer loyalty included items manufactured to custom size, such as with triple E–width hunting shoes and extra-long jackets, and the repair of leather footwear and canvas goods, which he mailed postage-free. By 1969, he tempted male and female hikers with a serious, high-quality hiking boot. A popular satire of the company catalog and style, Lisa Birnbach's *The Official Preppy Handbook* (1981), boosted L.L. Bean sales by 42 percent.

In 1988, Bean began selling discontinued merchandise at a liquidation outlet in North Conway, New Hampshire. He opened 28 additional outlets along the Atlantic Coast as far south as Williamsburg, Virginia; he also expanded north to Canada and west as far as China and Japan. The online site, debuting in 1995, spread marketing.

In 2001, Christopher J. McCormick, the company's head of marketing, replaced Gorman as company chairman, pushing catalog offerings to well-to-do sports enthusiasts. The addition in 1999 of the Freeport Studio line of designer goods for suburban women between 35 and 55 at first received a tepid response. But the line began to grow as female shoppers ordered functional A-line wrap skirts, comfortable Fair Isle and Norwegian sweaters, and a loosely cut alpaca-lined walking coat. Perhaps because Web-based images and listings sported more accurate color and descriptions, the Freeport Studio catalog made its last appearance in January 2002.

Subsequent years brought further innovations. The company added a traveler's line that featured jewelry organizers, shoulder bags, and wallets, and in fall 2010 launched a signature town-and-country series specializing in upbeat fabrics, hip sportswear, soft denims, madras shirtdresses, linen blazers, and buffalo plaid shirts for young adults. In 2011, facing a retail slump, the company instituted free shipping, a hedge against competition from Cabela's, Land's End, Orvis, and Bass Pro Shops. The catalog continued to grow with additions of fleece sportswear, Scots plaid flannel shirts, bush pants, tackle vests, boat mocs, robes and sleepwear, corduroy shirtdresses, blazers, multipocketed warden's jacket, barn coat, chinos, Shetland sweaters, and swimwear.

See also: Catalogs, Clothing and Fashion; Hunting and Fishing Attire; Mail Order.

Further Reading

Aaker, David A., and Erich Joachimsthaler. *Brand Leadership: Building Assets in an Information Economy.* New York: Simon & Schuster, 2000.

Gormon, Leon. *L.L. Bean: The Making of an American Icon.* Boston: Harvard Business School Press, 2006.

L.L. Bean. www.llbean.com

Labels

The marketing of name brands and signature styles dates to the rise of the mass consumer economy in the West during the nineteenth century. Around 1803, London tailors began touting upscale Savile Row shops by sewing trademarks on the inside of bespoke menswear. In 1852, Zhao Chunlan, a U.S.-trained tailor in Shanghai, made Western suits and jackets and reshaped out-of-date garments, which he marked with the original logos.

Paris couturier Charles Frederick Worth introduced the first designer label in fall 1857; in 1871, he introduced a new label from his signature, C. Worth. Louis Vuitton, meanwhile, chose the LV insignia for merchandise presented at the Exposition Universelle of 1867 in Paris. In 1906, dressmaker Lucy Duff-Gordon began marketing gowns, skirts, and lingerie internationally under the Lucile Ltd. logo. French dressmaker Jeanne Lanvin followed in 1909 by identifying her original women's and children's attire, the oldest fashion line still in existence. In the late 1980s, during the early years of capitalist-style entrepreneurship in China, Yin Meng became the nation's first private fashion label.

Department stores—Macy's and Lord & Taylor in the United States and Marks & Spencer in Great Britain—cut costs by distributing competitive fashion lines of underwear and children's clothes under the store brand. After

World War II, as the French attempted to regain national market share by boasting of their fashion primacy, Simone Pérèle placed the So French signature on handmade Parisian bras. At the same time, Pierre Balmain placed his name on original fashions.

By 1947, consumers could identify Christian Dior's "new look" with authentic labeling. The merchandising of distinctive styles encouraged the appearance of high fashion labels—Mary Quant in 1955 and Bill Blass in 1959. In rapid order, labeled fashions appeared under Cristóbal Balenciaga in 1960, Yves Saint Laurent in 1961, Issey Miyake in 1964, Oscar de la Renta in 1965, Halston in 1966, Polo in 1967, Calvin Klein in 1968, and Giorgio Armani in 1973.

In the 1960s, Balmain diversified European couture by selling fashions carrying the Jolie Madame logo to American stores. Quant adopted the same strategy with the Ginger Group line. Saint Laurent enhanced his marketing presence with new labels, YSL and Rive Gauche. Liz Claiborne surveyed shifts in fashion in the late 1980s with a computerized inventory that detailed the appeal of various lines marketed under the Ellen Tracy, Russ, Lizwear, Lucky Brand, Lizsport, and Juicy Couture labels.

Wedding dress niche marketer Vera Wang customized her label in 2004 to Simply Vera. In 2009, the Gap broadened its chain recognition with the sale of Banana Republic, BabyGap, GapKids, GapBody, GapScents, Forth & Towne, Athleta, and Piperlime fashions. In 2012, Marc Jacobs spearheaded a revolt against global goods merchandised under counterfeit labels, particularly Gucci and Burberry leather bags and Rolex and Omega timepieces.

See also: Couturiers; Fashion Design; Knockoff Fashions; Symbolic Colors, Patterns, and Motifs.

Further Reading

Hancock, Joseph. *Brand/Story: Ralph, Vera, Johnny, Billy, and Other Adventures in Fashion Branding.* New York: Fairchild, 2009.

Kendall, Gordon T. *Fashion Brand Merchandising.* New York: Fairchild, 2008.

Tungate, Mark. *Fashion Brands: Branding Style from Armani to Zara.* 3rd ed. Philadelphia: Kogan Page, 2012.

Lace and Tatting

Since the Renaissance, extravagant openwork in Western couture has permeated luxury fabrics and folk costume with airy filigree. The ancient Chinese and Egyptians improvised basic forms of knotting or string work for ritual costume. During the eighth century B.C.E., Phrygian women in Anatolia used a variety of tools—needle, shuttle, crochet hook, hairpin—to form cocoon fragments into *oya,* an edging popular in the Aegean region. Prospective brides won respect from future mothers-in-law by adorning elements of trousseaus and offering gifts of meadow scenes tatted (a lace-making technique involving knots and loops) in bright colors.

An outlet for imaginative design, a frame method called *lacis* involved the division of a grid into netting, a pattern of knots in use in the late 1200s in Western Europe. Lace making for mantillas and livery insignia flourished in the 1300s in Catalonia, sometimes with the use of gold or silver thread. Patterns advanced from rectangles to hexagons, a standard shell for internal webbing.

Lace in Apparel

Lace reached a height of artistry in Europe during the Renaissance. The looping, braiding, knotting, twining, and honeycombing of cotton, silk, linen, and metallic threads yielded flexible strips, trim, and insets for yokes, neck cloths, flounces, lappets, ruffs, piccadillies (broad collars), falling bands, cuffs, fans, and parasols. Less common materials involved stitchery with horsehair and straw.

Folk lace and cutwork graced Czech, Finnish, Hungarian, Belgian, Tunisian, and Irish apparel. In Cyprus, the Greek islands, and Turkey, Armenian *bebilla* (knotted lace) involved finger weaving and knotting into a sturdy filigree that resisted raveling. The method evolved from the decorative netting made by seamen for drawstring reticules.

Slovenian lace from Idrija involved the working of ribbon into mazes, a style similar to Russian lace for its meandering pattern. Maltese producers favored the equal arms of Maltese crosses. At Pag,

Croatia, fantasy edgings called "white gold" trimmed blouses and triangular headdress. Danish *hedebo* (cutwork) emphasized triangles, ladders, and wheels in satin stitch. In England, makers of Battenburg lace gathered tape into patterns for light filling.

In 1493, an inventory of the Sforza estate in Milan made the first accounting of lace as a wardrobe investment. The household of Elizabeth I of England in 1560 refers to a collection of partlets (front yokes) as models of Tudor filigree designs. In Cogne, Italy, strips of lace took shape on a drum, hoop, or pillow. At Cluny in France, weighted bobbins of wood, bone, or ivory maintained tension on each linen thread for sturdy, even stitches called tallies.

Mesh Lace

By the 1580s, fine dressing called for needle-and-thread technology that emerged from intricate Italian hand netting called *reticella* (mesh) and *Pottenkant* (pot lace), a stylized cap lace from Flanders featuring classic urns. Explorers in South America valued *nanduti* (webbing), shaped like palm leaves by the Guaraní of Paraguay. The people of Ceará, Brazil, learned a similar style, which they shaped on pegged circles on boards.

First cataloged in Venetian engraver Cesare Vecellio's book *Corona delle nobili et virtuose donne* (*Crown of the Nobles and Virtuous Ladies,* 1591), artistic patterns adorned precious garments, particularly ecclesiastical gowns and cottas, bridal veils, night wear, and infant dresses and slips. The producer drew threads from transparent linen to create a lacy geometric matrix over-sewn with buttonhole stitches in thread and gimp (cording). Popular star, rosette, ice crystal, and snowflake patterns in bas-relief centered handkerchiefs, which concluded in a framework of *merletti* (scallops), picots (loops), or *dentelle* (projections).

Seventeenth-century advances in *point de Venise* (Venetian needle lace) produced swirls, feathers, ferny tendrils, and floral designs featured in oil portraiture of royalty and aristocrats. Mythic elements—unicorns, griffons, deities, constellations—raised the price of handwork, often produced by convent labor. Colonists to the New World established lace making from Ipswich, Massachusetts, to Richmond, Virginia. In southern France, John Francis Regis, a Jesuit priest, became the patron of lace makers by evangelizing young peasant girls and convinced them to abandon prostitution and turn to decent industry.

In the 1700s, the braiding of coach lace for servant livery and military uniforms formed a reliable niche in trim commerce, as did the invention of a silk netting machine in Nottingham in 1778.

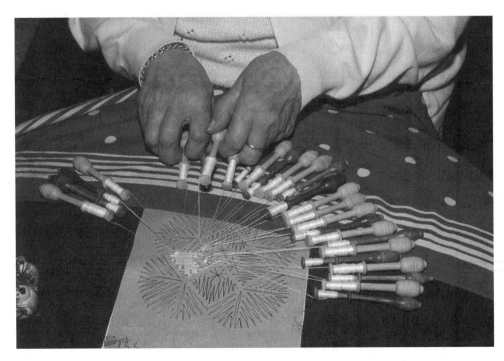

In fine Belgian tradition, a lace maker in Bruges uses multiple bobbins to weave an intricate pattern. Under a decree by Emperor Charles V during the sixteenth century, Bruges and Brussels became centers of the European lace-making arts and textile trade. *(Paul Kenward/Dorling Kindersley/Getty Images)*

England protected its handicrafts with import/export restrictions on lace from France, Italy, and Flanders. The French attempted the same restraint of trade by establishing an Alençon workshop staffed by Italian experts. The resulting handwork, known as tulle lace, remained the world's most sought after until the suppression of extravagance following the French Revolution of 1789.

In the nineteenth century, the French refined Chantilly, a black edging made from Grenadine silk. In northern Italy, knotted *puncetto* (pricking) maintained a simpler style formed of squares. Missionaries in Hawaii and China and on the American frontier taught tatting to indigenous costumers, notably the Oneida in Red Lake, Minnesota, and the Ojibwa and Mohawk in New York.

Handmade vs. Industrialized Lace

English inventor John Heathcoat introduced mechanized bobbin net or pillow lace in 1807, the beginning of the end of costly hand-tatted trim. Irish weaver Samuel Ferguson applied Jacquard technology to circular openwork in 1837. Simultaneous with industrial developments, a folk art called Youghal lace got its start in 1847 when a nun, Margret Smyth of Cork, Ireland, taught impoverished Irish women and girls to fashion a marketable trim that survived laundering.

While haute couture continued to feature Dresden duchesse whitework and Belgian rococo lace on expensive one-of-a-kind garments, recyclers of used clothing turned scraps into lace patchwork. During World War I, Belgian lace makers rewarded Allied troops with war lace, reproductions of unit emblems and coats of arms in filigree. Hobbyists in the 1930s made polka webs and wheels on plastic or wood frames fitted with pegs. In Australia during the 1940s, women popularized tatting as a pastime.

Synthetic lace introduced less costly methods of creating an ethereal filigree for aprons, day caps, and skirts. In Hudson County, New Jersey, in the late 1950s, Schiffli lace, a Swiss innovation produced by Austrian, German, and Swiss immigrants, involved the embroidery of a pattern on acetate. Chemical solvents dissolved the base fabric, leaving behind distinct stitchery, a "burnt-out" look. Other forms of chemical lace applied computerized patterns on fabric surfaces and heat or water to remove the undercoat.

See also: Collars; Elizabethan Styles and Fashions; Embroidery; Sumptuary Laws.

Further Reading

Jay, Hilary, Matilda McQuaid, Carla Bednar, and Nancy Parker. *Lace in Translation.* Philadelphia: Design Center at Philadelphia University, 2010.
Kraatz, Anne. *Lace: History and Fashion.* New York: Rizzoli, 1989.
Levey, Santina. *Lace: A History.* London: Victoria & Albert Museum, 1983.
Montupet, Janine, and Ghislaine Schoeller. *Lace: The Elegant Web.* New York: Harry N. Abrams, 1990.
Raffel, Marta Cotterell. *The Laces of Ipswich: The Art and Economics of an Early American Industry, 1750–1840.* Hanover, NH: University Press of New England, 2003.

Lacing

A classic closure method dating to prehistory, lacing preceded needle-and-thread stitchery as a means of securing hide wraps, chin straps, hatbands, hoods, infant swaddling, and shoes. Hunter-gatherers experimented with babiche (a coil of pocket string sliced from rabbit hide), vines, and roots for complex tying and netting and for securing footbags and fur cloaks. By combining lacing and knotting techniques with hole punching using an awl, Paleolithic tailors in present-day Kostenki, Russia, and Öland, Sweden, fashioned the first body-contoured garments and shoes.

In 5000 B.C.E., Middle Eastern leather and suede workers pierced slits into hide and overcast laces over one-piece footbags called turnshoes. One tanned cowhide shoe from 3500 B.C.E. found in Vayots Dzor revealed how crafters in southeastern Armenia fashioned the first gillie, a tongueless front lace-up shoe. A flexible footbag, the gillie illustrated the variability of lacing to alter fit.

A version of the gillie, the cuaran or pampootie from the British Isles around 3500 B.C.E., laced a raw stag hide around the foot with a twine or leather drawstring passed through slits along the throat and tied for security. The apparel of Ötzi the Iceman, buried in the Italian Alps circa 3300

B.C.E. and recovered in 1991, featured goat-hide leggings laced to the belt and deer-hide shoes over-stitched to bearskin soles.

Over the next 1,000 years, human technology replicated two-stage boots and leggings that tucked into shoes. South Africans made the sturdiest lacings from kudu leather. Hellenistic Greeks varied the Persian sandal with straps laced through the back of the tongue. Egyptians fitted Greek boots with loops through which to pass ties. Both Celts and Egyptian Copts displayed ingenious patterns of knot work or interlacing on metal belt buckles and diadems.

In Rome, senators fitted black straps through slits in the buskin, a low-rise boot. The front panel covered the lacing with a silver or gold crescent. Roman foot soldiers laced open-toed *caligae* (marching boots) to below the knee. To reflect the role of commander-in-chief, emperors chose parade boots laced in the style of infantryman's footwear. In Britain, quartermasters bought Celtic cowhide to supply airy netted caligae, the standard army footwear. Saxons laced boots tightly from toes to ankle and tied the thong securely over the arch.

Early Styles

After 300 C.E. at Agris in west-central France and around 500 at Sutton Hoo, a treasure site in Suffolk, England, disc brooches, a parade helmet, and shoulder clasps displayed interlacing as apparel motifs. The pattern retained its prominence on family coats of arms and military badges, such as the Croatian army insignia. After the First Crusade, European fashions of 1099 introduced the silk or wool crepe Byzantine *bliaut,* the first contoured apparel laced up the torso for use by both genders. The elegant female kirtle (dress), worn over a blouse, accentuated the shape of bust, waist, and hip.

An edict from Pope Alexander IV in 1257 banned extravagant lacings, but the fad for tight corsetry reached a height in 1350. In the early 1400s, civilian men adopted the army jerkin and leg wrap in cheap split sheepskin for everyday dress. For style, they secured lace tips in flashy metal aglets that directed ends into eyelets.

Renaissance church authorities in England, France, Iberia, and Italy declared lacings of shoes, sleeves, servants' livery, and courtiers' codpieces to be proof of exhibitionism. Patterns of passing cording, tapes, ribbons, or laces through holes varied from crisscross, double helix, and latticing to checkerboard, sawtooth, pentagram, train track, and webbing. In the 1500s, pregnant women tied aprons under laced vests and back-vented A-line jackets to conceal their bellies.

Female English riders laced buskins knee high, while men chose dress boots with laces and latchets (straps) that secured the vamp over the arch. Peasants and plowmen wore batts, or low, heavy lace-up brogans. Around 1640, male riders popularized bucket-top jackboots, dashing footwear featuring lacings and spurs. In the next decade, lacing of low-heeled boots gave way to buckles. For riding sidesaddle, women anchored lace-up calf-length boots by thrusting tapered Italian heels into the stirrups. During the same era, the French preferred high heels, broad toes, and suede vamps laced up the ankle.

Eighteenth-century girls' ensembles in Europe and North America featured the laced stays of adults. Women double-laced their ensembles by adding a day bodice, which tied across the front of a habit or blouse. In the mid-1700s, side-laced maternity bodices supported the back and facilitated breastfeeding. Laced kid leather shoes secured toddlers' ankles with front or side lacing. Austrian men popularized cavalier lacing on the broad-brimmed Khevenhüller, an aggressive cocked hat crisscrossed over the peak. French military dress acquired the plumed fur colback, a cylindrical hat laced from ear to ear.

A posthumous inventory of Thomas Lord Fairfax's wardrobe in Frederick County, Virginia, in April 1782 displayed the ubiquity of lacing to garments. His lavish apparel included two brown laced coats and matching waistcoats, laced vest in green silk, an Indian laced vest, and laced waistcoats in blue silk, and green, pink, and scarlet damask. As the popularity of ties increased, the future George IV of England advocated lace-up shoes in 1790. In his honor, cobblers restyled buckled boots with leather shoestrings, the forerunner of the modern shoelace.

Newcomers to the Western Hemisphere discovered the ubiquity of lacing among the Blackfoot, Naskapi, Creek, Ojibwa, and Washakie. Natives laced their apparel with babiche, and connected short pieces with a ring splice. Hopi maidens readied for marriage by lacing their hair into squash blossom–shaped coils over the ears. Cautious frontiersmen packed leather repair kits, which included babiche to replace worn boot, sled, and tent lacing, and netted snowshoes with sealskin thongs.

During the wars preceding the rise of the Emperor Napoleon, men's civilian styles adopted cavalry detailing in Prussian *blüchers* (or derbies) with bellows tongue and open lacing. The variable closure protected marching feet from constriction and swelling. From the Crimean War in 1853 through World War I, cordwainers laced leather tank boots. Outside bivouacs in the 1890s, female camp followers linked prostitution with thigh-high laced leather footwear.

Victorian dressmakers produced the first modern maternity outfits with contoured lacings over the bulging abdomen. In the 1850s, lacing altered the shapeless wrapper into the stylish redingote. The replacement of eyelet holes in boots with lacing hooks or studs in 1865 enabled the wearer to crisscross laces rapidly. The popularity of laced boots, such as the swaggering ankle-jacks of the 1870s, derived from the variability of shoestring configurations and the tightness of fit.

Modern Lace-ups

Into the Edwardian era (1901–1910), lacing remained central to Western fashion. Women supported their breasts with the bust bodice, a camisole laced back and front over a leather or white coutil corset.

In the 1930s, the American outdoor outfitter L.L. Bean manufactured laced moccasins, loafers, boots, and slippers. From 1940 to 1943, American bootmakers upped production by 40 percent to fulfill wartime orders for laced combat boots with a high-top buckled cuff and the fully laced corcoran (jump or paratrooper boot).

In the 1960s, conservative Western men dignified navy or charcoal business and dress suits with the black oxford, which laced over the tongue with a flexible under-web. For relaxing, they popularized the boat shoe, a leather weekender with four eyelets for securing a rawhide thong. The common unisex house shoe, sherpa-lined moccasins with thong lacing around the upper edge, combined the look and feel of outdoor and indoor footwear.

In the 1980s, couturier Gianni Versace and sister Donatella Versace reprised Renaissance flash with a youthful line of high-heeled boots and leather pants crisscrossed from ankle to waist. Teenagers echoed rap and hip-hop fads by wearing Adidas high-tops with the laces untied. In 2001, skinhead groups turned shoelaces into badges of violence, with yellow indicating bullies of Asians, pink for gay bashers, and white as advocates of white power.

See also: Boots; Fasteners; Leather and Suede; Prehistoric Clothing; Shoes, Men's; Shoes, Women's.

Further Reading

Polster, Burkard. *The Shoelace Book: A Mathematical Guide.* Providence, RI: American Mathematical Society, 2006.

Ravilious, Kate. "World's Oldest Leather Shoe Found—Stunningly Preserved." *National Geographic* (June 9, 2010).

Steele, Valerie, ed. *The Corset: A Cultural History.* New Haven, CT: Yale University Press, 2004.

Lanvin, Jeanne (1867–1946)

The inventor of children's haute couture, Jeanne-Marie Lanvin excelled at the refinement of female garments. A leading French couturier in the 1920s and 1930s, she founded the Lanvin fashion house in 1889, which became known for fine perfumes as well as women's clothes.

Born in Brittany, France, on January 1, 1867, to Sophie White and journalist Bernard-Constant Lanvin, she was the first of 11 siblings. At age 13, she received hands-on training from Paris millinery Maison Félix and began designing doll hats to sell to stores. Lanvin learned dressmaking in her early twenties from Parisian dressmaker Suzanne Talbot, who favored fluffy chiffon for hats and parasols.

After marriage to nobleman Emilio di Pietro in 1895 and the birth of daughter Marguerite Marie Blanche two years later, Lanvin studied the bold colors of contemporary artists Odilon Redon and Edouard Vuillard for dress ideas. With a ruffled and sashed wardrobe for Marguerite, Lanvin developed her career at age 42 as a designer of women's and children's apparel blending romanticism with modernism.

Lanvin's distinctive garments, which gained attention in such publications as *La Gazette du Bon Ton, L'Officiel,* and *Vogue,* blurred the line between fashion for girls and women by offering mother-daughter ensembles. A savvy businesswoman, she opened a boutique called the Heart House of Lanvin on the fashionable rue du Faubourg Saint-Honoré in Paris and followed with separate shops for swimsuits, casual wear, furs, lingerie, men's clothes, perfume, and home decor. Her World War I–era designs featured Asian styles in satin and velvet as well as the *robe de style* (chemise) that dominated flapper styles of the 1920s. By 1925, Lanvin employed 800 seamstresses to supply her shops in Biarritz, Cannes, and Nice.

In 1926, at a time when Lavin dressed whole families as well as film stars Marlene Dietrich, Ilka Chase, and Mary Pickford, the French government presented the designer a Legion of Honor for contributions to haute couture. Fashion mavens admired her use of bias cut, pleats, scallops, handkerchief hems, velvet medallions, and Aztec, Coptic, Persian, and Chinese embroidery, which Lanvin collected in a fabric library. In 1935, she presented a classic art deco gown in purple satin, with a slinky shape stabilized by geometric stitching around the collar. A matching cape with a broad shawl collar in ruched purple silk velvet intensified the monochromatic effect.

Lanvin's clean lines translated into patterns from Vogue for day dresses, suits and coats, sportswear and trousers, kimonos, and evening ensembles, such as the green harem pants outfit from 1935 and the black taffeta halter gown she designed in 1939 for her daughter Marguerite. Although World War II constrained her business, she continued making feminine attire in organza and chiffon and detailing sleeves and collars with ribbon, contrasting buttons, lace overlays, couching, and quilting. Her bold architectural lines influenced the 1950s styles of Cristóbal Balenciaga and Christian Dior.

At her death on July 6, 1946, the Lanvin fashion house passed to Marguerite and later to a cousin, Yves Lanvin. The company acquired the company L'Oréal Group in 1994 and the investor group Harmonie S.A. in 2001. Today, it remains the oldest label still active in both fashion design and merchandising.

See also: Fashion Design; French Clothing and Fashion.

Further Reading

Barillé, Elisabeth. *Lanvin.* New York: Assouline, 2007.
Lanvin House. www.lanvin.com
Merceron, Dean L. *Lanvin.* New York: Rizzoli, 2007.

Latino Styles and Fashions

A momentous blend of native and colonial influences, Latino attire identifies an enduring and resilient culture. New World styles limited indigenous fashions to purses woven of lianas, twisted yucca and raffia palm fronds, and banana stems netted by the coastal California Chumash from 2000 B.C.E. From the time of Christopher Columbus's arrival in October 1492, Spaniards in embroidered and braided silks marginalized the pagan natives, often naked and barefoot.

The invasions of Spanish conquistadores after 1519 introduced technically advanced materials and styles to the New World, including the semicircular wool mantle. According to ethnographer Núñez Cabeza de Vaca in 1542, ethnocentric Spanish adventurers congratulated themselves on importing a civilized wardrobe. The conquerors set caste parameters by barring natives and mestizos from wearing lamé, satin, and lace imported from European factories.

Plains Settlers

The pairing of serapes (blanket capes) and pants evolved from Maya and Aztec white trousers and tunics that men wore with leather huaraches or agave or maguey fiber sandals. Along the Pecos River, essentials of the Texas vaquero (herdsman)—bandannas, *tapaderas* (stirrup covers), and leather chaps hardened with horse sweat—shielded the neck from sun and the lower limbs from cactus spines. The sombrero (sun hat) made Plains life more bearable for the Tejano (Latino Texan). Based on a style from Córdoba, Spain, the saucer-brimmed straw hat with chin strap became the standard headdress of mariachi musicians and *charro* (rodeo) riders. Women feminized the look with ribbon, eyelet, feathers, and flowers.

Along the Mexican-American frontier, farm families raised cotton and sheep for clothing materials. Women bought cochineal carmine (*Dactylopius coccus*) imported from Oaxaca and collected yellow mulberry (*Maclura tinctoria*) to color men's short breeches and shirts. Plains riders dressed in cool cottons, long braids, and leather boots. For hard work, women chose low-neck blouses and full skirts accessorized with scarves and leather moccasins similar to those made by the Pueblo peoples of Arizona and New Mexico.

Merger of Styles

In the 1800s, the presence of Asian servants introduced the *china poblana,* a bicultural fashion similar in style to the sari worn by immigrants from India and consisting of a short-sleeved sackcloth *arpillera* (blouse), *rebozo* (shawl), and Mexican skirt. The folkloric costume standardized the white embroidered blouse and slip, a sequined skirt lifted coquettishly at the hem by a loop, a shawl with fringed bobbles, and satin slippers. In the plaza of San Antonio, Texas, cooks at outdoor cafés displayed the china poblana as an enticement to tourists seeking authenticity.

The creolized ensemble, devoid of cosmetics and corsetry, presented an elegant, forthright silhouette of the female form. Low-caste Latinas emphasized the ribbon-tied gown, waist cinch, and bolero jacket; transplanted Spaniards stigmatized North American peasant girls for displaying the shapes of full breasts and hips. In 1843, women in Monterey, California, set themselves above the laboring class with rich dress and severe chignons and buns of hair at the nape, symbols of social and moral control.

Among upper-class female immigrants to New Mexico and Alta California, the *vestidos de dama* (lady's outfit) in luxury materials—the lacy Spanish mantilla, corset, and carved *peinetón* (comb) in bound hair—contrasted the street Latina's functional, unrefined habiliment. Aristocratic girls began training in patrician wardrobe during childhood, when they learned to maneuver the delicate *porta-abanico* (folding fan on a necklace). Expensive ensembles of skirts, petticoats, and high heels served the middle class for Catholic confirmation, weddings, and *quinceañera* (fifteenth birthday) celebrations, a rite of passage featuring teenage girls in ball gowns and womanly hairstyles. Gifts of lockets and religious medals complemented the feminine tiara, a crowning that linked each girl with the regal mystique of the Virgin Mary.

After Spain ceded land to Arizona and New Mexico by the Gadsden Purchase of 1853, American and criollo (ethnically blended) attire gained influence over pure Latino fashions. Dismal carryovers from the Day of the Dead mythos—skeletons in black with white accents over facial bones and howling Lloronas in billowy nightgowns—contributed to Latino film and costume-party fashions. In El Paso, Texas, the exiled *revolucionario* (revolutionary) of the Pancho Villa era modeled the dashing *bandolero* (outlaw) look, romanticized by the unbuttoned white shirt, bolero, and waist sash. Media photos of Villa and his Mexican insurgents after 1910 showed the double *carrillera* (cartridge belt) crossing the shirt.

Post–World War I finery popularized Latino styles in niche markets, such as the rumba bodice (named after the Cuban dance), a ruffled dress or blouse in combinations of black and red as well as pink and yellow. Featuring African details, skirts fastened snugly over the hips and buttocks to dramatize the sexual pantomime of the dance. The tango, a posturing partner dance from Argentina that became a worldwide dance craze in 1912–1913, involved fancy steps, with the woman in a full skirt and her partner in straight-legged trousers. Male immigrants identified ethnicity with the pleated guayabera, standard dress for business and parties.

Modern Latino Dress

Latino apparel underwent decades of influence from European and U.S. fashions and Hollywood film, which stressed the bolero and pants outfit for men and flounced skirts for women. Surviving from Amerindian culture, unisex outfits featured leather huaraches, maguey fiber *ixcacles* (sandals), and the rectangular *huipil,* originally a sashed cotton tunic left open on the sides. Mestizo migrant workers in the U.S. Great Basin and California retained the serape for its convenience and multiple uses, including rainwear and infant wrap.

The Latino media and pin-up posters spiked interest in unique fashions and hairstyles attuned to late twentieth-century urban tastes. *Hispanic,* a lifestyle magazine founded in Florida in 1988, promoted the careers of entertainers such as Penélope Cruz, Ricky Martin, Andy García, and Benicio del Toro. In 1996, film producer Christy Haubegger issued *Latina,* a monthly survey of cosmetics and fashion for bicultural women. Cover styles featured celebrities Christina Aguilera, Salma Hayek, Victor Cruz, and Eva Mendes. Articles ventured into the tastes of Afro-Latinos and the wardrobes of noted role models, such as Tyson Beckford and Rosario Dawson.

The second-highest-circulating Latino magazine, *Latina* conferred beauty awards on the products that best complemented natural skin, hair, and nails as well as the color-blocking trends of cosmetician Victor Henao. Photo spreads and an online newsletter boosted youth awareness of celebrity fashion lines and accessories by Jennifer Lopez, Daisy Fuentes, and Sofía Vergara. Simultaneously, *People en Español* showcased the fashion looks of Latino singers and film and television stars Paulina Rubio, Juan Soler, and Carlos Ponce. Key to Latino media trends were the blended cultures and intergenerational celebrations of *latinidad* or *latinaje* (Latin-ness).

For haute couture, Latino designers gained a reputation for up-to-the-minute styling, as with Carolina Herrera's intensely feminine evening gowns and the minimalistic wedding gown that couturier Narciso Rodriguez made for Carolyn Bessette Kennedy in 1996. Mexican designer Christian Cota, a graduate of Parsons School of

Latina is the second-highest-circulating magazine aimed at the U.S. Hispanic community (after *People en Español*) and the most influential print-media vehicle of fashion and beauty marketing for bicultural women. *(Johnny Nunez/WireImage)*

Design, energized his collections with tribal textiles and hand painting and embroidery from the Yucatán for trapeze blouses and airy jumpsuits.

Experimental designs and textured fabrics have set Latino couture apart from competitors. Stylist Pedro Lourenço of Brazil applied crocodile textures and metallic flash to asymmetric dresses and pleated skirts and incorporated synthetic ties and a wood footbed into his strap sandals. Trendsetter Santiago Gonzalez crafts men's two-tone wallets, attachés, and duffels with textured ostrich and crocodile skin.

In 2006, the first Latino Fashion Week in Chicago, Miami, and Dallas featured five days of runway modeling. Key to the appeal were the photo shoots of Daniel Garriga and celebrities in ensembles and hairstyles influenced by Latino history and spreads in the magazines *Vanidades* and *Vox Populi.* Featured couturiers Noelia Cruz, Claudia Urrutia, Nelissa Carrillo, Ronald Rodriguez, and Sadia Pattison built the reputation of Latino fashion for the energy and color of silk suits, ruffled skirts, and printed chiffon.

Contemporary celebrations such as Cinco de Mayo dances and the Tex-Mex charro festival call for parade dress in tight silver-studded cowboy pants and short jackets with felt or straw sombreros and huaraches or leather boots. Rock concerts feature males clad *cholo* (street punk) style in tattoos, sleeveless shirts, and drooping pants, a cross-cultural fusion with African American styles. Message T-shirts among U.S. Latino teens picture the Mexican or Puerto Rican flag as well as portraits of Villa, Zapata, Fidel Castro, Eva Perón, and Argentine martyr Che Guevara sporting his signature black beret.

See also: American Western Clothing; Amerindian Clothing, Pre-Columbian; Amerindian Clothing, Post-Contact; Central American, Mexican, and Caribbean Clothing; Ethnic and National Dress.

Further Reading

Candelaria, Cordelia Chávez, Peter J. García, and Arturo J. Aldama, eds. *Encyclopedia of Latino Popular Culture.* Westport, CT: Greenwood, 2004.

Leonard, David J., and Carmen R. Lugo-Lugo, eds. *Latino History and Culture: An Encyclopedia.* Armonk, NY: M.E. Sharpe, 2010.

Root, Regina A., ed. *Latin American Fashion Reader.* New York: Berg, 2005.

Laundry

The cleansing of washable garments, laundering protects fabrics while removing stains, odors, and grime from apparel. The making of laundry soap after 2800 B.C.E. in Babylon involved the boiling of wood ash with animal fat, an ingredient later replaced by cassia oil. After 556 B.C.E. at Harran, Turkey, serving girls turned cypress and sesame seed oil and ash into a cleaning medium.

From the sixth century B.C.E., Greek grooming demanded a fresh, neat wool chiton. To keep fabrics spotless, the fastidious citizen depended on the labors of fullers, professional cleaners who soaked out stains and grease and brushed the nap. Linen garments received a thorough scrub with scouring sand. The Greco-Roman physician Galen admired the soap that Germanic tribes blended from goat tallow and birch ash, adding herbs for fragrance.

To maintain the wool toga for appearances at court, the theater or circus, or the Roman imperial palace, wearers sent garments to fullers, who collected urine from passersby for soaking garments in natural ammonia. After slaves trod wet clothing in a vat, they rinsed the apparel in water from public fountains before spreading pieces on a drying frame and bleaching them with a sulfur fire burning underneath. Fine woolens required brushing and arranging in a pressing frame to maintain shape.

Advances in Soap

In Britain, Scandinavia, and Eastern Europe, soap was available from Arab importers in the 600s C.E. until the technology itself reached the north. To the south, Iberian, French, and Italian soap makers relied on olive oil blended with barilla (saltwort) ash and fragrant blossoms. By the 800s, soap manufacturers did a heavy trade in Geneva, Liège, Marseilles, Naples, Savona, and Venice.

Arab formulas for olive oil and lye soap returned from Aleppo, Syria, with Christian crusaders in 1099. Soap makers in Castile, Spain, commercialized hard Aleppo bars. Spanish innovators aided washwomen with the addition of laurel oil from bay leaves, which contributed soothing, healing qualities for the launderer's hands. By 1370, the French replacement of animal fat with copra or palm oil and seawater refined the harsher recipes.

Late medieval washerwomen or itinerant whitsters, or linen bleachers, frequented communal washing stones along streams and knelt in laundry boxes to protect skirts and lower legs from mud and suds. Public washhouses offered laundry pools and a free flow of rinse water as well as drying racks and lines for pinning up wet wash with split twigs or carved clamps. After "bucking" (soaking apparel) in potash water (lye) or chamber lye (urine), workers scrubbed stained garments on washboards. With battledores, or beetling stones, launderers beat garments clean and spread rinsed apparel on grass and bushes to dry in sunlight. Soaking in lavender water yielded the Middle English term "laundry."

During the French Renaissance, the importance to status of cleanliness raised the value of laundry to fashionable people. For the first time in history, elegance began with a clean-smelling body and a spotless white linen shirt worn over impeccable underwear. Into the 1500s and 1600s, as aristocrats began changing their clothes on a daily basis, the increased need for soap brought prosperity to factories in Marseilles and Toulon as well as luxury taxes for the French treasury.

Laundry Technology

The invention of the grooved washboard in 1797 assisted launderers in removing ground-in dirt and grease from collars, cuffs, and knees. Around 1800, Antoine Labarraque, a French pharmacist, discovered the value of sodium hypochlorite bleach for disinfecting and whitening fabric. Homemakers passed used laundry water to the poor, who could not afford soap and bleach.

Urban women in early nineteenth-century England heated copper vats with small charcoal fires before boiling clothes in grated soap flakes and salt. The next step involved agitating a dolly stick (plunger) in the load to loosen ground-in soil and stains. The invention of corrugated zinc, copper, tin, or iron washboards in 1833 improved hand scrubbing of collars and cuffs. The invention of hand-cranked washing machines raised standards of cleanliness.

Mechanization threatened delicate fabrics from the agitation of wood paddles until their replacement by the rotating drum by James King in 1851. Soft liquid palm soap invented by William Shepphard in 1865 reduced problems with lumps and calcium and magnesium scum on clothes.

After one or more rinses and a soak in bluing (ultramarine) and starch water, the laundress concluded the task by cranking clothes one at a time through the rollers of a mangle or wringer. Ceiling racks on pulleys enabled the washwoman to dry the garments indoors. In Scutari, Turkey, during the Crimean War in 1854, nurse administrator Florence Nightingale set up an institutional laundry to cleanse the bandages, nightshirts, and caps of patients. The clean bedding of battlefield wounded constituted the debut of sanitized laundry in hospitals and other public institutions.

Following the 1849 California gold Rush, Chinese immigrants found work as launderers, a grueling job in steamy, airless quarters. By 1852, Asian arrivals from Canton rose from 325 to 20,000 a year. In San Francisco, nearly 90 percent of laundry workers were Asians, who survived exorbitant tax levies and other discriminatory measures. In the 1880s, Chinese Americans fought racist laws intended to drive them out of business; however, Chinese laundries continued to spread across the United States.

In the early twentieth century, Pine-Sol and Tide laundry detergent eased the task of washing clothes by boosting solubility in hard water with pine oil, isopropyl alcohol, and sulfonates. In the first half of the century, the gentling of all-purpose detergents with synthetic surfactants reduced wear on garments while dissolving grease and suspending dirt. The invention of the electric clothes dryer in 1915 ended the back-breaking job of carrying baskets of wet clothes to outdoor lines. Maytag eliminated hard rubbing by producing agitator washers in 1922.

Because synthetic surfactants cleaned well in cold water, homemakers after 1957 saved money on filling electric washing machines. In 1964, conservationists applauded biodegradable and phosphate-free laundry detergents requiring less wastewater treatment. The launch of fabric conditioning and softeners for the dryer ended the age-old problems of static cling and of stiffness and loss of texture in luxury fabrics from soap residue. In 1997, the U.S. Federal Trade Commission launched a fabric labeling system based on symbols covering water temperature, bleach, heated drying, ironing, and dry cleaning.

At the beginning of the 2000s, the replacement of knobs and control buttons with microprocessors, electronic sensors, and touchpads enabled energy-efficient laundry machines to gauge the temperatures and water levels for wash and wear, thermal and water-repelling fabrics, wool, silk, and hand washables. By 2003, the world consumed 9 million tons of soap and 18 million tons of detergent annually. The further concentration of detergent into smaller packages reduced weight and shelf space needed to stock supplies.

See also: Dry Cleaning; Ironing.

Further Reading

Maxwell, Lee M. *Save Women's Lives: History of Washing Machines.* Eaton, CO: Oldewash, 2003.

Mendelson, Cheryl. *Laundry: The Home Comforts Book of Caring for Clothes and Linens.* New York: Simon & Schuster, 2005.

Mohun, Arwen. *Steam Laundries: Gender, Technology, and Work in the United States and Great Britain, 1880–1940.* Baltimore, MD: Johns Hopkins University Press, 1999.

Lauren, Ralph (1939–)

An American trendsetter, designer Ralph Lauren turned elegant fashion into popular brand recognition with his Polo line of clothing and accessories, later expanded to include footwear, fragrances, and housewares.

Born Ralph Lifschitz on October 14, 1939, in The Bronx, New York, he claimed Polish heritage from his parents, Fraydl Kotlar and mural painter Frank Lifschitz. From wearing his brother's hand-me-downs, helping his father paint houses, and selling ties while attending the Manhattan Talmudical Academy, he advanced to stock boy at Alexander's department store before graduating from DeWitt Clinton High School and attending night classes at Baruch College of the City University of New York. After three years in the U.S. Army as a specialist in artillery, he changed his name to Ralph Lauren and married Viennese Ricky Anne Low-Beer in 1964.

Lauren began his career in the fashion industry selling Ivy League ties and button-down shirts for Brooks Brothers in New York, setting the tone for his later designs. After working out of a windowless office in the Empire State Building, at age 28 he opened a Manhattan tie shop selling original wide Italian neckwear under the Polo label, which Bloomingdale's and Neiman Marcus soon began marketing. In 1970, his full line of menswear—featuring wing-collar shirts, pleated slacks, tweed hacking jackets, and wide-lapel suits with natural shoulders—earned a Coty American Fashion Critics award.

A year later, Lauren launched a women's line featuring cashmere sweaters with man-tailored vested suits, patent leather boots, and alligator bags. His boutique in Beverly Hills, California, opened in 1971, made him the first American couturier with a freestanding store. Lauren began merchandising his famous short-sleeved mesh player shirt in 1972 under the familiar mounted polo player logo, the emblem of his $10 billion empire. His bias tea dresses, picture hats, and pinstriped suits for *The Great Gatsby* (1974) captured the essence of the Jazz Age. In 1977, Lauren costumed Diane Keaton in quirky hats, boots, and men's jackets for *Annie Hall.*

Lauren added clothes for infants, toddlers, and children to his designs in 1978. Three years later, his London store became the first European boutique to headline an American couturier. To project pure American style, he featured a polished prairie look in denim skirts over white petticoats topped with fringed buckskin jackets. The frontier theme extended into ruffly linen blouses and hooded capes. Men's looks covered the gamut from preppy cardigans and crested navy blazers to distressed bomber jackets with sherpa collars.

With the launch of Polo Ralph Lauren in 1986 on Madison Avenue in New York City, the designer increased the visibility of his apparel, which won him a Lifetime Achievement Award from the Council of Fashion Designers. He ventured into custom menswear, outfitting tennis players in the U.S. Open and Wimbledon and designing for television. By 2007, his label was flourishing on his signature linen slacks, safari jackets, jewelry, and watches.

At age 71, Lauren received a Legion of Honor award from the French government. His wearable women's clothes continued to spark global regard for their American authenticity and vigor, as exemplified by the vested knicker suit and a sparkly tunic over a handkerchief skirt in his 2010 collection. His men's RLX line, viewed on an iPad app, pictured male athletes in functional hoodies and cycling pants in innovative fabrics. In 2011, Lauren featured fringed coats, medallion belts, and Navajo shoulder bags alongside luxury denim in jeggings (jean leggings), watch caps, and tailored distressed jackets with prices reaching $2,000. His 2012 collection opted for an ethnic mix with Egyptian collars on halter gowns, Persian embroidery on evening jackets, glittery scrolling on vests, gilded boleros, gaucho hats, and Mexican serapes in traditional colors.

See also: Fashion Design.

Further Reading

Gross, Michael. *Genuine Authentic: The Real Life of Ralph Lauren.* New York: Perennial, 2003.

Mattern, Joanne. *Ralph Lauren.* New York: Facts on File, 2011.

McDowell, Colin. *Ralph Lauren.* London: Cassell Illustrated, 2002.

Ralph Lauren. www.ralphlauren.com

Leather and Suede

From Paleolithic times, rawhide, leather, and suede have supplied Asians, Europeans, North Americans, and Pacific islanders with basic apparel. Around 38,000 B.C.E., the earliest footwear involved the binding of undressed rawhide and rabbit fur strips to the instep and ankles with thongs to protect the sole and to enhance grip on ice. The Irulas of Tamil Nadu in southern India earned a reputation for snake catching and stripping skins of cobras, kraits, and vipers to sell to makers of exotic leathers. In North America, from 7000 B.C.E., the Anasazi of the Great Basin flaked stones to scrape elk hides for robes, which they associated with virility and bravery. For adornment, they added strips of rabbit fur and eagle and turkey feathers.

In 5000 B.C.E. in the Middle East, laced one-piece turnshoes took shape after leather and suede workers pierced slits into soles and uppers with an awl. The shoe took its name from the turning to the outside to receive overcast lacings. One recovered lace-up model dates to Armenian crafters in 3500 B.C.E., when the shoemaker produced a style similar to the modern gillie (lace-up).

The recovery of Ötzi the Iceman from a glacier in the Italian Alps in 1991 increased archaeological knowledge of Neolithic hide clothing dating to 3300 B.C.E. His outfit illustrated a sophisticated selection of animal hides for specific uses. He wore a goat hide coat and hemispherical bearskin cap with chin strap, goatskin shirt, goat leather loincloth, calf belt with calf tool pouch, chamois quiver, goat hide leggings laced to the belt, and two-piece deer hide shoes with bearskin soles over-sewn with laces. Over the next millennium, two-stage boots like Ötzi's consisted of leggings that tucked into shoes that could also fit into snowshoes.

Chemical Tanning

By leaving rawhide on the forest floor for months, hunters discovered that natural tanning from cork and willow bark, gumwood, fir branches, berries, barberry root, and decaying acacia, oak, larch, Lombardy poplar, and sumac leaves protected skins from putrefaction. The Sudanese preferred pods of the *Acacia arabica* tree.

Ancient tannery vats reeked from solutions of animal dung, brains, and urine, which laborers worked into hides with their hands and feet. In Mehrgarh, a Neolithic site in Balochistan, Pakistan, bacterial fermentation in damp chambers dissolved fat and meat and loosened hair and wool. From experience, tanners deduced that deerskin produced the finest grain, while goat and sheep produced the coarsest leather.

An Arab discovery of alum and ammonium or chrome salts mixed with egg yolk increased tawing (chemical tanning) technology. For turning deer, dog, fox, goat, raccoon, sheep, or woodchuck hides into alum, Hungarian, or white leather, the labor-intensive task required hand scraping with bone or stone blades on collagen fibers that the tanner painted with a lime and sodium sulfide paste. For the tanning process, Babylonian crafters reserved oil, myrrh, and gallnuts, an astringent plant abnormality caused by bacteria, fungus, or insects. Around 3000 B.C.E., Egyptian tanners in Cairo produced red leather with kermes, an insect dye. Sumerian leather crafters embellished their work with copper studs.

Hebrew and Turkish tanners originated the use of acorns and valonia (oak bark extract) for tanning, which required large vats to submerge hides in tannic solution for up to two years to prevent corruption and cracking. The leather-strengthening solution came into common use in oak-growing regions across the Levant and Iberia. After drying the hides, workers trimmed and shaved calf, deer, goat, lamb, and pigskins, and buffed the surfaces for suede or dressed them with oil, wax, and shellac to tighten and harden fibers and produce a leathery sheen called japanning.

Early Commerce

For some five centuries beginning around 500 B.C.E., leather was the material of choice for fishers, hunters, and travelers as well as the actors playing in Sophocles's tragedies in definitive leather buskins. Congolese tribes preserved snakeskins as long as 7 feet (2.1 meters) as shoulder decor and religious garments for shamans. The stoutest lacings and sandals in South Africa came from kudu leather, a lucrative trade item. Nubians made amulets from crocodile or hippopotamus leather.

In northern Africa, Egyptian tanners provided materials for gloves, loincloths and tunics, and shrouds. Decorative garments displayed cutout patterns. Shoemakers fitted sandals with toe posts and scalloped ankle straps. Around 335 B.C.E., the Macedonian diadem of Alexander the Great consisted of jewels attached to a fringed leather head strap. In 126 B.C.E., the Parthians of Iran manufactured long-sleeved leather coats worn over matching trousers. A braided sash thrown over the shoulder denoted rank.

Like the Parthians, the Romans turned leather crafts into valuable trade commodities. After 100 C.E., shoemakers made the first footwear designed for left and right feet. The Roman occupation of Britain from 43 to 410 introduced tanning to the Celts, who made shoes, clothes, and bags of tanned cowhide.

Medieval Crafts

Monastery curriers (leather specialists) acquired expertise in making suede for pouches and leather for sandals, belts, and short boots. Tanners situated

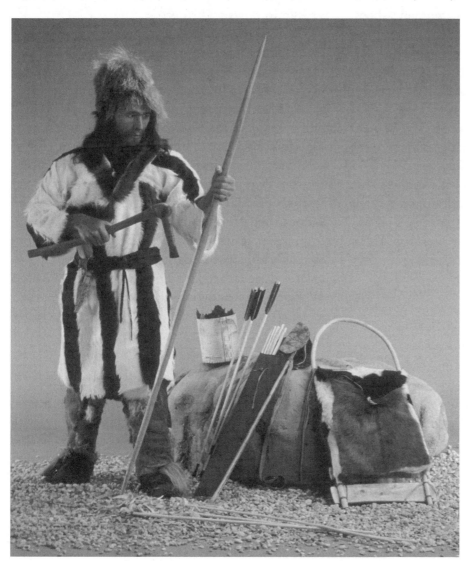

A human cadaver discovered in the Italian Alps in 1991—a 5,000-year-old male figure dubbed Ötzi the Iceman—shed new light on Neolithic hide clothing. As seen in this museum display, he wore a bearskin hat, goatskin coat and leggings, and deer hide shoes. *(Patrick Landmann/Getty Images)*

workshops and water mills on rivers and streams. They developed local styles in coloration and texture from the use of indigenous plants on hides delivered directly from the slaughterhouse. Austrian, Czech, French, German, and Slovakian hide dealers supplied calf leather to the crafters in England and Scotland, countries that produced little veal.

Around 1100, cordwainers (shoemakers) formed craft guilds to preserve their secret processes. A fast method for producing pliant leather for intricate apparel—buckled galoshes or overshoes, one-strap poulaines with long, pointed toes, and the thigh-high heuse riding boots popularized in the 1240s—involved sealing lime solution and hides in a revolving drum fitted with paddles to force the solution into the pores. Tanners sold large horse and bull hides for sole leather and smaller horse hides for the fancy vamps on women's shoes. Workers turned trimmings, called offal, from shoulders and bellies into welting and insoles. Cork covered in leather produced a comfortable shoe bed for dress, but an insubstantial basis for work and military footwear.

In the early 1400s, leather denoted refinement and savoir faire in dressing, particularly in Moorish Spain, where Islamic crafters flourished. Civilians adapted the military jerkin and leg wrap in cheap split sheepskin for daily use and tipped lacings with metal aglets for utility and flair.

New World Leather

The first encounters of Europeans with Amerindians revealed the presence in the New World of high-quality leatherwork in bear, deer, reindeer, and smoked elk for blankets, moccasins, and apparel, and snake and alligator skins for bindings. North America acquired its first commercial tannery at Swampscott, Massachusetts, in 1629, when Francis Ingalls, an English immigrant from Lincolnshire, set up tanning vats. As the towns of Boston, Charlestown, and Watertown took shape, tanners found work supplying the citizens with leather, which court-appointed inspectors began grading in 1638 to protect consumers from over-limed or partially tanned goods.

As herds of cattle, goats, and sheep increased

in Connecticut and imported cattle from Denmark arrived in New Hampshire, there were enough domestic animals to slaughter for their hides without risking famine. Colonial tanners and their apprentices in Salem, Massachusetts, stored sumac for use in dyeing and tanning. Plans called for tanhouses in each county to provide free workshops for curriers, tanners, and shoemakers.

By the mid-seventeenth century, crude dressings of hides with egg albumin, almonds, spermaceti, or blood began giving place to chemical tanning, the beginning of high-style footwear. Men favored bag breeches, a full cut of leather tied above the knee, as well as suede or leather waistcoats and square-toed lace-up shoes, which replaced pull-on boots. Women and men popularized high-heeled slippers in 1650 and topped leather uppers with silk embroidery, sequins, and grosgrain bows and rosettes.

Eighteenth-century oiled leather got its sheen from fish oil. Spotted or granular shagreen from rays and sharkskin received texturing from seeds of gooseweed (*Sphenoclea zeylanica*). Fine English kid and lamb still required the application of eggs, which London tanners bought by the million from Flanders and France. Elsewhere in the late 1700s, a demand for galluses or braces (suspenders) raised the price of African ostrich hide and morocco leather (goatskin), a fine material originated by the Moors with alum tanning and kermes dye made from insect scales. Vests and breeches sported zebra stripes and leopard spots, male decor intended to create a predatory air. The future King George IV of England advocated lacing in 1790, when shoemakers replaced the time-honored buckling of shoes with leather shoestrings.

Factory Goods

The Industrial Revolution introduced chrome tanning, which impeded rotting. During the U.S. Civil War, shortages of leather shoes, belts, holsters, and square-toed pull-on boots worsened in the South because of the dominance of manufacturing north of the Mason-Dixon Line. Slaves replaced durable work brogans with plantation shoes, a homemade footwear stitched together from odds and ends of leather. The lack of sturdy heeled shoes impeded runaways, who often arrived at Underground Railroad stations in tattered footwear held together with cloth strips or vines.

In the 1920s, orthopedic insoles, gripper soles, and rubber heels increased the life span of leather shoes for schoolchildren, workers, nurses, police officers, and servicemen. During World War II, rationing in the United States limited plain and exotic leather for belts and handbags; galoshes and cloth bags and belts were available, but sports shoes, dancing shoes, leather jackets, and hunting boots went out of production. On February 7, 1943, under Ration Order 17, the Office of Price Administration rationed leather, allotting each citizen no more than three pairs of shoes annually. Factories reduced leather embellishments, dropped the height of stacked heels, and issued styles in only four colors—black, brown, russet, and white. As war demands worsened before D-Day, on March 20, 1944, ration books cut allowances for civilians to two pairs per year.

The postwar boom in leather goods increased demand for chic sandals and belts, suede spikes, croc pumps and platform heels, and matching handbags. In the United States, the Indian Wildlife Protection Act of 1972 halted the skinning of exotic snakes to supply the Italian fashion industry. Oil shortages in the 1980s returned leather to competition, both in American and British shoe shops and in imports from Brazil, Italy, Korea, and Taiwan.

See also: Cobblery; Hides; Lacing; Shoes, Men's; Shoes, Women's.

Further Reading

Garnes, Jane E. *The Complete Handbook of Leathercrafting.* 2nd ed. Malabar, FL: Krieger, 1986.

Richards, Matt. *Deerskins into Buckskins: How to Tan with Natural Materials.* 2nd ed. Woodstock, VT: Backcountry, 2004.

Sterlacci, Francesca, and Joanne Arbuckle. *Historical Dictionary of the Fashion Industry.* Lanham, MD: Scarecrow, 2008.

Legal and Judicial Attire

From the beginnings of medieval law courts, attorneys and jurists have sustained their stature in society with sober dress. In most countries, standard judiciary attire has varied in type and color to symbolize levels of judicial purview. In London during the tenth century, the sheriff and court officials adopted gloves as marks of authority. After the establishment of Oxford University in 1096, the college of law settled on a uniform black gown for students.

In twelfth-century Persia, the Islamic legal community standardized loose ankle-length mantles of cotton or wool and ties to cover the head. British high court officials adopted a silk or taffeta cloak and hooded cowl in seasonal violet, red, or green. In 1334, Pope Benedict XII designated purple or scarlet for attorneys practicing in Paris. Fifteenth-century Italian and German judicial attire featured red caps and robes lined in red and decked in maroon scarves; the color indicated that passing judgment sometimes demanded blood atonement for felonies.

From the late 1500s into the next century, British judges abolished green robes from seasonal court attire and lawyers appeared before the bench in business attire. According to a dress code published in 1635, jurists held sessions in open red or black silk robes trimmed in white miniver or silk tufts. Accessories included a black cincture, starched winged collars, cotton or muslin ruffs, or lace yokes over batiste or lawn neck cloths and falling bands, forerunners of the jabot.

In Bhutan, Shabdrung Ngawang Namgyal, the Tibetan Buddhist lama unifier of Bhutan in the 1630s, issued the *Driglam Namzha* (system of rules), a dress code aimed at adding dignity to national dress. Men adopted a knee-length robe secured at the midriff with a cloth tie. Colored scarves reaching from the left shoulder to right hip identified authorities, with blue signifying royal counselors and assembly members, orange for ministers, and green for judges.

The Judicial Wig

After returning to the English throne from exile in France in 1660, Charles II introduced wigs for royal authorities and aristocrats. By 1685, wigs for everyday wear appealed to most of Britain's high social echelons. To protect dark fabrics from the whitening powder of bob-wigs, jurists covered their horsehair queues with bags. While civilian wig use waned, courtroom dress codes preserved traditional wig-and-gown apparel for judges.

Before the French Revolution in 1789, the judicial robe reached such proportions that it required a page to carry the train. After the collapse of the Bourbon dynasty, republican fervor stripped the aristocratic judge of ostentatious grand wigs and silk and velvet mantles. Likewise, Belgian and Dutch jurists abandoned high court pomp and adopted black robes with white banded collars. British courtroom attire universalized the gray or white periwig powdered with starch or wheat flour. The same headdress applied to colonial courts in Africa and the Western Hemisphere.

For the U.S. Supreme Court, which met the first time in New York on February 1, 1790, Chief Justice John Jay set the dress code—a wig and simple banded collar with an unpretentious black robe trimmed in salmon that marked his honorary Doctor of Law degree from the University of Dublin. U.S. jurists preferred less pomp but accepted as ceremonial dress a red robe varied at the shoulders with black and white velvet.

In the 1850s, judges and professors of law in Great Britain and its colonies tended toward black, a sober reminder of professional ethics. U.S. courtroom attire ceased to include wigs as out of date. Late in the nineteenth century, Chinese jurists topped the *shangfu* (court robe) with a winged hat and circular collar. New Zealand's barristers and solicitors heard cases clad in light blue. Italians accessorized black robes with white shirtfronts and shoulder tassels in silver or gold.

The Modern Jurist

At the beginning of the twentieth century, Britain's King's Counsel diminished superfluous fabric, reducing court tailcoat and silk gown to a businesslike silhouette. Lace collars gave way to starched bands. Scots retained elaborate attire, with appeals court judges in white with four red crosses on the torso and the lord justice in long white neck cloth and red robe trimmed in ermine with black tips. By mid-century, Indian and Pakistani jurists gave up wigs. In place of British regalia, Pakistani and

Malaysian court dress gravitated toward Muslim hats and Nehru jackets.

The twenty-first century introduced pragmatic reforms in matters of court dress. In May 2008, the Lord Chief Justice of England and Wales modeled a navy gabardine and wool robe designed by fashion consultant Betty Jackson with a stand-up collar, velvet placket and cuffs, and pockets. Gone were wing collars and wigs from family and civil proceedings. Only vertical bands in red, blue, or gold acknowledged judicial seniority.

With similar attention to modernization, Australian magistrates abandoned wigs in September 2010. As of 2011, New Zealand's tribunal code stressed dark suits, ties, shoes, and hosiery with a formal gown for judges. In contrast to less stringent judiciary dress codes, French and Swiss court officials, as well as those of Haiti, Rwanda, and Togo, honored centuries of pomp with black robes and white gloves, long white neck cloths, a shoulder scarf graced with ermine, and high court blue sashes and flat caps banded in gold braid. Palestinian courts obligated female attorneys to layer their courtroom gowns over Islamic dress. A head scarf, revealed only the face and hands.

Today, global court dress varies by country, ranging from elaborate medallions on Portuguese, Russian, Ukrainian, and Croatian judges and blue sashes on Estonian court attire to business suits on the lay judges of Norway and Greece. Canadian Supreme Court attire reflects British styles, but without wigs. On ritual occasions, jurists robe in red trimmed in white ermine over a small banded tie. Italian prosecutors and judges add gold-striped headdress to the red and ermine robe. In contrast, judiciary dress codes in Israel, Japan, and Mexico favor unembellished black robes.

Hong Kong and South Australian barristers attend superior court in a tailored black silk gown, bench wig, and cambric or lace jabot, the equivalent of the Malaysian waterfall cravat and the French magistrate's *rabat*. The throat adornment introduced on July 7, 1981, by the first female justice of the U.S. Supreme Court, Sandra Day O'Connor, involved consultation with English, South African, Canadian, and French outfitters. In the first-floor robing room of the U.S. Court, the jabot continues in use by justices Ruth Bader Ginsburg and Sonia Sotomayor, while male justices wear ties or bowties with white shirts.

See also: Robes; Wigs.

Further Reading

Hayward, Maria. *Rich Apparel: Clothing and the Law in Henry VIII's England.* Burlington, VT: Ashgate, 2009.

Rajan, Amol. "Objection! Judges Reject New Robes." *The Independent,* March 27, 2009.

Leisure Wear

The needs of modern consumers for comfort and style during free time fuel a global industry in leisure apparel. The antecedents in clothing and adornments are ancient. Throughout sub-Saharan Africa after 42,000 B.C.E., men wore a cool thong breechcloth, a style that later found favor among the Caribbean Arawak and North American Blackfoot, Huron, and Seminole. Chinchorro women of what is now Peru and Chile around 9000 B.C.E. worked and played in kilts fringed from grass, a cool, nonwoven material for everyday wear. In contrast, equatorial Amerindians of Ecuador and Pacific Melanesians preferred nudity and body paint.

The demand for relaxing apparel and hairstyles in Egypt in 3050 B.C.E. introduced the double-layer kilt and the shaved head topped with a blunt-cut wig for hot days and nights. Chinese Hanfu wardrobes after 1600 B.C.E. clothed men and women in knee-length tunics and open-crotch pants. Sashing and wrapped tops varied the fit for seasonal wear suited to family time and informal gatherings. Asian nomads created their own Bronze Age leisure wear after 1400 B.C.E. with felt socks, gloves, and slippers.

In Greece, unpinned chitons minus sword belts suited the Attic custom of peacetime urban dressing. Men cinched the Turkish linen tunic around the waist with a *zoster* (wide belt) and bloused loose folds above the midriff for a serene look. Around 175 B.C.E., Roman males adapted the combat boot as a soft-bottomed sandal sewn up the ankle with a hog bristle.

As the Roman Empire advanced over North Africa after 49 B.C.E., Libyans adopted the short tunic for wearing unbound and flowing. In the Atlas Mountains of what are now Morocco, Algeria, and Tunisia, the Roman traveler's cloak developed into the desert djellaba, or burnoose. The hooded cloak, a regional costume, shielded the body from sandstorms and sun.

Early Knits and Luxury Fabrics

In the early Middle Ages, German, Scandinavian, and British men found drawstring pants and mantles relaxing for day wear and sleeping. Copts knitted sandal socks to protect the feet from thorns. During a period of self-indulgence after 661, conservative Arab Muslims chose baggy apparel over more formal styles. Umayyad fashions engaged Persians in the luxury of relaxing robes and stockings made of satin and silk. By 1000, from Armenia and Anatolia as far west as Iberia, cotton underwear and hose softened Eurasian outfits.

The tenth-century invention of *bulgara cira* (Bulgarian silk velvet) introduced a lush material to Hindustani, Iraqi, Khurasani (Irani), and Russian wardrobes. During the 1200s, Florentine women popularized satin mules for wear on marble floors. Relaxation attire for Syrian men began with the *jubba* (robe) and in India with the dhoti, a soft cotton hip wrap.

Fourteenth-century knit gloves and silk glove liners eased stress on the hands of English horseback riders. The French coif shielded the neck from drafts, a common problem in dwellings lacking central heat. Southeast Asian men and women wrapped themselves in sarongs, leisurely draped body wraps woven from cotton, silk, or blends. West African mothers wound infants in gauzy slings that left baby limbs free for movement.

Spanish conquistadores found the Peruvian Inca unencumbered in fringed aprons, the Aztec in nonbinding sleeveless tunics, and Pueblo men and the Tarahumara of Chihuahua, Mexico, cloaked in cotton, linen, and wool serapes (shoulder blankets). Among the southeastern Swahili of Africa around 1550, the silk turban encouraged fashionable comfort among Muslim men. Moroccan noblewomen preferred trousers topped with a soft linen body wrap.

Late in the 1600s, French laborers initiated a trend in indigo denim pants and dungarees. Extended wear of denim pants by European sailors softened the fit in the seat and knees. In 1773, Captain James Cook's voyagers to Tahiti admired the native barkcloth poncho, a light shoulder wrap and rain cloak.

Tailoring the Leisure Class

During the Napoleonic era (1799–1815), trends in equestrian fashions dictated wide-lapelled dress coats, white shirts with cravats, linen breeches, and short hair for men and masculine spencers (single-breasted shrugs) and vests for women. In the second quarter of the 1800s, men's braces added stretch and security to ensembles of hip-length jackets over moleskin, linen, or wool breeches and pull-on boots. Split skirts simplified the seating of female riders on sidesaddles. For tranquil at-home evenings, fashionable European males adopted the silk velvet smoking jacket with soft rolled collar.

In the mid-nineteenth century, the leisure class in the United States, England, Switzerland, Chile, and Scandinavia browsed the racks of urban department stores by size and tried on outfits before full-length mirrors. For long shopping jaunts, consumers checked motoring coats, hats, and umbrellas at the store's cloakroom, met for breaks at store coffee shops and lunchrooms, and left packages for store delivery. For city strolls, women popularized high-button shoes and the gored walking skirt, a style featured in the June 1873 issue of *Harper's Bazaar*. In Nigeria, English visitors to Lagos admired the loose fit of men's cotton knee breeches paired with a wrap thrown over one shoulder.

By 1900, Edwardian leisure apparel freed the fashion conscious from tight, unyielding suits and overly arranged hairstyles. Blazers, flannel tennis slacks, wool singlets, sailor-collar pullovers, and lounge suits lessened the constriction of everyday attire for lawn sports and travel. In Australia, the *akubra* (bush hat) protected stockmen from inclement weather and heat. Makers of unisex crepe-soled shoes profited from the need for flexible footwear among boaters, golfers, and cyclists. Lingerie added sensuality to women's intimate wear with boudoir garments and foundation apparel.

After World War I, the United States employed a labor force of 165,000 dedicated to producing work and leisure apparel, including men's sports and hunting clothes. Tops in niche marketing, Burberry waterproof coats became a rainy day uniform for the British consumer. Elsa Schiaparelli paired knit tops with women's tennis skirts and cycling and golfing knickers. Nylon and rayon eased the fit of women's snoods, men's swim trunks, and children's socks and underwear.

By the 1920s, catalog shopping from Kays in Britain and Bloomingdale's and Sears, Roebuck in the United States pictured relaxed apparel and shoes on models. Buyers mail-ordered tennis skirts and biking and golfing knickers for women and Western jeans and OshKosh overalls for children. Shoppers in the Congo opted for silk shirts, zippered pants, and panama hats ordered from industrialized countries.

French couturier Coco Chanel debuted stretchy knits on women, who abandoned corsets for a natural silhouette. As pictured in *Vogue* in 1935, Lady Levi's introduced women to the mellow attire of cowboys and outdoorsmen. In 1936, *Harper's Bazaar* featured Man Ray's photographs of styles suited to lounging, water sports, and motoring. Manhattan couturier Claire McCardell Americanized comfort in shifts, wrap dresses, and ballet slippers. Home sewing became easier in Australia, Canada, Great Britain, and the United States with multisized patterns for infant sunsuits and children's play shorts.

Postwar Lifestyles and Leisure Couture

Man-tailoring in the mid-1940s introduced women to lounging pajamas and California-style pleated slacks. In 1950, viscose rayon raised the comfort level of men's slacks, Hawaiian flowered shirts, knit and bolo ties, swimsuits, and sleep shirts. Department stores increased the availability of women's rayon pajamas, stockings, intimate wear, and dresses. Wrangler promoted durable after-school clothes for children consisting of jeans and snap-front shirts.

Influenced by hippie counterculture philosophy in the 1960s, leisure dressing began overlapping with dress attire for dining out, concerts, shopping, and vacationing. Signs appeared in restaurant and boutique windows stating the dress code, which banned bikinis, tank tops, and bare feet. An unfortunate turn in design gave temporary status to less than flattering female Lycra pants, unisex bell-bottoms and shortalls, and men's double-knit disco or leisure suits with platform shoes, a flashy reprieve from business attire.

Italian couturier Emilio Pucci experimented with color-blocked poolside clothes, while American designer Geoffrey Beene complemented men's denim jeans with pullovers and jerseys. Spandex and panné (pressed) velvet added a touch of leisure to jacket and slacks sets and at-home dresses worn with matching slippers. The classic look, visualized on film and television, hastened the abandonment of national costume worldwide.

Office trends in the 1970s moved fashion away from formality toward polo shirts and soft tees with khakis or stonewashed jeans and the metrosexual pierced ear for males. In 1972, the Hudson's Bay Company offered Canadians expanded choices in gear for rough country hiking and hunting. Calvin Klein targeted the male wardrobe for revamping with wearable knits for after-hours unwinding. French style setters Ted Lapidus and Yves Saint Laurent promoted the bush jacket and safari suit, functional khakis long worn by men in Australia, Burma, and India.

During the 1980s, with the American "Me Generation" nearing middle age, the affluent of both sexes pampered their skin, hair, and nails at spas with massages, creams, polishes, and personalized color typing. As pictured in *GQ,* the modification of shirt-and-tie protocol with the turtleneck and leather jacket supplied men with more evening choices for casual business meetings. Microfiber, drip-dry nylon, Lizwear and Liz Sport separates by designer Liz Claiborne, and Ultrasuede coats varied women's wardrobes with more choices for relaxed dining and sightseeing.

The end of the twentieth century popularized leisurely board shorts, boonie hats, camo, chambray shirts, and A-shirts from Benetton, Banana Republic, Guess, and Old Navy. Comfortable outfits featured Velcroed® or zippered cargo pockets on pants, carpenter jeans, jeggings (a cross between jeans and leggings), and hoodies with kangaroo pouches on the front opening at left and right. Unisex running suits, fleece pullovers, and nylon zipper bags accommodated cell phones, keys, and cash.

In the twenty-first century, boho chic extends the fad in cowboy boots with tights, a practical, sturdy footwear when flip-flops or sandals are inadequate. Skinny jeans and jeggings limit pocket storage while increasing demand for nylon fanny packs, a lightweight accessory. Wrinkle-free denim, chinos, blazers, and coats in Tencel lyocell from Austria reduce ironing time. Blended cultural styles make available worldwide the West African *boubou* (caftan), Bedouin *thobe* (robe), Nigerian dashiki (tunic), Polynesian *pariau* (beach cover), Indian sari, Sioux moccasin, Caribbean guayabera, Aussie slouch hat, and Japanese kimono.

See also: Athletic Shoes; Denim and Jeans; Edwardian Styles and Fashions; T-Shirts; Unisex Clothing.

Further Reading

Blaszczyk, Regina Lee, ed. *Producing Fashion: Commerce, Culture, and Consumers.* Philadelphia: University of Pennsylvania Press, 2008.

Schoeser, Mary. *World Textiles: A Concise History.* New York: Thames & Hudson, 2003.

Scott, William Ramsey. *Dressing Down: Modernism, Masculinity, and the Men's Leisurewear Industry in California, 1930–1960.* Ann Arbor, MI: ProQuest, 2008.

Linen

The earliest cellulose fabric, woven of tough bast fibers, linen has clothed the world consistently for some 38,000 years. The first knotted or twined linen garments, which appeared in natural hues of ecru, ivory, gray, and beige, absorbed perspiration from the body. Found in the Dzudzuana Cave, present-day Georgia, east of the Black Sea, the earliest known shreds dated to 36,000 B.C.E., making linen preparation the world's oldest form of cloth manufacture. The spinning of flax thread in Central Asia, dating to 30,000 B.C.E., prefaced the long history of linen apparel and bags of hunter-gatherers.

By 5,000 B.C.E., flax growers in the Fertile Crescent and North Africa domesticated wild seeds to produce lint- and insect-free fabric. For its sheen and fresh texture, linen earned the name "woven moonlight" from Egyptians. From 4,000 B.C.E., the fabric served as material for everyday indigo tunics, embroidered robes for the priests of Isis, and shroud bandages for the dead.

Around 2000 B.C.E., enslaved fabric workers in the Nile Valley established the linen industry, producing Egypt's top nonedible trade item. Before Hebrew bondage in pharaonic Egypt around 1520 B.C.E., Joseph wore fine linen, a symbol of bureaucratic authority usually stored in a wood linen chest to protect it from mildew. After the biblical exodus, Israelites worshipped in the tabernacle, where linen provided curtains and the ritual coat, ephod (sleeveless apron), sash, and miter of Aaron, the high priest.

Classical Linens

Phoenicians honored their monarchs with linen garments dyed royal purple. Traders from Sidon and Tyre carried linen and flax seed to Greece and up the Atlantic coast to Brittany, England, and Ireland. In Palestine, Greece, Cyprus, Etruria, North Africa, and Crete, wild flax required lengthy retting (soaking) in ponds and streams. Fiber workers next heckled (combed) stalks and roots to remove seeds, pods, and unusable fibers from flax bast. Relics from Ur, Iberia, and Slovakia indicate the early adornment of linen with colorful wool embroidery.

Etruscans turned linen into dense fiber for armoring the right shoulder and making corselets (breastplates). From linen yarn, Greek worshippers of Demeter fashioned linen chitons similar to those worn by fashionable women. Greek women invented the linen pocket handkerchief and covered their sorrow with linen mourning veils. Greek men bound combat and surgical wounds in linen, which was softer and more easily removed than cotton. In the late fourth century B.C.E., Alexander the Great wore a linothorax (laminated chest guard) and turned a jeweled linen turban into a crown.

The Romans honored flax goods as *linum usitatissimum* (highly useful linen) for its application to durable towels, aprons, underwear, and scarves as well as for shrouds holding the remains of cremated corpses. Roman legionaries established linen factories in colonial Gaul, Spain, and Britain and developed apparel styles featuring linen tunics with cloaks of wool for warmth. Around 70 C.E., Pliny, the Roman encyclopedist, commented on extravagant female use of linen, on Nero's choice of Babylonian linen for his court, and on the veiling of German women in linen.

The laborious production of flax thread required up to 150 workdays. Yarn workers spun flax in damp underground rooms to encourage moisture in the fibers. The finest yarns went into the making of drawers and shirts, such as those worn by Jewish priests. After the collapse of the Roman Empire in 476, linen technology ceased to appeal to commercial investors, who preferred wool and cotton for easier profits. Arab tomb robbers seized linen wrappings from Egyptian mummies and used them to make garments.

New Uses

In the Middle Ages, among Arabs, Dutch, Huns, Vikings, Welsh, and Franks, linen provided the most elegant secular wear. The revival of linen for undergarments introduced the concept of "lingerie" to refer to the chemise, drawers, diaper, shift, petticoat, gown, corset, barber shirt, hosiery, and night wear, including that of Charlemagne. Some 54 English fairs sold flax for the weaving of linen and cotton blends worn by waiters, plowmen, carters, and shepherds. In the 1100s, women valued linen for neck cloths, wimples, cauls, neckerchiefs, and baby bibs.

Thirteenth-century armorers provided soldiers with quilted linen gambesons (jackets). A forerunner of the Kevlar bulletproof vest, the comfortable base garment separated chain mail and plate armor from the naked skin. Painters of the Holy Family depicted the Virgin Mary in a linen tunic and stole and the infant Jesus in linen swaddling.

During the Renaissance, fine cambric and gauze from Bruges, Belgium, and Ghent and Ypres, Flanders, dominated the upscale man's wardrobe in linen shirts, handkerchiefs, dickeys, and ruffled boot hose. The discovery of linen bras and panties at Lemberg Castle in Austria from 1400 attested to the fabric's popularity for soft, sturdy underwear that conformed to female curves. In 1578, Mary, Queen of Scots, purchased cutwork linen collars to add to her robes. After the opening of linen factories in Amsterdam and Haarlem, Holland, in 1595, exports to India and Japan spread European linens throughout Asia.

In the 1700s, northern Ireland competed with Holland at milling flax, soaking it in buttermilk for stretching in bleaching yards, and weaving linen duck and canvas for workers' smocks, aprons, and postal sacks. In 1711, Pictish Huguenot refugees Louis Crommelin and Jacob Dupre established the world's major linen fabric center at Belfast, which produced quality lawn, batiste, holland, cambric, kenting, and platilla. In 1760, the introduction of chemical bleach sped the production of pure white cloth for export to England for use in starched shirtfronts, frills, collars, and cuffs.

Scots-Irish immigrants to North America between 1770 and 1775 planted flax fields in New York, Pennsylvania, and New England. Dutch and Irish textile workers introduced European weaving methods and bartered with linen as currency. The Irish also sold heavy-duty glazed "bumpkin ware"—osnaburg, hessian, fustian, and buckram—for lining purses, shoes, hats, and suits. Technical advances in the power loom enabled linen weavers to balance tension on vibrating rollers to accommodate the inelasticity of flax.

Around 1900, linen came into style for the making of dusters, auto coats, and men's summer suits as well as the gaiter tops of high button shoes. After decades of replacement by synthetics, the reclamation of linen as a fashion material in the 1970s boosted income for flax growers throughout Europe, Britain, Russia, India, and China. Fashionable slacks, skirts, and blazers displayed the cool, soil-resistant fabric. Designer Ralph Lauren emphasized American tradition with linen shirts for women. In 2012, the introduction of linen knits in stretch blends, piqué, and waterproof fashions increased the availability of casual, urban, sporty, and sophisticated looks from a sustainable crop.

See also: Armor; Fibers, Natural; Lingerie; Textile Manufacturing; Weaving.

Further Reading

Bonneville, Françoise de. *The Book of Fine Linen.* Paris: Flammarion, 1994.

Collins, Brenda, and Philip Ollerenshaw. *The European Linen Industry in Historical Perspective.* New York: Oxford University Press, 2004.

Heinrich, Linda. *Linen: From Flax Seed to Woven Cloth.* Atglen, PA: Schiffer, 2010.

Lingerie

A subset of undergarments, lingerie refers to the sheer, frilly, or alluring female apparel that enhances women's appearance, self-confidence, and sex appeal. Until the 1830s, American women wore linen shifts, drawers, and chemises under outerwear to prevent chafing from homespun garments. The sale of sewing machines enabled manufacturers to apply tatted or lace edgings to cotton batiste and silk pantalettes to increase femininity.

The concept of intimate, enticing "unmentionables" developed in the 1890s alongside the introduction of birth control. Freed from reproductive imprisonment, women simultaneously escaped the punitive straps and lacings of corsets and embraced luxury. The gradual liberation of women from political and economic repression in 1920 sparked an interest in the sexuality of the female persona, a self-definition epitomized by the era's fleecy "liberty bodice" and lawn or muslin open-crotch drawers.

Three European advocates made conspicuous changes in undergarment design for women in the early twentieth century. French couturier Paul Poiret invented hobble skirts and dresses that accommodated natural curves and favored the replacement of rigid corsets with flexible, unboned brassieres. In 1906, fashion designer Madeleine Vionnet—the "queen of the bias cut"—popularized classic draped *déshabillés* (lingerie dresses) worn without foundation garments.

A contemporary of Vionnet in London, dressmaker Lucy Duff-Gordon—known by the fashion name Lucile—promoted slit skirts, draped tea gowns, and elegant lingerie to suit the tastes of the twentieth century. At salons in Chicago, New York, London, and Paris, under the Lucile Ltd. label, Duff-Gordon battled the ugliness of contemporary corsetry, turning Edwardian lace, ribbons, fabric flowers, black silk, and sheer chiffon in skin tones into nightgowns and intimate wear for trousseaus. In parallel, the International Ladies' Garment Workers' Union, organized in New York City in 1909, built consumer interest in Edwardian undergarments among working-class women.

Liberated by the exigencies of World War I, women experienced a dynamic shift in body aesthetics, reflected in fashion magazines and department store windows. Female shoppers sought lighter, airier materials for their garments, which they laundered by hand to dry overnight. One example, Caucasian flesh-colored stockings, appealed to the wearer of shorter skirts. Another, a cream-colored georgette robe with satin sash, rewarded women with at-home attire for lounging. In 1921, Lucile's lush, womanly wardrobes featured the breast-supporting bandeau and brassiere in peach, orchid, turquoise, lemon, and rose ash, two essential, slimmed-down foundation garments designed for the "New Woman."

Lucile rescued upscale lingerie from the belief that luxury exists only for the privileged. Her columns advocating both the sport brassiere and ultra-feminine lingerie appeared in *Good Housekeeping* and *Harper's Bazaar; Vogue* pictured her winsome afternoon dresses and robes worn without stays. Among Lucile's patrons for chic, sexy apparel were the stage hall star Lillie Langtry, ballerina Anna Pavlova, and president's daughter Alice Roosevelt Longworth. Meanwhile, readers of the Sears, Roebuck catalog were ordering her ready-to-wear brocade corsets as well.

Modern Merchandising

World War II made further inroads in liberating women's apparel. In 1946, Frederick Mellinger, recognizing the female need for a unique identity, invented the push-up bra and Wonderbra, the focus of his California fashion brand, Frederick's of Hollywood. The transformative power of the uplifted bosom affected teens, college coeds, and young unmarried women as well as older factory workers, clerks, and housewives, all of whom sought visual recognition of their womanhood.

Frederick's brassiere business expanded with catalog and personalized onsite merchandising of marabou mules, stockings, lace corsets, baby-doll pantie and strapless bra sets, camisoles, kimonos, and transparent honeymoon lingerie. By pampering women with risqué undies, Mellinger introduced middle-class women to seductive dressing in filmy peignoirs and nighties, bustiers, and body slimmers in siren red and black.

Victoria's Secret eventually nudged Frederick's from its position of dominance in American lingerie fashion. In the 1980s, merchandiser Roy Raymond opened his first shop in Palo Alto, California, showcasing quality intimate wardrobes in muted pastels for a variety of venues, from the grocery store and tennis court to the reception line. He selected a witty name implying that the prim fashions of Queen Victoria's time concealed private stocks of racy underwear. His lingerie actualized fantasies with stretch lace garter belts, bikini and tap panties, G-strings, halter bras, pants liners, and skin-revealing negligees in champagne silk. By 1999, Victoria's Secret sold $2.1 billion annually in lingerie.

Trendy Women's Wear

Raymond's target audience consisted of feminine dressers as well as professional women who chose to stress softness and appeal in their intimate wear. Vanity Fair, his competitor, upgraded standard two-strap bras with the V-back, a racer bra that featured wider armholes and narrower shoulder seams. Wacoal, a Japanese firm, fought the American challenger with a provocative nickel-titanium underwire bra that survived repeated washings. Although the underwire cost $30, twice the price of the average bra, Wacoal advertisers contended that quality lingerie increased the life of even delicate Lycra and lace.

Amid sexualized underwear and sleepwear in a romantic boudoir atmosphere, Victoria's Secret encouraged men and women to shop with confidence on the advice of nonjudgmental sales associates and supermodels Tyra Banks, Heidi Klum, and Gisele Bündchen. Although English/Spanish Web sites and televised fashion shows from Cannes stirred a conservative backlash against erotic thongs, garters, teddies, and feather boas, the company's boutiques flourished in London, Bogota, and San Juan, Puerto Rico.

The boom in spicy, flirty undergarments spawned demand for retro knickers and playsuits as well as makeovers of the utilitarian cotton and nylon briefs and pantyhose marketed by mainstream competitors Hanes, Playtex, Maidenform, Warner's, Fruit of the Loom, and Jockey. In 2012, Victoria's Secret sponsored the largest team in the history of the Komen Race for the Cure, a breast cancer education and research foundation.

See also: Brassieres; Corsets and Girdles; Gendered Dressing; Hosiery, Women's; Linen; Undergarments.

Further Reading

Fields, Jill. *An Intimate Affair: Women, Lingerie, and Sexuality.* Berkeley: University of California Press, 2007.

Néret, Gilles. *1000 Dessous: A History of Lingerie.* New York: Taschen, 1998.

Salen, Jill. *Vintage Lingerie: 30 Patterns Based on Period Garments Plus Finishing Techniques.* New York: St. Martin's Griffin, 2011.

Scranton, Philip, ed. *Beauty and Business: Commerce, Gender, and Culture in Modern America.* New York: Routledge, 2001.

Livery and Heraldry

Offshoots of military organization and rank, heraldry and livery promote family pride through the display of badges and coats of arms. Examples of official insignia date to the Egyptians, Macedonians, Hebrews, Goths, and Vandals. Chivalric insignia also identified relatives and staff of nobility, such as the boots embroidered with gold lions that King Henry I of England presented to his son-in-law, Roscelin, viscount de Beaumont, in 1113.

When Peter the Hermit led a mass of nationalities to Jerusalem on the First Crusade in 1096, he used a badge on their long surcoats to identify them as campaigners sworn to defend Christianity from advancing Muslim armies. English nobles embroidered a cross in white silk on the right shoulder of their surcoats with the Latin motto *Deo Volente* (God Willing). The soldiers of Christ copied the device in linen or worsted wool yarn. Variations in emblems identified French crusaders with the red cross and Flemish soldiers with the green cross. Troopers from the Roman states wore crossed keys, the papal symbol of Saint Peter on the Vatican coat of arms. Germanic members of the Teutonic Knights embroidered their badges with a black cross edged in gold. By the Fourth Crusade in 1202, Enrico Dandalo, the doge of Venice, had his hat embroidered with a cross to make it prominent to fellow campaigners.

Clans and Dynasties

Following the creation of chivalric devices for embroidery on shield covers during the first and second crusades, Henry II of England designed the first royal crest in 1154. Emblems or devices of fabric, fur, embroidery, appliqué, or enameled metal validated the authority of retainers on uniform coats and tabards. European knights wore embroidered insignia on the shoulder of their mantles, tabards, or *jupons* (padded sleeveless jumpers).

During the feudal era in Europe, families and clans identified individual armigers (members) graphically through escutcheons, abbreviated crests, beast shapes, geometric designs, distinct color combinations, and mottoes, such as *Dieu et mon droit* (God and my right), a French sentiment supporting the English concept of the divine right of kings. Crests appeared beneath a helm and its torse (plaited wreath), flanked by supporting honor guards, either bestial or human. For tournaments, the painting of rampant lions or stags and colored chevrons on shields identified competitors in the lists, where combatants rode in full body armor with visors concealing their faces.

Under the command of England's Richard I the Lionheart in 1191, individuals passed their crests to kin as part of inheritances. The Plantagenet badge, broom pods embroidered on official robes, served Richard as well as his brother John, Henry III, Richard II, Henry IV, and Elizabeth I.

Early heraldry required precious pelts for symbolism—black sable, gray vair (squirrel), and white ermine—edged or embroidered in official style. Knights marked themselves with the clan chief's crest engirthed with a belt and buckle emblem as evidence of fealty and service. Scots clansmen displayed their fealty with crested buttons.

In war, heraldic symbols became a rallying point for soldiers lost in the dust, smoke, and furor of combat. On June 24, 1314, Gilbert Clare, the earl of Gloucester, failed to wear his ensign at the battle of Bannockburn and died in captivity because the English thought him unworthy of ransom. Lords outfitted their retinues with uniform colors and furs, notably the black livery worn in 1345 by the brutal mercenaries of Edward of Woodstock, later called the Black Prince for his official color and his dark reputation.

The Liveried Retainer

The late medieval concept of patronage provided a system of benefaction by which barons and landowners maintained guards, artisans, and domestics—porters, inspectors, entertainers, launderers, stable boys, turnspits, and chimney sweeps. The term *livrée,* derived from *livraison* (allotment) in the 1300s, indicated that uniforms constituted part of the salaries of pages, guards, and retainers. Nobles extended the validation of coats, hoods and cockaded hats, knotted ribbons, epaulettes, corrugated leather rosettes, buckles, sashes, and saddle cloths to security guards and civilian dependents, as with the blue boar embroidered on the left shoulders of the yeomen of the earl of Oxford and the needlework on coachmen's pockets. Lesser members of a noble household wore abbreviated crests embroidered on sleeves.

In an era of peasant illiteracy, processions, royal progresses, funerals, and pageantry reminded the lowly of lordship and authority granted by the crown and church. In 1371, John of Gaunt, the duke of Lancaster, introduced the collar of esses (SS), a personal symbol that he awarded his nephew, Richard II. In London, uniform decor after England's triumph at the Battle of Agincourt on October 25, 1415, lorded over the French the victory of Henry V and his marriage to a French princess, Catherine of Valois, the mother of Henry VI.

Examples of mass production of insignias include the order of the duke of Buckingham in 1454 for 2,000 knotted bands, the heraldic symbol of the Stafford household and forerunner of the rib- and collar. In London, the Beefeaters and Yeomen of the Guard, uniformed in scarlet livery, wore a triple insignia—rose, shamrock, and thistle—honoring Great Britain and Ireland on the back and front of their tunics. Pursuivants (officers of arms), members of royal processions, wore damask silk tabards embroidered with the royal crest.

In a political use of heraldry, adversaries in the Wars of the Roses (1455–1485) promoted the wearing of badges of the feuding houses of Lancaster and York. Soldiers topped their armor with liveried tunics bearing the royal colors or the colors of the town where they mustered. In 1459, Margaret of Anjou awarded the swan badge of the Lancasters to soldiers to strengthen local loyalty. In 1463, Nottingham provided red jackets adorned with white fustian insignias in the shape of standing unicorns.

The bestowal of a metal chain of office or livery collar began in 1378 with the identification of Chamberlain Geoffrey de Belleville by Charles V of France with the *collier de la cosse de geneste* (collar of the broomcod). In 1484, Richard III dispatched a gold collar to James FitzGerald, the earl of Desmond, to win the Irish to the English cause. The bribe, sweetened with gifts of velvet doublets, gowns, and tippets, failed to rid Desmond of his rebellious tendencies.

The system of chain insignia extended to mayors in England and its colonies and to members of orders of knighthood, notably the Order of the Garter and the Order of St. Michael and St. George. The concept gained credence in other municipalities and spawned the Order of St. Michael in France, the Order of Vasa in Sweden, and the Order of Saint Sylvester and the Golden Militia at the Vatican. In 1802, Napoleon I decorated the Ordre national de Légion d'honneur with the profile of Marianne, a female symbol of liberty that appeared on a military pin, collar pendant, or pocket plaque worn with a red sash.

See also: Badges and Insignias; Clan Attire; Embroidery; Noble, Princely, and Chivalric Attire; Symbolic Colors, Patterns, and Motifs.

Further Reading

Cross, Peter R., and Maurice Hugh Keen, eds. *Heraldry, Pageantry and Social Display in Medieval England.* Rochester, NY: Boydell, 2002.

Fox-Davies, Arthur Charles. *A Complete Guide to Heraldry.* New York: Skyhorse, 2007.

Leslie, Catherine Amoroso. *Needlework Through History: An Encyclopedia.* Westport, CT: Greenwood, 2007.

Logging Attire

Historically, the style and workmanship of logging attire has reflected the rigor and danger of downing timber. When North American timbermen worked near rivers and deltas in the early 1800s, they needed breeches and footwear suitable for mounting horses, mules, and oxen. Canvas was the best material for waterproofing into "tin pants and jacket," the lumberman's rainwear when combined with a sturdy mackinaw, two wool shirts, a vest, one or more sets of long black wool underwear, gum boots, and a wool cap. Because belts increased the danger of being caught in tree limbs, loggers insisted on galluses.

Men packed their camp gear in dunnage (duffel bags). Bobbed or stagged pants without cuffs freed leg movement below the knee during escapes to prevent tripping in underbrush. Even in sub-zero temperatures, loggers rolled up the sleeves of their hickory shirts, denim shirts striped navy and white. All were available at the *wangan* (company store or commissary) in correct sizes to prevent loose shirttails and sleeves from catching in belts, gears, pulleys, spiked rollers, and sawteeth.

At the eighteenth-century logging sites in Bangor, Maine, leather goods had to be supple and regularly waterproofed to ensure grip on tracks, troughs, flumes, and skid roads. To prevent foot fungus, loggers slit boot sole arches to let water escape. Waistbands acquired stout metal clips for securing axes, froes, and handsaws. Goggles shielded the eyes from snow, sleet, rainy mist, and sawdust.

At the Saint Croix River valley in Minnesota during the 1830s, millponds provided fresh water that axmen heated for Sunday washing and laundry of underwear and socks. Loggers' wives purchased wool yard goods and yarn from John Rich, the founder of outdoor clothing manufacturer Woolrich, Inc., in Woolrich, Pennsylvania. In the 1840s, the company sold wool buffalo shirts featuring extra shoulder room for swinging axes. Holes burned by tobacco pipes and sparks from the chimney seemed minimal damage compared to the punishment of daily tree-felling.

Along the Great Lakes, heavy leather calked (spiked) boots with 42 cleats kept men steady while birling (turning and shifting) logs in the current. Nightly, the cautious workman greased the uppers and soles of his footwear with lubricating oil, bear fat, mutton tallow, or neat's-foot oil. Others coated boots with black paint or wax. When boots wore out, dependable firms restored them to usable condition.

For sleep, weary workers rolled up coats into pillows. By 3 A.M., the cook and cookees (aides) arose to dress in long aprons and begin heating water for black tea and oatmeal, crocks for apple "sass," and fry pans for bacon. Quilted rawhide pads served as oven mitts. In lieu of a camp doctor, the cook served as emergency medical officer by amputating fingers crushed by unexpected log jams and bandaging stumps of toes cut off when saws swung across the toes of boots.

During the Alaskan Gold Rush of the late 1890s, the 70,000 stampeders sailing for the Klondike out of Puget Sound, Washington, paid inflated prices for outdoor and logging apparel and thick leather gloves. Heavy-duty logging pants and bib overalls were in short supply. Snowshoes enabled trekkers from Dawson to navigate Dead Horse Trail up Chilkoot Pass to reach endless stands of valuable evergreens.

Until improvements in work conditions during the 1900s, North American loggers wore the same shirts, pants, red wool long underwear, and steel-toed boots for months at a time. By 1902, Smokejumpers forestry boots from White's Book Company offered a lighter, more flexible lace-up fitted with a Vibram sole and a two-inch strap at back for ease of entry.

After lumbermen unionized in 1905, protective gear increased safety; features included the canvas, felt, or leather shoulder pads under suspenders to protect the skin from the teeth on a crosscut saw.

During wet weather, lumbermen raised a "stink pole" (laundry pole) on forked stakes over fire to dry their boots, wool socks, and other apparel, which exuded steam, saliva from chewing tobacco, and the reek of sweat. Clammy hats set on the woodpile dried more slowly. Meanwhile, men darned their socks and patched elbows and knees with rawhide strips and lined up for haircuts on Sunday.

The provision of running water and laundry equipment to logging camps after World War I simplified grooming and improved hygiene. Heavy cotton White Ox gloves achieved fame among woodsmen and timbermen for improving finger dexterity and the hold on wire. Although the gloves lasted only a week, their low price per dozen pairs made replacement less problematic.

In the 1970s, research in Finland and Sweden developed more reliable logging apparel, including double-palmed gloves. For jackets and pants, high-tensile ballistic nylon shielded the skin from laceration. The same nylon padded pants to protect legs from the backlash of a chainsaw. Safety glass protected the eyes from slivers and shattering.

After the 1980s, the replacement of felt hats and cloth caps with brimmed hard hats of plastic or fiberglass saved lives. In New Zealand, fiber-padded leg wear yielded a 23 percent decline in injuries over a five-year period ending in 1988. Safety boots, face shields, and ear protection reduced the risk of injury from chainsaws, emery wheels, and flying chips. Waterproof and flame-retardant Kevlar gloves shielded the skin of handlers of dynamite and nitroglycerine.

See also: Protective and Orthotic Clothing.

Further Reading

Andrew, Ralph W. *This Was Logging*. Atglen, PA: Schiffer, 1997.

———. *Timber: Toil and Trouble in the Big Woods*. Seattle: Superior, 1968.

Heavey, Bill. "Cold Hunts, Warm Wool." *Field & Stream* (January 2001): 46–50.

Looms

- -

The apparatus for weaving yarn or thread into cloth, the loom promoted the interlacing of materials for human textiles. By setting up sticks and cords into a rectangle, the first weavers exploited the right angle as a means of webbing rushes and cattails into a plain checker. Unlike Pacific aborigines, who wove hammered bark cloth without a frame, Middle Eastern artisans set the warp or longitudinal threads between two horizontal bars for the entwining of the weft, knotted beige flax or natural white or brown cotton threads, forming a mesh.

From 6000 B.C.E. at the Catal Höyük settlement in south-central Anatolia, rudimentary looms advanced basketry to yield lengths woven of bast and flax at right angles and darned into shrouds. After 5000 B.C.E., pastoralists of Arabia and North Africa preferred the portable ground loom. Similar to a quilting frame, the harness placed the weaving process at eye level. The multiple-shuttle technology also served north Canadian netters and Carib hammock makers.

Prehistoric loom makers attempted to lighten the work of clothiers. A ground-looming method practiced in what is now Liberia involved staking warp threads in the ground and walking around the nexus to distribute thread. The Ojibway bag loom wrapped vertical supports with a fringe of natural fiber for the hand twining of weft, one of the world's oldest methods of fiber work. Innovators in India and Arabia eased the toil of weaving with the pit loom, which reduced cramping in the user's legs through a system of raising and lowering warp strands by a pair of treadles.

Primary Crafts

Around 5500 B.C.E., the warp-weighted upright or slant loom that originated in the areas of Serbia and Hungary forced the weaver to stand facing the warp and beat the cross threads into place with a wooden tool known as a sword beater. Technicians in Bali, northern Borneo, and Java straightened the weft with a bamboo or reed batten. Artisans set up operations on warp threads held tight to the heading cord or beam by stone, clay, or ceramic loom weights, such as those surviving from Anatolia, Crete, and Palestine and described in the epics of Homer.

The warp-weighted frame, which passed to Switzerland, Scandinavia, and Iceland and south to Greece, introduced unlimited vertical threading. Looms yielded the bast and flax fabrics that required no joining to complete robes and blankets. As depicted by a pottery drawing found in Badari, Egypt, and images of Queen Semiramis of Assyria, the long-lived technology of 5000 B.C.E. used a double-pointed shuttle to carry the weft back and forth through the warp, which weavers suspended from a rod.

Worldwide, forms of looming evolved during the transformation of natural fibers into clothing, as with the plain weaves of approximately 3500 B.C.E. found in West Pakistan. Around 3250 B.C.E., Andean hunter-gatherers at Guitarrero Cave west of Chimbote, Peru, evolved the twining or plaiting of cotton into knotless netting. They completed the primitive form of weaving on looms measuring 4 feet by 5 feet (1.2 meters by 1.5 meters). Among Fenno-Scandinavian Sami artisans from 3000 B.C.E., interweaving and stitching of the weft with colored threads and contrasting fibers fabricated borders for the piece.

Early Weaving Equipment

In China, during the legendary reign of Emperor Shi Huangdi in 2600 B.C.E., Queen Leizu became the "Silkworm Mother" for loosening the threads of steamed cocoons and weaving silk fibers on a loom. For matting, the Chinese loom guided threads across a wood block crisscrossed with saw cuts. Advances in East Asian and Mesopotamian shed sticks (crossbars) and Anatolian heddle rods after 2000 B.C.E. enabled the weaver to raise and lower odd and even warp threads to create intricate patterns.

The back strap loom, such as that employed by the Mesoamerican Maya, enveloped the weaver in a matrix held firm on two bars. For the delicate, gauzy linens of Egypt and India, a bent posture applied the toes against a back harness to control fabric continuity and prevent yarn breaks. A guide bar tamped threads into an even weave in back strap looming and the Egyptian mat loom, a Hyksos invention that crafters pegged to the floor around 1700 B.C.E. The Iban loom of Borneo and the Filipino Igorot frame produced a continuous warp yielding a tube of fabric.

Unique weaving fibers and tools developed in the second millennium B.C.E., including the banana stem fiber woven by the Chumash in the Santa Cruz Islands off coastal California. The Tiahuanaco of Bolivia guided weft threads into a matrix with a thin stick. Around 1200 B.C.E. in the area that is now Veracruz, Mexico, the Olmec interlaced cotton with plant leaves to make kilts and loincloths. Evidence from after 1000 B.C.E. at Voldtofte, Denmark, shows that Bronze Age weavers tamed the nettle (*Urtica diocia*) for looming with a twist at the spinning wheel.

At Mohenjo-Daro in the Indus Valley from the 800s B.C.E., cottage weavers built pit-treadle looms with heddle harness that shaped short-staple cotton into apparel. Around 400 B.C.E., primitive draw looms from Chu, China, introduced two-person methods of producing a continuous intricate design. The draw boy, the weaver's helper, worked the weaving gear from above.

Trade with the Mediterranean rim introduced loom terms to Republican Rome as early as 200 B.C.E. Conservative citizens judged the patriotism of women by their weaving skills and by the training of girls to produce clothing for the family. The warp-weighted loom depicted on the burial stele of 20-year-old Atta Altica Auniae at Burgos, Spain, indicates the feminization of weaving in the Roman Empire.

Innovation after 100 C.E. advanced Central African looming of raffia palm fronds and the cross-hatching of jute and flax into textiles in Madagascar. At Palmyra, Syrian weavers manipulated triple heddles to introduce the diagonal twill pattern. The mechanics of the Turkish treadle or pedal loom at Tarsus in 298 began replacing the warp-weighted loom. The horizontal treadle method turned cotton into a profitable commodity for sale in Moorish Spain, Sicily, the Middle East, Sudan, and Ethiopia.

In the early Middle Ages, treadle technology mirrored rigid log looms in the Western Hemisphere evolved by the Tarahumara and Tepehua of Mexico. The initiation of horizontal looming enabled weavers to sit during strenuous motions of casting the shuttle. By 400, weaving of uniform damask and tabby textiles turned the integral beaming of Syrian pit looms into moneymakers.

From 500 in the American Great Basin, Pueblo, Hopi, and Zuni evolved the fiber crafts of the ancient Basket Makers into weaving. Crafters sat at upright looms with legs outstretched and webbed rabbit fur strips and hand-spun dog hair and cotton fibers into tubes for blankets and wraps, kilts, and infant swaddling. Similar implements of fabric making flourished in Palestine, Phoenicia, and the Greek Cyclades. Tube weaving gave such value to women in the 790s that a tubular loom followed Queen Asa of Agder to her tomb in Oseberg, Norway.

In Ghana during the 1000s, the Akan, Ga, Asante, and Ewe peoples of the Volta River basin pioneered kente cloth, a traditional handmade fabric loomed in thin strips and whipstitched together. A century later at San in southeastern Mali, Bamanan women staffed the lengthy weaving and processing of *bògòlanfini* (mud cloth), a folk textile loomed on a narrow handheld frame to a width of 6 inches (15 centimeters). In Iceland, Greenland, Norway, Sweden, and the Faroe, Orkney, and Shetland Islands, vertical looms set up in Viking longhouses with soapstone weights produced hodden and wadmal padding from wool fleece.

Meanwhile, from Sicily to the Iberian textile market at Barcelona, looms turned cotton into trade fabric and apparel. In 1147, crusader Roger II stole Greek looms from Corinth and Thebes and abducted technicians and silk weavers to staff looming workshops in Calabria and Palermo. The precision of the draw loom applied the comber board suspended on leather leashes to shifting warp threads to weave a consistent texture.

Late Medieval and Renaissance Devices

Weaving proved so lucrative that the municipalities of Leicester, Northampton, Oxford, and Winchester, England, exacted a licensing fee and tax on guild looms. From 1368 at Jiangnan south of the Yangtze River, looming of raw cotton from North China contributed obscure techniques and mechanical refinements for the draw loom. Loom makers and repairers and weavers could earn more than 30 times the earnings of day laborers or agricultural workers. In the late 1400s, Flemish and Belgian loom technology refined the sheen and pile of velvet by adding a pile thread to the usual warp and weft.

In the 1590s, in the Pacific Northwest region of North America, the Chilkat loom produced leggings, shawls, aprons, and complex curvilinear blankets prized by the Tsimshian, Kwakiutl, Haida, and Nootka. Formed in vertical sections, the resulting fabric took shape on a heading cord of hide attached to uprights lacking a bottom frame. As warp threads dangled, the artisan contrasted natural goat wool with yarn dyed white, yellow, turquoise, and black. Hand weaving with a measuring staff distributed symmetrical sections without a shuttle. Goat intestines covered the advancing fabric to keep it clean.

Eighteenth-century looms increased industrial profits while lowering textile costs. In 1734 at Bury, Lancashire, inventor John Kay's flying shuttle passed the weft rapidly through the warp and increased the width of fabric that could be produced on one frame. The innovation outperformed the barrel loom, a cylindrical feed pierced with holes, which French inventor Jacques Vaucanson of Lyons perfected in 1745.

Looms in the Industrial Revolution

From 1770, weavers in Holland and Manchester, England, multitasked the Dutch engine loom and up to 24 automatic shuttles for simultaneous spooling of six varieties of ribbon. In the 1770s, vibrating rollers controlled the tension on linen to circumvent the brittleness of flax and speed the weaving of coach lace for fringe, military insignia, and livery. After 1775, tablet looms increased the complexity of weaves by pulling strands through the holes of punch cards.

The debut of English entrepreneur Edmund Cartwright's power loom in 1785 altered weaving from a cottage craft to an industry. Steam-powered looms in operation in 1788 at the Hartford Woolen Manufactory in Connecticut increased efficiency and consistency of the weave. At Pawtucket, Rhode Island, beginning in 1793, Samuel Slater, the "Father of American Industry," operated

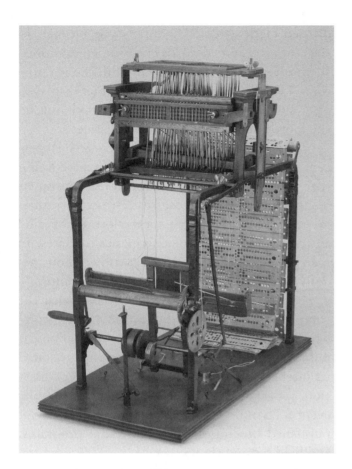

The Jacquard loom of the early nineteenth century, named for French inventor Joseph Marie Jacquard, automated the weaving of patterned fabrics by means of punch cards. Using punch cards to control operations presaged early computer programming. *(Science Museum/SSPL/Getty Images)*

10 percent of wool weaving involved a hand loom, much of it in Russia. More innovative technology increased the investment required to set up power looms. In Switzerland during the early 1950s, the first Sulzer loom required the formation of pellets, which projected the weft through the warp. Italian looms outpaced British models by weaving 15,500 square miles (40,140 square kilometers) in 1965 compared with 10,000 square miles (25,900 square kilometers) on looms from the United Kingdom.

In a late-twentieth century revival movement, a number of artisans returned to ancient and medieval looming techniques that revealed the beauty of slubs and irregularities in folk costume. The native Chilkat loom from the Pacific Northwest preserved the unique sectional weaving of goat wool, cedar bark, goose down, and Pomeranian dog fur. Cane looms reprised the frame weaving invented by the Salish of Washington State and the Guayos and Waiwai of British Guiana. In traditional style, weavers steadied the frame between their toes.

See also: Jacquard, Joseph Marie; Museums, Clothing and Textile; Textile Manufacturing; Weaving.

Further Reading

Essinger, James. *Jacquard's Web: How a Hand-Loom Led to the Birth of the Information Age.* New York: Oxford University Press, 2007.

Harris, Jennifer, ed. *5,000 Years of Textiles.* Washington, DC: Smithsonian Books, 2011.

Hecht, Ann. *Art of the Loom: Weaving, Spinning and Dyeing Across the World.* Seattle: University of Washington Press, 2001.

Mohanty, Gail Fowler. *Labor and Laborers of the Loom: Mechanization and Handloom Weavers, 1780–1840.* New York: Routledge, 2006.

Lord & Taylor

The oldest sophisticated department store in North America, Lord & Taylor shaped the shopping style of discerning women who demanded quality and elegance. Founded on April 28, 1826, at 47 and 49 Catherine Street in Manhattan by English merchant Samuel Lord of Orange, New Jersey, and his wife's cousin, financier George Washington Taylor, the company sold bolts of dress goods. The chain

looms with flowing water, which removed the added cost of fuel for steam generators.

At Westminster, England, after 1820, a loom named for French merchant Joseph Marie Jacquard simplified the patterning of matelasse, brocade, epangeline, and damask by guiding threads through holes in punched cards. Throughout the 1830s, mechanized weaving exported from England, Ireland, and Germany supplanted the cottage-loomed crafts of Syria and Turkey. Throughout southern Asia, however, hand looms continued to fashion sarongs, saris, and kimonos. In the 1890s, to retain handcrafts in the era of dobby loomed fabrics, King Ibrahim Njoya of Cameroon promoted the traditional weaving of *ndop* cloth on a treadle loom.

Industrialized nations created new specialties in loom setup and tuning, mechanical jobs dissimilar in skills from weaving. By 1913, less than established a reputation for distinction and classic good looks in women's dresses and suits, gloves, hosiery, cashmere shawls, and blankets.

After moving to a mansard-roofed building in an exclusive residential district at Broadway and Grand Street on the Lower East Side in 1861, Lord & Taylor acquired two more partners, George Washington Taylor Lord and Samuel Lord, Jr., the founder's sons. While selling custom-made clothing and infant layettes, the store survived the vicissitudes of the Civil War, including the draft riots of 1863.

On streets where fashionable matrons traveled by classy carriages, the company shared commercial surroundings with fancy goods purveyor Tiffany & Company, Macy's department store, and Benjamin Altman's emporium. Gas lighting introduced a flickering effect to merchandising on the second floor, the ready-to-wear department. In 1870, Lord & Taylor became the first department store to install steam elevators and offer personal shopping assistance.

Services for the Upscale Consumer

When Lord & Taylor occupied a five-story facility at Broadway and 20th Street, a segment of "Ladies' Mile," the owners dedicated its outreach to enjoyable shopping for understated apparel, shoes, and millinery. The chain expanded to Fifth Avenue between 38th and 39th streets, to Manhasset (Long Island), America's first branch store, and then to satellite stores in Boston, Philadelphia, and Washington, D.C. In 1891, the New York City Consumers' League honored Lord & Taylor for maintaining high standards for female employees, including lunchrooms, a rooftop promenade, choral singing and indoor baseball, and a gym offering fencing, gymnastics, and weight lifting.

The 10-story, 600,000-square-foot (56,000-square-meter) fireproof store enticed the wealthy to an atmosphere of carpeting, parquet, travertine marble, and fashionable dining at the tenth-floor restaurant loggia. In 1914, management promoted waists (blouses), silks, and Onyx hosiery inside the carriage entrance as well as French underwear, untrimmed hats, children's barbering, and long-term fur storage. At the northeast corner, smartly dressed clerks greeted shoppers one on one. In the coats and suits department, women examined themselves in new outfits before full-length mirrors. A French salon featured ensembles displayed on mannequins in glass cases. Hat modeling on the fourth floor promoted Parisian styles.

In 1916, the company invested nearly 10 percent of its $1.5 million in profits in advertising that pledged honorable service to the consumer. Young men could choose ready-to-wear casuals for motoring or English sport clothing. Period ads recommended circular stripes as the latest in men's silk hose. Discreet Pierce Arrow limousines delivered wrapped packages to patrons' homes.

In the 1920s, Lord & Taylor asserted that the company owed more to the consumer than warehousing mass-produced clothes to foist off on the public. To establish goodwill, the company stated its intent to shape taste through consumer education, appearance clinics, parades, and other public events. To build customer loyalty, Lord & Taylor published brochures, broadcast radio programs, and held fashion shows.

To appeal to artistic tastes, management hired a Russian artist to stage a model of St. Patrick's Cathedral made from handkerchiefs. As a result, the accessories department sold 20,000 handkerchiefs in one day at 25 cents each. In a public relations campaign, at the opening of the doors each morning, management appealed to patriots with a playing of "The Star-Spangled Banner." Oversized street-level windows enticed celebrants of winter holidays with Christmas and Hanukkah scenarios in impressive seasonal arrangements free of commercialization.

During the Great Depression, Lord & Taylor reserved the tenth floor of its headquarters for men's interests, including aprons and chef's hats for barbecuing and the home bar. Excelling at presentation, Henry Callahan earned acclaim for his designs and those of his protégés, Cuban designer Luis Estévez and William Carroll Pahlmann. In the store cellar, their crews completed displays of mannequins in realistic poses for elevating to street level by hydraulic lifts. An unusual spectacle used fans to blow bleached cornflakes, a simulated snowstorm intended to boost purchases of winter togs.

President Dorothy Shaver

Under the leadership of Dorothy Shaver, America's first female department store president (1945–1959), Lord & Taylor established a bureau of fashion and decoration. She modernized store publicity and advertising with photos of live models and appealed to young consumers with clothing for girls aged 12–16, later known as "Young New Yorker Dresses." The feminization of dressing tables drew buyers for mirrored and skirted boudoir accessories to hold hairpins, jewelry, scarves, makeup, and perfumes.

Buyers distinguished company stock by introducing fashions by Bonnie Cashin, Helen Cookman, Elizabeth Hawes, Muriel King, Vera Maxwell, Norell, Claire Potter, Adele Simpson, and Pauline Trigère. In 1938, Shaver offered American Design awards as a means of shifting shopper allegiance from French to American labels. Her innovations ranged from the retro evening dress with tiny back bustle or bow, copies of Wallis Warfield Simpson's wedding dress, and Nettie Rosenstein's crinkle satin evening gowns to figure skating costumes and the body-hugging zipper in coats, evening wear, slips, and robes.

At the onset of World War II, Shaver shifted from fashion to activism by honoring architects, artists, and inventors for joining the war effort, including William Pahlmann, who designed camouflage uniforms and gear for the military. In the absence of male window dressers, Shaver hired the first female designers to arrange displays.

After Shaver's promotion to chief executive officer in 1945, the department chain concentrated on customer service and suburban merchandising of "The American Look." Shaver described this style in an interview for *Life* magazine as the prominence of natural behavior, animation, ageless and confident fashions, and a fresh elegance in dress and makeup. She superintended the first branch store outside the city in Scarsdale, New York, and stocked such reliable labels as Ellen Tracy and Jones New York. The company cultivated foreign patronage by shipping merchandise to American ambassadors and assisting offshore customers with the purchases.

As staff development, Shaver offered workers free makeup and hair arranging each morning as a means of grooming clerks to company standards. With her elevation of the American Beauty rose as a company symbol and the signature logo, the president guided the store beyond the traditional parameters of retail. The store's prosperity earned Shaver the title of "First Lady of Retailing."

In 1968, president Melvin Emerson Dawley continued building the Lord & Taylor chain with stores in Atlanta, Chicago, Dallas, and Houston. He supported civic and cultural fund-raising by initiating an annual dinner dance and fashion show. In 1976, Joseph E. Brooks took charge and continued building stores in Florida, Illinois, and Michigan. He introduced the concept of investment dressing with the clothes of American designers Calvin Klein and Ralph Lauren. After incorporation with the May Company, Lord & Taylor added stores in Denver and Las Vegas to its 86 locations.

In 2003, Lord & Taylor revitalized its previous prestige with mascara bars, signature cafés, coffee bars, and a chain of restaurants under the name Sarabeth's. In addition to facility renovations, the company tempted a younger sophisticate by advertising upscale lines—Donna Karan ready-to-wear, Coach and Kate Spade handbags and Michael Kors sportswear manufactured in New York City, Juicy Couture casual apparel from Los Angeles, Joseph Abboud menswear from Boston, and Escada designer clothing from Germany—to tempt a younger sophisticate. In the 2010s, Lord & Taylor cultivated retro chic in its flagship store and also operated new stores in New Hampshire and New York and clothing and accessories outlets in Florida, Michigan, and New Jersey.

See also: Department Stores; Retail Trade.

Further Reading

Lord & Taylor. www.lordandtaylor.com

Marrone, Francis. "A Landmark Department Store." *New York Sun,* December 27, 2007.

Whitaker, Jan. *Service and Style: How the American Department Store Fashioned the Middle Class.* New York: St. Martin's, 2006.

Woodhead, Lindy. *War Paint: Madame Helena Rubinstein and Miss Elizabeth Arden.* Hoboken, NJ: John Wiley & Sons, 2003.